THE POLITICOS

1865-1896

by MATTHEW JOSEPHSON

A Harvest Book
HARCOURT, BRACE & WORLD, INC.
New York

CONTENTS

FOREWORD

IN a preceding work, I wrote of men who spoke little and did much. In the present work, touching other phases of the same historical period, I write of men who, in effect, did as little as possible and spoke all too much. The statesman and the captain of industry complement each other well: one talks, the other acts.

Outwardly, of course, the great party leaders of the age of Big Business that followed our Civil War filled the public eye handsomely enough— they played skillfully upon popular passion by that which they did or verbalized. Their time was picturesque, with its fierce (not always bloodless) partisan warfare, its rich scandals, its intrigues, its repentant reform movement, its desperate defense maneuvers. But in a sense deeper than most of them knew it was truly eventful. One might say that "they worked better than they knew."

It has been remarked that the political leaders of an era of purely capitalist revolution and growth, such as was the second half of the nineteenth century, though they have important historic missions to perform (worthy of objective analysis in all their aspects), seem less inspiring and romantic than the heroes of the revolutions against feudalism in the seventeenth and eighteenth centuries. Their annals are often an affair of greed and meanness, of mimic disasters, of big events and little politicians. But if they are seldom heroic, then at least they are often prodigiously comic—in spite of themselves—and "human, all too human." Only, the comedy seems greatly at our own expense.

My object has been to picture the Politicos as they were, the "key men" of politics, the professionals, singly and in combination, as they carried out their assignments, as they rose and fell and were supplanted, as power passed from the hands of one to the other among them—to picture them within the frame of their social world and real relations, observing the while the theory and practice of democracy exemplified by them in a decisive epoch of our republic.

During the 1930's, in the days of the New Deal, the nation experienced a form of party leadership and political action that was very different and decidedly more responsible than that of the Gilded Age of the Robber Barons and the Politicos. The country then passed through a prolonged state of depression and of crisis, whereas the earlier epoch enjoyed a carefree expansion over the land and in industry toward open frontiers. For several eventful years prior to World War II we witnessed the boldest political experiments we had ever known; precedents were broken, sweeping reform laws were placed on the statute books. Yet while there was visible change, there was also resistance to change, and there was much inertia and "recurrence," which stemmed from our past and was rooted in our bipartisan party system, that peculiar American institution which has dominated political government here for longer than a century. (The power even of a Franklin Roosevelt was checked in 1938 by a defensive alliance of bosses in both parties.) Men are born and die; Governors, Senators, Presidents come and go; but the party organization goes on long after them, and its inner circle, its state and county chairmen, its bosses, rule not for four or six years, but for a generation or for life tenure.

It was part of my intention in this work to determine how we Americans produced such a formidable, tradition-bound organization of professional politicians, forming the vital medium through which our democratic public life functions. The story of the rise and growth of our party institution is that of a distinctive social organism created by American customs and historical experience. We follow the development of the institution at local and national levels, observing also the individual destinies of the men cast in its mold.

In the early days of the republic the Founding Fathers trusted that the ingenious compromises of our Federal charter, reinforced by wise statesmanship, would achieve a nice equilibrium between the different classes and interest groups in the country. That plan looked well on paper. However, a democratic uprising against the rule of the patrician Federalists appears to have created the "party system," with its rival conventions and caucuses, and its component factions of ins and outs. The "party system," with its unwritten laws, became, in time, as stoutly anchored in American tradition as our sacred written charter, the Constitution itself.

Formed originally through the force of democratic passion, in the time of Andrew Jackson, the party institution in later years adapted itself admirably to a very different climate of opinion and a different form of society, that dominated by the post-Civil War plutocracy. In the historical period pictured in this book we find the industrial capitalists and the financiers triumphant over the farmers and the workers in the cities. Between 1865 and 1896 we perceive how the parvenus of industry, the "kings" of railways, the "barons" of coal, iron, or pork, steadily encircle and besiege the party organizations. In the end, despite the posturing and the windy rhetoric of the political orators, the whole bipartisan system—though having originated in a popular movement of opposition to the moneyed element—is fairly conquered and turned to account by the new masters of society.

By absorbing the "folklore" of the professional politicians, and examining their myths and taboos (as I have attempted to do here), it has sometimes occurred to me that one might possibly devise an informal manual or guide to the seeming "chaos" of our practical politics. The plain citizens of this country have long instructed themselves by observing the notable contradictions between the promises and the performances of politicians. Some of them have even learned to point out, in the speeches of the most voluble public orators, those matters which are passed over in silence, and often the most significant of all. If we accepted uncritically the terminology in which politicians justify their behavior, or that used by their apologists, then our own labor would be wholly academic. Yet how much that passes for history is still written in such unevaluated form.

Here, plainly, we enter a world full of delusions or mirage-like pictures, "painted villages" of cheerful peasants and soldiers, where things are eternally not what they seem. It would be wise, therefore, to apply a modern equivalent of the Socratic method; and take note always of the contradictions between "that which the political leader thinks and says of himself and that which he really is and does"; between the real moving forces of history and the rhetoric or "ideology" of public men. For paradox is a common form of amusement in public life: political leaders may be frequently heard mouthing one set of ideals or doctrines they appear to espouse with all their hearts (e.g., Liberty, or Justice, or Peace), while at the same time they may be seen to pursue practical ends wholly at variance with their professions of faith.

New York, 1963   MATTHEW JOSEPHSON

BOOK ONE

THE SPOILSMEN

CHAPTER ONE

THE TRIUMPH OF THE "DIRECTORY"

1865-1868

The talk and labor is of Reconstruction, for this is the engine by which they hold power; yet not a man among that great number . . . appears to know . . . what he means by Reconstruction. GIDEON WELLES

THE longed-for peace had come. The great military captains, Grant and Lee, Sherman and Johnston, vied with each other in gestures of magnanimity on the one side and conciliation on the other. Shaking off the stupor and frenzy of war, the Union and Confederate soldiers who were being mustered out at Appomattox instantly fraternized with each other.

After the iron days and nights of war, the call to peaceful, civil life seemed infinitely deep and sweet. There was so much to be done; there was so much work, chance, opportunity which the war and the victory itself opened up, in the farms and shops of the North even more than in the ravaged valleys of the South. The whole machinery of the country must be remade for the new age of coal and steam power which had come about even before men's eyes had grown accustomed to it. There must be greater arteries for the circulation of the new industry; a transcontinental network of railway track must be quickly laid; the production of iron must be doubled; new oil fields in Pennsylvania, copper and silver mines in Colorado and other mountain territories, must be opened up. Homestead farms, new towns and industries too, in the virgin prairies of the West along the moving frontier offered hope and fortune to the strong, willing men who had borne arms. To seek opportunity among the new resources that beckoned, to exploit these by their own untrammeled, individual efforts as freely as possible within the open continental market of America—here were the common realities, here for most men were the real fruits of the Second American Revolution. Finally, opportunity for work and enterprise was greater, more immediate, than ever before, because the barriers of the feudal land economy of the South which had dominated the policy of the nation for long decades were broken at last as effectively, as completely, as feudalism had been broken in England in 1688 and in France in 1789. In 1865 three-quarters of the American people set to work instinctively, planlessly, to build a heavy industry where there had been almost nothing of the sort, and to produce twice as much goods, food, wealth of all kinds, as they had produced in 1860. This had been their blind object and their end, though never mentioned in the dicta of party leaders or the terms of generals. Frustrated in this end, they had willingly taken to arms and halted not in the struggle with the enemy-brother until they had won.

Even the assassination of Mr. Lincoln, arousing momentarily horror, suspicion, and gloom, failed to shake for long the will of the people for repose after war, for swiftest return to the ways of peaceful labor after destruction. The Lincoln tragedy passed off in a fleeting mood of anger, bearing with it surprisingly little retribution; it was seen as the effect of insane intrigue rather than authoritative conspiracy, for had not Lincoln been the most conciliatory and merciful of the war-party leaders? But the new President too had proved himself a stanch patriot, and all seemed well. The press, most letters, and most memoirs of the time all tell of war weariness, of the passion for peace, for order, of immeasurable relief at the end of the long-drawn-out war.

This war weariness, combined with the nearly universal desire to embrace those chances of human betterment offered by the tremendous contemporary industrial and economic renovation and expansion, diverted men's minds at the outset from the perplexing problems of the peace settlement in the South. What was to be done with our 6,000,000 conquered rebels? How were we to treat with them? It was far less simple than treating with a subjugated foreign power. What was to be done with the colored freedmen? Were they to be given full civil rights? Few voices as yet spoke of conferring suffrage upon them. Here were engrossing, delicate race and economic questions; and public opinion seemed aloof, vague, or indecisive. But had not the military problem itself, during the war years, appeared utterly insoluble? Surely the questions of peace would be answered with reason and dispatch where the difficulties of war had been met at so fearful a cost.

The lessons of Northern blundering and dissension in wartime should have given warning of a frightful peace to follow. Disputes as to the restoration of conquered territories had broken out among the allied factions and classes on the Union side before 1865, but the need for military unity, the system of emergency-decree government, had muffled their dangerous echoes. Lincoln, the Moderate Republican, had put forth in December, 1863, a tentative plan for the restoration of semi-civil local government in three of the conquered provinces; Congress, led by the Radical Republicans Senator Wade of Ohio and Representatives Henry Winter Davis and Thaddeus Stevens, offered in July, 1864, a different, harsher plan in the Wade-Davis Bill, to which Lincoln gave a "pocket veto." Afterward leaders of Congress challenged the President's authority in this field with a vigorous resolution of censure, the Wade-Davis Manifesto. The successful election canvass of 1864 would seem to have supported fully the President's more lenient doctrines. Yet Lincoln did not deceive himself concerning the difficulties of Reconstruction in the South which were to be faced after the war. Stanton, his aggressive Secretary of War, had offered his resignation in a last interview before the President's death; and Lincoln, tears filling his eyes, as Stanton related, had said: "Stanton, you cannot go. Reconstruction is more difficult and dangerous than construction or destruction . . . you must help us through the final act. The bag is filled. It must be tied, and tied securely." [1]

The people were weary and indifferent; the soldiers themselves and their leaders were conciliatory toward the enemy. But the politicians were otherwise, and their hour had come again. News of General Sherman's gallant conditions of surrender offered to A. S. Johnston's defeated army brought at once a resounding public rebuke from Secretary Stanton and enforcement of severer terms by Congress.

What was, then, to be the diplomacy of peace in America? Despite the savagery of the war, the victors were disposed to be magnanimous. How was it that they were turned shortly toward a program of peace which involved subjugation of the conquered territories by

force for more than a decade, breeding hates fiercer than those of
bloody battle—hates flowing from daily petty oppression in civil life,
hence deeper, more malignant by far than the momentary, physical
emotion of war?

A brief season, a summer of calm before Congress convened, then
the war of words, the storm of partisan controversy broke in all its
force of towering and theatrical passion. The conquerors, yesterday
so firmly united, were today strangely at odds, even at blows
amongst themselves, over the disposition of the conquered. Against
moderate counsels which urged a speedy pacification of the rebel
States and promptest return from a degrading military rule to
"proper and practical relations with the Union," as Lincoln had
phrased it—these counsels coming chiefly from the circle of the Administration, the new President, Andrew Johnson of Tennessee—
strident voices of Northern "Jacobins," or "Radicals," were raised
in opposition, and cried for a Carthaginian peace. These now demanded in sternest, revolutionary tones a pitiless vengeance, the full,
forcible subjugation of the Southern former rebels, treatment of
their States as conquered provinces, continued suppression of their
civil rights, even confiscation of their lands—in short, the complete
breakup of their institutions, their customs, their society.

What demon had entered into the souls of the politicians at
Washington? What madness whipped them steadily to a pitch of
hate and fury which the people were so far from sharing or comprehending? What the true motives, the concrete interests, behind
their verbal bombardments, their legal batteries, their propaganda,
with which they conducted thunderous campaigns and skillfully
manipulated or flanked public opinion?

Peace had come, but there was no peace. The strident demands of
politicians and interested groups mingled discordantly with lyrical professions of patriotism, of devotion to the national safety. A peculiar,
distinguishing trait of the chaotic years of Reconstruction, it has been
said, was the marriage of the Protective Tariff and the Bloody Shirt.
The men who had borne arms no longer wished to fight, General
Sherman wrote to his brother, the Senator from Ohio. But he feared
that the politicians were ready to "prolong the war ad infinitum." [2]

II

Ours has been a jealous, quarrelsome republic of bourgeois, a strong element among its egalitarian citizens, in surprising degree, being ever suspicious of high authority, impatient of powerful leadership. The tone of political controversy is seldom polite or ceremonial, and the spirit of our popular tribunes often violent and vulgar in their partisanship, though Roman senators too were sometimes far meaner, far less dignified than conventional history pictures them. We have also among our people a tradition of eating up even great military leaders, chewing away the bay leaves of their glory—a tradition which is not without its virtues in a republic of free men. After every major war we have rent in pieces the autocratic power of the war leader or the President who served for a time as Commander in Chief. In the striking transition from war government to civil life in 1865 such a revolt, such a fate, was prepared also for the sagacious leader Lincoln.

Mr. Lincoln, as the rebel armies retreated in 1865, and especially in the several days following Appomattox, possessed the authority almost of an Augustus Caesar. As one of his contemporaries and partisans has recalled, he

stood triumphant in every public relation—chosen by an almost unprecedented vote to his second term, the rebellion conquered, the Union firmly re-established! Never since Washington's exalted position at the close of the Revolution, or his still more elevated station when he entered the Presidency, has there been a man in the United States of so great personal power and influence as Mr. Lincoln then wielded.[3]

For most of four years, the Administration, the "White House," had been supreme in our Government. Yet Lincoln was to have been assailed as Washington was assailed and humiliated. The terms of the Wade-Davis Manifesto of 1864 left no doubt on this score. His preferred course in Reconstruction after the war would have brought new accusations of "rash and fatal" acts; of striking "a blow at the rights of humanity and at the principles of republican government." The powerful autocrat of war, who for four years had exercised leadership in person or through his cabinet officers, would have been sternly admonished anew that the support of the Republican Party was "of a cause and not of a man"; that "the authority of Congress is paramount and must be respected"; that he must "confine himself to his executive duties—to obey and execute, not make the laws." But Mr. Lincoln, resourceful, patient, leader of his party, fell before the pistol of Booth, and the brunt of the party uprising prepared for him was to be borne by his successor.

The nation-wide political controversy over Reconstruction burst forth in the autumn of 1865 and raged for three years as a struggle first upon constitutional grounds between the two strongest branches of our Government, Congress and the President, then for ten years thereafter on other grounds, largely as a conflict between the two great parties. It was strife as unforgiving as the economic-sectional strife of the 1850's on the eve of the "irrepressible conflict." Its issues and terms at the period were as confused, as distorted, as contradictory, as those of any controversy in our recent history. Partisans of both camps were heard to appeal now to "eternal principles" and now to unreasoning hate, passion, and particular prejudice. They invoked the doctrines of the Declaration of Independence, of "natural rights," of universal liberty and equality, but turned also to time-serving bargains. They swore to defend sacred human rights, but stooped also to intrigues in the advantage of an interested group or party.

In short, the stormy epoch of Reconstruction, tragic and burlesque in turn, with its principal actors heroic and ignoble at once, its glimpses of idealism in partnership with fraud and chicane, with all its glaring contradictions between ideology and interest, between "eternal principles of truth and right" and class-economic necessities —this is a most fruitful period, a vastly instructive one for historical analysis. With its social circumstances strongly resembling and linked to those of modern times, this period may well serve as a point of departure for our inquiry into modern political institutions, which will seek always *the differences between that which men say and that which they mean in politics.*

In the struggle over Reconstruction, on one side men seemed to range themselves with those who would strengthen the Union, preserve the fruits of the victory over the secessionists, at once centralize and strengthen our federal form of government and extend liberty and suffrage to all men. On the other side were aligned apparently those sincere devotees of particularism and sectionalism who ardently cherished local liberties, States' Rights or home rule, all the protective rights granted by our Constitution to preserve men from despotic power and authority in the days before such principles became the subterfuge of corporate capitalism. Such general principles were certainly invoked by the leading spokesmen of each side.

But we soon see that the statesmen who championed universal suffrage and hence Negro suffrage, incidentally or concomitantly or with affected innocence were concerned as well with quite worldly things and pecuniary measures of enormous potency: with the defense of a new national banking system introduced during the war, with the repayment in gold specie of the national war debt, with a system of taxation known as the protective tariff, which had wrought epoch-making changes in everyday life. Their opponents, while espousing in general terms traditional local liberties and rights of self-government against a "grasping, centralized despotism," often—whether hailing from Ohio and Indiana or from Tennessee—show themselves indifferent or uniformly hostile to the new banking system, to the new mode of taxation, that is, the protective tariff; they are even largely unconvinced as to the "sacredness" of the war debt.

Finally, when we perceive how the leading statesmen of the struggle against slavery compromise in the end, exchanging, for instance, the concrete realization of Negro suffrage in the South for the mere formal or legal appearance thereof—eventually abandoning the Negro freedman almost wholly to his old masters—we begin to doubt strongly the truthfulness of the general principles and motives declared at the outset of the struggle. We wonder whether the *incidental* or concomitant objects in view were not the de facto ones, while the "eternal principles" invoked were but the de jure ones. We confront the profound contradictions between ideology and interest; between the mask and parade—the theatrical dueling of prejudice, associations of thought, patriotic sentiment, illusions—and the naked clash of different conditions of existence, different forms of property and economy, such as those of the town and country, of capital and landed property. Behind the marching songs and slogans of the Ins and the Outs, the epithets of "Copperheads," "rebels," "traitors," and the answering ones of "tyrant," or "Scalawag," we must grasp at the pecuniary objects, the genuine, concrete interests, the real stakes being played for, as in every historic social conflict.

Just as, in private life, we draw a distinction between what a human being thinks and says of himself, and what he really is and does, so, "and even more definitely in the struggles of history, must we differentiate between the phrases and fancies of the political parties and their true organic entity, their genuine interests, must distinguish appearance from reality." [4]

The Civil War was of course no pure and simple struggle over slavery or States' Rights. The preponderance of wealth lay in manufacturing rather than in agriculture after 1850. Practically all of the iron and textile manufacturing trade was in the control of the Northern bourgeoisie by 1860; over two-thirds of the banking capital, the greatest portion of the foreign shipping, more than three-quarters of the white population, mechanics and free farmers, were on the Northern side. Yet we must remember that the slaveowners of the South, carrying with them up to 1860 the agriculturists of the South and the West, had held a strategic balance of power for a generation, dominated the nation's policy, raised barriers of a feudal economy against the industrial destiny of the nation. The slave oligarchy held power and office, and under the system of party patronage established since 1828 used the very funds of the national Treasury to buttress their political power. They rebelled at last when these advantages could no longer be maintained.

When the slaveowners burst into insurrection, foreseeing the fatal turn of events, the Northern capitalist States moved to crush their rebellion. But also, once engaged in the conflict, the progressive bourgeoisie of the North sought not only to destroy the enemy but to complete their own revolution—the swift completion of the bourgeois revolution which had been begun in the eighteenth century. The Northern Whigs who for a generation under Webster and Clay— indifferent to the small cry of the Abolitionists—had shown an overweening appetite for measures encouraging to business, for a national banking system, for internal improvements of rivers and harbors and a protective tariff, for Pacific Railway subsidies and free homesteads —all the things which the Southern political power had barred—were led at last to join, adventitiously enough, in the struggle for "union and liberty." Whether Democrats or Whigs formerly, "the industrial classes, by a sort of instinct of self-preservation as it seemed to them, began to consolidate their votes in favor of the Republican party." [5]

But masses of people, free farmers and laborers, may not easily be led into bloody battle to endure hunger, torture, weariness, and death for a new banking act, or a 47 per cent ad valorem tariff upon imports. It was in the name of patriotism, freedom and equal rights for all men, and free soil—doctrines proclaimed sincerely no doubt by the more radical middle-class ideologues—that the liberty-loving Northern masses were stirred to action. "To hundreds of thousands of voters who took part in that memorable contest" (of 1860) and cast their ballots for Mr. Lincoln, as Blaine recalls, "the tariff was not even mentioned." Instead they were exhorted to aid free territory and resist the aggressions of the proslavery leaders of the South. But in the October elections in Pennsylvania, on whose outcome the whole national contest depended, the tariff was the real issue and had "a controlling influence not only in deciding the contest for political supremacy but in that more momentous struggle which was to involve the fate of the Union." [6]

Here, in accents which he made no effort to suppress, Curtin, the Republican candidate for the Governorship and the frank spokesman of the iron trade, asserted that Pennsylvania's sons were "pining for protection to their labor and their dearest interests." Indeed human liberty and the subvention of the iron trade became inextricably intertwined in his soul, so that he cried at once: "If you desire to become vast and great, protect the manufactures of Philadelphia. . . . All hail, liberty! All hail, freedom! freedom to the white man! All hail freedom general as the air we breathe!" [7]

Even while the fortunes of military contests in the Mississippi Valley or the Blue Ridge of Virginia were still in doubt, the political leaders of the industrial classes behind the lines in the North had quickly carried economic positions which decades of campaigning in peacetime had never gained. The immense orgy of spending, destroying, and producing precipitated by the war—the awarding of fabulous public contracts, the feverish rise of prices, the geometric multiplication of the national debt, and the quickened circulation of an inflated money—contributed to these ends. Moreover, the war party, as it sat in Congress sternly voting day by day measures supporting full military action toward crushing opposition, almost unchallenged, enacted a series of sweeping laws which entrenched in power the new dominant class and encompassed the ruin of the old regime as surely as had the laws of the revolutionary French Convention in 1789-93. Noteworthy was the drastic Morrill Tariff Act, which a practical Republican leader privately declared to Justin Morrill was the most important single piece of legislation of the century. The new national banking act of 1863 and the subsequent law of 1865, striking down state banks, were also the realization of a purpose pursued since Jackson had destroyed the United States Bank in 1836; they enriched enormously the financial and fund-owning class. Likewise the historic Homestead Act of 1862 threw open to settlement and exploitation by free capitalists and farmers the vast public domain of cheap land with all its forest and underground mineral resources, a movement which the Southern oligarchy had resisted tenaciously, and which a Democratic President, Buchanan, had blocked with his veto as recently as 1860. Significant also, and passed off as a military measure, was the Pacific Railway Act, the first large-scale subsidy to railroad enterprise, long championed by the Northern Whigs, whereby the Government advanced "loans" of over $54,000,000 in bonds to railroad promoters and awarded them outright land grants in addition of some 22,000,000 acres, that the eastern and western shores of the continent might be bound together at last. But most drastic of all, and surpassing any of the decrees of confiscation with which the revolutionary Convention in Paris struck at the old regime, was the confiscation of some $3,000,000,000 of property in the form of Negro slaves liberated by decree on January 1, 1863. This was done with the spirit of the General Franco of the Union armies: "Our duty is not to build up; it is rather to destroy both the rebel army and whatever of wealth or property it has founded its boasted strength upon." [8]

The new industrialist and financial class and the farmers of the North emerged the greatest gainers by far among the mixed coalition of classes which fought to win the social revolution underlying the War between the States. But no less triumphant and dominant was the war party itself, the youthful organization of professional politicians and officeholders known as the Republican Party, and the instrument of the great progressive bourgeois revolution of 1861-65.

A minority party in 1860, and victor in a three-cornered electoral contest, it knew during the war the intoxication of unchallenged power and fortune beyond calculation. Must this be relinquished? Its formidable adversaries had deserted en masse, leaving it in command of all the offices of the Federal Government!

It had the management of the gigantic war finances, through which it attached to itself the interests . . . of the great capitalists and bankers throughout the North. It raised revenues by a high tariff which placed thousands of manufacturers under debt to it and linked their fortunes also with its fate. . . . Railway financiers and promoters of all kinds had to turn to it for privileges and protection. Finally millions of farmers of the West owed their homes to its generous policy of giving away public lands. Never had a party had its foundations on interests ramifying throughout such a large portion of society.

And over all it spread the mantle of patriotism. . . . The promises of the Declaration of Independence had been fulfilled and the heroic deeds of the Revolution rivaled by Republican leaders.[9]

Of this national party, while the more numerous Free Soil farmers, the laborers, and the patriotic lower middle classes gave it numbers, the Northern capitalist class composed the right wing, and was the most persistent, articulate, resolute among the several partners. The business-minded Secretary of State, Seward, had said earlier that the political party was "a joint stock association, in which those who contribute most direct the action and management of the concern." [10] This was in a measure true by 1865—yet we must not assume simply that the fighting, crusading political party of Lincoln, Greeley, Sumner, and Stevens in its vigorous youth was wholly the alter ego, the "damned soul," or the entirely submissive concubine, of the Northern bourgeoisie. It had, as we shall see, by its very composition important and divergent reasons for existence.

In addition to considering the special interests of its biggest "stockholders," the management of the Republican Party faced after 1865 the problem of consolidating their victory and preserving the fruits thereof. American traditions, the peculiar form of our laws and customs which made the political party an unwritten, an unconstitutional arm of the Government, an institution in itself, with peculiar "institutional" interests of its own, an imperium in imperio—all these worked to the end that the successful war party should endeavor to perpetuate itself, to retain governmental power "for its own sake," even after its historic mission should have been fulfilled and need for its presence was seemingly ended. Thus "class motives" combined perfectly with "institutional" or party motives to the same end. Hence toward the close of the military conflict the party leaders looked with increasing anxiety toward the future day when the emergency war government must give way to civil government. Its managers scanned more sharply than all other items those acts of President Lincoln which restored conquered sections of the rebel South to the Union, and which promised to affect adversely its grip on the electoral situation. On this ground they were willing to assail Mr. Lincoln, and reminded him during the session of December, 1864, by a joint resolution of Congress that Louisiana and Arkansas, temporarily restored to the Union by him, were "not entitled to representation in the Electoral College."

This resolution reveals how even in the winter of 1864-65 the Republican Party leaders were secretly obsessed by the fear of becoming again a minority party. Even in the twenty-three Union States, only 55 per cent of the vote in the presidential election of 1864 had been Republican. The Democratic, antiwar vote was thus a big minority. What, then, if eleven unregenerate States were quickly returned to constitutional relations with the Union? They assailed Lincoln on this ground; they would fall upon his successor, too, should his policies threaten or jeopardize the retention of power by the war party.

Strong epithets, resounding appeals, in the name of patriotism and national safety do not necessarily frighten cool, hard-fisted capitalists.

The manufacturers and bankers of the Northeast could be depended upon by the war party in the peacetime that followed. But the simpler, more responsive masses of farmers and workers, especially those of the West who had fought for free soil, or "voted themselves a farm," could certainly be moved by such alarmist methods and held in line for years to come. As they cast about in search of policy, the war-party leaders determined instinctively to "prolong the war," to maintain the appearance of national danger. For them the problem of retention of power becomes at any rate the key problem with which the fate of the white rebel, as of the Negro freedman, is linked as the controversy over Reconstruction opens.

But in the war of words which now engulfed the new bourgeois republic—a war which also verged often upon coercion and violence —these material considerations, naturally, would seldom be referred to by the politician-ideologues. Yet this subterfuge, an occupational vice concerning which the reader has already been warned, must not be permitted to confuse our judgment, drawn from the historical perspective of today.

The era of Reconstruction has led to later controversies among American historians almost as twisted as those which marked the epoch itself. It seems evident that to get at the essence of what happened we must follow two threads of investigation: (1) that which touches upon all the action which the ruling political party takes in self-interest, that is, as an "institution" seeking to exist per se; and (2) the action taken in the interests of its most important allies, its "chief stockholders" and principal paymasters, the Northern business class, the class that was most articulate, reached and swayed all organs of opinion, that knew most surely what it wanted. The purely partisan or professional battles into which the Republican Party was plunged by its leaders immediately after the war, and which we take up first, in some detail, is therefore to be seen as only half of the story.

III

The outcome of the conflict between President Johnson and Congress over the policy of Reconstruction has often been treated as an instance of the victory of congressional over presidential authority in our Government. It might be described more accurately as the triumph of the Republican Party Organization over the Presidency.

Aided by the patriotic impetus provided by the war, and by an advanced development of parliamentary rules, of committee and caucus action, there had been formed in Congress a sort of "Mountain," a closely knit body of unflinchingly loyal and Radical Congressmen. Habits of prompt, concerted party action were formed; subcommittees and steering committees set policies for the party caucus. Party structure, in short, reached its most efficient organization in our history and, creating a solid phalanx, supported Lincoln's military action. Month after month, the "Mountain" voted to send new drafts of soldiers to the front, to raise fabulous sums of money by taxation and loans or by fiat, to crush secret or open opposition behind the lines—all measures that, by bringing to bear a merciless unremitting pressure upon the rebels, would wear down their armies. The keynote of acrid, militant patriotism was set in the House by Thaddeus Stevens of Pennsylvania, the aged Republican floor leader, chairman of the powerful Ways and Means Committee; while in the Senate Charles Sumner of Massachusetts, the old-time champion of Emancipation, outdid all the others in sounding the notes of a fanatical idealism suiting the rigors of the time. Nor did Stevens and Sumner desist willingly with the coming of peace from breathing rhetorical fury upon the defeated rebel. With this resolute, unforgiving spirit they entered upon the problems of Reconstruction.

The plan of Lincoln had envisaged executive control of Reconstruction so that the intervention of professional party politicians in so complex a problem might be eliminated. By this plan there were to be established temporary State governments in the South based upon a loyal nucleus of some 10 per cent of the voting population who should have accepted the Thirteenth Amendment freeing the slaves, taken an oath of loyalty to the Union, and repudiated the war debt of the South. When President Johnson in 1865 followed the harsher program embraced in the project of the leading Radical Congressmen (the Wade-Davis Bill), they in turn were seen suddenly to have moved to a more advanced position; in more and more positive tones, harsher doctrines of Reconstruction, by no means embraced as yet by a majority of their own party, were now an-

nounced by them. These proposed the continued forcible subjugation of the former rebels, the grant of all civil rights and privileges,
including the right of suffrage, to the Negro freedmen, and even,
according to some extremist spokesmen, such as Senator Ben Wade
of Ohio, the confiscation of rebel lands and their distribution to the
freedmen. Stevens, Sumner, Wade, and the other Radical leaders
knew their own purpose, but doubted strongly that the majority of
their party, with its Moderate Republican elements and its converted
Whigs and Democrats, could be brought over to their views.

The Radical leaders communicated with each other frequently in
the lull of the summer of 1865, and laid plans to capture the party
machinery in Congress. On August 26, 1865, Stevens, in a letter to
Sumner, privately advised that they must first "get the rebel states
in a territorial condition," so that Negro suffrage could "be easily
dealt with." He continued: "That, I think, should be our great aim.
Then Congress can manage it." Also, looking forward already to
the party elections of 1866, he added: "We need a good committee
on elections." The further plan was "to exclude all rebel state members until final reorganization"—according to Radical ideas.[11]

Charles Sumner, the New England "scholar in politics" who was
considered the foremost orator of the time, stood now at the very
height of his power. He was a man of "exalted moral fervor and
humanitarian idealism" who "lived in the empyrean and descended
thence with eternal principles which he discovered there and promul-
gated by preaching incessantly to his colleagues." [12] "It sometimes
seemed as if Sumner thought the Rebellion itself was put down by
speeches in the Senate," his friends felt.[13] However, though egotisti-
cal and dogmatic, and given to a pedantic form of oratorical eloquence, Sumner was a powerful ideologue in the service of his party.
That he believed single-mindedly and devoutly in the truth of his
chosen principles (like Robespierre, who also ignored intellectual
contradictions in his own policies) made him even more formidable
in a political contest.

Sumner encouraged the inflation of party feeling by his moral
fervor, while from his eyes, fixed on distant horizons, the meanness
of partisan maneuvers was happily concealed. For him, the Republican Party was holy; all who were not traitors to the Union and

humanity were bound to be with it. His triumphant party he decked with the glory of having established forever the principles and pledges of universal liberty and equality made by the Revolutionary Fathers.

Before the close of the war, Sumner advocated firmly the reorganization of the rebel States "on the footing of the Declaration of Independence," as he wrote to John Bright, "with all persons equal before the law, and government founded on the consent of the governed. . . . If all whites must vote, then must all blacks." [14] Sumner could weep at the lot of the Negro but "would filibuster to the end of the session to prevent the restoration to the southern whites of rights which were essential to their whole conception of life." [15] He also embraced at times the truly radical and logical doctrine of confiscation of the lands of the slave masters "as ancillary to emancipation"; the great plantations, he urged, "so many nurseries of the rebellion, must be broken up and the freedmen must have the pieces." [16]

In Thaddeus Stevens of Pennsylvania, the leader of Congress during the war, the victorious Northern bourgeoisie had their militant spokesman, a true radical of the industrial revolution.* Born during the term of President Washington, the Pennsylvanian was a wrinkled apparition out of the early days of the republic. In the 1830's Stevens, then a lawyer, had earned local renown through his fight for the establishment of free common schools in his State. He was a "commoner" to his public, a man of enlightened, even freethinking views. He believed himself a leader of the party of progress, a friend of the plain people, a champion not only of the black but of the white

---

* Much confusion has prevailed over the sense of the party name of "Radicals" given to the extreme wing of the Republican Party. They have been described as "radical" only with regard to Reconstruction in the South, and allied with big capitalism, railroads, national bankers, and railroad barons in the North, hence truly opposed to all that passes for "radicalism" nowadays. Such a view, however, is historically naïve and superficial; it ignores the phenomena of progressive and even revolutionary ideology which surges up with a new, conquering class of society, such as was the combined force of free farmers and new industrial capitalists. The new capitalism and the revolutionary sentiment of the Republican Party in its youth become so mixed that they cannot be distinguished from each other for the moment. Charles Sumner, the doctrinaire leader of the New England groups, for instance, saluted the proletarian uprising in France in 1848 as part of a world movement toward universal freedom, in which he was proud to participate.

masses. As a Whig and as a Republican, he had fought for the extension of universal suffrage, for free soil, for the opening of the public domain to the people, for all measures which might encourage industry and trade. To Stevens's mind, new railroads, new factories and foundries, all the busy, profitable industry of the North, were linked with the grand march of humanity toward a more productive and fuller life, while the world of the Southern plantation embodied the ways of sloth, backwardness, and darkness itself. To the aristocracy of the land Stevens had long ago dedicated his undying hate, a hate imbued with a fanaticism reminiscent of the French Jacobins.

Hate, fanaticism, as an instrument of party action toward a desired end Stevens well understood, as he understood and used the tactics of political intrigue and corrupt bargain. During his long career in local and national politics he had slowly become, by the force of his personality, his intellectual power, his fighting will, the pre-eminent party leader, as dominant over his fellow Republicans as was Henry Clay over the Whigs. For the sake of his party—"right or wrong, his party"—he would scatter confusion among his opponents, even if truth or logic buttressed the other side. "Throw conscience to the Devil and stand by your party" was an axiom widely attributed to him. To hold his followers in line, Stevens wielded patronage with a stern hand. Those who considered straying from "allegiance to principle" for the sake of "a few rations" he menaced with the fire and brimstone of party damnation. Hearing that President Johnson offered members of the war party certain Federal offices, he addressed a public meeting in the following terms:

I warn you to keep an eye on any professed Republican who consents to fill an enforced vacancy. . . . He is a moral leper whom you should not touch. He should be socially ostracized as unfit for decent society. Let him flit about in the twilight and hide his averted countenance from the light of day.[17]

Though a fanatic outwardly, this harsh and angry old man was possessed of much humor, and could turn in his public speeches from passionate eloquence or close-gripping argument to full mockery of his opponents. It has been held that Stevens's own business interests, as owner of an iron foundry, a newspaper publisher, and a lawyer friendly to the new railroads, colored his political doctrines. Yet Stevens showed himself far more tenacious and successful in accumulating political power than in accumulating gold. While scandal stained nearly all of his associates who labored with him in the midst of the legislative carnival for special interests, Thad Stevens's name remained impeccable. By his policy, the capitalists of the North were to be treated as allies worthy of high reward; but no less fondly were the interests of the masses of free Western farmers regarded so long as Stevens lived and ruled his party. To the alarm of great bankers, Stevens, as one of his last actions, delayed the resumption of gold-specie payment and spared the Greenback, so that the demand of agriculturists for inflated money and favorable prices might not be denied.

Then, full of a fire that seemed to consume him, Stevens knew how to appeal to the generous emotions of youth, calling to the masses of friends of liberty to aid him in his sacred cause. The issue of the time was no mere question of taxation or constitutional law, he declared in his speech at Lancaster in the summer of 1865:

Young men, this duty [of supporting Radical principles] devolves on you. Would to God, if only for that, that I were still in the prime of life, that I might aid you to fight through this last and greatest battle of Freedom![18]

In this same speech, before Congress convened again, he also sounded the keynote of the Radical campaign:

The whole fabric of southern society *must* be changed, and never can it be done if this opportunity is lost . . . How can republican institutions, free schools, free churches, free social intercourse exist in a mingled community of nabobs and serfs; of the owners of twenty-thousand acre manors with lordly palaces, and the occupants of narrow huts inhabited by "low white trash"? If the south is ever to be made a safe republic let her lands be cultivated by the toil of the owners or the free labor of intelligent citizens. This must be done even though it drive her nobility into exile![19]

The country would be well rid of the "proud, bloated, defiant rebels." The foundations of their institutions must be broken up and relaid, "or all our blood and treasure have been spent in vain."

The Southern States in his view should be treated as conquered territory, and not as States which had never left the Union and with which legal and constitutional relations could be speedily renewed. Hence only Congress, and not the President, had authority over the admission and representation of new States. The freedmen were each to be given "forty acres and a mule." He gave warning also: *"Let all who approve of these principles tarry with us. Let all others go with Copperheads and rebels. Those will be the opposing parties."* [20]

The Union had been saved by blood and iron; but now it becomes increasingly clear to the minds of the war leaders that the Republican Party must be saved and kept in power. This preoccupation filled the private correspondence of the Radical leaders, Stevens and Sumner, as we have noted. In his letter to the great English Liberal John Bright, Sumner had argued on high grounds of humanity, reason, and justice. But he had also mingled instinctively with these reasons arguments on grounds of *necessity*. Was the freedman, but yesterday a slave, intelligent enough to vote? But the question had become more "practical" than merely that.

Without their [the Negroes'] votes we cannot establish stable governments in the rebel States. Their votes are as necessary as their muskets. . . . Without them the old enemy will re-appear, and under the forms of law take possession of the governments, choose magistrates and officers, and in alliance with the Northern Democracy, put us all in peril again, postpone the day of tranquillity, and menace the national credit by assailing the national debt. To my mind, the nation is now bound by self-interest—ay, self-defence—to be thoroughly just. . . . Mr. Lincoln is slow in accepting truths. [21]

Even in their official reports and public declarations the partisan or "institutional" motives of the Radical Republicans showed their horns and cloven feet. Major General Carl Schurz, the German revolutionist who escaped to the United States after 1849, became famous as a journalist and an orator, and led divisions of German soldiers in the battles for the Union, was one of a number of Northern observers who were invited by the President to journey through the conquered States in 1865 and make impartial reports of conditions and prospects there. What Schurz saw led him to advocate before President Johnson the extension of the franchise to the Negro freedmen, though, as he admitted, "the masses are strongly opposed to colored suffrage." The question of fitness of the former slaves was considered secondary. He feared that the unrepentant white Southerners planned by one device or another to reintroduce their "peculiar institution," to limit and oppose free black labor. This was true enough, and one of the essential issues which the Republican Party ultimately abandoned. But, Schurz argued, by the introduction of Negro suffrage surveillance of the Southern States by the National Government would be made less necessary.

The whole problem of political and social reconstruction [could] be made simplified, if, while the masses lately arrayed against the government are permitted to vote, the large majority of those who were always loyal and are naturally anxious to see the free labor problem successfully solved, were not excluded from all influence upon legislation. In all questions concerning the Union, national debt and the future social organization of the South, the feelings of the colored man are naturally in sympathy with the views and aims of the national government . . . [vide Republican Party leaders]. While the Southern white sees in the national government his conqueror, the Negro sees in it his protector; while the white owes to the national debt his defeat, the Negro owes to it his deliverance.[22]

Schurz was not a native Yankee, he was a man of learning, and he was believed to be uninfluenced by sectional partisanship, yet, as President Johnson found out soon afterward, his voyage was secretly arranged and largely subsidized by Sumner and his Radical friends in Boston. Under a nom de guerre, Schurz's reports from the field had appeared also as propaganda in a newspaper friendly to the Radical program.

The intensity of the Radical educational propaganda was redoubled, before Congress opened, as suspicion spread of a change of heart in President Johnson. His Proclamation of Amnesty and Reconstruction, May 29, 1865, showed the Radical Republicans that he meant to pursue a conciliatory course of his own choosing, involving a loyal restoration of the Southern States, but under the control of their native white citizens who had recanted; his determination thereafter in adhering to this program, despite loud protests from the Radical faction, convinced Stevens that the President could not be turned aside, that the Radicals must therefore, as he wrote privately to Sumner, "be bold enough to lay the foundation of a party to take the helm of this government, and keep it off the rocks." [23]

In the last week of November, 1865, as politicians gathered in Washington for the opening of Congress, and for secret caucuses and conferences among themselves, Charles Sumner saw the President for a long private interview. He had admired Johnson, but now found him deeply "changed . . . and unreasonable" in his views. Sumner left him never to see him again, convinced that he was set like flint against the good cause, and that with the assassination of Lincoln "rebellion had vaulted into the presidential chair." [24]

Plans had been laid cautiously, and were unfolded at the Republican Party caucus. Schuyler Colfax, Radical partisan from Indiana, who had delivered an attack upon the Administration upon his arrival in Washington, was re-elected Speaker of the House. Whatever uncertainty may have prevailed among the majority of Republicans, initiative in action was taken brusquely by Stevens. He proposed that a Joint Committee of Fifteen of the two houses be chosen, to which all questions concerning admission of members from the Southern States were to be submitted without debate. This was accepted. The Joint Committee of Fifteen was intended to be something more than a tribunal dealing with admissions of members, as the President's advisers soon realized. Emergency tactics were spurred by reports of sporadic disorders in the South; the joint resolution establishing this committee as an engine of strategic power was railroaded through Congress on a strict party vote, even before the President's message was read. Stevens, "sharp-faced, grim-looking," had quelled resistance by Moderate Republicans and dominated the caucus.[25] Bold party intrigue and swift action had swept the Opposition off their feet and placed the Radicals in a commanding position for the contest with the President.[26] The President and his advisers thought the Radicals' moves too highhanded and too bold; their audacity was expected to rebound against them.

As a test case, a Tennessee Unionist, Maynard, a member of the House since the war—a man unquestionably loyal, like Johnson—presented himself for recognition, but was denied admission to Congress; his name was stricken from the rolls.

IV

Andrew Johnson, the "poor white," the self-educated tailor and political stump speaker from eastern Tennessee, had taken a most vital part in the coalition for the defense of the Union. In former years in the Senate he had denounced secession in terms more unforgiving and uncompromising than Seward's or Sumner's; as Military Governor of Tennessee during the war he had been an apostate to the majority of the people of his State, ravaged and bleeding, tragically divided by the very battle lines of the armies. "Treason is a crime and traitors must be hung!" he had cried in the heat of the civil struggle. Johnson's home, his family, his own life, had been frequently imperiled in the bitter, immediate struggle between brother citizens.

The eastern highlands of Tennessee held few Negro slaves; they were peopled by independent small farmers. The proportion of whites to blacks at the time of the war was said to be twenty-seven to one. This region was moreover the cradle of the Jacksonian agrarian Democracy, of which Johnson himself—in opposition to the plantation aristocrats—was an outspoken, even an extremist, leader for those days. For years he had fought for a Homestead Act in unison with Northern Whigs, so that the public domain might be thrown open to settlers. He was an opponent of slavery, as of secession, in its very home. He was a common man, the friend of common men, as he often boasted, and his plain, weather-beaten, lined workingman's face went to prove it. Among the several categories of former rebels to whom he refused pardon was the class having "over twenty thousand dollars in taxable property"—a distinction which aroused the derision of certain Republican opponents.[27] But while fighting secession, he was no Hamiltonian, but rather a stanch believer in home rule, in local government and local rights guaranteed by our Federal Constitution.

The President was disposed emotionally—when now the decision and responsibility descended upon him—to let the fighting cease, to receive the enemy in full fellowship again, to trust him, to leave him his liberties again. With regard to the question of suffrage in the rebel States, he was "conservative," as he was radical on other grounds; it must be decided, he believed with Lincoln, in a constitutional manner, that is, by option of the citizens.*

That Tennessee, a very large minority of whose citizens had paid a fearful price for their loyalty to the Union—as Johnson often proudly related—should be held even temporarily as conquered territory outraged his sentiments, and impressed him with the injustice being prepared for the white Southerners. On this ground he clearly opposed leaders of the North such as Stevens and Sumner, who also professed themselves friends of the common man.

On the other hand, the plight of the Negro masses, destined to slip back into a renewed and ill-disguised servitude unless thoroughgoing social reforms were decreed, Johnson regarded with something of the racial fanaticism of the Southern whites—if not with the stony indifference sometimes attributed to "poor whites" as a competitive labor group in the South. Of the political incapacity of the freedmen he was firmly convinced; he sought a realistic, a gradual rather than a precipitate, solution of this problem.

As the requirements of the President's proclamation were met in somewhat summary fashion by quickly called State conventions in the South, their "reconstruction" as provisional governments proceeded apace. The question of their representation in the Federal Congress Johnson cautiously did not raise at the beginning, leaving this for Congress itself to decide. Taking the position that he had no constitutional warrant to fix suffrage qualifications in the separate States by decree, he ignored all questions arising from the fact that Negro freedmen were excluded from State conventions, and that certain Southern States promised to bar Negroes forever from civil rights or suffrage by so-called Black Codes.

When the cry for Negro suffrage arose from the Radical wing among the Unionists in the North, Johnson became suspicious. He promptly saw a dark plot carried on in the name of justice to the freedmen, to fan race hate and race conflict, to fix an ignoble form of slavery upon white men. This was to be imposed from above

* The circumstance that a man who was no Republican, and differed from them on so many grounds, was nominated in 1864 for Vice-President arose from a habit of compromise long formed in our party conventions, and a desire as well to emphasize the policy of Unionist coalition of all loyal groups during the war.

on behalf of a despotic, central party organization, which, though having but a minority of the electorate behind it, grasped for a permanent rulership by fraud. Human liberty was synonymous with local liberty, consecrated by our federal form of government, or, as he said often in his public papers, "a government of limited powers, with a written constitution and with boundaries both State and National." Here was a new Hamiltonian conspiracy, dictated by professional politicians in league with massive financial interests such as he had opposed his life long, in the North as well as in the South.

Much injustice done to this old-fashioned Jacksonian Democrat by partisan writers has been repaired lately; his courageous, impetuous, and impolitic character has been much rehabilitated and restored by modern scholarship. Andrew Johnson throughout his stormy career was veritably a victim of history. In earlier life, his unflinching independence had made him a "bad" Democrat in the party sense; in later life, raised to the highest office by alliance with the Unionist Republicans, he proved to be no "good" Republican.

With every step, as his program unfolded, the new President had progressively alienated the Radical wing of the Republicans, who had originally counted him one of their own denomination and set him in office. They aimed to proscribe the Confederate leaders; the President pardoned most of them, excepting the prominent military men and firebrands; they sought to confiscate rebel lands, and the Administration's procedure barred this; they sought the enfranchisement of the Negroes, and Johnson's proclamations returned the power of this decision to the local governments of former rebels; they would have delayed the reorganization of the Southern States, under military rule, until the ascendancy of Negro voters would guarantee, as Sumner hinted, the permanent subjection of the historic party of opposition, the Democrats; Johnson's plan sought support among the Moderate Republicans, and above all tended to gain the adherence of a reunited mass of Democrats from North and South, already loud in approval, and promising soon in an early renewal of old party life to sweep the extreme war party from control of the Government.

And Johnson, himself an old-fashioned campaigner, from a region where political debate was part of the life of the people, also used the weapon of ideology, of eternal principles, in behalf of his moderate, constitutional program. In a first message to the Thirty-Ninth Congress, in December, 1865, he argued upon the issue of Reconstruction that the way of military subjection for an indefinite period would surely fail to end discontent, "would have divided the people into the vanquishers and the vanquished, and would have envenomed hatred rather than have restored affection." If military rule were continued, who could set precise limits for its end? He held that the States in question had in effect never left the Union, their pretended secession having been from the beginning null and void. Hence he would follow the spirit of the Constitution in "bringing them back into practical relations with the Union," and see to it that they renewed their allegiance to the United States as quickly as possible, resuming their functions as States of the Union. The risk that was taken in bringing the Southerners back into the fold and believing in their acquiescence was worth taking. He insisted that the late rebel States adopt the Thirteenth Amendment setting free the Negroes, but maintained that as respected the qualifications for suffrage in each of the States "the General Government should not interfere, but leave that matter where it was originally left—in the Federal Constitution." [28] The whole paper breathed an honest abhorrence of military oppression and of a headstrong government centralism strengthened by war and victory. Returning to peace, Johnson would also grant again even to the men whom he had treated as traitors during the war, whose hanging he had demanded, the right to local self-rule in the domains fixed by the Federal Constitution.

Thus within a year of Appomattox there were offered by different branches of the Government two opposing programs of Southern restoration—or rather two conflicting tendencies or philosophies, since the program of the Radicals was tentative, bided its time, and hoped for the summoning of a stronger public sentiment in the North, where no little approval was at first voiced for the conciliatory spirit of the President's message.

The fierce political warfare which was declared with the opening of Congress over the terms of the Southern restoration assumed the form of an extraordinary contest between the two strongest branches of our Government, over the issue of presidential or congressional authority. Though the lines of party were not clearly drawn at first— for the Northern Democrats too were Unionists—the question of Reconstruction soon became the ground of battle between the historic party organizations, the Whig-Republicans and the reviving Democrats. The leaders of the Moderate and Radical factions, Johnson and Stevens, were soon wrought to a temper in which each firmly believed the other capable of the foulest villainy and treason. Each appealed to his partisans in the name of high doctrines: "constitutional justice" and "local rights," or "universal liberty" and "national safety." Each believed implicitly in the ideological superstructure which had taken empire over his mind. While behind the parties and leaders the interest of classes and sections, of powerful economic groups, was concealed—until the hour came when ideology and leader, shield and sword, could be thrown aside.

President Johnson had estimated too lightly the imponderable forces arrayed against his idea of Moderate Reconstruction, forces bound up with the prolongation of the war spirit and war conditions in peacetime. Nor did Johnson know how to appeal to the liberal elements in the North. Opposed by the Radicals, he grew more determined, vehement, immoderate, one might say, in his pursuit of Moderate Reconstruction. He became, perhaps unwittingly, identified with the tenacious self-defense carried on by the surviving landowning class in the South, a class which had formerly detested him. In the North he was allied inevitably with sections of the Democratic Party which had supported the war indifferently, people who had actually preached ideas of "frugality" or strict constitutional observance during a time of national disaster!*

The leader of Congress, Stevens, on the other hand, was supported for the time not only by the loyal masses of the North but also by

---

* "The bourgeoisie never rules as a whole; apart from the feudal castes, who have still retained some part of their political power, even the big bourgeoisie, as soon as it has defeated feudalism, splits into a ruling and an opposition party— which are usually represented here by the bank [of England] on the one side and the manufacturers on the other. The oppositional, progressive fraction of the big and middle bourgeoisie then has common interests with the petty bourgeoisie against the ruling fraction, and unites with it in a common struggle." (Engels, *Campaign for the German Constitution*, cited in Marx and Engels, *Letters*, International ed., p. 148.)

the great industrial and financial class, which sought to consolidate its victory—although its members often felt revulsion for certain of the party leaders' "leveling" or "extremist" doctrines.

Here the special circumstances of the party conflict shaping itself anew must be remarked above all. We must note first how the dispute was deliberately provoked, how fuel was added to it, how the fire was fanned by unseen hands, until the masterly disorder plunged the President's program into ruin. Second, we must note that the controversy was so conducted that it gave a fatal, *sectional* twist to the issues involved, distorting them, diverting all attention from the far more fundamental, decisive questions of the time, which were being dispatched almost secretly and with a high hand by the ring of politicians who mated the President and seized control of the state.

V

The plans of the congressional leaders involved "delay, delay, delay" at the outset. Sumner and his friends intended that while the Joint Committee of Fifteen was at work, Congress should occupy itself with "theories." The discussion must continue for months; Sumner, as he declared privately, did not see how it could be stopped, nor did he wish to see it stopped. The single point to be reached was the *assertion of jurisdiction by Congress,* he held. So long as all speakers reached this point, it mattered not what roads they took, and he hoped that they would "all . . . speak and ventilate their theories." [29]

Stevens, opening the long debate on December 18, raised the questions of whether the rebel States had not "left the Union" and whether they were not to be treated as conquered provinces—questions which Lincoln had ridiculed as irrelevant. Congress alone, and not the President, he held, had authority to restore the "conquered provinces." The Constitution stated that "the United States shall guarantee to every State in this Union a republican form of government." But who were the United States?

Not the judiciary, not the President; but the sovereign power of the people, exercised through their representatives in Congress, with the concurrence of the Executive. . . . The separate action of the President, or the Senate, or the House amounts to nothing in admitting new States or guaranteeing republican forms of government. . . . Whence springs the preposterous idea that any one of these acting separately can determine the right of states to send representatives or Senators to the Congress of the Union?[30]

The last vehement words were clearly a shaft aimed at President Johnson, and deeply offended him, though he was not named. Stevens hinted broadly that severely protective laws must be enacted on behalf of the former slaves against their old masters, "else we had better left them in bondage."

The rumble of speechmaking in House and Senate concealed for the moment the most burning anxieties of the Republican leaders. This was certainly true of the question of increased representation from the Southern States which would follow their readmission. Before the Thirteenth Amendment had been adopted, the Negro or slave population was counted at three-fifths of its number in apportioning members to Congress; with this clause void, the freedmen without voting would permit the return of 30 additional Congressmen from the Southern bloc, instead of 18 as formerly. Had the war been fought that the unrepentant rebel, now busily enacting the first Black Codes, might return with power augmented by the death of slavery?

The Joint Committee of Fifteen on Reconstruction named at the outset by Congress included Stevens in its membership and a majority of eight Republicans of the Radical stripe. It began at once to hold elaborate hearings of witnesses from the South, with a view to framing an Amendment which would ostensibly establish civil rights for the freedmen. In reality, they sought an Amendment which, as they admitted privately, would be "a means of protection for the Government and the North," that is to say, for the Republican Party. This was to be done by granting additional representation in Congress to the Southern States in proportion as they granted Negro suffrage; while, conversely, their failure to do so would bring, as a punitive measure, a proportionate loss of representation in Congress. The Southerners were confidently expected to reject an Amendment which would inflict a mass of Negro Republicans upon them, and by which statehood was to be denied to them as long as possible. Thus a permanent shifting of the geographical balance of party power was to be incorporated into the Constitution. Beyond this, the Joint Committee of Fifteen, driven by Stevens, George Boutwell of Massachusetts, Justin Morrill of Vermont, and Roscoe Conkling of New York, intended to raise the issue of the Fourteenth Amendment and its new bill of rights before the country; it was to be a veritable engine of party warfare against the Opposition.

The measures of Reconstruction enacted by Congress were as promptly vetoed by the President, and a tug of war strange in itself, yet familiar under our government of divided authority, began after February, 1866. Hostility beyond accommodation by the most determined compromisers declared itself; high words followed in mounting rhythm, and one by one Radical Congressmen rose up not only to "ventilate their theories," but to heap abuse upon the President.

At length, threatened and calumniated, Johnson replied in kind. On Washington's Birthday, before followers who serenaded him at the White House porch, the harassed President promised that he would fight the "disunionists" who passed Reconstruction bills which were "legal monstrosities" as he had fought the secessionists. Their measures embodied once more the principle of taxation without representation. Some of them had spoken of removing the presidential obstacle. "They may talk about beheading," cried Johnson, "but when I am beheaded, I want the American people to be the witness. . . . Are those who want to destroy our institutions . . . not satisfied with the blood that has been shed? Does not the blood of Lincoln appease the vengeance and wrath of the opponents of this government?"

The terms of Johnson's speech were not uncommon for the partisan action of the time, nor stronger than those of his adversaries. The important charge which he made in his impromptu address was that the Radicals pressed for autocratic power to control a numerous class, the Southern Negroes, for their own political ends. The Joint Committee of Fifteen itself, he contended, was "an irresponsible central directory." [31]

The Radicals not only made violent reply, and even public demonstrations against the President, but also persisted in their strenuous efforts to muster a two-thirds majority in the Senate, which was accomplished on March 23, 1866, by unseating a Moderate Republican from New Jersey.

Stevens's uprising against the President was victorious. Thereafter all measures designed to cement control of the conquered territories by the Republican Organization were quickly passed over vetoes. A Freedmen's Bureau Bill, carrying with it appropriations of millions of dollars to be disbursed by faithful agents of the party, a Civil Rights Bill, nullifying the so-called Black Codes lately enacted by defiant Southern communities, were both repassed in March. On April 30, 1866, the Fourteenth Amendment to the Constitution was reported, debated rather briefly, considering its importance, altered at length in some details; it was passed by a two-thirds majority on June 13.

The Fourteenth Amendment, sent to the State legislatures for ratification in the summer of 1866, served as a kind of Trojan Horse by which the citadel of former rebels and Democrats was stormed. It was a most complex affair, in truth, cunningly made of several different kinds of material and paint. The first clause, the first sentence, in simple yet majestic terms was a latter-day bill of human rights: "All persons born or naturalized in the United States are citizens of the United States and of the State wherein they reside." Under this brave proclamation the Radical knights confounded the enemy and called to all true patriots and sons of liberty in the North to elect Radical Republican Congressmen in 1866. The second sentence, concerning "due process," "property," and "equal protection before the laws," also had a fair, brave sound, but was scarcely understood until many years after; this as well as other provisions bespoke the special and diverse interests which moved the members of the famous Joint Committee of Fifteen on Reconstruction. The provisions with regard to property, as well as those for asserting the validity of the Union war debt while forcing the repudiation of rebel debts, appealed especially to one important, farsighted group in the Republican community of interests, that of the Northern capitalists. Those making leading Confederates ineligible for government office and restricting representation in Congress in accordance with the grant of Negro suffrage by States undoubtedly satisfied the institutional needs of the Republican Party Organization. The whole thing, moreover, had an equitable air, applying to all sections of the country, but though all but six Northeastern States excluded even limited suffrage for Negroes, the colored population was so small in the North that no loss of representation would result there.

At all events the new law was a guarantee against the prompt adoption of an independent, moderate, presidential program which would have injured the prospects of Republican Party control of the state. Stevens feared only that the terms given to the former rebels were too mild, milder than the treatment which "a provisional governor of Tennessee—I mean the late-lamented Andrew Johnson of blessed memory"—would have meted out, as he drily asserted. In the storm of war partisanship which the Radicals maintained unabated for two years, the adoption of the obscure Fourteenth Amendment was brought about by 1868. When the embittered President and the minority of ten Southern States unwisely opposed the new constitutional law, the hands of the Radicals were but strengthened; the moderate elements of their own party, in alarm, turned to support the more drastic steps of the Radical program which followed.

Both sides now arranged to "go to the people" with their case. The congressional elections of 1866 made the most exciting political season since Lincoln's campaign of 1860. President Johnson made strenuous efforts to win the Northern people to his constitutional views and extricate himself from the dilemma of being a "minority President." An unusual step at the time, he embarked upon a long stumping tour in August by means of the new railroads, from Philadelphia and New York as far as Chicago. In his train, to demonstrate his loyalty to the Union, he brought with him the idolized General of the Armies, Ulysses S. Grant, as well as Admiral Farragut.

The extremist Republicans, in Johnson's view, showed no more regard for the Constitution "than for an old almanac." But the people too, when they are uneasy and emotionally disturbed, generally show incomprehension or indifference to arguments in the name of constitutional law. The President, who held at heart the strong views of a radical agrarian in opposition to the high protective tariff and to the concentration of wealth among national banks— policies encouraged by the war party—found himself obliged to be silent on these hidden issues; lest he multiply opposition to himself. Failing to develop these questions, which were to become so momentous for the independent liberal farmers of the Mississippi Valley, he failed to divide the Northern people upon economic lines, while permitting the sectional alignment to be held firmly against him. Moderate Republicans held aloof; at the same time, approval of his policies by Southerners and discredited Democrats was an extreme embarrassment. He found the press overwhelmingly hostile to him; fantastic rumors concerning his private character, his presumed plot to assume despotic powers, to overcome Congress by military force, to bring about the repudiation of the war debt (which bred panic among the business class), pursued him everywhere. The Northern mobs were suspicious, hostile, increasingly disorderly; and hecklers among them goaded the impetuous Tennessean into hasty or careless replies which did him no good.[32]

The "minority President" saw his power over patronage, the appointive power so vital to party management, steadily stripped away by his opponents. Stevens, ruling powerful committees and acting as chairman of the Republican caucus, not only exerted the pressure of the majority to block confirmation of appointments, but worked in close collaboration with heads of the Federal departments themselves. Even those cabinet members who sympathized with the executive were given to understand, Welles relates,

that they must conform to the theory and doctrines of Thad Stevens if they designed to preserve their Republican Party identity. . . . Most of the members of the Cabinet acquiesced or submitted to the usurpation. No appointments or nominations to office made by the Executive . . . were confirmed by the Senate, except the nominees first recommended or indorsed by Radical Members of Congress. Some of the Cabinet under these circumstances surrendered and made terms.[33]

Within the Cabinet the tenacious Radical Stanton, while Secretary of War, intrigued against the President persistently, not only to use the office-giving power for the Radical faction, but to control the army itself on their behalf.

As for the members of Congress, most of them, according to Gideon Welles, Secretary of the Navy since Lincoln's time, were

"small party men, creatures of corner groceries, without any knowledge of the science of government or of our Constitution. With them
all the great, overpowering purpose and aim are office and patronage." [34] Each Congressman knew that it was as much as his political
life was worth to defy the party caucus and its all-powerful chairman,
who terrified them with gloomy predictions of both Houses of Congress overrun with rebels, should they relax in their discipline. The
legions of Federal officeholders and postmasters, according to custom,
obediently paid their dues, an assessment upon their wages, to the
party's collectors and also labored in concert, unostentatiously, to
bring out the vote throughout the country wherever the fiery call of
the stump orator might not reach.

Finally, for the campaign of 1866, the Republican Party made
notable advances in the technique of organization. A new central
organ called the Congressional Campaign Committee was created at
Washington, with one member for each State, to control throughout
the Union the elections to the House of Representatives. The new
central committee, functioning constantly, watching the electoral situation in the congressional districts, "penetrated more deeply and more
continuously into local political life than could be done by the permanent committee of the national [party] convention," which
appeared in presidential elections solely.[35] Throughout the ranks of
the party the word was given that dissenters—so many moral lepers
—must be watched and reported as in the Church Militant; the party
which held but a minority of the total popular vote in 1864 must win
a majority, else everything was lost.

In the midst of the congressional campaign, race riots at Memphis
and New Orleans strengthened the hands of the Radicals and fed
their arsenal of vituperation. The blood of Memphis and New
Orleans must cry out, thundered Sumner, until it is heard and a
guilty President may suffer.

Roscoe Conkling, the young Radical Congressman from upper
New York and a picturesque orator, appealed not only to fears for
the national safety but also to the class interests of capitalists and
bondholders in the East, saying:

Do you want to give up your interests once more to this alliance, with two-fifths added to the old slave power? Do you want to bind your country hand and foot . . . ? What would become of it? What would become of the pension roll of soldiers and their widows and orphans? What would become of the public debt and the public credit? What would greenbacks, and five-twenties, and seven-thirties be worth? . . . Are you ready for this? Are you ready to put your rights, your property and the honor of the nation to be raffled for by the murderers of your children and the betrayers of your country?[36]

The masses of Union Army veterans too were brought forth to parade and demonstrate for the militant party. For what pensions might they expect with the return of the rebels to power? The Radical Republicans organized a most impressive National Soldiers' Convention at Pittsburgh in September, where the "Grand Army," with General John A. Logan of Illinois as its leader, began its long, stern campaign on behalf of ever greater and more generous favors for veterans, a feature of our politics for a generation. Here the political generals, Ben Butler and Banks, Schenck, and other leaders in "a tempest of anger" led the convention to declare that the President's

acts . . . have retarded the restoration of peace. If the President's scheme be consummated it would render the sacrifice of the Nation useless, the loss of her buried comrades vain, and the war in which we have so gloriously triumphed a failure.[37]

Oliver Morton, the famous wartime Governor of Indiana, who had momentarily accepted favors from Johnson but under pressure, like many conservative Republicans, turned to the other side, by the unrestrained violence of his oratory in 1866 fixed, perhaps better than anyone else, the style of the Bloody Shirt speech:

Every unregenerate rebel . . . calls himself a Democrat. Every bounty jumper, every deserter, every sneak who ran away from the draft. . . . Every man . . . who murdered Union prisoners . . . who contrived hellish schemes to introduce into Northern cities the wasting pestilence of yellow fever, calls himself a Democrat. . . . Every wolf in sheep's clothing . . . every one who shoots down negroes in the streets, burns negro school-houses and meeting-houses, and murders women and children by the light of their flaming dwellings, calls himself a Democrat. . . . In short, the Democratic party may be described as a common sewer and loathsome receptacle, into which is emptied every element of treason North and South, and every element of inhumanity and barbarism which has dishonored the age.[38]

Exhorted in such drastic terms to fight the rebel within, the electorate of the entire North and West delivered an overwhelming vote of confidence in the war party. The Republicans gained in 1866 the largest majority in both houses of Congress known to any party since Monroe's time, though it was true that ten of the former Confederate States were unrepresented.

Before the old Congress met again late that year, Stevens and his jubilant Radical comrades conferred in Washington; they felt themselves well vindicated and prepared to press home their advantage. Reconstruction of the South virtually as a subject province of the Republican Party Organization was the essence of their further plans.

The new Draconian Stevens Reconstruction Bill, passed over the President's veto March 2, 1867, ignored the provisional governments recently set up in the Southern States, dividing the conquered South into five military districts, and imposed a most rigorous army rule over them. This was to be carried out under the command of the General of the Armies, Grant—instead of the President. The traditional authority of the defeated Executive was then further hamstrung by a "rider" to an army appropriation bill which prohibited him from removing the General of the Armies. In effect, the military arm was made accountable to the central party leadership in Congress. The Supreme Court, which intervened now with one of its rare decisions on behalf of civil rights, *ex parte* Milligan, was simply flouted by the Radical leaders. Then by the celebrated Tenure of Office Act of March 2, 1867, the President was also forbidden to remove without out the Senate's approval civil officers whose appointment was subject to the confirmation of the Senate; and violation of the act was made punishable by fine and imprisonment. The President's enormous power of executive appointment and patronage was now virtually ended. On March 7, 1867, the new Congress empowered a committee to take testimony with a view to the impeachment of the President on the ground of "high crimes and misdemeanors."

The decrees which a machinelike Congress threw off one by one seemed born of the very madness of sectional hate or fear. Yet Stevens, amid high wrangling within his party over the unwarranted impeachment action, said repeatedly and coolly that it was "a purely *political* proceeding." [39] In this sense only can the management of the Southern communities also be understood. By dint of military control, and imposition of the so-called ironclad oaths, only Negroes, men who had borne no arms in the Rebellion, and newcomers called "Carpetbaggers" could participate in local government. Six of the ten rebel States were thus set up as territories which would safely register a Republican electoral majority. The political power of the old slave aristocracy seemed broken forever, with the proletarian Negroes unwittingly serving as loyal agents of the party of Northern capital.

"The talk and labor are of Reconstruction," Welles confided now to his diary, "for this is the engine by which they hold power; yet not a man among that great number of elected Radicals appears to know . . . what he means by Reconstruction." [40]

Party organization and party rule of the Government now reached perhaps its highest development in our history. Tumult and war passion had been artfully prolonged by these "masters of turbulence." After two years of postbellum political conflict, the brilliant, implacable old Stevens at the age of seventy-five ruled not only the South but the National Government, through a junto or "directory," as Johnson had correctly charged. From 1866 to 1868, the year of his death, Stevens as a sort of prime minister for Congress virtually ruled in place of the repudiated President, even holding the country's moneybags in his hands. The office of the House Appropriations Committee, of which he was chairman, was known as "Thad Stevens's room." Dying, Stevens handed to other leaders—unhappily, leaders of far different mold—a close-knit, militant party Organization, a superb machinery for party rule. This much had been well done.

VI

The off-year elections, chiefly of State officers and legislatures, provided some sobering thoughts for the Radical leaders in November, 1867. In the Mississippi Valley the realities of economic discontent showed themselves strongly; in Ohio the Republican Brigadier General Rutherford B. Hayes was elected Governor by but a hair's breadth, and a hardy, unashamed, reviving Democracy won the State legislature for itself. In the populous Northern States of New York, New Jersey, and Pennsylvania, by a strong recoil of public opinion, the legislatures turned Democratic also.

Among the farmers the beginnings of a postwar contraction—though it did not reach its climax until six years later—were already appreciated, and pointed to the injustice of a system of taxation and currency which seemed to discriminate against them as a class. While the Radical leaders preached universal liberty and equality, they had quietly passed in April, 1866, a law which inordinately hastened the repayment of the nation's huge war debt, and especially brought the swift retirement of the fiat paper money, the Legal Tender which Lincoln had issued during the war emergency.

The American program for repayment of the great war debt, far more rapid and drastic than that of Great Britain after the Napoleonic Wars, began to have the effect of a sweeping deflation. Prices of grain and other farm commodities, as well as of land, fell in 1866 and 1867. Credit grew scarce; a familiar cry of protest from the credit-hungry farm regions was heard, a protest which had been rising and falling ever since the days of Daniel Shays's Rebellion.

Moreover, popular resentment soon fixed itself upon the new national banks, and upon large bondholders, who sought repayment of the government obligations they owned in gold money of the pre-war parity. Money was being concentrated in the hands of the national banks, especially through the rapid retirement of Legal Tender by Secretary of the Treasury McCulloch. The national banks, which had bought low-priced government bonds during the war, received up to 9 per cent interest on these, then by depositing their government bonds as security, issued and loaned their own banknotes at from 6 to 8 per cent or more, so that many of them were said to be earning over 17 per cent per annum upon their own capital. The early return to the former gold-specie payment would virtually double the value of their government bonds.

The "Ohio Idea," which the Democratic Congressman George Pendleton championed, now won popular support; the war debt must be repaid in the selfsame Greenbacks which the bond-buyers had invested; moreover, the interest which bondholders received was to be taxed away. President Andrew Johnson favored such a course, and Jay Cooke heard alarming rumors in September, 1867, that he intended to dismiss Secretary McCulloch.[41] The Radical leaders themselves, Wade, Ben Butler, and Thad Stevens, actively opposed contraction and the repayment of the war bonds in gold money or its equivalent.[42] Jay Cooke, the "financier of the Civil War," and now the country's foremost banker, held himself at this time in closest friendship with the national Republican leaders, a relationship concerning which so much illuminating evidence has been left us. But even Cooke, whose policies were followed almost automatically by Secretary McCulloch, saw the wisdom of compromise, and accepted a modified program. Conservative and Radical Republicans combined in haste to pass the act of February 4, 1868, prohibiting further cancellation of the Greenbacks, while also holding in abeyance the debt-funding program.

The minor setbacks of 1867 gave pause to the Radical leaders. Then, with their eyes fixed on the presidential campaign of 1868, they determined all the more strongly to whip up new partisan tumult, to raise the alarm once more for the national safety. On August 2, 1867, President Johnson had finally dismissed Secretary of War Stanton, and appointed General Grant as ad interim Secretary, thus deliberately courting a test of the constitutionality of the Tenure of Office Act. In January, 1868, when the removal of Stanton was not confirmed by the Senate, a technical ground was opened for impeachment action, although the twelve hundred pages of testimony on Johnson's public and private life gathered by a Radical committee could produce nothing of an "illegal" or even questionable nature. The impeachment of the President, and his replacement by one of their own number, was to be the final step in the conquest of the state power by the Radicals.

The trial, prepared all through February, began on March 5, and dragged itself out with unbelievable rhetoric and melodrama until May 26. Day after day the Radical orators, with whom the more conservative and business-minded elements in Congress, such as Garfield and John Bingham of Ohio, were induced to join, rose to denounce the "criminal" President upon charges so farcical that men in their right senses could scarcely have made them.

Once more the tactics of "masterful turbulence" and verbal galimatias, which Blaine attributed to some of his colleagues, are clearly seen. The war of words is carried to new lengths. General James A. Garfield, a rising young Republican Congressman from Ohio, commented especially in private letters from the political battle front on the "insane love of speaking" which the Radical leaders showed in this national emergency. They had obtained consent of the Senate for virtually all of their followers to speak and testify at the trial of the President, and Garfield writes, "here we have been wading knee deep in words, words, words, for a whole week, and we are but little more than half way across the turbid stream." The fierce impeachers, he judges, would have abandoned all thought of impeachment if they were denied "an unlimited opportunity to talk." Here, for instance, was Stevens, reeling in the shadow of death, struggling to read words which could not be heard twenty feet off, and others giving two days at a time to "the worst type of Tennessee stump speech." [43] It was truly a circus parade in which the fanatical Boutwell, the turbulent Ben Butler, the "drunken" extremist "Zach" Chandler, then "Black Jack" Logan, Roscoe Conkling, Oliver Morton, and Charles Sumner, no less long-winded, airing their preposterous charges, filled the republic with more thunderous claptrap than it had ever known in the fourscore years of its wordy political life.

What was behind this farrago of hate, vengeance, and fantasy, evidently managed, guided, raised steadily to its fortissimo by shrewd theater directors?

Underneath the quarrel over Reconstruction, as we have come to see, lay great economic issues that had divided our people for generations and would divide them anew, issues which bore no resemblance to those mouthed so vociferously by the embattled politicians. The real issues embraced the whole profound change of direction in our postwar society. They touched the centripetal movement by which a partially organized, or weakly organized, "federal" union of States was being turned into a highly centralized nation; small enterprise, literally "cottage industry," was giving way to large-scale manufacture, which was to be encouraged, "protected"—that is, subsidized—by the National Government, protected not only against foreign competition, but also against the restrictions of local or State governments. Even our money was to be different, and national, now that the old State banks with their "wildcat" notes were to be taxed out of existence. On all these underlying questions, then—of taxation, of tariff, of the "centralizing" policy both in government and in economic life, of the stresses caused by the new social order growing up under Radical favor—almost no clue is given by the principal actors in the political drama before us, so that we are forced to scan always their private, unguarded expressions, wherever we may find them, to determine what they were truly engaged in doing.

The Radicals had enjoyed the sweets of power and unexpected favor for their economic interests. For all their doctrinary violence, they had held to their side the great moneyed groups of the North, interests which only recently had opposed unrestricted suffrage for white men in their own section. These groups—men of counting-houses, owners of factories, and all their train—were as yet a minority, a minority which had been consistently outvoted by the agricultural South and West for over thirty years. Neither the party leaders nor the business groups, then, had any wish to return to the hopeless minority fight which their fathers had made as Whigs. "To keep the economic questions in the background, until the Southern problem was settled, and their power secure," until their social revolution was completed, was therefore essential. "A campaign of denunciation and vituperation would accomplish this by keeping war hatreds alive. Against their political and economic opponents, unreasoning passion, rodomontade—claptrap rather than issues" would be most effective. Else, with war passion, fear, and sectional hate subsided, and normal times returned, both elements might suffer again "the discouraging experiences of pre-war decades," when so little headway could be made against the opposition and the peculiar inertia of our governmental system.[44]

But in the spring of 1868 we confront one of those moments when the two largest stockholders of the "joint stock company" fall into discord. The professional politicians, as they prepared the overthrow of the President, were plainly carried away by their lust for spoils.

They saw themselves in unchallenged control of all the Federal departments, and Ben Wade, the president pro tempore of the Senate, was already picturing himself in the White House and devising in his mind a new Radical Cabinet. By such logic the whole contingent of Republicans in the House had been brought to vote as a body for the impeachment resolution—many of them against their private convictions—and the Senators, who sat in judgment on the President, were also pressed to "let their conscience go." It was afterward said that each one feared lest he might not seem as "radical" as his fellows.

The party's powerful economic allies ended, however, by being thoroughly alarmed, not only at the turmoil that injured business, but also at the establishment of a precedent that would give a distinctly "South American" flavor to our constitutional Republic. Where would it all end if a few party managers, by organizing their followers in Congress, could overthrow the head of the Government almost at will? The prosecution of the President was not only high-handed, but rested on the most doubtful legal grounds. William Evarts of New York, one of the country's foremost corporation lawyers, conducted Johnson's defense most ably. The richest Republican patrons, such as the financiers Jay Cooke of Philadelphia and Hamilton Fish of New York, seemed to tremble at the thought of the "wild Radical" Ben Wade in the White House. Wade not only urged the free distribution of land to the Negroes, but aroused poor farmers and laborers against capitalists in the North, and championed even votes for women![45]

It was evident at this juncture that only the most unbridled and narrowly partisan ends might be served by impeachment. The power of President Johnson, even as a "negative" force, had been removed. In any case, he had but a few months left of his term of office, and by May, during the conclusion of the trial, the election campaign was well under way and victory for the Republicans, with a glamorous war hero as their standard-bearer, was a foregone conclusion.

At the last moment the hands of the extremists were stayed. Seven leading Republicans, including Lyman Trumbull of Illinois and the aged Fessenden of Maine, on the ground of principle had resisted the procedure from beginning to end. The defection of four more Senators at the last moment caused the loss by one vote of a two-thirds majority for impeachment. This unexpected outcome Radical leaders angrily attributed to Jay Cooke's uncommon powers of persuasion.[46]

But a presidential election now approached, and the party leaders, much like the French Directory after Thermidor, turned to new expedients for prolonging the conditions and moods of war as a means for prolonging their own power.

VII

At this moment Ulysses Grant, the "Savior of the Union," was the most popular and famous of Americans, the subject of unrestrained public ovations wherever he went. For more than two years the great soldier had cast an important shadow over the affairs and calculations of the politicians. His role as commander of the nation's military force, as well as his appeal for nearly 1,000,000 veterans of the war, was ever in the minds of the party leaders.

During the quarrels over Reconstruction both factions had wooed Grant. He knew nothing of specialized politics. A Democrat by vote before the war, he was thought to hold moderate views on Reconstruction. Like all men who are uncertain in their knowledge, he was shy, suspicious, and he took refuge in silence. While the partisan storms swirled about him, he felt compelled to hold himself aloof and appear to obey the orders of his superior, the President, like a good soldier. Thus, as the historian Motley said at the time, he played "the dumb, inarticulate man of genius," giving no clue to his ambitions, though all knew that the Presidency might be his for the asking.

But Grant's military aides and political mentors, such as the ambitious and wealthy Representative Elihu Washburne of Illinois, who had won him his first division command in 1861, left him no rest. His friend General John Rawlins, wartime chief of his staff, who had kept him sober during battle campaigns and pounded his ideas into Grant's head until Grant believed them his own, was another adviser who labored now to lead the war hero into the Radical camp.

With the dismissal of Stanton and Johnson's appointment of Grant as ad interim Secretary of War, the war hero's position became more difficult than ever. Though hitherto on terms of friendship with the

President, he was brought step by step to quarrel with him over the military administration of the South. In leaning now to the congressional faction, he seems to have been moved by reasons always obscure, and chiefly by instinct rather than conviction.[47]

On the eve of the impeachment trial, in January, when the Senate voted against the dismissal of Stanton and excited rumors of impending war between the President and Congress filled the Capital, Grant suddenly detached himself from Johnson's side and surrendered his office to Stanton. He then hurriedly returned to his permanent post at Army Headquarters, his for life at $20,000 per annum. Whatever the grounds for his action, Grant's resounding public rupture with his chief was all too timely, and it was accompanied by a most offensive letter to the President (dictated by the same General Rawlins) in which he accused Johnson of having sought to involve him "in the resistance of law . . . and thus destroy my character before the country." Rawlins, who was by nature a politician and, "having long foreseen the result of all the political complications, felt at last that the time had come" for rupture with the ill-starred President. "It was a stroke of political genius" whereby Grant became the logical, the inevitable candidate of the Republicans.[48]

During the uproar over the impeachment proceedings the military wing of the Radical faction had rushed into action. Stanton, restored to his office, slept at the War Department, while General Logan, now Representative in Congress, secretly called members of the Grand Army of the Republic together, formed battalions, and officered them. Sentinels in citizen dress were on duty every hour before the White House and the War Department building, while Logan slept on a cot beside Stanton.[49] During the trial of the President, the G.A.R. was apparently held ready to rise at a given signal to the defense of Secretary Stanton or Congress.

Patriotic Grant Clubs had been organizing themselves "spontaneously" at many points in the country since the autumn of 1866. Politicians in the field held the view expressed by one correspondent to Congressman Elihu Washburne, Grant's old sponsor, that "the soldiers hold the balance of power and will make the next President." [50] But more urgently after the alarming symptoms of discontent shown in the off-year elections of 1867, reports from the

"workers" in the field came in on all hands that a man was needed
for the national Republican ticket who could "bring out the vote."
The Middle West was apathetic. Similar reports came from the East.
"No civilian," as one party agent reported on November 7, 1867,
"can carry Pennsylvania, and without Grant our election would go
against us." [51]

But Grant had been silent, and the prominent Radicals among the
Republicans, such as Stevens, Ben Wade, Horace Greeley, and Sumner, had not only mistrusted him but on occasion assailed him. It was
his open and final break with President Johnson in January, 1868,
which made the Republican "directory" jubilant. When Thad Stevens
saw the General's insulting letter to the President he exclaimed: "He
is a bolder man than I thought him; now we will let him into the
Church." [52]

The thought of Radicals and even of most orthodox Republicans
was that the strategy of peace must bring about only such Reconstruction as would give "safety and power to the loyal." [53] But large
sections of the North, especially the Western Democracy of the
Mississippi Valley, showed indifference to the Radical fire bells;
they raised instead the most embarrassing questions concerning the
economic burden of the war debt, the high cost of "protected" manufactured goods, the taxation of bonds, the retention of Greenbacks
and an inflated money. Hence the Radical "directory" turned, though
not without misgivings, as our parties had often done before in
pursuit of their own interests, to the military captain as standard-
bearer. The use of a figurehead or symbol had long been part of
our political lore. In the unmilitary republic of jealous, democratic
bourgeois, where nearly all men owned arms, no one feared the army
"doughface" overmuch. Catechized and found safe enough by the
professional politicians—only the quality of his Radicalism left some
doubts—General Grant with all his aura of martial glory and successful patriotism was now borrowed for the propaganda campaign
against rebels and Copperheads.

"With Grant at the masthead," one enthusiastic Republican worker
had predicted, "the combined powers of darkness cannot beat us." [54]
The potential of Grant could be measured easily even before the

Republican National Convention opened in May, when an impressive Soldiers and Sailors Convention, called together by Logan, Commander of the G.A.R., nominated Grant by acclamation. An organized and highly interested support by nearly 1,000,000 voters was thus assured in advance. "Death to the Traitors!" was the slogan most often heard at the torchlight processions of the Boys in Blue. Also "Protection for Soldiers' Widows and Orphans!"

The crusade of the Republican Organization that year was to be highly colored with bunting, regimental banners, and military uniforms. That the directors of the war party would be able to continue by such means to gloze over the genuine social issues of the time was all too plain. The keynote for the approaching electoral tournament was sounded by Oliver Morton, the Middle Western party leader and orator, now Republican Senator for Indiana, at a festival of battle flags held by a gathering of Union veterans:

You have laid aside your arms, and have assumed the character of peaceable and quiet citizens, but your duties are not all performed. The great question now confronts you and must be answered, whether these precious flags are to be emblems of barren victories, whether the heroes in war shall become mere children in peace; whether they shall shamefully and blindly surrender at the ballot-box the great prizes which they conquered upon the field.[55]

VIII

The leaders of the war party were oblique in that they kept the economic questions in the background; in the name of patriotism, justice, liberty, they executed move after move which, at a glance, revealed all too plainly the overweeningly professional or "institutional" interest of party rule. A more lingering glance showed the devouring concern with pecuniary, class-economic objects only a little more masked and hidden beneath the vituperations against rebellion and the rodomontades of universal freedom. These significant contradictions may be traced even in the orations of the incorruptible Sumner.

No one questioned the earnestness of Sumner, who had been clubbed nearly to death in the Senate by the Southern firebrand Brooks for his antislavery speeches before the war. Long-haired, with careworn face and burning dark eyes, the immensely tall figure of the Massachusetts Senator would rise again and again as a martyr of the struggle against slavery and secession to make his familiar classical appeals for the rights of the freedmen. Then, at intervals, as in the congressional debates of February, 1866, one would distinguish suddenly notes intruding themselves which were in no sense academic:

Only through him [the Negro] can you redress the balance of our political system and assure the safety of patriot citizens. Only through him can you save the national debt from the inevitable repudiation which awaits it when recent rebels in conjunction with Northern allies [Democrats] once more bear sway. He is our best guarantee. Use him.[56]

To *use* the Negro, to save the national debt! Was it but for this mountain of gold looming ahead, $2,800,000,000 of it, that the incorruptible Senator and the "Great Commoner" of the House of Representatives, Stevens, together made their appeals to youth, to patriots, in the name of liberty and progress? Was it for the protection of cotton cloth, wool blankets, and iron ingots? Were these Republican ideologues hypocrites, or did they deceive themselves?

What undoubtedly happened was that the consciousness—one might say the subconscious—of the Northern politicians had long been colored by the whole social order from which they sprang and the mode of production, the way of life, to which they were attached by a thousand imperceptible ties. Their heads were furnished with general ideas, sentiments, prejudices, associations of thought, forming a whole ideological "superstructure." Instinctively they had learned to admire the thrifty, workaday, progressive ways of their own industrialists, artisans, and free farmers which had wrought an immense social revolution, and to loathe the economic backwardness, the "feudalism," of the Southern agriculturists. With the latter section and class, also, memories and images—slaves being dragged off to the auction block, a familiar sight in Washington before the war—were long associated with a cruel and alien way of life. The old cry for States' Rights, once raised by noble impulses, became detestable in their ears, while the dangers of such a Hamiltonian centralism as they championed in turn, under which new privileged groups might be nourished, were flouted. The new capitalism of the North seemed, in the youth of our industrial revolution, a friendly giant who richly paid free labor. The new banking and currency system, the distinctively protective form of taxation to be introduced, were but a small price to pay for national unity and human liberty, which seemed to depend upon them. Indeed they were vitally connected, intertwined, could scarcely be distinguished apart—in policy and action as in speech.

Meanwhile the leading Northern capitalists themselves, who were firm allies of the war party, were wont to express their thought in far more unequivocal form, not only in private correspondence, but in public. Thus in an open letter to the Boston *Daily Advertiser,* thereafter widely circulated as a pamphlet, Elizur Wright, an old-time Abolitionist and reformer, an inventor and manufacturer as well, declared in 1866:

> . . . I could easily convince any man, who does not allow his prejudices to stand in the way of his interests, that it will probably make a difference of at least $1,000,000,000 in the development of the national debt, whether we reconstruct on the basis of loyal white and black votes, or on white votes exclusively, and that he can better afford to give the Government at least one-quarter of his estate than have it try the latter experiment.[57]

Another equally candid Yankee millowner, Gardner Brewer, wrote to Sumner that the unrestricted suffrage of the colored people was wholly desirable from a selfish point of view, lest the Southerners uniting with Northern Democrats bring a long train of evils fearful to contemplate, such as

> a great reduction of the Tariff, doing away with its protective feature— perhaps Free Trade to culminate with Repudiation . . . and how sweet and complete will be the revenge of the former if they can ruin the North by Free Trade and Repudiation.[58]

These are characteristic expressions, characteristic of a great many made at the end of the war by protected textile manufacturers, iron, glass, salt, and copper producers, in the Northeast and Middle West, who formed nowadays a remarkably close alliance with the movement of Abolitionist Republicanism and with the misled Negro proletarians of the South.* To this powerful class the doctrines of centralism which Republican leaders boldly urged also made an irresistible appeal.

The Fourteenth Amendment, as we have seen, framed by the Joint Committee of Fifteen in all its ingenious parts, served as an admirable election-campaign battery in 1866 against President Johnson's party and was adopted in a tumult of partisan passions. Its first clause appeared to offer a bill of rights for the freedmen North and South, guaranteeing equality before the law and citizenship; its second clause controlled the apportionment of Representatives to Congress according to the enfranchisement of the Negroes; its third and fourth clauses excluded from public life the ablest Southern leaders, and enforced the repudiation of the rebel debt and the acceptance of the Union war debt. But few persons then living fully understood the cryptic meaning of the phrases inserted in the open section:

No States shall make or enforce any law which shall abridge the privileges or immunities of citizens of the United States; nor shall any State deprive any person of life, liberty, or property without due process of law; nor deny to any person within its jurisdiction the equal protection of the laws.

Ostensibly a humanitarian measure, offered as a charter of liberty and human rights, the Fourteenth Amendment was understood only many years after by jurists and historians as being actually, by virtue of its opening paragraph, "the Magna Charta of accumulated wealth and organized capital." [59] By interpreting the word "person" in its juristic sense of "corporation" or corporate person the Supreme Court was able in after years to depart from a policy of noninterference with State legislators and embrace the doctrine that it was "charged with the high duty of reviewing all and every kind of economic legislation by the states." [60]

Whereas previous Amendments (especially the Tenth) had largely

* That the Negro masses, pure proletarians, were lured by the promise of freedom and power to preserve the fruits of the war for Northern capitalists, and then, when no longer needed, were so monstrously betrayed, is one of the most extraordinary maneuvers in all the annals of bourgeois class politics, more remarkable even than the strange combinations of military castes or selfish clerical parties with poor peasants often effected in modern Europe.

defined, clarified, and buttressed the authority of State and local rights or privileges with regard to the National Government, the "Hamiltonian" war party now saw fit to reverse the process. Eighty years before, a nation of smallholders and merchants demanded freedom from foreign or central forms of authority. Now, foreseeing perhaps the approaching nation-wide scope of the new capitalism, they sought rather to protect the new large corporate "persons" by the aid of the National Government from oppression by the separate States. By the Tenth Amendment corporations were adjudged largely free of national regulation, and by the Fourteenth they were ultimately protected from local regulation. Thus it was truly a capitalist charter of liberties that emerged from the secret councils of the committee of congressional leaders before even any definitive plan of Reconstruction of the South and Negro enfranchisement. Representative John A. Bingham of Ohio, a conservative member of the Joint Committee of Fifteen, had actually tried to insert in the Amendment a supplementary clause to the effect that no State should "take private property for public use without just compensation." [61] But this had been voted down as possibly too transparent.

Many years later Roscoe Conkling, a member of the committee, explained that the Fourteenth Amendment was designed for the protection of white people as well as black; that the word "person" was not intended to be synonymous with "citizen," but was used in its juristic meaning of "artificial person" or corporation. Thus, arguing on behalf of Collis Huntington's railroad (San Mateo County vs. Southern Pacific Railroad Company) he related how, when the Fourteenth Amendment was first framed, many individuals and joint-stock companies were appealing for congressional and administrative protection against "the invidious and discriminating state and local taxes being enacted at the time." One express company felt itself oppressed by ruinous taxes and rules of damages in twenty-eight States; complaints were then also especially rife in and out of Congress, said Conkling, of oppression in respect of property and other rights made by citizens of Northern States who took up residence in the South.[62]

Speaking before the Supreme Court in 1882, Conkling said:

Those who devised the fourteenth amendment wrought in grave sincerity. They may have builded better than they knew. . . . They builded, not for a day, but for all time; not for a few, or for a race, but for man. They planted in the Constitution a monumental truth, to stand foursquare whatever wind might blow. That truth is but the golden rule, so entrenched as *to curb the many who would do to the few as they would not have the few do to them.*[63]

The politicians in those stormy years of Reconstruction were as men afflicted with dual identity: they were literally Jekylls and Hydes. As Dr. Jekyll, with a generous impulse they emancipated Negro slaves, swept away the feudal, landed order of the South; as Mr. Hyde, they deliberately delayed the recovery and restoration of the conquered States, whose economy languished during many years of disorder; imposed military rule; and established a network of Freedmen's bureaus and Carpetbag local governments which were subject to the central Republican Party Organization at Washington and paid tribute to the same. As Dr. Jekyll, they stirred the masses of voters to their support by use of a humane and libertarian ideology of a revolutionary American pattern; as Mr. Hyde, they planned and built coolly, at the height of deliberately invoked, turbulent electoral struggles and parliamentary storms, measures of high capitalist policy, to stand "not for a day, but for all time"; they worked to implant in the covenant of our society safeguards to property and capital which might hold against all future assaults.

Under entry of July 7, 1866, Gideon Welles wrote in his diary:

Congress accomplishes little that is good. . . . There is little statesmanship in the body, but a vast amount of party depravity. The granting of acts of incorporation, bounties, special privileges, favors, and profligate legislation of every description is shocking. Schemes for increasing the enormous taxation which already exists to benefit the iron and wool interests are occupying the session.[64]

So in the midst of the never-ending and resounding conflict with the Copperheads, the most worldly of the politicians pleasantly proceeded to enact a mass of innocent-seeming legislation: charters and grants for railroads, for land companies, special tariff duties, public contracts, pensions, appropriations. During the sessions of the historic

Thirty-ninth Congress, sitting from December, 1865, to the spring of 1867, and its successor, the Fortieth, from 1867 to 1869, a vast acreage of choice Western land, some 10,000,000 acres, was added to that which had been awarded earlier to Ames's and Huntington's Pacific railroads project during the war. There was time also to give 22,000,000 acres likewise to a vague new "Atlantic and Pacific" railroad, which years later turned up in the hands of Huntington and Jay Gould. Unresting lobbies employed by the Union Pacific, the Central Pacific, and the Pennsylvania railroads established most intimate working relations with the group of Republican politicians who were soon known as the "Railway Congressmen." These were rising business-minded statesmen who, such times as they were not waving the Bloody Shirt, labored to bring about the swift opening and exploitation of the public domain in the West, entered personally into little railroad promotions and stock-selling ventures of their own. The friends of the Pacific railroads promoters, according to Welles, were always in force at Washington, laboring to prevent any checking up of their actual construction on the one hand, and to obtain on the other hand ever new government subsidies with which to pay several times over the cost of the tracks they laid across the prairies.[65]

In this Age of Big Business which had been launched, with its transcontinental railways, its new stockyards, its oil wells in Pennsylvania, tales of miraculous, sudden fortune stirred the imagination of political leaders as well as private enterprisers. News of a 60 per cent dividend paid in 1867 by a branch of the government-aided Union Pacific—a company of which members of the Republican Party were said to be active sponsors—threatened at one moment to set in the shade the impeachment of President Johnson.[66]

The Railway Congressmen who managed the transfer of immense natural resources to friends and patrons of their party, amid frenzied land, town, and railway booms sweeping the country—must they refuse any part of the fortune they strewed about? For the famous "Christian Statesman," the pious Schuyler ("Smiler") Colfax, Speaker of the House, to have rejected the shares of Credit Mobilier offered by Representative Ames of Massachusetts would have been nicely scrupulous, but would it have been "smart"? When John Bingham of Ohio several years later was charged with possessing as a

free gift shares in the same fabulous corporation, he retorted simply
that he "only wished he had ten times more." [67]

Indulgent historians of the time have related that its ethics was
"confused," that the war period with its inflation of money and
profiteering by contractors was a solvent of public morals. But there
are indications also that many of the ruling party members were
settled and clear enough in their pecuniary canons. Senator G. F.
Hoar, who entered Congress at this period, describes with relish the
morals of the Radical demagogue General Ben Butler. During the
war the Yankee adventurer, serving as Military Governor of New
Orleans with a brutality still remembered there today, had seen fit
to make a requisition of $80,000 in gold upon a bank of that city,
a sum which was never afterward accounted for as having been paid
into the national Treasury. Years later the bankers employed one
of the most famous lawyers of the time, Edwards Pierrepont, to
bring an action against Butler, who was then a leader in Congress.
In the course of a conversation with Butler, Pierrepont observed to
him: "Your neighbors in Lowell will not think very well of it when
they see you riding in your carriage through the streets, and know
it was paid for out of money you have taken unlawfully from this
bank." Butler eventually settled out of court, paying back the stolen
money before trial came, but said to Pierrepont: "Well, you beat me.
But I want to tell you that you made one mistake. You said the
people of Lowell would not think very highly of me when they saw
me riding through the streets in my carriage and knew it was paid for
by the money of this bank. The people would think I was a fool for
not having taken twice as much." [68]

The Puritan conscience, as in many other fields, so in politics,
showed a remarkable elasticity in accommodating itself to new strains.
The young New Hampshire Yankee William E. Chandler, who appeared always as a Republican election "expert" in campaigns, was
to be seen moving about in his long blue cloak, wearing smoked
glasses, as he quietly distributed sums of $3,000 or $3,500 a month
to newspaper reporters, and negotiated for the purchase by the Republican National Committee of whole newspapers which were formerly Democratic.

In "dickering" with these fellows, Chandler asked himself on one occasion, "Can a man touch pitch and not be *defiled?*" But then, in the next moment, as he reports his purchase of a leading Washington (Democratic) paper, he answers his fluttering conscience: "*I am conscious of the correctness and purity of my own motives and do not dare turn away from this opportunity of demoralizing the Democracy.*" [69]

In a fervor of patriotism, and as a military measure, the statesmen had earlier made their vast grant of $50,000,000 in bonds for the Pacific railroads; then another fabulous grant for the Northern Pacific of 47,000,000 acres, which was less noticed. "I give no grudging vote in giving away either money or land," cried the Massachusetts Senator Henry Wilson. "I would sink $100,000,000 to build the road and do it most cheerfully." To encourage the opening and settlement of the Western lands, to bind the shores of the continent together, was a patriotic task. No less pressing and patriotic, by Whig-Republican lights, had been the encouragement, even the subsidizing, of home industry and manufacture. A leading Radical, Senator Zachariah Chandler of Michigan, had exclaimed: "I would raise a wall of fire between this nation and Great Britain. . . . I would not let a single pound of any article she manufactured come here during this war. . . . I am for the tax and the highest tax." [70]

The prosecution of the war against rebellion had been associated with a protective tariff levied against a hated England which profited and sought to profit further from our disaster. With the close of the war a cry arose from the Northeastern region that high tariffs were needed to pay the war debt, and an outburst of high Protectionism followed in 1866. The manufacturers as a class underwent a swift, remarkable organization for concerted propaganda and lobbying action. John L. Hayes, heading one of the first powerful lobbies in our history, that of the recently formed National Association of Wool Growers, advanced a scheme for keeping up the price of wool and woolen cloth; another group, supported by Bingham and by John Sherman in the Senate, maintained a monopoly of salt under the tariff, as David A. Wells, Johnson's Commissioner of Internal Revenue, demonstrated; [71] a copper syndicate with mines in Northern Michigan, in which the old warmonger Zach Chandler was interested, clamored for duties of 5 cents a pound on raw copper; the iron men of Pennsylvania demanded similar privileges, though iron was at $80 a ton here as against $32 in England. Each group, each promoter, clamored for Protection, for bounties, for appropriations.

These great benefits the embattled party politicians found it not in their hearts to refuse to their stanchest patrons and friends. While with one hand they carried unweariedly the sword of the patriot to the Copperhead, with the other they strewed freely government benefices among their allies. The dichotomy in Republican thought was perhaps best revealed in a G.A.R. slogan sometimes attributed to Senator James Henry Lane, the militant and picturesque Kansas Abolitionist. *"The old flag and an appropriation!"* he thundered at the conclusion of a speech in favor of soldiers' pensions. Not long after this (1866), with his mind unhinged, Lane committed suicide.

IX

Andrew Johnson, in the closing days of his term, stripped of power, his vetoes well-nigh futile against an overwhelming Republican majority in Congress, lifted his voice against the new, revolutionary principles "of government for the benefit of industry," principles as menacing to the welfare of the plain people as the rule of the old slavocracy. An enemy of large landholders, Johnson now opposed to the same degree the class which emerged from the war as large holders of government bonds. Gold in December, 1868, stood at approximately 150 per cent of parity in United States currency, the dollar being worth therefore about 66⅔ cents in terms of gold money; and Johnson, though knowing no more of finance than Lincoln, pointed out in his annual message at this time that the buyers of the "seven-thirty" war bonds had made their investment in depreciated Greenbacks then worth 50 or even 40 cents in gold. "The holders of our securities have already received upon their bonds a larger amount than the original investment," he argued. He would therefore tax away their interest, and use this money to pay off the principal of our burdensome national debt. Here was "a bold and shameless advocacy of repudiation," which alone showed, as a Republican spokesman, Blaine, has said, how much Johnson had merited impeachment. The President often attempted in vain to veto railroad charters and disguised grants to land-grabbing companies who would plunder the public domain. Johnson made further outspoken comment: that "an aristocracy based on nearly two billions and a half of national securities has arisen to assume that political control which the consolidation of great financial and political interests formerly gave to the slave oligarchy. . . . The war of finance," he predicted in a public interview, "is the next war we have to fight."

But it was too late. The opposition party had taken a course of twisted compromise; the independent President was to be hurled into the limbo of defeated politicians. Moreover, the "war of finance" had begun at once after Appomattox.

The policy of swift redemption of inflated debt and paper money which Secretary of the Treasury McCulloch pursued with the support of the Republicans had brought, as we have seen, the minor election upheaval in the off-year elections of 1867. "What bad news, sad news to-night," mused the pious banker Jay Cooke as he watched the election returns. "Pennsylvania and Ohio gone Democratic and the sad lessons of the war all forgotten. Well, God reigneth. His will and purposes will all be made known and enforced in good time." [72]

A last current of the Abolitionist Radicalism in Stevens and Wade had led them to advocate strongly repayment of the war bonds in Greenbacks—paper money. Even the conservative John Sherman of Ohio, who had been "as a lion" in defense of Cooke's financial policies during the war, appeared frightened and endeavored to halt a too drastic deflation. To an emissary whom Jay Cooke sent to him he said:

Our bonds do not state that they shall be paid in gold. That is no part of the contract. Our soldiers and sailors who . . . saved the Union were paid in greenbacks. . . . Our farmers and manufacturers who furnished materials for carrying on the war were paid with greenbacks. . . . Why then should the money lenders . . . who bought our bonds at a cut-throat discount during the war be singled out from all other creditors and be paid par in gold? . . . This logic has captured the people. Even if erroneous it is sweeping the country. When the issue comes the Democrats will go into power and carry out the change. They are sure to go further than safety warrants and financial panic and disaster are sure to result. [73]

The question of the national debt overshadowed all else in the minds of the well-informed citizen, though the statesmen evaded it. The problem of carrying the country toward rapid specie resumption and a sound gold basis, validating the mountains of paper profits left to the financiers as the outcome of the war, obsessed those likely to profit therefrom in 1867-69. Jay Cooke, the Tycoon of banking, was under fire in Congress, where resolutions of inquiry were aimed at his plans for new refunding operations; yet the imposing, white-bearded banker, on the defensive, persisted in his efforts to bend party leaders and newspapers to his will. Since 1866 he had apparently considered organizing the national bankers into an association, much like that of the wool and iron men, which might act in politics to defend their vast interests. This raised delicate questions. The young Assistant Secretary of the Treasury, William E. Chandler, already a wily political manager and wirepuller high in the national councils of the Republican Party, wrote Cooke December 2, 1867:

I very much regret that the organization in the interest of the banks of which you spoke to me a year ago has not been quietly effected ready for action. The banks need to bestir themselves to avoid hostile legislation and yet any organization effected now would . . . perhaps do more harm than good. This universal suffrage country will never see the end of attempts of demagogues to excite the poor against the rich, labor against capital, and all who haven't money against the banks who have it.[74]

Such a project of a defense organization for national bankers as the fertile Cooke privately discussed with his aides was reminiscent of Alexander Hamilton's eighteenth-century vision of a plutocratic class, cementing together the union of the States by their common interest in the national debt and the United States Bank.*

But Cooke ended by adhering to his more circuitous method of paying large contributions to the Republican Party chest, and making personal loans to leading politicians. Young Chandler, who became secretary of the Republican National Committee in 1868, also

---

* "The funds of the bank would create a class, or call forth one already in existence in support of the government. The stockholders of the [United States] bank would be even more united and more active than the holders of the funds because they would have more to gain." (H. C. Lodge, *Alexander Hamilton*, 12th ed., 1886, p. 102.)

pointed out to Cooke that "it would be a good investment" for him if money were supplied directly to help pay the election expenses of certain Western leaders of Congress, such as General Schenck and John A. Bingham of Ohio, and Logan of Illinois.[75] These leaders Cooke referred to always thereafter as "our friends in Congress."

After 1866 the Cookes besieged the war hero, Ulysses Grant, with their attentions. Henry Cooke, in the Washington office of Jay Cooke & Co., who acted as a public-relations manager for his brother, got himself into the confidence of the General, plied him with liquor, catechized him long before Thad Stevens and the Republican leaders did, and reported promptly to Jay that the great soldier was apparently conservative and "sound" on financial questions. Whereupon Jay Cooke answered him on September 9, 1867: "Tell Gen'l Grant from me that we all look to him to save to the country the legitimate results & fruits of the War." [76]

Grateful, but apprehensive, the leading financiers showered the conqueror of Lee with gifts and money prizes, much as the British bourgeoisie had rewarded Wellington after Waterloo. A fully furnished mansion for him in our largest city, Philadelphia, was paid for by A. T. Stewart, the dry-goods king, Adolph Borie, and other men of money; a sum of $100,000 was raised in New York by Henry Clews, the Wall Street broker, with the aid of Hamilton Fish, Moses Taylor, Edwards Pierrepont, August Belmont, Moses Grinnell, stockbrokers, bankers, war contractors, to pay for the mortgage on Grant's Washington home; and though Grant read almost nothing, a gift of a library to furnish his head richly, costing $75,000, was promptly donated by "fifty solid men of Boston." [77]

Under Grant, as the conservative financiers pointed out to the Republican Party leaders, there would be law and order, there would be above all "economy." While the Democrats and the opponents of the war against the rebellion would undoubtedly raise the banner of Repudiation, "and thus gain largely with the mass of people," the Republicans would gather the patriot and soldier vote. One Republican agent, commenting sadly upon Democratic gains in Ohio late in 1867, wrote to Grant's old friend and mentor, Washburne of Illinois:

After looking carefully over the field I know of but one man that in my humble judgment can beat this repudiation platform and that man is General Grant. . . . If we run Grant, we can generally count upon the soldiers' vote—they will vote for him to glorify themselves—feeling that to place him in the Presidential office will be an additional recognition of their own services . . . that is to say, they will prefer glory to repudiation. But with Chase or any of that school of politicians we will certainly be beaten. . . . The people are uneasy . . . and inclined to try a change.[78]

While Grant was being "let into the Church" in 1868 by Radical leaders and Logan, Morton, and other Western firebrands marshaled the soldiers' votes, leading national bankers and financiers in the East, whose class interests converged toward the institutional one of the professional politicians, organized themselves to raise "the sinews of war" for the same end. The managers of the Republican National Committee, Governor Edwin Morgan of New York, Washburne of Illinois, and Chandler of New Hampshire, held meetings in a Wall Street office where nabobs like A. T. Stewart, William E. Dodge, Collis Huntington, Cornelius Vanderbilt, William B. Astor, Hamilton Fish, and Moses Taylor were summoned to subscribe sums of from $5,000 to $10,000 each, sums then unprecedented. Certain war contractors linked to the Republican Party, such as Edwards Pierrepont of New York, who was believed to have given $20,000 on this occasion, were told as in 1864: "You have had a good contract, out of which you have made money, and we expect you to use a part of that money to assist to replace us in power." [79] But the bankers bore the brunt of the campaign levies.

CHAPTER TWO

THE SPOILSMEN

The party became a sort of church, which admitted no dissent and pitilessly excommunicated any one who deviated a hair's breadth from the established dogma or ritual, were it even from a feeling of deep piety, or a yearning for a more perfect realization of the ideal of holiness set before the believer.   M. OSTROGORSKI

ONE by one, as each Republican member rose in the Senate to speak his mind or to give testimony during the spectacular impeachment business of 1868, it was not his own voice that was heard but that of his party speaking through him. More than one of the younger statesmen present lived to confess in after years, as did James G. Blaine, that he had voted against his own conscience in obedience to party discipline.

The party decided, commanded; its leadership controlled, rewarded or punished, its members; it levied dues (assessments) upon its members and contributions from its patrons and clients either for political favor or for office. While President Johnson "swung around the circle" in his efforts to win the people by direct appeals, the ruling party's election agents worked far more effectively, under regional leaders, throughout the country to "bring out the vote" against his policy of Reconstruction. Agents of another department of the party could be seen with their black entry books in their hands, collecting from government workers throughout the Federal bureaucracy a regular tax upon their wages, whose aggregate sum would go to pay for the labor of those who "organized" the vote. General Grant, as candidate for the Presidency, in 1868 had the prestige of a military idol; he said nothing and his election was considered inevitable. Yet the old opposition party of the much discredited Democrats even in the North showed itself wonderfully hardy; in the "doubtful" States of Pennsylvania, Ohio, Indiana, certain technical activities by trained Republican Party strategists were believed indispensable up to the last moment; and without the party control of the Southern communities, which Thaddeus Stevens's Reconstruction laws had brought about, six Southern States would have been lost, and Grant himself defeated.

The party decided, commanded. Often charges were made during the Reconstruction debates, especially by Democratic opponents, that the ruling party was the device of the rich, the "moneychangers," the capitalists. But though capitalists in those days, as in other times, knew how to exert a decisive voice in public emergencies, the ruling party often vexed and disappointed the capitalists—as in the impeachment action itself, in its "excesses," or pursuit of its own special ends. Then neither of the great parties in the United States was a "class party." In the Valley of Democracy an Ohio Democratic leader, such as Senator Allen Thurman, would not appear at a public gathering without his red bandanna. But could the Democrats led by Mr. Tilden and Mr. Belmont, who made their presidential candidate in 1868 Governor Horatio Seymour of New York, allied by family to the great patroons and one of the wealthiest Americans, claim to be the party of the poor classes?

The political party antedated the arrival of true, large-scale capitalism in America. It was not invented by capitalism, though capitalists were able to turn it to their own account. Nor did the parties serve to bring about "government by discussion"; nor did they seek "truth" in their actions. The typical party leader, as one of the greatest of their line has said, often pursued purely party ends, even when "the righteousness of the cause and the strength of logical intrenchment" were against him.[1]

Yet the party was not recognized by our fundamental law, the Constitution; it stood outside the law while it worked everywhere to manage the popular will and government. It formed, as most Americans vaguely sensed, a fourth and decisive branch of government, "a government within the Government." It had its own rules (many of them secret), tactics, and ends; its own store of knowledge and experience. It was something "organic." It was virtually a tribal institution—as distinct as the church or the nobility in older lands—risen among the American people, rooted in the climate of the new democratic nation from the very beginning. But in the era after the Civil War—certain episodes of which we have examined in detail chiefly to notice better the institutional nature of the party operations —the party, the ruling party, was more jealous in its absolutism, more militant, more narrowly professional than ever before. The party was Caesar.

A "man on horseback" had just been raised to the Presidency by a grateful people. Would he be leader or led? Would he bend the Government to his will and ride down the demands of party men, as the two Napoleons had already done in their republic? It was as likely, under American political institutions, that he would be dragged from his horse should he defy his party. The fate of Andrew Johnson showed what might befall a President without a party.

The American people from the beginning have shown wisdom both in the realities and in the subterfuges of popular rule. Political "genius" has often been attributed to our eighteenth-century *philosophes*—the Fathers who were the architects of the Constitution. True, the Constitution was most cunningly and arduously wrought out of compromises between the powers of the sovereign States and those of the central Government, between the rights of individuals and the Government's requirements for safety and authority. But it required even more political "genius" for the people of the young republic to live under this cumbersome charter and to make it work.

The Fathers, with all their adroit checks and balances and provisions which would keep each part of the Government from winning power over the other part, may well have planned, it is supposed, "rather a government that could not do things than a government that could do things." [2] Certain of the founding Fathers, such as John Adams, in private even referred to our system as a "monarchical republic." As under the old Whig model of the British constitution, there was to be a popular, representative parliament at the core of the system. But the stronger checks set here against this branch reflected how troubled the Fathers were about the "vices" and "passions" of democratic rule; how soberly they thought of the differences between the poor and the rich; how they devised their awkwardly compromised and highly abstract document in order to oppose "interests" to each other, and above all in very fear of the masses of people, "the ever increasing class," as Madison said, "which labor under the hardships of life and secretly strive for a more equal distribution of its blessings." This charter, which was destined to be revered superstitiously as the ark of our covenant, was signed by its original authors with no little disgust and deep misgivings, especially on the score of its failure, according to Hamilton, to provide a "Crown," that is, a strong central Government.

Yet this cumbersome and suspect system was made to work at once, thanks to the existence of a unified, powerful caste of gentry who had for long years dominated the society. Parties or factions arose almost at once, based ostensibly on opposing views of the Constitution and of general government policy, but actually upon "the various and unequal distribution of property." * These by their action filled the gaps, the lacunae, in the new, artificial charter of government, and by making decisions or establishing precedents gave to it some life and unity.

In the aristocratic republic which had been designed in theory to avoid the "evils" of popular rule, the President was given enormous power, the small council of Senators too were to serve as "guardians of property against levellers," while the popular House was to remain a wholly inferior legislative body. The very mode of election of the President was to make him remote from the people, rather than their instrument.

Yet almost nothing in the Constitution seemed to work as planned. The system of divided authority, which meant in effect that one organ of the Government could ignore or obstruct what another was doing, led to Hamilton's effort to achieve unity of administration by cabinet or ministerial leadership. This evoked a jealous, passionate protest by Congress, which stubbornly asserted its prerogatives as the popular organ of the Government responsible to the people.

The want of unity, the divided character of the Government, led to an informal, extraconstitutional process which introduced unity and teamwork through the first, loose, party Organization. The fact that the Constitution, while designating the various government

---

* Madison continued, in the tenth number of the *Federalist:* "Those who hold and those who are without property, have ever formed distinct interests in society. Those who are creditors, and those who are debtors. . . . A landed interest, a manufacturing interest, a mercantile interest . . . divide them into different classes."

offices, told nothing of how men might be chosen for them also made the medium of the political party inevitable.

The Federalists were few in number and recognized each other easily. Their pretensions and excesses, as a ruling caste, united the opposition of fairly violent Jacobin clubs and levelers' factions as Anti-Federalists (Democratic-Republicans) under the leadership of the wary Jefferson, who welded them together into a more or less disciplined party of action.* Thus two great political parties were established in America, as in England, at the end of the eighteenth century. But Jefferson's more popular party, which promised to carry out the principles of democracy and obey the will of the people, soon showed a marked tendency in practice to take its leaders or officers from the same caste of gentry as the Federalists, and also to prolong its existence, to perpetuate its own power as a political party.

Following the enthusiastic "revolution" which thrust Jefferson into power, he found it necessary to set a new precedent by replacing certain men in national offices with his own supporters, arguing that "few die and none resign." But the Federalist President Adams at the last midnight hour of his term had already given to the judiciary, the third branch of the Government with its unexplored powers, a highly partisan character by appointing his own followers, including John Marshall, to permanent places in the Supreme Court.

For more than a quarter of a century thereafter, an aristocratic caste, a sort of political ruling family (known as the Virginia Dynasty), governed the republic with a mild sway. The era of Jefferson, Madison, Monroe, and the New England disciple of the Virginians, J. Quincy Adams, was that of an oligarchy of "wealth and talents," despite its original leveling pretensions. The Secretary of State usually passed as if by succession into the Presidency; the administrative personnel of the government departments, often held by men of skill, changed chiefly through old age or death. The permanence of the official class and of legislators was augmented further by the system of the caucus within the party Organization, composed of the members of the Federal Congress at Washington.

---

* Jefferson, knowingly or not, provided the legal outlets of party life for "varied discontents, which might have converted politics into a strife of revolutionary groups." (Ford, *The Rise and Growth of American Politics*, p. 126.)

These brought forward the names of the "regular" candidates to be elected to national offices. In the State governments, the legislative caucuses in the same manner nominated the heads of their State tickets as well as the Electors who, through the Electoral College, were to name the President.

Over this fixed scene, from which even the organized opposition of the old Federalist Party had vanished, a great current of change came after the second war with England. The people, increased almost threefold in number between 1800 and 1828, more aware of their power and rights, pressed anew for reforms long demanded: notably for manhood suffrage; for the safeguarding of local liberties against an arrogant ruling class, holding a central political control; for curbing the rising money power, favored once more by the Government's financial policies, which seemed identical with those of the revived United States Bank. In certain large States suffrage without property qualifications had been extended during this period; also the group of trans-Appalachian frontier States which had entered the Union extended suffrage widely through the cheapness of land-ownership. Thus it was a profoundly democratic, a "farmer-labor" uprising of very wide scope, originating at the frontier, in "the American forest," that found its leader in and pinned its hopes upon General Andrew Jackson, a settler of the new West.

The defeat of Jackson in 1824 by the caucus system, and the decision of the Electors to follow to the letter our constitutional law and elect Adams President—despite Jackson's great plurality over him—unloosed a storm of popular agitation which raged for four years and culminated in the fairly frenzied electoral campaign of 1828. The ostensible issues were raised by the necessity to overthrow King Caucus and by indignation at the alleged "corrupt bargain" whereby Henry Clay diverted his followers' support to Adams. "The most real issue in . . . 1828," however, "was one which was not stated at the time, nor generally perceived"; [3] it was the widespread demand for universal suffrage, the revolt against "aristocratic corruption" and the monopoly of political power by which a ruling class of officeholders named the only possible candidates for the Presidency. But even the immense enthusiasm evoked by the picturesque person of Old Hickory—an exponent of democracy by instinct rather than theory—would have been insufficient in 1828 to change the existing system had it not been for the intervention of the "politician" Martin Van Buren of New York.

The politics of New York were believed, even in the 1820's, to be "beyond the comprehension of any finite being." Here, as in the great neighboring State of Pennsylvania, where universal white suffrage had also been established, a new (or rediscovered), wholly democratic science was developed which concerned itself all year round primarily with "vote-catching," with the organization and management of unwieldy electoral masses, unable of themselves to act in concert. The shifty Aaron Burr, leading his faction against the clans of Governor Clinton, is said to have been Van Buren's great mentor in this science.* All emphasis was laid now upon partisan unity and management of masses, rather than upon doctrine or policy. Following Burr's tactics, Van Buren's election committees and agents scoured the remotest districts of New York State for votes. Party agents were bound to the leader by their passion for rank and place; and the term "Regency" applied to Van Buren's ascendancy in New York in itself signified the protective management of the commonwealth for its citizens.

Linking his ambitions to a "rising sun," Van Buren made elaborate preparations for 1828, to break up the solid Northeastern opposition to the Jacksonian party by winning New York. It is significant of the new nation-wide political party that organization for large-scale electoral warfare, by trained vote-catchers and office-seekers, was completed before the doctrines which the party advocated were clearly crystallized.

"*Could we only hit upon a few great principles,*" one of Van Buren's associates wrote him, "we should succeed beyond a doubt." The principles were soon found by the fertile Van Buren: they were

---

* "Aaron Burr's politics were learned in the camp. . . . When he, unhappily, turned politician . . . he adhered to the same [military] system. A party, he would maintain, in order to carry elections, must submit to discipline; must execute faithfully, and even blindly, the decrees of its leaders. Whatever is decided upon in the conclaves of the legitimate and recognized chiefs is LAW to the rank and file, which they must execute to the letter, on pain of proscription. (Parton, *Life of Andrew Jackson*, Vol. III, p. 122.)

"States' Rights" as against "Federal usurpation" under President J. Q. Adams.

To provision his own praetorian guard and to crush the Opposition effectively after his victory, Jackson introduced the "democratic principle" of rotation in office. Some 2,000 of the bureaucratic elite were "guillotined," amid scenes of despair on the part of the aristos and wild jubilation on the part of "King Mob."

Before Jackson's "reign of terror" by which the old bureaucracy was proscribed en masse, there had been during four decades of the republic only some 74 removals from office.[4]

Down to this period . . . the educated few had kept themselves uppermost. Cabinets, congresses, legislatures, governors, mayors, had usually been chosen from the same class of society as that from which the governing men of Europe are chosen. Public life was supposed to require an apprenticeship. . . . In short, the ruling class . . . was chiefly composed of men who had graduated at colleges, and had passed the greater part of their lives on carpets.[5]

This permanent bureaucracy which had kept the old political ruling class in power was overthrown.

The victorious party's members now had the "spoils" of office, leisure, security in which to labor in and out of season for the success of their Organization. The professional or "patronage" party had been forged in America, had become a part of the fabric of government itself, wholly unlike parties elsewhere which labored primarily for "class" or "ideas." The election contests thereafter, aside from their other social aspects, were fought by the two camps of Ins and Outs as a pitiless struggle, with the very existence of the mercenary soldiers at stake.[6]

A second distinctly democratic innovation introduced in the Jacksonian Era also set its stamp for ages to come upon American political life. Amid the popular excitement over Jackson, between 1824 and 1828 certain extra-governmental party gatherings or conventions had been held in various States, passing formal resolutions or manifestoes in favor of one candidate or another. This device soon appeared to many as far more "democratic" and convenient than the old informal caucus system of nomination; and by 1832 the inventive

Van Buren, desiring to run with Jackson for the Vice-Presidency, canalized all these sporadic local or State gatherings into a great *national* nominating convention of party delegates from each of the States, in proportion to the number of its votes in the Electoral College. This representative body of delegates, reflecting local and regional impulses throughout the nation, provided, it was felt, a truly democratic apparatus for the party, and gave a solemn, nation-wide sanction and "regularity" to the party's candidates.

We must note that the first truly national party convention of the Democratic-Republicans, in 1832, thanks to the skill of Jackson's Kitchen Cabinet of wirepullers, was arranged as a popular, "spontaneous" manifestation. The State legislatures willingly sent their party delegates to the national party assembly, for the new system answered a deep need, did away with a paradox created by the abstractions of our Constitution: that of holding popular elections of candidates chosen always in an autocratic manner. The humblest voter (by delegated authority) might now participate in the nomination as well as the election of government officers. The structure of party government now rose in representative and *federal* form, a counterpart of the constitutional republic itself. It had the design of a pyramid, based upon local party gatherings in districts, counties, States throughout America and tapering up to the hierarchy of the national nominating convention.

In appearance, following the outburst of radical democracy in Jackson's time, the masses of people now took part in party government itself by means of their popularly chosen delegates, who carried mandates "fresh from the people." In reality, the new institution, in which so much democratic pride was felt, brought about a remarkable formalization of the democratic process. It created a colossal elective pyramid, a vast mechanical structure of primaries, conventions, committees, whose workings, wheel within wheel, whose numerous details, committee business, advance arrangements, were far too complex to remain subject to the casual will or decisions of the masses of busy workaday citizens. Political action, which had been the concern of a comparatively few men of wealth acting in concert usually to safeguard their property interests and, thanks to property, having the leisure to do so, now became the province of a large number of (often propertyless) persons who had no other means of livelihood than their occupation with politics. In other words, the professional politician now appeared and simply relieved the poor or the busy citizen of the whole tedious, ungrateful business of democratic rule.

Certain parliamentary and managerial devices set up in 1832, such as the "unit rule," causing State delegations' votes to be cast in a bloc, and the requirement of a two-thirds majority of the nominating convention for choice of a candidate, had the further effect of giving a minority of the convention a great veto power. Meanwhile the complexity of the whole federated party rule, the numerous meetings, local or regional, and the elaborate preparations made necessary, brought about a certain division of labor as the work involved fell into the hands of specialists giving it all their attention. A real control, actually simplified and secretly centralized, shifted into the hands of permanent committees which conducted the representative local gatherings of the party delegates, and even the national conclave, like rehearsals. "It is hard to keep one's head through this mazy whirl of offices, elections, and nominating conventions," as Bryce comments.[7] Soon only the experienced, professional party workers could function, and were able to monopolize the party gatherings, representative in name only, bestowing elective offices on themselves and their friends. The great body of citizens, bewildered by the various stages of delegated authority, "abdicated."

The Jacksonian "revolution" coincided with a comparatively simple, happy, youthful period in our history, when the republic's social life, mode of production (over 70 per cent that of independent farmers), and conditions of individual liberty more nearly approached the ideal of radical political democracy than ever before or since. Widely extending the rights of the common people, overthrowing the official aristocracy, the Jacksonian movement even strove to create a mechanism which would register popular demands more accurately than before. In its receding tide, the "revolution" upon which so much enthusiasm and passion was spent, left us the spoils system, the professional political party, with its massive convention machinery which made the average citizen a "dummy" of the politicians and the parties. Here is one of those "recurring contradictions in popular government" by which "a mechanism established to register popular desire tends irresistibly to control it." *

II

It is a truism that the conquest of power and office generally changes, vitiates, a political movement. Leaders and officers of the party, were they ever so sincerely committed to a "popular" or "leveler's" or "agrarian" program, are now affected deeply by the dazzling advantages and privileges of official position, by the need for retaining these at all costs, and the haunting fear of losing them. In its new phase, a "conservative" rhythm comes over the former "revolutionaries"; the vision of state policy is obscured and distorted by the overweening preoccupation with office, with patronage.

Such a metamorphosis has been known in varying degree, of course, in all times, in all democratic states where the function of the political party is the manipulation of large numbers of masses of the population. Even in nations where the administrative bureaucracy is "frozen" and the majority party does not win official patronage as its prize, as in the case of the Social Democratic party (a true "class party") of the prewar German Empire, the growth of "professionalism" in leadership creates glaring contradictions between the principles or objects which called the party into being and its practical, day-to-day activities. The enthusiastic masses continue to believe in their leaders for a long time; or find it difficult to intervene directly, or to offset the technical knowledge, the strategic controls they hold—until some profound social crisis seizes the whole society.†

* "The invention is used . . . not to transmit power from the people to the government, but as a means of controlling the people; the power passes through such a mechanism downward to the masses and not from them upward to the government. The convention system, the result of an insurrection against dictation from officeholders, was not long a means for expressing popular wishes. The party management used it freely and deftly; it gave new opportunities for the skill of the professional political mechanic." The spoils system itself, "the effect of a protest against an office-holding regime, the result in some measure of the notion that the government was not for any official class but for the people . . . provided a means of financing party management; it furnished the sinews of war to party government." (McLaughlin, *The Courts, the Constitution and Parties*, pp. 123-25.)

† In a searching study of the morphology of the German Socialist party, written in 1910, picturing its early militancy, its vast organization, its final *"embourgeoise-*

But in the American republic of a century ago the victorious party not only took the administrative apparatus as its prize, the Federal departments, the customhouses, the post offices, but became at once the unifying "organic" element in the Government itself. The Government, so artificially divided, began to function like a well-oiled machine; the two houses of Congress worked in harmony with each other; the President knew in advance of their decisions, through the extralegal agency of the party; and through its district officers in the lower ranks or in the post offices or customhouses of distant cities, field contact was maintained.

The material advantages of party victory (in patronage), that of being the Ins, were so immense that the Opposition was driven in self-defense to organize itself, toward 1840, in the same pattern, as soon as it could rally from defeat. With the alignment of two great parties again, after echoes of Jackson's stirring struggle against the "money powers" died off, they were reconstituted as "Democratic" and "National Republican" (Whigs), "without an ounce of principle between them," the former President John Quincy Adams remarked. The Whigs, heirs to the old Federalists, were motivated, at bottom, by class and sectional views of property which generally clashed with those of the groups combined as Democrats; they favored a protective tariff which would encourage manufacture, "Hamiltonian" government support of canal and railroad projects; they even, timidly, opposed slavery. The Democrats, whose leadership was assumed chiefly by certain gifted Southern landholders, in combination with certain Northern groups, favored States' Rights, were predominantly proslavery and for Free Trade.

But the managers of both parties, especially the desperate Outs, were compelled to use indirection in preaching "principles" or raising "Live Issues" and concentrate all their attention upon building from the ground up a "machine" by which the election canvass

---

ment," Professor Robert Michels prophesied accurately its ultimate betrayal of socialist doctrine, years in advance of the event. He comments: "A period of political fear and persecution sustains the morale of party leadership, discouraging vain and selfish elements; whereas, periods of victory and peace lower the level of leadership." (*Zur Soziologie des Parteiwesens in der moderne Demokratie,* Leipzig, 1910, pp. 197-98, fn.)

might be efficiently organized. The national convention, by which unity and disciplined action might be enforced throughout the country, was copied from the Jacksonians, and stoutly advocated by experienced local Whig leaders, such as the young Abraham Lincoln, who in 1843 declared, in this connection: "A house divided against itself cannot stand." But to carry on the laborious routine, day-to-day fight from each small territorial unit to the national stage, to "shape public opinion" or win "voting cattle," the bait of patronage above all must be offered to the party "workers," first in the form of local, municipal, or State offices, then in the National Government if fortune favored.

In those days, a hundred years ago, the word "politician" became a term of reproach and scorn among the disillusioned but busy and good-humored citizenry. Politics was "the business of the office-holder" as agriculture was the business of the farmer, and philosopher-statesmen such as Jefferson and Madison no longer figured in party life, whose management seemed to have been given over to the more cunning of wirepullers, such as Thurlow Weed of New York and Simon Cameron of Pennsylvania. The party men pursued only "loaves and fishes"; their political organizations were seen, in one aspect, as machines, working from the central party management in a continual chain down to the far-spreading base of village and county units, a "mechanism working automatically and blindly." [8] On the score of opinions and principle, the party became as a church, whose members' minds were closed forever once they had taken its vows, "a sort of church, which admitted no dissent and pitilessly excommunicated any one who deviated . . . from the established dogma. . . ." [9]

By the tactical demands of the developed party institution, the prominent leaders, as it chanced, were characteristically men of most wavering and shifting principles. Such were Van Buren, Clay and Webster, Douglas, and even William Seward in the 1840's; and the parties, like the leaders, were prone to the most devious compromises; their platforms of declared resolutions of policy at national conventions shrank from decisive expressions of doctrine and any clear-cut attitude upon "Burning Issues" over which popular feeling divided itself intensely.*

The invention of the Dark Horse was in itself a remarkable product of our professional politics. Leaders who, despite their public squirmings, had become eventually associated with a given set of ideas, such as Clay, Webster, and Calhoun, were systematically passed over in the search for presidential candidates; and mediocrities who represented nothing, and owned few enemies, as they lacked friends and fame, were chosen in their stead. Then instead of clear resolutions of policy, which might harden or combine groups in opposition, slogans, even symbols, were employed as strategic weapons to divide the enemy or outflank him.

With an amiable, ignorant old Indian fighter, General William H. Harrison ("Tippecanoe") in place of the magnetic Henry Clay as their titular leader, and a Democrat, Tyler, as candidate for the Vice-Presidency (a measure of gross compromise in itself), the long-hungry Whigs in 1840 organized what was perhaps the most spectacular electoral canvass ever seen in a democratic society. They arranged a veritable carnival of torchlight parades and barbecues in which the masses of people, especially in the new Western States, joined for days at a time, as a great, spontaneous democratic holiday; the symbol of the Log Cabin, in which Harrison, like Jackson, had been born, was celebrated in rivers of hard cider, no less native, patriotic, and symbolic. To the cry of "Turn the rascals out!"—for the Democrats had grown mellow and corrupt in office—and to the tune of fantastic or meaningless songs, such as "Tippecanoe and Tyler Too!" the great opposition machine of the Whigs won a sweeping national triumph. George Julian, a member of this party and a Congressman from Indiana who participated in this campaign, said afterward:

---

* Thurlow Weed, who managed the Whig campaign of 1848, ascribed the successful election of General Taylor to his complete silence on any and all public questions. (Cf. Welles, Diary, Vol. III, pp. 249-50.) Seward, who occasionally played the role of a great agitator before the war, was believed never to speak from his own convictions. "My young friend," he once said ironically to an admirer, "we are warned to keep to ourselves what we do not believe. It is as well, frequently, to conceal what we do believe. There is apt to be public damnation in both." (Bradford, Union Portraits, p. 206.)

There was one policy only on which they [the Whigs] were perfectly agreed, and that was the policy of avowing no principles whatever; and they tendered but one issue, and that was a change of the national administration . . . it was idle to deny that on their own showing the spoils alone divided them from the Democrats and inspired their zeal.[10]

By the symbol of the Log Cabin and the spirits of hard cider the Whig managers cleverly and successfully appealed to the masses of people, actually touched deep chords of unconscious belief and principle—for the Democrats in their press had tactlessly derided Harrison as a low or common fellow.* This in peacetime was the highest use of doctrine or principle, namely, to outwit or outmaneuver or overreach the opposition party rather than to touch any profound social condition. For by now the historic American parties were not "credo" parties, as Max Weber has defined them, parties representing definite doctrines and interests or faiths in a church, or a monarchical or traditional aristocratic caste principle, or a rational Liberal Capitalist progress; they now paralleled and competed with each other as purely *patronage parties.*

"The mill has been constructed, and its machinery goes on turning, even when there is no grist to grind." [11]

A professional party, allied with New England textile factory owners who sought a protective tariff system, could detach masses of mechanics and farmers from the Democrats by cynical maneuvers, such as the dispensing of hard cider; a Democratic Dark Horse, James Polk, could for a time confuse issues by declaring himself "a better Tariff man than Henry Clay"; or Clay himself, while a Whig, might descend to a shameful compromise upon the extension of slavery, as in his "Alabama Letter." The leaders counseled usu-

---

* "We are surrounded by log cabins on wheels, hard-cider barrels, canoes, brigs, and every description of painted device, which, if a sober Turk were to drop among us would induce him to believe we were a community of lunatics or men run mad. . . . We never before saw such an exhibition of humbug." *Illinois State Register,* Springfield, June 5, 1840. (Beveridge, *Abraham Lincoln,* Vol. I, p. 270.) A Democrat further complained of the irrationality of the opponents: "We speak of the divorce of bank and state; the Whigs reply with a dissertation on the merits of hard cider. We defend the policy of the administration; the Whigs answer 'log cabin.' We urge the 'honesty, sagacity, statesmanship,' of Van Buren; 'the Whigs answer that Harrison is a poor man.' " (*Ibid.,* Vol. I, p. 272.)

ally, "Let sleeping dogs lie." Yet the underlying economic-sectional division pressed with all the greater force against the artificial limits of the patronage parties; the air of the 1850's grew heavier for the long retarding of social decisions, while the two political guilds dueled with each other for patronage.

The new Republican Party, under new and more forthright leaders, was launched as a great third-party movement in the North to succeed the discredited Whigs after their compromise over slavery in 1850 and their cowardly acceptance of the Kansas-Nebraska Act in 1854. In a time of approaching cataclysm, Seward, Sumner, Chase, and Lincoln now figured as men of principle, as progressive, popular leaders, and their party, outspoken in its opposition to the spread of slavery, combined with its main bloc of discontented Whigs smaller groups of Free-Soilers, Abolitionists, antislavery Democrats, and even repentant Know-Nothings (Anti-Catholics). Thus at last a fresh current of enthusiasm was brought into the sickly political atmosphere. After the promising Republican demonstration of 1856, the trained Whig organizers shifted quickly from their crumbling party into the new party which had taken the second place. For third and fourth parties, doomed to languish without hope of office or patronage, under the American system were inconceivable as a medium for professional politicians.*

The very choice of the moderate Western politician Lincoln, a Dark Horse—for he was then a figure of smaller fame than Seward or Chase—was dictated at the convention of 1860 on grounds of "availability," and decided in a hotel room in the small hours of the morning by machine leaders, such as Simon Cameron, the "Czar." Cameron, Weed, and other "bosses" promised to carry Pennsylvania and similar "strategic" States in return for the now customary pledge of the principal cabinet posts and government offices to their followers, pledges which Lincoln faithfully observed. The new and idealistic Republican Party in its platform declaration temporized upon

---

* In the politics of democratic states, conservative classes, knowing that they may save *their* system only with the aid of the masses who provide majorities "see themselves as obliged to dissimulate a democratic heart, by calling attention, as friends of the people" to the evils of the existing rule. (Michels, *op. cit.*, Introduction, pp. v, vi.)

the question of slavery, but made prominent display of Log Cabin floats in its canvass. The decisive victory in a three-cornered party contest, the most impassioned since 1840, was due in no small measure to the efficient army of political "workers" who had been gathered under its banner. These, at the behest of their regional commanders, Congressmen or Senators, flung themselves upon the spoils of office in 1861 all the more freely now that the Southern leaders retired from the Government by the act of secession. Lincoln, journeying to Washington in disguise before his inauguration, had escaped the assassins who perhaps then lay in wait for him; he did not, however, escape, for all the tragic emergency of civil rebellion menacing the country, the frenzied attack of venal Republican office-seekers, who clamored night and day en masse before his door for their reward.

III

In peace or in war, the office-seekers, parasitic and useful at once, must be fed, the spoils organizations whose ranks they manned must be sated. But in war the party spoils organization seemed literally to gorge itself with the blood of human beings.

In the all-important War Department, Simon Cameron of Pennsylvania, Lincoln's political benefactor, now throned, distributing to his friends valuable offices and war contracts entailing colossal profits to Pennsylvania's iron mills. Cavalry horses ready for the bone yard, rotten ships for transport, were purchased "to pay Cameron's political debts and cure old political feuds." [12]

The contracts for the defective Hall's carbines, which wounded the very soldiers who fired them, in whose financing the youthful J. P. Morgan was involved, the unseaworthy steamships of Commodore Vanderbilt, were contracted for through agents who were influential figures in the new Republican Organization. Cameron, the Secretary of War, was one of the partners of the Pennsylvania Railroad Company, while its vice-president, Thomas A. Scott, was made Assistant Secretary of War. Thus Cameron and Scott, while still owning stock in the Pennsylvania, saw to it that the very troops and horses who went into battle were carried in their railroad boxcars at exorbitant rates. While the Navy Department struggled to blockade the Southern coast, the newest or youngest of the Republican Congressmen, such as Blaine, haunted the door of Secretary Welles, to see to it that New England friends and New England shipbuilders and navy yards and "Blaine men" in Maine might be benefited properly.[13]

Tactfully, the President sends Cameron far away, as Minister to Russia, and the honest, unwearying Stanton in his place comes every morning to watch the bidding for war contracts with his own eye.[14] Yet the plundering process rises like a flood with the mounting appetites of acquisitive men everywhere behind the lines.

The war must go on; the Union must be saved in its darkest hour. But the friends of Seward, and his alter ego, the New York party manager, Thurlow Weed, must be "taken care of." And who is to name the recruiting officers in the western New York district, where conscripts are drafted and some are exempt—in return for large payments on behalf of substitutes? Who was there who could recruit divisions and handle funds for the Provost General more loyally than the friends of the rising Republican Congressman from Utica, Roscoe Conkling? [15]

During four years of the war, the appetites of the war-party followers had grown so monstrous that the patriotic Senator Trumbull cried out in deep anxiety that "the public treasury trembles and staggers like a strong man with a great burden upon him!" [16]

Three years of Reconstruction had made the Frankenstein monster of party organization more gigantic still. Presidential leadership, augmented by an exceptional Cabinet, had perforce become powerful, was visible and responsible to the people in its actions during the war. But the overthrow of presidential authority in Johnson's term had served to make the professional party command the dominant arm of our Government, its control behind the scenes exercised with *indirection* and therefore without immediate responsibility.

When the "strong, silent soldier" Ulysses Grant rode into power on March 4, 1869, his inauguration itself attended by a glittering military parade, relatively few men doubted that he would exercise leadership and tame his party. His glory was at its zenith, his character was a tolerably unblemished one, his arrival in the highest office brought high hopes and satisfaction in nearly all quarters. Grant represented order. "He was a great soldier, and the soldier always represented order," as Henry Adams wrote. We tend nowadays to forget a little unjustly Grant's inestimable military services to the North, whose Government had once searched frantically for an army leader. A "butcher" in war, Grant never retreated; he won. He had advantages of fame at the start of his term not possessed by Lincoln, also a plain man who had happened to "grow" in office. The "inscrutable Ulysses," with his morbidly reticent but unostentatious character, suggested moreover democratic virtue. The office of the President had come to him "unsought," as he said, hence it was assumed that he need make no entangling party alliances, would know how to choose and command able lieutenants, as in the war, and head a firm Government free of wirepullers and rid of squabbles.

"Let us have peace!" the providential man had said in a brief, meaningful phrase. The former rebels of the South remembered his impulsive magnanimity well, despite his break with President Johnson. The North, for its part, with Grant in power felt security from the fear which ever haunted it, and largely favored the extreme measures of Radical Republicans, the fear of new, bloody insurrection. Rarely had a statesman in our history, many remarked in 1868, confronted the people, Congress, the parties, with the strength of so much popular enthusiasm and popular sympathy behind him.

But the paltry results that followed, the confusion without end, the tragic disasters, the vulgar and comic scandals of the General Grant Era—how explain these? They make the story of a little man presiding over giant events, without genius, without plan. General Grant, in effect, bears out those who believe in a science of history. History, so to speak, provides the plan, seizes upon the General as a convenient figurehead for its larger designs.

Moreover, certain modern reinterpretations present Grant's civilian character in an unsparing light, yet one that traces consistently the logic of his fate. We see his failure in civilian life before fortune in war came to him. We see thereafter the "Lion of Vicksburg," the conqueror of Lee, in terror of Mrs. Grant and hiding his state papers from her at night. We see the hero and the fool; the kind father, the loyal friend, the hapless victim of flatterers and knaves; we see him ever obstinate and ever indecisive; dignified and slothful; now indolent, now roused to fury; but always no more than half intelligent; ever silent from agonizing uncertainty, and no wiser than the mythical man in the street. Essentially he was comic; not one of Plutarch's soldier-citizens, but rather a character out of nineteenth-century satire, out of Trollope or Mark Twain. His mediocrity was symptomatic, and typified the low-pressure quality of the Reconstruction statesmen here, which resembled strongly that of the canting political hypocrites of Queen Victoria's bourgeois kingdom or of the tottering Second Empire in France.

With Grant at the inauguration, a dashing company of his army staff officers in full regalia rode into power. General John Rawlins, General Horace Porter, General Belknap, Colonel Babcock, Colonel Badeau—all West Point men, like himself, except Rawlins—these with other lesser figures and relatives were his retinue of devoted friends and advisers. They injected their own particular note into public affairs, like the "political generals," Logan, Schenck, and Butler, who moved into the Republican Party with the Grand Army. Certain of these men acting as the President's secretaries and aides, or even as cabinet members, were still remembered gratefully for their brave war records; and if as a band of military adventurers they brought something of the spirit for "beauty and booty" into the government service, only an indulgent notice was given to their proceedings at the outset.

These men, together with certain old personal political adherents, such as Washburne of Illinois, who with but a few exceptions became the sole beneficiaries of high cabinet posts and administrative offices, surrounded Grant, protected him, advised him. They believed in him "because he succeeded," as Badeau, the court historian, told Henry Adams. Grant was to them "an intermittent energy, immensely powerful when awake, but passive and plastic in repose. . . . For stretches of time, his mind seemed torpid. Rawlins and others would systematically talk their ideas into it, for weeks, not directly, but by discussions among themselves, in his presence. In the end, he would announce the idea as his own . . . and would give the orders to carry it out with all the energy that belonged to his nature." They could not follow his mental processes. "They were not sure that he did think." [17] The gist of their advice now was apparently that he alone was to be President, and he alone was to be responsible.[18]

Another group who held large sway in Grant's intimate councils at the beginning were typically men from the highest ranks of our new financial society. The great Northern masters of industry and capital who were so prominently represented in Washington at the brilliant inaugural ball of March 4, 1869, in their fulsome gratitude had not only paid honors to and lavishly entertained the General, but also had given him rich money prizes. And Grant, who had so long been poor, stood in awe of them as owners of heavy financial artillery, listened earnestly and silently to the ideas of order and security which a Jay Cooke or a Hamilton Fish preached to him. To these men the advent of the General promised perhaps the end of a needless partisan turmoil. To them most of his inaugural address was directed, in which he promised that the financial policy of his government would be that of the patriot. "To protect the national honor," he said, the war debt must be paid in gold, adding also that "no repudiator of one farthing of our public debt will be trusted in public place."

The cabinet posts and all the Federal departments which were administered through them formed of course the central organ of party rule, the appointees acting in dual capacities as government officials and as commissioned officers of their party organization.

The appointments by a President at the outset of his term form the overwhelming concern of all party men. A tradition of a "geographical" distribution of the adminstrative government departments to points of strength in the party leadership on the one hand, and for purposes of building up support at weak points on the other, had been established for years. The loyal "friends" of the party in Indiana or New York must have one department as their reward; it was advisable usually to satisfy the patronage needs of the Far Western branch too. These rules Grant ignored.

In filling these places, in entering upon all the complex business of patronage distribution, Grant proceeded with the blunt, confident spirit of his siege operations in the war, and almost without benefit of the party leaders' advice. The recipients of his appointments were mostly uninformed almost up to the last moment, while his two experienced political advisers, Elihu Washburne and General Rawlins, were kept in terrified uncertainty of his plans, Rawlins actually becoming ill with fear. When the all-important cabinet appointments were announced, they aroused stupefaction among the professional party leaders and shame on the part of disinterested citizens.

Two personal friends, Washburne and the little-known Rawlins, were made Secretary of State and Secretary of War respectively. (Washburne was widely felt to be unfit for his high ministerial post.) The key place of Secretary of the Treasury was given to a man unknown in public life, the merchant prince from New York, A. T. Stewart, who had donated much of the prize money contributed to the General; another politically unknown capitalist, Adolph E. Borie, who had richly befriended Grant, was made Secretary of the Navy. Two other appointments, those of Judge Ebenezer Hoar of Boston as Attorney General and Jacob D. Cox of Ohio as Secretary of the Interior, brought men of ability and mark to the Cabinet; but they offended deeply in another sense, namely, that each was believed to be independent, honest, liberal, and unaffiliated with the inner ring of Republican leaders. Each of these virtuous men would be a thorn in the side of the party and the Administration.

The Republican leaders in Congress were both dismayed and disgruntled by so much awkwardness and by so little sense of political "forces" and values shown by Grant. But Grant was the President of their choice, the idol still of Northern voters, and it behooved them to proceed with caution. With more sorrow than anger—except in the case of the aged Sumner, aggrieved more than the others at being so little "consulted"—the Senate firmly refused confirmation to Stewart, the owner of New York's great dry-goods emporium, as Secretary of the Treasury. Stewart, formerly a poor immigrant, was pathetically eager for official honor; but though he offered to donate the profits of his business to charities for his term, the objection was raised (under an old law of 1789) that his direct engagement in commerce made him legally unqualified.

The President was clearly surprised and vexed; he endeavored to have the provisions of the old law disqualifying Stewart waived by permissive legislation of Congress. But this was refused. After a short, sharp contest, the conqueror of Lee's army, confused and faltering, made a sudden abject retreat. But somebody must be found quickly for the post. The appointment of a prominent man of business to one of the highest political offices, which Grant had attempted out of ignorance, was considered preposterous in those days. What was desired was a seasoned, specialized politician. Following a hasty conference, the party leaders modestly proposed for the Treasury one of their very own men, George S. Boutwell of Massachusetts, the most bigoted and partisan of the ring of Radical Republicans who had led in the impeachment of Johnson, as in all the harsh and devious business of the Joint Committee of Fifteen on Reconstruction. To this the President quickly agreed. He had been well disciplined by the party leaders.* So the Treasury would be far more accessible to the professionals than might be the case under a tyro such as Stewart. Boutwell also would favor the maturing plans of high Protectionists, whereas Stewart, a large importer, might have been expected to resist these.

With every step thenceforth Grant plunged further into unawaited and mystifying difficulties in his attempts to organize his Administration and in his connections with the men of his party. In a reshuffling of his Cabinet during the first few days, Washburne resigned and was sent to France as Minister; he had desired, as he explained, to serve but temporarily as Secretary of State, for the sake of prestige. To his place at length, almost against his will, came the dignified and dull grandee Hamilton Fish, long ago Governor of and Senator for New York, a conservative Republican who had contributed generous sums also to the Grant election campaign.

All seemed execrable confusion in the White House; executive officers knew not if they were confirmed or dismissed, and Assistant Secretaries acted in their place.[19]

Relations between the President and the great regional bosses who sat in the Senate, as managers of the national Republican Organization, were uncertain and secretly strained. By the "courtesy-of-the-Senate" tradition Senators would not confirm an appoint-

---

*Boutwell is "a good friend" and "feels kindly" toward the House of Cooke, writes Henry to his brother Jay. (Oberholtzer, *Jay Cooke*, Vol. II, p. 79, letter of Mar. 12, 1869.)

ment to a post office or a revenue post in any State which was disapproved by the Senators from the State in question. For obvious
reasons, the new President who fumbled toward leadership was advised to seek the repeal of the terrible Tenure of Office Act of 1867,
which had been leveled at Johnson as a Reconstruction measure and
as a means of having Congress exercise a joint control over executive appointments and removals. This he did, Senator Oliver Morton
of Indiana leading the administration fight for repeal, but the cool
resistance which was met opened the eyes of the "baby politician" in
the White House.

A powerful minority in the Republican caucus, headed by Senator
Roscoe Conkling, while tactfully avoiding an open break with Grant,
showed extreme reluctance to yield the executive power it had obtained. The Senate held fast, while the President for some days sustained a siege of the politicians by giving out no appointments to
office, hoping thus to force the Senator bosses to yield. For ten days
of uproar in March, 1869, the machinery of government at the
Capitol was blocked. "The city is filled with a hungry crowd, wanting offices," wrote Welles.[20] By unusually sharp tactics the determined
party minority held the other members at bay; then a Senate committee, visiting the White House for a conference, was reported to
have threatened Grant with the scandal of a resounding public break
in the party and unrelenting congressional opposition from the beginning of his term.[21]

Unquestionably the simple military man was baffled and appalled
at the prospect of such a destructive internal warfare as had been
waged against his predecessor, Johnson. A light dawned upon the
slow-witted soldier. With all his prestige, he was compelled to yield
to the Senators and accept as a peaceful compromise certain slight
changes of the Tenure of Office Act which restricted but little the
grip of the Senators upon executive power. Control of the patronage,
seized under pretext of a revolutionary struggle with a Copperhead
President, rested as firmly as ever in the hands of the party managers. Grant's "surrender to the politicians" in the first month of
his term, when he was regarded with almost superstitious reverence
by the population, was held to be an egregious blunder. Whatever
notions he or his military friends may have entertained of a "dicta-

torship" or of dominant presidential leadership—and few Americans, least of all Grant, were inclined to this—were now utterly abandoned.

It was a pregnant moment in the annals of party life. A President covered with "glory" shrank from a "constitutional" quarrel, and found it a positive relief to escape from a nightmare of party opposition, and to leave to the Senators a continued censorship (of disputed and quite doubtful legality) over the executive power of appointment and removal. Each Senator and Representative of the ruling party remained as a satrap with command of life and death over his own political province. Each was followed, as one Congressman wrote, "like a Highland chieftain 'with his tail on,' by a band of retainers devoted to his political fortune, dependent upon him for their own, but supported at the public charge." [22] The party managers entrenched themselves in effective control of the government apparatus for long years to come.

The outcome of the internal party struggle of March-April, 1869, remained somewhat obscure to the general public at the moment, the press actually reporting it as a "partial victory" for Grant; yet some commentators already prophesied that terrible mischief would follow; "Corruption, inefficiency, special favors, etc," would "marshal an army of professed politicians" in a powerful combination to undo Grant's presumed plans to introduce economy and order in the government bureaucracy.[23]

The general Government of the republic was at peace with itself; this much was achieved. Party "harmony" between the White House and the Capitol, so vital to the functioning of our divided government authority, was now established, in compensation for certain sacrifices by the captive President.

Grant himself, according to one view, now underwent an important "growth" as a politician. He learned that political action was far less simple than military operations; that to win victory in this new field he must lean upon "practical men" schooled in political warfare. As he had depended on Sherman and Sheridan for their technical military experience, so he must count now upon men who commanded whole divisions of political foot soldiers and deployed with myriads of voters in electoral campaigns, leaders such as Cam-

eron, Morton, Conkling, and Zach Chandler, rather than mere theorists and reformers such as Carl Schurz or Trumbull.[24]

The removal of Johnson appointees and the filling of Federal vacancies (so passionately awaited by the army of professional party
"workers"), it was announced by Grant, was to be done chiefly with
the advice of the Congressmen from the districts affected. Thenceforth an entente cordiale was maintained with the inner partisan
organization, most of whose leaders had first opposed Grant's wishes.
The new President's friends and relatives were confirmed in lucrative places and the loyal party camp followers proposed by the party
leaders, in turn, were all quickly named en masse by the President
and awarded the "spoils" of bureaucratic power. The conservative
Secretary of State found himself besieged by hundreds of office-
seekers or former soldiers, who arrived in trainloads, and were armed
with letters from their Congressmen or even with white cards from
the President,[25] as good for office as "vouchers" at a teller's window.

The Postmaster General, like Secretary Boutwell of the Treasury,
lent himself willingly to the requirements of the party chiefs. Plans
were laid now for the reshuffling of the Cabinet, so that within the
year the two or three department heads who were useless or, by their
independence, offensive to senatorial leaders were to be eliminated.
Grant also avoided formulating government policy, declaring that he
had "no policy to enforce against the will of the people," contenting
himself with executing the laws, hence leaving the congressional
leadership dominant. The "weakness" of the presidential office, which
had set in after Lincoln's death, became a tradition which endured
for a whole long generation.

The famous "Senatorial Clique" working behind the scenes and
behind the figurehead of Grant, now held absolute command over
the ruling party and virtually ruled the country. They had taken
over the national party machine which Thaddeus Stevens, through
his "directory," had built so well during and after the Civil War;
but the new leaders were men of an entirely different stamp. Their
ascendancy, the special nature of their rulership, was the most prominent feature of Grant's term of eight years and determined the whole
strange train of events by which the General Grant Era is remembered. The emergency of war and revolution and the need of na-

tional safety after the war had fashioned the party Organization into a more fanatical and disciplined band than ever before. But now the old ideologues who had led the movement were some of them dead; others, such as Ben Wade, "the wild Radical," were retired by the individual mischance of defeat; Sumner, Trumbull, and Schurz, inspiring orators of the antislavery cause, stood outside of the circle which had captured the President and controlled the party, and they entered more and more openly into opposition to both. The new commanders of the colossal party machine advanced nevertheless, as if automatically, in response to the blind instincts which had called them and their Organization into being.

I V

Revolutionary parties, like revolutions themselves, have their rhythm. Ardent, clear-sighted, strong in years of adversity or deadly struggle, they turn mellow and take their ease in the phase of success and plenty. The party of revolutionary capitalism, under the leadership of Lincoln, Fessenden, Stevens, Greeley, and the youthful Sumner, suggested positively Spartan virtue and idealism compared with the new leadership of a decade later.

In the political society of Washington, as in New York, an age of pomp and extravagance began after the war. Ladies' trains were 65 inches long, and their bonnets, if they were Senators' wives, were sometimes ornamented with huge diamonds. A Senator such as old Simon Cameron, who was a railroad-owner as well as a member of the Republican oligarchy, paid $1,000 a month for his quarters at the Arlington Hotel. The house of another of the oligarchs, Senator Zach Chandler of Michigan, blazed with lights from top to bottom, and his dining-table set for scores of guests was sometimes decorated in fantastic designs, such as "a miniature model of Pekin, with confectionery of all kinds and colors framed into temples, towers, minarets, and pagodas." [26] Visitors recalled the General Grant Era as having no polite conversation worth the name, and being but one long revel, White House dinners costing $1,500, those of cabinet officers having no means beyond their modest salaries being often little less sumptuous, with service of two or three dozen courses and six kinds of wine, and the chief subject of interest the gowns, the diamond necklaces, or the "sunbursts" worn by the great ladies of the day.

With the adoption of display, or conspicuous waste as an important development in practical ethics—for so, according to Veblen, the strong men showed their powers of consumption—there spread also a significant contempt for learning among the bluff soldiers, professional politicians, and hardfisted captains of industry who ruled the republic now. The President, it was noted by a Harvard professor, was "easily influenced by what one may call *second-class ideas*." [27] These were often skillfully set before him now by his chosen advisers, such as Zach Chandler, a huge, stout, bibulous fellow, bediamonded, with imposing fringe of side whiskers, "always ready to smoke a cigar, take a drink, play a game of cards or tell a good story." [28] What was the use, Chandler would explain, of sending "literary fellers" such as Motley and Lowell upon important foreign missions? And so their cultivated heads fell quickly—Grant even professed himself worried because Motley parted his hair in the middle—and a political General, a party boss from Ohio, or a simple livery-stable owner went to represent our Government abroad. Instead of the learned historian, a Robert C. Schenck went to the Court of St. James, disseminating there for several years his expert knowledge of draw poker. [29]

There was no dearth of orators to proclaim from the stump the ideology of the ruling party. But the ideas of national union, of universal liberty and veritable social progress, which Lincoln, Stevens, and Sumner had championed were now converted by the stentorian Oliver Morton and John Logan, Ben Butler, or the pretentious Conkling, to bellowings over the Bloody Shirt. This "line" had once possessed its utility, especially for the North, as a warning against recidivists of insurrection; but now, its usefulness outworn, the Bloody Shirt oration concealed but little the purpose of the oligarchy to hold state power, come what might, by prolonging the moods of hate and fear.

In the matter of Reconstruction Grant continued the policy of "holding down" the former rebels by military rule, and forcing steadily the adoption of the new Fifteenth Amendment, which di-

rectly conferred the vote upon the colored freedmen. In this field he
rarely moved without consulting Oliver Morton. For years the squat
figure of Indiana's wartime Governor, now floor leader of the
Senate, with the large, pale head and burning eyes of an invalid,
his long black hair and imperial, his fierce uptilted nose dilating
easily with theatrical emotion, could be seen eternally conferring
alone with Grant in the Blue Room of the White House.[30] Morton's
friends and henchmen soon filled the principal posts in the Southern
Carpetbag governments and helped hold these in the Republican
column. On the occasion of a message sent by Grant to Congress concerning a supplementary measure of Reconstruction in Georgia, he
was questioned as to the meaning of a certain phrase. He replied
simply, "I don't know what it means, Morton put that in." [31]

Another favorite adviser upon all matters of administration was
Roscoe Conkling, the Beau Brummell of the Senate. Quick and voluble, impressive in manner, Conkling spoke in the government councils with the voice of powerful financial groups of New York. By
1870 he had ingratiated himself thoroughly into the favor of the
President, and was awarded in the interests of his own personal Organization all the Federal patronage of New York, including the
rich citadel of the New York Custom House, which controlled the
bulk of the nation's commerce and import revenue. The other oli-
garchs of the war party, Cameron, Butler, Zach Chandler, wrung
patronage from the Executive almost at will, and reinforced thereby
their local or regional machines. To these men it became, for instance, a matter of intense concern that Jacob D. Cox, the Secretary
of the Interior, devoted the management of his department to reform
of the personnel and to measures of economy. Soon Chandler and
Butler were intriguing actively to bring about Cox's expulsion. He
had displayed his efficiency and honesty for a little more than a year
when there came a sudden note from the President in October, 1870,
in his most military manner, asking his resignation. This followed
a visit by Chandler to the Secretary's office, in which the latter
boasted that he, Cox, was to be removed.[32] Attorney General E. L.
Hoar in the meanwhile had been making very commendable appointments of good men for the Department of Justice and the Federal judgeships without heeding party chieftains' demands, and soon

Simon Cameron and others were after his head. On June 15, 1870, this worthy Yankee lawyer received a sudden message of dismissal from Grant, for no reason, he too becoming an early casualty of the Cabinet.

"What could you expect," said Cameron, laughing cynically, "for a man who had snubbed seventy senators?" [33]

The Department of the Interior and the Department of Justice, directed by complaisant men, became, like the Post Office system (directed by an obscure party hack) and the Treasury, the subject provinces of the party's proconsuls, who seemed to confine themselves wholly thereafter to the exploitation of the spoils system. Everywhere triumphant, these men could afford to cast aside the mask of a humanitarian ideology, and reveal themselves more fully by their overweening preoccupation with party business, by all their prosaic, day-to-day professional activities, as the pure spoilsmen they were.

No new ideas of policy, virtually no laws worth the name, nothing but a familiar jargon, trumpeted forth on every Fourth of July, as orthodox Republicanism, issued from the ruling group of Senator-bosses in all the years during which they dominated the President and Congress. And so after 1869, even the hollow subterfuge of being Radicals was dropped at last. The clique of Senators who, together, wielded the nation-wide patronage through the subservience of the President, and showed themselves as unswerving supporters of his "policies" (which were actually their own), became known more accurately as the Republican "Stalwarts," the most mercenary, the most professionally partisan element of their party.

A common pattern of development, of tactics and interests, stamped the Stalwart leaders. Whether they came from the recent frontier regions of the Mississippi Valley, like Morton, or the older cities of the East, like the foppish Conkling, or were originally illiterate tradesmen, like Zach Chandler, or tolerably cultivated men, like James G. Blaine, each one headed an identical regional or State machine, manned by his battalions of political followers.

Oliver Morton, perhaps the strongest of the Stalwarts, had long before (after 1856) organized the Republican Party of his State out

of the inchoate elements opposed to slavery "into a compact body
. . . well equipped for political warfare." [34] Indiana, a "strategic"
State in elections, whose action alone might swing the balance of party
victory, was ruled with a high hand during the war, and in peace
witnessed the rise of a regular party Organization which Morton ran
"as the country schoolmaster ran his school." According to local
authorities, he asked only that his orders be obeyed. "He controlled
the politicians as a showman controlled his puppets." They were his
"tools"; and Morton was "a practical mechanic who works well with
tools."

In Michigan the very fat, very rich, and very bibulous dry-goods
merchant Zachariah Chandler, one of the most belligerent of the
older Republican leaders, who had become Mayor of Detroit and
Senator before the war, also ruled over an irresistible machine for
managing elections in his State. For twenty years there were but
"Chandler legislatures" and "Chandler Governors" in Michigan,
while this "political Leviathan" directed his subordinates and his
local interests by means of an army of officials, Federal and State
job-holders, collectors, assessors, petty postmasters. These could all
be seen regularly making their march upon the State capitol in election seasons, "a retinue that might have been mistaken in its immensity for the Israelites who remembered longingly the flesh-pots
of Egypt." [35]

In neighboring Illinois the black-bearded volunteer General and
leader of the Grand Army of the Republic, "Black Jack" Logan, undermined the good Trumbull, replaced him, and assumed command
for twenty years of a State Organization of which it was said that virtually every office was for sale, and every form of special privilege
was on the counter to the highest bidder.

Everywhere the same tactics are seen. In populous New York,
where electoral management was so long a black art, Roscoe Conkling as United States Senator after 1867 simply succeeded by a series
of "strokes of state" to the leadership of the old Whig-Republican
Organization created by the masterful Thurlow Weed, the alter ego
of Seward. Arrogant and autocratic in his method, he directed a
large official army holding the many lucrative State offices and the
important Federal bureaucracy of customhouses and postmasterships

centered in the metropolis itself. From the unofficial headquarters of the New York Custom House, which alone employed then over 1,000 political "workers," the organization was run with the superb discipline and esprit de corps traditional in Empire State politics. Conkling said openly:

> We are told the Republican party is a machine. Yes. A government is a machine; a church is a machine; an army is a machine . . . the common-school system of the State of New York is a machine; a political party is a machine.[36]

Horace Greeley testified amusingly that in his travels throughout New York, as lecturer and journalist, he came upon hundreds of Senator Conkling's New York Custom House officials—supposed to be guarding the water front—far in the interior, traveling upon trains everywhere in connection with their party duties at local nominating conventions, committee meetings, and caucuses under the command of Conkling.

In Maine, as a protégé of the veteran Senator Fessenden and the wealthy Morrill brothers, long-time leaders of the State, the former schoolteacher and journalist James G. Blaine, still in his early thirties, had become Speaker of the State lower house and active head of the local machine, handling local patronage and power. By 1869 Fessenden was dead and Blaine had become a national figure in Congress, Speaker of the House—wielding enormous legislative power. Thus from "way down East" in Maine, where James Blaine's house in Augusta would serve many times as the unofficial headquarters for the Maine Legislature, and from Boston, where the scheming demagogue General Ben Butler created a praetorian band of Federal and local officials who toiled under him, to the new State of Wisconsin, where the Yankee lawyer Senator Matthew Carpenter ruled, and to farthest California, where the Radical Senator Aaron Sargent, ally of Collis Huntington's railroad octopus, directed duplicate organizations—everywhere the common pattern is repeated. It even springs to life in the newest Territory. But for the sustenance of these local or regional Organizations each leader vitally needed his share of the offices in the Federal Administration.

The boss was the nearly absolute ruler of his State Organization;

but in turn he was compelled, as regularly as the medieval lord of the manor, to nourish and protect his vassals and all his manor hands. For without their disciplined labor the substance of his power would vanish. The Senator-boss was in a sense enslaved to his ever hungry Organization; its quenchless appetite, like that of a legendary dragon, calling for ever more nutriment, more spoils, made for him "white nights" of torment over the problems of discovering patronage and favor enough to meet the demands of his followers, and days of unwearied search for all offices which might be turned to his army. There was not a little truth in President Lincoln's jest that before retiring for the night and after saying his prayers he invariably looked under his bed to see if the Senator from New York, then Mr. Harris, lay in wait for him.*

But what choice did Mr. Harris have in the matter? Even if a man were a thief, a brothel-keeper, a murderer, so long as he was a faithful member of the party Organization his leader might not only feel obliged to defend him from the consequences of his crimes, but be compelled even to obtain the sinecure of local government or Federal office for him.

For in each State the "active men" of the Organization worked together as a team; to the fortunes of the mighty Senator-boss, the lieutenant, the subleaders, were firmly attached; under the lieutenants, in turn, there labored in unison the heads of the local branches of the Organization, in each territorial unit of the State, divided in turn into counties and precincts. The rank and file of "workers," holding places as postmasters, revenue officers, United States marshals, or city or State officials, and State legislators or doorkeepers, were provided, like the subleaders, with security and leisure to act continually for the Organization with unsleeping vigilance at every stage of the whole ponderous democratic process. Holding the key

* In his novel *Eugène Rougon* Emile Zola gives a picture of popular politics in France which offers a remarkable parallel to contemporary American conditions. A cabinet minister is visited in Paris by a delegation from his southern constituency, uncouth provincials who make urgent demands for political favors. A friend present watches with some surprise the docility with which Rougon, brilliant popular leader in the Chamber of Deputies, assents to all of these exactions. Why, asks the friend, after they have left, does Rougon yield so readily to these loutish fellows who, for him, must serve as little more than pawns? But Rougon answers: "But I am nothing without them. *I am their pawn.*"

places of local and county committees, they together determined the choice of local primary conventions (leading to the State legislatures) and of Congressmen, as well as the State gatherings of the party, whose inner Organization determined the State-wide ticket, the Governor, the United States Senators, even the naming of a presidential nominee.

But the county bosses and district captains were usually "under obligations" to the State boss. In the New York Republican machine, for instance, one of Conkling's ten or twelve principal lieutenants, a rural leader, was said to have placed seventy-five local friends of his in public office in Washington and New York City immediately following a successful national election:

He puts men under obligations to him and commands their friendship and services. . . . He has appointees in the New York Custom House, in the New York Post Office, and in the New York City government.[37]

The State leader, through his lieutenants, maintained strict liaison with the local party officers, and thus intervened regularly in all local actions. While every form and process of popular, representative action was gravely gone through with, the boss stood by, designating the officers and committeemen at every step.

To hold power and to exclude from power the traditional enemy of the opposing party, the Republican spoilsman had, after the war, greatly expanded means for raising revenues. For many years, since State Organizations held nearly absolute control over elective or appointive offices, it had been customary for candidates to make payments into the party chest. A judgeship would be priced at $15,000, a seat in Congress at $4,000, a seat in a State legislature at $1,500. Thus the professional Organization raised up in the service of a political movement "had come down to an industrial concern for making money out of places; it bought votes, worked up this material into elective commissions, and resold them with its trade-mark to the highest bidder."[38]

But with the conquest of the national Administration, through the concerted efforts of the various regional bosses, as in 1868, infinite possibilities of enrichment were opened up for the Organization. The most valuable single piece of Federal patronage at this period was the great New York Custom House. When President Grant on July 1, 1870, at the wish of Roscoe Conkling, appointed the latter's adviser and henchman, Thomas Murphy, Collector of the Port of New York, he made Conkling one of the real rulers of the political Government. Murphy, an experienced Republican ward heeler of New York City, a notorious shoddy contractor during the war, and sometime business associate of William Tweed, helped Conkling to eliminate a rival leader from control of the Republican Organization. The administration of the New York Custom House was devoted thereafter entirely to supporting the needs of the President and the Stalwart boss. Grant's private secretary, General Porter, in communicating the President's views had written to Murphy: "I only hope you will distribute the patronage in such a manner as will help the Administration." [39] Murphy, who needed no urging, introduced almost at once more than 300 political foot soldiers into his office who were chosen solely in the interest of the Conkling Organization. When accused of creating excessive employment, Murphy replied stoutly: "There were certain people who had to be taken care of," and since "nobody in the party would say anything about his taking care of them . . . he would do it." [40]

Thereafter, the strongest lieutenants of the Republican Party in New York threw in their fortunes with Conkling, acknowledging him their liege lord. Among these were Alonzo Cornell of Ithaca, son of the famous philanthropist, Platt of Owego, the capable former druggist and county boss, and Chester A. Arthur of New York City, a veteran "worker" who had slowly risen through the ranks and through a labyrinth of committees to membership in the State executive committee of New York's political army. Amiable and tactful, a dandy known for his possession of a hundred pairs of trousers, Arthur, in 1871, became head of the great New York Custom House when Murphy resigned under fire.

Under Chester Arthur's skillful direction, 1,011 clerks and officials, the majority of them active members of the Republican State machine, not only toiled at preparations for primaries and elections, but also paid assessments upon their large aggregate of salaries to Arthur for the party chest. In these days the New York Custom House attained its highest phase of partisan usefulness after long

fame as a "nest of corruption." If there were an honest man in this
band who refused tips, gratuities, or bribes, or who did not practice
some petty form of blackmail upon importing merchants, then he
was seldom heard from. But how honorable and scrupulous were
the merchants, the businessmen themselves?

With the aid of spies or inside informers the experienced customhouse inspectors played for many years at a diverting game of
trapping large mercantile houses with undervaluations or short
weights, and by such measures wresting large fees from would-be
defrauders of the Treasury. Under the terms of the law then in
force, the entire value of an importation which had been falsely declared—not merely the amount of tax involved—was subject to for-
feiture, the moiety, or half, going to the head of the New York
Custom House as his fee and to cover legal expenses of collection.

In one instance Arthur's watchers caught the great metal-importers
Phelps, Dodge & Co. in a small difficulty involving several thousand dollars of import tariff, whereupon the whole shipment of
$1,750,000 of goods was declared subject to forfeiture. To escape
scandal and costly litigation, the old magnate William E. Dodge
reluctantly settled the threatened suit out of court, as advised by
Collector Arthur and his counsel, for some $271,017.23, the moiety
of which was divided between the special agent and the three leading
officers of the port, including Arthur and Alonzo Cornell, then Sur-
veyor of the Port of New York. An enormous fee for that day,
$50,000, was also paid to the eminent legal counsel employed in the
matter, namely, to Roscoe Conkling and Ben Butler.[41] Thus Arthur,
Conkling's lieutenant, operated what was the "boiler room" of the
Republican spoils machine. A Quartermaster General during the war,
he now served in the same capacity for his party. Sometimes he
earned for himself the princely income for those days of $40,000
per annum in fees. Not all of this wealth adhered to him, however,
for the political code of the time required an openhanded generosity
on the part of an officer of such means. It is related:

At State conventions, his suite of rooms was the caucus headquarters and
his cigars and other refreshments were hospitably offered and cheerfully
consumed. In addition, he was relied upon for contributions of money to

meet unexpected political exigencies, especially among New York City's district leaders.[42]

Then in addition Conkling could dispose of hundreds of post offices, United States Marshalships, and numerous other Federal appointments to all of his retainers hailing from various points of the Empire State.

Roscoe Conkling, unchallenged boss of the large, typical New York State machine after 1870, was himself a man of unique gifts. American politicians, according to Bryce's convenient classification, usually fall into two categories: orators, or "stump politicians," and Organization managers, or "desk politicians." Conkling throughout his public career held a national reputation as an orator, but he possessed to a remarkable degree the qualities of the latter type, the "desk politician," and made important contributions to the craft of professional politics in its very heyday.

The son of a prominent Federal judge, Conkling in his twenties had gone to Congress from western New York as a Northern fire-eater, a follower of Seward, who was his patron. Six feet three inches in height, yet well-proportioned and athletic in figure, with his piercing blue eyes, his handsome physiognomy, graced by wavy auburn hair falling in curls over his brow and a golden beard—Conkling's appearance alone made a political sensation, augmented by his romantic habits of dress, which favored cream-colored pantaloons, moon-colored vests, and fabulous silk scarves. To his natural truculence of temper, his studied arrogance in public, were added strong convictions of class and section, which made him a dramatic figure on the eve of the "irrepressible conflict." His speeches were carefully prepared, were delivered in his high, sharp voice with a tantalizing deliberation, which with the proud, uplifted jaw and nose accentuated his favorite tones of sarcasm.

Such bombast, such classic periods, one would think, bespoke but the inveterate dandy who looked for approval chiefly to the feminine contingent in the gallery of Congress—for so Washington scandal often whispered of Conkling. Yet in Conkling, for all his theatrical posing in public, there was concealed a consummate party manager. Under Grant, as under Lincoln, no government patronage within his purview escaped his hand; the lowliest of his retainers might count upon his unsleeping vigilance in their behalf. While his temper and haughtiness in public followed a Napoleonic model, not without its use in the rough and tumble of party life, tradition holds that Conkling in private commerce with his associates unbent and dropped his pose in favor of a charming candor, a cynicism mixed with camaraderie. It was as if to say:

Here we are, all men of the world together. Of course, we do rotten things in New York. You do rotten things in Baraboo. Politics is a rotten business. You know it. I know it. What's the use of pretending anything else? Nothing counts except to win. Well, we win, don't we? . . . What have you got? Full house on aces? Good as wheat![43]

Conkling and his Organization were extremely rich in post offices, in customhouse collections. In Pennsylvania, Cameron was no less richly endowed. At the Canadian border, in Detroit, the Federal Custom House was known similarly as "Zach Chandler's customhouse." In Indiana, Illinois, and Wisconsin, Senators Morton, Logan, and Carpenter too were rich in spoils, though these might take the shape of post offices principally, or departments under the Treasury, internal revenue offices which collected the excise tax upon whisky. In Massachusetts again, the subalterns of Boutwell and Ben Butler enriched the State machine with customhouse moiety fees. More, a special Federal Treasury official at Boston, engaged through Butler's influence to collect delinquent taxes (which would have been recovered in the normal course of events), turned half of the proceeds—sometimes in sums as high as $213,000, as single fees—principally to Butler's Organization of party "workers."[44] Thus the strength of all of the great bosses was rooted in rich bureaucratic spoils.

When the boss arrived at the national Capitol, for he was often directly crowned as United States Senator, his power in the general Government could scarcely be calculated, especially if he came from a populous and "strategic" State. Three heads of the party Organizations from three or four such important States, together with the weaker satellite States which were usually attached to each, could easily summon the strength to block or control national party conventions, eliminate or choose Presidents, and dominate legislation in

Congress. What single man, were he a great soldier, a President, a Supreme Court Justice, could hold out against them? If one searched for the true center, the real fountainhead, of national government authority itself, one need look no further than the dominant cabal of Senator-bosses heading the Organizations of New York, Massachusetts, Ohio, Indiana, Pennsylvania. It was to the combined power of these men that Ulysses Grant in 1869 had given virtually his own unconditional surrender.

CHAPTER THREE

THE SPOILSMEN IN POWER

I think our government is honestly and economically managed.   ULYSSES S. GRANT

THE General Grant Era witnessed the full flowering of the spoils system in our Government in stronger and purer form than ever before. For seven years, until they faced detection and punishment, the spoilsmen who invaded every branch of the National Government moved in the pursuit of "beauty and booty" solely. Gathered in overwhelming majority, with the great silent soldier present to keep order in the country, they needed to concern themselves with no threat from a beaten opposition party, no serious problems of national policy—such as troubled the prewar era—nothing, in short, but the uninterrupted use and enjoyment of the offices.

So far as the unhappy internal question of Reconstruction still faced them, the Stalwart bosses of the Republican Party, such as Conkling, Morton, and Cameron, and even moderate colleagues, such as John Sherman and Edmunds, saw to it only that Republican electoral votes and Republican congressional representation was forthcoming from the "reconstructed" States; and to this end military rule was continued—despite the mounting disorder it provoked in the shape of Ku Klux Klans and White Leagues—so long as the ruling party had a fighting chance to hold the conquered States.* The justification always was the "safety of the republic." Referring

* Following the election of Grant in 1868, army commanders of the military districts into which the Southern States were divided began to administer the so-called ironclad oath; only by swearing that he had held no office nor taken up arms under the Confederacy could any citizen hold office under the "reconstructed" government. Thus the Carpetbag or "Scalawag" governments, as agents of the Republican Party largely, were set up. In reaction, the whites turned to passive or secret resistance, to violence and terror, which, despite frequent intervention by the Federal military forces, dislodged the usurping politicians. With the abolition of the Freedmen's Bureaus in 1872, as a measure of compromise, the colored people sank again into tenancy or sheer peonage upon the land, an outcome which concerned the party of Lincoln almost in no way after 1876. The Negro had been "used" by the party of the North, and was abandoned, as Du Bois holds, when he was no longer needed. *Cf.* Du Bois, *Black Reconstruction*, Chap. XIV.

to a measure which concerned the support of one of the new Carpet-bag governments (in Georgia) a Stalwart, Henry Wilson of Massachusetts, blurted out before the Senate: "Law or no law, we want to keep this State government in power!"

Nor was there occasion or time to shape adjustments or reforms in the laws touching currency and taxation; these problems, especially in the matter of the mode of repayment of the national debt, protective-tariff duties, and refunding programs, were largely postponed—or treated in accordance with policies fixed amid the crisis passion of the war. There were certain questions of foreign policy, notably of enforcing settlement by England of our Alabama Claims, which were also postponed as long as possible.

Indeed there was little time for statesmanship, as one member of Grant's Cabinet explained—after he had been expelled. "It is . . . no figure of speech to say that diplomacy, finance, military, naval, and internal administration," he said, are ". . . relegated to such odds and ends of time as may be snatched from the greater cares of office." [1]

The saturnalia of plunder which developed throughout the Grant regime has often been attributed to the dominance in the republic of the new business class and their new pecuniary morals. This, however, is not a wholly accurate view. The new capitalists were, to be sure, among the "chief stockholders" and partners of the ruling party, and grasped wherever possible for government favor or protection; indeed, as a class, they achieved the fulfillment of "historic demands" in the decade after 1860. But while the capitalists held a controlling interest in the concern, they were not always able to exercise genuine control over their partners, the professional politicians. Nor had the capitalists in their own minds arrived as yet at any consistent smooth-working scheme of relations with the political Government and the men who held it in charge. For the capitalists themselves of the generation of "empire-builders" who followed the war, those for whom the concept of "community of interests" was yet unborn, it was a phase of unrestrained, pitiless competition with each other, often attended with physical violence as well as economic waste and destruction. The larger stakes played for in the boom period of giant industry were reflected in the increasing greed with which financiers and enterprisers besought the politicians for their specialized services.

The two major parties composed together a guild or "estate" of men trained in the specialized work of electoral management and organization. There were many points (marking the inward contradictions of the social system) at which professional politicians and men of business conflicted in their purpose. The entrance of businessmen into politics—even of a potent Dry Goods King such as A. T. Stewart—was then held unorthodox, and the politicians, jealous of their own interests, and by a code of professional solidarity, acted to exclude them. Men of property, on the other hand, had begun recently to use the word "politician" in the tone which implies "a necessary evil."

Venality had always flourished quietly in the republic; now the period of truly big business ushered in a phase of immense disorder. In response to the grosser tactics of bribery which showed themselves during the 1860's, the impulse of the professional politicians was to give regard to their own vested interests and allow the competing groups to *bid against* each other for their charters, lands, rights of way, and all sundry legislative services.

These were known as "the days of the Black Horse Cavalry" at Albany. The contest for possession of the Erie Railroad in New York, which ended with the comic-opera siege of Jay Gould and Jim Fisk in Pike's Opera House in 1872, had debauched the New York State Legislature for eight years as Vanderbilt and Gould vied with each other in paying greater and greater bribes. Gould, who appeared at Albany once with a valise containing $500,000 in Greenbacks, had the most frenzying and overstimulating effect upon the New York legislators—an effect injurious to his own real interest which it would take many years of disciplined machine leadership to eliminate.

In the national legislature as well, other clearly defined rivalries were freely exploited by the professional politicians. For many years Collis Huntington, on behalf of the quickly enriched group of Pacific Associates, was at war with the group which owned the Pennsylvania Railroad, headed by Thomas A. Scott. Each group sought new charters, subsidies, and lands for Western railroads. When the

Tycoon, Jay Cooke, undertook the promotion of the new Northern Pacific Railroad, the lobbying contest became a three-cornered one, which at moments seemed to bring moods of intoxication over Congress. In the parlors of the White House, in the corridors of the executive departments of the Government, one encounters Gould and Cooke intriguing, spying, and counterspying upon each other as they seek advance information and influence over administrative policy. But Jay Cooke possessed a supreme advantage: at the Washington branch of his bank, hard by the Treasury Building, the great party leaders habitually foregathered or came to deposit or draw money, or borrow it, sometimes upon security, sometimes without.

In another respect the pure spoils politician moved counter to the interest of the capitalists as a class. In local politics, municipal machines, such as the well-entrenched Democratic Organization of William Tweed, by the extravagance of their plundering preyed upon great property-owners to an alarming degree. The same excesses in municipal government were to be found elsewhere at this moment, notably in the shape of a Republican ring, including friends and advisers of President Grant himself, operating in the District of Columbia.

The simple old-fashioned plundering operations which the professional politicians carried on at customhouses and through the internal-revenue offices during the postwar period yielded much more boodle than ever before, which in turn provided greatly expanded sources of revenue, a large share being given regularly, habitually, even "patriotically," to the party chest. The party Organization thus became directly dependent in great measure, as we shall see, not only upon funds from the government Treasury, but—in most systematic fashion—upon fraudulent extortions from thrifty capitalists who imported copper, silks, and cloths, or manufactured whisky.

In short, the new capitalism gave an immense impetus to official and political venality—*blindly*, by its own disorderliness and fiercely competitive character rather than out of regard for its own deeper interests. A period of stability, the emergence of a "community of interests" among the dominant business class, would lend a different, soberer tone to the proceedings of the politicians.

For years the extortion process extended itself with increasing boldness, until the foremost property-owners of the country cried as with one voice for relief from the spoilsmen.

II

In the expansive postwar days, there fell to the hands of the Republican chieftains, aside from the traditional spoils of office, new resources vaster than perhaps any successful political movement had ever known. The distribution of the national domain, the Great West with its 3,000,000,000 acres in natural resources, whose wealth is still uncounted, had been begun during the war in accordance with historic Whig-Republican principles. It was continued after the war at an accelerated tempo as an immense "land-office" business transacted between the ruling party and its friends, through Congress and the Administration. The opening of the frontier to homesteaders and former soldiers was linked directly with the promotion of new government-aided Western railroads along whose tracks the settlers and town-builders set their stakes. The choicest sites, the most valuable resources, it was estimated afterward, were donated to the railroad promoters, four Western railroads alone receiving up to 1870 as much land as the States of Ohio, Illinois, Indiana, Wisconsin, and Michigan combined. The sum of $64,623,512 was loaned to the Western railroad-builders, chiefly to the Ames-Durant and Huntington groups, by the Pacific Railroad acts of 1862 and 1864.*

At the outset the new Railroad Barons cultivated direct relations

---

* From a partial list covering a decade of the war party's legislative grants to railroads alone we may grasp the scope of the government largesse (in acres):

1862	Central Pacific	6,500,000
1862	Central Branch, Union Pacific	265,000
1862	Kansas Pacific	6,000,000
1862	Union Pacific	9,650,000
1864	Burlington & Missouri	2,441,000
1864	Sioux City & Pacific	45,000
1864	Northern Pacific	42,000,000
1866	Oregon Branch, Central Pacific	2,127,000
1866	Oregon & California	2,500,000
1866	Atlantic & Pacific	22,672,000
1866	St. Joseph & Denver	470,000
1869	Denver & Pacific	800,000
1870	Oregon Central	1,000,000
1871	Branch Line, Southern Pacific	2,500,000
1871	Texas Pacific	13,000,000

with the members of Congress. Oakes Ames, the wealthy Massachusetts plow-manufacturer who undertook to build the eastern half of the Union Pacific, sat as a Republican member of the House from 1862 to 1873 continuously, and so exercised direct persuasion among the brethren of the party. Collis Huntington, promoter of the Central Pacific (western half of the Union Pacific), came to Washington personally, bearing with him in a trunk such cash as he and his associates had raised, some $200,000, which was entirely exhausted for "legal expenses" in obtaining a prized Federal charter. The astounding charter of the Northern Pacific, carrying with it ultimately some 47,000,000 acres of Northwestern land, was also obtained during the war through the direct appeals of patriotic gentlemen.

After the war, however, the activities of the Railroad Barons underwent a certain organization. "If you have to pay money to have the right thing done," Huntington had said formerly, "it is only just and fair to do it." He learned to his sorrow that direct bribery, such as he had practiced for years, was wasteful and uncertain as well as costly. Jay Cooke believed similarly that "politicians should [not] throw obstacles in the way of what was just and right . . . when capitalists were ready to raise money."[2] Through the employment of skilled lobbyists and claim agents, who had long infested Washington but who now embraced larger undertakings in railroad grants and land jobs, Huntington, Jay Cooke, and Ames worked indirectly, but in a more constant and systematic fashion, to "explain things," to "educate" and "convince" the great body of national legislators.

A clamorous, competing crowd of flashy men, and sometimes worldly women (such as Mark Twain has pictured), now besieged the Capitol in force, buttonholing the politicians everywhere, plying them with liquor, cigars, and money. Lawyers, journalists, or former politicians themselves, the lobbyists knew the ways of the government and the party machinery, and operated with a freedom and effectiveness which the land-company promoters or embryonic Railroad Barons could not assume. Under the head of "legal expenses" the lawyer for the Crédit Mobilier, the holding company controlling the Union Pacific, expended $400,000 between 1866 and 1872, in a manner which he refused to divulge afterward to a congressional committee of inquiry. Between 1862 and 1873, Huntington's railroad spent some $1,900,000, none of the sums being recorded by vouchers, except under the head of "general legal expenses." These sums were chiefly handled by the well-known lobbyist General Franchot, employed at a salary of $30,000 to $40,000 per annum, and residing permanently at Washington.

At night in his hotel, Franchot would entertain the legislators, arguing as follows: "Huntington is a clever fellow; vote for his bill," he would say to them. And Huntington, coming in, would protest laughing: "Put your liquor and your cigars away. Sit down and give them good solid reasons why this should be done in the public interest." [3] "Solid" or "substantial" reasons usually meant only one thing. For the Cookes, Henry, brother of the Tycoon, wormed himself into the intimacy of President Grant, was appointed Governor of the District of Columbia, and as a member of the Kitchen Cabinet watched carefully over the legislators and cabinet members. After Jay Cooke entered upon the huge Northern Pacific project in 1869, Ignatius Donnelly, an eccentric Western politician and former Congressman, served as his chief lobbyist; while a statesman from Minnesota, who had been given a share in the Northern Pacific pool, operated directly upon the floor of Congress.[4] Meanwhile, a whole team of lobbyists worked for the wily Tom Scott, head of the Pennsylvania Railroad, with whom were associated Cameron's friends, the ironmasters and railroad men of Pennsylvania, J. Edgar Thomson, Fenton, Morrell. It was Scott who wrested from Congress in 1871 the last of the gigantic railroad land grants, that of the Texas Pacific, 13,000,000 acres.

By working indirectly, the railroad undertakers found that they could keep the "greed" of the legislators more easily within bounds; that they might discreetly combine forces, as Jay Cooke and Huntington sometimes did; that they might exercise a continuous surveillance over Congress and its important committees and even endeavor to control the strategic standing committees. The lobbyists increased their professional experience with the years, so that by the end of Grant's term we find at least one of them making an offer to guarantee by written contract "for a fixed sum" of $60,000 a year the cooperation of his "friends in Washington." [5]

But the Railway Congressmen themselves showed constant improvement for a time. Some of them were actually trained by the railroad lobby to act with understanding of the railroad's special requirements. "Mr. X can do us some good," Huntington explains in one letter. "There is so many things about our business that he does not know." But Mr. Kasson (of Iowa), a very prominent Republican statesman, "is a very able man, has been able to do us much good, and he has never lost us one dollar." [6]

Through the machinery of the central party command, the process of concentrating control of the mass of legislative business in the hands of standing committees had been developed until it held virtually a power of life and death over lawmaking. Behind the personnel of the House and Senate committees stood of course the secret party caucus, which expressed the will of the party Organization; that is to say, of its leadership overseeing all the committee appointments. In the Senate, for many years, nothing could apparently be done without the approval of the Stalwart cabal of Oliver Morton, Roscoe Conkling, Zach Chandler, and Simon Cameron, who by their grip on the administrative patronage could make or unmake the careers of their satellites. As to the working controls of the lower house, the private papers of Jay Cooke—who devoted half of his life to winning advance information and government favor—yield us much knowledge.

"There are three men in the House," wrote Henry Cooke to Jay Cooke, "whom I deem it very important to make our *active* friends. General Butler, Logan and Schenck. The latter we have already. Butler & Logan *you* must see." [7] All three were famous volunteer army Generals and Republican stump orators stationed at the top of the Radical hierarchy and members of the most powerful standing committees. Schenck, then the leading man of the Ohio machine, for years chairman of the all powerful Ways and Means Committee, was soon to become our Minister to England under Grant, busying himself there with the errands of railroads and banks, and the financial conspiracies of shaky gold-mining concerns.

Logan, who was soon to enter the Senate as the unchallenged boss of Illinois, showed an overweening interest in railroad promotions of all sorts, in Indian land ventures and internal-revenue schemes.

As for Ben Butler, Henry Cooke urged his brother to see to it that this dangerous and noisy Congressman was given a retainer as corporation counsel for the Northern Pacific Railroad! One of the Cooke lobbyists, W. E. Chandler, himself a member of the inner circle of Republican wirepullers and campaign managers, informed the banker that Butler was irritated at not having been consulted. "So am I Mr. Cooke's friend," Butler had exclaimed audaciously, "but I do not always go on the principle of 'Love me—love my dog.' Besides Jay has said nothing to me of this." [8]

But in the huge "bear garden" of the House of Representatives, who was so fitted to oversee the distribution of the national domain and the disposal of government privileges and grants as the Speaker himself? Here among the mob, chiefly of ignorant, crossroads politicians, there were ever clashing currents and trade winds so to speak, stirred by factions debating on behalf of competing interest groups.

Happily, for six years of the eventful Grant regime, a brilliant parliamentary leadership which imposed order among unruly spirits, and enforced the Republican Organization decrees as irrevocable law, was embodied in the youthful Speaker of the House, Blaine of Maine.

After a thorough training in the "regular" party politics of his State, James G. Blaine, by his uncommon natural gifts, played a leading part in the wartime Congress, which he entered in 1863. His tall, erect figure, his face, not handsome like Conkling's but full of special character, with its prominent, intelligent nose, its fine dark eyes and flashing smile, marked him out as much from the crowd of new statesmen as did his formidable gifts for public debate. Then his resourcefulness, his readiness of thought, his personal "magnetism," his delightful sense of humor, soon gathered about him countless friends, admirers, followers, to whom for a long time Blaine embodied nothing short of genius.

No lawyer, and without means of his own, Blaine nevertheless lived by politics; indeed it was said of him that he ate, drank, breathed politics. His utterances, private and public, show him a great technician or master of tactics among the new professionals of party life; he knew the patronage value of each department of the Federal Government, and coming from farthest Maine, he remembered precisely the strength and weakness of counties in Ohio or Indiana and their electoral history and habits in bygone years; he remembered the names of men whose hands he had shaken for an instant, precedents, all the devices of parliamentary law. All this practical intelligence, "smartness," unresting energy, and power over men Blaine throughout his life devoted to the ends of party orthodoxy.

He had apparently resolved from the beginning to succeed by being "strictly the organ of his party," a function which he ascribed admiringly (in his famous eulogy of Garfield) to the great congressional leaders Clay, Douglas, and Stevens. Each of these "believed his party always right, but right or wrong, . . . his party." The leader moreover must know not merely how to strike, but where to strike and when to strike. "He often skillfully avoids the strength of his opponents' position and scatters confusion in his ranks by attacking an exposed point when really the righteousness of the cause and the strength of logical intrenchment are against him." [9]

Here, in these approving terms for other leaders, we see expressed Blaine's sense of his own mission; the leitmotiv of this American politician who towers over his fellows as party leader during a whole long generation, his career one which can dispense with both righteousness of cause and logic. Blaine had been bitterly poor in his youth, and he hunted success grimly. But poverty in our frontier society, as he said hopefully, was indeed no poverty. "It is but the beginning of wealth, and has the boundless possibilities of the future always opening before it." Success was no impossibility to one of Blaine's caliber, and the possession of money was of course the unmistakable sign of success.

Undoubtedly Blaine possessed a clearer understanding than most of his fellows of the meaning of the mighty economic revolution which was in stride during his time. Like Henry Clay before him, he was obsessed with the Manifest Destiny of the country; his speeches dwelt often and again upon the "boundless possibilities" for wealth and expansion which rose before the citizens of the great republic of the West. Indeed they were characteristically studded with facts rather than with bombast such as an Oliver Morton used. He stood always a little apart from the extreme Radical and Stalwart factions—though without giving them needless offense—looking

beyond the naked spoilsmanship of his fellows, his attention fixed
upon the practical details of protective tariffs, banking and railroad
legislation, rather than upon those of military oppression or Negro
suffrage. Men of capital deeply engaged his respect, for though he
himself was a generous rather than an avaricious man, his need of
money was his Achilles' heel, and his pursuit of it his secret torment.
According to the cruel memoirist Welles, Blaine acquired a reputation as "a speculating member of Congress" from the start.[10] His
friendships not only with New England politicians and financiers but
also with the Pennsylvania boss, Simon Cameron, led apparently to
fruitful investments in coal and iron lands and even well-chosen
town lots in Western Territories, so that while still a young Congressman his way of living grew ample, his home was a fine
Washington mansion.[11] Meanwhile in his private correspondence he
expressed himself as thoroughly hostile to extremists, was Moderate
rather than Radical in his Republicanism, and alluded unkindly to
"agitators and premature reformers" as "cocks that crow at midnight, heralding no dawn." [12] Early in his career Blaine had shown
himself a champion of Sound Money, and this we are told by his
official apologist contributed greatly to his final elevation as Speaker
of the House by the party caucus in 1869.

No man since Henry Clay, it was often remarked in the years that
followed, had controlled the unwieldy, often uproarious lower house
so easily as Speaker Blaine. He was at home standing above the disorderly crowd of legislators, dominating, scolding, caressing, yet
always ruling with an air of fairness. He commanded obedience; he
helped the awkward parliamentary machine to function, by his keen
faculty for steering the debate and prompting action. But in presiding over the House, Blaine's methods were at times "most unconventional," according to press comment of the time. Sometimes,
tradition sanctioned the Speaker's leaving the chair temporarily to
another member while he took the floor or told certain men what to
do, in the case of a measure which specially concerned him. But
Blaine did this probably more often than any other Speaker before
him, though always with tact and discretion.[13]

The power of the Speaker in Blaine's day, presiding as he did at
the bottleneck of all legislative traffic, was second only to that of

the President under our system. He was a symphony conductor who lent significant form and rhythm to the House procedure. His gavel was as omnipotent as the auctioneer's as he recognized or refused members, bills, motions, hastened or delayed events, raised questions of rules or procedure, called or obstructed votes, and appointed the members of the standing committees which reported out or "buried" legislation. The Speaker usually followed the party "line" in appointing members of committees; yet the value of each appointment to oversee appropriations or railroad legislation must be measured against a thousand thrusts and pressures of lobbyists and party factions.* During the years of Blaine's chairmanship the nation's capital experienced a land-office boom in grants-in-aid, franchises, and subsidies to allies of the ruling party; and the Speaker's role in endeavoring to preserve harmony, in befriending and strengthening, or choosing between, the new interest groups which so often bid against each other for government privilege, was as arduous and trying as it was unique and decisive. Henceforth his days and nights, as Mrs. Blaine relates in a letter to her son, are curiously filled "with wool and cotton manufacturers to meet in Boston, dinners, breakfasts and lunches." [14] †

* The fierce competition of the new Railroad Barons at the Capitol was a potent force for disorder, against which the able Speaker strove to prevail. Thus Huntington, competing with Tom Scott for a right of way to a southern transcontinental route, writes to his partners: "The R. R. Com[mittee] of the House was set up for Scott, and it has been a very difficult matter to switch a majority of the committee away from him, but I think it has been done." (*Pacific Railway Commission Report*, Huntington to Colton, Mar. 4, 1876.) He remarks elsewhere that although the committee favors Scott, it is "commercial," and he doubts not that it can be "convinced."

† The "smartness" or subtlety of Mr. Blaine is supported by numerous anecdotes. One of the best of these touches the formidable Ben Butler, known then and always as a champion of "soft money." When Blaine became Speaker, Butler made known at once his wish to be appointed a member of the important Committee on Appropriations, and to gain this end he appeared one morning at the door of the Speaker's room. For Blaine to have refused Butler point-blank would not merely have been tactless, but would have invited reprisals from a dangerous antagonist owning a pair of leather lungs. Blaine knew what Butler had come for, and had his page inform Butler that he was out of his room and would shortly return, and please to wait. In the meantime he jumped out of the window, rushed about, visited and consulted with various strong men of the party, and added sufficient party support to himself to eliminate the statesman from Massachusetts, who meanwhile haunted his anteroom hour after hour. When Butler finally saw Blaine, it was too late; the committee had been named in accordance with the approval of the other party chieftains. *Cf.* Hoar, *Autobiography*, Vol. I, pp. 201-202.

Far more precious after 1861 than other favors in the gift of the ruling party were the indirect subsidies to home manufactures under the guise of mounting protective-tariff duties on imports. Ever among the most prominent and persistent friends of the war party were the industrialists and their agents, who, with their appetites whetted by the historic gains won in wartime, besieged Washington incessantly for more and greater favors of the same sort. Led by the first alert organizers of industrial associations or lobbies such as John L. Hayes, the New England textile capitalists and the Pennsylvania-Ohio iron men formed a united front and maintained close liaison with an important section of the Republican Party. The cleverer and more learned politicians who could read trade reports and account sheets and write tax laws—Morrill of Vermont, John Sherman and John Bingham of Ohio, Henry L. Dawes of Massachusetts, William D. ("Pig Iron") Kelley of Pennsylvania, and finally Blaine himself —had grasped apparently from the start the material relationship between the price-raising features of the tariff system and the values of iron lands and mills. While professing an overwhelming, special regard for the soundness of the government finances, and the need of revenue to repay its war debt, these respectable gentlemen—certainly Sherman, Morrill, and Blaine—found reward (almost painless and without risk) in the pleasing labor of heaping high the profit margins of manufacturers of wool, cloth, glass, marble, copper, and iron products.

Some years before, in a wartime speech of March, 1865, Blaine, as a disciple of the New England Protectionists, had cleverly pointed out that the protective tariff was a form of taxation which while bringing large revenues to the Government would "leave the burden . . . inappreciable to the public." [15] Thereafter a pertinacious propaganda, fostered by Horace Greeley in the powerful New York *Tribune,* spread the gospel of tariff taxation as the "most patriotic way." The protective tariff in time became consecrated in the speech of the Republican ideologues as the "historic American system," although such a system had been stoutly resisted by the American people during most of the threescore and ten years of their history before 1860. Indeed Thad Stevens himself, out of regard for the sentiment of the farm population, had tactfully opposed fresh increases of the tariff in 1866. But with the sweeping victory of 1868 behind them, the Protectionists returned to the fray, asserting that they sought primarily the "protection of American wages," while elaborate plans for elevating the tariff level to new notches were laid in 1869. When certain Moderate Republicans noting an important but scattered protest from farming communities and importing merchants, proposed mild downward revisions of the tariff schedules, Protectionists like Kelley and Bingham retorted with fury, habitually accusing their opponents of being friends of "British" or "rebel" Free Trade doctrines.

Such accusations were directed even against one of the war heroes in Congress, General James A. Garfield of Ohio, during the early stages of his political career. Once he had said that he regarded Protection as "a temporary war measure," and though he later modified his views so as to allow for a "reasonable" continued protection of iron mills (prominent in his own Ohio district), his unorthodoxy was not readily forgotten or forgiven. Recognized as one of the rising young personalities in the House since 1865, an attractive speaker who even possessed some learning, Garfield was marked for advancement and enjoyed the warm personal friendship of Blaine. But when in December, 1869, the announcements of committee appointments were made by the new Speaker, it was seen with surprise that Garfield was not named chairman of the Ways and Means Committee, a most important post which had been unofficially promised him. Instead, Dawes of Massachusettes, whose opinions were less widely followed, was named for a place which held the strategic power of decision over tariff duties.[16]

The bitterly disappointed Garfield, then in a reformist phase of his career, was left to ponder upon the meaning of this heavy reverse, this significant delay in his climb of the political ladder, and after much reflection ultimately changed his views in a remarkable degree toward the orthodox.[17] "I have no doubt I should have had the Ways and Means but for the fact that I have positive opinions and have frankly and squarely expressed them,"[18] he wrote privately at the time. The iron men of the Mahoning Valley, he says, "want a representative that they can own and carry around in their pantaloons pocket."[19]

A close scrutiny of Dawes's previous voting record would have shown what Blaine fully understood, as he quietly struck Garfield's name from his original list, that the Massachusetts Congressman was leagued with the textile lobby. Under his management a purported tariff-reform measure emerged in 1870 which was an epic of picturesque logrolling, directed chiefly by the inveterate lobbyist Hayes, who played one local interest skillfully against another, but who also had "spent considerable sums in various ways *peculiar to Washington*." [20] Inspired by these proceedings, a Democratic humorist in the House, S. S. ("Sunset") Cox of New York, in a light mood introduced resolutions against "free sunshine" by which all windows, shutters, and curtains were to be kept forever shut. "For the sun is a 'foreigner.' He comes from abroad and we must . . . gratify these Pennsylvania gentlemen who have a monopoly of this article of coal." Then he continued further his illuminating discourse on logrolling, which once convulsed the country in its prosperous, tolerant moods: "Michigan steals on copper; Maine on lumber; Pennsylvania on iron; North Carolina on peanuts; Massachusetts on cotton goods; Connecticut on hair pins." It was "reciprocal rapine." Finally, he exploded to Speaker Blaine: "Stealing by tariffs, Mr. Chairman, is as De Quincey proved of murder, a fine art." [21]

The changes in legislation urged by those friends of the war party who would benefit most by them were adopted without serious question. Again and again intricate schemes for money-making were brought forward and incorporated immediately in tariff acts.* Here too, as in the "orgy" of land grants, in the enactment of tax laws there was carried on a happy, unrestrained, though unobtrusive distribution and sharing of wealth among the friends of the war party, proceedings over which the Speaker presided urbanely.

Railroad legislation, however, held the enthusiasm of the three Congresses presided over by Blaine between 1869 and 1875. In the session which preceded Grant's election certain bills had been intro-

---

* The steel duties of 1870, for instance, caused an intense scarcity of steel rails for transportation, and a price level about 100 per cent higher than in England. Andrew Carnegie and others launched themselves at once into the manufacture of Bessemer steel, a most profitable industry virtually subsidized overnight by the war Republicans.

duced which looked to the regulation of the Pacific railroads, the cost of their construction, and the rates they charged. Other measures also were considered which would assure the repayment of the large sums of money which the Government had loaned. In some alarm, Oakes Ames, head of the Union Pacific, bestirred himself to win friends in Congress, and in the winter of 1867-68 distributed his first discreet gifts of free shares of Crédit Mobilier "where they would do the most good," that is, among prominent Senators and Representatives. With the transcontinental line completed in 1869, amid nation-wide celebrations, both Ames and Huntington organized "junkets" for politicians, who traveled over their lines at a cost of $10,000 per private train.

Their imaginations aflame over the exploits of the Iron Horse, the politicians gladly invested in "options" for railroad securities which cost them nothing and brought fabulous profits. Soon many were swept into the contemporary speculative "craze" for railroads and, like James G. Blaine himself, were busied buying and selling shares or bonds of new Western lines or branch lines, chartered and subsidized overnight by Congress or by State legislatures. The rush was on for "strategic" positions, as in town-lot booms, for the occupation and promotion of small lines which would offer competition to the larger trunk lines and win enormous prices for their stockholders.

The session of 1868-69 created rumors which spread far and wide until even from Paris our Ambassador, Elihu Washburne, who while in Congress was long known as the "Watchdog of the Treasury," sent a warning to his friend Blaine:

I may be deceived but I don't like the look [of the political situation] at this distance. . . . I am delighted not to have seen your name among the junketeers on the Pacific Railroad. Keep clear of all entangling alliances.[22]

Ignoring such advice, the brilliant Speaker pursued his favorite railroad schemes with the deepest relish. From his strategic post he could watch over the operations of the railroad lobbies large and small. Most important of the railroad enterprises which at this moment sought government aid was Jay Cooke's ambitious Northern

Pacific Company, with whose chief political agent, Henry Cooke, Blaine remained in closest contact.

"Blaine . . . had valuable suggestions on the Pacific Railroads and legislation. He says that if we manage our case with discretion we can get a handsome money subsidy from Congress"—so run the confidential reports of Henry to Jay Cooke, October 16, 1869; and on November 1, 1869: "You must see and satisfy Blaine. I have been working up the idea of a government subsidy with him and others." [23]

Nor do the possibilities of smaller operations, feeder and branch lines, escape his sharp eye. One of these, the Fort Smith & Little Rock, continuance of whose Arkansas land grant depended upon congressional sanction, faced a trying moment when Mr. Julian of Indiana moved suddenly for an amendment to the bill renewing its grant, an amendment which would have been most offensive to its sponsors.

Blaine himself, in one of his letters to the Boston stockbroker Warren Fisher, which reached public fame when published among the Mulligan Letters in after years, describes the services he performed in the crisis. He writes on October 4, 1869:

It was on the last night of the session. . . . The House was thin . . . and Julian's amendment was likely to prevail if brought to a vote. Roots and other members from Arkansas . . . were in despair, for . . . if the Arkansas bill had gone back to the Senate with Julian's amendment, the whole thing would have gone to the table and slept the sleep of death.

In this dilemma, Roots came to me to know what on earth he could do under the rules for he said it was vital to his constituents that the bill should pass. I told him that Julian's amendment was entirely out of order . . . but he had not sufficient confidence in his knowledge of the rules to make the point, but he said Gen. Logan was opposed to the Fremont scheme, and would probably make the point. I sent my page to Gen. Logan with the suggestion, and he at once made the point. I could not do otherwise than sustain it, and so the bill was freed from the mischievous amendment moved by Julian, and at once passed without objection.

At that time I had not seen Mr. Caldwell, but you can tell him that without knowing it, I did him a great favor. [24]

Blaine had moved in time to block a "mischievous amendment" when no one else could do so, or knew how; with the help of General

Logan, thank heaven, the day was saved for the Arkansas proposition, and he reminds Mr. Fisher and also Mr. Caldwell, a New England financier of shady reputation, of his timely service. Soon he has formed a useful business friendship with Fisher and Caldwell, who admit the Speaker into a sort of silent partnership in their schemes upon terms which he assures them are only "too generous." The influential Speaker receives handsomely printed bonds and stocks in an uncompleted railroad which he is to sell to his many friends at generous commissions.[25] He promises his partners that he will be no "deadhead" in their venture—for by now he often uses railroad lingo.

A few weeks later, and we find Blaine offering to Jay Cooke as a "great bargain" a block of securities in the same Arkansas railroad, the Little Rock & Fort Smith. In this letter, November 10, 1869, he brims over with the intoxication of the pure stock salesman, and offers Cooke working control over a "Napoleonic" combination of competing and connecting lines. To refuse Blaine is embarrassing, as Henry Cooke explains to Jay, for he is "a formidable power for good and evil" to all the projects of the House of Cooke.[26]

Blaine in his private character was a man of high moral scruples; and unlike certain of his confreres, a devoted husband and an affectionate father. His appeal to Cooke was therefore accompanied by a modicum of moral hairsplitting by which he unconsciously justifies his behavior to himself; the transaction in question must in no sense be considered a bribe, he implies clearly. All legends concerning Blaine to the contrary, there is absolutely no evidence that he ever pocketed bribes. It was a case simply of offering invaluable services, in his high government capacity, to powerful interests who were seen, by his own lights and his party's, as the proper logical beneficiaries of government largesse.

I may say without Egotism, that my position will enable me to render you services of vital importance & value—services for which I cannot desire or accept profit or gain to myself. I am willing however and ready to do all for you in my power at any time you may desire. . . . *I am willing to serve you where I am absolutely debarred from any participation in profits. Are you not willing to aid me when you can do so with profit to yourself at the same time.* Just how your subscription to the enterprise will aid me I need not explain—*Sufficient that it is so.*[27]

Jay Cooke, however, after due reflection, wisely concluded not to trust Blaine's judgment of the securities Fisher and Caldwell had handed him; since the Speaker was plainly in need of money, he judiciously increased the loan standing in his name.

The busy years passed; Speaker Blaine remained constant at his post, his gavel tapping out cheerfully the transfers now of slices of the public domain to his party's friends, now of large indirect subventions in the form of tariff schedules. Under his alert leadership the chief Republican leaders of the House, Logan, Bingham, Kelley, Garfield, and others, collaborated in this historic task as a matter of conviction. The husbandry of continental railroads, and of territories as large as whole European nations, was a new, an extraordinary field for American politicians, usually occupied with finding places for fourth-class postmasters or lighthouse-keepers; it was not surprising that they moved at times with something of dizzy uncertainty, as if intoxicated at their incredible good fortune.

The members of the small, impotent Opposition in Congress looked on this scene with emotions which ranged no doubt from disgust to despairing envy. Until one day a Democratic spokesman, Stevenson of Ohio, arose in the House to heap bitter, unheeded reproaches upon the majority party, intimating also that Speaker Blaine himself "was not what he ought to be." Certain grievous suspicions also moved this member to say at last that he felt that "the House of Representatives was like an auction room, where more valuable considerations were disposed of under the Speaker's hammer than in any other place on earth." [28]

III

Meanwhile, the band of military adventurers who with Grant's arrival in power fastened themselves in key places of the administrative bureaucracy moved generally in ways peculiar to themselves. While the experienced party leaders worked like Conkling to perpetuate their party's power, or like Blaine to create order, even efficiency, in lawmaking, and to secure to their strongest allies among the capitalists "the legitimate fruits of the war," these soldiers of fortune were possessed purely by the gold fever of the times. They fomented disorder and danger wherever they worked. They knew nothing of lawmaking and less of civil administration; they knew nothing of political ideology, or electoral management. Yet, by their favor with the President they overran the Government, acted with increasing boldness and extravagance, until the ruling party which had so gratefully taken them into its bosom must needs in very self-defense cast them adrift.

Blaine himself sensed early that these hangers-on of Grant's Kitchen Cabinet were exceeding the frame of their usefulness, the military glamour they brought to his party. He described them privately as men solely "bent on *loot* and booty, and ready for any Mexican invasion or Caribbean annexation, and looking to excitements and filibustering and possibly a Spanish war." [29]

Grant's White House staff had "nothing but uniforms," it was remarked. The leading personage was his wartime friend and adviser General John Rawlins. Once the bright star of the army's general staff, Rawlins was no sooner installed as Secretary of War than he conspired with Cuban insurrectionists to wrest Cuba from the hands of Spain, even if it brought the exhausted country into a new war. Desperately poor and in ill health, Rawlins accepted from the hands of the Cuban rebel junta a block of bonds of some $28,000 in face value, realizable only in the event of annexation (as Secretary of State Fish learned from detectives).[30] Rawlins also pushed vigorously the strange intrigue whereby Santo Domingo was to be annexed, as soon as certain American business groups and political friends of the President had established themselves in a position to profit thereby.

Rawlins died of tuberculosis within a year of his appointment, and Grant appointed in his place another soldier, the affable, handsome, auburn-whiskered General William W. Belknap. Soon Belknap and his wife astonished social Washington by the affluent style in which they lived and entertained in an era of luxurious and fashionable display. From accomplices appointed to lucrative army posts came regularly shares of their loot, such as the sum of $12,000 paid annually to Mrs. Belknap by a trader at Fort Sill, Indian Territory—these moneys being squandered upon balls and banquets and silken dresses. Then also military appointments and other army posts and favors within the purview of the Secretary of War were sold right and left, as was afterward learned, and the proceeds paid to friends of the Secretary.[31]

Among Grant's personal retainers were also General Horace Porter, his private secretary, who afterward improved his station by connection with the Vanderbilt railroad dynasty; Major Frederick Dent, his brother-in-law, also a secretary and aide-de-camp; the shifty Colonel Adam Badeau, who acted as the presidential historian; and the stout, ruddy, black-eyed, mustachioed Colonel Orville E. Babcock, who had also served as his military aide, assistant secretary. Then some favorite civilians: the New York ward heeler Thomas Murphy, with whom Grant liked to "talk horse"; Henry Cooke, appointed Governor of the District of Columbia; and Boss Alexander R. Shepherd, former plumbing contractor, now jeweled, free-spending, breezy leader of the Washington Public Works Ring.

Of all these men, Babcock, thirty-three years of age, a graduate of West Point with a good war record, soon exerted the strongest influence over Grant and was the very soul of the Kitchen Cabinet. He presided over the anteroom leading to the President's office, receiving or rejecting visitors, expediting the labors of the patronage, showing Grant always a most indefatigable personal attention and devotion. Babcock was a gay dog, a dashing, resplendently uniformed character out of Italian operetta; he both diverted the President and filled his slow-working mind with suspicions of opponents or designing men, which in itself furnished evidence enough of his infinite loyalty to his chief. The honest, conservative Secretary of State Fish, who for years strove almost in vain against Babcock's power, commented in his diary that the man was a double-dealer, a mischief-maker, a counselor who told lies to the President, brought false rumors to him, induced him to sign letters which suited designs of his own or of men more designing and powerful still, and got him to authorize other letters which Babcock wrote to the same ends.[32]

He had a fine flair for romantic and desperate intrigue. Establishing confidential working relations with the Stalwart party leaders (to whom, as private secretary, he was immensely useful) and at the same time with nearly all of those who might be said to form the

Republican demimonde, the leading organized rings of marauders who by grace of political protection preyed upon government departments and public alike, the ambitious Babcock actually played a leading part in the nation's affairs. He might have gone far indeed were it not that his immoderate appetites for clothing, drink, and fornication—all to be satisfied at the cost of the public Treasury—led him to ever more brazen adventures and needless risks.

The first ideas of policy which occurred to the military minds in the White House circle as promising luster for the new Administration were of foreign conquest or annexation. At the very start, the spreading insurrection in Cuba absorbed the attention of Secretary of War Rawlins as well as our Minister to Spain, General Daniel Sickles. Meanwhile two shady American adventurers, who acted in collusion with the President of Santo Domingo, Baez, as well as with a financial and shipping syndicate seeking concessions, approached the Grant Administration with a project for sale of the West Indian republic to the United States. Grant was interested at once to a remarkable degree and sent Colonel Babcock, July 17, 1869, to Santo Domingo as his confidential agent, though without diplomatic authority to obtain a report on the situation. Upon Babcock's return in September, Grant simply announced to his Cabinet that his private secretary had brought back a treaty of annexation.

The cabinet members were consternated, Secretary of State Fish being especially embarrassed, since he had been scarcely consulted. Yet Fish, though reluctantly enough, began steps to complete the negotiations for Santo Domingo; while the enthusiasm not only of Babcock, but of Ben Butler and John Logan, General N. P. Banks, and other Stalwart politicians close to the President, was gained, apparently, by promised concessions of free water-front land in Santo Domingo's port. Babcock returned to Santo Domingo in November, maintaining close contact not only with the Dominican intriguers but with the American promoters of the scheme. Meanwhile news of the negotiations, leaking out, made a sensation in the press, and plans were hastened to win the approval of the Senate, Grant himself paying a personal call upon Sumner, chairman of the Committee on Foreign Relations, shortly after New Year's Day.

Schemes of conquest fermented in the rooms of the White House, in every Federal building; cabinet members and minor officials previously poor and unknown became remarkably affluent overnight. In the entourage of the President and at the Treasury itself certain bold spirits laid deep plots in 1869 to corner the very gold supply of the nation.

Though the Grant Administration was pledged to early resumption of specie payment under the old gold standard, the enabling legislation which had been passed thus far, in 1866 and 1868, left enormous discretion to the Secretary of the Treasury, while the contentions of Sound Money and Greenback spokesmen in Congress created extreme uncertainty and confusion from time to time in the money and credit market. As always before and everywhere, the great bankers who hoped to share in large debt-refunding operations hovered about the Treasury and the White House to learn what they could in good time. "Give us promptly and in advance all the information you can about the feeling of the President & Congress," Jay Cooke would write to his brother.[33] Advance knowledge of amounts of money to be borrowed, interest rates, changes in the price of gold—all this was sought incessantly by the personal approaches of the competing financiers, Jay Cooke, August Belmont (who represented the Rothschilds), August Drexel, and now the newcomer, Jay Gould.*

At the Treasury, the inscrutable Boutwell appeared to be following a policy of drift; the price of gold and money rates continued to rock mysteriously from season to season, a condition which always favored the designs of practiced speculators. In Wall Street, which had its own ways of learning things, it was charged openly that the Secretary's moves were sometimes "conspicuously more advantageous to certain 'friends of Government' among the speculators . . . than to men engaged in legitimate business." [34]

Now the "Mephistopheles of Wall Street," Jay Gould, flushed with his recent triumphs over Commodore Vanderbilt in the Erie wars, matured carefully his grandiose scheme to conquer the money and exchange market. His own motives, as he insisted to President

* The business of "keeping a step ahead of the market" obsessed the bankers. "It's the only way to work and be sure of success. It's old Rothschild's way," Henry Cooke wrote to the Tycoon. (Larson, *Jay Cooke*, p. 232.)

Grant, were pure and patriotic, since with the rise of gold and consequent cheapening of the dollar, exports of American grain would expand.[35]

The President, according to his habit, freely accepted the hospitality which Gould and his partner Jim Fisk pressed upon him, the use of an Erie Railroad private car, of one of Fisk's palatial river boats on a journey to Boston. Gould meanwhile gathered certain of the counselors and relatives of the President into his conspiracy. Abel Corbin, the former government claim agent, lobbyist, and real-estate operator who had recently married Grant's sister and often lived with the President's family, was made a partner at the start by being given shares in the pool operation of the Erie Ring. But most important of all, a member of the clique of military adventurers, General Daniel Butterfield, appointed at Gould's urgent recommendation as Assistant Treasurer and so heading the New York Sub-Treasury, was bound to the plotters. Here too the intervention of Babcock, who urged the appointment of Butterfield, was shown later to have been a decisive factor. Thus when Boutwell worked to depress gold and raise the paper dollar by sales of gold, or when he paused in such operations, the wires were evidently tapped.[36] The plotters whispered that the President himself was in their hands; a part of their gold store, they pretended, was earmarked for Mrs. Grant, though actually held in the name of Corbin.

The strange destructive tug of war between the bulls and bears in Wall Street's gold room continued during the summer of 1869. By September 23, 1869, the price of gold, accumulated by the Erie Ring between 140 and 144, mounted abruptly above 150, while legitimate commercial houses, who would need foreign currency for imports, and large banks were on the verge of panic over the great losses faced in their future commitments. Still the Treasury did not move and remained "neutral," though Greeley in the *Tribune* had warned the country of the sensational conspiracy and both Grant and Boutwell were definitely informed, while leading financiers clamored for the sale of government gold to break the "corner." Then on Black Friday, September 24, Gould by his tremendous buying operations carried gold to a high price of 162½. Among the mass of trapped firms "short" of gold were two hundred and fifty leading bankers and merchants of New York, including Jay Cooke & Co. The Cookes, in their distress, hammered at the Government for rescue, Jay Cooke learning on September 23, "Something will be done." Grant and Boutwell in precipitate haste had sent orders for the release of gold to Assistant Treasurer Butterfield in New York.[37] The conspirators thereby knew this even earlier, and were in time to unload when a consortium of Wall Street bankers with government assistance attacked the gold ring. At noon of Black Friday gold underwent a gigantic collapse from 160 to 133. The ignorant Boutwell seemed "astounded by the suddenness and terribleness of . . . his action," which, rescuing one faction, ruined the other, though the uncanny Gould escaped scot-free. The gold raid, the ensuing panic in the country, and the unpleasant exposures following the congressional investigation by Garfield's committee (which dared not probe the evidence it took) offered gloomy lessons upon the character of the ruling party. The investigation, as Garfield related, led from "the dens of the Gold Room, some of the offices of the Sub-Treasury . . . and perhaps . . . into the parlor of the President." [38]

Although the President himself was proved more ignorant than guilty, his Administration had easily been overpowered by the conspirators to the loss of the whole country. That the financial policy of the Government might be swung at will by privateers of the money market, with the aid of a needy army officer in the Treasury, was an evil omen at the very start of the Grant Administration, as Henry Adams wrote at the time. But in the ranks of sober, respectable capitalists it caused a veritable shudder of fear.

Little disturbed by these events, the young military aides of the President thrust themselves again and again toward the richest centers of government patronage, while Babcock steadily extended his working arrangements with the party's lower elements. How far they might go was shown in the case of George K. Leet, formerly a minor member of Grant's staff and a clerk in the War Department. With the aid of the ubiquitous Colonel Babcock, Leet won a letter of introduction from the President to the head of the New York Custom House. From him the young man readily obtained a large portion of "general-order" warehouse business of the port for a new firm which he formed. Imported freight which could not be claimed and shipped to its consignees on the day of arrival was, by this arrangement, mostly sent to the warehouse firm of Leet & Stocking. But when in 1870 Conkling's henchman Thomas Murphy was placed in charge of the New York Custom House, Leet insisted on having his warehouse made the officially designated one, in fact a monopoly, a request which seemed to carry with it the approval of the White House.

Soon handling charges were raised to exorbitant levels, yet the largest shippers and importers must act through Leet, else mysterious inconveniences and delays followed. Though Leet resided in Washington after 1870, his firm was reported to be earning more than $50,000 a year, and in one year as much as $260,000. It is notable again that large- merchants began to pour complaints into the office of the Secretary of the Treasury; shipping business was in some measure also diverted from New York.[39]

In almost every affair of the time, in every plundering foray, the hand of Babcock is seen busily fishing for gold.

Most lucrative, for instance, was Babcock's informal partnership with the municipal ring in Washington. Congress in 1871 created a Territorial government for the District of Columbia, with a Governor and a legislative council, and Grant at once chose Jay Cooke's brother Henry to be its head. Cooke was also nominally president of the District's Board of Public Works, but its vice-president and real directing genius was Boss Shepherd, who now undertook a costly rebuilding and renovating program for the Capital, with a control over contracts which the contemporary Tweed Ring in New York might well have envied. Streets and roads were paved and graded, swamps drained, parks laid, statues flung up everywhere, while a new local machine, supported largely by Negro voters, voted at the will of the American Baron Haussmann swollen appropriations and assessments upon property-holders. The "pigsty" capital was transformed by Stalwart Republicans into a thing of ponderous neoclassical beauty, but now rumors spread of magnificent real-estate "jobs," extravagances, and contract swindles. By 1874, the capital staggered on the verge of bankruptcy with a debt of over $17,000,000.

Also active in the District Ring, though behind the scenes, were found, as usual, Ben Butler, Zach Chandler, and the new Secretary of the Interior, Columbus Delano, an Ohio Stalwart politician. Even the popular, upright Congressman James Garfield was believed to be implicated in one of the ring's subsidiary projects, that of the De Gollyer-McLelland construction company, for whom he acted as legal counsel while serving as chairman of the House Appropriations Committee. The sponsors of this last venture conducted in 1872 a strong lobby before Congress for a pavement contract involving $700,000, some $72,000 of which was expended in advance to "influence" politicians. In the letters and telegrams exchanged among the interested parties was the following:

The influence of Gen. Garfield has been secured by yesterday's, last night's, and today's labors. He holds the purse strings of the United States, is chairman of the Committee on Appropriations, and the strongest man in Congress. . . . The connection is complete. I can hardly realize that we have Gen. Garfield with us. It is a rare success and very gratifying, as all the appropriations for the District must come through him.[40]

Garfield was paid the large retainer of $5,000 for his services. He had nothing to do with the De Gollyer lobbying action itself; yet it is instructive to see how so well-intentioned a character becomes helplessly involved, year by year, in the nets of the spoilsmen.[41]

When, in the troubled panic season of 1873, mass meetings and petitions of injured property-holders led to exposure of the depredations of the District Ring, Shepherd faced ruin, and with the aid of his cronies, Babcock, Butler, and Delano, boldly intrigued in Congress to the end that the Federal Government might assume the District's debts. Henry Cooke, under fire, timidly resigned the Governorship, and the President after some meditation named in his place the actual contriver of all the mischief, Boss Shepherd himself.

As the army of occupation spreads itself over the Government, Colonel Babcock, through his continual, confidential supervision of the Executive Department, performs the most vital services for the leaders of the spoilsmen. From his strategic post, he systematically protects and advises customhouse extortioners, Santo Domingo filibusterers, the District Ring, the Black Friday plotters, above all, the managers of the vast organized internal-revenue conspiracies. Whenever scandal or rumor points to him, the great party leaders in the

Senate rush to his defense; he is a man who at all costs cannot be sacrificed.

And through the years the "figurehead" President, incarnation of administrative ignorance, his strength and his berserk will sleeping, trusts his lively, handsome, popular secretary with the most touching, affectionate loyalty. Was Grant himself, after all, personally honest, as those who knew him still insisted? Was he aware of all that went on as he brooded or nodded silently over his innumerable cigars in the White House? The fiercely partisan attacks soon leveled at his Administration certainly shook his judgment, which was never strong for civil affairs. Soon he lived in the "fog" of political battle, believing none but the practical commanders who defended him and who were supported by him in turn. Moreover, the tragicomic blunders and Gargantuan follies of the Grant regime bespeak a triumphant, confident stupidity; they have a form which could not possibly be achieved by a knowing rascal. What did the former tanner, the unsuccessful storekeeper of Galena, know of the niceties and proprieties which must be observed in gigantic financial transactions, in the costly public administration carried on by an army of 100,000 Republican bureaucrats? What scruples or nice compunctions had he ever acquired which cynical leaders like Conkling or Morton or Ben Butler could not laugh away?

IV

It is high time that we cease to think of the spoliations of the General Grant Era as "accidental" phenomena, as regrettable lapses into moral frailty, arising in an age of transition, of emotional release after war. We must turn rather to examine the systematic, rational, organized nature of the plundering which was carried on at this time.

Have not men always been frail, and quick to embrace temptation? Why then do periods of governmental sobriety, marked only with petty official venalities, alternate with periods in which "corruption" takes on a vast scope?

The Grant terms recall the epoch of Walpole's ministry in England, when a tumultuous economic expansion and revolution and "corrupt" patronage politics developed simultaneously. In contemporary France it was paralleled almost exactly by an industrial and real-estate boom, by scandalous "excesses" in administration and public-works programs—like that of Baron Haussmann in rebuilding Paris. Likewise in Bismarck's Germany, after the Franco-Prussian War (of 1870-71), in spite of a long-established, trained bureaucracy there were not a few sensational administrative and financial frauds. In all these great nations of the capitalist era, war, in itself a social-economic symptom, was followed by disordered, heightened economic expansion, and strain upon the apparatus of political government. But in the decade after the Civil War in America, the process assumed Brobdingnagian proportions which were connected with the special tribal character of our political institutions and which earned for the period a historical reputation as "the nadir of national disgrace." [42]

Here there is more resolution than "laxity." In the United States the very nature of the traditional political organization, its inveterate patronage character, which demanded public office for purposes not explicitly stated—that is, for keeping the party Organization itself entrenched in power—left a shadow ground, a no man's land, between legitimate and illlegitimate, legal and lawless action, where the professional soldiers of politics were used to act, to move warily, keeping ever to shelter, yet with no want of firmness and determination. Swallowing whatever Sunday-school qualms they might have known, they performed tasks of the highest utility. These professionals, usually politicians of the second rank, when placed in actual charge of government departments became expert in their threefold task of: first, facilitating (for all the cumbersome process of democracy) the plans of large private enterprisers where they required government aid; second, gathering a share of the proceeds from such services for themselves, their friends and colleagues; and finally, the business of diverting a heavy portion of these extraofficial honoraria to furthering the continued power and prosperity of the common party Organization. Such were the men who sat at the elbow of the President; and by 1871, they formed a majority at his very cabinet table.

The very presence of an honest, intelligent official seemed to give rise to the most absurd difficulties. The dismissal of Jacob Cox from his office of Secretary of the Interior in the autumn of 1870 was a case in point. In his department great land claims, railroad grants, cessions of Indian territory, were reviewed, validated, or nullified; and Cox, committed to civil-service reform—a dawning idea—had exercised an unpleasant surveillance over the minor officials in his department. Cox's gravest sin had been that of opposing a certain very dubious claim known as the McGarrahan Claim, based on an alleged Mexican grant of 1844, and covering many leagues of California soil now known to hold a goodly store of silver. Federal officers had often ruled against it; courts had repudiated it; yet in the winter of 1869-70 it showed amazing vitality under the proddings of two great Republican chieftains, Ben Butler and Zach Chandler. Defying the secret maneuvers of these gentlemen, Cox had actually taken steps to patent the land in question in the name of other, more valid claimants. Promptly steps were taken by the party managers to push the old McGarrahan Claim in Congress, while Grant was pressed to undo his Secretary's order. According to recently published evidence which entirely verifies rumors in the press of the time, Grant was furious with Cox, saying, "I shall have a new Secretary of the Interior." Grant ordered that Cox should issue no patent in the matter and leave the whole affair to Congress, though it lay under the jurisdiction of the Department of the Interior. Cox protested vehemently, saying that he had labored faithfully to keep his department "free from fraud and corruption," and that if his efforts in that direction were not sustained, he would desire to be relieved from his office. The President related to Fish that Cox's remark had "cut him severely." [43] Cox's letter of resignation thereafter contained an allusion more cutting still to the fact that his handling of the Indian Service patronage had been "peculiarly distasteful to many influential gentlemen in both houses."

Garfield, a friend and admirer of his fellow Ohioan Cox, wrote him at once: "The worst fears of the country are realized. . . . It is a clear case of surrender on the part of the President to the political vermin which infest the government." [44]

In the House, sometime later, the case of Cox and the McGarrahan Claim was aired, with high words from Garfield defending his friend and even the cause of civil-service reform. Ben Butler, Logan, and Bingham of Ohio, the party "regulars," however, responded with most violent language which bespoke the real temper of the House. While charges of forgery, swindling, and perjury were flung about, the House members with equanimity voted 110 to 92 to sustain the

McGarrahan Claim as "perfect." Garfield, commenting upon the horde of Carpetbaggers in Congress who rode in the "McGarrahan train," avowed to Cox that he "was never more disheartened, never more disgusted with the course of legislation." [45]

There is evidence that a handful of leading politicians in Washington, among them Garfield, seeing men like Cox defeated and driven from public life, suffered periodic distress of conscience and considered keeping their skirts clean by quitting politics. What was most painful now was that the great majority of party men showed themselves as absolutely one with the spoilsman leaders.*

Columbus Delano, shrewd (too shrewd!) Ohio machine politician and former Congressman, soon ruled the Department of the Interior in Cox's place, in perfect accord with the Babcocks, the Ben Butlers, the Zach Chandlers. While he held office, Jay Gould and Collis Huntington had little ground to complain that their Western railroad lands were not provided for. In the meantime, John Delano, son of the Secretary, appeared at the department at times to press certain spurious land claims in his own right with no little success,[46] although that was to make for a subsequent cabinet crisis. But what Delano excelled in was in devoting the resources of his department to needs of his party Organization, a vital labor in which some of the more conspicuous cabinet members sometimes showed timidity. The ambitious Boutwell, Secretary of the Treasury in the following year (1872), determined to stand for the Senate, and so acted nowadays with circumspectness, giving rise to dissatisfaction among the professional party "workers." That season one of these men, from Iowa, made bitter complaint to the party management against Boutwell, who was most unfavorably compared with Delano during the presidential campaign for Grant's re-election:

The cabinet . . . should remain right in Washington ready to give us all the aid they can. Boutwell must either place in our hands his department [the Treasury!] or someone else should take it. . . . They have got enough legitimately in the Treasury Department to take us through. . . .

* However, the former theologian received an "education" which hardened him. It was undoubtedly his great and intimate friend Blaine preaching a realistic philosophy of popular rule—tactics, and "management, management, management"— who buoyed him up most in dark hours and laughed away his attacks of squeamishness.

From the Interior Department I get good accounts all the time. *If we had Delano at the head of the Treasury we would go through and nobody would be hurt.*[47]

Such men were light of touch, and their operations "hurt" no one. Alas, there were never enough Delanos! But wherever they labored, they saw to it that the wealth which accrued to the plunder rings was contributed systematically to aid in the preservation of party power.

As a rule—to which the Grant Era shows striking exceptions—the actual division or distribution of government money and plunder was not managed by the conspicuous cabinet members themselves, standing at the head of departments, or by high officers in the Administration. Men with careers and ambitions usually looked the other way. This complicated and specialized work was usually overseen by men in the "Minor Cabinet," underofficials who seldom aspired to the Senatorship or an Ambassador's role, remained long in office, became expert at their work, and pursued it largely undisturbed over long years as the great war party's Organization rolled happily in the clover of official power. It was these men, unknown to the public, seldom mentioned in the press, who composed the party's demimonde, living and working always in the twilight ground where spoils and public moneys were gathered, divided, and allotted for the cost of campaign struggles throughout the Union year by year.

Several years later James G. Blaine wrote Garfield a series of intimate letters containing advice and warnings which, written by so profound a student of practical politics, in the very heat of struggle, plot and counterplot, despite their fragmentary character and partial suppressions make altogether the most brilliant realistic manual of American popular rule we have ever had. In one letter specifically Blaine defined the whole section of the party which dominated the Government completely from 1869-77, the "Grant Stalwarts," comprising the Southern Carpetbaggers, "with the machine in New York, Pennsylvania and Illinois," as "rule or ruin leaders." He warned Garfield:

"I think I am not wrong in saying that this section contains all the desperate bad men of the party." [48] They would seek loot anywhere; they were ready even for a foreign war or invasion as a legitimate means of continuing political power for a clique.

At this moment, in 1880, when a very imposing political banquet was tendered in New York to a certain Dorsey—one of the shadiest members of the party's demimonde—in honor of his practical efforts in the late campaign, Garfield puzzled over the meaning of this "curious" affair which aroused ugly gossip in the press; but Blaine, with his wonderful knowledge of the whole complex machinery, clarifies the President-elect at once. The "true intent and meaning of the Dorsey dinner," he explained, was to enable Mr. Dorsey to make certain "demands which will in the end center in the Second Assistant Post Master Generalship, through which channel, in my judgment, there are cunning preparations being made by a small cabal to steal half a million a year during your administration." Blaine closes with a solemn and significant warning, repeating the substance of previous reminders: "I again beg you to keep yourself free from all possible commitments as to the *minor cabinet* which in the P.O.D. [Post Office Department] is even more important than the major." [49]

Thus, writing in 1880, in the closing days of the General Grant Era, Blaine gives us the key to the working of the party's underworld. It was the Minor Cabinet, the Assistant Postmaster General, Assistant Treasurers, the chief clerk of the Treasury, the collectors of revenue, and their like who actually controlled the seizure and the distribution of booty. Inconspicuous, yet placed in strategic posts, each usually represented a geographical division of the party's Organization; that is, one hailed from the Indiana machine of Oliver Morton, another represented the Cameron dynasty in Pennsylvania, or the Conkling Organization in New York, or Logan's "crowd" in Chicago. And whether the operation involved a construction ring, a post office, a customhouse, or an internal-revenue affair, or collaboration with building contractors or private business interests, the party's chiefs seemed always to know the character of the operation and accurately enough the sums realized, as may be perceived from Blaine's letter above.*

---

* Thus, Attorney General F. C. Barlow at New York, requested by the collector for his party to furnish $1,000 out of his salary of $6,000, sent only a check for

Was it not "holy work" done to keep the glorious party of liberty, union, and victory in power?

For years, ever since Lincoln's term, there had been rumors of a secret Whisky Ring operated by certain large distillers in combination with Federal officials to defraud the Treasury of excise taxes. But after 1870, with Grant and the Stalwart Republicans in undisputed power, the Whisky Ring activities became bolder, grew in fact to gigantic proportions. The structure of this peculiar ring, spreading through many States, living in the half-world between legitimate and illegal activities yet essentially an organic outgrowth of the professional party Organization, follows perfectly the suggestive description given to such things by Blaine and establishes the pattern for all the later rings that arose successively in place of those overthrown.

The grand director of the Whisky Ring during Grant's term was Brevet General John A. McDonald, a veteran of indifferent war record, and more lately a claim agent and speculator in any "venture" where political-military influence might count for something. In the autumn of 1869, when the whole country was shaken by the Black Friday money panic, he had come boldly to Grant, with whom he was acquainted, asking for a letter of introduction to Jay Gould and Jim Fisk. This Grant had refused, but instead appointed the man at his request (and upon Babcock's advice as well) as Supervisor of Internal Revenue at St. Louis, a responsible post at the decent salary of $3,000 a year, having jurisdiction over Missouri, Kansas, Arkansas, New Mexico, and Texas collections. At the moment, it is important to note, there were signs of revolt in Missouri, where Senators Carl Schurz and B. Gratz Brown showed symptoms of turning independent and opposing the annexation of Santo Domingo. These two, and other local leaders, protested vehemently to Grant at the unfitness and ill repute of the man McDonald, who was placed in their midst; but the latter proceeded at once, with Grant's blessing, to organize a following in Missouri which promised most faithful support of the Administration. Thus the point of departure is the

$120, declaring that as an honest man he got no more than his salary. *Cf. Nation*, Nov. 17, 1870, p. 329. But the party managers, by previous experience, counted upon larger proceeds from this office.

political mission.[50] In his internal-revenue district McDonald took charge at once of current operations by which distillers, in connivance with government men, passed in false reports of the quantity of spirits they manufactured or rectified, and also regularly issued forged internal-revenue stamps; so that usually from a distilling center like St. Louis three times as much whisky would be shipped as paid a tax.[51]

Not for nothing had McDonald been an admiring observer of Gould's and Fisk's monopolistic forays. McDonald had the acumen to extend his operations in the same manner. Both distillers and officers were "organized." Honest officials were compelled to serve him; distillers who resisted were blackmailed into partnership through petty prosecution for minor or pretended infractions of the law and thenceforth assessments were regularly levied upon them. The ring formed contacts in the more important distillery centers, such as Milwaukee, Chicago, Peoria, and Indianapolis, and hence working agreements with Federal men and politicians holding sway over those districts.

A distinguishing feature is the way in which the whisky organization paralleled geographically the chief centers of Stalwart Republican strength. In Milwaukee E. W. Keyes, the local boss, and Senator Matthew Carpenter of Wisconsin, the Stalwart associate of Oliver Morton, were said to have entered the alliance.[52] In Illinois the regional machine, directed by Logan, was suspected generally of working closely with the ring. In St. Louis the ring purchased a newspaper, the *Globe*, and had the collaboration of its owner and editor, William McKee.

Business thrived wonderfully; and soon a responsible, experienced business manager was engaged at a large salary to oversee the nearly nation-wide operations of the ring from its headquarters in St. Louis.

Earlier, the Whisky Ring had kept confederates within the Treasury Department at Washington who gave warning against inspections or investigation. Now, behind the impassive back of Secretary Boutwell and of Richardson after him, the chief clerk of the Internal Revenue Department, William Avery, supported by numerous assistants, acted as a silent partner and informer. But also, from the White House itself, the audacious Orville Babcock worked to protect the cabal. The leak was always through the President's office, where reports of complaints or intended inquisitions were brought first of all under the eye of Babcock. Secret telegrams would fly from the President's secretary to the manager at St. Louis, giving warnings.[53] Then Babcock in person would make mysterious journeys to St. Louis, receiving diamonds worth several thousand dollars, cigar boxes containing bills of $1,000 each, hotel accommodations, rare liquors, even the soft ministrations of a "Sylph." [54] For money rolled in faster than men could spend it; within a period of four years taxes variously estimated at from $2,700,000 to $4,000,000 were diverted from the Treasury, and of this approximately 40 per cent, between $1,000,000 and $1,600,000, went to higher government officials and to regional bosses, in various cities and States, who upon demand got large contributions from the ring on behalf of Republican campaign committees.

It was this phase of the ring's activities, its vital function in the nation-wide party machine, that reveals its organic political character and form, embracing the co-operation of the Kitchen Cabinet from the White House, important officers of the federal civil service and the most powerful of the Senatorial bosses.

McDonald, in his not wholly accurate but very suggestive confessions, published as a campaign document in 1880, insisted that there was an understanding between the President and the members of the ring that their gains "should constitute a campaign fund to advance the interests of the administration." [55] McDonald's statements, though having a great deal of plausibility, are not credible unless checked against other evidence which appears at the trial of the ring members. It was not true that Grant knowingly participated in the ring activities and profits, nor even that he accepted without remuneration McDonald's gift of a costly team of carriage horses and equipage. But the statement of McDonald's bearing upon the political inception and the objectives of his organization is of an eye-filling truth that has neither been noticed enough nor been effectively challenged:

The original intention of the organizers . . . was to make the ring co-extensive with the nation, with headquarters in all the large cities, for the purposes of raising a campaign fund with which to advance the interests of President Grant in his aspirations for a second term . . . the money received from the distillers and rectifiers was used according to the original intention of the members, until Grant's re-election, when, the purposes of the organization having been accomplished . . . it was decided to continue the appropriation of the revenue and to make the members of the ring the beneficiaries of the fund. *During congressional and municipal campaigns, however, a part of this fund was always used in the interests of the Republican candidates.*[56]

For years the Internal Revenue offices at St. Louis became something of a national center for party politics; at moments the whole Western wing of the Republican Party subsisted upon its parasitic suborganization in the whisky trade. Faced with a hot campaign, a great Senator would telegraph to McDonald's headquarters for new levies upon the distillers, so that a congressional district should not be "lost" or so that even a State might be "saved." McDonald insisted that none other than Oliver Morton made a hurried trip to see him in St. Louis at the height of the campaign of 1872, in order to replenish the war chest of Indiana.[57] These leaders, in turn, defended the ring members, "in the party" interests, as McDonald put it.[58]

The Republican Party for nearly two decades after the war was a mighty patronage organization, deriving revenues and profit from the sale of offices and assessments upon the wages of its army of place-holders. It received in addition handsome endowments from leading bankers and industrial capitalists who needed its services and who were favored by its policies. But in an important degree the party's established suborganizations and parasitic rings, by diverting a steady stream of funds from the earnings of private citizens as well as the public Treasury, made the party *autonomous and self-supporting*. In this sphere of activities, the greed, the irresponsibility, of a whole wing of officials made them increasingly a menace; their excesses were increasingly a subject of the deepest anxiety to the party's moneyed allies.

The ruling party, in short, pursuing special "institutional" interests of its own, was not the satisfying, responsible, controlled instrument of the capitalist class which some men hoped for. For this unexpected, lush overdevelopment of the spoils system, confusion in the minds of the dominant economic class itself was to blame. The more far-sighted of these tended to an opposition within and without the ruling party; the others, outweighing them in power, still felt themselves for a long time unable to forego the immense conveniences of political venality.

V

Ruled by a half-dozen party chieftains, the monstrous military-bureaucratic machine rumbled on, in control and enjoyment of all the political government functions of the republic. For more than a decade after the Civil War it continued unabated its military or Carpetbag rule of the conquered Southern States. And if men who remembered our American libertarian tradition protested at the stationing of five Major Generals and 20,000 soldiers in the South and the disfranchisement for so many years of Southern whites, or at the harsh acts of repression which Congress authorized in 1871, they were denounced in the name of patriotism, and reminded that the Republican Party had won the war and saved the Union. To the loyal soldiers the party gave pensions, to farmers free soil. To the capitalist class of the North, who were among its strongest friends, it distributed the more important largesses in land resources and tariff subsidies. If smaller people, "petty bourgeois," and especially the spokesmen of farming communities sometimes protested at monopolies in railroads, or salt, or wire nails now showing themselves for the first time in the 1870's, if sober, honest, enlightened citizens of the middle class counted the cost of bureaucratic corruption—even great merchants the prey of customs rings—the party leaders confronted them at once with the specter of upheaval and disunion. For the futile, limited opposition from the enemy party, the Democrats, was for long years stamped with the official onus of "rebel" and "Copperhead."

But more important were the protests, murmured at first, then stronger, of a faction of liberal or idealistic men within the Republican Party itself. Here were found the ardent Abolitionists and libertarians: Senator James Grimes of Iowa and Representative George Julian of Indiana; Senator Trumbull of Illinois, Lincoln's old colleague; the eloquent German-American leader General Carl

Schurz; the brilliant war hero, and learned Federal Judge Walter Gresham; and above all the now disaffected, implacable old Senate leader, Sumner of Massachusetts. They were appalled by signs, omens, of catastrophe and crime. Julian professed that he was "disquieted by all the signs of bribery." Trumbull had resisted the impeachment of Johnson, warned his party of excesses in Southern Reconstruction, and moved for inquiries into ugly nests of corruption which were now heard of on all sides. Carl Schurz ardently, and sometimes Garfield timidly, fathered a Civil Service Reform Bill in Congress. And in July, 1870, the scrupulous Grimes, a leading Radical during the war, was writing to Trumbull of the Republican Party: "Like all parties that have an undisturbed power for a long time, it has become corrupt, and I believe it is to-day the most corrupt and debauched political party that has ever existed. . . . I will no longer vote the Republican ticket, whatever else I may do." [59] And Judge Gresham of Indiana, whom Grant admired as a soldier, and to whom he offered a high cabinet position in 1869, declined this unconditionally, explaining in a letter to his law partner, "I am disgusted with the whole thing . . . the Republican party is an infernally corrupt concern, and I don't care how soon it is broken up if the Democracy don't survive it." [60]

Against such prominent malcontents within the camp the party leadership moved with tremendous energy, to enforce "party regularity" and discipline. The highhanded Oliver Morton, who was closest to the President, and in the Senate dominated the Stalwarts much like Stevens before him in the House, would fiercely expound the party credo over and again. Gesticulating, swaying in his chair, for he was now paralyzed from the waist down, this iron-willed political fighter, whom all eyes followed—with his pale face full of pain, his flowing black hair and beard, his sickly, heavy-lidded black eyes and quivering nose of a bulldog—could be heard thundering immitigably against those who urged pacification of the South and amnesty. For the Negro and Carpetbag organizations, the "loyal" State governments, were almost his special province, which he knew made safe Republican dominance. He would defend with equal vehemence, in a jumble of partisan jargon which then and thereafter passed for the philosophy of Stalwart Republicanism, the rigid party control of official patronage. Against Independents and would-be reformers he would cry in his grating voice, which could be heard from his chair to every corner of the Capitol: "I hold the Republican Party superior in importance to any man who is a member of it . . . *this is a government of parties.*" In the civil service of this government men must be appointed only with "regard to politics." [61]

A very moderate civil-service reform measure in response to often voiced complaints, one allowing the most absurdly meager appropriation for its execution, confronted Congress early in 1870 as a small shadow. But there it met the withering attacks of John Logan, who described it as "the most obnoxious bill . . . that has come before this House." [62]

In the Senate the uproarious Zach Chandler shouted: "What are they howling for reform for? We have it now. There is hardly a man who is setting up his cry for reform who is not a corrupt scoundrel or a thief." [63] And Morton, whose campaigns were warmly supported by the Whisky Ring, declared smugly that "the civil service of the government was as well managed as any civil service in the world." [64]

Those who charged their party with corruption, those who pressed reform here and resolutions of inquiry there, were "traitors" and "Copperheads" who should be read out of the party, he implied. They would make possible the return of the Democrat to power! Calamities, awful acts of God were possible, too. An earthquake, the Chicago fire! But Morton prayed that they would not return again.[65] Then he launched himself usually into a tirade against those who instigated atrocities against freedmen in the South, who burnt Negro schools, churches, women, children. Blaine and Conkling too were cynical adepts in waving the Bloody Shirt before dissenters within.

Perhaps no one reached such extremes of partisan cruelty as the very Rabelaisian Senator from Michigan, Mr. Zach Chandler. He it was who called down upon those who opposed Stalwart policy not only the plagues of Egypt, but even the curse of nuptial sterility. For his part, Democrats might writhe forever in barren beds, so that there might be no more Copperhead children. In a campaign speech at Detroit, Chandler spoke for about two hours and wound up his speech by turning to his right and there addressing the ladies (of whom the meeting was composed by half) as follows: "and if any of you ladies are married to a Copperhead husband, let him sleep alone"![66]

CHAPTER FOUR

PARTY PURGE

1871-1872

The Reformers by profession, the "unco guid." They are to be treated with respect, but they are the worst possible political advisers—upstarts, conceited, foolish, vain, without knowledge of measures, ignorant of men, shouting a shibboleth. . . . They are noisy but not numerous, pharisaical but not practical, ambitious but not wise, pretentious but not powerful! They can be easily dealt with. . . . I could handle them myself without trouble. JAMES G. BLAINE

HIGH in the ranks of the Republican Party were numerous men who were increasingly revolted by the violent excesses of all kinds, the plundering or the privateering, which went on under the dominant Senatorial Clique, the new Stalwart "directory" that ruled in the name of Grant. Certain of these dissidents kept their disappointment secret. Men of conservative or moderate spirit, they acknowledged the might and social convenience of party organization, dared not attack it openly, and trusted that in remaining by the side of their mad brethren they might stay their hands and prevent worse things befalling the republic than those they witnessed. Others among the dissenting minority, who had distinguished themselves during the social upheavals of recent years by the generosity and humanity of their views, Sumner, Trumbull, and Schurz—the last of the progressive, idealistic Radical Abolitionists who were left—could scarcely restrain their indignation. Their counsels were spurned by the new regime. Their temper made them awkward allies at best in an epoch of complacent acquisition and corruption. To them it seemed a question but of waiting until war hatred had died down, and of finding a clearer issue upon which they might have a fighting chance to appeal to the country—without being proscribed as "rebels." But war hatreds were kept alive as long as possible by the Carthaginian peace which the dominant leaders and the President imposed; and new ideas of foreign adventures, of seizing Cuba and Santo Domingo, even of wresting Canada from England, were entertained for the sake of further beclouding real issues.

In the first category, that of would-be preventers of evil, was Hamilton Fish, the rather cultivated New York grandee, an anomaly in Grant's Cabinet, and lending it social distinction. He was one of the few political personages in the entourage of the President who did not try to appropriate the columns of the Capitol or the very stones of the Treasury Building. For his unusual scruples with regard to the public property, Fish has ultimately won a certain historical notoriety, and merited perhaps the literary monument recently raised to him by pious hands. To be sure, he was very rich and old when he came into high office; as one who had feasted long and well he was surfeited with the fleshpots for which the simple spoilsmen lusted. As a man of inherited wealth, a leader of the old Whig Party which formerly defended public order and finance against popular uprisings in New York of Barnburners and Locofocos, Fish was naturally at odds with the dangerous extremists in the ruling party, whose excesses he, as a conservative old Dutch Knickerbocker, a prudent bourgeois of the old school, sought patiently to curb. Although not a colorful Secretary of State nor a party leader like Seward and Blaine, nor a diplomat of unusual finesse, he labored steadfastly to delay disastrous actions or at least to prevent "something worse." Often, as he silently witnessed appalling blunders and thievish conspiracies and described them in his voluminous private journal, he conveys to us in restrained tones his true horror and dismay. Often his heart sinks, and his resignation is ready; but Grant would plead with him earnestly to remain by his side: "We need you and your wife." For social reasons, he and Mrs. Grant could not possibly have dispensed with the imposing Mrs. Fish, no less decorative than her husband. But more important, as the worthy Ebenezer Hoar told him at the moment of his own dismissal from the Cabinet, Fish was "the bulwark now standing between the country and destruction." Fish must "under all circumstances . . . hold fast." [1]

In 1870 and 1871 the tiny republic of Santo Domingo, with its 100,000 Negro inhabitants, became the accidental issue for a spectacular struggle which opened a first breach within the ruling party. To Colonel Babcock, as to President Grant, who heard his glowing reports, Santo Domingo offered alluring possibilities. Behind Babcock, as we have seen, stood the thieving dictator Baèz, some Yankee fortune-hunters and guano importers, then Ben Butler, Logan, and a few other spoilsman leaders. But what *business* was there in Santo Domingo, sober, respectable citizens and newspapers asked themselves with disgust in the spring of 1870. The whole hinterland of our own United States still formed a huge, untouched colonial empire, perhaps the richest in the world; the country literally hungered for foreign capital to bring railroads there, to build cities, steel mills, and steam engines. Why, then, Santo Domingo?

But though the moment was unripe, President Grant (spurred by his friends) had set his heart upon this shady adventure in imperial expansion as a measure of national policy, perhaps the only policy which appealed to his whole fancy. Beyond Santo Domingo, and a possible naval base there, lay the scheme of advance toward an Isthmian canal and its defense. Early in January, 1870, Grant had gone personally to call on Sumner and invite his aid for the proposed treaty of annexation, as chairman of the Senate Committee on Foreign Relations. Sumner had then made only an enigmatical reply, promising that as a good Republican he would give the question his "most careful and candid consideration," a reply which Grant had incorrectly assumed signified agreement. The interview was comic in the extreme. After it was over, both men disagreed violently in their reports of it, each accusing the other of bad faith. When we note, according to the account of one person present, that the President in his deep ignorance addressed Sumner as head of the "Judiciary Committee," to which he believed his treaty would be committed by the Senate, we are little disposed to give credence to his recollections.

What happened was apparently a fantastic dialogue, in which neither man listened seriously to the other. After the little President had made his formal request, the Senator, who was already secretly alienated from him upon other grounds, stared into the distance, and began a pompous harangue upon his own grievances concerning the award of patronage to his political friends. He himself was worried and sore because he was not being "consulted," because his own allies were being removed from office, for even the incorruptible Sumner could not exist without political aides. He related afterward that he had formed no clear idea of what treaty Grant was talking about.[2] Yet large events followed this strange meeting. What Sumner learned, immediately afterward, in studying reports of the Santo Domingo venture impelled him to gird on his sword and buckler and lead from the floor of the Senate a memorable and furious demonstration of insurgency against the Executive and against the majority of his own party.

After Ulysses Grant, the tall Massachusetts Senator, of the flowing mane, romantic gestures, and silver tongue, was perhaps the most famous of living Americans. During the Civil War and for the years afterward, the impassioned Abolitionist had dominated our foreign policy. In him the motives now were mixed: those of the idealist who embodied in himself always the golden principles of the Declaration of Independence, the champion of oppressed peoples, learning now that American warships by a show of force sustained the power of the "puppet" dictator Baèz in Santo Domingo, that the whole affair reeked of corruption and knavery; and the motives of the politician declining in influence and authority, the very substance of his power threatened by the slighting of his retainers. He was but little deferred to in high councils of the party these days; his views of the Alabama Claims were rejected in the English negotiations; his friend John Motley, Minister to England, was being undermined and was expected to be supplanted, as he understood. Other political friends in office were threatened with removal at the will of the Senatorial Clique, and of Ben Butler, to whose thieving henchmen the Federal patronage in Massachusetts was being handed over, while Sumner's own wishes were flouted.[3]

Moreover, the President had sent his military aide to negotiate a secret treaty without consulting *him*, Sumner! (What if Sumner had known also that Grant had allotted $150,000 from the secret-service fund to the support of the Dominican dictator in collusion with whom Babcock acted?)

Grant, who was never cast for the role of Caesar, was nevertheless by his ignorance doubly dangerous; alternately he cringed before the political chieftains who hemmed him in, and in a casual, unthinking way affronted the very spirit of our democratic laws. It needed but a few nervous twinges of the egomaniac, the creature of rostrums and public stages, in Sumner to transfer rebuffs for himself to the composite person of Congress, the sovereign will of the American people, insulted and injured by the cabal of a ruthless military Captain. Was not the Senate vested with the treaty-making power? The last thought became an obsession in the slowly clouding mind of the aged political warrior, whose brain, as many persons believed, had been a little unhinged ever since the clubbing he received from the secessionist Brooks, before the war.

Hardened by Sumner's unrelenting opposition, the Senate Foreign Relations Committee reported adversely upon the Santo Domingo treaty, March 15, 1870. In open debate on March 24, 1870, Sumner delivered the first of a series of powerful attacks upon the Administration's foreign policy, exposing the folly and the incalculable future cost of Santo Domingo annexation. There followed a distressingly bitter struggle of three months within the party. The President, in the tenacious mood of the battles before Richmond, now used his office to lobby for senatorial support, repeatedly offering patronage as a direct bribe in return for votes, according to Carl Schurz and others.[4] Insults flew back and forth; scandals concerning the Santo Domingo conspirators were aired in the press, and before a Senate committee Sumner, uttering overheated words which reflected upon Grant, demanded that Colonel Babcock be cashiered.

The country was indifferent or comprehended little; conservative leaders were quietly hostile to the treaty; the Senate, slowly aligning itself with Sumner, instinctively maneuvered to maintain its grip over the Executive, as in the struggles over Reconstruction with Johnson, while leaving Sumner and his friends to bear the burden of the battle. At the end of the long-drawn session, June 30, by a tie vote, the President's treaty of annexation failed of ratification.

A spectacular and undignified enmity between Grant and Sumner was now born, and Grant showed vindictive traits; privately he menaced Sumner with physical violence and abused his sympathizers; while Sumner was no less implacable, his roaring against the little General being audible from his home up and down Pennsylvania Avenue. A renewed message from Grant, urging action upon Santo

Domingo annexation in the session of December, 1870, was preceded by the cutting off of political heads; the dismissal of Motley from London was ordered; patronage arrangements were made to defeat Sumner's allies in the Senate, such as Carl Schurz, Senator from Missouri, whose re-election was to be blocked by the action of the Whisky Ring men. Then, on December 21, 1870, Sumner, before thronged galleries, in his worst and most extravagant style, delivered himself of a resounding philippic against Grant and his political field marshals upon the theme of the "dance of blood" which intriguers and military conspirators were initiating in the name of Manifest Destiny.

Previously in a public interview he had told a tale of "young military men the President had gathered about him," who had taken a notion that "there was a good speculation in Dominica," while Grant had unwittingly been pressed into their scheme, until the coast of the Bay of Samana, at Santo Domingo, had been staked off into lots marked "Cazneau," "Babcock," "Baèz," and one or two particularly large ones marked "Grant." [5] His information he claimed was derived from a naval officer who had seen such charts.[6] Now he warned the President not to earn for himself the fate of Andrew Johnson, "not to oppress a weak and humble people, not to exercise war powers without authority of Congress . . . not to forget that there is a grandeur in justice and in peace beyond anything in war." [7]

Sumner's fire-bell ringing had alarmed public opinion. Brought before the Senate again by Grant's stubbornness, the Santo Domingo treaty could not be saved. Apathy or caution ruled the Senators. Then, more momentous foreign questions raised by the Franco-Prussian War and the ensuing settlement of the Alabama Claims against England demanded all the attention of the Senate and the State Department. The Stalwart leaders, Oliver Morton and Conkling, assailed Sumner with cruel personalities; but what was more important, they held over the old Radical hero the threat of sternest disciplinary measures. These were carried out pitilessly on March 8, 1871, when the secret party caucus voted to depose Sumner from his place as chairman of the Senate Foreign Relations Committee. This high committee post, which bore with it an international prestige, was conferred upon Simon Cameron, the Czar of Pennsylvania. The filibusters in Santo Domingo and Cuba might well take heart once more. In a mood of vindictiveness, the President also struck off the well-groomed head of Sumner's friend, Motley. General Schenck, the breezy poker-player from Ohio, became Minister to England.

The public "degrading" of Sumner by his party was a shock not only to many old Republicans but to the whole country. Sumner's name for nearly a quarter of a century was synonymous with self-denying devotion to the Union, with a revolutionary militancy which recalled Cromwell's Old Ironsides. From this crushing blow of his demotion his spirits never fully recovered.

Most men ceased now to expect miracles from the Grant Administration. Was the revolution "devouring its sons"? The ideologues who had represented a certain disinterestedness in the service of their party's policies were the ones who were systematically proscribed in the prolonged "Thermidor" which was carried out in 1871-72. For these men who in other days had most stirred the hearts of liberty-loving citizens of the North were precisely the faction which was ranged now in a desperate opposition to the command of the dread party caucus. But, as if to show that ideas could now frankly be dispensed with by the party machine, the Senate whip, Oliver Morton, made a speech warning all men of the fate of Sumner, and called down anathema upon those who had entered the opposition within the party, for no sin greater than this was known in all the politician's manual, as he repeatedly explained. Though the decision of the party might be squarely against a man's "personal wishes and choice . . . against . . . convictions of right," he must honorably abide by it. Else how could the party exist as an organization, how could a government of parties exist? [8]

Sumner was *crazed*, they whispered now. It was true that the choleric Sumner labored as one overwrought by illness or neurosis much of the time; he roared "like the Bull of Bashan," rolled his tragic eyes and worked his features wonderfully. But even if Sumner had cooed like a turtledove, the mere fact of his insurgence against party unity was enough in the minds of the new leadership to convict him of political insanity.

The storm over the tiny West Indian republic was the warning symptom of growing cleavage within the ruling party. A handful of dissident Republicans, though pitifully few, had fought by the side of Sumner and even gathered for the moment the support of the Democratic minority in the Senate.

These independent Republicans had represented for many years such intellectual force and moral earnestness as their party still retained from its age of *Sturm und Drang*. They were, characteristically, men who read books, studied especially the enlightening pages of the London *Economist*, preached ideals of a rational, middle-class liberalism and—perhaps what was most characteristic of them—were decidedly wanting in party orthodoxy. Above all, they believed the American republic could dispense with the spoils system, through which a dreadful command over the party caucus was exercised. The position of the independent Republicans toward 1872 was both interesting and perilous.

"Grant has read me out of the Republican Party," wrote one of these men, Carl Schurz, to a friend in October, 1870.[9] The old Prussian revolutionary leader had refused the President's plea for help in the Santo Domingo treaty; coming to the White House afterward, he found the door closed to him.

Carl Schurz, the outstanding independent of our postwar politics, who in his best phase acted usually according to his knowledge, his convictions, rather than according to the party line, was for this reason the butt and target of "regular" politicians. This unaccountable political waywardness was attributed to his being a foreigner, a German—though few Americans could equal him in mastery of the English language. Henry Adams, on the other hand, as a passive spectator, thought Schurz's independence made him an "ideal statesman." He was certainly more completely and peculiarly identified with emergent movements of reform during the darkest 1870's and 1880's than any other political figure.

The independents were essentially libertarians, as hostile to protective-tariff schemes as to dangerous foreign adventures; as for the issue of Reconstruction, in a mood of reaction to so many protracted disorders, they were weary of military rule, and favored a more statesmanlike course of conciliation and amnesty nowadays, such as the unhappy Andrew Johnson had taken. Then Schurz, like many other public-spirited persons, became alarmed at the Gargantuan growth of the party spoils system. Aware of the strong progress being made in the German Empire and in England toward an efficient, distinguished civil service, Schurz worked night and day to found a political movement which would purify the American government bureaucracy, and turn the republic at last into the wonderful middle-class millennium which he visioned.

On a few rare occasions since the Jacksonian Era, forty years before, men had risen in Congress to advocate ideas of civil-service reform. Schurz in March, 1869, made a notable speech proposing a system of appointment to the government service according to merit, determined by competitive examination rather than by partisan interest. In the following session of Congress, Schurz introduced a Civil Service Reform Bill, but saw it buried in committee all that year. Nevertheless men who were grown hopeless, and especially young men, saw a light in civil-service reform, which after the clash over Santo Domingo became the battle cry of the Independent movement. For only by way of civil-service reform, they believed, could the dreadful patronage power be removed, a power which already held a sword suspended over the heads of men like Carl Schurz and Lyman Trumbull.

II

The phenomenon of the reform movement is as native to our politics as the tendency to corruption. The one appears regularly to beget the other. In early agitation for civil-service reform its chief exponents—Schurz, Trumbull, and George William Curtis—were soon supported by an element of the wealthiest and most respected citizens. For men of wealth were in truth divided in their councils. Most of them, desiring the freest scope for their competitive instincts, privately enjoyed the conveniences of the spoils system, as a "practical necessity." On the one hand they preached respect for law and order, for the authority of the state; but on the other hand it was felt that such principles were not to be "too vigorously emphasized." Corruption should not be "too strongly condemned, nor spoils politics too vigorously assailed." For, while theoretically indispensable, "these were instruments of control under the given situation." [10] But during the winter of 1871-72 a cause célébre, the explosion of the Tweed Ring scandals in the nation's largest city, gave special scope to the movement of reform.

During the long years of drought, while the party of Lincoln "battened at the public crib," vital fragments of the opposition party, much diminished and discredited in its national pretensions, had survived—nay, flourished—in the citadels of certain municipal machines. Thus the practiced demagogues of Tammany Hall retained for generations their grip over the polyglot proletarian mass of New York City.

A great proportion of the immigrant arrivals in the land of milk, honey, and gilded pavements clung to life in New York's frightful slums, comprising one of the most ignorant, violent, *lumpen* proletariats in the modern world. For this rabble, traditionally, the rulers of the city's dominant political organization provided bread and even circuses in the form of annual clambakes and excursions. Tammany agents, meeting their poor Irish and foreign brothers at the dock, gave them advice and aid, food baskets, beer, and even work; in return the new arrivals permitted themselves to be inducted—sometimes at the rate of 1,000 a day—as citizens and "voting cattle" into the Democratic Party. Boss William M. Tweed, who had risen to supreme command of the Tammany machine, was, like Robin Hood of legend, ever generous to the poor. On Christmas Day of 1870, he gave $50,000 to the people of his ward, and $1,000 each to the aldermen of the various city wards to buy coal for the needy. "Well, if Tweed stole," it was said, "he was at least good to the poor." [11] Like their predecessors, Tweed and his partners, Sweeny and Connally, had long levied upon the numerous brothels, saloons, gambling dens, and criminal associations, through the city police and the courts. Commanding the preponderance of voters who ruled at the polls, they earned tolerant support of the leaders of society, business, and professional life, who also must dwell with some security in their city. The State Republican leaders themselves, men like Thurlow Weed and even the virtuous Horace Greeley, must wink at them if they would have the convenience of the great city. The elegant Democratic Governor, Horatio Seymour, and the even more distinguished Samuel Tilden and the lordly August Belmont had controlled the

Democratic National Convention in 1868, thanks to the aid of Tammany, who sometimes by their strategic power dictated the names of presidential candidates, as well as Governors.

In 1869 and in 1870 Tilden had worked faithfully to hold the important chairmanship of the Democratic State Convention in their interest, throwing his influence in the nick of time to the Tweed Ring. Nevertheless, amid the public excitement of the last party gathering, the wealthy Mr. Tilden had had his pockets picked, a measure of justice which aroused merry comment. "Mr. Samuel Tilden . . . got, we hope, a realizing sense of the company he keeps when he opens conventions . . . for Mr. Tweed, and Mr. Hall, and Mr. Hoffman," was the dry comment of Edward Godkin's *Nation*.[12] When some early murmurs against the excesses of the city government arose in 1870, Boss Tweed, Connolly, and "Brains" Sweeny easily obtained the endorsement of the most respectable capitalists and bankers of the city, including John Jacob Astor and Moses Taylor, who certified to their "correct and faithful" administration of the city funds![13]

Yet the contradictions of the system were becoming unbearable to other respectable capitalists. As in the case of Mr. Tilden, they were having their pockets picked at the very moment when they lent their cheerful support to the thieves.

By 1870, the depredations of the ring went far beyond a "necessary evil"; they were no longer an "instrument" for governing voting cattle, but an immense piratical monopoly. By the operation of public-works schemes, they plundered $1,000,000 a month from the city treasury, earning more in a year than Mr. Vanderbilt; they had added some $50,000,000 to the public debt, controlled banks, embarked with Jay Gould and Jim Fisk upon perilous, unsocial schemes to corner railroads and the money market, as in the Black Friday affair of 1869. The Tweed Ring must go. The men of money, previously divided, were now as one in believing that the day of retribution, the day of reform, was at hand. In *Harper's Weekly* the editor, George William Curtis, attacked with his pen, while the brilliant Tom Nast with his pencil directed a murderous fire upon the thieves. Incriminating documents were found in plenty, and turned over to the leading newspapers of the city; mass meetings of citizens were organized by the very friends of Messrs. Astor and Taylor, who had endorsed Tammany yesterday but formed the Committee of Seventy today. William E. Dodge, the copper merchant, who was having his troubles with spoilsmen of both parties, and whose company was charged in Congress with giving bribes to customs inspectors, was one of the leading reform speakers; William F. Havemeyer, the sugar magnate, whose employees were also often accused of conniving with corrupt Federal officers, was another fighter in the revolution; while the financial wizard and corporation lawyer Samuel Tilden somewhat tardily took the leading part in the crusade against his former allies, since he was accredited with having "an intimate knowledge of the Ring and its methods." [14]

The deep Tilden, who had neither sanctioned nor shared in Tweed's audacious schemes but who, like his confreres, found the ring in the end an encumbrance, perhaps also a bar to further ambitions, now organized an elaborate plan of exposure and prosecution, and flung himself upon the Tiger "like an avenging angel." [15] The ringmasters were tried, arrested, or put to flight; the Tammany judges were impeached. The public was appalled at the whole story, and the Democratic Party was weakened and beaten that year. But Samuel Tilden, who had earlier shown "only a general interest in reform," as he himself said, had won national fame, and now united the dissenting factions of the stricken party under his leadership into a great reform Organization of his own. [16] He had created, out of precedents and materials at hand, the very pattern of American bureaucratic reform.

Certain aspects of the often related Tweed affair must be underscored before we leave it. The masses of the people had been highly indifferent to reports of the Tweed Ring spoliations; indeed, they were traditionally friendly to the Tammany leaders and heartily prejudiced against "reformers." Tweed himself held that the majority of his supporters could not read what was said of him, but ascribed his disasters to Tom Nast's pictures, which required no reading. Men like Tilden, the richest of corporation lawyers, a master of financial speculations, with the aid of numerous grasping capitalists, such as Havemeyer and Dodge, had finally aroused the sober, law-abiding middle classes and also won enough popular support to bring about a political upheaval. These were the same men for whom the political spoilsmen had been most serviceable in the past, "practical necessities" or "instruments of control." But when these spoilsmen became ever bolder, waylaid their superiors, and practiced an increasingly large extortion upon the quickly gained fortunes of the Tildens, Havemeyers, and Dodges—picked their pockets, so to speak—then the anger of the great New York capitalists knew no bounds. They turned and smote their former allies hip and thigh, harried them into prison, exile, or death.

Such sobering, undeceiving conclusions upon the reform uprising in New York are no sudden fancy or invention of our own, but suggest themselves from the evidence of informed but private comment at the period. It was customary, in the vulgar speech of the time, that men like the multimillionaire Tilden (who organized one of the first stockmarket "corners" in 1860) "stole," though of course in perfectly high-minded and legal fashion and in quantities imposing enough to bring him honor. Even Horatio Seymour, formerly Governor of New York and Democratic candidate for the Presidency in the last campaign, who was a great landowner and capitalist as well as a consummate politician of the old school, used precisely such expressions. Commenting upon the overthrow of Tweed and the appearance of a reform movement in a letter to Samuel Tilden, Seymour says with exquisite justice and wit: "Our people want men in office who will not steal, but who will not interfere with those who do." [17]

III

"An age of reform" had begun, the Independent Republican Senator Lyman Trumbull proclaimed.[18]

While sensation followed sensation in New York's Tweed Ring affair, the contagion of reform spread to the national capital. Complaints and petitions in goodly number came now from the richest patrons of the Republican Party themselves. The Dry Goods Nabob, A. T. Stewart, protested several times to the President and the Secretary of the Treasury that he was being despoiled by those whom he had patronized; he was the prey of the Custom House Ring at New York, with its warehouse monopoly which acted "to annoy, vex and deplete" most importing merchants.[19] William E. Dodge announced at the same time that his firm, after suffering "obstruction and damage" in New York at the hands of the Federal ring, was diverting its metal shipments to other ports (where the minions of Chester Arthur and Conkling might not with impunity levy upon them). In addition, the most respectable lawyers, financiers, merchants, and trade associations of the metropolis, among them August Belmont, Brown Brothers, W. and J. Sloane, and Arnold Constable, protested at having their books seized, open extortion practiced upon them, and small irregularities magnified into occasions for blackmail by the "workers" in the Conkling machine.[20]

In the Senate Carl Schurz began to speak for a group of rich, prominent citizens when he urged that an end be made of rotation in office under partisan control. As he said, under the spoils system the whole machinery of government was literally pulled to pieces every four years, the business of national legislation subordinated to the distribution of plunder among partisans, and the men who had learned the duties of their offices dismissed as soon as they had mastered them. Alluding to the warehouse and custom frauds in New York, he demanded, Why is nothing done?

But the fact remains that this scandalous system of robbery is sustained—is sustained against the voice of the merchants of New York—is sustained against the judgment and the voice of the Secretary of the Treasury himself. I ask you how is it sustained? Where and what is the mysterious power that sustains it? The conclusion is inevitable that it is stronger than the decent respect for public opinion, nay, a power stronger than the Secretary of the Treasury himself.[21]

Schurz's words were aimed clearly at the Senator-bosses and the spoilsmen rings upon which they based their control of the party caucus. The pressure of public opinion was rising, and the protests of the great New York merchants, whose cause the German American reformer pleaded so powerfully, were even more insistent. Nevertheless, it was the ineffable Roscoe Conkling himself who, in December, 1871, introduced in the Senate the resolution of inquiry that authorized an investigation of his henchmen at the New York Custom House. Then, with a cool effrontery that baffled the authors of the resolution, Schurz and Trumbull, the New York boss supervised the appointments for the select committee of investigation, and saw to it that it was composed chiefly of persons friendly to his interests.

The novel ideas of reform had met with so much favor that early in March, 1871, a provision had been incorporated in an act making appropriations for sundry civil expenses which authorized the President "to prescribe such rules and regulations for the admission of persons into the civil service" as would "best promote the efficiency thereof," also to appoint an advisory board, later known as the Civil Service Commission, which would establish rules for examining into the fitness of candidates for the government service. President Grant himself expressed approval of this measure, and appointed the well-intentioned editor of *Harper's Weekly*, George William Curtis, chairman of the new commission. But the men of Congress were suspicious, and grudgingly refused that which was most important, appropriations of money with which to carry on the work of reform. The first measure of civil-service reform, sponsored by Schurz and Trumbull, was adopted as a transparent dodge—the Stalwart politicians amusingly enough took credit for it as their own handiwork. Curtis soon found to his distress that the rules recommended by him were never carried into practice by the Grant Administration at any point.

The chieftains of the ruling party nevertheless showed increasing irritation and alarm at a movement which threatened their whole system of authority. During the winter of 1872 they harassed the independents unmercifully, and provoked numerous clashes in Congress. Again and again did Roscoe Conkling, displaying his broadest sarcasms, inveigh against the reformers for having their own party's "every little fault and shortcoming dragged into the light," while Zach Chandler, in his own homely style, heaped contempt upon the "newfangled notions." When Curtis, on behalf of the new Civil Service Commission, offered its first timid sketch of a merit system for choosing government officials, urged the classifying and grading of services, the elimination of assessments, and also reported that a vast sum, fully one-fourth of the Federal revenues, was lost in collection, he was challenged vigorously, indeed ridiculed, by Oliver Morton, the Republican whip. Morton sharply opposed measures for a broad investigation of the government service as utterly needless, saying:

There seems to be a disposition on the part of some people in this country to become professional reformers; to have it understood that they are
the reformers par excellence; that they, above all others, hate corruption,
and that they make it the business of their lives to hunt down those who
are corrupt.[22]

Morton, for his part, would not permit them to monopolize reform. He would gladly accept the proposed changes in rules "whenever you . . . [could] carry on a government without regard to
politics." But was this not absurd on the face of it? He who had
"climbed the political ladder," would never "slap the faces of the
friends who had helped him and call it virtue." His friends, he
vowed, could continue to "call on him." He would not refuse them
what aid it was in his power to give.[23]

The rancorous quarrel in the Senate in 1872 broadened, touched
the subject of amnesty to former rebels, passed even to fierce dispute
over the Franco-Prussian War. Yet at every shift, the point at issue
was identical: a group of men challenged the party command, proposed measures which threatened its authority, and were visited in
turn with wrathful condemnation for their awful heresy.

Popular feeling in America had moved strongly against Louis
Napoleon's cause in the recent war; and Sumner and Schurz, aware
of this (Schurz especially seeking to influence the German vote),
suddenly aired a scandalous report that our War Department, under
suspicious circumstances, had sold arms to the French Government.
A resolution of inquiry was brought forth again. But Morton, tirelessly on guard, leaped to the attack. Schurz, he thundered, while
still a member of the Republican Party, sought but to dishonor and
destroy it.

Yesterday Carl Schurz had been a brave Republican captain; but
now he "betrayed his principles"; he was as one who would "bite the
hand that fed him"; he would hold treasonable commerce with the
enemy, with the Democrats, the Ku Klux Klan; he was "a traitor"
and must leave the party.

Schurz, in a graceful retort which made appeal to the liberal and
idealistic sections of the people, exclaimed: "He [Morton] has never
left his party. I have never betrayed my principles. That is the
difference between him and me." [24]

Lyman Trumbull, also singled out for excommunication, showed how the systematic charge of "treason" and demand for party discipline was brought in answer to every appeal for the correction of some abuse. This minded him of Patrick Henry's speech describing the surrender of Cornwallis at Yorktown, "where the only discord which disturbed the general joy was the cry . . . through the American camp: 'Beef! beef! beef!' " set up from among hungry Continentals, more intent on their bellies than on glory. "So now when the country was reeking with corruption, and an investigation was proposed, it was met [by the gentleman from Indiana] with the cry of *"Party! party! party!"* [25]

Not to be outdone, Conkling insinuated seriously that Schurz had been in contact with foreign spies (from whom he had derived his information), and cunningly offered a resolution, to be added as a rider to a bill before the Senate, by which "any Senator who had acted in collusion with such foreign agents" might be liable to fine and imprisonment. To which the poor Schurz, beside himself with passion, shouted that he and Trumbull were being proscribed because —and here the cat was out of the bag—they opposed the planned renomination of Grant, upon which the perpetuation of the ruling clique of politicians hung.

Two American Senators whose only aim was to investigate abuses, were met by one of the spokesmen of the administration flourishing a statute threatening them with fine and imprisonment. . . . Let it be known . . . that he who was in earnest, setting his face against those in power to detect fraud and punish violations of the law, had before him the prospect of a dungeon! [26]

But the "dungeon" which the domineering Morton was preparing for Sumner, Schurz, and Trumbull was really nothing other than expulsion from the Republican Party. The party Organization came first, and all its members must abide by its decisions, or leave its ranks in public disgrace. Morton, in effect, pronounced a doom upon the insurgents—Sumner, Schurz, Trumbull—stripping them of all party support and patronage.

With ambition to win the balance of power between the two older parties, the organizers of the so-called Liberal Republican Party used the whole debate over the French arms affair only as a pretext for arousing the people. Its climax came with Sumner's terrible oration of May 31, 1872, against the Grant Administration, the long, passionate speech with which the dying Senator virtually closed his public career.

Like one of Plutarch's Romans, the veteran Massachusetts states-man cried out against the decline of the nation's morals. Reviewing the history of his party, he exclaimed: ". . . Alas! how changed. Once country was the object . . . once principle was inscribed on the victorious banners." But now were we not moving to an open des-potism? A member of the President's official household (General Babcock), describing himself as "Aid de camp of the President of the United States" had attempted to negotiate a secret treaty of an-nexation at Grant's wish—over the heads of the Senate, which alone had such powers. Grant accepted gifts, vast gifts, and rewarded the donors with offices. The Presidency had become a "perquisite"; the President had sought to open the Treasury to the richest man in the country. He surrounded himself with a ring of military officers who attempted to rule the country with unspeakable arrogance. The coming Republican National Convention, at which the renomination of Grant was prepared, would be ruled by a combination of "the Great Officeholder and the Great Officeseeker in one" with "the Military Ring, the Senatorial Ring, and the Custom House Ring." Grant was a "Caesar with a Senate at his heels." "On what meat does this our Caesar feed?" Sumner quoted in peroration. His heart grieved for the Republic. "Save it from Caesar!" [27]

At first few had listened. The inner circle of Senators were furious and showed scant respect for the orator, Conkling, Carpenter, and Chandler consulting each other in loud voices which rudely inter-rupted the speaker. But as the hours wore on, word spread through the capital, and soon the populace filled the galleries to bursting. Citizens and Senators alike were once more fascinated by the trans-ports of the old orator. Cheer upon cheer followed his periods.

IV

It is difficult to convey now something of the excitement, the in-fectious enthusiasm, which once gripped the young and old heads who launched the Liberal Republican or "Mugwump" party of 1872. Men of principle who had sought careers in politics, and intellectuals who had had none as yet, were transfigured with hope—though they afterward denied this in the most shamefaced manner. The prime object was first to block the re-election of Grant, with whom the fate of the Stalwart machine was linked. Further objects were to introduce the new ideas of civil-service reform, to pacify the South at last, to effect order and economy in government finances, bring about reductions in the protective tariff (to which much current corruption was attributed), and in general to renovate and purify our political life. The mechanical, meaningless party "lines" would be sundered; out of the debacle of the old corrupt Organization, political leaders would arise who represented ideas, issues, in a government of discussion, untroubled by wrangles over the spoils of office from year to year; a way would be open at last to careers for men of talent and education.

Youth was to the fore in the new crusade. Charles Francis Adams, Jr., and Henry Adams, who had been busily attacking the Erie Ring with their pens, offered their services to Carl Schurz, while trusting fondly that their father, Lincoln's strong, wise Minister to England, would be chosen as the leader of the political-moral revival. Likewise the young, successful journalist Whitelaw Reid, assistant editor of the New York *Tribune*, supported his master Horace Greeley, who, turning upon his past, made a resounding break with the official party in favor of reform and amnesty. Other young men of letters in search of careers were Horace White, independent and able editor of the Chicago *Tribune*, Henry Watterson of the Louisville *Courier*, and Murat Halstead of the Cincinnati *Commercial*. Then there was the poet William Cullen Bryant, the Free Trader David A. Wells, and the wealthy New York reformer Oswald Ottendorfer (New Yorker *Staatszeitung*), Charles W. Eliot, the progressive young president of Harvard University, each of whom gave his blessing to the cause of civil regeneration. In short, there were persons of culture and wealth, representatives of the more responsible capitalists and of the decent middle class—and none of your "hurrah boys" or loafers, who usually made up the mass of the regular party demonstrations.

At a large preliminary mass meeting for the Liberal Republicans

in Cooper Institute, New York City, April 12, 1872, it was observed
by eyewitnesses that

*the audience was composed of that sober, thoughtful middle class, equally
removed from wealth and poverty,* which one has seen in the same room
on all great occasions since 1860, such, in short, as was there at the first
emancipation meeting in 1862, and at the reform meeting [against the
Tweed Ring] last spring.[28]

In later years Henry Adams, who with his brother participated
much more actively in the organizing of the bolters' party than he
afterward allowed, was to make mock of the innocence, the confusion,
and the limited vision of this reformers' crusade. What, for instance,
was the old wirepuller and bribe-taker Reuben Fenton, the Senator
from New York whom Conkling had overthrown, doing in this
galley? What were these whisperings behind the scenes of numerous
Republican malcontents?

Four years later, when asked to give work and money to a similar
independent uprising, Henry Adams privately upbraided Carl
Schurz, reproaching him with unmistakable bitterness for much of
the political "jockeying" which had been carried on at the first
Liberal convention.[29]

Jockeying? At an assembly of reformers!

Presidential nominations and the campaigns therefor are usually
prepared far in advance. Technically speaking, the group of actual
organizers of the "bolt" from the established party was composed
almost equally of amateurs and political crooks. What obsessed their
thought from the beginning was the plan of making practical "combinations" which would end in an actual victory and not mere
twaddle. Thus if New England, where ardor for reform was supposed to be strong, could be split away from the Republican column
and joined with Democratic strength in New York and the Middle
West, where discontent at the ruling party was also mounting, it
would be enough to win. The subtraction of the minority of Independent Republicans would virtually neutralize the advantage held
by the party in office. Generally, the Democrats still showed amazing hardiness, holding many city and regional organizations and running, despite the sectional passion of the day, but 10 per cent behind

the Republican vote. The Democratic wirepullers, therefore, hovered about the Cincinnati Liberal Republican Convention, eager for Mugwump aid, offering advice, bargains, promises, in return for their own demands. Unrepentant in their lust for party victory, they had shown an overweening disposition for compromise and bargain in 1868, when their leaders, with Tammany support, forced a conservative Eastern nominee, Seymour, upon a radical-inflationary platform demanded by the Western wing. In 1872 they showed the same disposition in a form more shameless still.

The "better element" had trusted that the veteran diplomat of wartime, Charles Francis Adams, Sr., as head of their movement might unite the Democracy with his own Liberal Republican support in a strong bid for power. But that impeccable and independent Yankee had gone off to Geneva to preside over the Alabama Claims conference, leaving a declaration that only "an unequivocal call" committing him to no political bargains whatsoever would be accepted. Failing of Adams, there was Lincoln's friend, the honest Trumbull of Illinois, or at least his neighbor, Judge David Davis, who both offered unsullied names. But the professionals were already hard at work in the wings, the very enthusiasm, earnestness, and disorder of the large Cincinnati convention covering more effectively their cool operations.

The first too clever move, naming Carl Schurz as chairman of the convention, removed the chance for this powerful speaker to advance his views and his candidate, who was Adams. Then there followed the adoption, at the instance of the wirepullers, of the harsh unit rule, making a two-thirds majority mandatory and placing the strange, rudderless mass meeting at the mercy of a firm minority faction. It was "an extraordinary proceeding," as Schurz protested vainly, showing that the reform movement "was virtually in the hands of a set of political tricksters, who came here not for reform, but for plunder." [30] The platform as finally compromised was plainly a bargain for the support of the notorious Protectionist Greeley and his newspaper, the *Tribune*, since the issue of tariff reduction, which most of those present associated with civil-service reform, was postponed and evaded. The outcome of the Liberal Republican Convention was as astonishing as it was melancholy.

"Marse" Henry Watterson, the colorful Kentucky editor, has left in his memoirs a hilarious account, yet only a little overdrawn, of the nocturnal negotiations carried on in a hotel room among the "Quadrilateral" of four young editors, including himself, Horace White, Murat Halstead, and Whitelaw Reid. By these, acting as go-betweens, the presidential nomination was donated to Adams in the first place, and to Trumbull as a second choice. But Reid, an ambitious "kingmaker" in his twenties, ended by hoodwinking the other mischief-makers and joining in a heavy, last-minute thrust of the professional element. The two leading candidates were outflanked, and Horace Greeley, with Senator B. Gratz Brown of Missouri as his running mate, was chosen to head the Liberal ticket.

Greeley was soon afterward also nominated by a dead-hearted Democratic Party convention, at which Tammany sachem and Southern Bourbon alike were resolved, come what might, to ally themselves with the reform party.

Greeley, though an ornament to his country for thirty years past, was felt to possess an unfitness for public office as extensive as his craving for the same. His baby face with its fringy white side whiskers, his white plug hat, his umbrella, became at once the target of the pitiless Tom Nast, then at the height of his destructive power. The candidacy of Horace Greeley evoked a prolonged outburst of ridicule from the Republicans. He was a delightful journalistic phi-losopher, who brimmed over entertainingly each morning with ideas which contradicted those of yesterday or last week. While personally honest, he declared himself opposed to civil-service examinations as arrant nonsense, and had been too often used and hoodwinked by New York's most knavish political conspirators to serve as a proper medium for a reform movement. He had been the editor of the in-cendiary *Tribune* during the Abolitionist campaigns, and had ended by signing Jefferson Davis's bail bond and calling for universal amnesty. He was for "$100 a ton duty" on pig iron, and so he was "boiled crow" to his Democratic and Mugwump allies, all tariff-reformers. He had said, "All Democrats may not be rascals, but all rascals are Democrats," and now he was the standard-bearer of the "seditious" party. In short, though his qualities as a publicist and humanitarian, a champion of labor, a friend of the common man, had endeared him to millions of readers, he was, as Roscoe Conkling pointed out at once, a political impossibility, "grotesque and harmless . . . a man of oddities, flattered by many and most of all himself." Garfield wrote to a friend:

> Was ever the like known in the history of politics . . . ? If the nomination [of Greeley] . . . would result in dissolving both parties and raising up a fresh organization free from the traditions and involvements of last year, I could rejoice but now everything is thrown into doubt and uncertainty.[31]

The opportunist maneuvers of the Cincinnati reform convention were seen as the crudest, the most transparent devices for "combining" conflicting classes and groups. It was reasoned thus: The Democrats would carry the South; Greeley, with his cry for Protection, would carry Pennsylvania and New England; his friendship for labor would win the population of the great cities; and his reformist promises would perforce bring in the trusting Liberal Republicans. It was, in short, "a pure politician's dream"—only, too extravagantly perfect to come true.

The reformers were inconsolable at the outcome of so many good impulses in a nomination which left them all too exposed to the powerful opposition party. The "convention of idealists and professors and sore-heads," as Conkling had named it, had produced nothing but jockeying, combinations, bargains. Schurz must needs wrestle much with his conscience before he agreed even to campaign for the Liberal-Democratic combination. He, "the most industrious and least energetic of men," as Joseph Pulitzer called him, was chiefly blamed for the fiasco. This "lost leader" is usually pictured, after the convention, as weeping aloud while he plays at the piano mournful German lieder: *"Mein Herz liegt am Rhein."* *

The young men of "talent and wealth," who had hoped that a road was being opened for their return to public life, as in the days of the Virginia Dynasty, folded their tents and stole silently away,

---

* "There was reason for their gloom. Most of them free traders, they had nominated a high protectionist; idealists, they had been circumvented by the least responsible and reputable elements in the convention; hoping for Democratic support, they had selected the candidate least likely to appeal to that party." (Fuess, *Carl Schurz, Reformer*, p. 193.)

Henry Adams recalls; in their expiation, they offered their services to railroads and banks. An ill-organized revolt of middle-class reformers, as Schurz himself confessed, had been outgeneraled, and the whole Liberal Republican movement "dragged down to the level of an ordinary political operation."

V

The "regular" Republicans in 1872 were the embodiment of unity and discipline in action. The full force of their Organization was devoted especially to making examples of the Mugwumps in their party by defeating them wherever they stood for office. The question of support for General Grant was made "a test of Republicanism and a cause for political excommunication." [32]

Moderate members of the party noted with no little alarm the fate of their "apostate" brothers. Though John Sherman, James Garfield, G. F. Hoar, and George Edmunds, men of light and learning, believed with Blaine that Grant was an unfortunate burden for their party, they held their tongues. Thinking of his professional future, one by one each silently bowed his head and bore the yoke of party regularity. In private Garfield said that such men as Cameron, Chandler, Morton and Conkling, "by whom the Administration seemed to be run, constituted the worst feature in Washington politics. And yet most of them [Republicans] will support him [Grant] if they must. Frankly I am of that number." [33] Moreover, the nimble Blaine, who absorbed himself thoroughly in the machinery of politics, assured Garfield that civil-service reform was a humbug. [34]

Another capable and moderate Congressman, G. F. Hoar, son of a distinguished Yankee family, whose gifted cousin Ebenezer had been so heartlessly expelled from the Grant Cabinet, soothed his own elastic conscience by assuring himself at this time that he "could do ten-fold more good" by staying within the Organization "than people with ten times his ability and capacity who have left the party."

Still other party men remained faithful seemingly out of professional or technical pride in their work. The expert William E. Chandler, who acted usually as a permanent secretary at the Washington offices of the Republican National Committee, was

privately disaffected, yet once more agreed to manage the confidential work of spending campaign funds where they did most good.
"I am a fool for going into this campaign," he wrote, "but I love
my party and cannot help working for it." [35]

President Grant was renominated unanimously at an automatized
convention in Philadelphia, and the affair celebrated with well-
rehearsed cheering. "As to platforms and parties," the blunt-spoken
General William T. Sherman once wrote to his brother John. "Of
course I regard these as mere traps to catch flies." [36]

The Republican platform not only pointed smugly to its leader's
support of civil-service reform, but even referred to a modest downward revision of the tariff schedules made by Congress in the last
hours before the opening of the electoral campaign, May 30, 1872!
Tea and coffee had been placed on the free list, thus creating the
"free breakfast table" for which there was some popular demand.
The free list was extended—to prevent more drastic reductions—a
very moderate "horizontal" reduction of 10 per cent, having a very
unequal effect, being made for most manufactured articles. At the
same time the income tax was quietly erased from the books. These
were Fabian tactics, which without changing the protective system in
any real sense, by lowering the government revenues unwisely and
freeing luxury articles from taxation would soon afterward inevitably pave the way for renewed tariff increases along purely Protectionist lines.[37] Nevertheless the Republicans confronted the embarrassed Democrats with a record, adventitious though it might be,
of a small start toward tariff reform. Aside from the one question
of extending amnesty in the South, the platforms and candidates of
both parties, by their evasion of issues or their subterfuges, canceled
each other.

The campaign was prosecuted with the utmost vehemence. Recent
disorders in the South, especially in South Carolina, the menacing
rise of the Ku Klux Klan in answer to military rule, were incidents
used once more to fan war passions and fears of disunion in the
Northern masses. The mind of the spoilsman leader, Oliver Morton,
dominated the Republican army. In the Middle West it was said that
"Morton was fighting like Macbeth for his very existence. . . . In
his grim calculations the only way to keep the Republican party

united was to keep the passions and animosities of war at red heat."
According to the New York *World*, the Republican Party's continued
attempts to "heighten the misery and increase the degradation of the
South" reflected but the "dark passions that rule Morton's heart." [38]
Everywhere he called upon men to preserve the fruits of victory, to
show "gratitude to the soldiers and sailors of the republic," to uphold "the protection of American industry . . . the honor and dignity of labor"; "and covering all like a shield—'The Union must be
Preserved!' " [39]

In the East Roscoe Conkling outdid even Morton in vituperation
for the former comrades who bolted. In his familiar poses of scorn,
drawing himself up to his full height, he would clip out slowly the
words of his unvarying song of hate. What were the Reformers?
They were but *soreheads:*

> A war of mud and missiles has been waged for months. . . . Every
> thief and cormorant and drone who has been put out—every baffled
> mouser for place and plunder—every man with a grievance or a grudge—
> all who have something to make by a change, seem to wag an unbridled
> tongue or drive a foul pen . . . traitors to their party . . . gnawed by
> ambition and cupidity . . . madness drove them on.[40]

But from their partisan passion the Stalwart orators could turn
quickly to practical appeals to the more solid portion of their public
to "let well enough alone." At Chicago, now rising from the ruins
of its terrible fire, Oliver Morton forecast to small property-owners
new disasters to come should the Democrats triumph; an inevitable
depression would follow and "a hundred thousand people would
lose their homes." Thus the tradition that prosperity was Republican
took vigorous root after the war. And Conkling warned all those
who held the securities of the country, and property-holders in
general, not to swap horses and "run the risk of a Democratic President now." [41] In pointed appeals to the merchants and bankers of
New York, Conkling declared:

> If the name and the character of the administration of Ulysses S. Grant
> have been of value to the nation, no one knows it so well as the men who
> represent the property, the credits, the public securities and the enterprise
> of the country.[42]

The Republican managers once more attempted to rally the powerful moneyed interests who had been their patrons. "Who knows what
Greeley might do?" murmured Zach Chandler, the chairman of the
Congressional Campaign Committee, to Jay Cooke. And Zach's wily
lieutenant, W. E. Chandler (of New Hampshire), pursued Cooke,
now for $5,000 to win a State in an early election, now for $10,000
to save New Jersey for the Secretary of the Navy. Did the Cookes
care to see the naval account lost to their bank?[43] And Cooke, as he
himself said, groaning, was ridden to death "like a free horse," giving
up, according to some reports, as much as $50,000 in all to safeguard
the new government-aided Northern Pacific project.[44] *

The moneybags, as Bowles now wrote, were "everywhere conservative; and though you could prove all day to busy wealth-seekers
that the President made rascally appointments, accepted gifts,
stretched if not broke the law . . . they would reply 'General
Grant is a safe man.' "[45] Various manufacturers, merchants, and
bankers cheerfully lent their aid to Grant. Yet their part in this campaign was not so decisive as that played this season by professional
organization and experience. Most capitalists, for one thing, thought
that the politicians in 1872 were imposing on their credulity in hinting that the absurd Greeley might win if they did not "shell out."
In the intramural correspondence of the Republican professionals
one reads many a complaint of the suspicious, flinty spirit of the
capitalists. The party secretary, William E. Chandler, worried over
the "October States" and the poor impression their results might
make, approached the Union Pacific group with urgent pleas. Here
again for special reasons large gifts were obtained. General Gren-
ville Dodge, who worked both as a member of the Republican
National Committee and as an executive of the Union Pacific, do-

---

* Much apprehension ruled at this moment in financial circles, which uneasily
sensed but could not measure the onrushing economic crisis. On the other hand, Jay
Cooke and his partners, now so terribly involved in the Northern Pacific scheme,
with its deficits and overdrafts, lived secretly in the nightmare of approaching bankruptcy. For the Tycoon the re-election of Grant and the Republicans was "a matter
of life and death." (Larson, *Jay Cooke,* p. 389, citing Cooke Papers, Jay Cooke
to H. Cooke, Apr. 5, 1872.) If Greeley were beaten, he had the promise of profitable government loan-refunding operations. Yesterday Cooke had supported the war
Government; today his existence hung upon the favor of its successor. To cover,
perhaps, the very weakness of the firm, he was driven to make more lavish contributions than ever to the party fund and to show a bold front everywhere.

nated over $30,000, but insisted that he could do no more.[46] "I find it utterly impossible . . . [to raise money] by contributions from private citizens and business men," wrote an Iowa party manager to William E. Chandler.[47]

In the autumn crop-moving season that year, money was scarcer than ever; a growing depression in Europe caused the shutting off of credits by bankers here. It seemed useless to try to "force our friends to wake up in this fight, to spend their money," commented General Dodge. "The Government and the ones directly interested in the fight," he contended, must bear the burden.[48]

In Indiana a Democratic Governor, Thomas A. Hendricks, was elected in October. Oliver Morton in his desperation had sent his own lieutenant from Indianapolis to New York for fresh funds, claiming that "estimation of our needs is at least $15,000 too low." [49] Yet he had suffered a serious defeat. More money must be raised, then, through officeholders and indirect party affiliates. Throughout this campaign one hears the ceaseless cry for an increase of assessments. As Grenville Dodge somewhat callously hinted, the government departments must furnish the sinews of war this year. "Our enemies charge us with everything . . . they lie by wholesale. I am in favor of having the game as well as the name." [50]

A careful study of the 1872 campaign by a contemporary has shown that political assessments upon officeholders may have attained now their greatest volume. The National Campaign Committee of the Republican Party was "a committee for Extortion, sending out assessment demands by the hundred thousand." The axe was swung mercilessly to enforce collections of from 2 to 6 per cent of salaries in the New York Custom House, close to two thousand dismissals having been made in the three years preceding the presidential campaign.[51]

Most vital of all, however, must have been the aid furnished by the organized rings connected with the Federal departments. In the emergency, the greater portion of cash for the war chest came not from bankers and manufacturers but from the suborganizations of the party affiliated with customhouses, from Treasury officials and officers of other Federal departments. From warehouse monopolists, Indian traders, and contractors money donations arrived. Above all, succor came from the great Whisky Ring, which General John McDonald operated from his St. Louis headquarters, as he piously declared, in the interests of a Republican campaign fund. Senator Morton, in great trouble, had come personally to McDonald, and obtained on one occasion some $20,000 for Indiana alone.[52] In all, $55,000 was expended to save this strategic state in 1872, according to its famous boss.[53] Then later, according to the testimony of another member of the ring, William Grosvenor, calls went forth for new and unusual assessments upon all the whisky distillers themselves, at the order of "a very prominent Senator." [54]

It was fortunate that the Republican machine was still somewhat autonomous. With far more lavish supplies of money than their opponents, the Republican managers were able to offset the apathy of capitalists in a lean year, to dominate the press and the stump, and to transport with dispatch, wherever the need arose, mobile masses of voters.

Though Greeley and especially Schurz made able public speeches and the Liberal-Republican-Democrat group conducted their campaign upon an unusually high level, the press treated them all with contumely; the most fearful prejudice against Greeley and his reformist allies, skillfully spread at the time, has persisted to this very day.

The old Indiana Radical George Julian, standing for re-election to Congress as a Liberal Republican, has related, for instance, that Morton all but incited the Negroes to murder him. He concludes regretfully: "If I had consulted my own selfish ambition I would have chosen a different course, since I knew by painful experience the cost of party desertion." [55]

When, early in September, Charles A. Dana of the New York *Sun* broached queer rumors of a great railroad conspiracy involving the Union Pacific and leading Republican members of Congress, such as Blaine and Garfield, the most violent counterblasts drowned his charges from one end of the country to the other. Dana's tales, which were cited by Horace Greeley, were branded by a leading Republican spokesman as "one of the vilest and boldest pieces of rascality in the way of wicked journalism I have ever seen." [56]

Following his defeat, the aged Horace Greeley sank wearily into a final and fatal illness. "We have been terribly beaten. . . . I was assailed so bitterly," he commented, "that I hardly knew whether I was running for the Presidency or the Penitentiary."

It was a glorious victory, the great soldier outrunning the Native Philosopher by 750,000 votes, or a full 20 per cent of the popular vote cast. In the Electoral College, Greeley had gained but 6 out of 37 States, Senator Morton's Carpetbag organizations holding 7 of 10 States in the South. Louisiana, however, voted Republican only according to the "Custom house count." [57] In the North the strong-holds of Republicanism, commanded by Conkling, Morton, Cameron, and Logan, emerged with sweeping victories.

The Republican Party was now well "purged." Its old Radical, idealistic leaders were dead, expelled from public life, or if they still held office, like the tragic Sumner up to 1874, ostracized. "The public is not ready to support us," wrote Henry Adams to Carl Schurz, as he contemplated the disaster which had befallen the first civil-service reform movement.[58] None were left to challenge the power of the machine, whose command was more absolute than ever before. "There is virtually no opposition to the Republican party," James A. Garfield wrote to a friend in December, 1872, as Congress convened again. The reformers were crushed to earth. "The Democracy are stunned, perhaps killed by their late defeat, and there seems to be no limit to the power of the dominant party. If to its great strength," he continued thoughtfully, "it shall add, as I fear, arrogance and recklessness, it will break in two before the next administration goes far." [59]

CHAPTER FIVE

PANIC, SCANDAL, AND A CLOSE SQUEEZE
FOR THE WAR PARTY

The demoralization of war—a spirit of gambling adven-
ture . . . a grasping centralization . . . assuming to
control the industries of individuals by largesses to fa-
vored classes . . . wrung from the body of the people
by taxation . . .   SAMUEL TILDEN

THE electoral results of 1872, which were much more decisive than
four years earlier, showed that to most Northern people Grant
had made so far "a safe sort of President"—as the Republican orators
commonly described him. They showed that most Americans were
still suspicious of a change of regime to a political "combination" in
which former rebels might play a leading part. The opposition party
had indeed given too great hostages to fortune, made too many
weird bargains and promises.

The people had spoken. General Grant and the Stalwart leaders
were content with the mandate they had received. To the latter it
meant that their methods had been vindicated. The victory was,
after all, a clear sanction for the spoilsmen.

Almost everywhere the organization leaders, commanding their
clans of "workers" and vote-catchers, had triumphed at the polls.
Dizzy with success, they could afford to exclaim in the manner of
Roscoe Conkling: "Well, we win, don't we!"

The brief shrill cry for reform seemed to die suddenly, as if
strangled in the throats that had raised it.

Never were "professors," "idealists," or Independents more thoroughly discredited; never did well-intentioned theorists and amateurs seem more ineffectual than in 1872. For years Carl Schurz still
carried on his crusade in the public press and from the lecture platform, his comically long, lank figure, his earnest bespectacled face
with its pompadour and bristling black beard, becoming the familiar
scarecrow symbol for popular caricature of the Don Quixote intellectual in politics. George W. Curtis, Whitelaw Reid, John Hay,

Henry Adams and his brother Charles, also longed to "do something," but generally sang in despair at the darkness which engulfed our party politics. A growing tradition of the ineptitude of intellectuals for the direction of our society took strong root in the rough, practical era of General Grant and flourishes to this very day— though it would undoubtedly have puzzled the *philosophes,* Franklin, Jefferson, and Madison, who built a strong republic out of revolutionary chaos.

The President thenceforth appeared to listen to none but the Stalwart bosses, to whom he felt himself wholly indebted. Mr. Curtis's recommendations for improvements in the civil service were treated with unconcealed indifference. It is true Grant did make some facesaving requests to Congress for enabling legislation in this regard; but the Republican Congress after the elections pretended deafness and gave neither authority nor money for the work. Mr. Curtis, humiliated by these rebuffs and the President's veiled resistance, resigned in 1873 as chairman of the Civil Service Advisory Board. A few months later Grant in an official message announced that "if Congress adjourns without positive legislation on the subject of 'civil reform' I will regard such action as a disapproval of the system, and will abandon it."

But the legislators did nothing, and Grant soon after named Ben Butler's notorious henchman William A. Simmons to one of the richest posts in the government service, that of Collector of the Port of Boston. Simmons was a man of pure life, and a devout Methodist; but his appointment enraged the better element of Boston, who were preyed upon by Butler's ring, and to whom Simmons was known to be "a practiced adept in manipulating the lowest class of voters, and in carrying elections by dubious means." [1]

"There is a good deal of cant about civil-service reform," Grant remarked privately some years later. All he had learned about practical politics in four years showed that a centralized control of the machinery of government must be fostered by a systematic partisan use of the patronage power if elections were to be won and power retained under our elaborate democratic processes. Thenceforth the mere protests of respectable elements at administrative waste or plundering tactics seemed but to harden or anger him, as members of his Kitchen Cabinet noted. Nearly all vacancies in Federal departments, cabinet posts, even the places of Supreme Court Justices, were consistently filled with men a grade lower than those who had previously occupied them.

Above all, Grant's appointments strengthened the great regional machines in the more important States, those of Cameron, Conkling, and Butler in the East, of Morton, Zach Chandler, and Logan in the West. The accelerated process of centralization which party life now underwent gave to our politics more than ever a character of *automatism*. For almost a decade more, to the end of the General Grant Era (which may be said to have lasted actually up to Garfield's death in 1881), the chief business of statesmen seemed to consist in dispensing jobs and privileges to their followers, their thoughts always fixed upon the calendar of committee meetings, caucuses, and primaries, of office vacancies to be filled. With the South relatively peaceful, especially after 1877, and few significant or Burning Issues of public policy being raised, political experts and technicians could concentrate upon carrying out an elaborate division of labor in their specialized fields, until the man seemed to be replaced by the machine, while the political government seemed to regulate itself largely in committee rooms and secret conferences rather than in halls of eloquence and logic such as Clay or Webster had graced. Men of light and learning shunned politics; men of talents and wealth in these days of an immense capitalist transformation had, by all odds, mightier careers open to them in other fields.

Mechanized, secretive, corrupt as our party politics appeared in the epoch after the Civil War—though not all knew this—the Age of Big Business which was ushered in with the war and which extended modern capitalist methods of exploitation at breakneck speed to every corner of the American continent seemed, by contrast, filled with high and golden adventure, beckoning all men with red blood in their veins. The country had literally "no time for thought," Henry Adams has said trenchantly, while it tripled and quadrupled its steam power, built its railway network, plowed its prairies, and raised up its new cities. Men were aware of the new steel mills which were opened to the brave music of brass bands in Pittsburgh, of the Golden Spike celebrations which marked the completion of Pacific railroads—milestones in the hurly-burly, planless program of a vast industrial revolution. Men were aware for one moment, and rushed on the next moment to new enterprises and chances which overwhelmingly absorbed them.

The new captains of industry who now headed great corporate groups organized for manufacture and transport were little concerned with the majesty of the political state. They asked only that it guarantee them the right to embrace whatever opportunity they chose and whenever the opportunity presented itself. Internally, the long-established government tradition of "weakness" or laissez faire favored the success of the new capitalist class. No inherited institutions of nobility, church, or military class disputed their conquest of the free, continental market; the existing system of taxation, which was not onerous, on the other hand distinctly favored their advance.

The "weakness" of the Government—save for its military strength in the South—was a boon, making for a capitalist paradise, while the increasing strength of party organization, for all its bureaucratic corruption, cost little and was an immense convenience. To be sure, the expansion of capitalist enterprise more and more touched points where the general interest was involved, where matters of special public privilege, franchises, or rights of way entered into the speculative designs of the rising class of super-businessmen. At these points, the highly centralized party institution, with its branches in each State, could be turned quickly to account; the big enterpriser need not concern himself with masses of voters, but could go directly to the managers of the party institution and treat with them plainly, or even speak "sharply" to them.[2] For though they did not partake of the active management of parties, the industrial barons were more than ever, as Seward had said, "chief stockholders in the concern," having the right to demand that it heed their interests closely. Year by year the alliance between large capitalists and professional politicians grew closer. Though an inferior order of men nowadays, the politicians were useful mercenaries, and needed sharp speaking to only when they plundered their business allies as well as the public.

As for the masses of people in America, surely they were no more evil or corrupt than others. Culturally the strain and exhaustion of a great industrial revolution (never properly estimated here) shows itself for a time in a toughening of the human fiber; an age of violent change brings few great books, little magic.*

The generous passions which had been summoned by the struggle for the Union seemed to subside in the calmer years of plenty and industry. Americans, especially those who were recently arrived, remembered instinctively how hungry and naked most men have been through long centuries. Unquestionably they had far greater material opportunities here than most Europeans have ever known, and they rushed headlong to meet them. The busy shopkeeper at his crossroads, the intelligent mechanic, the small pushing tradesman, might ponder now and then over the question of the tariff; probably less often over that of currency, which was even more technical; and perhaps hardly at all upon problems of national policy. The moment they thought of confronting and acting upon such questions, a "fatalism of the multitude," as Bryce terms it, seemed to grip especially the more numerous classes of the population. A later student of political realities has defined this reaction as a sense of the remoteness of the government with relation to the individual vote.[3]

Nor did there exist such sharp and clarifying alignments of the population into classes according to mode of production, or the marks of feudal privileges, which might have worked to polarize our parties. Indeed the classes were in constant flux, were *mobile:* the worker today was a master tomorrow, owning his own land and ani-

---

* "In those days a fatality hung over the intellectual generation that came to manhood. They saw how peace brought its special horrors; steam-power and railroads . . . functioned with a quite primitive brutality. They saw all recognizable landmarks swept away by the new economy. The more imaginative of the young men, who had been educated to literary and political tastes, viewed with dismay the scenes of scarred barrenness of 'anarchy-plus-the-police,' and could make nothing of it. They had the conviction that they belonged to another century or another climate; that they had been born too soon, or perhaps too late." (Josephson, *Portrait of the Artist as American*, Introduction, p. xvi.)

The idealistic New England school, in its decline, wondered sometimes if the fruits of the struggle for human liberty had not been stolen. Of the younger men who did not feel themselves "disinherited" and driven to exile, Mark Twain caught something of the legend of the Gilded Age: poor settlers dreaming of the railroad which was to run through their acres, lobbyists and politicians conjuring up unheard-of appropriations. Walt Whitman sometimes chided the republic for its want of "soul," but as a true seer also saluted in the *Democratic Vistas* its "practical, stirring, worldly, money-making, even materialistic character" as "parts of amelioration and progress . . . *needed to prepare the very results* I demand." (Italics mine.)

mals, or even his own tools. Urban laborers or "proletarians" were less than 30 per cent of the population in 1870. The spaces of the frontier were in effect a safety valve, though perhaps not so potent as Turner believed in diverting periodic social discontent during cyclical depressions. Then, among the great mass of newly arrived immigrants, racial, religious, and language motives worked powerfully; and our professional politicians, who were unblushing materialists, ceaselessly labored to exploit these, using them on the one hand to mitigate emergent class motives and on the other to make "combinations." Democratic agents agitated the poor Irish Catholics of polyglot New York City against "upstate" Republican bigots, so that they might vote for the millionaire Tilden. Republican agitators worked vigorously upon the special needs or fears of progressive German settlers in the West, so that they might vote for policies favorable to great Eastern bankers. The little man, the man in the street, upon whom the government apparatus seemed to weigh but lightly, was largely indifferent and uninformed—up to Election Day. Concerning the peccadilloes of the politicians, when he heard of them—there were jokes and legends enough—he was good-humored, with a tolerance born of the wealth and the abundance of opportunity still present or existing as an ample margin at the earlier stage of our capitalist era.

This mood could change sharply in years when the locusts came.

II

The ruling party, when on March 4, 1873, its titular head and chief ornament, Ulysses Grant, delivered his inaugural address, was more powerful than ever as a vote-gathering and patronage organization. It was also more disposed to use this power without stint. The more affluent and successful a party, the less it heeds its most conservative counselors. Disturbing rumors suggested nowadays that the senatorial oligarchy intended to keep "Caesar" Grant perpetually upon the throne. The very unchallenged power of the party offered a certain menace even to those groups whom it most befriended. Emboldened by long rule, the professionals committed excesses and crimes, whose costs were often chiefly borne by the wealthiest patrons of the party itself. These might protest to the boss, but he felt himself obligated to defend his henchmen. Certain public frauds, as we have seen in the affair of the Tweed Ring in New York, would go too far, and bring retribution. Then, this done, a new series of frauds would sprout quickly: Post Office Rings, in place of Whisky Rings, or land-jobbing operations in place of post-office schemes. Prominent citizens who made complaint to Senator Conkling or Senator Cameron would encounter only a shrug of the shoulders, a laugh. Important business groups were also irked by the politic compromises of the Republicans upon the harassing currency question, and by their misrule in the South, which was "bad for business" and kept this whole region in poverty. Yet the Republican managers insisted upon these tactics, lest they lose their legislative majority—and what then would befall the Pacific railroads or the protected iron trade?

No less disturbing were the dissensions and jealousies of the great chieftains, behind a façade of party discipline; while bound together, their lips sealed, like partners in crime, they waged ceaseless intrigues against each other which created special problems. Greed and jealousy whipped them toward grievous errors.

The great financiers and industrial captains who were "silent partners" of the ruling party, though profiting from the complaisance of their allies, often groaned at their wasteful blunderings; other moneyed groups in the competitive society, who were less privileged, were tormented by a rankling sense of the injustice they suffered from the political friends of their rivals. Coveting similar privileges, rather than an end of the corrupt system, they too created friction. In short, the great party institution, in the very fullness of its power, suffered from serious occupational diseases as well as from the strain of conflicting demands upon it which revealed how imperfect it was as a social instrument.

The party leaders were but human, and the presidential "itch" or "virus" wrought mischief among them. The dream of arriving at the plain, low-slung White House troubled their days and nights. Only a few men out of a generation might become First Citizen of the republic, but great numbers never ceased to aspire. The hankering for the throne, turning men who were sane into men transported, became the hidden comedy, the age-old joke of our democratic political life. James Blaine in a letter to Whitelaw Reid, which was full of the esprit and philosophy he could often command, explained at length what he knew of the ordeals as well as the grandeurs of the Presidency, to which men aspired though it might "kill them" to win it. All Presidents in the past, Blaine concluded, had been made miserable—yet he too, he admitted, "would enjoy being made miserable after the pattern of those illustrious predecessors." [4]

No less did Conkling, Morton, John Sherman, and others bend every effort, open or secret, that they might at last be likewise "made miserable." Their rivalries had long been at work in painful contrast to the courtesies which they showed each other in public. As they intrigued in the "court" of the President, in his Cabinet, in the cloakrooms of Congress, for advantages in patronage, their rivalry from muffled contests more than once broke into open feuds, while each occasionally forgot the all-important Republican task to which he was assigned by Providence, and concerning which no real disagreement existed.

Conkling and Blaine in fact had been deadly adversaries ever since a debate in the lower house in April, 1866, over a matter of petty patronage connected with the Provost Marshal's department. Conkling had attacked the officer in question, and Blaine had upheld him, taking the occasion also to twit Conkling for alleged irregularities during the war. Then, in his domineering manner, a very mountain of conceit and pride, all swelling with anger, the member from New York had said among other cruel things:

If I have fallen to the necessity of taking lessons from that gentleman . . . God help me. . . . If the gentleman from Maine had the least idea how profoundly indifferent I am to his opinion on the subject which he has been discussing, or upon any other subject personal to me, I think he would hardly take the trouble to rise here and express his opinion.[5]

To which Blaine in highest spirits made an unforgettable retort:

The contempt of that large-minded gentleman is so wilting, his haughty disdain, his grandiloquent swell, his majestic, super-eminent, overpowering turkey-gobbler strut has been so crushing to myself and to all the men of this House, that I know it was an act of the greatest temerity for me to venture upon a controversy with him.

The House was convulsed with laughter, but Blaine, raising his hand for attention and with characteristically animated mien, dwelt upon the reports current in the press that the "mantle of the late Henry Winter Davis," famous wartime orator, had fallen upon Mr. Conkling, reports which had lately given added pomposity to his strut. He continued:

The resemblance is striking. Hyperion to a satyr, Thersites to Hercules, mud to marble, dunghill to diamond, a singed cat to a Bengal tiger, a whining puppy to a roaring lion. Shade of the mighty Davis, forgive the almost profanation of that jocose satire![6]

Blaine had clearly come off best in this passage at arms in the old rhetorical style; he would have extended his hand to Conkling and lived at peace with him thereafter. But Conkling was a good hater who forgave no injury; to the end of his days he nursed his grudge against Blaine, maintaining a more or less secret intraparty feud which was to embarrass not only the career of each but the fortunes of their Organization itself.

Behind the curtain drawn over the party councils there was to be seen now a growing cleavage between two factions competing for dominance of the Republican Organization. On the one side were the "Stalwarts," Conkling, Morton, Cameron, Zach Chandler, very close to the Administration, receiving the largest share of executive favor, and paying almost exclusive attention to manning the Federal service with their helots; in the other camp, more moderate, more studious politicians were numbered, soon labeled "Half-Breeds" by their opponents, and including notably Blaine, John Sherman, Garfield, George F. Hoar, William B. Allison of Iowa (a new arrival), and George Edmunds of Vermont, men who, if they too must needs give a sharp eye to their supporting clans, were known at least to devote part of their time to the framing of laws, to the study of prosaic budget reports and tariff schedules. Within each camp personal ambitions or fears also brought now petty conflict, now a shifting of allegiance. But the division was clear: while the faction led by Blaine and Sherman seemed usually to possess larger views, more responsible to the interests of influential and thrifty citizens in the community, that of Conkling and Morton was narrower, more intolerant toward the South, more knavish in its systematic relations with the divers plundering rings within the government service.

During the quarrel between Sumner and the Stalwart Republicans, Oliver Morton had written to his wife: "They hate Sumner, but they hate me more." [7] In the Stalwart camp, Morton and Conkling each strove to overreach the other in managing an ignorant and complaisant President toward his own ends, or they would quietly combine to undermine a common enemy within the party.

Blaine, while seeing no harm in his own peculiar course, would have liked to "liquidate" the Stalwart faction, in whose excesses he saw a danger to country and party alike, and to whom he ascribed "all the desperate bad men, bent on loot and booty." They were as vicious and detestable as the "noisy" and "pharisaical" reformers. [8] But how dispose of the hated rivals without wrecking the Organization itself? How expose them without exposing oneself?

When certain revelations concerning Blaine's connections with a government-aided railroad—leading to sensational upheavals—were made one day, it was whispered that Morton himself had instigated the publication of these matters in order to injure Blaine, the original exposures having come from an Indianapolis banker close to Morton. [9]

III

Some fifteen Republican statesmen had been subject to "calumnious" attacks during the late campaign on the score of their presumed relations with the Crédit Mobilier, the holding company which built the Union Pacific Railroad. Business jealousy and a thieves' quarrel among the promoters themselves preceded the outburst of scandal touching the political leaders. As Congress convened again in December 1872, it was the very men accused, Speaker Blaine and Representative Garfield, who moved for a formal investigation of the charges.

What purpose had the majority party, which could easily have blocked such a resolution, in introducing it? Such moves are rarely accidental but follow deliberation in the party caucus. For one thing, the Railway Congressmen implicated in the Crédit Mobilier "campaign lie" were confident that they were dealing with a small petard, and that they could prove that no corrupt intent, no possible bribery was involved here. It would be a splendid thing, then, to clear the skirts of the majority party at the outset of a new term. Blaine himself, who was erroneously charged with having taken ten shares of Crédit Mobilier stock from Oakes Ames knew well that he could refute his accusers, serving his own and the party's credit handsomely. Perhaps plans for further interesting railroad legislation waited upon the successful outcome of the investigation which, at any rate, was to be carried out by a preponderantly Republican committee, its chairman being Representative Luke Poland of Vermont. Finally, the accused statesmen conferred together and made plans for each to give testimony, varying in detail, but agreeing generally in context.

We know for instance that a few days prior to Oakes Ames's appearance before the committee, early in December, 1872, Garfield saw him privately, and they compared notes on the statements each was to make concerning dealings with each other. Yet the most carefully planned rehearsals have a way of going wrong at the public première.

Ames, the millionaire plow-manufacturer, felt sincerely that public esteem as well as profit was owing to him for having carried out the daring transcontinental railway enterprise from which, as he declared, "the capital of the world shrank." He had thought it as natural that he should sit in Congress, a deputy for his own railroad interest, as that Huntington should employ lobbyists for his own part of the Pacific railroad system. And then what meager sums were involved in the accusations of political bribery! Out of the millions which both roads had expended for "legal expenses" and lobbying, and out of the enormous loot—reckoned at between $44,000,000 and $50,000,-000—which was their profit, only some $65,000, representing 343 shares of Crédit Mobilier stock, was traced to the group of politicians involved in the sensational trial of 1873. These shares had been placed in trust with Oakes Ames five years earlier by his partners, to be disposed of in small lots of from ten to twenty in order to make "friends of the Union Pacific" in the House and Senate.

It was a case of needy Congressmen who, in a period of nation-wide boom and gambling, were approached by their colleague Ames with the offer of a good speculation, which was in effect a gift horse. How could they well refuse? Ten shares of Crédit Mobilier, selling in the market at $200 each, could be subscribed for at $100 each, or a total of $1,000; if they were wanting in cash, Ames would "lend" them the sum needed at current interest rates, and dividends—Ames promised enormous special dividends to come—would retire the debt and leave a profit into the bargain.[10] In fact, dividends paid out to the Crédit Mobilier stockholders from July 1, 1867, to January 1, 1869, amounted to more than 341 per cent in terms of cash; although not all the politicians on what may be called Ames's preferred list who had accepted the contract from him held on and received the full reward. Several sold too soon; others became frightened and canceled their agreements.

Early in 1868, at the very time these contracts were being made, a bill was introduced by a Western Congressman which was hostile to the Pacific railroads, proposing closer control of their construction costs and freight rates. "We want more friends in this Congress," Ames wrote in alarm, February 22, 1868, to his associates. It was difficult, he said, to get the Congressmen even "to look into this law" unless they had "an interest to do so."[11] When the bill in question came to a vote, amid the furor over Andrew Johnson, Ames's investment clients quietly helped to bury it.

Later, toward 1870, a faction among the railroad promoters, that of Durant and McCombs, had become suspicious of Ames's transactions in the shares donated for political work, charging that he appropriated a part for himself. Suit was brought, incriminating letters were published, and the names of leading Republican captains were besmirched, men who in the code of the time, and of our own time as well, were profoundly convinced that they had done nothing to compromise either their honor or the public interest. But the crash of Crédit Mobilier stock and reports of a gigantic inside swindle gave the case unexpected prominence.

Ames too to the very end protested his innocence of any evil intention, answering all questions concerning his deals with forthright candor. Blaine's denial that he had ever accepted any stock was supported by Ames, and the brilliant Speaker was triumphantly vindicated at the outset. However, questions of Blaine's profitable connection with the construction ring of a Union County branch road, the Dubuque & Sioux City, whose land grant he and Representative

Allison helped to renew, were never brought up at this hearing, being held irrelevant matters. The other prominent Congressmen—Garfield, Kelley, Bingham, Dawes—Vice-President Colfax, and Vice-President-elect Henry Wilson gave testimony which sounded increasingly confused or uneasy as public interest in the committee hearings grew. Either they had not understood Mr. Ames's proposition; or they had merely accepted a "loan" and repaid it; or they assumed that they had made a "legitimate" investment; or, as in Colfax's case (most surprising of all), they had known nothing whatever of the matter.

The Poland Committee soon appeared responsive to the restless reform currents afloat at the time, and therefore disposed not to "whitewash" the Crédit Mobilier people or the Railway Congressmen too easily.[12] Mr. Ames's position began to seem hard. His tone changed. He appeared hurt and troubled. Was he, "the only honest man" there present, to be made the "victim," as Ben Butler, his counsel, cried? He drew forth a "memorandum book" and now, quoting chapter and verse, contradicted the testimony of various witnesses. The Christian Statesman, Vice-President Colfax, was caught in the most humiliating contradictions. Colfax, who had long been an aspirant to the Presidency, was formally adjudged to have sworn falsely. Garfield and Kelley, who claimed to be victims of "misunderstanding," as well as Dawes, Bingham, and Wilson, were considered to have acted without corrupt intent but with "indiscretion," and were mildly censured by their judges. A resolution recommending the expulsion of Oakes Ames from Congress, and likewise of Representative Brooks of New York (Democrat) and Senator Patterson of New Hampshire, was brought in by the Poland Committee. Two Vice-Presidents were heavily damaged; reputations rolled in the dust; alarm and shock were felt throughout the country; and yet also a manifest widespread sympathy, according to the press!

In the case of Garfield, careful study dispels the idea that this earnest, sensitive, but unwary politician acted from corrupt motives. But that so palpably honest a fellow should be involved in a shady transaction, from which he evidently tried to withdraw too late, that he should then give contradictory testimony, or reveal little or nothing at the time of the trial to clear himself, "in order not to injure his party or fellow members"—all this points clearly to the nature of the company and the mischance into which a former theologian in politics might fall, as well as to the discipline imposed upon members of the party machine.[13]

No instances of direct bribery were found and only mediocre sums were involved, though there was a great deal of lying. The actual meaning of the inquisition as some understood it at the time was that only the smaller, the least discreet personages on the fringes of the railway contingent in Congress had been punished or censured; the "careless fellows," as it was said, "who openly took on a few shares of stock for their cousins and sisters, hoping to turn an honest penny." "The paid lawyers who had been elected with Union Pacific money," who had jammed through "clauses" in midnight sessions of years gone by but never owned the stuff, went unscathed.

Who were these magicians? From evidence we have cited, former Representative Robert Schenck, now Minister to England, John Logan, Blaine himself, J. A. Bingham, Ben Butler, who acted as Oakes Ames's counsel while still a member of Congress, were the most active among them. They were the "leviathans," as a Democratic Congressman hinted, who were caught in the net of the committee; and little wonder that they could not be "landed." *

In Congress the vote for expulsion was with some effort turned into a motion of censure, at the instance of the unscathed Representative A. A. Sargent of California, known in after years as the Senator for the Southern Pacific Railroad. The vote was close and the maneuvering of the Speaker counted for much in the final outcome. It was noticeable that Blaine three times left the chair to advise and lead the forces opposing the expulsion of Oakes Ames and company. Earlier, when Stewart, lawyer and lobbyist for the Crédit Mobilier, addressing the House in a fiery speech had refused absolutely to reveal sacred "professional secrets," Blaine had led the applause, and accompanied Stewart arm in arm from the rostrum. At the last instant, with an adverse decision impending, Speaker Blaine delayed the count long enough for the arrival of a scant majority of Railway Congressmen, to turn the tide.[14]

* Interview in New York *Tribune*, Jan. 30, 1873.

These very nights that followed the House sessions, an intimate member of the Speaker's family circle relates naïvely, Oakes Ames, "man of honored ancestry and stainless name, the modest hero of the great Pacific Railroad," sat silent, stunned, wretched, "before Mr. Blaine's library fire with his head bowed on his breast, while the younger man [Blaine], alert and intent, applied himself indefatigably in and out of the house, arranging for his defence as for that of the other men who were implicated with him." [15]

For as surely as Blaine knew himself to be honorable, so were they all, all honorable men. Blaine, who knew the world, might well have pondered the habitual injustice of mankind. Must honor be measured only by quantity in our society? Was it just that a prominent statesman (Colfax) who had accepted $1,200 "sent him by an admirer" should be stripped of his position and banished by scandal from public life, while a small syndicate of private citizens who contrived, by the "planned mismanagement" of the Pacific railroads, to distribute $44,000,000 among themselves were accorded the envy and admiration of all the universe?

Most politicians in those early days were but children in the realm of finance. Though they played a high part in making great transfers of the public domain to private hands, they themselves were destined to go always relatively ill-paid and needy, their modest earnings quickly dissipated, their smallest peculations advertised to all the world. In the meantime, George Hoar of Massachusetts, through a Senate committee, was bringing in a report which dealt with the construction and management of the Pacific railroads themselves. Those who built the eastern half of the system were shown to have realized "in cash value, at least $23,000,000," or but little less than the total money subsidies advanced by the Government.[16] The Huntington-Stanford syndicate was shown afterward to have appropriated almost as much, through the identical device of construction and holding companies. Yet, though the two Pacific railroads were now thought to be ruined, no prosecution threatened their projectors, who were instead honored and celebrated as paragons of Yankee pioneering enterprise, men who had "spanned the continent with a great highway of civilization" or "extended civilization 2,000 miles to the westward."

The initial plans of the party managers with regard to the Crédit Mobilier "calumnies" had not come off well, and a number of the party leaders now licked their wounds; yet the inarticulacy of the public seemed like forbearance, and recovering their aplomb as well as possible, the ruling party continued in pursuit of its further plans. Only a few days after the vote of censure on the Railway Congressmen, in March, the Republican majority, prodded by Ben Butler, with an insolence that could only have come from a sense of supreme command of the situation, introduced and passed the famous Salary Bill ("Salary Grab Act") of 1873. The President's salary was to be doubled, cabinet officers' and Supreme Court Justices' salaries were likewise raised, while members of Congress also increased their own honorarium by 50 per cent, to $7,500 a year, this to be retroactive for two years, making an outright gift of $5,000 each. Although there was something of logic in such a measure which would render statesmen less hungry and less easily prey to temptations, a veritable wave of indignation swept over the country, and the recent Crédit Mobilier comedy was almost completely forgotten.

Puzzled by the charges and countercharges of the Crédit Mobilier episode, the honest yeomanry of the nation grasped clearly, however, the meaning of the "back-pay" steal, and their resentment was stubborn and unabated during the off-year State elections of 1873 and the congressional elections of 1873 that followed. The ruling party Organization showed clear signs of the arrogance and madness of power, as some had predicted, and must reap the fruit of its folly. To top it all, the sudden explosion of the financial panic of 1873, a catastrophe of unparalleled force, changed the climate of the country, aroused the people more than ever, shattering political illusions and party loyalties alike.

IV

The thunderbolt which announced the coming of the cyclical depression upon a grand scale was the failure of Jay Cooke & Co. (with whom so many Republican leaders were intimately connected) on September 18, 1873. While men literally refused to believe this news, terror ruled in the financial markets as well as among politicians whose unpaid notes lay in Cooke's strongboxes. The leading bankers and brokers who had been close to railroad jobbers followed Cooke in their collapse; runs spread to commercial and savings banks believed to be burdened with unsalable railroad securities; money went into hoarding; and during the remaining three months of 1873 more than five thousand business houses closed their doors. The financial panic then transformed itself into an industrial depression, the most intense and destructive the young republic had experienced.

The bursting of the American bubble of speculation had followed upon a period of frenzied railroad-building in the past four years which had reached a pace three times faster than ever before known. With this uncontrolled expansion of transport—often into unpopulated areas—went an equally planless increase of investments in all heavy industries, notably iron and Bessemer steel mills. The high prices, high profits, of the time and the great war savings in the hands of capitalists, the surplus funds of European financiers—all pressed into the American industrial expansion with quenchless optimism—assumed the form of fixed instead of circulating capital and created a "glut" of "ill-digested" securities in the world's money centers.

Jay Cooke's difficulties, as with dwindling reserves he turned over more funds to the giant railroad project whose profits lay ever in the far future, were but symptomatic of the generally weakened position, warning signs of which had earlier been noted in European markets. In the West a violent "Granger" agitation, begun five years before and reaching a climax in 1872-73, showed that the settlers, who had first welcomed railroad expansion at all costs, were up in arms against the "railroad robbers." Then the scandals of the Erie Railroad, the Tweed Ring, the swindle of the Crédit Mobilier, had all combined to prompt a flight of "timid" capital, especially on the part of European bankers.

As the movement of expansion had been unbridled in the American paradise of free capitalism, so the movement of retreat and deflation met with no brakes or controls worthy the name. The country desperately needed more credit, capital goods, railroads, machinery—but who would wait now until such "frozen" assets yielded their return? The economic cataclysm was something which passed all understanding so far as the statesmen of the reigning party were concerned, men who had spent their days and nights chiefly in haggling over government places. The spectacle of the business crash stupefied them; and their behavior in the crisis would have made for superb comedy were it not that so many workers by tens of thousands in the meantime must walk the streets in hunger, and so many farmers in almost equal number must abandon home and lands under the hammer of the auctioneer.

On the Sunday following the downfall of the House of Cooke, the little President and his Secretary of the Treasury, William A. Richardson (replacing Boutwell, who had passed to the Senate), hurried to New York to confer there with leading businessmen and financiers. Accompanying them was the strong man of the Republican Party, Senator Oliver Morton, who, as he related, "saw the crowds of bankers, brokers, capitalists, merchants, manufacturers, and railroad men who throughout that day thronged the halls, corridors, and parlors of the Fifth Avenue Hotel, beseeching the President to increase the currency by every means in his power, and declaring that unless the Government came to the rescue nothing could save the country from bankruptcy and ruin." [17]

The Government's financial system and policy were cumbersome at best, a rigorous, inelastic debt-retirement program leaving it but weak resources with which to meet a great emergency. One faction among businessmen, suffering from immediate shortage of credit, clamored loudly that the Government must "issue" more currency to overcome the panic and hoarding movement; while another, no less resolute, insisted that it was this very power of issue, that is, of the inflation of currency, which led to the flight of gold in an emergency. Indeed the President, listening to conflicting advisers, made contradictory announcements: that he favored issuing "reserve" Greenbacks and also resumption of specie payment—in short, inflation and contraction at once! At one moment he would make the useless observation that the panic was "a blessing" in disguise; at the next he would recommend an increase in the coinage of silver—forgetting that a Coinage Act of 1873 had suddenly terminated the minting of silver.[18]

A fierce debate raged throughout the country by 1874 over the question of whether the American currency system was to be "hard" or "soft," gold or paper. It was the historic, traditional form which political controversy between opposing classes and regions had taken in America ever since the eighteenth century. The money question, cutting across party lines, became a Burning Issue, creating a nightmare for the professional politicians—most of whom understood nothing of it all—and overthrowing all their careful schemes for purely partisan issues and "combinations" by which elections might be won.

To the farm population of the Mississippi Valley and the prairies farther west, the problem was terribly clear and admitted of only one solution. Money itself seemed to them to have become suddenly unbearably "dear." They had cheerfully contracted debts during the war years and the postwar years, when bumper crops had flowed in a prodigious ever swelling stream over the new railroad lines. Wheat had sold at $1.25 a bushel when they had bonded themselves for immense quantities of new farm equipment and accepted the mortgage loans freely offered them. Now that wheat had fallen to half its former value moneylenders pursued them for repayment at ruinous rates. Throughout the nation's hinterland, over its broad granaries, the "little people" and almost all who traded with them thus formed now a huge, disadvantaged debtor class, clamoring with one voice, as in the days of poor landholders of Italy under the Gracchi, for the increase of prices which alone might relieve their sufferings, and which required a preliminary inflation or debasement of the circulating money.

The people of the West were in the position of colonial producers exchanging cheap, abundant food and raw materials for finished or manufactured goods usually made and financed at the Eastern seaboard. But while the value of their own goods fell in the world market, the internal price level of manufactured goods was relatively sustained at a comparatively high, inflexible point by a protective tariff; railroad and warehouse tolls remained fixed by monopolists, who were now the bêtes noires of the American yeomanry; bank-interest rates of Eastern "Goldbugs" and "Shylocks" also ranged from 8 to 18 per cent; but in times of crisis such as the autumn crop-moving season of 1873 financing was utterly unobtainable. In the Western States the Grangers, the Greenbackers, and the men of the new Farmers' Alliance (which embraced some 1,500,000 members by 1872) opened a formidable onslaught upon the railroad-owning and banking class which contributed to the panic not only among capitalists but among politicians as well. The politicians assembling in Washington had heard the debtors' doctrines of inflation sounded again in the familiar refrain of the 1830's and the 1860's, a music which was destined to attain higher and higher crescendos in coming years, in which the struggle between Haves and Have-Nots assumed its old pattern, its traditional American form and ideology.

As in other national emergencies, Hard Times and the money issue in the 1870's disrupted party lines, upset all calculations of electoral balances and political quantities in a manner which impaired the very usefulness of the biparty system. The Democrats, since the Civil War, were the more inchoate of the parties; in the East, especially in the New York Organization, which by its electoral numbers weighed so heavily in the national party councils, Samuel Tilden represented financial interests more conservative, more devoted to the gold standard, than any Republican faction. South of Mason and Dixon's line were former rebels, Bourbons, yet predominantly agriculturists at odds with their party's New York wing. But in the Mississippi Valley, the stronghold of the old Jacksonian Democracy, there were leaders who had followed Old Hickory in their youth, and who figuratively put on a red bandanna handkerchief whenever they mounted the public stump. Senator Allen Thurman of Ohio, leonine orator of broad frame and craggy head, had always used this fashion since the 1840's; and he with Governor Thomas Hendricks of Indiana and Senator Dan Voorhees, the "Tall Sycamore of the Wabash," George Pendleton, and other old Jacksonians (who were usually dubbed "thieves," "demagogues," or "repudiators" by Eastern conservatives) now leaped into the fight for "shinplasters," Greenbacks, and prosperity.

Fortune smiled upon these vociferous agrarian leaders during the 1870's; and a curious phenomenon was now seen in the Mississippi Valley. To the canny Middle Western Republican bosses Morton, Logan, and Zach Chandler, who felt the rising pulse of their constituents, there came premonitions of dire defeat, and they were seen to veer sharply to agreement with the Western and Southern Democrats! Morton, with his eyes fixed upon the presidential succession, now ascribed all our economic troubles to the "fanaticism about a return to specie payments." [19] He led the fight within the ranks of his party for a moderate inflation by reissuance of the Legal Tender. Fearing disaster at the polls in 1874, Morton and his faction actively fostered an inflationary act in Congress that was "an anchor thrown desperately to windward" by the beleaguered Republicans.[20]

Within the administration party, however, Roscoe Conkling, who was closely connected with great New York bankers, worked tirelessly to block the inflationists. Among the so-called Half-Breeds John Sherman (who had held mortgages at 8 and 10 per cent on Ohio farm lands) also led the resistance to demands for an increase of paper money. This prudent moneylender and accumulator of securities exclaimed during the Senate debates of January, 1874, with a callous cynicism: "Will there not always be men in debt? Will not always men, with bright hopes, embark too rashly on the treacherous sea of credit? Will there not always be a demand upon you [Congress] for an increase?" [21] And Garfield, one of the party's more learned ideologues, raised the hopes of frightened State Street by his all too clever appeal for a stable money medium as being in the sole interests of labor—"To them the country owes the splendor of the position it holds before the world more than to any other equal number of our citizens." [22]

Before so complex and technical a problem, upon which nevertheless whole sections and masses of the people expressed the most passionate opinions, the politicians showed themselves wavering, divided, frightened. At the national Treasury itself the situation was most perplexing. A goodly part of the circulating currency still consisted in Mr. Lincoln's irredeemable Legal Tender, or Greenbacks, of which more than $400,000,000 had been outstanding recently. Under broad discretionary powers given by previous acts of Congress, Secretary McCulloch had reduced this sum through specie payments to $356,000,000 in 1868, when Congress had halted the deflationary movement and ordered the Legal Tender to be maintained again at $400,000,000. This left a paper-money "reserve" of $44,000,000 in the Treasury, concerning whose disposition no two politicians were agreed. Actually the "reserve" was smaller, since, during the money squeeze of 1873, some $26,000,000 of it had been quickly reissued by the Treasury to meet current expenses—*illegally*, some charged—though with little result.[23] To bankers and financiers, the very existence of this wartime fiat money in our circulation, and the precedents under which Congress might again extend the debasement of currency, were anathema, created endless uncertainty and menace for all values in the future. While the agrarian element demanded more paper money, the leading financial groups in the Northeast clamored as loudly for its elimination and quick resumption of the gold standard in order that "confidence" might be renewed at last.

At such moments we feel the whole patronage party institution at strain, as it faces contradictory demands—on the one hand, to appease its allies in the countinghouses, and on the other, to hold the foundation support of its agitated, suspicious electoral following. Exercising the greatest parliamentary skill, John Sherman, chairman of the Senate Finance Committee, steered the inflationist movement toward a "victory" which was in truth but a most heavy and dark compromise. The inflationary bill of April, 1874, which Sherman completely supervised, permitted an increase of $46,000,000 in the note circulation of national banks, against the security of government bonds; also the issuance of the $44,000,000 "reserve" Greenbacks was authorized, though most of it was already "unlawfully" issued to meet the Treasury deficit. Thus the bill was hailed by the inveterate compromiser, Sherman, as bringing a "moderate" inflation of our money, though it actually added but 5 per cent to the circulating Legal Tender. Sherman meanwhile assured his friends that the act would do no harm and much good in preventing worse measures.

When the bill came to the President for his signature, delegations of conservative capitalists, filled with painful excitement, besieged Grant for a veto. They would brook no careful, cowardly compromise with the "repudiators." Grant sent word that he "sympathizes strongly with the business interests."[24] Actually, as he described in after years, he suffered the most painful perplexity and spent many hours arguing the case for each side to himself and slowly answering his own questions. Within his Cabinet there was a significant division of opinion also, the more conservative men favoring Hard Money, and the purely professional politicians, such as Secretary Delano, an opportunistic increase of Greenbacks. "A veto will certainly injure the party," exclaimed the latter at a cabinet conference in April, while Hamilton Fish, the old Knickerbocker millionaire, countered: "I dissent utterly from that view. The honest sentiment of the country . . . will sustain it [the veto]."

Almost at the last moment, April 22, 1874, with a final change of heart, Grant sent the inflation bill back with his veto. This surprising action was at once celebrated as a most "courageous" gesture on behalf of Sound Money and the views of conservative bankers. Republicans from financial New York reported that a perilous load had been "lifted from the hearts of sober men in the city." [25] And Grant, showered with the blessings of mortgage-owners and bank depositors, was for a second time acknowledged in the Northeast as the savior of his country.

Grant's veto of a Republican bill represented "a turning of the corner" for the country, as Senator G. F. Hoar of Massachusetts remembers.[26] The Republican Party committed itself anew to its pledges of specie resumption made in 1869, at a moment of rapprochement with conservative financial groups. But party chiefs of the Western wing like Morton and Logan, who fought in the trenches every year for the people's vote, murmured their dismay at consequences which would follow in Western States.[27] The President had shown high courage indeed—greater courage hath no man!—to court defeat at the polls for the sake of high capitalist policy.

The Republican Party leaders might have spared themselves the pains they took in designing compromises. In the 1874 congressional elections the people moved in a manner which has always been known technically as a Tidal Wave. The campaign machinery of the war party had floundered badly; opposition had risen to irresistible proportions, and foreshadowed clearly a change in the Administration also in 1876. Wrath long accumulated during Hard Times over the Crédit Mobilier exposures and the "Salary Grab" bill was sharpened by the swing of the ruling party to a conservative policy, bringing to the House of Representatives a sweeping majority of Democrats for the first time since 1858.

The people had spoken. The party of the Outs, sometimes characterized by the more bigoted Republican leaders as the party of "Free Trade, Repudiation, Whiskey, Ireland, Democracy, Falsehood and the Devil generally," [28] would be in position to thwart legislative action during the remaining years of Grant's term. Meanwhile the Lame Duck session of the Forty-third Congress was still to sit up to March, 1875, and action might still be taken before the dark forces of disunion and "rag money" descended upon the Capitol.

Early in December, 1874, upon the assembling of Congress, a month after what could only have been seen as a great popular mandate for currency expansion, a Senate caucus was called together and named a committee of eleven to shape new financial legislation. Sherman was made chairman, and the other members were chiefly drawn from the most orthodox of the Republicans, prominent among them Conkling, Boutwell, Sargent and Allison; with Morton and Logan in apparent opposition. After much bickering, the decision was made to support a Resumption Bill providing for the return to specie payment within four years. These Republican leaders, moving directly in the face of a mandate from masses of small property-holders, farmers, and debtors, worked amid a pall of gloom over the ambiguous clauses of a currency bill which was at last, after so much "masterly inactivity," to redeem their party in the eyes of wealthier allies. They acted, one of them said, as if "they might as well be hanged for sheep as for goats." Already defeated overwhelmingly at the polls, conciliation having failed, they "had nothing to risk by a move in sound-money legislation, and possibly much to gain." [29] "John Sherman fully appreciated . . . that the business interests of the country demanded a return to specie payments as speedily as possible." [30]

Among the elaborate provisions of Sherman's bill was one which provided for the vigorous extension of the national banking system, an increase in the circulation of national banknotes, and a corresponding reduction in Greenbacks, until they stood at $300,000,000; the redemption of Greenbacks in coin was to take place after January 1, 1879.

This measure brought a certain improvement and flexibility to the semicentralized national-bank system fostered during the Civil War; it extended vastly at the same time the privilege and profits of the national bankers. An enormous and perpetual power of discretion was also given to the Secretary of the Treasury "to use surplus revenues from time to time," and to "issue, sell and dispose of bonds" for the purpose of accumulating gold, so that the country's credit might be held thereafter firmly linked to the international gold standard. There was also much in this bill which was Delphic and subject to conflicting interpretation, so that as Senator Thurman (Democrat) said aptly, "no one could say whether it was a contraction or an inflationary measure." But this too was not without design. Sherman, who wrote and managed the passage of the Resumption Bill, and after whom it was named, was admittedly under the constant advice at this time of August Belmont, agent of the Rothschilds in the United States.[31] By the driving tactics of Speaker Blaine in the House, and a "strict party vote," this measure was swiftly carried, January 7, 1875. In the Senate even Morton and Logan, who had recently proclaimed everywhere their paper-money credo, now voted for it with stolid discipline. On this day, in "death-bed repentance," the Republican Party became openly, rather than with indirection, the party of conservative business.[32]

The politicians of a defeated Congress in its final death throes usually show their real hand. These men, in their desperation, looked only to conservative bankers and protected manufacturers who had been their patrons, for a vital future support which would one day bring their return.

While the barbarian Democrats waited impatiently at the gate, the Forty-third Congress continued its deliberations until midnight of March 3, 1875. To the Resumption Bill which finance capitalists advocated, they coolly added a tariff act which answered fully the demands of the manufacturing capitalists. On the pretext that the force of the depression made the Government's revenues insufficient, the moderate tariff reductions of 1872 were now suddenly repealed, the old high protective scale restored upon manufactured goods, while taxes on tobacco, spirits, molasses, and sugar—all articles of popular consumption whose taxation the common people bore most heavily—were sharply raised. The tariff act of 1875 was an appropriate and mocking gesture with which a body of statesmen identified in greatest measure with Custom House, Whisky, and Railroad rings and Carpetbag machines bowed itself out.

V

Hard Times had raised unpleasant class-sectional issues harrowing to professional politicians. They revived also after 1873 the lively ghost Reform, whom the Stalwarts thought to have laid with the defeat of Mr. Greeley.

When in depression the profits of enterprise are meager, the same groups of businessmen who have been wont to look good-humoredly upon bureaucratic wastefulness and corruption as a convenience, or a necessary evil, think twice of the matter, and soon come forward with heavy moans and dire complaints of extortion. Shepherd's Public Works Ring in Washington, Butler's and Conkling's men in Boston and New York, looted the public Treasury—but they also preyed upon private property as well!

In Boston, for instance, Ben Butler's man John D. Sanborn had been appointed to aid the Treasury Department in collecting delinquent taxes, after 1872, under the moiety system. He had gone bluntly to the internal-revenue officers at Boston, presented his contract with the Treasury Department, and demanded and obtained their list of delinquent taxpayers. The collection of sums requiring no effort whatsoever, and which would have been received in the normal course of events, he thereafter credited to himself, pocketing half, or fees totaling $213,000 within a single year, in the interest of the Butler machine. Such schemes were typical of Butler's fertile brain; but among the victims were prominent corporations, including large railroads, who promptly made public their knowledge of the corrupt practices they suffered from.

Whenever public criticism was voiced against some high government official, the political methods established in Grant's term had required usually that he be replaced by someone more practiced or useful still in the partisan spoils system. Secretary Boutwell had been much assailed; when the Massachusetts Legislature elected him to the Senate early in 1873, Grant appointed Assistant Secretary of the

Treasury William A. Richardson, a shifty Boston politician, in his place. Richardson, facing the crisis in 1873, soon proved lax and incompetent; and when the uproar arose over the Sanborn contracts, which he had authorized, his head was demanded and his resignation was ready in turn. By all usage Secretary of the Interior Columbus Delano, the Ohio wirepuller, who aspired to the Treasury, should then have been named in Richardson's place. Indeed powerful party influences worked behind the scenes to promote Delano to a post where he might have opened wide the strongboxes of the Treasury to his party—"without hurting anyone."

But the vital Treasury post touched the purse of great capitalists, and Delano, moreover, had committed himself to the Western Greenback "heresy." The tactics of depression and the approach of national elections now forcibly suggested a move toward Sound Money—to restore business "confidence"—economy in administration, and housecleaning. Thus Grant, by one of his inexplicable volte-faces, named a Western Hard Money man, the Kentucky Unionist General Benjamin H. Bristow, as his new Secretary of the Treasury, June 1, 1874.

An officer of Grant's Army of the West, of military figure and sweeping mustachios, not only was Bristow distinguished as a soldier but also he had recently served the Department of Justice ably as special counsel. He was an accomplished lawyer, ambitious, scrupulous, and surprisingly enough, a strong champion of civil-service reform. Bristow's entrance into the Grant Cabinet was widely applauded —though Tammany politicians might have characterized it with one of their memorable paradoxes upon the wisdom of "pandering to reform."

For some years a sober element in the Republican Party, looking toward 1876, had been quietly pressing for a house-cleaning which would dispose of some bad men "without tearing too much up," as Chandler of New Hampshire phrased it.[33] Bristow now threw himself into this task, which evidently required a superhuman diplomacy. In his department he found at once appalling inefficiency and dishonesty which truly troubled his middle-class-reformer's soul; from one-third to two-thirds of Federal collections were lost, as confidential reports showed, the higher figure applying to the recovery of excise taxes upon spirits. Then he came suddenly face to face with the far-spreading evidence of the great Whisky Ring and its systematic affiliations with his own party. During the hard times of the past two years alone, some $4,000,000 in taxes had been stolen. Every important distillery center seemed to be connected with the national ring; and yet Bristow's predecessors, Boutwell and Richardson, had shut their eyes to the alliance between their officials and the distilleries.

By his financial conservatism and vigorous economies, Bristow within a few months attained national prominence. He therefore felt strong enough to attack the whisky conspirators.

All through the autumn of 1874, Bristow sent inspectors into the various revenue districts and gathered evidence. In December, 1874, he attempted to send inspectors into the district of John McDonald, Grant's friend and political agent at St. Louis. But an unseen hand moved against him. Before the Treasury inspectors could reach the St. Louis headquarters of the ring, the President's private secretary, Orville Babcock, knew of their purpose, and from the White House telegraphed the secret warning which he signed "Sylph," in remembrance of an attractive courtesan of St. Louis whom the whisky men had provided for him. When Bristow's men arrived to examine the records, everything was in marvelous order.[34]

Bristow now moved to change the personnel supervising the different revenue districts in his department, as a means of gaining easier access to their records. By this order McDonald was to be shifted to a post in Philadelphia. At this, McDonald hastened to Washington, saw his confederate Babcock, and made a large payment to him; then he was admitted to the President at once, and made loud complaint that party interests throughout the West would be injured if he were ousted—which was perfectly true. Grant then revoked Bristow's orders, thus keeping McDonald at St. Louis.[35] The reformist Secretary was blocked, felt discouraged, and moreover was aware of subtle backstairs intrigue which aimed at unseating him.

Indeed it was, in some measure, desperation at the very persistence with which Babcock and the wily Delano sought to undermine or eliminate Secretary Bristow that led him, during the winter of 1874 and the spring of 1875, to redouble his efforts. Mistrusting his own Internal Revenue detectives, for informers were all about him in his own department, he now planned his attack with utmost caution. He changed the ciphers used in department dispatches, set elaborate traps, and finally planned, when all was in readiness, concerted raids to be sprung at distillery centers throughout the country for the purpose of seizing books and records. Even so the conspirators were partly warned.[36] McDonald and company sent in their resignations, the distillers were already half finished with clearing out their excess stocks and destroying their records when Bristow's secret police fell upon them, May 10, 1875. McDonald and his secretary-confederate, Joyce, were indicted in June; bills were found against 350 government officials and distillers, mostly in St. Louis, Milwaukee, and Chicago.[37]

In designating the extremely energetic Bristow to institute some house-cleaning in the Treasury Department, President Grant had worked better than he knew. But Bristow had begun by exposing the boldest, the most gigantic government frauds since the Yazoo land claims in the early days of the republic.

"Let no guilty man escape," Grant said tersely to his Secretary of the Treasury when the mass of evidence was brought before him. But the development of the case brought managers of the regional Republican machines in Wisconsin, in Illinois, in Missouri, into the net of the Federal prosecutors. Finally it penetrated to the mansion of the President himself, where his private secretary, the irrepressible, audacious Colonel Babcock, in liaison with all the conspirators, directed a secret intrigue which aimed to discredit and overthrow Bristow himself.

Grant, who had felt it expedient to bring about economies and eject thieves from the government service, suddenly recoiled. The scandal in the press, the moves to prosecute his intimate counselor Babcock, now seemed successive blows aimed at himself, his Administration, and the Republican Organization. Throughout the country the element of Independents who had supported Greeley in 1872 appeared delighted with Bristow's probing; indeed Secretary Bristow had occasion to engage certain reformist Republicans (with whom he seemed openly identified), such as former Senator John B. Henderson of Missouri, to aid in the trial at St. Louis; and rumors came in November, 1875, that these men would stop at no injury to the central party Organization: that they would prosecute the President's brother, Orville Grant, his brother-in-law, Fred Dent, the Republican National Committeemen of 1872, and Ulysses Grant himself!

The old palace guard of the "court party," relatives of the Grant family, the Kitchen Cabinet, all combined to poison the President's mind against the reformer in their midst. Bristow was plotting with the band of soreheads and even rebels "to indict the whole Administration."

At a cabinet meeting in October, 1875, Secretary Bristow had shown Grant the Sylph telegrams of Babcock; the Colonel, called in to explain them, admitted that they came from his hand, but brazenly asserted that they referred to other routine administrative matters. Such a defense satisfied no one but the determinedly complaisant Grant. But alone with the President, Babcock had protested his innocence, then, as in a Dumas romance, declared that "a woman's honor" was at stake. Holding the President's ear continuously, he cajoled and diverted him; he fed his suspicions at the outcry being raised against his Administration. Bristow was *ambitious!* The disaster being prepared for the ruling party Bristow and his friends would use to seize control for themselves.

Indeed Babcock left no stone unturned, affirmed his innocence in telegrams and violent statements, raised the alarm vigorously, and called the strong men of the party to his side for mutual defense. Senator Logan now besieged the President with complaints that Bristow was but carrying out "a raid" upon his Illinois province.[38] When Bristow's chief aide, Treasury Department Solicitor Bluford Wilson, came to Grant with further evidence against Babcock, he found that Zach Chandler—who had lost his seat in the Senate and now graced the Cabinet as Secretary of the Interior—hung about the office of the President and would not leave Wilson alone with him. From Maine and New Hampshire to Wisconsin "the best men of the party" clamored against Bristow and Solicitor Wilson, protested that the Whisky Ring prosecution would lose them the elections in 1876.[39]

Thus everything disposed the President to confine the prosecution to the ousting of petty officials and the punishment of fraudulent distillers, while sparing figures high in the party Organization. His own "line" was expressed clearly in the matter of a Federal judge, one of his own appointees, concerning whom charges of corruption were published in July, 1875, and whose resignation was demanded. Grant then wrote to his Attorney-General Edwards Pierrepont:

> I do not feel so well satisfied . . . that a change will be necessary and even if such a change should be necessary in the end, I do not wish to contribute to the triumph of the enemies that are now assailing the Judge —the *Sun,* the *Tribune,* etc.[40]

Upon this ground Grant, whatever he knew or suspected, was now stubborn in his resolve to shield Babcock, who still worked in the White House by his side.

During the trial at St. Louis, the special government attorney, John B. Henderson, passing the bounds of discretion, made allusion to current suspicions that Babcock's complicity touched the President himself. Why had the Treasury official, Douglass, permitted the President to interfere in the case? "What right has the President to interfere with the honest discharge of the duties of a Secretary of the Treasury?" he had exclaimed. At once Grant, exerting his full influence, had demanded and obtained the dismissal of Henderson from the government service.

Collector McDonald, McKee, Avery (chief clerk of the Treasury Department), were all duly tried, found guilty, and sentenced to prison terms. But with the resourceful Babcock it was less simple. He struggled for delay; he demanded a military trial, with his shifty friend General Belknap, the Secretary of War, to preside over it. Failing in this, he engaged powerful counsel, paid for by subscriptions of loyal Republicans, who used every trick of legal defense; his detectives even rifled the papers of the Treasury Department, meanwhile, in an attempt to steal the evidence incriminating him.

The trial of Colonel Babcock, as chief confederate and "inside man" for the whisky conspirators, beginning in February, 1876, was in fact a trial of the inner Organization of the Republican Party. Before his cabinet members Grant, usually so impassive, could no longer conceal his mounting worry and excitement. To Hamilton Fish he complained that "his secretaries and clerks, his messengers and doorkeepers," were taken from him, that "the prosecution was aimed at himself and they were putting him on trial." [41] It was with difficulty that the President of the United States was withheld from rushing across the country to make a personal deposition on behalf of his friend in a criminal trial—instigated by his own Government.

The meaning of all these episodes was illuminated sharply by an extraordinary speech made by one of the convicted criminals, the actual business manager of the Whisky Ring, Joyce, who after denouncing his prosecutors called attention to the hateful "miasmic" tide of reform which now threatened to engulf all that was fair and bright in the nation; he pictured himself as one of the great martyrs of history for the cause of his party; and predicted vengeance and final humiliation for the fanatical, mad reformers who had wrought all the present mischief. [42]

Behind the scenes a tremendous tug of war ensued, upon whose outcome hung all advance preparations for the presidential nomination—involving plans for a third term for Grant; or a direct Stalwart succession; or a shift which would further the aspirations of Speaker Blaine; or, worst of all, the triumph of the reform element, to whom the embattled Bristow had become a hero and a Daniel. The Stalwart chieftains, Logan, Morton, Conkling, and Zach Chandler, and Blaine too, were fully aware that their whole system of control was endangered by the peril to Babcock. For in his confidential capacity he had been a link which connected with all the parts of the whole: he had been involved in the Santo Domingo project, as in the public-works adventures of Boss Shepherd's Washington ring; he was connected with Gould's Black Friday gold conspiracy, with Leet and the New York Custom House frauds; his activities reached to plunderers, safebreakers, statesmen, courtesans, and railroad masters as well. Hence the intrepid editor Samuel Bowles in the Springfield *Republican* assured his readers that the case of Babcock assumed universal proportions, involving not only Grant and the whole party machine but also the railroad magnates of the East, Tom Scott and Jay Gould, as well as the Whisky Ring of the West. The whole system was at stake, and if Bristow should be ousted, as was widely rumored, it would be the triumph of the "subtly pervasive and potent" influence of the railroad men, combined with the whisky thieves, over the "plain voters" and "reform leaders." [43]

By all accounts the Treasury Department's prosecution was hampered by obstructive action of the Federal Government itself. An order of immunity offered by Secretary Bristow and his counsel which would have permitted the taking of state's evidence was deliberately revoked by President Grant himself in January, 1876, thus sealing forever lips which might have spoken freely not only of Babcock but of the great Middle Western bosses, Senators Carpenter of Wisconsin, Logan of Illinois, and Morton of Indiana.

The climax of the trial was the President's deposition in favor of Babcock's character, sworn to before the Chief Justice and presented in lieu of Grant's personal appearance at St. Louis. On February 24, 1876, the trial ended in Babcock's acquittal. He alone, among the many whisky conspirators, had been spared, though his retirement was now inevitable. The rescue of Babcock from the penitentiary was hailed by Stalwart Republicans as nothing less than a great victory for their party.

The President thereafter was a blind old lion who grew furious with all who goaded him, especially those who affected the hateful style of reform. He consumed much of the remainder of his term in vindictive strokes at Bristow's aides, who had labored faithfully to recover large sums of money due the Government, but who were now systematically dismissed. From Bristow he was long completely estranged, treating him with contemptuous ill will, but delaying his enforced resignation for purely political reasons.

The closing months of Grant's second term were of nightmare quality as the Democrats, present in force in Congress, determined to press inquisitions in all directions. His Administration had "outraged every rule of decency," Henry Adams observed, "but scores of promising men whom the country could not well spare were ruined in saying so." Grant seemed to most men a sad, puzzled figure. Tom Nast, following a personal visit, thought: "The President was overwhelmed . . . wherever he turned some new dishonor lay concealed." [44]

In the spring of 1876 his Administration approached utter breakdown, as new scandals surged up on every hand.

Early in February, while the party Organization fought to the death to save Babcock, report came that General Robert Schenck, our Minister to Great Britain, and one of the foremost of the "regular" Ohio Republicans, had suddenly resigned and left London in full retreat before officers of the law. After helping to spread the fashion for draw poker in society, he had publicly sponsored a worthless mining stock, the Emma Mines, his name being used in its prospectus as a director; but what was most galling, he had "sold short," or unloaded his own fraudulently acquired shares, before the bubble burst for the deluded British investors. Only the plea of diplomatic immunity and immediate departure had spared him indictment and trial.

The country was still vibrant with the shock and alarm of these affairs when news came to the White House that a congressional committee had found "uncontradicted evidence of malfeasance in office" by General William Belknap, the Secretary of War. A favorite of the President, an ornament of the Cabinet since 1870, for years the handsome Belknap and his wife had lived upon the proceeds of the sale of army trading-posts. Before action for his impeachment could be taken, Belknap, accompanied by Zach Chandler, on March 2, 1876, hurried to the White House in greatest agitation, and impressing upon the credible Ulysses that he had become involved in an illegality through an action of his wife—once more a woman's honor was being shielded!—asked that his resignation be accepted.[45] "He spoke of his dead wife," Grant explained afterward. "So I wrote him a letter accepting the resignation." The House Democrats were in an uproar over the President's effort "to rob an American Congress of its right to inflict punishment . . . on a publicly convicted criminal."[46] The Republicans appeared distracted; only their majority in the Senate prevented a technical impeachment following the long House committee inquisition into the War Department affairs, which stretched throughout the summer months of the presidential campaign.

Department by department, virtually the whole Federal Government came under the fire of "resolutions of inquiry" by a Democratic House of Representatives. The "horrors" of the Navy and the Interior (under Delano) were shown to have been but little less fearful than those of the War and Treasury departments. Day by day high public officers who had been the honor of their country and party fell from their stations, and successive, bewildering shifts were made in the Cabinet, until the unhappy Hamilton Fish was the only one who remained to the end.

Every day the independent press of the country bombarded the Republican Administration and "Grantism," spreading large the tales of shame which the opposition party gathered for it. Scandal upon scandal, like explosive blasts, shivered the great war party from top to bottom.

Yet those hardy spirits Oliver Morton, Roscoe Conkling, Simon Cameron, and Zach Chandler seemed undismayed as they prepared for the approaching presidential tournament, and busily, as always, transacted characteristic "deals," "arrangements," and "combinations," as if they had learned nothing.

Before a New York State Republican Convention that spring, George William Curtis had dwelt strongly upon "the low tone of political honor and morality," and concluded by giving warning:

> The unceasing disposition of the officers and agents of the Administration to prostitute the party organisations relentlessly . . . has startled and alarmed the honest masses of the Republican party.[47]

But Morton and Conkling were not overly fearful of the "honest masses" of their party. They still affirmed in private, as Senator George Hoar heard, that they might hold power by continuing "to bribe the people with the offices created for their service." [48] What concerned them more seriously was the ill will shown by respectable and affluent elements in the community who had always patronized their party, the Republican swing to financial conservatism having been offset by exposures of the heavy public cost of the spoils organizations. Of no less concern was the steady loss of Carpetbag strongholds in the conquered South, between 1872 and 1876. To hold these positions, or to regain them, it would need literally terror and violence. It was in such terms, quite apparently, that the Stalwart strategists calculated upon the future.

VI

The revival of the old Democratic Party during the turmoil of the early 1870's was an astonishing phenomenon, and a commentary upon the vitality of the two-party system. Slowly the old Democratic local Organizations rewon lost territory, overcame their own errors, threw off the onus of Copperheadism, and began to take their place on a nation-wide rather than a sectional basis—as the war hatreds subsided—confronting the Republican Party as an orderly, dependable, even conservative partner in the traditional regime of party rule.

In the South the Republican military-bureaucratic misrule, which brought little real good to the party's Negro proletarian allies, permitted the old ruling class to recapture by 1876 all but three States: South Carolina, Florida, and Louisiana. In Louisiana, where the Scalawags were cleverly encouraged to quarrel among themselves, spectacles of dishonest elections, disorder, and bloodshed, leading up to the New Orleans insurrection of September, 1874, ended by wearying the whole country. Once more the bluff General Phil Sheridan sent his troops to the State legislature, in January, 1875, and ejected the white "banditti," as he called them, and pacified the region by force of arms. But such moves now served as boomerangs. With public anger over Sheridan's highhanded tactics shown even in New England, the breakdown of the old Radical program was seen at hand. Through the breaches already made by legal or illegal opposition, more and more former rebels appeared to take their place on the Democratic side of Congress.

So far as the Northern States were concerned, the war-party leaders feared more than all else the possible loss of two or three large States, which, combined with the nearly Solid South, might make for the speedy recapture of the National Government. The rise of Samuel Tilden as a resourceful leader of the Democrats in New York, heading a unified, energetic reform Organization patterned after the machines of the Republicans, seemed to fill the cup of their misfortunes. The old Democratic Party now offered itself to the national electorate under responsible auspices, as a fully equipped, rival concern.

Among the prominent Republicans, James G. Blaine had been less harmed thus far by recent catastrophes than the senatorial leaders closely identified with "Grantism." In the House the dazzling Speaker of yesterday now led the minority Opposition in purely defensive maneuvers. Master parliamentarian and nimble wit that he was, Blaine employed himself chiefly in harrying and fencing with the enemy, until "he soon had the whole Democratic side of the House floundering in . . . a maze of bewilderment." [49] But now, as the new session of the Forty-fourth Congress began in December, 1875, Blaine, brimming over with ambition, prepared a master stroke which would both baffle and confound the Opposition and arouse the whole country in a sense most desirable for Republican Party ends.

A veteran Democratic Representative, Samuel Randall of Pennsylvania, had introduced at the opening of Congress an Amnesty Bill removing legal disabilities from former Confederate officials who were still under the ban. In view of the sentiment shown lately even in the North concerning the Louisiana atrocities, only mild opposition was awaited, especially from Blaine, who had at times shown an intelligent spirit of conciliation. Yet he announced his intention of offering an amendment to Randall's Amnesty Bill, an amendment which would exclude Jefferson Davis from its privileges.

On January 10, 1876, according to plans prearranged with his supporters, Blaine stepped into the aisle before expectant and crowded galleries. A born actor, with powerful voice and passionate gestures, Blaine gave himself to an enraged harangue against the "lost leader" of the South, "the author, knowingly, deliberately, guiltily, and wilfully of the gigantic murders and crimes at Andersonville." In a chord of anger and hate he cried:

> Some of us had kinsmen there, most of us had friends there, all of us had countrymen there, and in the name of these kinsmen, friends, and countrymen, I here protest . . . against calling back and crowning with the honors of full American citizenship the man that organized that murder.[50]

Never before had Blaine spoken with such heat and such abandon. But the alarm must be raised at all costs against the creeping tide of the Democracy; terror and hate must be released again and the tocsin of "patriotism" sounded anew. He continued:

And I here before God, measuring my words, knowing their full extent and import, declare that neither the massacre of Saint Bartholomew, nor the deeds of the Duke of Alva in the Low Countries, nor the thumbscrews and engines of torture of the Spanish Inquisition begin to compare in atrocity with the hideous crime of Andersonville.[51]

Blaine had "looked and acted like a tiger springing upon his prey"; he had baited the hot-blooded "Southerners . . . as skillfully as the matadore enrages the bull." [52] Little wonder that General Benjamin Hill of Georgia unwarily made a hot riposte which bristled with "Confederate loyalty," and bespoke an unregenerate spirit of secession living still in the bosom of the Democracy. The Democrats, including moderates among them from the North, were thrown into confusion, many of them feeling unable, amid the sultry passions deliberately brewed by the Gentleman from Maine, to show themselves voting in favor of Jefferson Davis. Blaine's maneuver was considered extraordinarily clever at the time, causing the defeat of the Amnesty Bill, diverting attention in great measure from the frightful scandals of the civil Government. Blaine, in short, had raised the old banner of the Bloody Shirt, and shown its still potent propaganda possibilities for the approaching contest. The Republican horde in its darkest hour had found a voice, a leader, perhaps a savior, one who was little touched as yet by the plagues which beset his blemished rivals, Grant, Morton, and Conkling. Hope revived everywhere among the gloomy crowds of officeholders, and on the night of his speech, at a reception by Mrs. Hamilton Fish, Blaine was literally mobbed by admirers, men and women alike.[53]

Garfield, after the debate on the Amnesty Bill made a trip to New England in March, while "the horror of the Belknap scandal" still weighed on his soul—but was able to verify the success of his friend's tactics. He found, to his delight, that the Northern bourgeoisie were thinking less of whisky pirates and War Department depredations and more of the return of old Jeff Davis and his friends as a menace. Garfield confided smugly to his journal that the Bloody Shirt speeches represented "sound strategy" that made of the revived fear of "rebelism" and disorder a useful sedative against present ills.[54] So the gasconading of Blaine, soon emulated by Morton and Conkling in most bitter fashion, drew a protective veil over the inner rottenness of the regime, and served to shore up its crumbling defense walls.

To the mass mind of the North, with its simple fears, Jim Blaine appealed as a fighting leader; numerous State parties declared him their choice for the Presidency, and the "Blaine Legion" now grew gigantically in the winter of 1876. But by his very eminence the brilliant gentleman from Maine exposed himself as the target of adversaries and rivals. A government director of the Union Pacific Railroad, J. C. S. Harrison of Indianapolis, Blaine soon learned (in February), was making most damaging charges against him; he alleged that $64,000 had been advanced to the former Speaker by the malodorous railroad, against nearly worthless collateral consisting of bonds in the Little Rock & Fort Smith Railroad. An Indianapolis newspaper published the story, April 11, 1876, adding that a prominent local banker possessed secrets which would forever "blast the prospects of a certain candidate for the Presidency." [55] Some held Oliver Morton, rather than vengeful Democratic intriguers, to be the instigator of this new prosecution. Garfield, as he noted in his journal, thought that it was "a plot on the part of Conkling, Dorsey and Cornell." [56]

Blaine's temperament was an audacious one. Before he could be threatened by an investigation, he took the offensive himself, rising to a question of privilege and making, April 24, 1876, a sweeping denial of the rumors in the public press, giving as his evidence testimonial letters from the heads of the Union Pacific Railroad, including the obliging Tom Scott. The picture of honor falsely attacked and defending itself in "manly, truthful" fashion is always a touching one. Even the reform group, who saw in Blaine an alternative to the Stalwart leadership, held that he had "vindicated himself completely" and that the affair was "an invented scandal." [57]

Yet the House committee, inspired with its Democratic mission, continued detective work in the irregular affairs of the Pacific railroads. The trail led to transactions which touched Blaine, who was credited widely in Washington not with small peculations, such as those of the Crédit Mobilier Congressmen, but with serving as the "auctioneer" of immense land and railroad rights. Finally, on the morning of May 31, 1876, while Blaine attended a meeting of the subcommittee in charge of the railway hearings, there appeared a quiet-spoken witness whom he knew, one James Mulligan of Boston, formerly a bookkeeper employed by his business partner, the broker Warren Fisher. Mulligan contradicted Blaine's assertions, stating that one of the directors of the Union Pacific, Elisha Atkins, had assured him that it was true that Blaine had received $64,000 from the Union Pacific, through Tom Scott, against the nearly worthless collateral of Little Rock & Fort Smith bonds. Mulligan had also some letters in his possession between Blaine and Fisher.[58] At this point, Blaine is said to have turned pale and hurriedly urged the Republican member of the committee to move an adjournment.

That very afternoon, according to diverse accounts, Blaine pressed the railway directors, Fisher and Atkins, to obtain from Mulligan the letters in his possession. Failing in this, the statesman is said to have gone in person to Mulligan's hotel room, interviewed him alone, and implored him in the most moving terms to have mercy upon "his wife and children"; then, having obtained temporary possession of the letters, according to Mulligan, refused to return them, holding that they were his private property and were not "relevant." To the congressional committee he also brought depositions of two prominent lawyers to this effect.[59] The inquisitors of the Judiciary Committee were blocked for the moment and adjourned to June 7, 1876.

Blaine's position was not easy in the early days of June, with the party nominating convention approaching. His defense had been legalistic and obstructive purely, at a time when the public was morbidly sensitive upon railroad affairs. Moreover, selections from copies of the Mulligan Letters, as they were known, were appearing in Dana's scandalmongering New York *Sun* and making a queer effect. What was to be done? Should he refuse to divulge the letters, he would be suspect; should he publish them voluntarily, he would undoubtedly be injured, as Garfield who saw them judged—and this at a time when his agents were gathering convention delegates for him in State after State.[60] *

The excited Capitol had heard that Blaine would rise again (to a question of privilege) on June 5. Again tense throngs hung upon the words and gestures of the magnetic Gentleman from Maine as he stood at bay. He now called all men to witness that he was a man much persecuted by partisans who aimed at him rather than at the Union Pacific. Were not two members, a majority of the subcommittee which sought to try him, former Confederate soldiers and unregenerate "rebels"? Within his rights as a citizen, he had defied the House to compel him to produce his private letters, but having vindicated that right, he went on:

> I am not afraid to show them. Thank God Almighty I am not ashamed to show them. There they are [holding up a package]. There is the very original package. And with some sense of humiliation, with a mortification that I do not pretend to conceal, with a sense of outrage which I think any man in my position would feel, I invite the confidence of 44,000,000 of my countrymen while I read those letters from this desk.[61]

Thereupon, with superb aplomb, he proceeded to read from the letters as he pleased, in an order of his own, with occasional suppres-

---

* Blaine's embarrassments were augmented not so much by evidence of bribery as by the complexity and irregularity of his business operations. As Speaker he had used his position to form strategic business relations with railroad promoters, and sustained himself in good style by active sales of securities in branch lines which were to be absorbed by the great trunk-line systems. Cf. Oberholtzer, *Jay Cooke*, Vol. II, p. 152 ff. Blocks of securities in new railway ventures were sold usually in several categories: mortgage bonds, land-grant bonds, and stocks. As brokerage commission, Blaine held back a portion of these, which, however, varied according to the terms he was able to arrange.

When the railroad bubble burst toward 1872, Blaine's clients found themselves with heavy losses, some of them greater in proportion as the statesman-broker had held back land-grant bonds which normally went with their subscriptions. In short, they looked at Blaine as "one who took in his friends," as Rhodes puts it bluntly.

A careless rather than a wicked man, Blaine extended himself to raise money and reimburse certain of his aggrieved clients, as well as to prevent disclosures. Thus in 1872 he had induced Tom Scott to relieve him of $150,000 in Fort Smith & Little Rock bonds, now nearly worthless, which found their way in most irregular fashion into the Union Pacific treasury. The services of the Speaker, as we may perceive, were valued at very high rates by the great government-subsidized roads. Cf. Russell, *Blaine of Maine*, pp. 277-78; Rhodes, *History of the United States*, Vol. VII, pp. 194-98.

sions or running comments, so that the whole made no decided effect
of any kind, while the ingenuous, disarming candor of the witness
aroused inevitable sympathy. But for the curtain of his performance
he had devised a still more brilliant stroke.

Some days earlier a friend of Blaine's, perhaps prompted in his
action, as was said, had cabled to London to ascertain the address of
Josiah Caldwell, one of the original promoters of the Little Rock &
Fort Smith, urging him to telegraph the chairman of the House
Judiciary Committee, Proctor Knott, that he had given no bonds
directly or indirectly to Blaine—thus further corroborating testimony
already given by the Railroad Baron Tom Scott. This had been done
by Caldwell. But Chairman Knott had not made public the adventitious telegram when it arrived on June 1. Caldwell, in any case, was
known to have departed for London while the sheriff searched for
him and was a poor character witness.

Blaine, taking advantage of the oversight, now advanced down the
aisle of the House upon Chairman Knott (Democrat) and asked him
point-blank if he had not received a cable message from an important
missing witness. Knott seemed to parry the question for a moment,
admitted then that he had received such a dispatch.

Mr. Knott: How did you know I got it?
Mr. Blaine: When did you get it? I want the gentleman from Ken-
tucky to answer when he got it.
Mr. Knott: Answer my question first.
Mr. Blaine: I never heard of it till yesterday.
Mr. Knott: How did you hear of it?
Mr. Blaine: I heard you got a dispatch last Thursday morning at eight
o'clock from Josiah Caldwell completely and absolutely exonerating me
from this charge, and you have suppressed it.[62]

At this palpable hit there was a roar of applause, "wild, long and
deep" from the entire House and the galleries. All business was
suspended amid a bedlam evoked by the finishing blow which the
accused had apparently delivered the enemy. Though he "threw
dust in men's eyes," told "six distinct falsehoods," and was in no
sense "exonerated" by the prearranged telegram in question, he
diverted attention effectively, and his judges themselves were mo-

mentarily baffled. It was "one of the most extraordinary exhibitions of histrionic skill," said Proctor Knott, "one of the most consummate pieces of acting that ever occurred upon any stage on earth." [63] Nothing that was said, no further evidence brought forward—and there was much—could make his legion of partisans believe that he had not triumphantly vindicated himself once more. Though, as the *Nation* now thought, he had shown but the "pluck" of a "faro-banker," his "wonderful audacity," his "great charge upon Proctor Knott," was a "signal victory." [64]

A wrangling Judiciary Committee resumed its attempts to try the formidable Blaine, then postponed its hearings. The matter of the Mulligan Letters was still pending as final preparations for the Republican National Convention were completed. On Sunday, June 11, a day of overwhelming heat, Blaine suddenly sank to the ground in a dead faint at the door of a church he attended in Washington, a victim of strain and overwork. In the illness that followed he evoked more than ever the sympathy of the masses of people, whose eye he always filled—though at least one skeptical newspaper, Dana's New York *Sun*, announced the news as "Blaine Feigns a Faint." [65]

A few days later, his supporters at the Cincinnati convention learned with profound delight of their chief's remarkable and most timely recovery. It was better so, for there was much to do.

VII

The spirit of the 1876 Republican nominating convention was a grim determination to win the Presidency again at all costs, to hold the Administration breastworks with all its patronage in the face of the reviving Democracy. Somewhat tardily, Grant had stopped the third-term movement in his favor, which had aroused unrest; and his legatees, who were to carry on what passed for the principles of Stalwart Republicanism, were considered to be Roscoe Conkling and Oliver Morton. Conkling controlled the strategic New York delegation with its heavy convention and electoral vote—though Samuel Tilden had defeated his State machine two years before; Morton possessed some Middle Western strength but, most of all, the Southern Carpetbag and Negro contingents. Benjamin Bristow's cause was supported by a scattered but remarkably enthusiastic host of reformers and liberals, such as Schurz and George William Curtis; but this faction had incurred the undying hate of the spoilsmen. Finally, the important State of Ohio had a Favorite Son, General Rutherford B. Hayes, who had recently won a notable campaign for the Governorship, a contest in which he had defeated the vociferous champions of paper-money inflation.

Blaine was admittedly the strongest runner, against whom the whole field contended, with strength spread over the populous Republican regions from Maine and Pennsylvania to Iowa, and even the new far-off State of Washington. The whole logic of his career pointed to this hour, and his plans had been carefully laid. The Mulligan Letters, however, had disturbed them, and implacable jealousies within the party raised also the important issue of party unity and discipline.

Colonel Robert G. Ingersoll, renowned lecturer and orator, made the nominating speech for Blaine, which became a children's classic of unexampled bombast and rodomontade, but which contained nevertheless some candid, even ingenuous allusions to current political troubles. As to certain railroad transactions, Colonel Ingersoll thundered that the Republicans of this convention "do not demand that their candidate shall have a certificate of moral character signed by the Confederate Congress." It was a key to the ideology which would be exploited in the approaching campaign. But, he continued, the people

call for the man who has torn from the throat of treason the tongue of slander—for the man who has snatched the mask of Democracy from the hideous face of the rebellion. . . . Like an armed warrior, like a *plumed knight,* James G. Blaine marched down the halls of the American Congress and threw his shining lance full and fair against the brazen forehead of the defamers of his country and maligners of his honor. . . . In the name . . . of those who perished in the skeleton clutch of famine at Andersonville and Libby, whose sufferings he so vividly remembers, Illinois—Illinois nominates . . .[66]

This stupendous galimatias, which did not fail to make a virtue of vice and necessity, enchanted the assembled political "workers," who would have chosen their leader on the spot. But the eulogians of Conkling, Hayes, and Morton must needs take their turn, and as Blaine himself noted regretfully, "the hastening shades of evening" delayed events.

The early balloting showed Blaine far in the lead, with at first 285, then more than 300 votes, or within close call of a majority. Morton, Conkling, Bristow, and Hayes each had little more than a third of his strength, or in the neighborhood of 100 delegates each, but as they held their followers firmly, Blaine's cause could not gain, and the convention remained in deadlock at the sixth ballot. Then came the recess, and traditional bids and offers by the managers of each candidate as they pressed for a "break" to their side. Blaine's people could not deal with the Bristow or Hayes contingent; while as for Morton and the implacable Conkling, it was a relished opportunity to destroy the "smart" Gentleman from Maine. Then, no doubt cautiously, the party directorate recalled the repentant advocacy of civil-service reform in its new platform and contrasted this with the recent ill odor of the leading aspirant. It was appreciated that the Democrats would make hay with the disasters of the Grant regime, and their leader would be the conqueror of Boss Tweed, Samuel Tilden. At this crisis, which required the strategy of party "harmony," the Ohio politicians under John Sherman made skillful maneuvers in favor of their Dark Horse, Governor Hayes, who had offended almost no one and who would outrage neither the reformers nor the Stalwarts.

After the feverish consultations of the recess, the New York delegates, who were believed to have been let out of prison on bail furnished by the Custom House Ring, were sent rushing by the adroit Chester Arthur to the Hayes "band wagon," while Oliver Morton's battalion of spoilsmen instantly followed suit.[67] * The conservative

---

* The dangerous cleavage in the party reveals itself clearly: Blaine possessed leadership of half of the party, but the other half was as resolutely held by his enemies, the Stalwarts. At the last moment, Simon Cameron of Pennsylvania, according to testimony left by Oliver Morton, "borrowed" some of Morton's delegates to hold off a Blaine stampede. In return, Morton and also Conkling agreed quickly to give up the race and divert their following from Blaine at all costs. It was Zach Chandler, with his Michigan delegates, who precipitated the first "break" in favor of the Dark Horse, Rutherford B. Hayes, reflecting the strategy of the party's Inner Circle. Cf. Foulke, *Life of Oliver P. Morton*, pp. 400-01.

Hayes of Ohio, "a third rate nonentity, whose only recommendation is that he is obnoxious to no one," as Henry Adams wrote at this time,[68] was the perfect answer to a delicate problem of party harmony. The action of the convention, however, in the opinion of the young John Hay, writing to Blaine on June 17, 1876, represented "the greatest personal tribute . . . which has ever been given to a public man in this country." [69] He had all but won the prize, though his frailties were known to all the nation. Although defeated by fairly sharp practice, Blaine, with the discipline of his calling, soon joined with his rivals Morton and Conkling in stumping the country against the menace of the "rebel" power.

VIII

The revival of the party of the Outs by 1876 in a nation-wide sense was virtually foreordained. With most of the Republican chieftains, of both the Blaine Half-Breed and the Stalwart factions, now widely discredited, and the old leadership all but restored in the South, it was generally assumed by experts that the old-time opposition party could scarcely be prevented from winning the national Administration. As we have seen, in the person of Governor Samuel J. Tilden, sixty-two years of age, a figure out of the Van Buren epoch in New York, the Democrats had found a Northern leader who worked effectively to fuse their inchoate party into a militant unit.

This learned corporation lawyer of weak health and subtle, diffident manners, who liked good living, with books, fine wines, and men of letters as his favorite companions, possessed a mighty fortune, most of it quickly acquired during the Civil War by methods which were coldly astute rather than prepossessing. Before he had become known as the Great Reformer, he had sometimes been hailed also as the "Great Forecloser." [70] He had been the preferred adviser of great railroads and their owners, Gould, Jim Fisk, and William Tweed. In forty years he had attained an uncanny knowledge of political craft, and moving quietly through caucus meetings and cloakrooms, came to be credited with exercising a "most subtle and mysterious influence" over the affairs of the whole State.

He, who had his pockets picked by the Tweed men, had turned

upon them at last, as some observers held, when he knew "by signs in the sky that the storm, which would *not* 'blow over,' was getting ready to break." [71] In the upheavals of 1871-72, the New York Democrats had been purged and defeated, to Roscoe Conkling's profit—but Tilden, who had overthrown his party, "had not fallen, Samson-like, under the ruins." [72] Rallying the dissenting factions of the New York Democracy into a great reform Organization of his own, during a season of depression and rampant discontent, he had raised the cry of "Turn the rascals out!" swept Conkling's Republican machine out of office, and had himself elected Governor with what was then an unheard-of plurality of 50,000 votes.

Tilden had appealed successfully to the "sober middle class"; he had also among his supporters new capable political lieutenants, such as his chief aide, Daniel Manning of Albany, newspaper proprietor, banker, and city boss; also Abram S. Hewitt, the cultivated iron-master, who was son-in-law of the famous Peter Cooper; and divers ambitious young lawyers in search of a career, such as Charles S. Fairchild and William C. Whitney, who had worked brilliantly in the Tweed Ring prosecution. Finally, Tilden gathered to his side a chastened Tammany Hall, now headed by Honest John Kelly, but boasting still its large proletarian following and its vote-gathering machine. These diverse elements, combined under the banner of Reform, Tilden, once in possession of State office, managed to satisfy and hold in leash according to the time-honored formula of patronage distribution.

Samuel Tilden must be credited with having established the modern pattern of reform as fixing governmental economy—rather than any change in the social status—as its goal.

During 1875 he completed his secret studies of the New York State Canal Ring, which had looted many millions in public funds by manipulation of public-works contracts. Arrests, indictments, and suits for restitution were vigorously carried out; and these new exploits in "saving the taxpayers," added to the earlier ones, aroused the highest pecuniary enthusiasm in thrifty middle-class breasts throughout the Eastern States. Thus Samuel Tilden, who was suspected of "a willingness to purchase reform at any price," became the embodiment of bourgeois administrative virtue, and rode easily at the crest of the opposition tide mounting throughout the country after the Crédit Mobilier and Whisky Ring scandals.*

In each capitalist democracy, as Friedrich Engels has noted, though the rulership is held by capitalists predominantly, divisions arise among powerful rival groups, divisions determined by their special material interests. Thus in America finance capitalists, with notable exceptions, such as the lately fallen Jay Cooke (who had gone beyond his depths into politics), were cooler toward the Republicans than "protected" industrial capitalists. These men, like the great lay Democrat Belmont, were suspicious of Republican demagogy on the Burning Issue of specie resumption; the gold standard could never be attained quickly enough to please them. Still another aggrieved faction among rich capitalists—and with good reason!—were the *importing* merchants, or processors. They suffered deep injury, as they believed firmly, under the protective tariff. Abram Hewitt, for instance, who entered the House of Representatives in the 1874 Tidal Wave, had long felt that the famous iron mills of Cooper & Hewitt, located on the eastern seaboard at Trenton, New Jersey, could not compete much longer with the rising mills of Pittsburgh and Ohio beyond the Alleghenies unless coal and iron ore could be imported cheaply and free of duty.† To the tariff, with its system of special privilege, was also widely attributed much of the current bureaucratic plundering.

On the score of civil-service corruption and waste a farsighted group of capitalists—a minority, to be sure—were now fully resolved to bring to an end the notorious spoils system. The ill fame of the Tweed Ring and the whisky conspirators had spread as far abroad as countinghouses in Hamburg and Frankfort and Amsterdam, where bankers who were invited to finance American enterprises showed sometimes an absurd alarm at the dangers which public plunderers

---

* *Cf.* Alexander, *Political History of New York State*, Vol. III, pp. 340, 341 ff. Alexander notes contemporary reports that Tilden's policy of pardoning criminals was considered excessive. Nine confessed criminals would be set at large so that evidence against a tenth might be conclusive—this in the Tweed Ring case, as in the Canal Ring case.

† *Cf.* Nevins, *Abram S. Hewitt*, pp. 261-63. The biographer does not notice the reflections of Hewitt's trade position upon his "liberalism."

offered to business in the great republic of the West. In their correspondence with American agents and promoters, they dwelt upon the *sauber* bureaucracy founded under Bismarck, and exhibited such fright at tales of ruined railroads and revenue scandals that capital flotations for some seasons actually became difficult here.

Hewitt, by his intelligence and wealth, quickly assumed a post of leadership in Congress, and in 1876 made a vigorous statement of the Democracy's renovated ideology:

The spirit abroad is the spirit of reformation. The people are determined to bring back that better era of the republic in which, when men consecrated themselves to the public service, they utterly abnegated all selfish purposes . . . when Franklin with his modest income and uncourtly costume . . . was held in more honor than the proudest ambassador of the proudest empire . . . when members of the Cabinet were selected because they were statesmen, "honest, faithful, capable," and not because of their skill in managing party politics; when to be summoned into the public service was a priceless honor and not an opportunity for private gain.[73]

But beyond the Northern capitalist groups who gave increasing adherence to the reviving Democratic Party, there were other, diverse components. In the agricultural Middle West remnants of the old Jacksonian Democrats, under leaders such as Hendricks, Voorhees, and Thurman, who preached the blessings of paper money, summoned new strength during the Hard Times. In the South the old white plantation aristocracy, who gathered again the reins of regional power, as agriculturists, stood also some distance from their Northern brethren in the party which sought Hard Money. Finally, in the great city machines, where the poorer laborers and proletarians and recent immigrants flocked to the Democratic standard usually—in Cincinnati as in New York—there was a numerous element and its characteristic leadership which recked little of civil-service reform and economy. These four diverse classes, whose lines conflicted so sharply, must be welded together if the old Democratic Party after nearly twenty years of defeat was to make a bid for power against the ruling Republicans as an efficient rival concern. In truth, the Southern and Western wings of the party had no love for Mr. Tilden and his ways; but their gnawing hunger for Federal office led them to suppress their doubts and defer to his leadership.

During the Hard Times after 1873, Tilden called for a return to old principles of democracy and "limited" constitutional government; he championed again the doctrine of States' Rights as against centralization, to which, in its oppression of local and individual liberties, he plausibly attributed the ills besetting the nation. "What the country needs now," he said, "is a revival of Jeffersonian democracy, with the principles of government and . . . the high standards of official morality which were established by the political revolution of 1800." And, alluding to the old struggle between the Federalists and the Jeffersonian party:

The demoralization of war—*a spirit of gambling adventure, engendered by false systems of public finance; a grasping centralization absorbing all functions from the local authorities, and assuming to control the industries of individuals by largesses to favored classes from the public treasury of money* wrung from the body of the people by taxation—were then, as now, characteristic of the period.[74]

Tilden, who had been something of a Harpagon, and who had used his individual rights with noted ruthlessness, managed to appeal at the same time to two different classes: to the equality-loving masses, and to the more prominent persons injured by the "grasping centralization" of political adventurers pursuing a "false system of public finance." Little wonder that the man who made such skillful appeals to diverse groups, and who promptly received the presidential nomination at the hands of a united and fortified Democracy, aroused Republican managers to a pitch of desperate fear.

The tide of discontent in the great plebiscite of 1876 was already running strongly to the Outs, and foreshadowed an inevitable cyclical change of parties within our biparty institution. The Outs were clearly now under the more conservative and responsible leadership, and offered once more a most convenient check upon the power arrogance of the Ins, who, long debauched by the fleshpots of office, had forgotten their higher duties. Rutherford Hayes predicted in Oct. 12, 1875, in his diary: "Defeat in the next Presidential election is almost a certainty." [75]

Between the two parties, as usual, no clear social issues were raised. The platform of the Democrats, written by the journalist Manton Marble of the New York *World*, was a magnificent literary invocation to civil-service reform; whereas the Republican promises, though having a forthright sound, seemed only a little more vague. Hence Rutherford Hayes, who with John Sherman and Garfield stemmed from the moderate Ohio wing of his party, had added to it more positive expressions in his letter of acceptance of the nomination. The spoils system, which had flourished for more than forty years, Hayes said, "ought to be abolished. The reform should be thorough, radical and complete. We should return to the principles and practices of the founders." He too!

The Dark Horse from Ohio, himself a man of inherited fortune in railroad securities, showed an interest in "clean bureaucracy" no less devoted than Tilden's. A Puritan by nature, brief-spoken, stubbornly honest in the manner of the old-fashioned middle class, Rutherford Hayes had become the compromise choice of the dissentious and desperately frightened party Organization. Through his voice the Republicans promised, it was observed, a "better and much more substantial civil reform than the Democrats." On this score claims were neutralized, as upon the muffled but deeply felt tariff and money questions. Each party accused its opponent of cowardice in such controversial matters—and both were right, it has been said.

But though the outspoken tone of Hayes on the matter of civil-service reform troubled the minds of professionals, hope was roused in Republican breasts by the reappearance of the battle-scarred old chief of spoilsmen, Zach Chandler, as chairman of the Republican National Committee. "Just think of a Civil Service Reform party making Zach Chandler chairman of the Executive Committee!" exclaimed Godkin of the *Nation*. Chandler and his experts now left no stone unturned to ensure the victory of reform after the Republican pattern; all corporate allies, recipients of land grants and railroad charters, were promptly levied upon. Although political assessments had been officially forbidden, Chandler's circulars soliciting "voluntary" contributions for the "laudable purpose of maintaining the organization of the Republican Party," went out to all officeholders receiving more than $1,000 a year. In the State Organizations of the party, such as that of Pennsylvania, the circulars ran:

Our books show that you have paid no heed to either of the requests of the committee for funds . . . we look to you as one of the Federal beneficiaries to help bear the burden. Two per cent of your salary is ——. Please remit promptly.

At the close of the campaign we shall place a list of those who have not paid in the hands of the head of the department you are in.[76]

Mr. Tilden was feared by his opponents as "a wonderful organizer and manipulator," having large wealth and being utterly unscrupulous in its use.[77] From his library, which he seldom left even to address his followers, he wrought in silence and secrecy throughout the tense campaign. His elaborate vote-catching organization was believed by those who did not know him better to be provisioned out of Tilden's own "barrel," containing upwards of $10,000,000. In any case a prolific literature relating in detail all the evils of the Grant regime was steadily sown about the country.

Moral denunciation alone did not frighten the veteran Republican managers overmuch; but the real scarcity of cash in these lean times hurt. Where were the Whisky Ring men, who at emergencies in the past came forward so generously to "turn" close election districts? Alas, McDonald and his mates sat in the penitentiary. In August Oliver Morton hurried to see Governor Hayes, and warned him that Indiana was all but lost. The remedy? *"Money and speakers.* Money to pay men to travel and organize—to print and circulate documents." Asked by Hayes how much would be needed, he replied that it would be twice as much as in 1872: "one thousand dollars to a county will do it, or ninety-four counties, one hundred thousand dollars." [78]

But presumably the money was not raised. In its October elections Indiana, with its Favorite Son, Hendricks, standing as Tilden's running mate, went Democratic; and the tension among Republican officeholders everywhere grew maddening. It was now that the Minor Cabinet, described for us by Blaine, moved into action. A new plunder ring, this time quietly working in the United States Post Office system instead of the Treasury Department, assumes a leading part in the emergency, as a new suborganization within the party, headed by

Senator Stephen Dorsey, a Carpetbagger from Arkansas, and Thomas Brady, the Second Assistant Postmaster General. Commanding un-limited funds, the Post Office Ring and its agents set to work in co-operation with leading party managers, such as Chester A. Arthur, Collector of the New York Custom House, to carry strategic States, especially those which might still be held in the South.[79]

Rutherford B. Hayes and his most active lieutenant, John Sher-man, have been pictured as worthy and prudent characters among the Republican politicians of their era. Yet even the mild Hayes in his private writings reveals a strain of the Know-Nothing spirit which many Middle Western Republicans inherited from the 1850's. He suggests a smug conviction that Republican social order meant rule by the "better element" of prosperous farmers and patriotic former soldiers; a notion which James Bryce found prevalent still in the 1890's. Hayes's third gubernatorial campaign in Ohio, in 1875, had in fact turned frankly upon the animus against Catholics and immi-grants. "It is owing to emigration West," he writes with anxiety, "that Ohio and Indiana are not Republican. Catholics are taking the places of Republican farmers and soldiers." [80] For this civil-service reformer too, in the last resort, all means to win, even terror and force, might be justified by a little accommodation of the puritanical conscience hidden by his curtain whiskers.

The underlying issues of the campaign were Hard Times and the money question. Hayes and his chief adviser, Sherman, though bent upon currency contraction and early resumption of specie payment, took strenuous measures to ignore such questions, tactics in which the conservative Tilden imitated them.

To conceal this end, the cue which had been given by Blaine in his January Bloody Shirt speech was to be followed as a means of beclouding issues. This much Hayes indicated clearly in a letter to Blaine, September 14, 1876, when he commented upon the fearful strength which the Greenback "heresy" had assumed in the States of the Mississippi Valley, where most people hoped that the party of the Outs, despite its silence on the question, would "do something" for them now. It was imperative to kindle again sectional fear and hatred, terror of disorder and rebellion. "Our strong ground," Hayes wrote Blaine, "is the dread of a solid South, *rebel rule*, etc., etc. I hope you will make these topics prominent in your speeches. *It leads people away from 'hard times,' which is our deadliest foe.*" [81]

The Republican stump orators Blaine, Morton, Conkling, and above all the stentorian Ingersoll now outdid one another in sounding all the notes of a fanatical patriotism which might effectively "lead people away from 'hard times.'" The slogans of Ingersoll were in keeping with the grand design:

> Every man that endeavored to tear the old flag from the heaven that it enriches was a Democrat. Every man that tried to destroy this nation was a Democrat. . . . The man that assassinated Abraham Lincoln was a Democrat. . . . Soldiers, every scar you have on your heroic bodies was given you by a Democrat. [82]

Union ballots must still preserve the work done by Union bayonets, as Oliver Morton held. The cry of the Bloody Shirt, ever louder and wilder, was raised against the Democrats who cried scandal. New York, Indiana, Ohio, important sections of the North, might be lost. But in the last-hour struggles to hold the remaining Carpetbag strongholds in the South—where the naked bayonet alone might decide the outcome of the national election—the war party's violent slogans gave a deeply needed sanction for even military force.

On October 17, 1876, following riots in South Carolina, President Grant answered the call of the Republican Governor Chamberlain with a proclamation of insurrection and the dispatch of Federal troops. Thus two weeks before Election Day, some thirty-three companies, nearly the whole defense force for the Atlantic seaboard, were rushed into South Carolina. The United States Marshals and soldiers who thereupon oversaw the election returns acted, of course, as armed *political partisans*, in South Carolina, as in Florida and Louisiana;

> the soldiers . . . who are now making arrests for "intimidation" in South Carolina, and who are to preserve order at the polls on election day, are really an armed force in the service, and acting under the orders of, one of the parties to the political contest. [83]

In Indiana the independent Republican Judge Walter Gresham wrote to a friend on the eve of the elections, October 24, 1876, to voice his anger at the use "of bayonets in connection with the election . . . a dangerous thing. I am afraid of such precedents. How long will it be before the same thing is resorted to in the North!" Would not Hayes be "counted in," he wondered.[84] The "working" Republicans, as the *Nation* observed later, from Zach Chandler down, had the use of the army and the navy, "either for physical interference or moral influence on their side." [85] A majority of the voters, over 4,200,000 in all, might vote for Reform and Tilden, but could he be installed in office in the face of such overwhelming force, whose open use the whole propaganda of terror, the treacherous alarm of a "new rebellion," had plainly prepared?

CHAPTER SIX

DEFENSE OF THE SPOILS SYSTEM

Parties are not built up by deportment, or by ladies'
magazines, or gush! ROSCOE CONKLING

ON March 4, 1877, Rutherford B. Hayes was sworn in and installed as the nineteenth President of the United States. To accomplish this result had been no easy task for the Republican Organization. As to the electoral battle itself, we must award the palm to the Republicans for sheer cheek and coolness under fire. During the three months' interregnum that followed the election, the Constitution, the government apparatus, public opinion, and business confidence had labored under acute strain, while none knew certainly who was to be the new Chief Magistrate. And in the closing phases of this strange post-electoral dispute the unity of the Republican Organization itself had shown signs of breaking, a development which was an evil omen for the future.

Most historians who have discussed the crisis of 1876-77 have, with Rhodes, applauded the extraordinary calm with which the masses of people accepted the settlement of the disputed election, "effected peaceably and according to due process of law under conditions, which, in nearly every other country, must inevitably have led to civil war." [1] An inherent vagueness in the American Constitution, the multiplicity of governmental authorities it revealed, again sorely tried the patience of the citizen. Yet the American people as a whole showed a moderation in action, a reverence for law, which, as Walter Bagehot commented at the time, offered singular contrast to the statesmen's violence of speech. What has not been commented upon sufficiently is the real indifference that gripped the mass of people as to the final outcome. This points to their instinctive understanding that it was but a contest between two great patronage parties neither of which broached the deeper issues of the time; hence those who had risen to arms in 1861 were now perplexed, but pacific. Those Southern politicians who talked most menacingly in public showed themselves in private, however, alert for compromise at the last—for a consideration.

The tortuous solution of the Hayes-Tilden election, for whose sake both parties abandoned mere scruples, was indeed a travesty upon representative, constitutional government. It is true also, as was often said, that Mr. Tilden should have been declared President according to the rules of the game, but was overreached by superior skulduggery on the part of his opponents. It does not appear likely, however, that the country was "near to civil war." What is most striking after longer reflection upon this colossal political comedy is the similarity of motives and methods in both of the great political "cartels" and their common material interests—which led to a peaceful settlement and bargain. Nay, in the last hours, though the leaders might beat their breasts in public and swear in the name of eternal principles and sacred covenants their unyielding resistance, they virtually competed with each other in seeking to lose rather than to win!

Early on the night of November 7, 1876, it was known that the party of the Outs had carried by a clear margin four important Northern States: New York, New Jersey, Connecticut, and Indiana. With almost all of the Solid South now counted as Democratic, the commander in chief of the Republican armies, Zach Chandler himself, had at last gone to bed wearily at his headquarters in the Fifth Avenue Hotel, New York, giving up his cause for lost. On the morning of the eighth (as for several days thereafter) nearly all the press conceded the election of Mr. Tilden; though the Republican New York *Times*, in a late city edition of November 8, contended that "the result . . . is still in doubt." Thus far its tabulation of electoral votes showed 184 for Tilden and 181 for Hayes, this counting South Carolina and Louisiana as Republican. But Florida had not been heard from. "If the Republicans have carried that state as they claim, they will have 185 votes—a majority of one."

In the early morning hours of November 8 something further had happened that aroused the sinking hopes of Republicans. From Democratic State Headquarters in New York, Senator William A. Barnum of Connecticut had sent an artless inquiry to the office of the New York *Times* for last-minute news concerning the elections in

South Carolina, Florida, and Louisiana. One of the editors, a certain John C. Reid, had therefore come swiftly to the surmise that the Democrats were still doubtful of these States, and had as quickly calculated that if they could only be held for Hayes, then all was not yet lost. He rushed at once to Republican National Headquarters, where he encountered W. E. ("Bill") Chandler, the veteran campaign paymaster, just returned from a field trip, "a small man wearing an immense pair of goggles, his hat drawn down over his ears, a greatcoat with a heavy military cloak, and carrying a gripsack . . . in his hand." [2] Reid, an intense partisan, relates that he informed Chandler of his suspicions, and urged that the Republicans should "keep their heads up." Together they had rushed to rouse the big, fat Zach Chandler, asleep in his hotel room above.

What followed tells us much of the force of the Republican Party Organization as a militant institution, resembling certain church orders at this moment rather than a political party. Though the field marshal himself was in his nightshirt, rubbing sleep from his eyes, he quickly grasped the possibility of saving the day. At once telegrams shot forth to lieutenants in the field, to Carpetbag bosses in the disputed States:

Hayes is elected if we have carried South Carolina, Florida, and Louisiana. Can you hold your State? Answer immediately! [3]

The warnings to "beware of fraud" and to "hold" their States meant only too clearly that they must *withhold returns*. To the party's agents in Florida went the further message:

The election of Hayes depends on Florida. W. E. Chandler has gone to Florida to see you with full powers to act and make terms. You can put a man in the Cabinet or elsewhere if you choose to demand it. Do so and get a friend where he can help you. Don't be modest. Agree to carry the State through the three counts and you have your own terms in your hands. [4]

Bill Chandler, expert distributor of party funds, had departed at once for Florida, authorized by Zach to do "whatever he thought necessary."

While days passed and no President was yet decided upon, the

Republican leaders now made confident predictions of victory. The party's Inner Circle, meanwhile, moved swiftly in accordance with a concerted plan. A credit was opened in a Philadelphia bank. Following William Chandler, Department of Justice detectives went to Tallahassee, Florida; then, by November 9, 1876, came Thomas Brady, the Second Assistant Postmaster General (and head of a newly formed plunder ring), with a force of special agents of the Post Office Department, bearing cash with which to "hold" Florida. Other trusted agents directed themselves toward Columbia, South Carolina.[5]

All through November Bill Chandler sent repeated telegrams in cipher for money and help. On the thirteenth he wired: "Have Arthur [head of the New York Custom House] send Republicans acting with Democrats." On the fifteenth: "Florida needs eminent counsel and help. Can you send $3,000 and $2,000, making $5,000? Danger great here." [6] Then soon afterward he reports cheerfully: "The mails are unsafe as well as the telegraph, and I don't want to write about the election here—*we shall be all right*." [7]

In South Carolina a very heavy force of Federal soldiers had been kept on hand, and an adequate one also in Florida. Through General Sherman, Grant sent on November 10 further orders that the armed forces should be vigilant to "preserve peace and good order, and to see that the proper and legal Boards of Canvassers are unmolested in the performance of their duties." [8] The Republican agencies busied themselves at the holy work of checking up on the White Leagues and the Ku Klux Klan, who invariably intimidated and "bulldozed" Negro Republicans. In both these States, where military protection had been effective, returns seemed close, and it was possible quickly to repudiate enough ballots to reverse small Democratic majorities.

But in turbulent Louisiana the problem was more difficult; a Tilden majority of almost 9,000 out of some 207,000 votes, an excess of well-nigh 10 per cent of the Democratic ballots, must be overturned by the canvassing board. Louisiana was to be the ground of final battle. But the devoted Republicans did not flinch at this task.

On November 10, following the first swift measures in Florida and South Carolina, President Grant invited a number of prominent Republicans to go as "visiting statesmen" to observe the canvass of the votes. Hewitt, chairman of the National Democratic Committee, thereupon asked a similar delegation of prominent Democrats to go to New Orleans to watch the Republican statesmen. In the Republican delegation John Sherman and Stanley Matthews of Ohio were understood to represent Hayes directly; these, with Garfield, who was also present, started with the assumption that except for intimidation the State "would have been carried for Hayes by the Negro vote." Republican agents not only opened and examined the returns from each parish, but at once also entered into delicate negotiations with the Carpetbag officials who still ruled there. This is shown by their communication to John Sherman, as follows:

New Orleans, La.
November 20, 1876

Sir:

We have carefully considered the arguments advanced by you in our interview. Your assurance that we shall be taken care of is scarcely specific enough. In case we pursue the course suggested by you we would be obliged to leave the State. Will you therefore state in writing who we shall look to for the fulfillment of these promises.

Respectfully,
D. A. WEBER,
JAMES E. ANDERSON [9]

To which Sherman made reply that neither Hayes nor himself, nor the country at large, could ever forget their services, should they "stand firm." He felt justified "in assuming responsibility for promises made," and guaranteed that the two gentlemen would be provided for "as soon after the Fourth of March as may be practicable, and in such manner as to enable you both to leave Louisiana should you deem it necessary." [10] Supported by the Republican "visiting statesmen," not to mention regiments of Federal soldiers, the Louisiana Returning Board proceeded to accept the testimony of perjurers, thieves, and prostitutes, and to throw out the ballots of whole parishes, until over 13,350 Democratic votes were canceled and a Hayes majority of over 4,000 was produced. [11] The great Republican raid upon the Southern provinces, which the two Chandlers had initiated, was finished by December 6, 1876. A fait accompli had been registered. An unquestioned defeat had been turned into a legally doubtful case, whose merits must thereafter be determined by a predominantly Republican Government.

The Democratic statesmen who had followed their rivals to New Orleans complained, protested, and delivered an opposing report. Wells, the Republican Carpetbagger who had supervised the Louisiana count, had then kindly offered Louisiana to the Democrats for a consideration of $200,000.[12] The favorable certificate of the State of Florida had likewise been offered for a sum of $200,000, which, as Tilden remarked, "seemed to be standard." But according to numerous accounts, the Democratic managers and agents moved too slowly, or even bargained for cheaper offers of as low as $30,000 for the electoral votes of a single State—which would have delivered the Presidency. A subsequent congressional investigation of Democratic cipher telegrams wrung confessions from Colonel Pelton, Tilden's nephew, that he had engaged in "dalliance" with members of the Returning Boards, though it was merely "to bribe men to do their lawful duty." While the competition between both sides had been sharp, the Democrats were continually inept and behindhand, or even stingy, the money in some cases arriving definitely too late.[13]

In early December, from each of the three disputed Southern States there arrived opposing certificates of the electoral vote, one Democratic, the other Republican. The pious Rutherford Hayes was convinced by John Sherman, a fanatical partisan, that only white "bulldozing" had deprived him of a clear majority in the first place. His own supporters had completely outmaneuvered the enemy in the first phase of the strange post-election struggle. Moreover, widespread reports in the press during December referred to Democratic attempts to purchase the Presidency—a transaction considered easily within Mr. Tilden's great means.

The second phase of the contest was a constitutional or legal struggle at Washington. The lower house, with a Democratic majority, sought to follow rules and interpretations which would have raised Tilden to the White House; the Senate, with a Republican majority, sought to further Hayes's candidacy. The Constitution provided that the president of the Senate must read the certificates of electoral votes by States, and "the votes shall then be counted." But by whom should they be counted if there were two sets of returns? By a joint rule, since 1865 either House alone could repudiate a State ballot that was believed questionable. But the Senate on December 8 had hastily declared that the joint rules were no longer in force.

For almost seven weeks the contest was deadlocked in Washington, the country waiting with growing uneasiness while politicians maneuvered or engaged in stupefying constitutional debates. The Republicans, with Garfield their spokesman, now showed themselves champions of States' Rights, holding the local returns sacred (!), while the Democrats asserted the power of the National Government to "go behind" the (falsely) authenticated returns. The leaders on both sides, searching for a formula of compromise, amid interminable wrangling finally shaped an Electoral Count Bill in January, 1877. This provided for a tribunal or commission of fifteen, composed of five Representatives, five Senators—their total number evenly divided between the parties—and five Justices of the Supreme Court, the fifth Justice to be the Independent, David Davis of Illinois, while the four other Justices were understood to be divided evenly in their partisan connections. These were to judge finally of disputed returns, where the two houses of Congress disagreed. The Republicans had feared this solution, Sherman and Morton opposing it bitterly as favoring a Democratic victory of 8 to 7, because of their apprehension of Justice Davis's views. Suddenly on January 25, 1877, agreement on the Electoral Count Bill was reached.

The intervention of Roscoe Conkling at this stage was most curious. A relentless partisan in politics all his life, he now acted in late January to aid the Democratic cause by urging acceptance of Justice Davis and the Electoral Count Bill as a magnanimous solution which averted the danger of civil war. "He who ruleth his own spirit is greater than he who taketh a city," he cried in an excess of disinterested patriotism. It was the Democrats' turn to be jubilant—until the following day, when news came that Justice Davis had determined to resign from the Supreme Court and accept the Senatorship for Illinois, offered to him after a long contest in that State. The sudden defection of Davis, who plainly had dreaded the responsibility thrust upon him, overturned all the nicely balanced plans for the Electoral

Count Commission of fifteen, whose personnel had been arrived at through the most intense scrutiny by both parties. The fifteenth, the deciding commissioner, must now again be chosen from the Supreme Court bench, according to the terms of the bill. The choice fell inevitably upon Justice Bradley, a Republican appointee, and according to his known record far less likely to be disinterested than Davis.

Rage and dismay now overcame the Democrats at this unexpected turn of the wheel. Then partisan excitement rose to new crescendos when rumors spread that Roscoe Conkling, acting in collaboration with the Tilden managers, would lead a revolt against his party, switching enough votes in the evenly divided Congress to offset the final Republican advantage.

In Conkling, at this trying crisis, the elements and motives were mixed. The lifetime habit of party loyalty was suddenly wrenched by the realization that with Hayes's election, the rival Half-Breed faction would be dominant, and the promised civil-service reform to which Hayes was irrevocably committed would be as death to his machine and to his own political fortune. His New York State Organization had behaved most sluggishly in the recent campaign, as if convinced that it could survive a salutary defeat at the hands of its opponents far better than a poisonous reform at the hands of its friends. Undoubtedly as a piece of wishful thinking, Conkling had asserted openly his belief that Tilden was legally elected.

Yet in the end, the party suppressed the threatened Conkling revolt, and what seemed the last, unexpected obstacle was hurdled.*

For the Democrats all seemed lost as the Electoral Commission voted mechanically 8 to 7 in favor of Hayes upon the question of the disputed Florida and Louisiana returns. A glimmer of a chance still lay, however, in filibustering, in parliamentary obstruction. As the vote upon the ballots, State by State, prolonged itself in Congress up to the last days of February, it became more and more certain

---

* One of the melodramatic legends of the time holds that the lovely Kate Chase Sprague used all her wiles to persuade him to remain faithful in his Republicanism. Her own motives were felt to be those of personal vengeance. Mr. Tilden, eight years before, had thwarted the movement at the Democratic convention to nominate her father, Chief Justice Chase, for the Presidency. *Cf.* McClure, *Our Presidents and How We Make Them,* pp. 268-69.

that no President could possibly be named before March 4. What would happen then? Moods of panic swept over the politicians, as over the money markets, while reports were heard of men drilling and armies of 100,000 raised overnight by long-haired journalists such as Marse Henry Watterson for a march upon Washington.

In these last grave hours an irresistible fellow feeling brought the leaders of both parties—who still publicly challenged and dueled with each other in Congress—to explore together, in secret, the possibilities of a final bargain.

And meanwhile what of Samuel Tilden, potent leader of the opposition party, sustained in his claims by some 4,300,000 voters, 250,000 more than Hayes had mustered? Would he press on to the brink of a revolution for the sake of his often announced and cherished principles, which demanded the freeing of individual enterprise from a "grasping centralization"? Intimate pictures of him at this juncture by John Bigelow, his friend and aide, and in the private journal of Abram Hewitt, his lieutenant, show the leader to be a worn invalid, indecisive, brooding. He secluded himself, and maintained a painful silence, giving no clear intimation to his managers, certainly not to Hewitt, as to what his real wishes were. He could have called forth powerful demonstrations from his followers by a clear message; he could have carried on a resolute obstruction, which according to Blaine's statement would have forced the Republicans to retreat.[14] Instead, "Mr. Tilden devoted himself more than a month to the preparation of a complete history of the electoral counts" from the earliest days of the republic, in a half-hearted attempt to clarify the issues of the time, so his biographer, Bigelow, relates. Privately, with a curious fatalism, he expressed the conviction that the Republicans, President and army behind them, would never permit a fair settlement, and would "count in" Mr. Hayes. He advised procrastination, then finally yielded to the appeals of Hewitt, Bayard, Thurman, and other Democratic leaders for the Electoral Count Bill, as a settlement that would at least relieve the anxieties of "the suffering business classes." For what did Mr. Tilden, who had opposed the War between the States, want with a revolution? Did he not also perhaps reflect, as Mr. Hewitt, the ironmaster, remarked, that the passage of the Electoral Count Bill alone was "worth five hundred millions" to the country's business?

Much has been made also of Mr. Tilden's "patriotism" and "noble self-abnegation." But Hewitt, one of the chief participants in the great constitutional comedy of 1876-77, has left us in passages of his journal an idea of more explicit interests involved:

> To violence of any kind Mr. Tilden was by nature strongly opposed . . . his intimate connection with many great industrial and corporate enterprises would naturally lead him to a conservative course of action.[15]

The firebrand Watterson also understood this conservatism in Tilden and in Abram Hewitt, whom he pictured "with one hand upon his heart and the other hand in his pocket" declaiming: "I would prefer four years of Hayes's administration to four years of civil war." For, as between the opposing pretensions of each of these conservative gentlemen, Tilden and Hayes, and their parties, industry was halting, capital was idle, labor was unemployed, the country's affairs were paralyzed. "Make an end! Raffle for it!" was the sensible demand that came from property-holders of both parties. Garfield wrote to Hayes:

> The Democratic business men of the country are more anxious for quiet than for Tilden. The leading Southern Democrats . . . are saying that they have seen war enough and do not care to follow the lead of their Northern associates, who as Ben Hill says, "were invincible in peace and invisible in war." [16]

In the deadlock of late February, when filibustering seemed likely to stop the functioning of our lawful Government after March 4, the day was saved by the refusal of a large number of Southern Democrats to follow the lead of their angry Northern brothers. "If we are saved," Garfield commented in a letter of February 25, 1877, "it will be by the Southern rebels." [17]

On the following morning, February 26, 1877, at nine o'clock, Garfield was among the prominent Republicans who attended the historic secret conference in a room of Wormley's Hotel between leaders of the two parties, called by Judge Stanley Matthews, representing Hayes. "Matthews' talk led me to believe," Garfield relates, "that there had been former consultations and that a compact of some kind was meditated." [18] From the veiled words of Abram Hewitt's diary as well, we perceive that the Democrats had at last agreed to cease their obstruction to the formal completion of the electoral count, and abandoned all claims to the Presidency. For their part of the bargain the Republican spokesmen promised on behalf of the new President that the Federal troops which enforced the constitutional Amendment giving Negroes the full rights of citizens would be removed from the South. Thus the legal ground on which the Republican claim to office rested was abandoned, since the Carpet-bag governments in Louisiana, Florida, and South Carolina must immediately give way to those of regular Democrats and former rebels.

The Republican Party turned back to their masters the former slaves whom they had pretended to liberate—though at every stage all concrete measures to this end, the distribution of land and tools and capital, had been systematically avoided. All pretended adherence to the great emancipation principles of Lincoln and Sumner—the whole ideology of universal human rights which had been the declared goal of postwar Reconstruction, and the issue between the two parties—was now forfeited by the Republicans. The hour had come at last when the Republicans and their Northern capitalist allies no longer needed to "use" the freed Negro as a pretext, or as an ally, for the forcible control of the political government.

The "gentlemen's agreement" secretly transacted between Hewitt, Lamar, Watterson, and Randall for the Democrats and Matthews, Sherman, Garfield, and others for the Republicans at Wormley's Hotel, restored "home rule" to the Southern ruling class, and permitted the peaceable inauguration of the Republican President six days later. A few days passed, and a sudden, strange, political migration was seen. The last of the Republican Scalawags were in full flight from Southern cities; virtually all of the members of the Louisiana Returning Board arriving hurriedly in Washington, where they settled down in the offices of the new, reformed Government that President Hayes and Secretary of the Treasury John Sherman were erecting.[19] *

* "All the members of the Louisiana Returning Board received lucrative offices mainly from the United States Treasury Department." The *Potter Committee*

II

President Rutherford B. Hayes approximated what the French would call *un brave bourgeois*—an honest citizen. Even more God-fearing than John Sherman, his fellow statesman from Ohio, he held that the Republican Party "must mend its ways," but at the same time exhibited a devotion to "Republican principles" that shines with a beautiful self-righteousness in the many pages of his long diaries. He had sanctioned Sherman's devious operations in Louisiana as, after all, so much "holy work" done in the name of Republican orthodoxy, justified by many rebel "atrocities" against Negro rights and constitutional law. He had thereafter even furnished money from his own pocket for the legal defense of one of the members of the Louisiana Returning Board, and tolerated the transfer of this gentleman and his brethren from Louisiana to safe berths in Federal department offices. Then, by a presidential order of April 10, 1877, he removed the regiments of soldiers from Columbia, South Carolina, and from Louisiana, thus honestly fulfilling the secret pledge given by his friends at Wormley's Hotel, and ending the anomaly of dual governments in those States.

To men such as Conkling, Morton, and Zach Chandler, who headed the opposing wing of the party, this decree was a bitter draught, and, as Conkling reminded all men, it served to remove the very legal ground for Hayes's election to the Presidency. Oliver Morton, expiring of his last fatal illness, was to pass from the scene this year, 1877, bearing his secrets with him. Zach Chandler, too, another of the famous wartime Republicans, had not long to live. The news that President Hayes was appointing Independents and reformers—and, worst of all, Carl Schurz, to his own post of Secretary of the Interior—filled his cup of bitterness to the full and helped to destroy his health. He cried aloud at the ingratitude of the man for whose elevation to office he had done more than anyone else, indeed more than could easily be explained. "Hayes has passed the Republican party to its worst enemies," he said.

Early in 1879, in the midst of a vituperative speech touching the

Report, p. 48, gave a voluminous list in 1879, Chairman Potter observing of Sherman: "We are all to believe in the right of what we earnestly desire."

bitter intraparty feud of the moment, the old spoilsman fell to the platform under a heart stroke. One might say that Zach Chandler died with a curse upon his lips for rebels and reformers alike.

"He serves his party best who serves his country best," Hayes had declared virtuously during the late campaign. With the planless Reconstruction of the South ended, and the Carpetbaggers retreating upon Washington, he wrote in his diary on April 22, 1877: "Now for Civil Service Reform." The honesty of Hayes had a quality of stubbornness that meant trouble, but possessed no glamour that called to public sympathy. He had embraced the views of Schurz, who believed with all the fervor of a fanatic that if only honest men could be appointed to public office all our political evils would be at an end. For such were the limits of the reform doctrines that flourished between 1870 and 1890. Hayes's Cabinet, with Sherman placed perforce in the all-important Treasury Department, William Evarts Secretary of State, Carl Schurz Secretary of the Interior, Wayne MacVeagh Attorney General, was the most brilliant and honest one since Lincoln's second term, its members conceived as the directors of an almost impartial bureaucracy. But such an allotment of the very sources of national patronage enraged, nay, drove to the verge of madness, the great Senator-bosses. Blaine had wanted a cabinet post for his henchman Frye of Maine; Simon Cameron had wished his son Donald continued in the War Department, where Grant had recently placed him; Logan had sought in vain a cabinet post for himself; and Roscoe Conkling demanded the Postmaster Generalship for his lieutenant Representative Thomas Platt, but had seen this bestowed upon David Key of Tennessee, a former Confederate soldier!

Soon Conkling never spoke of the President in public without a sneer, also referring to him as "His Fraudulency"; while his friend Dana in the New York *Sun* termed Hayes the "de facto President." It was no question of mere personal discontent for the Senator-bosses, but rather a matter of the very basis of existence of the professional Organizations which they headed. Hayes's reformist policy promised mortal blows to the whole system of party authority, and so there soon burst upon him a revolt, driven by all the wrath and hate of a faction among his own party's leaders. The tormenting effects of this internecine warfare, so little understood by an indifferent public at the time, are shown clearly enough in many a passage of Hayes's diary. The campaign of slander and intrigue Hayes was equipped to bear, thanks to his stolidity and self-righteousness. He replied seldom to attack; his acts veered from petty punishment of opponents to stubborn inaction and silence; thus he failed to arouse public interest in his policies, while steadily losing control of his party in Congress. The four brawling years of Hayes's Administration tell us of all the miseries that honesty and good intentions may precipitate in America's professional politics. To the danger of a Government without a President in 1877, there was soon added the embarrassment of a President without a party.

The most influential class in the community was now sorely divided upon the question of government reform. One faction more and more decidedly dreaded the evil example of Grant's harrowing Administration. A leading Western capitalist and political figure wrote to Sherman:

In the administration of the executive departments of the Government there are so many important reforms to be effected that it is needful that especial pains shall be taken in the selection of the President's constitutional advisers. They should all be men . . . free from all suspicion of . . . personal and partisan interests. . . . The plighted faith of the Government—the financial credit of the country, are all involved in it, for it is manifest that no permanent revival of business—no steady application of labor and capital can be hoped for until important reforms are effected, and an administration shall be organized on principles widely different from those which have governed the present one.[20]

Here was the view of sober, economical men, who had suffered not only from the wastefulness and open plundering of Whisky and Custom House rings, but from the vacillating, demagogic games of the statesmen as well. Yet on the other side, unspoken, vague, lay the equally deep convictions of powerful groups whose chances and purposes seemed as much favored by the very instability and vendibility of the political government. This was the heyday of violent conflicts among captains of industry and barons of railroads, as each struggled to eliminate his competitors from the spreading continental market for steel, or oil, or transportation. In this very year a furious railroad rate war broke out between the trunk lines that reached from New York to Chicago, as William, the son of Cornelius Vanderbilt, sought to destroy two great opponents. Nor did Tom Scott of the Pennsylvania Railroad, nor Collis Huntington, desist even now, amid so much public scandal, in their unremitting, secret duel for special privilege behind the very walls of Congress. Where force and chicane fought for such imperial prizes as immense railroad monopolies, none of the principals, defying society itself, considered for a moment submission to the authority of a strengthened or purified government bureaucracy. Instead they moved by habit and preference among the shadowed recesses of the spoils organizations, counting in the last resort, as did Gould, Scott, and Huntington, upon the constant availability of government favor, and their own skill and experience in purchasing it.

The outcome of this obscure competition between the advocates of permanent reform and the friends of a convenient "instability" in government administration was scarcely clear at this season, when President Hayes announced his first decrees of civil-service reform, May 26, 1877. In a letter to Secretary Sherman—who himself was striving secretly to placate certain of the Senator-bosses—Hayes declared that "the collection of the revenues should be free from partisan control, and organized on a strictly business basis . . . the party leaders should have no more influence in appointments than other equally respectable citizens." This statement of opinion was followed by an executive order of June 22, 1877:

No officers should be required or permitted to take part in the management of political organizations, caucuses, conventions, or electoral campaigns. Their right to vote or to express their views on public questions . . . is not denied, provided it does not interfere with the discharge of their official duties. No assessments for political purposes on officers . . . should be allowed. This rule is applicable to every department of the civil service.[21] It should be understood by every officer of the general Government that he is expected to conform his conduct to its requirements.

Hayes's announcement still had the nature of a mere expression of opinion. For Congress continued its sullen indifference to the whole business of reform.

At all events, Schurz now labored to establish the merit system in the Interior Department, while the thrifty John Sherman actually dismissed useless clerks from the government pay roll and, using information that Bristow had previously collected, took steps to investigate the offending customhouses, including the one at New York, fortress of the Conkling machine.

The Secretary of the Treasury was an intensely "practical" and conciliatory Ohio politician, whose measures would perhaps have been mild enough to raise no enemies against his own advancement; but in the Cabinet, as Secretary of State, sat William Evarts of New York, the brilliant corporation lawyer, with his bright gray eyes, his sharp nose, and his witty but too voluble tongue, urging on the President and forcing Sherman's hand. Evarts, who was no purist in politics, belonged nevertheless to the faction of New York capitalists who were burdened by the excesses of the Custom House Rings; he had formerly brought numerous petitions on behalf of merchants who had been victimized, and had come to represent the Independent or anti-Conkling minority of New York Republicans.

The customhouse which Chester Arthur and Alonzo Cornell presided over was most vulnerable. Though Collector Arthur was, oddly enough, given an opportunity by Sherman to advise as to the personnel of the commission that would investigate his department, the chairman thereof, John Jay of New York, showed himself reasonably independent; his report, though judicious, verified the widespread suspicions of bribery, underappraisals, and political assessment along the water front.[22] Factions of merchants and injured business interests, who with the general community suffered losses, were now loudly demanding that the customs department be run like "a commercial house," or, as the professional politicians termed it disgustedly, "*like a factory.*" At any rate, the Jay Commission's report, part of which was compiled in secret hearings, when handed to the President on May 24, 1877, led directly to his strong reform order of June 22.

Although Conkling's lieutenants, Collector Arthur and Naval

Officer Cornell, were not charged with dishonesty so much as with "laxity" and the direct use of their department for the management of political organizations, caucuses, and conventions, their removal by Hayes during the summer of 1877 seemed inevitable. Hints were conveyed to them that their resignations would be most welcome, but nothing happened. Apparently the Conkling Organization in New York was to bear the brunt of the reform movement at the outset, and this on the eve of an important New York State Republican Convention, at which a struggle for control was expected.

From Cornell and Arthur down to the humblest precinct captain of the army that bivouacked all over the State, all the New York Stalwarts understood now the desperation of their cause. All their power based itself on the operation of the patronage in Federal and State offices. The State had recently been lost to Tilden's Democratic reform Organization; were Federal patronage now lost in addition, the Republican machine would be an army without supplies. Thousands of trained "workers" who toiled for the canvass all year would become casualties; the following of the lieutenants, Cornell, Arthur, and Platt, would vanish; then Conkling himself would soon pass from the Senate. Leader and led clung together in their extremity. Would the "Oneida Chieftain" raise the banner of revolt within the party, among all the professional brethren who must be ruined by "reform"? As chairman of the State organization, Alonzo Cornell now openly defied President Hayes's order (that Federal officials were to refrain from party management) by formally calling the New York State Republican Convention to meet at Rochester on September 26, 1877. The whole country, and especially leaders of regional machines and myriads of professional politicians, watched for the signal from New York.

III

The great Senator returned at this moment from a brief European tour, receiving a most impressive and boisterous welcome, apparently from the whole metropolis—one of the first of the planned demonstrations for notables at New York Harbor—in which tugs and steamer whistles made jubilee in Conkling's honor. The object of his voyage, it was rumored, was a visit to Mrs. Kate Chase Sprague in Paris.[23] At once he went into conference with his lieutenants, who concluded with him that their case was truly desperate. The "axe is suspended" over the heads of Conkling's assistants, as if for "trading" purposes, Dana's New York *Sun* presumed; that is, suspended until it could be seen what course, loyal or rebellious, they would take at the impending party convention. But the Stalwarts now decided quickly that bargaining was out of the question. Concessions to the enemy would be a breach in the larger defenses. They were besieged in the strongholds where Conkling had ruled like a feudal monarch for seven years. From his office alone "the popular government of the Commonwealth of New York had been directed," as Elihu Root remarked in after years. Mayors, Congressmen, Senators, even Presidents had been named there. Retreat was impossible to his nature, as to his circumstances.

With a cool audacity worthy of other freebooting characters of the time, a Jim Fisk or a Commodore Vanderbilt, Conkling and his mates quickly made plans for the coming convention at Rochester that would discredit and defeat the reformers among them, who were backed by the national Administration. Throughout the State, ward captains and county leaders organized the naming of delegates to reduce or eliminate the "reformatory" element led by George William Curtis, the editor of *Harper's Weekly*. The nominations for the State ticket were fixed in advance; steering committees, resolutions, "keynote" speeches, even the last details of the convention hall claque, were made ready beforehand. Tom Platt, Congressman from Owego, and a veteran machine leader, had some literary pretensions and prepared two speeches, "one full of vindicative [sic] hostility and the other mild and non-committal." [24] Conkling read them both and selected the fire-eating speech, "which sounded like his own stuff." He rewarded Platt by making him chairman of the convention.

It was to be a spectacular demonstration against the National Government, upon whose success depended the whole balance of power over the nation-wide party Organization.

In a great hall at Rochester, September 26, 1877, the solemn party convention opened, its assembled host of humble political "workers" arriving from all corners of the Empire State, "seekers after loaves and fishes," all silent and praying. Chairman Platt, the "Machiavelli of Tioga County," sounded the keynote, a withering attack upon the Republican President in Conklinian style. Platt, in defiance of the purists, sang the praises of "the working and fighting soldiers of our political army," who toiled "from sunrise to sunset" for the success of their party, only to see the fruits of victory stolen from them by ingratitude. Maledictions were hurled upon the contemptible "political Pecksniffs and tricksters" who shouted for "reform . . . a sweet morsel rolled under [the officeseeker's] tongue." Contrasted to these insults to members of the Administration and their policy were significant encomiums for the "glorious" but "modest" Grant, then upon his celebrated world tour, whose subsequent career clearly figured in the plans of the Stalwarts for a "restoration." Platt concluded meaningfully: "Fellow Republicans . . . It is no time to relax or despond. . . . What *we do now and here* . . . is for all time." [25]

Angry protests from the minority at this unheard-of denunciation of the party's own President, and motions for the ousting of Platt, were voted down by an uproarious but concerted majority, which sustained the chairman's "scorcher" as voicing its real sentiment.

George William Curtis, a round, short man of gentle, intellectual face and soft, musical voice, rose to answer Platt. In his youth he had been a member of the Brook Farm Community, a friend of Emerson; then, after years spent at a German university, he had returned to serve as a crusading Abolitionist and an idealistic follower of Lincoln. In his career as a journalist he had become known for stainless honor, having devoted his modest earnings over a great part of his life to repaying losses incurred by others in a publishing venture in which he was once a partner. It was he who had most opposed Conkling's candidacy for the presidential nomination in 1876, asking every week in *Harper's:* "With what great measure of statesmanship is his name conspicuously identified?" He had also threatened to expose Mr. Conkling's "professional relations"—this was a thrust below the belt—"to causes in which he was opposed to attorneys virtually named by himself, before judges whose selection was due to his favor." [26] But despite his ability and distinction, Curtis's spirit of moderation and fairness obviously unfitted him for the contest with Conkling's band. He entered the arena like some poor early Christian.

In a long, moving speech he appealed to the convention for an endorsement, thus far withheld, of the President's liberal Southern policy and his steps toward reform of the civil service. Curtis described the confusion and degradation of the Federal departments, pulled to pieces every two or four years for partisan motives, its workers increasingly exploited and demoralized. Men like Conkling, he argued, were responsible for the demoralization of our government service. Curtis did not believe that "any eminent Republican, however high his ambition, however sore his discontent, hoped to carry the Republican party against Rutherford B. Hayes." He prayed that those present "might yet see the Republican party fulfilling the hope of true men everywhere, who look to it for honesty, for reform, and for pacification." [27]

The great gathering had listened to Curtis at times with scant respect; but Conkling, gently waving a fan against the stifling heat of the day, watched him closely, his judgment swayed by an ungovernable hate, the notable weakness in his equipment as a stump and cloakroom politician. "Conkling had been waiting for Curtis," writes Alexander, the historian of New York politics, "as the American fleet waited [later] for the Spanish at Santiago." [28] Once or twice his carefully managed entrances and exits had brought strong, carefully managed "spontaneous ovations" from delegates "eager for his leadership." [29] But in the evening session of September 26 an overwhelming throng, swollen by anticipation of a sensational address, greeted the arrival on the rostrum of the chieftain's familiar, towering, and perennially romantic figure with a resounding volley of cheers.

Nature had lavished upon Conkling "superb gifts of mind and person. He was of commanding, even magnificent presence, six feet three inches tall, with regular features, lofty forehead, and piercing eyes—blond and gigantic as a viking." [30] It was difficult for a man so superlatively handsome not to be vain, and his bearing, his delivery, his clear, harsh voice, did not conceal his egregious vanity, while it showed, too, something of the genuine contempt he felt for the crowds who followed him. Conkling appeared always, as he himself once related, "to take account of *the spaniel-like element* of human nature." [31]

Here was only a State convention, Conkling reminded his hearers as he began, and the head of the National Government was not a candidate before it. Nor could Conkling believe that the national Administration would ever wish or attempt to coerce a State convention, or introduce "matters foreign to our duties," or issues upon which opinion was divided and silence preferable. (The platform resolutions were thus to preserve an insulting silence as to "Mr. Hayes," his policies and even his title to the Presidency, then still subject to widespread attack.)

Warming to his work, the orator then argued, with an air of virtuous indignation, that only intervention by a certain faction "with somewhat of menace and truculent dictation," and hints of chastisement if certain resolutions were not forthcoming, was the cause of present discord. He bridled at the notion of a "despotism" exercised from Washington; he descanted for some minutes upon the eternal value of human liberty, and then with steady, even pace mounted to an epopee, easily one of the most significant in the political literature of this period:

Who are these oracular censors so busy of late in brandishing the rod over me and every other Republican in this state? . . . Who are these men who, in newspapers and elsewhere, are cracking their whips over Republicans and playing school-master to the Republican party and its conscience and convictions? They are of various sorts and conditions. Some of them are the man milliners, the dilettanti and *carpet knights* of politics.[32]

As he spoke these words, Conkling's nostrils were dilated, a wide sneer disfigured his lips, his eyes flamed, and he bent to one side, to get a full view down the aisle of George William Curtis, pointing a long finger at the hapless reformer, as one of those present

whose efforts have been expended in denouncing and ridiculing and accusing honest men who, in storm and in sun, in war and peace, have clung to the Republican flag and defended it against those who have tried to trail and trample it in the dust. Some of them . . . have attempted to belittle and befoul Republican administrations and to parade their own thin veneerings of superior purity. . . . Some of these worthies masquerade as reformers. Their vocation . . . is to lament the sins of other people. Their stock in trade is rancid, canting self-righteousness. They are wolves in sheep's clothing. Their real object is office and plunder. When Dr. Johnson defined patriotism as the last refuge of a scoundrel, he was unconscious of the then undeveloped capabilities and uses of the word "Reform!" [33]

Upon this last sentence Conkling's delivery was indeed theatrical. His auditors remembered how slowly he drawled, with the "r's" rolled, the sibilants hissed: "When Doc-tor-r-r Ja-a-awnson defined patr-r-riotism as the law-s-s-st r-r-refuge of a scoundr-r-rel," and so on. Thus, abandoning himself to his hate, lunging and stabbing at the "new and strange tenets for Republicans," at the "apostates," the "betrayers," who had cast "truthless aspersions" upon the glorious Grant (applause) the orator made an unforgettable picture for the crowd, painted with all the colors of personal invective and derision. The nonsense over civil-service reform, he exclaimed, was but "a Chinese war of noises." Looking again toward Curtis, whom he described cruelly as the editor of a family journal "made famous by the pencil of Nast," he delivered a most revealing and memorable observation upon reformers:

They forget that parties are not built up by deportment, or by ladies' magazines, or gush! [34]

The coterie of reformers he pictured cleverly to his simple hearers as "a newly announced upper class of Republicans . . . an order of nobility or gentry," who would exploit unjustly the labor of their humbler brothers in the party. Then, as Mr. Curtis had drawn a parallel between his own long services to the party and Mr. Conkling's, the Senator alluded to this, placing his left hand behind his back, his right upon his heart, and with a mocking sneer, saying: "The member from Richmond did me honor overmuch." He closed in militant fashion with a citation from a legend of the medieval crusaders: "Let the future decide between you, and let it declare for him who carries furthest into the ranks of the enemy the sword of the cross." [35]

The mob of professionals were appeased by so much blood, though hisses in goodly number were mingled with the stormy cheering. Curtis, like other respectable characters there, was shocked; as he wrote to Professor Charles Eliot Norton, it was hard to put out of mind

that man glaring at me in a fury of hate, and storming out his foolish blackguardism. I was all pity. . . . Conkling's speech was carefully written out, and therefore . . . no one can imagine the Mephistophelean leer and spite.[36]

Conkling, however, must be commended for having provided us with one of those historic moments when all cards are laid on the table, as befits a meeting of men among men in politics. He had spoken only of the truths and realities of their profession as all the plain "workers" knew them; he said only what everyone knew when he charged that silk-hatted reformers and "hypocrites" with their "gush" had never won an election, and never done anything for the masses of the people. The "stanch old-time Republicans" saw ingratitude and factionalism aimed solely at the regular New York Organization; hence they turned the convention into "a demonstration, hostile, fierce, contemptuous," against the ruling President at Washington.[37] They cheered to the echo the name of Grant, whose third-term campaign it now suited the design of the Conklinites to broach. A complete Conkling slate was quickly voted by the Rochester convention; Cornell and Arthur, who had defied the orders of the President, bluntly refused to resign their Federal posts. The reformers under Curtis hurried to call protest mass meetings of respectable citizens, but the Conklinites continued their way irresistibly, paying little heed to such censure.[38]

The answer of President Hayes, silent under so much insult, was to send to the special session of Congress, which opened October 15, 1877, the names of two distinguished businessmen who were to supplant Cornell and Arthur: L. B. Prince for Naval Officer, and Theodore Roosevelt, Sr., for Collector.

In the cloakroom of the Senate Conkling now campaigned in earnest, and speedily won the sympathies of his fellow Senators. What was at stake here clearly was the "courtesy of the Senate," the custom by which the Senator-bosses accorded each other final sanction over the appointments by the Administration in their regions and States. Thus by this long-established code even Blaine, now risen to the upper house, supported Conkling's demand in the caucus, urging in public debate that civil-service reform must be imposed in some other manner and at some other time, but not in order to overrule Senators and oust "good, capable, honest and experienced officers" at New York.[39] With a magnificent esprit de corps all the Senators were impelled to defend their traditional privileges, upon which the local Organization machinery was based. Conkling's powerful appeal to his colleagues to preserve the "dignity of the Senate," to protect 4,000,000 citizens of New York from "dictation," was heeded by a majority of 35 to 21. The spoils system, which so many sound, conservative commercial personages now sought to supplant with an impartial bureaucracy and which even stronger interests, though less vocal, wished to retain, was thus prolonged in its life for many seasons to come. A thrill of joy went through Conkling's legion, and the courage of his officeholding lieutenants was renewed. The President noted in his diary:

> In the language of the press, "Senator Conkling has won a great victory over the Administration." . . . But the end is not yet. I am right, and shall not give up the contest.[40]

The executive arm must needs bide its time now; at the close of the session of Congress, in July, 1878, with Congress adjourned, it struck again to suspend Arthur and Cornell, pending the approval of the coming Congress. While Theodore Roosevelt, Sr., had waited to assume his office he had died suddenly, an incident which contributed perhaps to the conviction and persistence with which his son thereafter pursued the cause of civil-service reform. Arthur was personally popular, and though new investigations were carried on, and new turmoil raged in the press, it was widely believed that the proposed changes had some partisan motive behind them, designed to strengthen a faction opposed to the Conkling machine in New York. Secretary Sherman himself had been collaborating in friendly and "practical" fashion with Arthur up to this period, so far as certain political appointments were concerned, though perhaps without knowledge of the President.[41] The cause of reform was being directed in a dull, halfhearted, and inefficient manner; the President was without support; and there was much reason to believe that re-

newed attacks by Conkling in the Senate would again carry the day
for the spoilsmen.

Sherman, who had been winning national prestige at this same
period by his remarkable management of the national finances, now
suddenly changed his tactics and threw himself openly into the
struggle against the New York machine and the Stalwart wing of the
party. A further program of economy and retrenchment, a swing to
a true conservatism of policy such as he visioned, even his own climb
to the role of a leading presidential candidate for 1880, were in
peril. Confusion and discord had ruled long enough; and he used
all his resources and skill to best the Oneida Chieftain, turning
the methods of the spoilsmen upon them, canvassing and actively
lobbying in the Senate himself, diverting the patronage to the
strengthening of anti-Conkling forces in the New York party.*

At length on February 3, 1879, when half the term of the new
President had gone by, the hard-fighting Conkling came to grief.
"Senatorial courtesy" wavered and gave way as his colleagues tired
of the dangerous intramural struggle. In vain did Conkling, according to his wont, produce from his pockets damaging private letters,
which he exhibited at Senate committee conferences, to show how the
President and the Secretary of the Treasury had caused Arthur to
appoint deserving friends of theirs to office. Godkin has left us a
mocking account of the foray:

> The . . . excitement among the henchmen was painful to witness. On
> the one side was their "gifted leader," well combed and neatly attired,
> his brain full of the facts in the case, his coat-pockets crammed with damn-
> ing letters, surrounded by piles of law-books, a curl of scorn on his lips,
> and his torso bursting with "sarcasm." On the other was the shrewd and
> wily Secretary of the Treasury, working as he had never worked before,
> pursuing the Senators to their lodgings and constraining them to support
> the Administration for this once. . . . On Monday, the opposing forces
> closed in deadly conflict, and the reports which have crept out represent

* Sherman besought General E. A. Merritt, who was to succeed Cornell, to be
"active and efficient" in this "warm contest"; he was to gather "evidence of discontent at Albany with . . . Mr. Conkling"; and to bring "local influences to
bear" upon both Senators from New York. (Sherman Papers, Letterbook, Jan. 18,
1879.)

the Conkling onslaught as one of the most shocking scenes of "sarcasm" and "scorn" ever witnessed in a legislative body.[42]

A narrow majority of the Republican Senators had clung to Conkling's cause to the bitter end; but enough Democrats had used the opportunity to widen the confusion and cleavage in Republican ranks by aiding a President whose title they still challenged. Conkling's very tirades against Hayes were believed to have offended numerous members of his own party, who now hastened to confirm the removal of his henchmen.[43] It was a serious defeat for Conkling and the old spoils system he defended, but no surrender followed.

IV

While the President struggled and floundered in his efforts to impose government reform "on business principles"—as he explained to his new customhouse appointees—the divided Congress wrangled most bitterly; the rival parties themselves were each sundered by jealousies and factional strife, Stalwarts against Half-Breeds in the Republican Organization, Tilden followers against Tammany men or unregenerate former rebels in the Democratic camp. The whole scene gave an effect of the unreality of partisan politics and its total divorce from the underlying social issues of the time; also of the absurd impotence of the political Government under which the country appeared to stagger without goal, without direction. Yet when a profound and "irrepressible" conflict of class forces arose within the society in the late 1870's, and caused unprecedented disorders, the apparently "weak" political Government suddenly showed unexpected strength, its jealous political captains held their tongues, while force and guile and unheard-of energy were called forth to suppress the common dangers.

In cyclical economic depressions in the past, the discontent of the minority class of urban labor in the United States waxed for a time; but then almost at once, energetic workers from the East seemed to be "drawn off" into the Great West, with its ample areas of free or cheap land. After the Civil War, in an era of rising wages, a promising trade-union movement and class party was fostered, especially in New England, by intellectuals such as Albert Brisbane and Wendell

Phillips. In depression usually the labor unions became weakened, their members scattered over the broad country, their leaders turned to practical politics within the established parties, even under men like Ben Butler, who championed the eight-hour day, inflation, the suppression of contract labor, and the exclusion of the Chinese. In New York and in Middle Western cities a few thousand followers, chiefly Germans, embraced a pedantic form of international socialism (much disapproved by Marx and Engels themselves), which gained but a meager following amid the bewildering mobility of American economic life.

But while the ill-manned, ill-piloted ship of state wallowed on, the depression following 1873 prolonged itself, undoubtedly sharpened by the deflationary policy of the Government and the banks—so ill-suited to the country's ultimate enormous need of construction and industrial expansion. According to some contemporary reports wages fell from 37.5 to 60 per cent between 1873 and 1877; [44] 3,000,000 were unemployed.

In the farm regions poverty and bitterness were universal as wheat sank to 50 cents a bushel, and corn was used for fuel, while mortgage debt seemed to "grow until it devoured the land." [45] Though one-third of the nation's land resources was still untouched, the planless advance of industrial and railroad construction had to be paid for in some manner; successive cuts of 10 per cent and increases of the labor load by the leading railroads and coal operators spread a spirit of desperation among workingmen, and a sudden revival of labor action in new, secret form followed. In the anthracite fields of Pennsylvania, the terroristic Molly Maguires organized themselves among the Irish miners and flourished for years in the form of a conspiratorial organization, until suppressed by methods as melodramatic and conspiratorial as their own. But among the railroad workers, whose strikes had often been frustrated, the Trainmen's Union, comprising engineers, conductors, brakemen, and firemen, was organized more rationally, but with no less violent impulse. On July 17, 1877, at the lowest ebb of the depression, came the opening of their strike at Martinsburg, West Virginia, a junction of the Baltimore & Ohio Railroad, the movement soon spreading to Pittsburgh and throughout the Middle West.

The method of the strikers was revolutionary, involving seizure and control of towns and railroad yards at strategic points of the network, effecting blockades of freight movement; it was carried forward with the tremendous energy of the American labor movement in its youth, and reached its first goal at once: the stoppage of the railroad system upon a nation-wide scale.

The politicians, quarreling over the spoils of office, no less than the industrial captains, who were plunged in competitive duels, gazed with stupefaction at the convulsive movement among the masses. Strikes and riots so concerted and of such size had never before been known in the republic. Business activity was paralyzed; 100,000 union men threw down their tools. It was, as Rhodes, the son of an Ohio coal operator, remembers, a "social uprising" that

seemed to threaten the chief strongholds of society and came like a thunderbolt out of a clear sky, startling us rudely. For we had hugged the delusion that such social uprisings belonged to Europe and had no reason of being in a free republic where there was plenty of room and an equal chance for all.[46]

But then, until recent years the country had never known of railway monopolies extending over 1,000 miles of track, and employing under their single command whole army divisions of workingmen.

The intervention of State militia on a large scale in New York, Pennsylvania, Maryland, Ohio, Indiana, and Illinois brought not relief, but mounting violence and destruction instead. In Baltimore the infuriated people completely routed State soldiers, who had opened fire on them indiscriminately. In Pittsburgh, where the Pennsylvania Railroad yards were in possession of the workers, most of the local militia, when called out, fraternized with the workers. On July 21, reinforcements from Philadelphia, "including many young men drawn from the leading families of the city," were brought to Pittsburgh and induced to fire into the crowds, killing outright a score of men and women. The people thereupon rose as one man, drove the State troops into a railroad roundhouse, and besieged them there. The whole city of coal and iron was then given over to rioting and incendiarism, the conflagration of railroad yards, warehouses, and factories reddening its skies. "Hell is open and the lid is off," the alarmed press reported.[47]

Among the workers were many former soldiers, who sometimes maneuvered in good military order and knew how to use artillery, as at Pittsburgh. Their leaders, unknowns, seemed to spring up from nowhere and were imbued with a simple revolutionary impulse, expressed in manifestoes of the time such as the following, summoning all workers to a meeting in Indianapolis

for the purpose of sympathizing and taking action with our starving brothers in the East who are now being trampled under the feet of the railroad bondholders. Everybody invited that believes in equality and justice to all mankind. Let us all have a hand in breaking the backbone of this railroad monopoly.—By Order of The Committee.[48]

It was class war stirring the lower layers of society, even terrifying the politicians, as John Hay of Cleveland noticed with dismay. Owners of important properties organized themselves in many cities into Committees of Public Safety. At Indianapolis the war veteran General Walter Q. Gresham, now a Federal judge, ordered United States Marshals to arrest all strikers who molested trains operated by a Federal receiver and so under the jurisdiction of his court. Then Gresham, who was known as a liberal, joined with Generals Benjamin Harrison and James Wilson in the work of the Committee of Public Safety.[49]

From this year dates the beginning of a most vigorous intervention of the courts in labor disputes. The militia as then organized was felt to be inefficient and undependable; an obvious need dictated the rapid construction of large arsenals in the principal cities.[50]

At the start of the strikes the most frantic appeals for Federal aid had been dispatched to the President at Washington. Thomas Scott is said to have telegraphed every hour for two days on behalf of the Pennsylvania Railroad, and demanded that the regular army be doubled. Other railroad masters expressed themselves with similar alarm or vehemence upon the apparent slowness or deliberation of Hayes. After a quick survey of the situation—for use of the national army had never been known in industrial disputes, and only sparingly in local disorders—Hayes issued a proclamation calling on the people to disperse and threw the full force of the United States Army into West Virginia, Maryland, Pennsylvania, and Illinois, upon the demand of their Governors.

The Federal troops imposed order, and the President noted in his diary: "The strikes have been put down by *force*." "Regulars, . . . it [the mob] knows to be a machine," wrote Horace White, a prominent liberal journalist, "the most terrible of all the machines invented by man, . . . which . . . when it strikes, strikes like the flail of destiny, without remorse, or pity, or misgiving." [51] Horace White, Carl Schurz, and Tom Scott all united in stressing the weakness of the militia and the need of a large standing army if we would escape the horrors of the recent communes in Paris. The historian Rhodes, whose financial fortunes suffered this year, recalls private gatherings of respectable people in western Ohio who discussed earnestly the revolutionary scenes of 1877, and invariably gave their blessings to the "quiet unassuming man in the White House who saw his duty clearly and never faltered." The State power often had a semblance of fearful weakness in America; but now, as Rhodes concludes in his terrifying account of the great strikes of 1877: "It was seen that the federal government with a resolute President at its head was a tower of strength in the event of a social uprising." [52] The great railway strikes had been defeated by their own misdirected violence. [53] The spirit of labor solidarity, the possibility of concerted nation-wide economic organization, however, now became something more immediate than before. The Knights of Labor, organized in 1869, grew by great leaps, assuming the form of a militant industrial union movement, having only an indirect or sometimes secret affiliation with one or the other of the political parties.

The politicians, on the other hand, once the crisis had passed, strove more industriously than ever before to mitigate the sharpening class divisions. In several State conventions that year of both great parties, labor planks, so called, "sufficiently vague to bear a double interpretation by the friends of order and by the mob," were adopted. [54] Meanwhile, the leading stump orators for many years to come evaded the issue with an intense prudence. Sometimes a Conkling, in answer to hecklers who spoke of "the chasm between capital and labor," answered with rasping irony that this chasm was but a "sar-casm," and the "most dangerous of the country's enemies" were those who contended that there was actually an issue between the "two great partners, capital and labor." [55] The opinion of liberal reformers was almost identical with that of Conkling: E. L. Godkin, an intense libertarian, declared that "every American citizen is a fully equipped man, standing squarely on his own feet and abundantly competent to make his own bargains," while hotly resenting movements to "pamper" unemployed malcontents.

American history, since the founding of the republic, had embodied always a more purely economic and secular development than that of probably any other nation, in the highest degree free of the restraining force of feudal and clerical institutions. It had been indeed a more or less naked economic struggle, as James Madison had long before foreseen, in which the less fortunate classes sought constantly and jealously to raise their condition to the level of the more fortunate. This prime motive of a society in which Homo economicus was clearly dominant was but slightly susceptible to alteration by hieratic, mystical, environmental, or racial interests. Yet for this very reason, and out of their own engrossing concern with purely secular ends, the professional politicians strove to divert and warp the latent class conflict by the most ingenious tactics of ideology. Differences of race, language, and religion were pounced upon, and also special regional influences showing themselves as media by which the great patronage parties might successfully work against the ground swell of class interest.

Whereas in Europe the alignment of political parties was fixed nowadays, as Bryce said, by "the fears of the Haves and the desires of the Have-Nots," in America the party chieftains pursued deliberately their superhuman chess game, whereby they sought "combinations" of classes and groups. New alarms of Southern rebellions in one region, the call to race hatred and fear in another, drew fast sectional or racial lines, which distorted or concealed the underlying development of class movements in political life.

The industrial proletariat in America, periodically wooed by high wages, divided by language and race increasingly, and alternately tempted and confused by the mobility of our class structure, faced special political difficulties unlike those of the European masses, who formed everywhere their great Social Democratic parties at this hour. As they groped toward unity, the American workers could show high courage in industrial combats; but in the political field they were led inevitably to divide themselves between the established patronage parties.

Nor must we overlook the skillful ideological flanking movements carried on by demagogues and stump orators, such as Blaine. When the Bloody Shirt seemed to have lost its potency in making the people forget Hard Times, Blaine, making a lightninglike shift, began to deliver thunderous speeches before the Senate upon "the menace of the incalculable hordes of China" to American workers. This was a Live Issue to white workers along the Pacific Coast, whose wages were undercut by Chinese contract labor, and who, as in San Francisco under the lead of the "Sand-Lotters," carried on murderous riots against the Chinese. Thus by supporting a Chinese exclusion bill Blaine gained many adherents in the Far West, while endangering little the party's strength in the East. As for Mr. Blaine's friends, the railroad-builders, who counted almost overwhelmingly upon Chinese contract labor, they were helped by the accident of divided authority in our Government—since, for years, Presidents regularly vetoed Chinese exclusion bills that were approved by their own parties in Congress.

Then, turning eastward to New England, the magnetic Blaine knew how to win the favor of a most numerous and miserable section of the city workers, the poor Irish. He would say nothing for the eight-hour day, but by his fierce verbal onslaughts upon Great Britain was able to carry a large racial group over to his party.

Such maneuvers, widely copied by other professionals, directed to dividing, detaching, or neutralizing sections and wings of the lower classes, showed an unusual awareness—rather than indifference—to underlying economic issues and class forces.

Then, as if this were not enough, the party orators never failed to preach the current version of the "American dream" that directed the mind of the luckless or discontented worker toward the glittering chances of the frontier. The ideology of individual enterprise at the frontier Blaine himself expressed probably more convincingly than anyone else at the time:

The poverty of the frontier, where all are engaged in a common struggle and where a common sympathy and hearty co-operation lighten the burdens of each, is a very different poverty—different in kind, different in influence and effect, from that conscious and humiliating indigence which is every day forced to contrast itself with neighboring wealth on which it feels a sense of grinding dependence. *The poverty of the frontier is indeed no poverty. It is but the beginning of wealth, and has the boundless possibilities of the future always opening before it.*[56]

Professional political experience seemed endlessly fertile in raising Live Issues that provided escape from class conflict toward some tentative equilibrium between the privileged and the discontented. For the leaders of the great patronage parties the essence of tactics lay in the legerdemain of pretended compromise, whereby these uncanny political illusionists played for the moneyed support of one class and the votes of the other—so long as momentary points of common interest between the classes could be improvised and enduring differences ignored. By these shifts the rise of a class or "belief" party of workers, as a medium for the regeneration of society, was undoubtedly long delayed. They did not, however, wholly prevent the emergence of a "belief" party speaking for another powerful, numerous, more articulate class at this period.

The pattern of a purely economic class party, one of the first in modern America, was fashioned by the dirt farmers of the Mississippi Valley, hardened and united by their common misfortunes and ready to assault the rulers of society and their political managers alike.

V

Late in August, 1879, John Sherman, quitting his arduous and somewhat mysterious labors in the Treasury at Washington, returned to his native State for a visit and spoke before 3,000 people at the Toledo Opera House. He, whom August Belmont, his most intimate financial counselor, had recently called "the noblest son of the noble State of Ohio," was greeted with a warmth unusual even in his own varied experience. At sight of Sherman's trim, slender figure and wise, eager little head, a storm of hisses arose. The people shouted jeers and insults at the tops of their voices: "You are responsible for all the failures in the country"; "You work to the interest of the capitalist"; "Capitalists own you, John Sherman, and you rob the poor widows and orphans to make them rich." [57]

What plague had befallen western Ohio? What ill winds were sweeping the broad Mississippi Valley these days? From the inner slope of the Alleghenies to the foothills of the Rockies a vast political storm raged, and its lightning played about the heads of the veteran chieftains of both parties. Sherman's State, the home of Pendleton's Ohio Idea of inflated paper money, had seen the founding of a new nation-wide political party whose organizing convention, in this same city of Toledo, February 22, 1878, brought together deputies from twenty-eight States, including fractions of all the dissenting groups in the country, from Grangers to Utopian Socialists and woman-suffrage advocates. It was a mass movement, chiefly of the American peasantry, if we may call them that, which proposed now, as General James B. Weaver of Iowa said, to lead the people back to "the old-time Democracy of Jefferson and Jackson, and the pure Republicanism of Abraham Lincoln and Thaddeus Stevens." [58] The new National Greenback Party of 1878 was a spontaneous, nonprofessional political movement which, upsetting native traditions, struck as a third party at the established system of party rule itself.

The doctrine of money inflation was an economic leitmotiv which was often sounded in the American past, in the 1780's, in the 1830's, after the Civil War, and echoed the uprisings of landed debtors as far back as ancient Greece and Rome. The warning notes had been heeded after the war, between 1865 and 1869, when Thad Stevens resisted a swift and cruel deflation of the national debt desired by the owners of securities. In the 1870's the same theme was sounded even louder than before from the farming regions of the country, as commodity prices pursued a prolonged downward course.

The first impulse of protest had brought the rise of the Grangers as a nation-wide association of Reform, Independent, and Anti-Monopoly groups. Laws regulating the railroads, whose burdensome and arrogant rate-making policy now made them as detested as they had at first been welcome, were passed by certain Western State legislatures. The State courts had then largely nullified such measures of control. Jay Gould had come, and from the rear platform of his special train menaced the farming communities with the total removal of transportation service should they persist in their hostile action. Yet the farmers of the Middle West had continued their efforts at direct political intervention on their own behalf after 1873. Even in California, where Collis Huntington and Leland Stanford controlled all the mountain passes, a furious local revolt brought the victory of an Anti-Monopoly Party Governor, Newton Booth, and later his election to the Senate.

During the period of deflation the farmer's task had become simply that of making two blades of grass grow where one had grown before. Two bushels of wheat must be raised to pay back each dollar of debt contracted in more favorable and flourishing times. It was now that the meaning of the hastened repayment of the war debt, carried out at fearful cost to the debtor class, "the little people," and linked with the disastrous fall of land and crop values, was grasped throughout the country. Was it just, as Senator Voorhees of Indiana had often cried, that a $1,000 bond which had been worth $500 in gold should be paid in gold at its face value? During the "blight" which overhung the farm lands in the 1870's the men and women who had recently pushed to the farther prairies of the Mississippi Valley, in the western half of Kansas, Iowa, and Nebraska, found credit and money almost unobtainable. In these evil seasons the self-reliant and far-wandering American farming class, now producing fabulous crops which filled the markets of Europe and the Orient, searched its soul and pondered over the mystery of money and credit.

They had set up a cry for more circulating paper currency, for "soft money," and the politicians had driven forward the resumption program. In their hope of inflation, the farm leaders had lately fixed upon the medium of silver, now being produced in enormously increased quantity in the Far West, and found that the mints had been closed to the coinage of silver by the law of 1873—now that the value of silver too had declined, as against gold. They had voted for the Democrats as the party of Outs in 1874—despite the conservative Eastern leadership of that party—and these too had failed them. They had clamored for inflationary measures and witnessed the "midnight passage" of Sherman's Resumption Bill in 1875. They had given a national majority to Tilden in 1876 and had seen the Hard Money candidate, Hayes, installed by chicane, while the mistrusted Sherman, according to a now transparent design, was named to administer the national finances. Hence the various dissident groups in the Middle West and on the Pacific Coast, taking up the Ohio Idea of increased Greenback currency, came together at last, during the stormy days of the great strikes of 1877, in a movement toward unity and action through an "independent" party favoring, in general, "cheap capital and well-paid labor," free silver coinage, and a graduated income tax.[59]

Amid great difficulties, in 1877 Sherman had carried on with a most ambitious refunding program by which some $235,000,000 of the Federal debt bearing higher interest coupons were converted into loans bearing 4 per cent. At moments the alarm of the great strikes had caused delicate negotiations with foreign money centers to be broken off, while moneylenders inquired frantically if a social revolution were in progress in America against the Government itself.[60] With considerable business craft Sherman had effected, nevertheless, his refunding and gold-gathering campaign in conjunction with a great international syndicate of bankers, supported by Belmont, acting for the Rothschilds, Drexel, and Morgan, the Seligmans, the National City Bank, and Levi Morton of Morton, Rose & Co. The success of these transactions was partly due to the secret manner in which they were handled; but this in turn gave rise to scandal and angry protests against the omnipotent Secretary. Sherman was "indiscreet, in permitting concentrations of the bulk of his deposits with a single bank," in which he was sometimes charged with having some interest. He granted "undue favors" to the banking syndicate.[61]

But perhaps furthering his elaborate plans more than anything else was the providential arrival of bumper crops in 1878 and 1879, produced by the aggrieved farmers themselves at a time when Europe suffered from scarcity, which at last brought a "favorable" export balance and permitted the accumulation of foreign gold currencies. The vast toil of millions of farmers, then 70 per cent of the population, was to pay for the Civil War in gold, replenish the national savings after the depression, and furnish the source of capital for powerful railroad and manufacturing monopolies rising under a favoring tariff wall.

But in the face of the spreading rural agitation among millions of

smallholders in 1877, the chieftains of the Republican Party preserved a troubled silence or hid their heads, ostrich fashion. In each
party an important wing was infected with the cheap-money "heresy,"
as it was called. The "silver movement" in its first onslaught broke
across party lines, and won the support of trans-Allegheny Republicans and Democrats alike. Early in November, a bill for the "free
and unlimited coinage of silver at 412½ grains" per silver dollar
was introduced by Representative Richard ("Silver Dick") Bland of
Missouri, and passed in the lower house by an overwhelming vote.
Garfield, now the minority floor leader, had opposed and voted
against this measure "alone among the Ohio delegation, and almost
alone in the Mississippi valley," as he himself noted.[62] It was Abram
Hewitt, the Eastern Democratic leader in the House, who carried the
burden of the attack even more boldly against the inflationists in his
party. The rank-and-file politicians no longer responded to the whip.
The economic cleavage in Congress fell according to mode of production—according to whether one's constituents came from counting-
houses or wheat fields; but this division bore also a particular sectional and geographical character provided by the American environment.

As Bland's bill reached the Senate in November, 1877, it carried
an ominous clause which repealed the whole Specie Resumption Act
of 1875. Panic spread among moneylenders, and Belmont, in constant
touch with John Sherman, wrote to inform him that the bankers'
syndicate would be obliged to cut off its credits to the Government
of the United States. The Bland Bill was to "the whole civilized
world . . . an act of repudiation . . . and cast a stain upon our
national credit," wrote Belmont. Then later, November 29, he
warned Sherman that "capitalists and banks on both sides of the
Atlantic will not buy a bond at par *in gold*" with a silver dollar worth
about 90 cents as the Legal Tender of the country.[63]

The blind uprising of labor had been suppressed by the Administration's use of force on behalf of the railway and factory owners. Now,
in the face of widespread agrarian discontent, even more baffling,
the President was ready to veto the Bland Silver Bill in order to
"save our financial honor." But canvassing quickly showed that the
veto would be promptly overruled in both houses of Congress.

Therefore Sherman, who was the strong man of the emergency period in 1877-79, labored indefatigably once more to effect a compromise which might appease both sides.

In the Republican Senate, the astute William Allison of Iowa, chairman of the Finance Committee, now labored to amend the silver bill in all its vital parts. Quarreling Senator-bosses swallowed their jealousies and lent warm co-operation in a common cause. Allison enjoyed for long years the friendly regard of his dirt-farming constituents, but at the same time, as Chauncey Depew said of him, he was one of the few Western politicians whom Eastern financiers trusted. "He could grant to an adversary an amendment with such grace and deference to superior judgment that the flattered enemy in turn accepted a few suggestions from the master" without comprehending the extent of his blunder.[64] The tactics of Sherman, Allison, and their adviser, Belmont, were shaped toward escaping an "unlimited coinage," which might ultimately cause a genuine inflation, and granting instead a "limited" silver coinage of $2,000,000 a month as minimum and $4,000,000 as maximum. The Bland-Allison Bill would provide its own embarrassments in the future; but under conservative auspices, by keeping silver at a minimum, the resumption program would be safe for years to come, as Sherman hoped; the bondholders could breathe easily again.

"The amendments to the Bland bill reported by Mr. Allison from the committee on finance," wrote Sherman complacently, "completely revolutionized that measure." [65] And President Hayes observed in his diary: "Belmont, the agent of the Rothschilds, fears the effect of a veto—prefers the bill should be approved, *bad* as he thinks it is." [66] Sherman was enabled, despite its passage, to continue undeterred with his huge refunding and gold-buying program, so that by the end of December, 1878, he was ready for resumption with a hoard of almost $200,000,000 in gold coin and bullion. On the first business morning of 1879, none came to reclaim gold for government notes—since none doubted the Government's ability to pay—and the dollar stood at 100 in terms of all the world's gold currencies.

Yet the compromise of 1878 had only fanned the anger of the rural voters and brought to Sherman in person, in Toledo, the greeting of jeers and insults noted earlier. From Maine to California the Greenback and silver "craze" swept over the farming masses. The leaders, embittered by repeated deceptions, championed the agrarian idea of a "managed currency"—as it would be properly called in the twentieth century—by the great sovereign governments of the world.

"Inflate the currency," said one picturesque Greenbacker, Solon Chase of Maine, "and you raise the price of my steers. . . . Resumption means falling prices and shrinkage of wages." [67] And from the other side of the country Allis, the Wisconsin spokesman of the smallholders, argued also that "we were prosperous while the currency was abundant [during the Civil War], and the reverse when the currency was depleted." This was later held to have been a "false" prosperity; but were not *real* railroads, buildings, and factories, and machinery created? Were these not *tangible* improvements? So Allis, Weaver, and the other farm leaders argued. The evil was that the benefits of these improvements did not circulate sufficiently, were not distributed or "used" enough. Yesterday, "we were employed in earnest and useful work, and had a good paymaster," who had much currency.[68] Now all was woe and poverty. Hence more currency we must have. Such were the arguments from a concrete, pecuniary interest which sometimes led excited Western orators in the 1870's to describe the Greenback as "almost a cure-all of these evils. . . . Standing alone in its majesty, it is almost the summum bonum of human financial wisdom."

But the concept of currency inflation by silver coinage or Greenback also underwent a refining process, acquired an ideology which attached to it the egalitarian spirit of eighteenth-century revolutions. In one sense the preference for paper money was no less crass than that for gold money; but in another the silver and "rag-money" movements, though taking a peculiar form from American conditions, envisaged a juster scheme of distribution of worldly goods and chances. Greenbackism, it was often observed then, "was the American counterpart of the radicalism of Europe." It "was a doctrine of universal suffrage of wage-earner and farmer"; it purposed "to take away from bankers and middlemen their control over government and credit, and thereby to furnish credit and capital through the aid of government to the producers." [69] In another and most significant sense, as Frederick Turner has said, it turned the doctrines of the Western settlers from a fixed belief in the policies of laissez faire, in the supreme importance of individual and local liberties and rights, to new doctrines which advocated the intervention of the National Government on behalf of the masses of laboring and producing people. Departing at last from their unmitigated individualism, the frontiersmen believed with Weaver, a leader from the recently settled Iowa, that money must be "nationalized." The Greenback Party must take "national" action, strike at nation-wide monopolies and railroad pools, and "privileged classes of creditors." The answer was not in "less government," as Jefferson would have urged, but in the Government's taking over "control" of money from the bankers, as Weaver held, and in the "rigid regulation of interstate commerce and transportation."

Lacking all patronage, the Greenback Party became an immediate menace to the professionals. Its chief recruits came from the lodges of the Grangers and the new Farmers' Alliances in the West, though it numbered also in its varied following iron-manufacturers who suffered because of the fallen value of ore lands, anti-Chinese Sand-Lotters in California, and temperance advocates from Kansas. While the press, the bar, and the pulpit, as Weaver said, all thundered against the strange new creed, an astounding initial success was won by the Greenbackers in their first concerted campaign during the off-year elections of 1878, when 1,060,000 votes flowed to their party, 14 Greenback Representatives, including General Weaver, being elected to Congress.

The Greenbackers in the upheaval of 1878 had missed by a narrow margin their hopes for capture of the balance of power in Congress as a third party. In some measure they had contributed, by drawing strength from the Western Republicans, to the sweeping victory of the Democrats, who after 1878 for the first time since the Civil War held a majority in the Senate as well as the House. The professional politicians in Democratic uniform asked not, as they needed not, Greenback collaboration. The third party's promising beginning soon appeared curiously like an abortion.

How could they maintain a nation-wide party organization without the sinews of war? In the early agrarian campaigns they were unorganized and without leaders "except for localities." They were "poor and needy and in debt," as professional politicians shrewdly reported from Indiana.[70] One of the Greenbackers complained:

> There is no money to pay the ordinary and necessary expenses of a campaign. There is no press to advocate organization, to lead public opinion; and the whole army of anti-monopolists . . . is yet at sea.[71]

Whenever the factions of Greenbackers and Anti-Monopolists, who were creating a genuine Opposition in the political field, halted in fatigue, or whenever their vague, contradictory program met with waning enthusiasm for reform—then the unsleeping, officeholding, mercenary soldiers of politics returned to the attack.

The curse of middle-class parties, or "petty-bourgeois" parties, as the Greenbackers would be defined under the Marxian formula, is that their grievances against their social oppressors (the large capitalist undertakers) involve largely matters of *degree* or size of accumulation. The drive among small undertakers to seek larger profits, to eliminate competitors and become large undertakers themselves, is the poisonous element that corrodes their parties.

Sherman's harsh process of deflation worked to restore financial "confidence," though at fearful cost, and at the terms of the moneylenders; it led soon to a cyclical expansion of credit and speculative optimism. By a happy conjunction of events, the crop disasters in Europe in 1879, coupled with swollen harvests in America, marketed at most favorable prices, revived trade suddenly; railroad construction and manufacturing, which had languished for six years, boomed again on an enormous scale, and town and farm lands also boomed, while millions of settlers resumed the epic march, now to the farther, arid, Western uplands of the Mississippi Valley, to Colorado and the Dakotas and deepest Kansas. With the downward movement of prices checked at last, in 1879, and wheat worth more than $1 a bushel, a protest aimed essentially at low prices for farm products weakened; the forgetful American farmer suddenly regained his traditional optimism, befitting a land of unplumbed natural resources and boundless opportunity. In such smiling seasons reform became a dreary subject, and the crowds at the Greenback meetings dwindled to a fourth their usual size.

General Weaver had been an ardent Abolitionist, a Radical Republican, a war hero. Though he might safely have climbed the ladder of the great war party, his earnest nature had disposed him first to independence, then to desertion of the Republican "church" and the embrace of an agrarian radicalism that brought down the fiercest condemnation upon his head. He was no violent Jacobin, and of course no "anarchist," as the Eastern press insisted, but rather a rigid Middle Western Puritan, given to an oratory of florid eloquence. The position of his small phalanx of Northern Greenbackers in the Forty-sixth Congress between an overwhelming Democratic majority and an equally hostile Republican minority was an unhappy one, which no leadership could have rendered effectual under our system. Nast caricatured Weaver as Bottom, with an ass's head, crying eternally and uselessly: "I object!"

The theme of green or silver floods of money sank low again for years. The gaunt, ascetic face of General Weaver, the "lost leader" of the agrarians, assumed a habitual air of disappointment.

VI

During the term of Hayes, an interval rich in class conflicts, the central government authority appeared significantly "weak" and deeply divided—except when strikes arose or private property was in peril. Years were passed in loud wrangling between the party leaders and between the President and Congress, while no legislation worth the name was enacted—an outcome not wholly unforeseen. Neither of the major parties broached any vital issue of the time, and both parties on the whole successfully resisted efforts to improve them carried on by reformist factions from within.

The distinguishing feature of the period between 1877 and 1881 was the manner in which each party seemed absorbed with casting out its own devils—a form of dialectical struggle within the American party system itself. "Reformers" contended with spoilsmen, President Hayes and Sherman against Conkling, Tilden against Tammany Hall in the rival party, not because of any fundamental difference in social outlook, but in order that a tradition-bound, nearsighted, greedy patronage system might be replaced by some form of efficient administrative conservatism.

President Hayes was widely discredited because the majority of his own party would not follow him; the Republican Party itself was discredited by its long career of scandal and stood now as a helpless, disorderly minority in Congress. James Garfield, who served in the thankless post of Republican floor leader, advised the President earnestly on March 1, 1879, that "if he wished to hold any influence he must abandon some of his notions of Civil Service." The politicians nowadays seemed maddened by the unpredictable disposition of patronage. Hayes's election, Garfield himself confided, to his journal, had been "an almost fatal blow to the party." But on the other hand, the much stancher reformer J. D. Cox now told Garfield that

the President had utterly failed to accomplish anything in the way of civil service reform and . . . had pursued no system that could be defended by any class of politicians.[72]

The Democrats, on the other hand, possessed an overwhelming congressional majority after 1878, a high point in the slow postbellum revival of the older party. Their Western leaders, with an eye to the popular anger at railroad monopolies, had earlier introduced a bill for the partial regulation of the two Pacific railroads, the most vulnerable of the great corporations that had risen out of the war.

These had steadfastly refused to pay even current interest upon the large government money subsidies advanced for their construction, their indebtedness for principal of mortgage bonds (due in 1895) and interest being estimated at $65,000,000 by 1877. To the dismay of Huntington and Gould, a Sinking Fund Bill which would establish a schedule for the retirement of this debt was resolutely pushed in Congress by Senator Thurman of Ohio, until in its final shape it faced closing debates in the Senate in the spring of 1878.

The lobbies of the railroad captains, which up to recently had been competing with each other for new land grants and subsidies, now composed their quarrels and joined hands in defensive action. During these dark days, Huntington and Gould dared not leave Washington. "Every year the fight grows more and more expensive," Huntington groaned in his private letters to his partners.

By Sherman's Resumption Bill of 1875, and his subsequent fight to "save the country's financial honor," the Republican Party had already entered its phase of decided conservative policy. In 1878, the party's Senate leaders, especially James Blaine, Aaron Sargent, and William Allison, by their powerful efforts to turn aside attacks upon the railroads gave to their party a bias more conservative still.

How cruelly changed, cried Sargent of California, was the spirit of the Government toward the Pacific railroads! In time of war their construction had been a patriotic task, the one means of safeguarding our Pacific possessions. "Now we hear only curses and threats . . . against those who accepted . . . our smiles and promises, and the Government resolves itself into a hard creditor that makes Shylock respectable." To Blaine also, the support of the Pacific railroads project had been "a large, patriotic, Union-saving" venture, designed "to hold together in strong political union the great communities that bordered the two oceans . . . with hooks of iron if not of steel." [73]

So much was familiar ideology, but Blaine proceeded further to voice doctrines more interesting still. Thurman, the old-fashioned Jacksonian Democrat, had contended that the Pacific railways really proposed paying nothing, and would in any case be utterly unable to do so if no annual sinking-fund provision were enforced by law. Such cynical views Blaine opposed with the utmost energy; he was now not merely the patriot, he was the optimist par excellence. With detailed factual knowledge, such as he usually brought to his speeches on railway finance, he dwelt on the immeasurable future of the continent, and the boundless wealth as well that would fall to the Union Pacific. How could anyone predict that the Union Pacific would not repay when due the total sums borrowed?

There were moments when Blaine's devotion to his great land could scarcely be distinguished from his patriotism to the great Union Pacific. It was as a matter of constitutional principle, however, that Blaine advanced the thesis that the Government could not seek to control the railroad corporation further than the literal terms of the original contract and charter given. Against the government regulation demanded by the Western Radicals he protested passionately:

If we have anything to boast of in this country, it is that we have limited the powers of government, and one of the highest and most sacred limitations upon the powers of government is that they shall protect the contracts made by agreement between parties . . . and they shall not impair and destroy them. Ah, there is not one law for a contract to which individuals are parties, and another law for contracts where the government is a party. . . . This is a government of granted powers. It derives all the powers it possesses from the people through the Constitution. It has no power to impair the obligation of a contract . . . nor to reserve such powers of altering contracts.

Here is our once Radical Republican now opposing a "grasping centralization" of the government power. Once he had enthusiastically advocated the power of the Government to donate immense public grants to individual enterprisers, upon given conditions. But though these conditions might be evaded or nullified, the Government of "limited powers," as he now conceived it, had no redress, and no right to control its ward from squandering the heritage. Then with many a humorous thrust or taunt at the politicians who had been "punching and knocking and harrying and twisting" the poor railroad corporations, for fear of having nothing else to do, Blaine offered a little amendment of his own to the Thurman Sinking Fund Bill, which in effect dangerously weakened its provisions. Such an amendment, as his Democratic opponents loudly clamored, would be "prussic acid," the "poisoned drop" that would be the death of the proposed legislation.

Allison of Iowa, a veteran parliamentary horse-trader, now rose with more subtle objections still. The real problem, as he gathered from the feelings of the dirt farmers in his constituency, was that of the reduction of freight rates. He, for his part, longed to see the time when the Government could use its power to compel "these railway corporations to reduce their rates." Now if harsh terms are imposed "to hasten the payment of debt," how can the clamor of the people for lower freight rates be answered . . . "how can we with any face go to these corporations with a law compelling them to reduce their rates of traffic or rates of fare?" [74] Allison would have let Mr. Gould and Mr. Huntington off lightly today, that they might be the more easily disciplined or punished tomorrow!

Thurman's Sinking Fund Bill, which was eventually passed after several years of masterly obstruction, helped only a little toward recouping the Government's railroad investments. But in the contest over its provisions Blaine had shown once more his pre-eminent powers as an ideologue. He had announced a credo of liberty for corporations—liberty from government interference—which was to be the basis for the conservative political thought of the age.*

The Democratic majority plainly tried to make capital of the pursuit of railroad reform in a season of unrest. But in the year that followed, its members brought discredit upon their party also, and by their excesses made it appear even more unmanageable and demoralized than the beaten Republican minority. The conservative Northern leadership of Samuel Tilden was flouted. Under the pressure of former rebels determined to free their section forever from military supervision of elections, obstructive or "sniping" tactics were used, which forced obnoxious riders on ordinary appropriation bills, bringing presidential vetoes and after a time threatening almost complete stoppage of the process of government. One such rider, indeed, refused appropriations for the Federal army itself, and, as Garfield charged, buried "both the Army and the memories of its great services to the Union in one grave." [75] In the Senate, however, both Blaine and Conkling grasped their opportunity to tell the country that the party that had been banished for eighteen years sought to signalize the return to its "birthright of power" by striking down the gallant old army.

Conkling, who had suffered heavy defeats in the intraparty struggle, now commanded the attention of the entire public as he raised the "Southern question" once more in speeches on April 24, 1879, and denounced the "revolutionary" procedure of the former Confederates. The Northern masses were being stirred again by the waving of the Bloody Shirt; their minds were being prepared also

* Mr. Blaine, in the opinion of his colleagues, also performed other and more particular functions. Senator G. F. Edmunds, the conservative Republican leader from Vermont, wrote privately toward 1880: "It is my opinion that Mr. Blaine acts as the attorney of Jay Gould. Whenever Mr. Thurman and I have settled upon legislation to bring the Pacific railroads to terms of equity with the government, up has jumped James G. Blaine, musket in hand, from behind the breastworks of Gould's lobby, to fire in our backs." (*Harper's Weekly*, Oct. 11, 1884, p. 664.)

for the approaching elections, as the truculent Conkling in his spectacular and sarcastic style baited the Southerners in Congress almost to physical violence, before tense crowds in the galleries, among whom was always noticed nowadays (when Conkling spoke) the beautiful Kate Chase Sprague, wife of the alcoholic millionaire and former Senator, Sprague of Rhode Island.

For many seasons the intimacy between the Senator from New York and the lady who at times attempted the role of a Madame Roland in Republican Party politics had been a source of gossip. In August, 1879, their rumored liaison was heralded in the newspapers, the story of Sprague having found the Senator in his home at Narragansett and driven him forth with a shotgun creating a minor political crisis.

The President himself in his diary noted with relish his enemy's embarrassment:

The Conkling scandal is the newspaper sensation of the time. This exposure of Conkling's rottenness will do good in one direction. It will weaken his political power, which is bad and only bad.[76]

There followed a period of discreet retirement and rupture of relations with Kate Chase, during which Conkling nevertheless held, undiminished, the loyalties of his admiring henchmen.

The Stalwart machine in New York had lost its fortress, which had been the New York Custom House; it was on the brink of extinction. But its leaders wrought in silence new and bolder schemes of attack and diplomatic alliance. While Tammany, under the lead of John Kelly, now broke in two the Democratic Party by bolting and nominating its own State ticket in opposition to the Tilden reformist wing, Conkling's Republican lieutenants labored in perfect harmony. Conkling then, issuing from his politic retirement to serve as chairman of the Saratoga party convention, "moved on the city at the head of a determined phalanx" of his followers.[77]

By rigid machine action Alonzo Cornell, whom the President had dismissed from his Federal post at the Port of New York, was nominated for Governor, while Chester Arthur, who was named chairman of the Republican State Committee, was placed in line for elevation to the United States Senate.

In November, 1879, thanks to much-bruited collusion with Tammany in the three-cornered fight of the gubernatorial election, the whole Conkling slate was elected to office. It was an amazing triumph and vindication over the "man milliners," and held utmost significance for the national political tournament next year. It was in fact "a triumph for nobody except Conkling. He had put into the highest State office a personal adherent, whom the Administration had stigmatised by dismissal." [78] In the face of bitter protests from the press, the pulpit, and the White House itself, and the condemnation of a large wing of his own party, this man who embodied what Elihu Root named in his honor "invisible government" had returned to dominate his great State and cast his full shadow over the national party.

Since 1877 Conkling had been, with Cameron of Pennsylvania and Logan of Illinois, privy to carefully laid plans for the "restoration" of Grant, and the renewal of Stalwart control of government offices, and all that went with it in Whisky and Custom House rings. These plans were furthered by the world tour of the little soldier, who, though much disliking the tiresome ovations he received in foreign lands, was warned by his political advisers to remain aloof and outside his troubled country. Hope once more beat high in the breasts of fierce spoilsmen, while the prospects of reform—"snivel service," as Conkling called it—seemed more dismal than ever.

President Hayes had shown no capacity for such large-minded leadership as might have tamed the political hordes and aroused the enthusiasm, or at least the interest, of the public for his cause. His administration of the civil service was inconsistent, by all accounts, and his reforms were little more than "expressions of opinion," which not all members of the bureaucratic force heeded. But how could the President be consistent when the strong man of his Cabinet and now leading presidential aspirant from Ohio, John Sherman, used the methods of the spoilsmen to advance his ambitions? Sherman, upon the request of Chester Arthur, in the autumn of 1879 appeared on the stump in New York to advocate the election to the Governorship of the same Cornell whom he had removed from a high Federal office!

Rutherford Hayes, as he faced a welcome retirement from a stormy and unrewarding term, was forced to confess in all truth:

There can be no complete . . . reform of the civil service until public opinion emancipates Congressmen from all control and influence over government patronage. Legislation is required to establish the reform. No proper legislation is to be expected as long as members of Congress are engaged in procuring offices for their constituents. . . . I must do the best I can, unaided by public opinion, and opposed in and out of Congress by a large part of the most powerful men in my party.[79]

As the old war party prepared for new marches upon the electorate, it was evident to practiced eyes that rings of contractor-plunderers once more fastened themselves upon certain government departments—with the help of certain officials in the so-called Minor Cabinet, political veterans appointed through the influence of Cameron, Logan, and Conkling. Hayes and Sherman had sought to eliminate Warehouse and Whisky Rings, and to effect certain economies and improvements in the Treasury, in accordance with business principles. But like an army of termites, expelled from one sector the spoilsmen had simply marched into the undefended Post Office Department, in 1876, the very year of the great Whisky Ring trial.

Returning from their post-election intrigues in the South in December, 1876, the two Western spoilsmen, Stephen Dorsey and Second Assistant Postmaster General Thomas Brady, had arranged a "combination" that controlled the new mail contracts established recently by Congress under the so-called Star Route system, providing for some 134 stagecoach and pony routes in unsettled parts of the Southwest. The conspirators had followed the practice of presenting, according to law, the "lowest bid" unfailingly, then, this obtained, by collusion with post-office officials who were their partners and with auditing officers of the Treasury Department as well, they exacted payments thereafter of three to ten times over the contract sums, in return for "expedited" or "more frequent" services, or pretended improvements, which were usually nonexistent. It was one of the largest, most businesslike "operations" in the history of the Federal service, having, like the Whisky Ring, its business manager, its political protectors, and government officials as partners.

In the case of some twenty-six contracts, for instance, calling for an original payment by the Post Office of $143,169 per annum to the mail contractors, the returns were raised to $622,808 per annum, on the grounds of increased number of trips per week and shortened time per trip—though the public had noticed almost no change whatsoever. Increases of almost $1,000,000 in all were obtained, and of this it was widely believed that $500,000 went to the ring members, who regularly and generously paid very large contributions therefrom to the Republican chest, especially for close campaigns in "doubtful" States.[80]

Rutherford Hayes had shown an active dislike for the company of thieves in the Federal service. He had taken pains, so far as executive supervision was concerned, to set the Federal departments upon a responsible, businesslike footing. When, at the end of his four years' term, secret reports of the whole Star Route Ring, showing "corruption and wrong-doing . . . of a very extensive kind" by "prominent officers," reached his successor in the White House, the latter commented briefly: "I am surprised that it could have so long escaped the notice of President Hayes's Administration."

Once more, after four years' struggle for reform, an important department of the Federal Government was being quietly tapped to furnish cash for the ruling party's nether world. The spoilsmen's organizations entrenched themselves, perpetuated themselves under new guises, apparently defying all effort to dislodge them.

CHAPTER SEVEN

THE DOWNFALL OF THE SPOILSMEN

1880-1881

*My God! What is there in this place that a man should
ever want to get into it?*   JAMES A. GARFIELD

AFTER 1879, the sun of prosperity shone again over the land; rich
harvests were marketed at good prices. A striking phenomenon of
the early 1880's was the vigorous resumption of the westward mass
movement of immigration after a momentary halt. At the western
limits of the central plains the legions of immigrant wagons were on
the march again toward the arid uplands which had formerly been
known as the Great American Desert. Between 1880 and 1890 the
population of Iowa rose 17 per cent, and that of Kansas 43 per cent;
but that of Nebraska, now filling up its western half, increased 134
per cent, Colorado 112 per cent, and the Dakotas 278 per cent. It was
the second great wave of settlers toward regions where "a poor man
can live richer," and where a diligent farmer could "soon become a
very nabob." [1]

While industry also moved forward again, in a magnificently
youthful fervor of construction, political thought floundered; the
professional leaders clashed in mimic battles which bore no conceivable
relation to the needs of the hour: those of conserving the diminishing
public domain, planning the exploitation of the soil, regulating the
monstrous growth of private enterprise and attendant maldistribution
of wealth—in short, righting the balance that swung ever against
free farmers and laborers.

Even hard-fisted men of business were much puzzled nowadays
by the windy rhetoric and the false heroics of spoilsmen leaders like
Roscoe Conkling. These embodied long after their time had passed
the most ancient arts of official corruption; they imposed upon their
bands of followers a form of tribal loyalty no less ancient, and held
them entrenched in the government system, like some fixed military

class that retarded "progress" and flouted all "business principles." From their brawling dissensions all meaning seemed to have fled. Their leadership, moreover, seemed unequal now to meeting the demands for privilege which were being made by the strongest class in the community, the industrial capitalists. This failure in itself spoke of inward decay in the old party institution and the need of a political rebirth. To men who cared nothing for political speeches, and thought chiefly in terms of bank deposits and steel ingots, it seemed that an end must be made somehow of the eternal wrangling over post offices; party authority must become more responsible to the needs of finance and industry; party Organization itself must be turned to better account.

"It seems to me the great duty of the hour for Republicans is to quit quarrelling and try to get together," Whitelaw Reid, the tall blond young man who tried to fill Horace Greeley's square shoes nowadays, wrote sensibly to John Hay.[2] Reid and his friend John Hay, two intellectuals of the younger Republican generation, had married heiresses of gold-mining and railroad fortunes respectively; each sought impatiently a political career open to talent and wealth; each looked with dismay at the continuance of old-fashioned corruption and party theatrics. Yet the conflicts of the rival chieftains in 1880 promised to be more shockingly bloodless, more opera-bouffe than ever before.

With the blooming of the lilacs in the "presidential year" all attention shifted to the preliminary preparations for the national party assemblies. President Hayes had announced his determination to retire, which none seemed to regret, and the Republican Party in 1880 was thenceforth divided into three parts, mainly under the separate banners of Grant, Blaine, and Sherman, the leading aspirants.

John Sherman, the clever Secretary of the Treasury who had dominated the Hayes Administration, was now at the height of his fame, and the promise of conservative statesmanship that he bore drew strong support from the banking and financial community as well as from his henchmen who owed their offices to him. Sherman shrewdly claimed credit for business recovery, saying in a speech at New York, October 27, 1879, so that all bondholders and bankers might hear: "The Resumption Act was a Republican measure, supported, advocated and voted by Republican Senators and Members." [3] And again: "The Republican party proposed . . . the resumption act as the best remedy for the evils that followed the panic of 1873. . . . It now declares its purpose to hold fast to what it has done." [4]

Blaine, who had seen the Presidency wrested from him in 1876, filled the eye of the public as much as ever. His strength was widely distributed; his "magnetic" personality raised up Blaine Legions in Oregon and California as well as in Maine, or in Pennsylvania, where he was born. Among cultivated and wealthy young Republicans, such as Whitelaw Reid, John Hay, and Henry Cabot Lodge, there was a conviction that intelligent statesmanship might be awaited still from this experienced party leader, despite the doubts that had often been raised of his public morals. Blaine himself, measuring the dissension within his party and aware of the prodigious preparations made for a "restoration" of Grant by his enemies, was apprehensive, both as to his own candidacy and as to the chances of his party that season. Yet the very menace of the Grant-Conkling movement brought frantic appeals from Moderate Republicans that he enter the fight, if only to defeat the party's "bad men."

The unwritten law forbidding a third term weighed upon the Grant movement. Yet for this reason the Stalwart bosses who proposed to rule the country again in his name made efforts long in advance and with unheard-of thoroughness to ensure his renomination. During his retirement they had advised Grant pointedly to go abroad. For twenty-six months the little American Ulysses toured the world, the object of an unprecedented hero worship characteristic of the nineteenth-century masses in Japan as well as in England. The American press, especially Gordon Bennett's New York *Herald*, kept the American public fully informed of the royal honors paid Grant and of his triumphant progress from continent to continent, so that when he arrived at last in San Francisco, patriotism and mob spirit in the form of monster parades and reviews throughout the country burst all bounds. For Grant had become a symbol of something, as the Stalwart managers perceived—perhaps of the average man, at all events a symbol as potent almost as the Log Cabin itself.

But horrors! He had returned too soon, in September, 1879, eight months before the party convention. It was the ennui and homesickness of Mrs. Grant that had led the iron soldier into this error. From his friends, Conkling, Logan, and the other Stalwart bosses, came letter after letter begging the traveler to remain away yet a little while longer.[5] Recollection of the catastrophes of Grant's Administration was being stimulated again in the unfriendly press.[6] Soon the Grant managers literally hustled the former President off on a visit to Cuba and Mexico. If he would only leave the field to them, they assured him, they would have the party nominate him by acclamation. Actually, they were compelled to labor night and day to keep alive the boom for the "silent genius."

The Conkling Organization had rallied from defeat, stronger than ever. At its State convention in February, 1880, for the purpose of electing and instructing delegates to the approaching national party gathering, the most arrant bulldozing tactics came into play when Conkling demanded a resolution requiring each delegate to pledge his acceptance of the majority's candidate, as in a party caucus, so that the entire State vote might be cast as a unit at Chicago. This resolution was "steam-rollered" despite the active resistance of a minority of 19 pro-Blaine delegates, led by Judge William Robertson of Westchester County. A public outcry arose at the New York boss's tyranny; Robertson promised, at all events, that he would disobey the Organization's decree.[7]

In similar manner the Pennsylvania machine of Don Cameron, the son of old Simon, and the Logan machine in Illinois rode roughshod over opposition, pledging their States to Grant and joining hands with Conkling. Propaganda was spread to the effect that a spontaneous, irresistible public sentiment demanded a third term for Grant; but privately it was pointed out to the professionals that only by a "restoration" which would give them back their complete title to the entire Federal patronage could they rescue themselves from political limbo. Thus the triumvirs, Conkling, Logan, and Cameron, at the head of a well-disciplined and well-nigh desperate body of over 300 delegates, arrived at the Chicago party convention with all but a majority of the nominating votes.

Commonly the national nominating convention resembles as much a market place as a representative parliament of the party government. Each "movement" or State delegation is passionately attached to its chosen candidate, or Favorite Son, but the ambassadors laboring on behalf of the candidate come together by a common understanding not only to win but also to negotiate or trade. Only one man can win the nomination, but the others in consenting to lose may win a rich Federal department, a Treasury, a Postmaster Generalship, customhouses. Hence the gathered politicians swarm and buzz like flies, as James Bryce observed, at recesses, in all the corridors and near-by hotel lobbies.

But the 1880 convention in Chicago, meeting now "at one of the most splendid barns that was ever constructed" showed a most curious restraint upon such horse-trading. The lines of deep partisan feuds that rent the party were drawn tight. Anti-Grant Clubs, with their banners decrying hero worship and military rule, looked as unforgiving as the Stalwarts. The reformers' contingent, the "man milliners" of politics, still present in some force and as hostile to Blaine as to Grant, added their own shrill notes to the bristling bitterness of the scene.

The long-time deadly enmity between Conkling and Blaine forbade all thought of terms or bargains between them. Meanwhile an intense rivalry had also sprung up between Blaine and Sherman, Blaine's agents having "raided" Sherman's Ohio bailiwick, and humiliated him by removing some of his Native Son delegation. For all his scheming, "Uncle John" stood before the party convention with Ohio something less than solid in his favor. So much factional discord and crossfire between the leading rivals led to a remarkably firm deadlock, which had been anticipated to some extent by sharp students of politics.

Some even felt premonitions of disaster. Mrs. Blaine, who was deeply informed, wrote to her son in August, 1879:

. . . I am so deeply disgusted with American politics, our whole system of popular government, with its fever, its passions, excitement, disappointment, and bitter reaction, that any sphere, however humble, which gives a man to his family, seems to me better than the prize of high place.[8]

There were wheels within wheels; fertile minds turned to thoughts of a Dark Horse. If strategy should dictate the choice of a Moderate Middle Western Republican, then James Garfield (among a group of lesser figures), as President Hayes himself observed privately, would be a more "available" compromise candidate from Ohio than Sherman; one who owned fewer enmities. Earlier in the season a Pennsylvania capitalist, Wharton Barker, who enjoyed managing presidential booms and tariff legislation, had quietly pressed Garfield for permission to launch his campaign.[9] But by the discipline of his profession and rules of seniority, Garfield found himself obliged to act as the nominating orator and campaign leader for his immediate superior in the Ohio Organization, John Sherman. According to the account of witnesses, a secret understanding was reached by the two men. "I am older, of longer service, deserve the first chance," Sherman is believed to have said. "You must help me—until my prospects are gone. If I cannot have it, you are a possibility—and I would prefer and promise in the last resort to throw my support to you."[10] *

In short, Garfield had, after some soul-searching, thrown off the presidential fever, officially rejected proposals for his own candidacy, and laid plans to enter the Senate—while understanding clearly that if a Dark Horse were necessary at the convention, he would be the most prominent choice for that role. Yet he had allowed himself to be inveigled by the crafty Sherman—in return for a promise of promotion to the Senate—into attending the convention as a leader of the Ohio delegation.†

It was a most difficult position, especially for a man as vacillating as James Garfield. His very participation at Chicago would provide its embarrassments; but failure to aid Sherman with all his power

---

* This account of Sherman's commitment to Garfield as an alternate is also borne out by an entry in Garfield's Journal, Feb. 18, 1880.

† Garfield at any rate admired Sherman much less than he did Blaine. On May 25, 1880, before his departure for Chicago, he called on the Secretary of the Treasury to learn what strong points of his public life the latter wished emphasized in the nominating oration. Sherman, according to Garfield's entry in his diary, then confessed that "the chief characteristic of his life from boyhood up had been courageous persistence in any course he had adopted." *Courageous persistence!* Garfield had earlier described the man as one who habitually "studied the popular current, floated with the tide and drifted with the wind of popular opinion." (Smith, *Life and Letters of Garfield*, Vol. II, p. 957; Vol. I, pp. 475-76, letter to Conrad, Jan. 3, 1871.)

would also lay him open to the charge of treachery, ruining his prospects in his home State. Garfield outwardly possessed many attractions; he was handsome, of massive and yet graceful figure, with a huge, leonine head, and a resonant voice. The deep inner weakness of his character, a fatal want of insight and decision, led him eternally to fall between two stools.

II

When Garfield arrived at Chicago on May 29, 1880, the preconvention trading and "dealing" in votes or advantage had reached its possible limits. Grant had over 300 pledged delegates, and Blaine something less—each short of a majority—while Sherman was a poor third with about 100 pledged votes, and three other lesser Favorite Sons, Washburne, Edmunds, and Windom, with negligible support hoped to figure in a compromise. But the dangerous news of the hour was of a secret understanding among the Stalwarts by which the convention was to be led to adopt the so-called unit rule, whereby each State's total vote would be cast without dissent for the candidate approved by the majority. It was to be a coup d'état virtually assuring the prompt selection of Grant by suppressing the scattered minority votes, which in many State delegations were usually for Blaine. Garfield and the Ohio politicians, sensing the perilous emergency, at the last hour effected a hasty alliance with the Blaine delegation and the minor candidates, for the sole purpose of defeating the unit rule.

In committee and on the floor of the convention, Garfield assumed the lead of the combined anti-Grant forces, pleading forcefully against the "tyranny" of Conkling's faction. In contrast with the arrogant New York boss, Garfield showed his habitual moderation in debate and made a most pleasing effect upon the convention. By a close margin the unit rule was defeated, and by a forced compromise the third-term faction accepted the independent Senator George Hoar of Massachusetts as temporary chairman of the convention. The Stalwart movement had met a decisive check at the outset, had been forced to relinquish a measure which was sure to give them victory. Moreover Garfield, rallying the opposition at this moment—it was one of the high points of his public and party career—had strength-

ened and justified the rebellion of the independent minority in Conkling's home State. These were mortal blows, and it was not in
Conkling's nature to forget them.

During the public debates a well-posted claque had greeted Garfield's appearances with warm demonstrations of applause. The Senator from New York in disgust sent him a message written upon a
scrap of newspaper: "I congratulate you as being the 'dark horse.' " [11]

The hours devoted to framing a suitable platform for the season's
canvass provided comic relief amid so much dire partisanship. Platform resolutions condemning polygamy and Chinese immigration,
and (once more) charging the Democrats with sedition, were approved by the convention, which also declared its "sympathy" with
civil-service reform, though as an appropriately vague expression
offered from the floor rather than officially through the Resolutions
Committee.

At this a certain obscure Carpetbag delegate from Texas, one
Flanagan, arose with the historic remark: *"What are we up here for?
I mean that members of the Republican Party are entitled to office,
and if we are victorious, we will have office."* There was hearty
laughter and applause; the Texas delegate had expressed the true
desires of the great majority of deputies assembled from thirty-eight
State machines, and only in a spirit of good fun were they led to
adopt the civil-service resolution.

On the evening of June 5, the fourth day of this stormy convention which some feared might be the scene of the breakup of the
Grand Old Party, the various candidates were at last put in nomination. Roscoe Conkling over several weeks had been preparing his
supreme oratorical effort for what he called the "Austerlitz of American politics." At this time even the chieftains of great machines had
been impressed with the possibilities of mass appeal through literary
efforts, such as Ingersoll's Plumed Knight speech for Blaine four
years earlier.

Conkling, in most impressive style, opened with verse concerning
the man who now hailed simply from

Appomattox
And its famous apple-tree.

"Never defeated," Grant could "grandly win" New York and all doubtful States; unjust assaults had but "seasoned and strengthened his hold upon the public heart." Referring to recent social upheavals and appealing to timorous capitalists of all sorts, he cried: "Perils and emergencies will search in vain . . . for any other on whom the nation leans in such confidence and trust." Grant had shown that "communism, lawlessness and disorder, although it might stalk high-headed and dictate law to a whole city, would always find a foe in him." Then, turning to the professional "workers," he reminded them that Grant had "never betrayed a cause or a friend." Thus far the orator had reasoned effectively, from partisan political motives. But as he gained passion he turned inevitably to unsparing mockery of his opponents, to whom he now gave mortal offense. Through Grant, Conkling meant to uphold the faith "not only against the common enemy"—the Democrats—but all pretended reformers and purifiers of politics, "against the charlatans, jayhawkers, tramps and guerrillas—the men who deploy between the lines, and forage now on one side and then on the other." He went out of his way also to give mortal offense to the Blaine forces as he said pointedly, in an allusion to the unpleasant Mulligan Letters: "We shall have no defensive campaign. . . . We shall have nothing to explain away. We shall have no apologies to make." Blaine, without being named, was pictured as an artificer, while he said of Grant:

Without patronage and without emissaries, without committees, without bureaus, without telegraph wires running from his house to this Convention . . . he is a Republican who never wavers.[12]

We must recall the voice, the magisterial presence of the orator, and even his sinister reputation, to comprehend the reaction, in wave upon wave of uproar, which his words evoked from the delegates, gallery claques, and 10,000 spectators.

After witnessing this demonstration, the next orator, Garfield, began by saying aptly that the "assemblage seemed . . . a human ocean in tempest." In the highly rhetorical style of the time, though more reasonable and conciliatory than Conkling's, he continued:

I remember that it is not the billows, but the calm level of the sea, from which all heights and depths are measured. . . . Gentlemen of the

Convention . . . When your enthusiasm has passed . . . we shall find below the storm and passion that calm level of public opinion from which the thoughts of a mighty people are measured.

The heart of Garfield's speech for John Sherman lay in his appeal for party harmony as a means to victory. How should victory be accomplished? Surely not by assailing "our Republican brethren"? "In order to win victory now we want the vote of every Republican,— of every Grant Republican and every Anti-Grant Republican, in America,—of every Blaine man and every Anti-Blaine man." [13] Garfield, while performing thoroughly the duty that would lead him to the Senate, was inevitably calling attention to the possibilities of himself as a compromise or "harmony" candidate who might compose the factions. The subsequent outcome, and accusations by enemies, have lent color, while giving no proof, to suspicions of duplicity on · his part.

In the balloting, which began on June 7, no candidate possessed a clear advantage at the start, Grant having 304, Blaine following closely with 284, and Sherman running a poor third with 93. Some 75 votes were also distributed among three Favorite Sons. Of this last group, 34 votes for Edmunds were from the Mugwump reformist faction, who could be won neither to Grant nor to Blaine. This deadlock, long foreseen, in which the leaders could neither negotiate with each other nor gather enough remaining strength from the rest of the field to win, continued with no sign of a break for two days, through thirty-four ballots. Garfield had had from his friends the honorable mention of one or two votes on certain ballots. They were at work covertly, ready for the chance if it should come, and apparently in close touch with Blaine agents. On the thirty-fourth ballot the Wisconsin delegation, which had voted steadily for Blaine, suddenly switched 16 votes to Garfield, making 17 for him. It is remembered that he rose to his feet to make a point of order, agitated, almost incoherent, perhaps to give a formal refusal to his nomination. But the chairman of the convention, Hoar, quickly overruled him before he could proceed. "I was terribly afraid," Hoar relates, "that he would say something that would make his nomination impossible." [14]

On the following ballot Indiana with 27 and a scattering of other delegates went to Garfield, giving him 50; the effect of his rapid gains—while Blaine and Sherman declined and Grant held firm— suggesting a "boom." Then on the thirty-sixth ballot came word by telegraph of the release of the Ohio delegation at Sherman's order, accompanied by the "stampede" of the whole Blaine column, and Garfield was nominated by 399 votes as against 306 for Grant.[15]

The Stalwarts had gone down without striking their colors; they had not joined hands with their opponents in naming the compromise candidate in the end. The selection of Garfield had been forced by Blaine as a means of averting his own extinction at the hands of the triumvirate of Stalwart bosses. "I should much prefer to see the party defeated with Garfield or some other candidate to winning with Grant," Blaine is reported to have said.[16]

As a corollary to these interesting proceedings there came the quick nomination for the Vice-Presidency of Chester A. Arthur of New York, Conkling's first lieutenant and handy man. Conkling, invited under the system of compromise which governed the convention to name his man for this office, had refused, and had commanded Arthur in haughtiest tones to drop the proposal as he would "a red hot shoe from the forge." [17] Arthur, the "Gentleman Boss," and former cus- tomhouse collector, showed some spirit in resisting his leader as well as concern for the future of his party. With a certain humility he pleaded that the Vice-Presidency was a greater distinction than he had hoped for, and he would accept it even "if only a barren nomina- tion" resulted. Moreover, the other satellites of the New York Or- ganization approved of his course, and longed for peace after fierce strife. To Conkling it was bitter gall; "like taking a suit of old clothes in lieu of the English mission," the Nation said with relish.[18] Moreover, he appeared to have lost control over his own followers in the general disaster. The party would need Arthur's services if it hoped to capture New York in the coming election; above all it would need all his tact to win over the "sulking Achilles."

For Garfield, as he awoke from the excitement of the fantastic con- vention which gained him a presidential nomination at so little cost, the outlook was dark. He was clearly under the heaviest obligations to Blaine; but this did not simplify his relations with the Stalwart wing of the party. Garfield in winning had contributed to the defeat of the Grant leaders, one of whom, Conkling, was known to be "the implacable enemy of anyone who had successfully crossed his path." [19]

Garfield was an "angle-worm" to Conkling and his friends; but to Sherman, Chester Arthur was a "burlesque" as a running mate. The breach between the factions in the party seemed irreparable. The compromising manner in which it chose its standard-bearers seemed sickening to disinterested men.

III

The two great patronage parties toward 1880 had achieved a remarkable state of equilibrium. This almost exact balance, which would require during the next decade but a slight movement of public opinion, the smallest turn of a screw, to effect victory for one side or the other, was undoubtedly the result of their common nullity of program, their identity in objective and group relationships, and the degraded character of public leadership. During this phase, when Burning Issues and true class interests are dormant, the veritable indifference of the public seems as marked as the excitement of the professionals seems feigned. In our politics the changes in personal fortune or in those of factions are largely irrelevant, except that beneath the theatrically agitated surface they bespeak the slow, all but unconscious, transformation of the old party institution in its painful evolution toward new directives and new tactics. It is well to scan the surface and the texture of this change.

The Democratic Party after 1877 had completely conquered the Solid South, following the departure of the Federal troops. A decade of "peaceful" Reconstruction, according to the Radical plan, had sown more undying sectional hatred than four years of slaughter; the Negro and the white masses alike had been betrayed by the political bargain of 1877. Control of political offices, which formerly in the South had been, in great measure, a hereditary privilege of the older and richer landholding caste, was now democratized in exactly the sense that it was democratized in Republican Chicago and Cincinnati: a lower grade of professional politician, whose strength was based on local office and plunder, largely displaced the old aristocratic leadership. But aristocrats and commoners alike combined in removing or neutralizing the Negro suffrage. Henceforth the Solid South cast its 138 or more electoral votes in successive national contests on the side of the old revived party of Martin Van Buren.

North of Mason and Dixon's line, the Democratic Party based its strength in patronage upon certain city machines, as in New York City and some of the large Middle Western towns. It needed now only the winning of two or three large States, out of the two dozen in the North, to make for national victory; and after the Tidal Wave of 1878 the fates seemed propitious.

Yet in the vital New York State sector of this party also a disgraceful quarrel over the spoils of office suddenly rent the party in two. Tilden's reformation of Tammany had been so superficial that within two years of his term as Governor, the Tiger ruled again over the polyglot metropolis of New York. The Tilden faction, moderates and reformers, were defied by the men of Tammany in 1879, so that the State government had been won by Conkling's men. At the nominating convention in Cincinnati in 1880 Tilden, on the ground of ill-health, declined to stand again for the Presidency. A contest by Tilden would have given the electorate a chance to repair the Republican wrongs of 1876; but it might also have thrown light on the somewhat bungling Democratic attempts at "stealing" ballots.

Bent upon winning at all costs, the Democratic Party managers, like the Republicans, hit upon a compromise candidate—General W. S. Hancock, a hero of Gettysburg. This was almost too cagey. With the Republicans offering a former Union Brigadier General, the party which had so often been accused of disloyalty offered, in turn, a far more distinguished Union General of much higher rank and military fame, though of no known capacity for political or administrative life. Then, to carry the "doubtful" State of Indiana, its governor, William H. English, was nominated for the Vice-Presidency.

In their announced political programs the two parties were as similar as in their routine corruption and their paltry internal dissensions over patronage. The Democratic Party declared itself "the friend of labor and of the laboring man," while the Republicans promised to pass tariff legislation which it was alleged would primarily raise the wages of labor. When the Republicans accused their opponents of favoring a downward revision of the tariff to the loss of protected capitalists, Hancock hastened to reply that under his party "the manufacturing or industrial interests of the country . . . [would] have as much protection" as under the Republicans. The tariff, he maintained in a public address which had been written for him, was "a local question," a statement which had much truth, but which aroused widespread ridicule at the time.[20] On the issue of money, which caused so much periodic excitement among the farmers and the lower middle class, the two platforms canceled each other.

Following the cue given by Secretary of the Treasury Sherman, the hopeful Republican ideologues claimed credit for the current economic recovery. Then by an easy step of exegesis, they claimed further that the fine weather of 1879 and 1880 was somehow ordained by a Republican Administration. Sherman said:

We gratefully acknowledge that Providence has been on the side of the Republican party, or rather that, having sought to do right, we find ourselves supported by Divine Providence.[21]

Ingersoll, with a trifle more of hyperbole, offered in its extreme form the legend of the G.O.P. as the provider of prosperity:

I belong to the party that believes in good crops; that is glad when a fellow finds a gold mine; that rejoices when there are forty bushels of wheat to the acre. . . . The Democratic party is a party of famine; it is a good friend of an early frost; it believes in the Colorado beetle and in the weevil.[22]

A pleasanter, more traditional vein of ideology was the revival of the Log Cabin symbol, already used for Harrison and Lincoln. That General Garfield had been born in so politically perfect a mansion was a happy accident that his supporters freely exploited. Nor was a vacation jaunt on an inland canalboat, in his boyhood days, overlooked in the season's literature and oratory which played upon the folklore of the self-made man risen "from canal boy to President," a legend associated with the most fervent of American dreams.

At this very moment, much more pertinent doctrines were being offered in good earnest by the young National Greenback-Labor

Party, whose nominating convention was held in Chicago on June 9. It proposed an eight-hour day for labor, a graduated income tax, national regulation of railroads and of all interstate commerce, and both silver and paper currency inflation. It denounced also the attempts of the two major parties "to stir up sectional strife as an effort to conceal monstrous crimes against the people." [23] But farmers who had voted against the low price of wheat and corn in 1878 abandoned the Greenback cause after the "boom" of 1879-80, the total vote of this party for James Weaver declining to 300,000, or less than a third of the votes in the previous congressional elections.

The 1880 campaign embodied certain new elements as well as the familiar and traditional ones. Garfield, whose growing conservatism had been noticed with favor by high financial interests, determined that he would avoid controversial interests and devote his speeches to "a solid South and the business interests of the country." [24] We find him now systematically cultivating the support of certain of the richest industrialists and bankers.

But these men were no longer simply wealthy patrons, hoping for a reflected glory or some modest special privileges, as in the past. They thought now in terms of the effect of general party policies upon the rising monopolies they controlled. Here were no longer dry-goods merchants or rich country bankers, but men like Jay Gould, who controlled the Union Pacific Railroad, Chauncey Depew, the vice-president and political manager of the Vanderbilt family's New York Central Railroad, William and John Rockefeller of the notorious Standard Oil monopoly, and Levi Morton, perhaps then the second banker in New York—Morgan being of course first—and head of the great Anglo-American banking firm of Morton, Rose & Co., which became the nucleus for the modern Guaranty Trust Company. These were men who were concentrating the nation's productive wealth rapidly in their few hands, were hailed already by an admiring press as "nature's noblemen," the uncrowned kings and self-made masters of enormous aggregations of American capital.

On August 5 Garfield made a memorable visit to New York for diplomatic reasons, at a time when the outcome seemed desperate. He saw William Walter Phelps, James Blaine's wealthy friend and patron; he went to the home of Whitelaw Reid, and met Jay Gould there, the man whom ten years earlier he had denounced to the whole country for his part in the Black Friday gold conspiracy. "Jay Gould came in," Garfield writes in his journal, "and we had a conversation on the campaign. I think he will help." [25] Upon the same visit, at a secret meeting, he saw Levi Morton, from whom he sought a "special fund" to be administered by Morton for the purpose of carrying New York, which he declared to be "the darkest spot." [26]

Later, pursuing the large capitalists more systematically, more directly than party leaders had ever attempted before, he wrote to one of the party agents in Indiana demanding that this man approach a "Mr. Rockafeller" [sic] of Cleveland. "Do you know his state of feeling toward me?" he queried. "Is it such that I might safely invite him for consultation and talk freely with him about Indiana and ask his coöperation?" It was not about "the raising of means," Garfield hastened to add—using the indirect word with the scruples of a former theologian—that he wished to see the notorious monopolist. And Garfield's correspondent in Cleveland, Amos Townsend, hastened to reply in alarm, September 3, 1880:

> It would not do for him to visit you, as it would be reported and *cut* like a *knife* in Pennsylvania. He is however, *all right* and will do what he can for your success. It is *risky writing* and you will be wise to keep your hand off paper and keep out of all complications.[27]

Garfield took pen and paper again, however, and reported that two Indiana bosses, William W. Dudley and John C. New, desired the assistance in the canvass of Rockefeller's force of five hundred oil-selling agents located all about Indiana.[28]

In September, after the surprising defeat of the Republicans in Maine, came the voluble and oily Chauncey Depew from New York for a private interview with the prospective President. He promised the help of his "friends" the Vanderbilts, and Garfield, hearing this, fairly shouted for joy, as Depew remembers.[29]

A novel element also was the first intervention in a national election campaign of Mark Hanna of Cleveland, a robust millionaire of coal, iron, shipping, and banking. Hanna's Republicanism, as Herbert Croly relates, was at this time ardent and "innocent." Yet he brought certain fresh impulses to politics. Already locally famous in western Ohio, Hanna is said to have originated the idea of a Business Man's Republican Club, organizing the main body of Cleveland's capitalists as an auxiliary political association, to lend their prestige to the one party rather than to the other. Besides raising generous sums of money, Hanna arranged torchlight parades of businessmen, which he led in person; the idea of similar clubs now spread to many other cities.[30]

At this stage of American party politics, however, the aid of businessmen alone could not win for the Republicans if unity and harmony among the professional leaders were not achieved. When after laborious efforts and negotiations all summer some outward "harmony" was established, Grant and Conkling consented to work together for their party in Ohio. Grant had promised to visit Mentor, the candidate's home not far from Cleveland, and Conkling, it was reported, hesitated to join him. There is a legend that Mark Hanna, present at the conference of mighty leaders in a railroad train, brusquely persuaded Grant and Conkling to go, and accompanied them to the famous presumed scene of reconciliation with Garfield, September 28, 1880.[31] Thus instinctively this businessman in politics with blunt common sense attacked the problem of chronic discord in the dominant party—which alarmed all businessmen, and which to him should simply have been adjusted long ago on a basis of costs and profits.

IV

The pursuit of "harmony" by the Republican candidate was the inward drama of all that summer's political madness. At this time one of the key men in the party situation was Levi Morton, the Croesus who had come to New York as a poor Yankee farm boy from Vermont.

Avid of public glory, by lending himself first to Conkling's and then to Platt's counsels, Morton rose eventually to be Governor of New York, an Ambassador, a Vice-President—though the final honor he pursued so feverishly always eluded him. In any case, through Morton's hands passed most of the funds raised by the very rich New York capitalists, a large and increasing portion of the total "means" available. The outcome in New York depended on him. But the great banker would not move until the chief of the spoilsmen, Conkling, gave the command. Supreme voice in the electoral contests, especially when so close, still centered then in the nationwide professional Organization and its generals. Money alone would be ineffective unless the trained political soldiers who knew how to distribute it so as to catch votes would co-operate wholeheartedly. And without the promise of such unstinted aid Garfield, headed for defeat, could not have the contributions of the capitalists themselves. Here was the agonizing problem which possessed the unhappy presidential candidate after June.

The final stand of the "Stalwart 306" delegates pledged to General Grant's third term was more than a sentimental or romantic gesture in homage to the war hero; it was an evil omen, a threat, as clear as if a black flag had been run up, that unless terms were soon made with the Stalwarts, they would by their resistance, overt or passive, bring about the defeat of their own party.

Garfield had previously shown a respectful interest in the aims of the liberal middle-class spokesmen who had agitated since 1872 for civil-service reform. Moreover, he was the colleague of Sherman and the Ohio Half-Breeds, who out of principle or secret ambition had struck such heavy blows at the Stalwart machine in New York. Nothing was more infuriating to professional officeholders and party "workers" such as Bill Chandler, Chester Arthur, and Thomas Brady—who had helped to capture Southern States in 1876—than the prospect of being kicked out immediately after having lifted a President and his friends to power. On the other hand, the influence of men like Carl Schurz, Samuel Bowles, and George William Curtis, the "man milliners" of politics, was increasing among reasonable and intelligent groups of voters; and in a close election their Independent minority might decide the results between the two parties in New York State. Thus Garfield felt compelled to placate the Independents, or Mugwumps, while making ceaseless efforts to appease the wrath of Conkling. Then he must instantly swing about and mollify the suspicious Blaine Legion, for was it not Blaine who clearly had dictated the nomination of Garfield at the time of the Chicago deadlock? The papers and letters that Garfield and his heirs have honestly bequeathed to us give a wonderfully illuminating picture of the moves now made in the presidential drama of 1880.

With the diplomatic situation so involved, Garfield's advisers all reflected their intense anxiety. Immediately after the convention Whitelaw Reid, the editor of the New York *Tribune*, wrote:

> . . . I beg you to make no promises to anybody. . . . I . . . have seen such misfortunes resulting from hasty promises by Presidential candidates that I am specially anxious to impress the point . . . please don't make any journeys or any speeches.[32]

These close observers knew Garfield well and feared his wavering. The Ohio littérateur John Hay especially feared his want of "gall" and begged Reid to provide something of this! Yet late in June, while besieged by advice and dangerous gossip, the candidate made a journey to Washington, as discreetly as possible, where he saw and consulted his brother in arms of many years in Congress, Blaine, in "a full, long and cordial talk."[33]

Blaine was on intimate terms of friendship with Garfield; but the "magnetic man" had "too great faith in management," as Garfield noted in his journal. However, Blaine clearly possessed the power of quick decision and the fighting spirit that the candidate lacked. His advice was invaluable, though before the election, to disarm criticism and rivalry, Blaine quite evidently held himself at a distance.

Then the uneasy candidate went to the length of calling on Conkling at his hotel, but found him absent, and left a note making an appointment for the next morning. Conkling returned the call, found Garfield out, but learned that Garfield had been seen riding publicly in a carriage with Carl Schurz, the bespectacled, blackbearded German devil of reform.

Conkling was beside himself with choler; and Whitelaw Reid hastened, pen in hand, to warn the candidate that the "working politicians" must not be frightened into believing that under Garfield the same things would happen to them as under Hayes. The Conkling men now looked upon Garfield with suspicion; he must repair this evil in his letter of acceptance.[34]

Garfield now swung about to conciliate the spoilsmen. The titular head of the Republican National Committee was this year the venerable, wealthy, and honest Marshall Jewell, former Governor of Connecticut. The real managing head was General Stephen Dorsey, a war veteran, a former Carpetbag Senator from Arkansas, and now henchman of the Illinois boss John Logan, whose ill will was allayed by this appointment. Dorsey, we must remember, was now also a senior partner in the post-office plunder ring of the Star Route contractors, directed by the Second Assistant Postmaster General, Thomas Brady. Thus he had a serious stake in a Republican victory. Brady and William W. Dudley, both of the Indiana machine, gave invaluable services, as did Chester Arthur in New York. But it was the cynical, hard-fighting Dorsey who carried the brunt of the contest in Indiana and New York, which strategy chose as the ground of battle; and Garfield recognized this by various effusive expressions of gratitude. Dorsey was "a man of great ability" Garfield privately believed.[35]

Garfield's letter of acceptance, which appeared in July, was a performance showing the work of many hands. The candidate made painful attempts to please all factions, Stalwart and Half-Breed, reformers and plunderers. What Garfield intended is set forth in a very candid letter to Blaine, June 29, 1880, wherein he referred to the problem of the civil-service plans as a "wretched business." He said to Blaine:

I believe in party government, and that the spirit and doctrines of the Republican party should prevail in the Executive departments. But I do not wish to do anything which will alienate the doctrinaires from our support. Now please give me your best thoughts on the subject.[36]

Garfield had also written, asking for suggestions, to Carl Schurz, Hayes, and Chester Arthur.

Nevertheless the reformers, such as Godkin of the *Nation*, were "cruelly disappointed" by the letter of acceptance and found Garfield on various grounds "without dignity" as "without backbone." [37] But neither were the Stalwarts conciliated. Mere words were nothing to them.

Blunt warning came now from William E. Chandler, who wrote that Conkling and his friends in New York must have personal assurance that they would not be "outraged" anew, as they had been by

President Hayes. "The state of New York is . . . vital and it is worth while, perhaps to stoop a little in order to conquer much." [38] Garfield writhed at the notion of a penitent journey to New York; he hesitated, he objected earnestly. Should not the bosses come to see him at his home in the Ohio village? But from Dorsey came a command in an unmistakable tone, that

it is a duty which you owe to yourself and to the Republican party to be here on the 5th of August regardless of what Mr. Jewell says or Mr. George William Curtis or Mr. Anybody else. . . . I insist that a conference with Governor Cornell and Senator Conkling is an absolute essential to success in this campaign . . . they want to know whether the Republicans of the State of New York are to be recognized . . . or whether the "Scratchers" and Independents and "feather-heads" are to ride over the Republican party of this state as they have for the last four years. They . . . can only be satisfied by a personal conference with you. [39]

With many a groan Garfield prepared to leave, but wrote confidentially to Blaine on July 30:

My dear friend, you must stand by me. Many of our friends . . . think there are evidences that a few leaders in New York meditate treachery and say that the visit will either prevent it or so develop it that the country will understand it and place the responsibility where it belongs. Of one thing you may be assured, there shall be no surrender to any unreasonable demands. I will do nothing to compromise myself or the noble men who stand up to the fight. . . . I want you to find the exact situation, if possible before I arrive, I want you to know how large a force C has behind him and just what the trouble is. [40]

The belief persisted at Republican headquarters that the Conkling-Grant faction would gladly see Garfield, and Blaine, who stood behind him, defeated. All through the summer Whitelaw Reid had been reporting to the candidate that Conkling spoke of him with unrestrained bitterness, swore that Garfield meant to cheat him. If Conkling were pulled into the campaign it was only to be "by main strength." [41]

On the way to New York the candidate addressed large crowds from the back of his train at various stops. A sympathetic figure and pleasant-spoken, he gave no sign of his inward torment. This one reads now pityingly in almost every line of his journals and letters, which reflect how he is alternately warned, coaxed, and threatened by his chief counselors and nose-pullers. It is an unforgettable picture of a future President that Garfield makes as he asks himself each night in his diary if "any harm had been done" by the noncommittal remarks he permits himself to utter in public. In those days there existed still an old, hypocritical tradition which demanded that a candidate should not appear to seek his office and should not campaign too openly for himself.

His mission to New York in August, earlier mentioned under another head, was twofold: to raise more funds for emergency purposes, and to outflank party disaffection. At Albany Governor Alonzo Cornell, Chester Arthur, and Chauncey Depew had climbed on board his train and accompanied him to New York, where he arrived on the night of August 4. He was taken at once to the Republican stronghold at the Fifth Avenue Hotel, and that night saw various rich benefactors of the party.

On the next day at noon, August 5, was held the open peace meeting in the Fifth Avenue Hotel parlors, before 200 prominent citizens, with short addresses from Blaine, Logan, Sherman, and others. But "My Lord Roscoe" was not there! Garfield notes that the New York chieftain's friends "were embarrassed and somewhat indignant," though they gave signs of zeal and enthusiasm now for the work in hand.[42] Thomas Platt, who was present in Conkling's place, had a totally different impression, recalling that the "chagrin, mortification and indignation which were manifested" at Conkling's conspicuous absence emanated from Garfield.[43]

It was on the following afternoon, August 6, that the all-important private conference with Conkling's field marshals, Platt, Arthur, Crowley, and Levi Morton (the "angel" of their organization), took place. Out of this long interview, at which Garfield maintains he gave no "mortgages" upon his political future, entirely conflicting reports have come. Platt, describing the meeting in great detail, relates that the first business was to pacify Garfield for the insulting absence of Conkling, intended plainly as a disciplinary measure. The New York machine leaders did not propose to "bear the brunt of the battle in the campaign" unless they came to an agreement about the "recognition" of the regular Republican Organization of New York. Garfield, on the other hand, felt obliged to show grateful "recognition" as well of the anti-Conkling Republicans from New York—the faction led by Judge William Robertson, who voted first for Blaine, then for Garfield, at the convention. But on this score, according to Platt's account, he promised solemnly to consult the Stalwart leaders and be guided by them in naming all Federal officials for their State. Then the matter of raising money to carry on the canvass was disposed of, Morton being named chairman of the committee on finance, and being promised in return special government favor in handling refunding bond issues.[44] Another version by "one of those present" holds that one important cabinet post was promised the Conkling machine.[45] "No trades, no shackles," Garfield noted in his diary, after it was over; also he writes a few days later to Reid: "Do you know how Arthur, Platt or Cornell are feeling since the conference? I do not hear from either of them. My letters indicate that the New York trip did no harm and much good." [46]

Apparently Garfield did not assume that his promise to "consult" and "be guided" (in accord with his private views on patronage expressed earlier to Blaine) constituted a firm contract. His sympathetic biographer, Thomas Clarke Smith, also holds to this view. Yet it is inconceivable that the sort of men with whom Garfield conferred, Platt, Arthur, and Cornell, would have let him out of the hotel room, according to another and more pertinent view, without pinning him down at least to the promise never to interfere with their control of New York's Republican Organization. "Garfield knew the sort of men with whom he was dealing," and for their services there was only one form of payment.[47]

One is led inevitably to the simplest conclusion about all these secret negotiations, which the historians have overlooked: that Garfield, given his character, must have made pledges of an equivocal character. Their fulfillment depended upon whether the New York men "worked hard." To corroborate this view there is the evidence of continuing mistrust—despite all pledges exchanged—up to the closing weeks of the campaign in September and October, reflected by Tom Platt:

"Have you any faith in Garfield?" asked Platt of his chief. Conkling made a wry face, sneered, and replied, "Not much, but we will try him out." [48]

At last, however, things began to move; Conkling, a compound of brilliance and petulance, came forth from the tent in which he had lain sulking and lent his voice in public speech for his party. Though he did not flatter the candidate, or even name him, it was pleasant, for a change, to have him turn his powerful sarcasm upon the enemy party. Yet in private he continued to express his mistrust of "men from Ohio bearing gifts."

With Stalwart approval, money flowed freely from financial New York. Thomas Platt also raised funds by assessing State and Federal officers at New York; and at Washington, Brady, the Star Route plunderer, pressed the post-office and other department clerks for their tithes. Indiana's "workers" were clamorous for money, ostensibly in order to prevent the Democrats from importing floaters. Overriding Chairman Jewell of the Republican National Committee, Dorsey drew most of the funds on hand and plunged into the struggle for "vital" Indiana. Garfield followed the fray from close by, urging on the professionals as in the following letter:

My dear Hubbell:
Please say to Brady that I hope he will give us all the assistance he can. I think he can help effectually. Please tell me how the Depts. generally are doing.[49]

To Brady, this sounded like an appeal to him to use the profits of the Star Route contracts, as he maintained afterward, though there is no evidence that Garfield so intended his message, or knew of Brady's secret at the time. Garfield also exhorted Dorsey, as the fatal day approached, not to "relax any grip anywhere." He concluded: "I rely greatly upon your calm equipoise which has shown itself so often and so well hitherto." [50]

Dorsey, Brady, and the former lieutenant of Oliver Morton, William W. Dudley, waged a glorious fight for Indiana, thanks to the money provided by assessments, plunder rings, and New York bankers. It was well so, for floaters' prices ran high that year.* As Dorsey related candidly in a public interview several years later:

Well, we had a big campaign fund. . . . There was spent in Indiana about $400,000, not a nickel of which came into my hands. The Republican organization there was as good as it can be, and the credit of it is due to John C. New and Colonel William W. Dudley.

By these methods the threatened Democratic lead in Indiana—"venal" Indiana!—was cut to a Republican majority of a bare 7,000 votes.

In New York, as Dorsey further related, the sole chance

"lay in concentrating all our powers in New York and Kings Counties—that is, the two cities of New York and Brooklyn. Well we did so. We cut down the Democratic majorities more than 75,000 and the State was carried by 20,000. You want to know how this was done?" he concluded. He smiled and was silent.[51]

Garfield was elected by the scant margin of 10,000 votes, but the capture of three large and doubtful States, New York, Indiana, and Ohio, furnished a majority of 215 electoral votes, against 155 for Hancock. Garfield could scarcely have ignored the methods by which victory had been gained.

As if to remind him, his jubilant comrades presented Stephen Dorsey, the architect of victory, with a monster banquet and testimonial at Delmonico's restaurant in New York on February 11, 1881. Ulysses Grant, Henry Ward Beecher, and the Vice-President-elect, Chester Arthur, vied with each other in praising Dorsey for his artistry. Arthur, who may have eaten and drunk too much on this occasion, alluded in a playful and somewhat mystifying fashion to the "secrets" of the late campaign:

Indiana was really, I suppose, a Democratic State. It had been put on the books always as a State that might be carried by close and perfect organization and a great deal of—(laughter [and cries of "soap"]). I see the reporters are present, and therefore I will simply say that every-

---

* The "floaters" were the men who, in close elections, voted according to the highest bid.

body showed a great deal of interest in the occasion and distributed tracts and political documents all through the State.[52]

The banquet and Arthur's queer speech received too much attention in the press and caused heart-searching in the councils of the President-elect. What did it all mean? Was it not but a way of calling attention to the just claims of the Stalwart spoilsmen in return for vital services given? Garfield confided to his journal that it was all "a curious affair," whose whole significance he could not quite understand. Soon William E. Chandler and Blaine enlightened him by warning letters as to the Stalwart design of "building up" and defending Dorsey's place in the party hierarchy. Blaine wrote, February 13, 1881:

I am afraid the true intent and meaning of the Dorsey dinner was to enable him to make demands which will in the end modestly center in the Second Assistant-Postmaster-Generalship, through which channel there are cunning preparations being made by a small cabal to steal half a million a year during your administration.

It was the Minor Cabinet they desired to hold against assault, Blaine warned him now very seriously, and while referring here to previous cautionings on this score he concluded: "I again beg you to keep yourself free from all possible commitments as to the minor cabinet which in the Post-Office Department is even more important than the major."

V

The winter season, interlude between the election and the inauguration of Garfield, was one of fabulous intrigue, fabulous even in the quarrelsome annals of the American republic. Behind the scenes, while the public heard only confusing or distorted reports, Guelphs and Ghibellines fought without quarter for control of the new government.

Blaine, who was always "a power in the land," as Uncle John Sherman said, had played his usual lively role in the stumping of the last campaign, while holding himself at a discreet distance in public from his friend Garfield. Once more he had failed to win the coveted nomination for the Presidency, owing to the jealous strife between the factions. Yet, though he himself could not have won, he had played the most decisive part in "making" the President. According to the rules of party life, his claims upon the Chief Executive were boundless; and those who knew the secret of Garfield's kindly and wavering nature were aware that Blaine's would easily become the dominant voice in the councils of the new Administration. Blaine "ate, drank and breathed" politics; Blaine "would be the power in the Cabinet," his friends generally assumed.[53] The logical course for him would be to consolidate his position and unify the party nationally under his own leadership. These were the first moves.

A long friendship, though an unequal one, linked these two politicians. Garfield was sometimes critical of his friend and told himself that he must not do "too much complacent yielding" to his friend's aggressive demands.[54] But in truth he knew himself to be under the heaviest debt to the former Speaker, and soon ended by yielding anew. After the scandal of the Crédit Mobilier, it had been generally expected that Garfield would be demoted from important committee memberships in Congress; but Blaine, who had also been slandered, had protected him sympathetically like a fellow sinner. Seven years before Garfield had written the Speaker in profuse gratitude that

those of us who have been the special objects of assault during the last year appreciate more highly than you know of the courage and manliness with which you stand by them. I am sure you will never have occasion to regret it.[55]

Very shortly after his election Garfield in a personal interview offered Blaine the leading post of his Cabinet, that of Secretary of State, but asked that the appointment be kept secret for a time, so that they might more easily face unforeseen eventualities. On December 20, 1880, Blaine accepted the post in an effusive letter declaring:

You need no pledge of my loyalty both in heart and in act. . . . Your administration must be made brilliantly successful and strong in the confidence and pride of the people; not obviously directing its energies to reëlection, but compelling that result by the logic of events. . . . To that most desirable consummation I feel that, next to yourself, I can contribute more influence than any other man. I say this, not from egotism or vain-glory, but merely as a deduction from an analysis of the political forces which have been at work in the country.[56]

There followed a busy correspondence between the two men, Blaine not waiting any longer to give directives and outline policies.

Blaine's letters show his tremendous shrewdness as a craftsman of politics; with their unusual gift of expression, worthy of a great literary artist, and fresh from the battlefield, they make up an extraordinary treatise on the practice of American party government.

Blaine not merely allied himself but "merged" his political fortunes with Garfield's. "I believe with you as President," he writes, on December 10, 1880, ". . . I could do much to build up the party as the result of strong and wise policy." He then proceeds to analyze the composition of the party itself, which, he holds, must be unified and controlled before anything can be accomplished. The Republican Party, he says, contains three sections, like Gaul. The first is the "Blaine section," most important because its support comes from the populous and stanchly Republican States and districts, whereas the supporters of Grant (the Stalwarts), coming from the Carpetbag States, are stronger in party nominating conventions than in elections. This Blaine section was now Garfield's to command. He continued:

> The second section is the Grant section, taking all the South practically with the machines in New York, Pennsylvania and Illinois—and having the aid of the rule or ruin leaders.

Here was the most disreputable element of the party. Now for the sake of larger interests, with which Blaine now identified himself, he argued frankly that they must be destroyed, though it was not easy:

> These men are to be handled with skill, always remembering that they are harmless when out of power and desperate when in possession of it. . . . Of course it would not be wise to make war upon them. Indeed, that would be folly. They must not be knocked down with bludgeons: they must have their throats cut with a feather.

The third section were the "unco guid," the reformers by profession, the worst possible advisers, concerning whom he spoke with his habitual deep-grained cynicism. These were all

> upstarts, conceited, foolish, vain, without knowledge . . . of men. . . . They are noisy but not numerous, pharisaical but not practical, ambitious

but not wise, pretentious but not powerful. They can be easily dealt with, and can be hitched to your administration with ease. I could handle them myself without trouble.

In a subsequent letter, no less illuminating, Blaine gives Garfield lessons upon the geographical distribution of the party patronage through the allotment of the various government departments. The Secretary of the Treasury, for diplomatic reasons, should be taken from the West; he must be "identified with an agricultural community." Blaine's old comrade in arms, Senator Allison of Iowa, was the logical choice, since

the nine Republican States that begin with Ohio and end with Kansas . . . [contain] the very heart of the Republican party, and your administration must nurture, develop, and sustain the party in those States.

Of the selection of Wayne MacVeagh, a Republican from Pennsylvania, as Attorney General he said in his vivid language: "There is no other Cabinet stone in your hand that will kill so many political dogs at one throw." [57] He even looked farther ahead to future elections and advised the appointment of W. E. Chandler, the veteran wirepuller and Machiavelli of election campaigns, as Solicitor General, because he possessed "the singular faculty or series of faculties that would make him extraordinarily useful to any President." [58] Blaine finally promised to restrain his own selfish interests and limit himself to a healthy criticism of his chief; but soon this was forgotten as he threw himself heartily into his favorite game of "managing" everything and everyone.

In Blaine's letters we have essentially a proposal of alliance between a giant of politics and a pygmy who is President. But more significantly, we have also a clear analysis of the alignment of party strength; a plan, albeit a dangerous one, for unifying the party; and in many passages also the vision of a powerful Administration that would spread prosperity over the country "from above."

Easily the mental superior of his confreres, Blaine looks far ahead, plans a more efficient party Organization—one in which the plunderers and bravos are to be stripped of influence. In a more farsighted and statesmanlike manner Blaine would serve our heavy industries, especially coal and steel, by new tariffs; he would seek expanded foreign markets in South America and Central America. But how could these and other great ends be certainly achieved if the party government were still dominated by men like Conkling, who could not see "beyond a custom house or a post-office," and who alarmed the country with their brutal partisanship? By his friendships nowadays with the mightiest of capitalists, such as Andrew Carnegie, Stephen B. Elkins, W. W. Phelps, Blaine had become enriched, thought in terms of larger enterprises and larger interests, and moved away from the old evil company of the "desperate bad men" of the party, whose methods now seemed outmoded. It was Blaine who warned the President concerning the new plunder rings forming among the Stalwart spoilsmen. To "build up the party," according to his new visions, these men and their leaders must be eliminated. But to eliminate them one must wrest from them the spoils of office.

Garfield's disposition was to conciliate the quarreling sects and admit "all Republicans . . . in full fellow-ship." The danger from the Conkling Stalwarts, now symbolized by the number (306) of the delegates who had gone down for Grant at Chicago, was that they might act as a separate faction, a party within the party, harrying, overturning, menacing until they gained their ends. Even Blaine urged attempts to conciliate the opponents at the outset, the better, afterward, to "cut their throats with a feather."

The Stalwarts thrust forward the "angel" of their machine, Levi Morton, as their candidate for command of the Treasury Department, which had been "pledged" them, they asserted. Garfield refused this as impolitic, in view of the Western sentiment against "Wall Street," with which Mr. Morton was identified; he offered him the Navy portfolio instead. The Stalwarts complained bitterly of being betrayed; they suspected the ascendancy of Blaine and accused him of seeking their complete destruction. They brought pressure from every direction upon the President-elect. The war over the offices was on full blast this winter, fiercer than at any time since Andrew Jackson had begun the spoils system fifty years ago.

Blaine's faction in turn warned Garfield that he must stand firm, that is, resist the common enemy. John Hay wrote to him boldly: " 'One thing thou lackest yet'; and that is a slight ossification of the heart. I . . . fear you will try too hard to make everybody happy—

an office which is outside of your constitutional powers." [59] Whitelaw
Reid, in the thick of the New York intrigues, filled the President's
mind with bad reports of Conkling and his wicked men. "They
[Conkling's faction] . . . mean to be your masters, and when you
submit they will like you well enough. But they don't trust you. . . .
It is always 'this man Garfield.' " It seemed impossible, he reported,
to "keep Conkling reasonable." [60]

Blaine precipitated the battle for the extermination of his enemies.
Abandoning the feather for the bludgeon—for rumors of Blaine's
acceptance of the State Department appeared in the press on December 28 and 29, 1880—the Blaine Legion broke the temporary truce
by attacking the Stalwarts in their stronghold of New York. During
a contest for the junior Senatorship, then open at Albany, Blaine
actively fostered the candidacy of Chauncey Depew against Tom
Platt. Blaine had invited Depew to "interfere" in the race; the Blaine
candidate, by holding the balance between Democrats and Stalwart
Republicans, could obstruct Conkling's program of control.

Then, following up this threat, Blaine in an unsigned editorial in
the New York *Tribune*, January 3, 1881, written as if "by authority,"
declared that the President-elect was taking no part in the senatorial
contest, but added that

the incoming Administration will see to it that the men from New York
and from the other States, who had the courage at Chicago to obey the
wishes of their Districts . . . and thus finally voted for Garfield, shall
not . . . lose by it. The Administration . . . will not permit its friends
to be persecuted for their friendship.[61]

This was taken as plain warning that the anti-Conkling leader,
William H. Robertson, who had defied the machine's discipline and
bolted with his Independent following to Blaine, would be protected.
To Conkling it meant only that the Grant men need expect no quarter from this Administration.

To secure his election to the Senate, Platt was driven to "bargain"
for the votes of Depew, pledging that he would not oppose the
award of "their fair share of patronage" to the bolters and would
confirm the appointment of the insurgent Robertson, even if he were
nominated by Garfield for the Cabinet.[62] Platt was believed to be

disposed to "set up house for himself," and, it was felt, was thus detached from Conkling, the doomed leader.

"At any rate we shall show that Mr. Conkling doesn't own the State," Whitelaw Reid wrote to Garfield, January 1. And in a letter to John Hay, his close friend, Reid admitted that he was directing the campaign to build up a Blaine machine in New York. "What we now look to is a broadening of the machine, with our fellows in and a united party, minus Conkling, who won't last forever!"

During this wearisome, unresting struggle, which Garfield had hoped to avoid, many lists of cabinet members were made up, changed, thrown away. When he offered the New York machine an alternate department, Garfield would be refused, the subject of his appointment usually dreading the vengeance of the spoilsmen should he disobey them. New negotiations and intrigues followed, dragged themselves along into February, up to the very eve of the inauguration. Levi Morton had been at the point of accepting the Navy Secretaryship, instead of the Treasury, but Conkling and Arthur, getting wind of this, routed him out of bed at four o'clock in the morning and forced him to refuse it. Another time Blaine's lieutenant, Whitelaw Reid, brought secretly to Washington one Thomas James, a Stalwart Republican who had made an honest record as Postmaster at New York. Without Conkling's knowledge he was led to accept the Postmaster Generalship, and then spirited out of Washington back to New York, and kept in hiding. Thus a professed compromise slate, with some pretext at geographical representation of the principal Republican States or wings in the Cabinet, was completed at the last hour.

Conkling sensed that his following was breaking up under these heavy blows, while Federal patronage seemed largely out of his control. Without a loyal cabinet officer directly responsible to him, attached to his fortunes, he could scarcely hold his command. On March 3, 1881, with Vice-President-elect Arthur and some other henchmen who supported his protests, he visited Garfield at his hotel, where a stormy interview took place. Conkling launched himself upon a fantastic tirade of sarcasm, while the future President looked on in silence and felt that the Senator was acting a part in a play.[63]

Outwardly some calm was preserved. Inauguration Day came and went and saw a weary, bewildered man deliver a noncommittal address to the nation. Garfield in truth had no appetite for the maddening contests over office, the sieges by mobs of place-seekers. He gathered bitter fruits and bitter knowledge of what the role and the life of a President were to be.

But the struggle renewed itself as the new session of Congress opened, spreading from the closet to the open chambers of the Capitol. Conkling's position was now truly desperate; his followers were leaving him; he needed a large share of government places, departments, customhouses, consulates, all. Thus he came to a new conference with the President, pressing his claims tirelessly, bitterly. Garfield, as he relates, adopted many of the Senator's proposals as to minor appointments, agreeing to award nine Federal posts to Conkling henchmen.

"But I told him I must recognize some of the [anti-Conkling] men who supported me at Chicago." [64] For these, Conkling suggested foreign appointments. But would not that be tantamount to "exile"?

At this point Conkling asked him what was to be done about the Collectorship of the New York Custom House, actually the most important administrative post outside of the Cabinet itself; and the President replied amiably that this matter could wait for another time. They were in partial agreement now, and the names of nine new Federal officials satisfactory to the New York boss were sent to the Senate on March 22, 1881.

The newspapers of the opposing faction that evening spread the alarm that Garfield had sold out to the Conkling machine. Not only the Blaine Legion but also reformers thundered at the President as one who lacked backbone and yielded to the thieving spoilsmen of his party.

That night, while the President was at dinner, Blaine stormed in. He had risen from his sickbed on hearing the bad news, and now "expressed great distress at the New York appointments," as Garfield's journal records. He returned after dinner, and the two men held a long private discussion until midnight, in which apparently a fateful decision was reached.

On the following day the Senators, especially the Stalwarts, were awakened by a thunderbolt. By a new order of the President the ruling Collector of the New York Custom House, General Merritt, was brusquely moved to another post, and Judge William H. Robertson, long the leading rebel against the regular New York Organization, was named in his place. Thus the all-important office, of which Conkling had inquired with a feigned casualness three days earlier, and concerning which he had a pledge of "consultation," was, by a sudden hostile move, torn from him and delivered to his enemy.

After being pulled in all directions Garfield had finally been convinced by his "magnetic" Secretary of State that it was useless to try to conciliate Conkling. The nomination of Robertson was considered an extraordinarily "bold action" for so habitual a compromiser as Garfield; it was characterized in the press as "James G. Blaine's private vengeance." [65] It must be noted that Collector Merritt had been awarded his post in place of Arthur after hard fighting by the civil-service reformers in Hayes's Administration; and that according to the code of reform he, as an able official, should have held office during good behavior, instead of making way for a leader of the Blaine faction. The presence of Robertson, the ambitious enemy of Conkling, at the head of the New York Custom House meant nothing less than utter ruin for the Stalwart machine.

All sorts of great personages, long harassed by the spoilsmen, now demanded that Garfield use his authority "to make an end of Conkling." Jay Gould and Chauncey Depew acted in connivance with Reid, the Blaine lieutenant in New York. And Uncle John Sherman, while expressing fears that the unresting Blaine might "meddle" too much in all departments of the Government, none the less urged the President to an outright rupture with the New York boss—a man whose mind never rose above "a custom house or a post-office!" First, try all means of conciliation, but this failing, he wrote:

The only way is to give him blow for blow. . . . Hayes could have crushed him but would not. If Conkling opens on you as he did on Hayes, you ought without delay or hesitation to do what Jackson did with his senatorial enemies, strike them back through their friends. [66]

The breach was inevitable; it was unfortunate that instead of having his throat slit with a feather Conkling's head should have been taken with an axe, in the end. It was unfortunate also that the

President should have moved without warning or "consulting" the New York Senators, Conkling and Platt, hence, as his opponents justly charged, violating the gentlemen's agreement of August 6, 1880, at the Fifth Avenue Hotel, and other promises given or implied.

The rival leaders of the Moderate or Half-Breed Republicans, Blaine and Sherman, were now in agreement upon immediate ends. Sherman, since his term as Secretary of the Treasury, was intensely absorbed in banking and investments of his own, and envisaged an improvement of partisan politics. Blaine, too, having risen in the social scale, was bent on building up the party, as he said, "by strong and wise policy" that might lead to higher things than mere post offices.

Carthago delenda est! The Stalwarts must be destroyed, root and branch. In the opening days of the new Administration, the Secretary of State gave himself with ardor to labyrinthine domestic intrigues for the patronage. The pawns who were officeholders were moved back and forth, in order to "widen the breach between Conkling and Platt," or to detach Conkling's supporters from him one by one. If the President considered for a moment pacific measures toward the opponent, then Blaine came down upon him, accused him of the blunder of "chivalric generosity," insisted upon ruthless or vindictive steps, even the recall of Conkling men already nominated to Federal offices.[67] There was deep bargaining; there was doing and undoing. Under the alternate hammer blows, thrusts, and pulls of the Blaine and Conkling faction all the civil service gains under President Hayes were soon swept away.

The finishing stroke, seizure of the great New York Custom House from the Stalwart machine, involved an actual breach of faith, according to the usages of the time. But this meant nothing so long as it paved the way to the reconstruction and unification of the Republican Party under the unchallenged domination of James G. Blaine.

The righteous anger of the Stalwart faction at seeing themselves "betrayed" and knifed once more, under the pretext of reform, passed all bounds. The naming of Robertson as Collector for New

York they understood as a deliberate "intolerable insult." Even the judicious Vice-President Arthur said to his friends:

Garfield has not been square, nor honorable, nor truthful with Conkling. It is a hard thing to say of a president of the United States . . . spurred by Blaine, by whom he is easily led [Garfield] has broken every pledge made to us; not only that, but . . . in a most offensive way.[68]

The Grant Republicans cried havoc; cabinet members rushed to resign or changed their minds at the last moment; partisan newspapers, such as the New York *Herald* and the New York *Sun*, leveled accusations of double-dealing at the Administration, in terms likely to turn their readers to murderous violence.

The heavier the firing, the more Blaine cheered on the hapless, bewildered President, saying in a hurried note: "Yr. work today creates a splendid impression." (It was more properly Blaine's work.) Or again: "you must be as firm and resolute as if you were fighting Chickamauga over again." [69] Blaine's friends, such as John Hay, dropped in to bring encouraging reports from the field, and Garfield would say bravely: "Robertson may be carried out of the Senate head first or feet first. . . . I shall never withdraw him." [70]

Conkling, meanwhile, roused up the Senators to war upon the Administration for their ancient prerogatives of "senatorial courtesy" in Federal appointments. Once more the conscript fathers heard tirades against the Chief Magistrate from verbose Roscoe, whose wrongs moved him to transports of sarcasm. Before a Senate caucus committee he spoke hour upon hour with an eloquence never before surpassed, also brandishing from time to time damaging letters, with which his pockets, as usual, were crammed and which "he prayed to God, he might never, in self-defense, be compelled to make public." A little urging brought forth one document in question, a letter (described above) wherein Garfield tried to prod the spoilsman Brady for campaign funds to be raised by assessment.

Busy citizens paused at their labors to look with uncomprehending wonder at the madness of the statesmen in the Capital. Occasionally some intelligent comment appeared, such as that by E. L. Godkin, who held that the President was compromising the cause of reform despite his good intentions. He was fighting a New York boss while permitting a Maine boss to replace him.

He has been in office now for two months trying to restore "harmony" and satisfy "claims," and recognize "wings" and "sections" by making appointments without regard . . . to fitness, and he has simply produced deadlock and confusion and disappointment among politicians, and disgust among the taxpayers.[71]

It became clearer now, with every day, that the long reign of Conkling was about to end. He could no more move his colleagues in the Senate to split the party, as under Hayes, and paralyze the Government at the beginning of the term, for the full power of the Administration and all Blaine's party influence were thrown into the senatorial contest.

Rumors of disaffection within the New York stronghold were spreading. Whitelaw Reid claimed to have heard from Lou Payn, one of Conkling's handy men, that the Senator had abandoned his old-time ambitions for the Presidency, and intended to retire at the end of his term in 1885 in order to practice law and recoup his fortunes. He now contemplated, in reality, only a harrying, guerrilla action, the sort of destructive opposition in which he excelled above all others. Though this meant disastrous division in his party, and loss of his State, he cared little. "Platt, Payn, and the rest, of course, do not like this prospect," continued Reid's confidential report. "Whether Mr. Conkling has any political future or not, *they think they ought to have.*" Garfield must hold firm while the enemy will "every month become more and more powerless. I really believe you have him where there is a chance to make an end of him, and of the corrupt, insolent and bullying elements which he has carried into our politics," wound up the editor of the *Tribune*.[72]

But in the White House, the tormented President, beset by office-seekers and unstrung by the babble of quarreling partisans, exclaimed to Blaine with deep emotion: "I have been dealing all these years with ideas . . . I have been heretofore treating of the fundamental principles of government and here I am considering all day whether A or B shall be appointed to this or that office." Later he exclaimed:

"My God! What is there in this place that a man should ever want to get into it?" [73]

Garfield's will hardened when he learned suddenly from Postmaster General James of the discovery of the Star Route frauds and grasped the awful extent of their plunderings. Men high in the party's Inner Circle, all of them members of the Stalwart faction, such as former Senator Dorsey and Thomas Brady, and even Platt (though indirectly), were implicated. It would provide, as Attorney General MacVeagh pointed out, one of the greatest political scandals in American history, at the very outset of the new term, and would undoubtedly lose the party its majority in both houses of Congress at the next election.

With a troubled heart the President gave the order to clear out the Post Office Department and prosecute to the utmost. Dorsey, caught in the net, now appealed for clemency to the man whom he had elected to office "almost single-handed," as he declared. Garfield had expressed fulsome gratitude toward this man and had hesitated gravely before ordering his indictment. At first disturbing rumors of a "new Crédit Mobilier" spread in the press; then, as arrests were made of minor members of the ring, some of whom confessed their guilt, the full scope of the affair burst into view. Over $4,000,000 had been stolen from the Government during the past five years, it was estimated.

On May 9, 1881, the sentiment of the Republican caucus showed that with Democratic help the Senate would act to ratify the nomination of Robertson as Collector at New York. This marked a historic reversal of the tradition of "senatorial courtesy."

The misfortunes of Garfield, the unrelenting aggressions of Blaine, the fall of Conkling, the exposure of the party's plunder ring—all these came together and were linked with profound changes in the internal nature of party government, for which men had waited overlong.

Thomas Platt, the junior Senator from New York, who was surpassed now only by Conkling and Arthur in influence over his State machine, was caught in a most awkward position. He had risen to the Senate by a bargain with the Blaine men, in which he promised not to oppose their action in awarding patronage to the New York insurgents. On the other hand, he must stand and fall with his chief, Conkling. He had made too many crafty bargains. Therefore, in order to extricate himself from an intolerable position, he proposed, as he relates, that he and Conkling resign the office of Senator and seek vindication by re-election by the legislature in New York— such as they had won before by the successful contest of Cornell for the Governorship in 1879. Conkling, who looked only to glorious victory or self-inflicted political death, was attracted by the idea; and on May 16, 1881, the nation was startled at hearing of the voluntary resignation from the Senate of Thomas Platt and Roscoe Conkling. It was a sensation of many days, and was caricatured mercilessly by Tom Nast, who showed the decapitated Conkling strolling about, carrying his head in his hand, while the smaller Platt did likewise, crying *"Me too!"*

The Half-Breeds and all the Blaine Legion were jubilant, feeling that Conkling and Platt had lost face and set the Senate itself against them, or had sawed off the limb of the tree on which they sat. Blaine exclaimed in a hurried note to the President concerning his splendid victory: "Glory to God! Victory is yours, sure and lasting." The Senate now quickly confirmed all the Garfield nominations, May 18, 1881. In the meantime the unresting Secretary of State went in person to New York to command the Blaine Republicans at Albany in the fight against the Stalwart Senators.

The dreary struggle shifted to New York, where for two months Conkling and his lieutenant lobbied away before the legislature at Albany in their dismal campaign. Vice-President Arthur himself, in defiance of Garfield and Blaine, went to New York to aid them in their contest. People pitied the once haughty Conkling as he stood pleading every day for long hours with small local politicians for their votes, men whom he had invariably treated as his lackeys. Day after day the legislature droned on, its balloting hopelessly deadlocked as Democrats and Half-Breed Republicans combined in opposition to the old machine. But in the last week of June the hopes of Conkling and his colleague were destroyed—not by reason of the belated wave of reform that swept over the party Organization, but by a stepladder!

The Honorable Thomas Platt, Tioga County's pious churchgoer and paterfamilias, dwelt in a room of the Delavan Hotel in Albany, whence he continued to direct the legislative struggle from close by, when one night a Half-Breed Assemblyman quietly placed a stepladder before Platt's door, climbed up, and peered through the transom. After him a dozen or so of the pro-Blaine legislators, softly treading in stocking feet, and suppressing their chuckles, one by one climbed the ladder and gazed their fill.

Upon the following day, all of Albany whispered of the affair, and it was but a question of hours until the newspapers would flaunt the gossip, as at once they did, of "an unspeakable female" seen in the arms of the former Senator.[74] On the day preceding publication of the domestic scandal in Albany and New York papers, Platt withdrew from the contest for the Senate—as he stated to friends, in order not to embarrass Conkling's chances. This news appeared simultaneously with other arresting information on July 2, 1881.

On this day, at the height of the turmoil over offices and corruption in Washington, Garfield prepared to leave for a vacation journey to New England and proceeded to the Union Station, accompanied by Secretary Blaine. Unnoticed by them, a small, idiotic, wretched man who had formerly been a Republican appointee to a clerkship, followed quietly at their heels. Blaine was speaking with his usual animation of great future plans of foreign expansion by which American industry would be directed to the conquest of Caribbean and South American markets—plans to which he prepared to give himself with all his ardor, during the long years in power before him—when the crazed Guiteau approached closer and discharged his pistol into the President's back, crying out: *"I am a Stalwart and Arthur is President now."*

BOOK TWO

THE REFORMERS

CHAPTER EIGHT

INTERLUDE

1881-1884

. . . Arthur had no "faith in reform" but was simply yielding to popular sentiment.   G. F. HOWE

DURING the long agonizing of the President in the summer of 1881, a powerful revulsion of feeling swept over the public and changed the political climate. From its mood of apathy or knowing cynicism public opinion veered to intense sympathy with the stricken Garfield; it expressed itself in demands for the punishment of the clique of Stalwart bosses whose partisan excesses had loaded the pistol of the deranged assassin. Then also, as with one voice, all classes of the community, even including the great railroad capitalists, clamored for those hitherto unpopular reforms in the government service which only a small, intellectual minority, the "man milliners," had advocated for a decade.

In Guiteau's possession had been found an inflammatory issue of the New York *Herald* attacking Garfield and Blaine; also his strange letter to the people announcing that his action was intended to unify the Republican Party and save the country. Though Guiteau was plainly insane, it was seen by many reasonable people that his insanity differed only in degree from that of certain statesmen of the period. A morbid public interest in all the details of the President's lingering death, as well as in the trial and hanging of the madman, was transformed into a popular demand for the proscription of the New York Stalwarts. Under the stormy condemnation of all the people, who wept copiously over Garfield's bier, Roscoe Conkling was banished from public life. The most violent of the old party chieftains, whose tactics and principles had certainly prolonged the turmoil over offices that had brought Garfield to an untimely grave—though he was not alone culpable—now abandoned his attempt to return to the Senate, and retired into private life and the practice of a corporation lawyer. Conkling's last years were passed in a bitter obscurity, from which he seldom emerged. Walking the streets of New York during the blizzard of 1888, he came to his end among the terrible snow-drifts, alone, silent, almost forgotten.

The Stalwart wing of the party was now doomed, and internal peace was in prospect. Platt too was retired in disgrace, though he was to show himself the owner of many political lives. But by the accidents of the traditional party diplomacy, Chester Arthur, Conkling's chief lieutenant, was to become President upon Garfield's death!

Blaine had projected tremendous visions in his talks with Garfield, on the very morning of the assassination, "of a united America, reciprocity, arbitration, trade, glory, and the rest." [1] He had counted on ruling the party and the government for eight years. What a fearful miscarriage of great designs! The horror with which he viewed the sudden reversal of fortune, after so successful a fight to clear the field of his rivals, may have been mingled with some wordless regrets at his own indiscretions. For was not he too, though indirectly, unwittingly at fault, and the cause of his own bitter undoing? Blaine, like his wife, prayed during the summer, while hope remained, for Garfield's survival: *"Because he lives we shall live also,"* wrote Mrs. Blaine in one of the flashing phrases of her letters. [2]

But on September 19, 1881, all the bells of the land tolled for the passing of the martyr of spoilsman politics. Chester Arthur was sworn into office, and James Blaine made the decision to retire from his post in the Administration. From his library in Augusta, where he now worked quietly as a historian, he watched his successor in the State Department reversing his own half-begun policies of foreign expansion and trade penetration; he scanned closely, as always, the tides and the skies of the political ocean in which he must swim to the end of his days.

The American republic was almost the last of the great modern nations to begin the patently necessary work of rationalizing its governmental bureaucracy in a scheme of impartiality, of fitness for office and stability in tenure. Behind the Jacksonian system of patronage there had stood a certain jealous libertarian defense of the individual citizen against the fixation of a governing or administrative class, against the coming of the Great State. The stabilized or permanent bureaucracy generally suggests the supremacy of the state, the settling of a regime of fixed status and hierarchy, which was traditionally unpleasant or unsuited to the still fluid American society. While Imperial Germany under Bismarck and Imperial Britain had found the creation of an efficient bureaucracy useful in preserving their empires, the play of the hieratic party system in America had resisted it almost too long and held the prize of official power at stake between two parties.

But the more developed, the more complex a society becomes, the more advanced and large-scale its modes of production and enterprise, the more insistent grows the demand for equity to all groups in protection, policing, taxgathering, and the administration of all functions left to the public domain. To render the civil service more efficient technically and more impersonal does not imply a step forward in democracy, but rather, as Max Weber has shown, indicates the necessary strengthening of the instrument of the extension of capitalism in every sphere, "with its desire for equity . . . regular procedure of justice, *the protection of acquired rights.*" [3] *

A historic contempt for the bureaucratic career had governed men in the young republic of the West, where for so long there had been so much free land and so much of free natural resources to enrich them quickly. But where the government service remained chaotic, the party Organizations, in compensation, had developed extremely strong, concealed bureaucracies and controls within themselves, which provided such stability as was needed. In the end, patronage politics had gone to such grotesque extremes—especially at the moment of the killing of Garfield—that the cry for civil-service reform, which had originated among a minority of intelligent capitalists and petty bourgeois, had been taken up by the whole nation. The leaders in both great parties, who had delayed this house-cleaning for the sake of their own tactical necessities, now hastened to bow to the popular voice, which was felt in a new "landslide" of votes for Democratic Congressmen in 1882.

* Weber, in his penetrating study of types of rulership, attributes the rise and extension of bureaucracy to the fixing and legitimization of class structures in society.

In the year that followed Garfield's death both parties co-operated in passing a Civil Service Act, the Pendleton Bill, which gave, though "with statesmanlike caution," as George Hoar said, legislative support to reform. It was, if not perhaps "the Magna Charta of civil service reform" in America which Ostrogorski has called it, at least the beginning of a sea change in the system of party government.

In the months that followed, some 14,000 officials, a good fraction of the mass of Federal employees, were placed under the merit system, and made more or less immune to removal for political cause and to the levying of political assessments upon their wages. Half of the postal officials and most of the customhouse workers came under the control of the Civil Service Commission, which was established as a permanent feature of the executive branch. Both parties claimed credit for the act, only a few candid voices, such as that of the cynical Senator Ingalls of Kansas, arguing against the scheme as a subterfuge through which each side hoped to cheat the other.[4]

We know that the politicians did not abandon at once their attempts to control patronage; many years were to pass before a "nonpartisan" service was achieved. Yet a first blow had been struck at the old party regime, and important shifts in tactics and principles of party command were thereby made necessary.

Within a year of the enactment of the Pendleton Bill, the new Civil Service Commission was able to report that although government workers were not yet safe in declining to pay party assessments, a considerable drop in such levies was indicated.[5] The stream was drying up a little, though it never stopped flowing. In the years that follow one notes an unwonted shortage of funds in the party that has so long held Federal office; the operations of government-contract rings and political plunderers are also diminished, causing new losses to the war chest. The party leaders are compelled to look elsewhere for a primary source of revenue. The fashion for civil-service reform that marked the 1880's, therefore, ushered in more brilliant and more devious forms of corruption, spreading through State and municipal governments. It brought also the intervention of the "businessman in politics" over against the professional leader, at a time when the business class was impelled to make tremendous new economic demands upon the people's representatives.

"My God! Chet Arthur!" men had exclaimed at the thought that Conkling's lieutenant, the "Gentleman Boss," would rule in the White House. Chester Arthur had risen by slow stages through the ranks of the political army. For twenty years he had devoted himself to gathering and awarding the spoils of office; one saw him in smoky hotel rooms, where brandy and cigars were dispensed freely, patiently conferring and negotiating with committees, chairmen, agents. Such a training in the arduous business of New York's political demimonde now appeared to stand the new President in good stead. It had developed in him a truly discriminating diplomacy, a suppleness in judging of the appetites, weaknesses, and ambitions of the men surrounding him. Though he had entered office under a cloud, the beneficiary of Guiteau's pistol, he acted from the start with remarkable tact and grace. Of necessity he separated himself from the disgraced Conkling, and strove to moderate the intestine strife of factions in his party. In the comedy of reform that must now be enacted in deference to an aroused public opinion he played his part with surprising ease. In some ways he impressed himself upon the minds of important businessmen especially as the most effective President since Lincoln.

The man who four years before had been dismissed from the New York Custom House owing to his spoils politics backed the Democrat Pendleton's Civil Service Act, and signed it on January 16, 1883. Its program was then carried on from the start, with tolerably good faith. The querulous disappointment of General Grant, of Conkling (in retirement), of Platt, is a measure of the moderation and conservatism with which Arthur made appointments to his Cabinet and to subsidiary posts. Robertson, the storm center of Garfield's short term, was retained in office as Collector at New York, despite the bitter complaints of Arthur's friends.

One of the first and most painful duties that devolved upon the Stalwart party manager, now elevated to the White House, was the prosecution of the Star Route Ring, inherited from Garfield's term. What made it more difficult was that Stephen Dorsey, the field marshal of the Republican National Committee in 1880, had been eulogized by Arthur at a public testimonial banquet. Among other members of the ring was Brady, Second Assistant Postmaster General, who had collaborated in many a political battle with Arthur. The confession of one of the members, M. C. Rerdell, private secretary to Dorsey, in June, 1881, had shown how large had been the conspiracy in fraudulent postal contracts; it was rivaled only by the whisky frauds under Grant. Though President Arthur felt repugnance for the task, knowing well the vital part these men played in the national Republican Organization itself, he ordered his Attorney General, Brewster, to prosecute "with the utmost vigor of the law."

Dorsey, Brady, and the six other postal officials and mail contractors who were indicted underwent trial in February, 1882, all pleading "Not guilty." They were defiant and indignant; they defended themselves powerfully. Tremendous legal obstacles to proper indictment in the District of Columbia were raised, partly through the advice of Roscoe Conkling. Distinguished Republican lawyers, among them Robert Ingersoll, made emotional pleas for the defendants. Constant attacks were made upon the judge, the grand jury, and the prosecution; the jury members were approached with bribes. Confessions by ring members were recanted. Government witnesses became undependable, or hard to be located, owing to the incompetence of the government counsel or failure to provide indemnification for them. The jury failed to agree after a trial of many months.

In September, 1882, a new trial was ordered. Nine months later, following a process that was little more than a succession of mob scenes—with appeals to patriotism, denunciations of rebels, the intimidation of the state's witnesses, and testimonials by cabinet members favorable to the conspirators lending the highest color to the affair—the jury brought in a verdict of "Not guilty as indicted." We are led to conclude with a historian of Arthur's term that the President and his official family could not find it in their hearts to do more than a modicum of their duty toward their old partners.[6]

How can the leopard change his spots? Or professional Stalwart politicians prosecute their former colleagues in more than a half-hearted manner? In swinging to reform, Mr. Arthur showed as much moderation and practical wisdom as he used to show in quietly rewarding his political allies. Government and party system could not be improved too suddenly and drastically. Nevertheless, the open stealing from the till of the Government was sharply reduced after the famous Star Route trials. The officialdom of the party separated itself from large-scale revenue frauds. Only an overzealousness on the part of certain officers sometimes showed itself on behalf of the Grand Old Party. William ("Machiavelli") Chandler, now Secretary of the Navy, caused some stir by the manner in which he awarded large shipbuilding contracts to John Roach, a warm patron of the Republican Party campaign. But in the matter of the Roach shipyard contracts the system of patronage had become already both more refined and more restricted than before. This too contributed to the drought suffered by the ruling party in 1882 and 1884. Businessmen had grounds for satisfaction in the improvement in our taxgathering institution brought about during Arthur's term.

In numerous ways Arthur commended himself by a conservatism favoring bureaucratic sobriety and economy in government. The politicians now searched busily for new outlets in the way of spoils. By 1882, under the ponderous system of taxation retained since the Civil War, the surplus revenues of the Government were swelling. But instead of reducing taxes by means of a revised tariff schedule, Congress had steadily increased pensions to war veterans and miscellaneous appropriations for public works; in the spring of 1882 the Forty-seventh Congress voted the unheard-of appropriation of more than $18,700,000 for a Rivers and Harbors Bill. This last act Arthur vetoed with a ringing message, holding that its purposes were not for the "common defense or general welfare" and were "beyond the powers given by the Constitution." Such a move made a most favorable impression in high quarters, though the politicians resented it and by a quick combination between the parties overrode the veto.

With the curious problem of surplus revenues embarrassing the Treasury and offering temptations for the party leaders, Arthur in a further message cautiously advocated measures "for the relief of industry and enterprise from the pressure of unnecessary taxation." The only logical direction which this could take was in the reform of the overdeveloped protective tariff, under which industrialists now benefited so remarkably. While the Government acquired unwieldy surpluses of funds locked in the Treasury by unnecessary taxation, protected industries such as Carnegie's steel companies were reporting profits of some 200 per cent per annum upon their invested capital.

Once more agitation for the reform—that is, for the lowering—of the tariff became widespread toward 1880-82. In the Mississippi Valley spokesmen for Free Trade now vied with the most rabid champions of Greenbacks or silver-money inflation in denouncing the iniquities of monopolists "subsidized" by tariffs, and claiming universal gains to accrue from the elimination of Protection. In the East scholars such as William Graham Sumner and Arthur Latham Perry on behalf of the new Free Trade League made powerful arguments for their cause and gained thousands of ardent converts, so that their clamor nowadays overruled even the cry for civil-service reform.

The idea of an expert commission to review the tariff problem impartially and propose a plan for rational and "scientific" change had been often advanced, resisted as often, and was finally approved by President Arthur in a message of December, 1881. At this time many protected industrialists no longer opposed tariff revision, but wished only assurance that it would be done moderately, by their friends, while preserving the main features of Protection.[7]

In the spring of 1882, under authorization of Congress, Arthur named a body of nine "civilians" as a commission to report upon a plan for "a judicious tariff or a revision of the existing tariff." Here too was cause for satisfaction among large industrial interests. John L. Hayes, the astute secretary and lobbyist of the National Association of Wool Manufacturers, was named chairman of the Tariff Commission; Henry Oliver of Pittsburgh represented the iron and steel men. Other men acting for kindred protected interests were selected to round out the committee, thanks to the pressure that lobbyists and Protectionist Senators such as Morrill and Sherman exerted on the President.[*]

In a period of transition, the former boss of spoilsmen in the White

---

[*] The surveillance that John L. Hayes exercised over the personnel of the Tariff Commission is shown by the following: "General Butler is a wool manufacturer has requested Sen. Jones to see President on appointments tariff commission. Post him further." (Morrill Papers, telegram from J. L. Hayes to Morrill, May 17, 1882.)

House seemed to bring a momentary order and dignity into the Government, along with policies strongly desired in respectable quarters. Methods were changing; leaders groped for new issues related to the economic realities of the day, while abandoning the old war cries. Even Blaine from his seclusion announced himself a convert to the cause of civil-service reform, in 1882. He too would now correct "the evils arising from the distribution of an overgrown and unwieldy patronage," and to bring this about advocated an increased tenure for civil appointments. Such a conversion was called by unforgiving commentators but "the traditional tribute paid by vice to virtue." [8] With Blaine calling for the reform of the spoils system, and a lieutenant of Roscoe Conkling in the White House occupying himself with the problems of the reform of the protective tariff, people might well rub their eyes and ask themselves what surprises the political circus masters had in store for them.

II

In commenting on the President's Tariff Commission, authorized by an act of May 15, 1882, the new Senator from Rhode Island, Nelson Aldrich, explained that

there was a representative of the wool growers on the commission; there was a representative of the iron interest on the commission; there was a representative of the sugar interest on the commission; and those interests were very carefully looked out for.[9]

And why should not sugar, demanded Aldrich, "which represents three hundred millions of invested capital," receive representation?

Here was heralded, as Aldrich's biographer has written, a new concept of government, one might say, a new political "line." The younger leadership rising through the Republican Party's transition, typified by the young Nelson Aldrich, now thought in terms of great economic groups, where the elder statesmen thought invariably in terms of geographical sections and political clans. A man like Aldrich thought imaginatively of "sugar" or "iron" as "a social and political entity, as a vast assemblage of interests, an economic commonwealth . . . which he was willing to treat with." [10]

The oratory of the Elder Statesmen had played upon the swords and roses of war, the doctrine of universal liberty, the menace of rebellion in the South. The new men made speeches that bristled with facts; their heroes were pig-iron ingots and steel rails, matches, and mountains of glassware. From the outset certain of these young men, notably Nelson Aldrich, William McKinley, and Thomas B. Reed, determined to quit the hoary themes of Radical wartime Republicanism and devote themselves to studying the schedules of tariffs, the statistics of imports and exports, which were a mystery, a jungle, to the other statesmen.

McKinley, the young soldier and lawyer, had the conventional mold of a Republican. As a mere boy he had been one of Ohio's volunteers in the war, and had risen to the place of Major; he was handsome, affable, and fluent in public speech. But what was more important, he climbed quickly and lightly through the ranks of his party, because he represented so earnestly the *industrial* interests of his Ohio district. Upon his first arrival in Washington he memorialized Congress on the needs of the iron men of Canton, Massillon, and Youngstown, as his eulogist tells us:

McKinley's resolution to specialize upon the Tariff . . . was a natural one for him to make. His father and his grandfather were both manufacturers of iron, an industry which depended heavily upon the protective tariff. The counties of Stark, Mahoning, and Columbiana were rich in coal mines and well filled with furnaces, mills, and factories for the manufacture of a variety of objects. In East Liverpool there were potteries employing a thousand men, a new and thriving industry. . . . Capital had been invested with the expectation that the Government would continue to guard them against foreign competition.[11]

McKinley at once took his place at the side of the old Protectionist leader Pig-Iron Kelley, becoming a member of the important Ways and Means Committee in 1880. His discourses upon his favorite theme, delivered with a fervor and self-righteousness that won widening attention, usually began: "I speak for the workingmen of my district, for the workingmen of Ohio, for the workingmen of all the country."

Thomas Reed of Portland, Maine, the large, stout young Congressmen of nimble and ironic mind, also represented aggressively the textile-manufacturing interest rather than a clique of spoilsmen. While McKinley rose to prominence as an orator, Reed, a man of superior intellectual power, excelled as a parliamentary leader in Congress after the manner of Blaine; whereas the close-lipped, cold Aldrich usually eschewed public appearances and worked by preference in the privacy of closed committees, caucuses, and conferences.

Aldrich, the strongest of the new leaders, had been successful as a grocer, then as the president of a large bank in Providence. This "sound young businessman" had entered politics originally as a reformer on behalf of people of substance, the rich taxpayers of his ward, to resist the impositions of local plunderers. Then, engaging the support of the party Organization, the "keen, aloof," and rich young man, had himself sent to Congress in 1878, and to the Senate in 1882. With all these new men, local Organization politics had been a means to an end, rather than, as in the case of men like Oliver Morton and Conkling, an all-absorbing profession—their purpose being always a more efficient deputyship.

Aldrich would say candidly: "Most people don't know what they want." In the turmoil over the protective tariff Aldrich worked skillfully for decisions in favor of the manufacturing interest. He stood generally for a union between manufacturers and workingmen, against the agricultural population. Characteristically, Aldrich would, for instance, support the manufacturers and weavers of wool as against the producers of wool, the farmers. Then for many years this latter-day patrician could "command the solid support of the classes that signed checks and contributed to the exchequers of political parties." [12] His henchmen at home could take care of the "Purchasables," whose votes create legislatures.

President Arthur's Tariff Commission submitted to Congress in December, 1882, a surprisingly intelligent report based on hearings and evidence taken in all parts of the country from many industries. Without doing violence to enterprises flourishing under the existing system, the commission planned certain moderate changes, eliminating the more glaring instances of favoritism and inequalities that brought undue hardships to the consuming public, and bringing about a moderate reduction of about 20 per cent in the tariff revenues. [13]

It drafted a tariff bill simplifying many schedules, but aiding manufacturers considerably by reduction of duties on raw materials and relieving consumers a little by reductions on necessities such as sugar and molasses. The commission's report, cautiously commended to the attention of Congress by the President, mounted up to nearly four thousand pages of evidence, tables, and statistics. But most Congressmen, with the exception of men like Aldrich and Reed, were notoriously incapable of digesting such a report.

"Your Congressman is a swine," Henry Adams quotes a cabinet member of this period as saying to him. One must go to him with a stick and "hit him over the snout." Congress took the proposed bill in hand, and proceeded to draw another of its own devising, the "Kelley Bill." The Senate Committee on Finance disregarded both projects and drew up a bill of its own, with which it planned to confront the House. In the meantime lobbyists descended like a flock of buzzards upon Washington, crowding all the hotels that winter, pulling, tugging at the statesmen in the name of all the diverse, conflicting interests that employed them. In the confused free-for-all that followed, all the "harmony and symmetry" which John Sherman had applauded in the Tariff Commission's bill was thrown to the winds, as committeemen in both chambers wrestled with long schedules and with the unblushing and unending demands of lobbies for sugar, iron, wool, glass, marble, and a hundred other trades.[14]

At this time the two leading industrial lobbies organized upon a permanent footing were those of the National Association of Wool Manufacturers, directed by John L. Hayes, and the American Iron and Steel Association, directed by James Swank, its secretary, and dominated by the Pennsylvania metal-manufacturers, Joseph Wharton, Wharton Barker, Samuel Fenton, and Daniel Morrell. John Hayes, repudiating the commission report which he had signed, pressed for higher duties, instead of lower ones, on woolen goods; Swank worked tirelessly toward similar ends among the Congressmen for the iron interests. In the meantime Henry Havemeyer of New York, described by Aldrich proudly as "the largest sugar refiner in this country, one whose influence upon legislation has often been properly felt," besieged both chambers and the White House in the name of the industrial monopoly he was building.[15]

These lobbies had for long years been perfecting their relations with strategic committees of Congress. They maintained constant contact with committee members, such as Senators Justin Morrill, Sherman, Aldrich, and Representative Kelley; they advised, gathered information, distributed the speeches of friendly statesmen, aided in election campaigns. And not seldom agents like Hayes and Swank were able to block one committee appointment or further another. What they agreed upon now was the urgent need of haste in passing a bill at the Lame Duck session of Congress, which was to end in March, 1883, since the elections of the preceding November had once more reversed the Republican majority at the Capitol.[16]

The average petty politician in Congress knew little about and cared less for the economic and social effects of tariff legislation. By the excited competition and pleadings of interested groups he could perceive that special privileges even greater than those of the land and railroad rights given for the asking in the 1860's were now at stake. What were these but vast "subsidies" which the iron and textile lobbies fought for day and night in the corridors of the Capitol, subsidies sanctioned by the authority and power of the Federal Government?

That new "rights of way," though in a more subtle and seemingly honorable form, might be won for the steel, sugar, or textile enterprises of giant size dawned upon the politicians who were now being courted so passionately. Their field of operations, which had recently been sensibly restricted by the civil-service reforms, was now enlarged again and given new scope in the name of American labor and American enterprise. In many a district new and powerful relationships were being cemented that held glittering prospects for the future. Thus there was hastened the process of logrolling,* well known for long years, but now to become the most prominent feature of our economic statesmanship. Confusion was increased as a politician singly or as a member of a clique demanded preference for the industry of his own "deestrict" before he would accord favor to another industry or section. A Congressman from Massachusetts would not desist in his opposition until woolen cloth was granted higher rates; but

---

* "I cannot move this log of my own unaided strength. You help me roll mine, and I'll help you roll yours."

McKinley of Ohio would grant nothing to wool unless increases in duties upon iron and steel were also accorded. To overcome the many bottlenecks that developed in the drafting of the season's financial legislation, the process of logrolling was brought into play, especially in the closing hours of the session. The tactics of the industrial lobbyists strongly encouraged logrolling. J. L. Hayes, the leading lobbyist of the age, wrote to Senator Morrill, head of the Finance Committee, numerous messages such as the following:

> I am informed that the iron men deem it of the utmost importance that the duty on *wire rods* should be 1¢ a pound, and this is all that is needed to secure the heartiest support for the bill. Is it not possible for you to yield this to them and secure friends for our woolen interests? [17]

In this fashion the various innumerable items of the tariff schedule were rolled up higher and higher. It was a conflict, it has been said,

> between the restrained ambitions of intelligent industrialists, set forth in the [Tariff] commission's report, and the unbridled acquisitiveness of the average business man, for whom by the pressure of the lobby the government was made to serve as an agency to fatten profits. On no previous occasion had the conflict been so obvious. [18]

In the last stages of the legislative struggle the two houses were deadlocked over separate tariff bills. A majority of the Democrats in the House, under the leadership of John Carlisle of Kentucky, indignant at the "audacity" of the Kelley Bill, tried to filibuster during the last days; while the Democratic Protectionist Samuel Randall of Pennsylvania carried a minority faction of his party to the aid of the Republicans. Joint conference between the two houses was necessary at once if any bill at all were to be completed in the few days that remained. Thomas Reed, the new Republican general, now executed a brilliant parliamentary maneuver. By having the Republican caucus pass a special House rule which required only a simple majority (instead of a two-thirds vote, as normally) to take the tariff bill from the table, unlimited debate was finally stopped by February 27, 1883. Then, by further provisions of Reed's rule, the tariff bill could be withdrawn from the table only to have its controverted points judged by a small joint committee of both houses of Congress, a committee that was dominantly Republican and Protectionist. Thus only one kind of bill could be evolved in the committee, and no effective public debate would be possible. It was, according to a happy comment of the time, like "the Irishman's dream of a gun which should fire so as to hit the object if it was a deer and miss it if it was a cow!" [19]

Within a mere twenty-four hours the Joint Committee rewrote the whole long tariff measure as a "mongrel" bill, a mixture of hasty increases and insignificant reductions of duties, and it passed in the midnight hours of the Lame Duck session—before an overwhelmingly Democratic House of Representatives could enter the gates. A great many of the provisions raised duties instead of lowering them, as the popular sentiment demanded, by the ingenious and dishonest device of changing classifications. Rates on bar iron and iron ore and steel rails, which the Senate had lifted above the scale of the House measure, were raised anew in the committee; the same was done for woolen cloth and marble. In defiance of popular mandates, a compromise tariff, having scant regard for the government financial problems, had emerged, but nevertheless one in which the manufacturing interests received the lion's share. The logrolling politicians, led by Aldrich in the Senate—who dominated the joint-committee negotiations—and Reed in the House, had cemented closer ties than before with the industrialists of the country, accelerating the movement toward a still stronger protective system for American manufacturing capitalists. Thomas B. Reed, the cynical humorist of the House, had reason to congratulate himself (as he did in his diary, on March 4) upon his brilliant parliamentary coup d'état by which the proposed tariff reform was turned virtually into a general increase of rates.[20]

III

During the period of transition, while the professional leaders groped for new tactics and a new "line," and others constrained themselves to "pander to reform," as they amusingly put it, there were stealthy reversions to the old tried and tested principles. While showing himself as decorous as possible, Arthur, by long training, had learned that elections were not won by the "gush" of "man milliners," but only, as he explained once in a private conversation, *when all the men in politics* are pleased and satisfied and set to work with enthusiasm for the ticket. They bring out the votes, and if you trusted these elections to business men and *merely respectable influences,* the Democratic Party would get in every time.[21]

Around the jovial celibate in the White House a cabal of the traditional kind was soon formed, which explored thoroughly the chances of capturing dominant sections of the party government through presidential influence, assuring in advance the renomination of the incumbent. Covert steps were taken to place in office here and there Stalwart friends of the President's faction. In Ohio Sherman found that the spoils system was being used quietly to undermine his own position, while at the same time some furtive efforts were made to discredit Blaine in investigations which impugned his motives in relations with certain South American states.

In New York Arthur made an open attempt to win back the Organization power that Conkling had lost. Governor Cornell had had an honorable record in office, and sought re-election in 1882. In 1881 he had broken with Conkling and Arthur when he had advised them to make terms with Garfield. Later he had defied the machine leaders again when he vetoed a suspicious measure reducing tax levies upon Jay Gould's New York Elevated Railways. Conkling, who was believed now to be Gould's corporation counsel, had come forth from his obscurity to lobby for the bill. When it finally failed of passage over Cornell's veto, Conkling and Gould had marked Cornell for defeat at the approaching party convention.

Arthur's able Secretary of the Treasury, William J. Folger, who had been prominent in New York as a lawyer, a judge, and a member of the Stalwart Organization, was induced to run against the more popular Cornell. He was well understood to be the "Administration's man"; all the power not only of the President but also of the Treasury Department was used in the drive to nominate him. By "rule-or-ruin" tactics worthy of Conkling, and by a slim margin of votes, Governor Cornell was eliminated. As Alexander relates:

In their efforts in Folger's behalf delegates were coerced, and efficient officials at Albany, Brooklyn, Utica, and Ogdensburg, removed in the middle of their terms, were replaced by partisans of the President. Even after the patronage packed convention assembled the questionable methods continued. Gould's agent hovered about Saratoga. To secure the election of a temporary chairman by the State committee, Stephen B. French, an intimate of Arthur, presented a fraudulent proxy.[22]

The purpose of running Folger for Governor was to have a firm grip on the New York Organization for the next presidential campaign. But the public, still shocked at the Garfield tragedy, was outraged anew by the crude machine tactics used at Saratoga. In any case the State party was split, its disgruntled factions, either as Independents or as Blaine men, bolting the ticket in great numbers. The Democrats, sensing their opportunity and composing their own quarreling factions, had seized upon the banner of Reform, and placed at the head of their ticket the obscure but reputedly honest former Sheriff and Mayor of Buffalo, Grover Cleveland, who was elected by an "avalanche" of nearly 200,000 votes more than Folger.

This crushing defeat showed how clearly the President, in his attempt at national party domination, had overreached himself and lost control of his own State. The Conkling band was in fragments. In Pennsylvania and Ohio as well, in 1882, Republicans were rebuked for their errors by Democratic Tidal Waves, which so often took place in the purely congressional elections. In the lower house, after March 4, 1883, 200 Democratic Representatives faced little more than half as many Republicans, while the Senate remained Republican by 3 votes. Arthur's halfhearted efforts to revive the dwindling Stalwart faction were fruitless. They had earned him the enmity of the reformers, while the professionals were little satisfied. Moreover, they cleared the way for the return of the party's strong man, Blaine.

The logic of events, as Blaine the historian would say, even with darkened prospects, made him after 1882 the unchallenged leader of his party, behind whom the quarreling wings could unite at last. Far from being forgotten after his withdrawal from the State Department, he ran the danger of being "boomed" prematurely for the next presidential nomination. Therefore he had followed for two years the well-established tactics of aloofness. His devoted aide, Whitelaw Reid, had warned him not to accept any favor at the hands of the accidental President, such as the position of Ambassador to Great Britain.

It would be to become a dependent of Chester Arthur, instead of the greatest independent political force in the country. To go quietly to Augusta, take care of your health, have a good time and take your fair share in political campaigns, as they come along, is to garner and increase that force.[23]

As if the astute Gentleman from Maine needed this advice. The remnants of the Stalwart bands had been left to defeat themselves in 1882, while the Blaine Legion avoided errors. The mighty Senatorial Clique of Reconstruction days was gone, Oliver Morton, Zach Chandler, and Simon Cameron being dead and Roscoe Conkling banished from public life, while Logan, his Senatorship lost, sued for terms with the Blaine faction. Only the "noisy but not numerous," the "pharisaical," reformers of the type of Schurz and Curtis opposed Blaine vigorously; and these men he now tried to flank by announcements of his conversion to civil-service reform.

Blaine's views had broadened greatly since the days when, as Carl Schurz charged, he had "wallowed in spoils like a rhinoceros in an African pool." It was true that he had once lived by his wits as a needy adventurer in the midst of the national "barbecue." But today, as he wrote in his *Twenty Years of Congress*, history of the triumphant career of the Republican Party, he seemed more and more the spokesman, friend, and prophet of an arrived and all-powerful class, the captains of industry. Their achievements he celebrates in many a page of his once popular history, which was written in the mood of optimism fitting for, and on the whole justified by, an expanding cycle of capital. What Blaine repeatedly envisioned was that the country's population, which now stood at over 50,000,000, would be doubled, as it had been in his youth, and reach 100,000,000. But the chief credit for the nation's immense material growth Blaine claimed for the Republican Party. To extend the process, to continue the eternal expansion of American enterprise abroad, had been his preoccupation as Secretary of State. Now he apparently turned more and more to the idea of making Protection the peculiar credo of his party, of making the Republican Party frankly the "party of businessmen."

The very importance of Protection to special interests had often led to its being avoided as a Burning Issue in political campaigns, in favor of simple questions like the "rebel" or the exclusion of Chinese immigrants. For tariff schedules were a question of financial and taxation policy, which only a small part of the public and few enough stump politicians could grasp. The nice adjustments of the tariff were usually left to the stealthy parliamentary legerdemain of congressional committees and interparty bargains. On this complicated and dangerous issue the Democratic Party, since the war, usually avoided committing itself, subject as it was to much internal disagreement on the question; neither were the Republicans themselves committed too openly thereto, owing to the animus of their Mississippi Valley voters. Yet Blaine, like the newer Republican leaders, despite the complexity of the whole subject, favored taking up Protection as the essential and characteristic Republican doctrine. In a sense this would hasten the transformation of the G.O.P. from a purely "patronage party" into a "belief party"; there would be the perceptible shift— especially marked since civil-service reform had begun—from spoils policies to a politics of "interest" and "class."

Discussions at this period between industrial capitalists and Republican leaders often turned on the question of changing the old slogans of innocent partisanship. James Swank, the secretary of the American Iron and Steel Association, wrote to Senator Justin Morrill:

The right of the black men to vote and have their votes counted should be strenuously insisted on, of course, but besides this we need not longer, I think, wave "the bloody shirt," but rather as vastly more politic, press the tariff issue upon our Southern brethren.[24]

Blaine, watching the parliamentary struggle from his retirement, had also kept a sharp eye on the interests of capitalists. On February 19, 1883, he wrote to Whitelaw Reid of the New York *Tribune*, which served nowadays almost as his personal organ, of his fear that the pending tariff bill might not be protective enough. The iron and steel men were being "pushed mercilessly to the wall," he protested.

We need one of your old fashioned bugle blasts in The Tribune, for the protection interest, strong, aggressive, cogent, as you know how to write. . . . The bill as the Senate is perfecting it with Beck's leave should be mercilessly slaughtered by Republicans in the House—and will be if you say so boldly in The Tribune.[25]

Henceforth Blaine constantly urged Reid to fight openly for the protective system as the great issue before their party. He would say: "I wish you would agonize more and more on the tariff."

Against the chances of jealous discontent rising among the masses of people at the open marriage of the party to trade associations and monopolists, the Republican spokesmen possessed an old recipe. The purpose of increasing Protection was as much the sheltering of American labor as of American capital, according to Garfield and Pig-Iron Kelley. The veteran Kelley, returning from a recent journey to England, spent himself willingly in describing the plight of British workers. He had seen how women and children toiled for ten or twelve hours a day at the grimy furnaces of Birmingham, where iron nails were manufactured, a sight, as he warned, "not calculated to inculcate Free Trade doctrines in the minds of any one." [26]

Even the philosophers of the time, after the manner of the English evolutionist Herbert Spencer, not only condoned but celebrated the captain of industry (who was soon to be the master of monopolies) as "nature's nobleman" and the true specimen of the survival of the fittest. A whole school of academic pundits propounded now the politics of individual profit-seeking. The good things of this world— including lands, mineral wealth, and special privileges—were being distributed according to merit, while poverty was the reward of indolence and vice. Outstanding economists at this time, such as Professor J. Lawrence Laughlin, praised the effects of the protective tariff, and eulogized the Vanderbilts and Goulds as "benevolent" promoters of human prosperity and progress; while another philosopher, Professor John Bates Clark, urged all his readers to ignore surface phenomena of strikes, lockouts, and class conflicts, and observe how the finer forms of self-seeking ushered in "God's kingdom in the industrial world." [27]

During the controversy over the tariff act in February, 1883, certain attacks had been made by Free Traders upon the motives of one

Joseph Wharton of Philadelphia, the largest manufacturer of nickel in the country, who was believed to be buttressing his monopoly by new duties. Wharton replied bluntly in the terms which were now general currency:

I have supported and aided the Government more than it has supported and aided me. I am not a pauper nor a lawyer. . . . I am one of the men who create and maintain the prosperity of the nation and who enable it to survive even the affliction of wrong-headed and cranky legislators.[28]

The leadership of Blaine, the convictions and interests of new leaders such as Aldrich, tended to make the party of Lincoln the efficient instrument of the dominant business class, the "party of business." But while such a tendency declared itself now more and more openly, and the times furthered it, there were historic and traditional forces that resisted the process, and for some years to come retarded the full flowering of a purely capitalist ideology and politique.

The sorry episodes of Grant's, Hayes's, and Garfield's terms, with their disgraceful factious strife and scandals of plundering public officials, did not as yet dispose all factions of businessmen to trust politicians with great sums of money. While some groups "bled" themselves freely, others known to have immense wealth were notoriously stingy and suspicious. (It was firmly believed at this time that more than half the money given to a politician for special service was wasted or "stuck to his fingers.") Still other factions, resenting extortions, pressed determinedly for bureaucratic reforms that would make government officials trustworthy and impartial. Finally, another and most serious obstacle was the revival or renascence of the rival professional organization, the old Democratic Party. In their stronger and stronger drive for official political power, the Democrats left no stone unturned in reaching out to propitiate and combine the support of different and even mutually antagonistic sections and classes. For though both parties habitually avoided class politics, both were extremely sensitive to those differences in kind and degree of property which the old Federalist, James Madison, had said were "the most common and durable source of factions." Moreover, the eager Democrats competed powerfully for capitalist support; loudly their leaders now proclaimed that they were even more devoted to the salutary prosperity of the business class than their adversaries. Besides, there were certain special reasons and even important grounds of convenience to which may be attributed the very widespread anticipation or desire for a "change" toward 1884.

CHAPTER NINE

THEIR MAJESTIES' OPPOSITION

No harm shall come to any business interest as the result
of administrative policy so long as I am President . . .
a transfer of executive control from one party to an-
other does not mean any serious disturbance of existing
conditions.   GROVER CLEVELAND

WITH the end of the General Grant Era of unbridled spoils politics, there followed a transition period (1882-96) when disparity of strength between the two great cartels of professional politicians disappeared. The death grip which the war party, the party of Union and Universal Liberty, had held upon the offices was relaxed; while the moral handicap which the Opposition had long borne, the traditional curse of disloyalty during the preceding epoch, was sloughed off. Moving abreast of their rival operators in all the political horse races that were run during this interval, the Democrats became accustomed, once more, to official power in the National Government, became, in short, the accredited party of Opposition.

For some years, since 1874, the revival of the Democracy had been foreshadowed by off-year victories. Once more they showed a disposition for mustering the larger popular votes. Or, to put it in another way, the Republicans had shown a tendency to offend the sensibilities of the people, while showing greater tenacity and cunning than the Democrats in clutching at national power. Hence for a generation the legend had grown up that Democrats were naturally stupider than Republicans, and permitted their opponents to profit by their habitual "blunders." *

The years intervening between the martyrdom of Garfield in 1881 and the election of McKinley as President in 1896 saw a swift, sure growth of the industrial system, an unparalleled advance in the economic organization of American society.

---

* Bryce in traveling widely in the United States during the 1880's received the impression that the Republicans included, in the North at any rate, the more prosperous classes and especially those who had the advantage of superior education.

This transition is usually termed the Age of Big Business, of centralized "pools" and "Trusts," and is distinguished by the crystallization of giant monopolies in coal, steel, oil, and railroads. Our politics, however, by a singular contrast, for the next four terms showed a regular alternation of government control that gave an outward effect of fluctuating authority and weakness after twenty-four years of unbroken single-party control.

The new phase of balance between the two parties, while devoid of great leaders or inspiring measures, assumes immense interest and teems with new political inventions once we peer beneath its surface manifestations.

For many a year the most naïve of the Republican stump speakers had been going up and down the land warning their countrymen of the evils and the blight that would follow a Democratic victory. There would be, as John Carlisle, the Democratic Speaker of the House, once summed it up ironically, nothing but prostration for our manufacturing industries and derangement in our finances; our currency would be debased, our credit as a nation destroyed. Confederate Brigadiers would mutilate our Constitution, abolish the Supreme Court, deprive the former soldiers of their pensions, undo the work of the Civil War.

Yet for all the moans of Republican Jeremiahs, the people brought about calamitous overturns in State after State, until in 1882 the very heavens had seemed to fall in upon the long-sinful Republicans. In nine States north of Mason and Dixon's line, even including Pennsylvania, Democratic or reformist Governors were elected to office; the support of the once contented and loyally Republican mass of farmers in the Mississippi Valley seemed to be crumbling away. Greenbackers and agrarians, deserting their independent third party, voted Democratic tickets. The Republicans had sown the wind and reaped the whirlwind, as many of their own adherents sorrowfully commented. The successive episodes of brutal dissension among their leaders, the hypocritical attempts at reformation, ending always with fresh national scandals—such as that of the recent Star Route conspiracy—had long sickened the minds of men.

Blaine himself felt a certain pessimism this season concerning the prospects of his party. His son Walker, who worked by his side nowadays, reflected this in an intimate letter, saying that "father is the only candidate for the Republicans. . . . But I doubt much whether the Republicans can elect anybody." [1] The party managers thought no more of running for the Presidency some mediocre Dark Horse; and the delayed nomination of Blaine, as the strongest leader of his party and a superb campaigner, was seen to be inevitable.

His influence over the national party gathering would be the determining factor in 1884, as four years earlier in 1880, and as it would be again in 1888, during a period of twelve years when the sway of "Warwick" Blaine was dominant among Republicans; ". . . If he cannot himself be President, no more can any other Republican without his assent," wrote Mrs. Blaine to her daughter at this time. [2] But in 1884 the candidacy of the former Speaker of Congress, who for years had resisted legislation for civil-service reform, provided special embarrassments.

The American people, especially the numerous lower middle class, with their long-developed tradition of personal liberty, taught for a century in every school reader, felt themselves not so much tyrannized over as seriously irked on many sides. The arrogance of the new railroads, which charged all that the traffic would bear, tried their patience. But while the farmer bent monotonously over his furrow, stared at a landscape without vistas, the bought politician rode about the world on his free pass. The free pass brought mountains of petitions to Congress in the 1880's from angry middle-class farmers, causing greater bitterness than more thoroughgoing evils, such as monopolized warehouses and elevators.

In 1881, there began the powerful pamphleteering by Henry Demarest Lloyd which familiarized the country with the Standard Oil and other monopolies. Lloyd connected the rise of monopolies with railroad discrimination, saying:

The forces of capital and industry have outgrown the forces of our government. . . . The movement of the railroad trains of this country is literally the circulation of its blood. Our treatment of the "railroad problem" will show the quality and calibre of our political sense. . . . It may indicate whether the American democracy, like all the democratic experiments which have preceded it, is to become extinct because the people had not wit enough or virtue enough to make the common good supreme.[3]

Lloyd, who was himself a man of independent wealth, and had virtue and much wit rather than anything of revolutionary fire, said at this time: "The Standard has done everything with the Pennsylvania legislature except to refine it." He continued later on the same score:

> Rings and bosses are rising to the top in the evolution of industry as in that of politics. . . . A few individuals are becoming rich enough to control almost all the great markets, including the legislatures.[4]

Mounting tariffs, rising prices, the arrogance of monopolies during a minor depression setting in in 1882-84, sorely tried the patience of the people. "Scratch a monopoly and you will find the Government underneath" was one of the sayings of the time. But would the Republicans change the Government? In the grain- and corn-growing regions many converts were being won to the creed of Free Trade or tariff reform; toward 1882 distressed Mississippi Valley farmers turned from Weaver's Greenback gospel to the Democratic Opposition, believing that it would "do something" for them.[5]

With disgruntlement so general, the danger was apparent to some keen eyes that the "status character" of the long-ruling, decadent Republican Party, their tenacious grip on power in the face of popular opposition, might of itself be a cause of disaster to the country. Would it not be preferable that Liberal Capitalist, middle-class, agrarian, and labor discontent should be canalized into the party of the Opposition? This alone, as the clever Kentucky journalist Henry Watterson wrote privately to a confrere of the enemy party, would mean an important *"invigoration which the transfer of power peacefully from one party to another will give to our republican system."* [6]

The strong silent men who acted for the "massive interests moving obscurely in the background" of public affairs missed nothing of the signs and omens visible in the sky. It would be absurd, it would be the height of naïveté, to presume that they were not disposed to turn to their account, as before, the peaceful return to power of the official opposition party; or that they overlooked that which Watterson saw at once in such change: a means of invigorating, even a braking device adding stability to, our republican system.

For many years Gould and Huntington had maintained "friendships" among the Democrats. In the rich Huntington-Colton correspondence there is sometimes mention of "beating a Republican with a Democrat," because, as Huntington explains, "people think our hand is over the one and under the other." Or again

I notice that you say of —— he is a wild hog; don't let him come back to Washington, but as the House is to be largely Democratic, and if he was defeated likely it would be charged to us, hence, I should think it would be well to beat him with a Democrat.[7]

Jay Gould's confession of political faith had already been announced during investigations of the Erie Railroad in New York: "I was a Republican in Republican districts, a Democrat in Democratic districts. But everywhere I was for Erie!"

The very prospect of widespread bureaucratic reform, eliminating the most accessible and venal public officials, held no real terrors and even provided certain gains.

For reform of all kinds was in the air of the 1880's. Reform was the Live Issue of the day wherever opinion was articulate, wherever thoughtful Americans paid attention to political affairs. A symptom that the "inexhaustible capabilities of the word Reform," as Conkling would say, were being exploited more than ever before was its popularity nowadays among the younger arrivals in the lower ranks of politics. But the type of reform that made the most fortune was that which Carl Schurz's and George William Curtis's preachments advocated, that which centered upon the purification of the civil service, and in truth evaded completely the great questions, the great dangers to democracy raised by monstrous railroad and industrial monopolies. Here once more was a Burning Issue which cut across the lines of division of classes and sections of the people, combining the divers groups of the community while ignoring the enduring differences over which they conflicted. The idea that bureaucratic reform, such as England and Germany had carried out, would cure our political ills was now warmly supported by respectable and wealthy taxpaying citizens, the dominant classes who ruled public opinion. Carl Schurz, now editor of the New York *Evening Post* (which was subsidized by the new railroad grandee, Henry Villard), wrote thunderous editorials by which he strove every day to "save American youth" from the example of a Blaine. It was no coincidence that types of aristocratic American youth who were prepared to climb the political ladder, such as Henry Cabot Lodge of Boston and Theodore Roosevelt of New York, nowadays enlisted under the banner of civil-service reform in all local contests.

But it was the Democratic Party of the Outs that now held obvious advantages in the race to offer civil-service reforms, and there the new movement made the most rapid headway. In New York's corrupt old city machine the followers of Tilden, public-spirited capitalists or lawyers such as Abram Hewitt and William C. Whitney, now arose as leaders to dispute successfully the shameless power of Tammany. And from western New York there came rumors of a "God-sent" leader of reform, Mayor Grover Cleveland of Buffalo.

I I

Within a year of reaching office, the "Veto Mayor" of Buffalo, though a raw recruit in government service, blocked numerous fraudulent measures on foot among the politicians, two of these alone touching sewage and street-cleaning contracts saving the taxpayers of the middle-sized, provincial city approximately $1,000,000.[8] In the manner of Rutherford Hayes, this "ugly-honest" Mayor was reported to have said that "public officials are the trustees of the people." [9]

An honest man had arisen, or at least one who demonstrated that he could be so while in public office, and soon people looked upon him with wonder and awe. Though he busied himself prosaically as a strict inspector general of street-cleaning and sewage accounts, his fame spread in the Empire State. To economical taxpayers the possibilities for further use of such reform ardor seemed not to be despised, and a movement was begun which catapulted the obscure Cleveland like a meteor into State and national leadership such as, by his own admission, he was ill prepared for.

On other grounds as well, the stout, beer-loving "man of the people" who toiled for so many years as a small-town lawyer possessed interesting possibilities. McElroy, an early biographer who was a confidant of Cleveland, relates that from his first years of activity in local politics he was used even by the Republicans in the role of peacemaker, because he "was in close touch with the masses before he began much contact with the classes, and . . . easily maintained sympathetic relations with both without offense to either." [10] As McElroy explains it to us, Grover Cleveland's combination of attractions and virtues was such as could now scarcely be dispensed with:

> When political troubles arose in the people's section, they would send for Cleveland, "who would sit down among the brothers of discontent, play with them, drink with them awhile, and then peacefully settle their controversy."

For the Democratic Party splendid chances were opened in 1882 for the capture of the Empire State, when the Conkling-Arthur machine outraged the electorate by their dismissal of Cornell and the dictation of Folger as the Republican candidate for the Governorship. In like manner the army of Democrats was woefully divided: New York City was riven between the Tammany Hall contingent and the Tilden Organization, which, under the leadership of Abram Hewitt, William C. Whitney, and H. O. Thompson, had built up the County Democracy as a reform machine. Upstate, in the central cities around Albany, Daniel Manning, Tilden's lieutenant in chief, shrewd and imperious newspaper-owner, banker, and boss of Albany, directed another and probably the dominant wing of the State party; while a fourth faction supported the aspirations of Roswell Flower, a wealthy grain and stock-market speculator who was a member of Congress, and promised to contribute "generously" to his own advancement. Yet at the last moment these competing factions were persuaded by a common lust for office to coalesce, with a fair semblance of unity, around Cleveland, the independent "outsider" from western New York—as their most "available" candidate. Thus, stoutly supported by an organized band of office-seekers, and rallying to his cause all the indignant reformers and Republican bolters in the State, the virtually unknown and untried Cleveland was elected Governor by a Tidal Wave.

Cleveland exemplifies the legend of the self-made man by his laborious climb from poverty to glory and success. His was the success, as Nevins apologetically explains, of "typical" rather than of exceptional or brilliant traits. It was a time when "character" (which Cleveland had in good measure) was desirable in public office—if intellectual power could not be found. "The nation in 1885 needed a man who would typify Reform, and Cleveland proved to be the man." [11] This exceedingly homely fellow of common mold now becomes the figurehead of the reviving Democracy, the container of political virtue, the hope of the reformist frenzy that sweeps over the middle class.

We have seen also how the nation was overready for a political "change," albeit one that in Cleveland's conception would do "no harm . . . to any business interest"; and toward this end the hungry Democrats had formed themselves behind the burly hero of reform as a solid, vote-catching machine that matched the best specimens of Republican organization. At the head was Daniel Manning of Albany, like Cleveland a huge, stout, iron-jawed fellow, but one who possessed superior cunning in political management, "the machine incarnate," as Carl Schurz called him. Manning's clever young associate and aide Daniel Lamont became Governor Cleveland's private secretary, discreetly overseeing or advising upon every move. The lieutenants of the old Tilden Organization thus surrounded and helped the new leader with all their resources. William Whitney, the brilliant, handsome young corporation lawyer who had recently married into the Standard Oil clan, "type of the successful New Yorker who mingled business with politics," brought the advantages of intelligence and wealth, much as Whitelaw Reid and John Hay provided these for the Blaine Legion. At the lower end of the system, the breezy Hubert Thompson, a successful adversary of Tammany Hall in New York, using their own beer-hall methods, provided contact with the people in the streets. [12]

An increasing agitation for reform in local and State government during the 1880's was also the result of an internal evolution in the relations between capitalist enterprise and government. Under our

Federal system, a most vital part of the police, administrative, and judicial authority is allotted to the State and city governments. Their authority embraced the power of incorporation; of taxation; of the regulation of industries, including banks, insurance companies, railroads, and public utilities. The distribution or control of many kinds of natural resources, rights of way, monopolies, and public franchises were likewise in control of the local or regional political governments.

During the economic revolution of the Civil War and the Reconstruction Period, when joint-stock companies became more numerous and multiplied in size, their undertakers had rushed upon the State legislatures and city councils with their demands for all forms of public privileges. The distribution of such privileges brought a carnival of disordered corruption and bribery in State legislatures and city councils far exceeding anything known in the earlier days of the republic; insatiable appetites of adventurous and farsighted entrepreneurs were equaled only by the endless chicane of small, local politicians. The lurid contests of the Erie Ring and the Vanderbilts for public grants and franchises in older States such as New York, or of the Pennsylvania Railroad in Pennsylvania—when whole legislatures repeatedly sold themselves to one side, then broke their contracts and sold themselves to the other—were exactly duplicated under the regime of Governor Leland Stanford in new California. The whole system for many years, through the 1860's and 1870's, suggested the utmost disorder in public economy. There were such frequent instances of "strike bills" or blackmail legislation that a man like Huntington or Jay Gould could say with some justice that he bribed politicians "in order to prevent them from robbing me of my property." These were "the days of the Black Horse Cavalry," as Elihu Root, the corporation lawyer, has said, when local lawgivers seemed beside themselves with greed. The shadowed uncertainties of such a system provided special chances for skilled corruptionists such as Jay Gould, but also involved considerable disadvantage by their burden and tax upon the whole community.

During the General Grant Era, when the attention of powerful regional bosses was fixed largely upon the distribution of national government resources and grants, few beginnings had been made toward bringing about order in the relations of private corporations and local legislatures. The business system itself groaned under such costs, until there emerged as healing agencies for the bleeding body politic, and filling identical functions, the reformer and the specialized boss of local politics. Appearing to be dialectical opposites in politics, they were yet identical.

The reformer proposed his economies, his impartial arbitration of competing claims, needs, demands for government protection or franchise; the latter-day specialized State or city boss, in contrast to his old-fashioned, rhetorical, and purely patronage-seeking predecessor, directed in sober and efficient manner the traffic in the multifarious local political business our form of government requires. The new type of boss, such as Platt, Quay, and Foraker (whom we shall discuss under another head), now negotiated in much more secretive form—as a consequence of his dubious legal position—his transactions with the railroad and municipal franchise-owning corporations, the insurance companies and banks, who might be affected by legislation and who needed to buy a certain amount of political power.[13]

It was no longer a matter of political leaders who used the power of patronage over an army of followers, and of rich capitalists who casually acted as Maecenases for famous statesmen for the sake of extending their "influence"; it was a matter of firmer, more direct and "businesslike" relationships. As the economic function of the State boss in his bureau or clearinghouse of political privilege became more fixed and specialized, party funds became more extensive again —depended less than ever upon assessments of public officers, and overwhelmingly upon regular and large contributions from the big corporations within his bailiwick. "This alliance between the political machines and the corporations—particularly those who operate railroads or control municipal franchises," as Herbert Croly has said, "was an alliance between two independent and coördinate powers in the kingdom of American practical affairs." The captain of industry now fully turned to account the existing democratic institution of the party organization, and brought about what Croly calls "the peculiar, unofficial organization of American industry and politics." [14]

When in 1882 the middle-aged Grover Cleveland as Governor, and Theodore Roosevelt as an Assemblyman, came together to Albany, the corporate-political alliance so well described by Croly was being perfected, despite many difficulties. The young littérateur in politics, Roosevelt, has recorded his surprise at the complexity and baffling legal appearance of many of the bills arriving before legislature and Governor in these days. Both men in their different ways, and at their different stations, with no little bewilderment attacked the same problems: Roosevelt impetuous and incautious, Cleveland unimaginatively patient and methodical in dealing with masses of detail.

Cleveland advocated a general reform, along civil-service lines, of the State administration, but was scarcely able to make a beginning of this task; and it was still an untamed jungle when Theodore Roosevelt became Governor nearly twenty years later. The young Assemblyman began by collaborating with the Democratic Governor, but ended by expressing vexation at and disappointment in him. A number of reform bills which Roosevelt introduced or fathered, in his first ardor, were among the accumulation of "thirty-day bills" piled on the Governor's desk and dismissed with irritating vetoes. This was done, Cleveland would say, not because he was opposed to their principles, but because they were imperfectly drawn and would lead to "prolonged and expensive litigation." [15]

The reformist Governor delivered some vigorous blows at Tammany's leader, Honest John Kelly, during disagreements that developed at the outset of his term. It was a time when Tammany was unusually weak in New York City and was being largely outmaneuvered by Hubert Thompson and Whitney, leaders of the city's rival Democratic organization, the County Democracy. In the meantime, when serious charges of fraud were brought against Thompson himself, as the newly appointed Commissioner of Public Works, Cleveland could do nothing. Thompson was indicted by a grand jury, and was described as a "smaller Tweed," Assemblyman Roosevelt charging him with an "overwhelming series of irregularities and extravagances." Nor in a similar case, when Sheriff Davidson, a New York City anti-Tammany boss and like Thompson an ally of Daniel Manning, was under fire for having disposed irregularly of $85,000 from the public funds, could Cleveland be persuaded to do anything. Measures aimed by Roosevelt and his fellow crusaders at the wrongdoers were struck down by the Governor on technical grounds. It was seen then that powerful members of the party's patronage machine, which Daniel Manning of Albany was building skillfully behind Cleveland's broad back, could not be spared, least of all on the eve of a presidential nomination.

George William Curtis had led Republican bolters to vote for Cleveland; and observers commented . . . "Curtis knows now that his idol has clay feet." [16]

What was really taking place was, in effect, as Theodore Roosevelt afterward intimated, that Cleveland contributed to the building of a "reform machine" to replace the odious and disgraced Democratic machines. Cleveland publicly fought John Kelly and Tammany's notorious plunder organization, earning the applause of the country. Bills that struck at Tammany were acceptable, while punitive measures against Chairman Manning's henchmen came to an untimely end in gubernatorial vetoes.

Cleveland's appointments showed a perceptible, though discreet, yielding to the needs of the party machine. In a very forthright interview, shortly after his elevation to the Governorship, he said on this subject that it was "unfortunate for the Democratic party that this 'boss' system exists. While it does exist it becomes a necessity—a disagreeable necessity, I assure you—for me to recognize it." [17]

The government reformation was to proceed, then, within the limits imposed by the "disagreeable necessities" of the boss system: reform was to respect professional Organization and its proprietary interests; Organization was to accord reform a certain decorous respect in return.

Cleveland suggests a rugged, personal honesty; he was temperamentally awkward in the Jesuitical maneuvers of politics; he was unhappy, tactless, and disagreeable when yielding to requests for appointments from Daniel Manning, the chairman of the State party. The fact that he so yielded, and with such evident reluctance and irritation, is in itself a revelation of the irresistible and fateful strength of the party system.

Because of the aura that hung over the sturdy reformer from

Buffalo and the vigorous revival he seemed to have brought to the New York Democracy, men tended to overlook the deep instinctive conservatism of his character and his whole earlier way of life. Those biographers who have overemphasized his bachelordom, the colossal beer-drinking bouts, and the free living in Buffalo's taverns ignore the habits of hard work and thrift, the puritanical scrupulousness about money, and the laborious savings and prudent investments by which this typically bourgeois character gathered a small but adequate capital in middle life. In this way he was easily led to accept—though ignorant of national issues and economic science—the Hard Money and gold-standard convictions of the banker Daniel Manning, which were native to Eastern capitalists.

We find him now also, in pursuance of ulterior ambitions, induced to speak at a banquet of the powerful New York Chamber of Commerce on the subject of the businessman's interest in politics. The question he posed on this occasion, before the rich men of New York, was "whether enough care was taken to send champions of this all-important interest to the Legislature"; at which "the responsible men of the metropolis caught the significance of the reference and rose in vigorous applause." [18]

But in the spring of 1883 an incident occurred that illustrated even more strongly the unusual possibilities of the reform spirit which this ponderous conscientious "inspector general" brought to our politics.

The elevated railroads of New York City, then controlled by Jay Gould, the Mephistopheles of American finance, were permitted by charter to charge a 10-cent fare except in certain rush hours, when passengers had to be carried at 5 cents. Owing to Gould's unpleasant, monopolistic ways, popular agitation had brought about the passage in the State legislature of a bill fixing the city's elevated-railroad fare at 5 cents for all hours.

But the "Great Obstructionist," as Cleveland was afterward called, decided firmly that he must veto the Five Cent Fare Bill; and to his contemporaries his arguments appeared (as they do to certain of our own) "irresistible" on legal grounds. The proposed law, said Cleveland, would revoke rights granted previously by State charter; it impaired the obligation of a contract, thus violating the Constitution of the United States; and though the Governor was "not unmindful . . . that this bill originated in response to the demand of a large portion of the people of New York," he would stand firm in preserving the honor and faith of a great State.[19]

Since this veto, middle-class minds have applauded in Cleveland a statesman who could rise above "good politics" and the insistent clamor of a people enraged by Gould's mean tyrannies and meaner public service. Andrew White, the distinguished president of Cornell University, observed with relish that Cleveland had overcome his "sympathies for the working people" and showed "not the slightest germ of demagogism"; while Theodore Roosevelt too was convinced that the bill in question was, after all, unwise, and that "a mischievous precedent" was avoided by the veto.[20] Nevins concludes that Cleveland's vetoes were usually better than his appointments; that is to say, his defensive or negative actions were better than his attempts at advance or reconstruction. He celebrates the veto of the Five Cent Fare Bill as an instance of political "independence" and "courage," adding also that such defensive action offered inducements to "timid" capital to make further investments in street transportation.[21] There is little doubt that the responsible men of capital fully "caught the significance" of Cleveland's vetoes.

Truly, Cleveland was "God-sent" for them too. If the spirit of reform spread widely, much of the waste of lobbying and bribery might be spared by the large corporate groups. Without urging or prodding, such "courageous" statesmen as Grover Cleveland would defend to the last breath the property rights of corporations under the law, while leading a veritable crusade for reform, designed to regulate a disorderly official corruption. Jay Gould must have pondered seriously upon the merits of a type like Cleveland, with his reputation for bluff honesty, as against the conveniences of such known quantities as Conkling or Blaine.*

When the quadrennial tournament between the two parties began in 1884, it was seen that throughout the Northern States people of the "better sort," people who had money and property, would be turning about to vote for the Democracy and its "thrifty steward."

* A popular tradition holds that "the reformer is one who gives to the capitalist for nothing that which the real politician holds for a price."

Whitelaw Reid, in a very blue report to Blaine, informed him that in the clubs of New York "it was hard to find any one who was going to vote for him." [22]

III

The Republican nominating convention at Chicago in 1884 was an almost unexceptionable demonstration of harmony. Even Tom Platt, who had now recovered much of his aplomb and quietly gathered in the reins of the New York Organization, spurned the "ad interim" President, Arthur, and supported the nomination of Blaine. When the handsome young Joseph B. Foraker, soon to be Governor of Ohio, rose to play his part for Sherman, Ohio's Favorite Son, many felt that his words pointed to the great man from Maine rather than to Uncle John:

> We not only want a man who is a pronounced Republican, thoroughly tried in the crucial tests of experience, but we want also a man whose very name will allay instead of exciting the distrust that disturbs the industrial interests of this country. He must, of course . . . be a friend to human liberty, to equality of rights . . . but there is one thing in which our platform reminded us today he must not believe, and that is a substantial reduction of the duties on iron and steel and wool.[23]

The failure of President Arthur's design for his renomination, through supporting a presidential cabal with patronage, was pathetic. At the same time he had done high services for reform without pleasing its friends. Despite his fulsome talent for diplomacy, he had fallen between two stools, and was to be remembered afterward chiefly for his elegance of dress, his good table, his fine wines, his ready quotations from Dickens. The one jarring note at the Chicago proceedings was the presence of a sullen band of the "unco guid," as Blaine contemptuously called them, the "noisy but not numerous" and "pharisaical" Mugwumps.

Once more Carl Schurz, the grizzled crusader for civil-service reform, led a minority delegation which believed unalterably that the elevation of Blaine would be a "terrible calamity" for the country. These men named Senator George Edmunds of Vermont, whom scandal had never touched, as their candidate. The strength of this faction came chiefly from the "aristocratic liberals" of Massachusetts,

Charles Francis Adams, Jr., Josiah Quincy, Leverett Saltonstall, Moorfield Storey, Thomas Wentworth Higginson, Charles Eliot, and the young Henry Cabot Lodge. From New York came a strong array of Independent journalists, numbering Curtis of *Harper's Weekly*, Godkin of the *Nation* and New York *Post*, and the "silk-stocking" Assemblyman Theodore Roosevelt, who now attended his first national party convention.

Foraker, who was in Ohio a good example of the advanced type of machine boss, recalls the first unpleasant impression which the band of reformers made upon orthodox Republicans. Lodge, Roosevelt, Curtis, were men with eyeglasses, who "had their hair parted in the middle [!], banged in front," their cutaway coats tightly buttoned in English style. Curtis particularly, "with his intensely intellectual John Bull face" and "mutton chop whiskers," gave the effect of an Anglomaniac and created amusement, exceeded only by the figure of Roosevelt, "a rather dudish-looking boy with eyeglasses and an Olympian scowlet-for-a-cent." [24] Civil-service reformers not only got their ideas from the detested British but, according to the legend that Conkling and others assiduously spread, they differed peculiarly from hearty, red-blooded Republicans in being "neither male nor female," but probably eunuchs.

There was in truth an Anglophile spirit, caught by "Fire Alarm Joe" Foraker, which is to be seen as well in the intimate correspondence of the two literary politicians, Lodge and Roosevelt. The theory of Good Government, the ideas of having "good men in politics," of purifying the civil service, of introducing higher standards of education in national and local governments, had of course been the obsession and "cure-all" of Carl Schurz for nearly twenty years. The circle of Lodge, Roosevelt, Whitelaw Reid, and William C. Whitney undoubtedly played with the further idea of having our politics dominated or given leadership by young career men of wealth and intelligence, as in England. Moreover, the tone of domestic administration was to be further improved by their rather boyish martial spirit, calling for a strong-handed, "brilliant" policy in foreign relations, which was to win new national glory for their country. It was such an amalgam of political theory that filled the many pages of correspondence between the two aspiring students and party apprentices, Lodge and Roosevelt.[25] But whatever their hopes may have been, they were cruelly dashed to the ground by the behavior of the "Blaine convention."

At mention of the magic name of Blaine in the nominating speech of June 5, 1884, the convention became "a mass meeting of maniacs," as Godkin wrote.[26] Whole delegations mounted their chairs and led the cheering; men tore off their coats; banners were waved; women became disheveled and hysterical; the uproar became a Niagara of sound which engulfed the poor schemes of the reformers. Schurz and Curtis and the Yankee Mugwumps quickly came to the decision to bolt their party if the Democrats should have the decency to nominate Governor Cleveland.

The young intellectuals present were no doubt plunged into despair. Roosevelt left in a rage for a ranch in the Dakotas, feeling that there was no really "honorable course" within the Blaine party. While Roosevelt experienced a *crise de nerfs* and calmed himself by punching cows, Lodge also suffered torments of conscience when his old mentor, Carl Schurz, pleaded with him to "follow a noble impulse" and abandon party "regularity." However, the gifted pupil soon came to his decision to support Blaine, saying:

I regard my action as the only honorable course to take. . . . By staying in the party I can be of some use. By going out I destroy all the influence and power for good I possess.[27]

To leave the party was truly an act of fearful apostasy, still! It was like turning upon the officers of your regiment in Prussia, or setting yourself against the men of your public school in England; it was to defy the historical institution of the American tribe, and its almost mystic oracles of order and authority.

Soon the Boston man of letters was so far converted to "regularity" that, as a Representative in Congress, he set to building his own personal machine of Federal appointees. Young Roosevelt's wrath also cooled quickly. Coming East at the urgence of his friend for a private conference whose details are lost to us, he was persuaded that independent action meant but ruin and barren fruit. Then, having "the political asset of self-hypnosis," [28] he publicly announced to his small following in New York his sense of obligation to support the choice of the party convention. Roosevelt's partiality for civil-service reform, according to his very penetrating recent biographer, derived chiefly from "middle class prejudices," which were now tolerably curbed.[29]

IV

The naming of Blaine as the Republican candidate, and the news of Mugwump disaffection, made Governor Cleveland the most "available" standard-bearer for the opposition party. At the Democratic convention in Chicago, various Favorite Sons were quickly passed over: Speaker Carlisle of Kentucky because he espoused a low tariff, and Governor Hendricks of Indiana because he stood for Western "rag-money" radicalism. Manning, the model State boss, with Tilden's approval overcame Tammany opposition to his candidate; in the night hours at Chicago, he made a "deal" with Samuel Randall, the conservative Pennsylvania leader, promising the latter all Federal patronage for his State. In the meantime another powerful machine boss of the modern type, Arthur P. Gorman of Maryland, was won over by William Whitney, thus bringing about the speedy nomination of Cleveland by a sweeping majority on the third ballot. Clever management from beginning to end gave the effect of an irresistible "boom" for Cleveland, who only two years before had been unknown outside of Buffalo, New York.

The Cleveland campaign, as Allan Nevins has described it, was "a far-reaching moral movement to awaken men from old lethargies and fix their eyes upon some new city in the heavens." [30] In all fairness, it must also be called the fine creation of three masterly wire-pullers, Manning, Whitney, and Gorman. Its hard, routine labor was performed by a well-led, well-disciplined mass of unregenerate Democratic office-seekers, who had long wandered in the desert but saw as a mirage on the horizon before them the offices of the Federal Government.

Although Senator William Barnum of Connecticut, an aged iron-manufacturer and party hack, was titular chairman of the Democratic National Committee, his associate, Gorman, was the head of the National Executive Committee and the directing genius of the campaign. Gorman was a man of many sides, intelligent, quick-witted, strong-willed, and unusually attractive in appearance. In 1852, as a boy of thirteen and a page in the Senate, he had begun to absorb his political science. In the rough-and-tumble politics of his native Baltimore, where local elections were often decided by the skillful deploying of mobile gangs of thugs from one balloting station to another, Gorman had become a past master of electoral strategy. From a State office having access to the public treasury and controlling much patronage, that of Director of the Chesapeake & Ohio Canal, Gorman had risen to be the absolute boss of the Maryland Legislature, enriched himself rapidly, and in 1881 engineered his own election to the United States Senate. Although respectable elements in Maryland showed horror at Gorman's brazen tactics of bribery, he had also "a faculty . . . of inspiring confidence in the moneyed interest," which ended by silencing opposition.[31] It was Senator Arthur Gorman, now beginning a thirty-year reign in the Democratic Party, to whom command of the "far-reaching moral movement" for reform was entrusted.

Daniel Manning, the New York boss, who acted as Gorman's chief lieutenant in the campaign, has been pictured by one of his proud underlings as a tremendous power who died prematurely. Manning, for all his imperious manner and bull voice, was cunning enough to resort to much detective work, including the use of spies and counterspies; he was methodical, organizing accurate lists of doubtful men and sections, and elaborate pre-election canvasses, according to an improved technique which showed almost day-to-day fluctuations in the contest. When it was feared at the last moment that the Republicans would steal the returns in their upstate New York strongholds, offsetting the Democratic lead in the city vote downstate, Manning was able to set up overnight, at enormous expense, a large organization of responsible watchers, who literally saved the day.[32]

Whitney, like John Hay, as Henry Adams mockingly related, was an example of a young American intellectual who, having married a great fortune, participated in the fascinating but costly game of President-making. This brilliant pupil of Samuel Tilden had worked intermittently behind the scenes of New York political contests for twelve years. His function now, thanks to his connection with the Standard Oil clans, and one which in many ways anticipates that of Mark Hanna later, was to serve as a liaison officer between the mightiest corporations and Trusts and the national party Organ-ization. William Whitney, who was to gratify every ambition, satiate every taste, gorge every appetite, in Henry Adams's description, and yet swing the country at his will, threw himself into the Cleveland campaign with all his characteristic nervous intensity.[33]

In their Inner Circles and canvassing organizations the two tradi-tional parties were identical and well matched. The Republican chair-man was Blaine's friend and business patron, Stephen B. Elkins of West Virginia. A former Territorial delegate from New Mexico, Elkins had wrung millions from the "operation" of old Spanish land claims; then, removed to the East, he had married an heiress and figured as a leading actor both in Wall Street and in Washington. As strategists and regional bosses, Don Cameron of Pennsylvania, John Logan, who was the candidate for the Vice-Presidency, and Platt of New York worked harmoniously with their former Half-Breed adversaries for a common victory. In an electoral campaign, the Ins always have all the advantage over the Outs, as Arthur Gor-man observed at the time. "Machiavelli" Chandler was now Secretary of the Navy and used his department forces actively in the campaign. The Commissioner of the Pensions Bureau, Colonel William W. Dudley, a veteran of Oliver Morton's old Indiana spoils machine, likewise sent scores of officials from his bureau into Indiana and Ohio, at government expense, and their efforts to dragoon the soldier vote he personally superintended.

Serious though (because of civil-service law) more furtive efforts were also made to gather the tithes of Federal officeholders, through assessment headquarters quietly set up at Washington. But thanks to the Pendleton Act of 1883, many thousands of Federal officials were now safe under the merit system, and hardened their souls against the demands of the Republican Party tax-collectors. William Chan-dler's private correspondence in this "season of reform" is composed of a long and entirely sincere lament over the actual scarcity of cash.[34] This Republican poverty at a time when the Democrats were unusually affluent was the most prominent and unusual feature of the 1884 contest.

Far from appealing to the hearts and minds of the citizens in a duel over principles and doctrines, both adversaries were circumspect and wary to the point of boredom. Into the fires of the great "moral movement" that season, New York's sterling hero of reform was cautious to throw as few brands as possible. Under shrewd advice, he assumed a politic silence, by which the chances of having his words twisted and used against him were lessened. Blaine, a genius of the debating forum, a dramatic stump orator, spoke often and vigorously without saying anything that arrested attention. In his letter of acceptance he discussed as usual the growth of the country's manufacture and agriculture under Republican rule (described in terms of geometrical sums), and predicted still richer harvests to come. He concluded:

Nothing stands in our way but the dread of a change in the industrial system which has wrought such wonders in the last twenty years, and which, with the power of increased capital, will work still greater wonders of prosperity in the twenty years to come.[35]

Indeed Blaine strove as he might to raise alarm among capitalists on the score of Protection. Repeatedly, according to tactics he had long planned, he warned his public of the evil days which had already begun—by citing the financial panic of May, 1884—as a consequence of anticipated change in our tariff system. Persistently Blaine strove to bind the business class to his party.

But this device and the tactics of alarm failed notably. The Democrats persistently refused to give battle on this ground; their platform had consisted of the most Delphic utterances on all controversial points such as Protection; they had "straddled" the issue, the ardent Free Trader Henry Watterson complained; and in truth, as George William Curtis concluded, "the platforms of the two parties are practically the same." Both parties proposed the regulation of the wicked railroads, for which there had been insistent demand for ten years. Both parties alike favored administrative reform. The Democrats denounced in furious terms the corruption of the Republicans, but the Blaine Republicans now baldly claimed credit for instituting the first civil-service legislation!

Democrats went to pathetic extremes in countering the charges that their party proposed any measures whatsoever which would in the least degree change the fundamental, existing scheme of things.

The few words that Cleveland had to offer dealt with dismissing the fantastic claims of opponents on this score. To the capitalists of the country he promised: "No harm shall come to any business interest as the result of administrative policy so long as I am President," adding that "a transfer of executive control from one party to another does not mean any serious disturbance of existing conditions." [36] The new Democratic leadership outdid the Republicans in wooing men of capital. To James Bryce, witnessing his first American presidential campaign, the maneuvers of the politicians passed all understanding:

. . . the odd spectacle was presented of Republican orators advocating a protective tariff . . . and hardly any Democrat referring to the subject except to say that he would not refer to it. Both sides declared against monopolists and the power of corporations. . . . Both promised to protect the rights of Americans all over the world, to withstand Bismarck in his attacks on American bacon, and to rescue American citizens [of Irish race] from British dungeons. [37]

In the last resort, to determine the social difference, or rather nuances, between the two great political cartels, we must examine their finances, the vital sources of their revenues. These varied in both cases from levies by local officers upon gambling-dens, brothels, and cafés—brothels were Democratic in New York and Republican in Philadelphia!—to the sale of nominations, State and Federal, implying almost certain election by the machine leaders, and assessments upon job-holders. But with the beginning of civil-service reform the old sources of party revenue were somewhat diminished, and a very marked increase in "impersonal" contributions by the heads of large corporations took place at this time—impersonal in the sense that the donors had predominantly financial rather than friendly or honorific motives.

"What about this man Cleveland?" wrote James J. Hill, the Western railroad-builder, to Tilden. "He is all right," replied the corporation lawyer. [38] Hill thereupon sent Manning $10,000—and telegraphed his associates in the West "to get busy" for Mr. Cleveland.

On the Republican side, evidence through the existing Blaine papers is scant; but it is well established that the large railroad masters Vanderbilt (through Depew) and Gould aided the Blaine cause, Jay Gould, according to rumors at the time, yielding up $50,000 to a last-minute appeal. Andrew Carnegie, Stephen Elkins, and William Walter Phelps were among the financiers of heavy industry who were directly concerned in the protective-tariff system; the American Iron and Steel Association came forward as generously as ever to the Republican side; and the Standard Oil again made its donations through Henry Flagler. Platt, Henry Clews, and Levi Morton as usual gathered a large chest from the New York bankers and stockbrokers; while John Roach, the shipbuilder who held government contracts, though not ranking with the others named above in wealth, gave, according to his own statement, $15,000 to the Republican National Committee in 1884.[39]

For the Democratic treasury we have Cleveland's own memorandum, candid though incomplete, showing that the party of the Outs had more distinguished and more generous financial support than ever before in its long history. The largest recorded payments are: William H. Barnum, $27,500; Edward Cooper and Abram S. Hewitt, $25,300; Representative William L. Scott (of Erie, Pennsylvania), $24,000; Oswald Ottendorfer, New York publisher, $18,000; Roswell Flower and D. Willis James, $16,000 each; William C. Whitney, $15,250; Arthur P. Gorman, $14,908.25; Daniel Manning, $13,675. Then smaller donations of approximately $10,000 from James J. Hill, the Western railroad-builder; Levi Leiter, the Chicago merchant; Addison Cammack, the notorious Wall Street speculator; the Straus brothers; and numerous others in smaller sums—the total footing up to $453,000. But "it is . . . fair to assume," as McElroy, Cleveland's confidant, concludes, "that even the grand total of almost half a million dollars does not tell the whole story of the campaign funds of the Democrats."[40]

There came always last-hour appeals for the purchase of the floating vote, as Frank Kent has described them, payments for which are never listed by either party. In this connection Hudson, who served as an aide to Manning, alludes, for instance, to a further special contribution of $70,000 by Messrs. Cooper and Hewitt.[41]

There were bankers and finance capitalists on both sides of the contest; there were coal and iron industrialists on both sides; finally, in the case of Henry Havemeyer of the Sugar Trust, and the Standard Oil men, the practice of making contributions to both parties was now openly reported. The Rockefellers, Flagler, and Archbold were closely connected with the Republican Party; but their business associate Henry B. Payne, and Payne's son-in-law William Whitney, were even more directly occupied with Cleveland's campaign. Only this faint nuance is perceptible: that the extreme, insatiable advocates of the protective tariff appeared to lean toward the Republican leader, while the Eastern iron-manufacturers, such as Cooper & Hewitt, disadvantaged by their distance from Western ore fields and the tariff upon imported ore, definitely favored reduction in tariff; the dry-goods merchant Isidor Straus was a Free Trader, but William L. Scott, the grasping coal merchant, who is remembered chiefly for the terrible lockout of his workers ordered in the winter of 1889, is seen subsequently to be playing an obstructive part in Democratic plans for a lower tariff.

With the parties now well matched in every respect—financing, Organization, platform, ballot-box stuffers, and thugs—and with the Democrats, while owning the Solid South in advance, also fighting on even terms in at least a half-dozen large Northern States, the outcome hung clearly upon elliptical or fantastic turns of chance, the seizure of a pawn. The urbane and disillusioned Henry Adams, at the height of the battle, wrote to an English friend:

We are here plunged in politics funnier than words can express. Very great issues are involved. Especially everyone knows that a step towards free trade is inevitable if the Democrats come in. For the first time in twenty-eight years, a Democratic administration is almost inevitable. The public is angry and abusive. Every one takes part. We are all doing our best, and swearing at each other like demons. But the amusing thing is that *no one talks about real interests. By common consent they agree to let these alone. We are afraid to discuss them.* Instead of this the press is engaged in a most amusing dispute whether Mr. Cleveland had an illegitimate child, and did or did not live with more than one mistress; whether Mr. Blaine got paid in railway bonds for his services as Speaker. . . . I have laughed myself red with amusement over the letters, affidavits, leading articles and speeches which are flying through the air. Society is torn to pieces. Parties are wrecked from top to bottom. A great political revolution seems impending. Yet, when I am not angry, I can do nothing but laugh.[42]

V

Where there are no issues, where there are no decisive, clarifying divisions of class interest, the necessity becomes more imperative for the professional party managers to engender artificial differences; to invent enthusiasm, passion, and frenzy; to set factions among the people, upon any pretext possible, to tearing and smashing each other to pieces. The canvass of 1884 was a succession of dramatic national spectacles and mass demonstrations into which men in all walks of life, and even women, were drawn by the contagious excitement. While such real issues or interests as were at stake were suppressed or beclouded by the balanced parties, adventitious issues were raised instead, touching on the personality and the "moral character" of the competing leaders, who were exposed to a pitiless glare of publicity. The Independents, or inveterate reformers, in particular, following Schurz's lead, drew lessons from Blaine's public career which showed that his election would be a terrible moral example for our young people. This was the heavy handicap which many Republicans had foreseen in undertaking the candidacy of Blaine during a season of reform.

"The paramount issue this year . . . is moral rather than political," Mr. Curtis announced at a great meeting of Republican bolters in New York, which was designed to swing all doubtful voters in the Empire State to the Democratic Party.

Taking the Democrats at their word, the Republican strategists chose this very moment to explode a moral bombshell in the midst of their rivals. Copies of Buffalo newspapers arrived in New York bearing a colorful account of sinful strayings by the bachelor Cleveland, in his youth. Maria Halpin, the Buffalo widow who had "loved too well" Cleveland and others, had been delivered of a child, the sire unknown, whose charge Cleveland had agreed to assume. The woman, who was given to drink, blackmailed Cleveland from time to time; and in the end, for the child's safety, the future statesman had removed him from the mother. In press and pulpit excited debate over the grand affair now brimmed over, as in the days of

Henry Ward Beecher's trial. Republican ministers held large audiences in thrall while with an evangelical fervor and a Victorian profusion of detail they drew lurid pictures of the Democratic leader as a "libertine" and "moral leper" who sought to introduce himself into the highest office of the land. A pall of confusion and gloom now fell upon the old party of Andrew Jackson.

The hardened sinner himself behaved well; he showed a desire to state his case manfully, claiming no superior domestic virtue but only a pardonable frailty, following which his conduct had been correct and just. His supporters, attempting some rather stumbling dialectics in his behalf, tried to explain away "Grove's" *péché mignon.* Godkin in the *Nation* wrote:

> We are not defending incontinence. Chastity is a great virtue, but every man knows in his heart that it is not the greatest of virtues, that offences against it have often been consistent with . . . the qualities which ennoble human nature and dignify human life and make human progress possible.[43]

But the jubilant Republicans from Maine to California would listen to no moral hairsplitting that condoned Democratic incontinence, and declared that they would be content with nothing less than a Chief Magistrate who embodied the most flawless chastity—a virtue in which Mr. Blaine was held to have outshone all the rest. Certain desperate Democrats, hoping to fight the Devil with fire, provoked rumors which reflected scandalously on Mr. Blaine's private character and, circulating rapidly by word of mouth, bewildered the public even further. But Mr. Cleveland is credited with having ordered such methods stopped, holding that the other side "can have a monopoly of all the dirt in this campaign." [44] Moreover, the gossip concerning Mr. Blaine's domestic morals was proved to be quite baseless.[45]

The grotesque debate over the sexual issue extended itself, causing impending industrial conflicts and class issues and the economic depression to be forgotten. The Democrats meanwhile were greatly out of countenance—until one of their friends, a veritable philosopher, at a gathering of Mugwumps in Chicago, set the whole matter in its proper light. Inasmuch as Mr. Blaine, the impeccable papa, had shown himself weak and dishonest in public life, while the naughty sinner, Mr. Cleveland, had shown the utmost honor and capacity in office, "we should elect Mr. Cleveland to the public office he is so admirably qualified to fill and remand Mr. Blaine to the private life which he is so eminently fitted to adorn." [46]

In the midst of this "vilest campaign ever waged" there arrived at Democratic headquarters in New York a large packet of new Mulligan Letters, specimens of the private correspondence of Speaker Blaine and his friends the railroad projectors. Certain of these documents, when read beside the ones published in 1876, were more devastating than anything in the earlier installment. Besides illustrating further Blaine's lapses from official decorum at the time when he was Speaker, they revealed, as in the case of the letter to Warren Fisher dated April 18, 1876, and preceding by a week Blaine's theatrical "vindication" of himself in Congress, how he had arranged to have his business partner copy and sign a letter of Blaine's own composition to be used as testimony in his favor. *"Burn this letter"* was the closing request of Blaine; but Fisher, using his own discretion, had preserved it, so that together with several others no less damaging to the Republican candidate it had fallen again into the hands of the embittered Mulligan. Gorman and Manning, the Democratic strategists, held back the new Mulligan Letters for two weeks, then in mid-September, when the fight was at its hottest, released them and broadcast them through the press.

The round of accusations, slanders, countercharges, and denials continued ever stronger, whipping up public feeling to a dangerous pitch. But in addition to this, the unprecedented size and character of all the parades, the "Chinese business," organized throughout the country by both sides, seemed to illustrate the pure professionalism which had seized both parties. The American people had always instinctively loved these vast folk demonstrations; and the politicians used them to keep up the "boom" of the canvass. A Republican "businessmen's" procession of 16,000 would be answered by a procession even more imposing of Democratic lawyers, merchants, and artisans numbering 40,000.[47] The shouts and songs answered each other stridently:

> Blaine! Blaine! James G. Blaine!
> The con-ti-nen-tal liar
> From the state of Maine,

was countered by

> Ma, Ma! Where's my Pa?

alluding to Cleveland's youthful indiscretions. Or another marching cry would be sounded:

> Five-five-five-cent fare!

by the Republicans—touching the Governor's veto of legislation favored by working people. But the Democrats would chant in defiance:

> Burn this letter! Burn this letter!
> Burn, burn, oh, burn this letter![48]

As the campaign approached its climax, it was seen that it would be unusually close, and the election experts of each side, Chandler and Gorman, conceded victory to the other. While carefully avoiding fundamental social issues and points of controversy, and characteristically cutting across fundamental class divisions, the leaders of both sides devoted their final strokes to detaching special nonpolitical factions or groups from one another. Intrigue met intrigue in the maneuvers for the support of organizations of ministers, Prohibitionists, Catholics, or labor unions. Although the third-party movement had entered a decline and the Greenback-Labor contingent now planned to vote largely for the Outs in 1884, the old demagogue Ben Butler, long in disgrace, had introduced himself as the presidential candidate of the skeleton party, and with the funds of the Republican National Committee, secretly supplied him by William Chandler, tried to capture enough of the New York Irish Catholic vote to defeat the Democrats.[49] The Democratic managers, on the other hand, probably intrigued with St. John, candidate of the small Prohibition Party which, offended at Republican rebuffs, proposed to divert some of rural New York State's votes from the Blaine column.[50] Although such measures tended to cancel each other, Blaine's appeal to New York's 500,000 Irish-born voters, as a habitual baiter of John Bull, was highly feared in Democratic headquarters. Responding to urgent calls by his party managers, the Gentleman from Maine, pale and weary unto death, but as magnetic as ever, returned suddenly from his Western speaking tour to lead the battle for New York in person. Here, in the closing hours of the contest, occurred an incident which gave the advantage in the maneuvers for factions to the Democrats.

By prearrangement, a delegation of Protestant ministers called on Blaine at Republican headquarters at the Fifth Avenue Hotel, on the morning of Wednesday, October 29, 1884; their spokesman, the Reverend Dr. Samuel Burchard, addressed Blaine at some length in terms which included the following immortal phrases:

> We are Republicans and don't propose to leave our party and identify ourselves with the party whose antecedents have been *rum, Romanism and rebellion.*[51]

This poetic but deadly alliteration was missed by the fatigued Blaine, who was usually so lightning-quick of thought, but not by the watching scouts of Senator Gorman, noting down every word of Burchard's address. Overnight Gorman's fliers were posted everywhere, informing the Irish Catholic masses of the mortally insulting words of a bigoted Presbyterian minister, which had passed without reproof in Blaine's presence. The mood of the Irish and other Catholic people in New England and New York, previously cool to Cleveland, quickly veered to a frenzy of anger against the Republican leader—at a moment, five days before election, when it was too late to repair the mischief.

But so far as popular sentiment was concerned, Blaine piled Ossa on Pelion that very day when he attended the great banquet offered in his honor by the two stock-market buzzards, Jay Gould and Russell Sage. This dinner at Delmonico's restaurant, at which Blaine was given an ovation by two hundred of New York's Money Kings, has been remembered usually under the title of Belshazzar's Feast. In the glittering ballroom, decorated with rare flowers, where delicate food burdened the groaning tables and the choicest wines flowed, the masters of capital did too great homage to the man who had served them so long and so well.

Here were Jay Gould, Cyrus Field, John Jacob Astor, Levi Morton, D. O. Mills, Jesse Seligman, Cornelius Bliss, Henry Clews, Henry Havemeyer, John Roach, and many another multimillionaire or monopolist. To these the guest of the evening addressed himself with a fervid encomium of all money-making and wealth-getting activity. The total increase of wealth in the Empire State during the past twenty years Blaine, with his ready figures, estimated at some $4,500,000,000.

. . . I am sure, gentlemen, that the Republican party is not arrogant nor over-confident when it claims to itself the credit of organizing and maintaining the industrial system which gave to you and your associates in enterprise the equal and just laws which enabled you to make this marvellous progress.

But what would happen to "you men of New York with your wealth and your just influence" if the Republican system of sound money and Protection were reversed? He gave warning: "If these policies are to be reversed you will have to recast your accounts and review your ledgers." [52]

After the dinner, the real purpose of this festival—which Blaine had attended despite the risk—was revealed. The orator and his hosts retired to the back rooms of the restaurant, with the doors closed to the press, and took up a collection of emergency funds.*

On the following day the Democratic press of the East seethed with fury against Blaine. Joseph Pulitzer, recently arrived in New York, had made the *World* the most daring and sensational newspaper of the time. At this moment when an economic depression caused widespread unemployment, his headlines cried:

* Such funds would be devoted chiefly to "getting out the floaters." Despite the whipped-up excitement of the campaign, thousands of free citizens in "strategic" or "doubtful" States had formed the habit of looking on the proceedings with a trained indifference. They must be rounded up, paid, fed, marched to the polls with their ballots in their hands so held that the district captain could see the ticket (which had been printed and furnished by the party Organization). *Cf.* J. B. Bishop, "The Law and the Ballot," *Scribner's Magazine*, February, 1888. According to Ostrogorski (*Democracy and the Organization of Political Parties*, Vol. II, p. 345), not only immigrants and "voting cattle" were so dealt with after the Civil War, when vote-purchasing was said to have vastly increased, but shrewd Yankee farmers in New Hampshire and Indiana waited as floaters for their $5, and money for every member of the family or farm hands. No real secrecy at the polls existed until after 1892, when many States introduced the Australian ballot.

THE ROYAL FEAST OF BELSHAZZAR BLAINE AND THE MONEY KINGS
BLAINE HOBNOBBING WITH THE MIGHTY MONEY KINGS
MILLIONAIRES AND MONOPOLISTS SEAL THEIR ALLEGIANCE
LUCULLUS ENJOYS HIMSELF WHILE THE COUNTRY SORROWS
AN OCCASION FOR THE COLLECTION OF A REPUBLICAN CORRUPTION FUND

Underneath, covering the whole front page, was printed McDougall's powerful cartoon showing the statesman at the sumptuous table, surrounded by fat capitalists with huge "sparklers" upon their shirt fronts, while a poor skeleton of a citizen, with his ragged wife and child, begged with arm outstretched, for crumbs.

In the closing days of this intoxicating campaign the agents of each party raged at each other with a passion and a fanaticism which ended by infecting the whole people. Edmund Burke, the great Whig philosopher, writing in 1770 about the evils of the two-party system which took root at that time in England, declared in a passage of most brilliant insight that the true source of mischief lay in the working of a "double ministry," the one a sham set before the public, the other, the real one, holding actual power of administration, controlled by a cabal working behind the scenes. The interests in control behind the scenes, Burke argued, "contrive to form in the outward administration two parties at the least, which, whilst they are tearing one another to pieces, are both competitors for the favor and protection of the cabal; and, by their emulation, contribute to throw everything more and more into the hands of the interior managers." [53]

More than a century later, in the great republic of the West, the form of events showed the justice of Burke's remarks concerning the behavior of parties and the fictitious passions they engender, when once more the interior managers seemed to have so "contrived matters that the people have a greater hatred to the subordinate instruments than to the principal movers."

The truth concerning the outcome of the historic Millionaires' Dinner at Delmonico's has been much overlooked. These Money Kings, who calculated the value of each dollar, knew Mr. Blaine well, knew well the Republican Party and knew well the Democratic Party. They listened to Blaine's pleas without enthusiasm, and then gave disappointingly little. According to a statement by Stephen

Elkins some years later, the greatest disappointment in the affair "consisted in its failure from a financial point of view, campaign contributions from the millionaires present being much less generous than had been expected." [54] Thus the Money Kings pronounced a doom over the "glorious" Republican leader.

Apparently they were tolerably willing to risk the reform of the civil service and the peaceful transfer of power to a party that promised in no way to disturb the business interests of the country. More than one of the millionaires present, such as Havemeyer and John Roach, who might both certainly be included in the interior cabal, paid contributions to the Democrats as well as to the Republicans. According to further accounts, other great capitalists who had long been faithful Republicans felt inclination and confidence to "switch." "The representatives of four large firms in New York, approached by the Republicans in the final weeks, declared 'they couldn't stand Blaine,' and this year gave $5,000 each to the Democratic National Committee for Ohio." [55] J. S. Clarkson, the powerful Iowa boss and newspaper-owner, who played an important part in the Republican Party management, declared that *"it was Republican business men voting against their party* [in 1884] *who defeated it in New York, Connecticut, and New Jersey."* [56] Voting against "their" party, or withholding their funds from it, they appeared at any rate to act in such a manner that the final measures that seal victory in a close electoral contest were not taken.

According to private discussion among Republican leaders subsequently, John Logan, the candidate for the Vice-Presidency, had urged that arrangements be made to "control" a block of several thousand "Independent" Democratic votes in Kings County (Brooklyn, New York) which were offered by one Joseph O'Brien, a Democratic State Senator. But nothing was done about this, either because it was considered an unnecessary effort or because there were no funds for the affair. [57]

On Tuesday, November 4, rain fell, an unpleasant sound to rural Republican ears; at the polling stations the Democratic agents and watchers were present and active in surprising force. Indeed it was afterward rumored that they were too forceful in the region of the metropolis, as at Long Island City, where Greenback-Labor votes were counted for Cleveland. Cleveland carried New York by the extremely slight plurality of 1,149 votes out of 1,167,000 cast, while winning also the Northern States of Indiana, New Jersey, and Connecticut by slim margins, with a total plurality in the country which was only 25,000 more than Blaine's vote.

The result of the canvass was in doubt for several days; fears of another disputed election were felt; and ugly reports were heard that Jay Gould, who was then the country's favorite bogeyman, was delaying and falsifying the returns by his control of all the telegraph lines and the Associated Press. Crowds rushed to besiege the massive Western Union Building, chanting: "We'll hang Jay Gould to a sour apple tree." From the safety of his yacht on the Hudson River, the little bogeyman telegraphed congratulations to the winning candidate on Friday, November 7, 1884, in a message fraught with all the deeper meaning of the season's stormy political tournament:

Governor Cleveland: I heartily congratulate you on your election. All concede that your Administration as Governor has been wise and conservative, and in the larger field of President, I feel that you will do still better, and that the vast business interests of the country will be entirely safe in your hands.[58]

CHAPTER TEN

THE COMEDY OF REFORM

*To have said and done nothing is a tremendous power;
but it should not be abused.*　　　TALLEYRAND

THE "peaceful revolution" that had cost the country so much shock and strain brought to a halt Republican control of the executive department of our Government, uninterrupted during a whole generation. Under our system of a "plebiscitary presidential republic," as it has been called, the administrative powers lodged in the Presidency are so important that the ritual significance of a miracle always attaches itself to the inaugural ceremony when the parties change place. And in the case of Mr. Cleveland's inauguration popular curiosity was enormous. His entrance symbolized the peaceful transfer of power from the party that had come to occupy a status position to the party of the Outs. It marked also the complete return to civil life of the former rebels, and the burial of the old war hatreds.

Though the campaign of 1884 had been fought, as usual, over irrelevant questions, those touching the copulative habits of the one candidate and the prevaricative habits of the other, we would be wrong to conclude from this that deeper yearnings were not also involved. Where the major social issues are so cunningly neutralized by the parties it is difficult to measure how many people desire tariff reductions and a lower cost of living, how many farmers wish for an improved distribution of credit, how many liberal bourgeois desire a reform of the civil service, or how many of the men of wealth press for policies that we have defined as those of a rational Liberal Capitalism. Undoubtedly these motives, in an unformulated or even unspoken manner, entered into the struggle for a political "change"; this was suggested by the manner in which the so-called Independent vote swung decisively to the Democrats.

Thus, for a season, the excesses and internal dissensions of the Republican politicians, ending in the murder of a President—administrative scandals such as that of the Star Route Ring, the spectacle

374

of public office being sold to highhanded railroad and industrial monopolists—had all focused sufficient popular anger on the Ins to undo their organizational advantage, and to base large hopes upon the Opposition.

The very stout, very bluff-looking man from Buffalo, as he made his inaugural address undoubtedly carried with him the goodwill of most of the people. Even the radical agrarians of the farther Mississippi Valley shared the widespread conviction which Henry Adams privately expressed at this time that "a step toward free trade, at any rate" would be inevitable. Even greater numbers of the people agreed with Henry Watterson that the change and overturn that Mr. Cleveland symbolized would bring at the least a certain "invigoration . . . to our Republican system."

The noncommittal platitudes voiced by the new President should have afforded a clue to the future and set at rest too great anticipations, were it not that such ambiguity was held to be part of the established technique of American statesmanship. The Chief Magistrate appealed for a spirit of mutual conciliation between the parties. He intended, he said, to surround himself with the best and broadest minds, which would shun "extravagance and waste," would not harm business interests, and would show that a transfer of executive control meant no serious disturbance of existing conditions. So far as tariff and taxation policy were concerned, he envisioned only the "readjustment" of irksome duties, having "a due regard to the interests of capital invested and workingmen employed in American industries." He said further on this score in his first annual message to Congress: "The question of free trade is not involved, nor is there now any occasion for the general discussion of the wisdom or expediency of a protective system." He was strictly committed to civil-service reform. But his concept of reform was narrowed down to "economy" and "the application of business principles to public affairs."

Boldly embarking upon a sea of trouble, Cleveland set to work purging the Federal Administration and extending the rule of civil service, begun under Arthur. Energetic, full of "backbone," and disposed, as Tilden said, rather to do a thing badly himself than to permit anyone else to do it well, this forthright and honest steward gave himself up wholeheartedly to the formidable administrative task that had been left to him. At once he collided with a solid wall of political realities.

The Federal patronage had always been the very source of party power; to remove this beyond the hands of the Democratic Party managers was to weaken the party's very capacity for successful action. From the beginning a fairly frightful struggle over the award of offices raged behind the scenes of the new Administration.

In his very choice of his Cabinet Cleveland had been obliged to bow to the authority of the party's national committee. By the "geographical" principle, which the old political philosopher Blaine has defined for us, the cabinet officers were intended to strengthen the revived party in the different sections. Secretary of State Bayard was the veteran Senator from the Border State of Maryland; the Secretary of the Treasury, Daniel Manning of Albany, New York, suggested the influence of Tilden and the New York machine; William F. Vilas of Wisconsin, as Postmaster General, represented an attempt to extend the party influence in the Middle West; William C. Endicott of Boston, as Secretary of War, brought a New England capitalist and railroad director lending social grace to the Cabinet; while L. Q. C. Lamar, as Secretary of the Interior, the old-fashioned, absent-minded Senator from Mississippi, appealed to the former Confederates in the party. On the other hand, William C. Whitney, under whose spell Cleveland had plainly fallen, as Secretary of the Navy was an added counselor from the New York Organization, rewarded for his large personal contribution to the victory. Only Senators Bayard and Lamar had achieved a national reputation previously; the selection of Boss Manning as the person to reform the much-abused Treasury Department was sharply attacked; while Whitney's elevation was ascribed by Schurz to his being the son-in-law of Henry B. Payne, of the Standard Oil Paynes, and to the money he had given the party. Finally, the stationing of the silent, wise little Daniel Lamont as the President's private secretary, ever at his ear and at his side, seemed to complete the dominance of Tilden counselors in the White House, and left the impression that the party's "saint and martyr" would manage everything.

A secret quarrel soon developed, however, between Tilden and

Cleveland, into which Manning was soon drawn. Tilden was in poor health, but was determined to direct the financial policy of the Government through his devoted friend and former lieutenant Manning, who had taken the Treasury post somewhat unwillingly. The President's first expressions in favor of Sound Money and opposition to silver inflation, as well as Manning's conservative measures to undo the effects of silver coinage, had been directed by Tilden entirely. But soon afterward, within the year, Tilden, who was on his death-bed, made no secret of his alienation from the President. Manning, too, according to repeated rumors, was offended, chiefly over the question of spoils; he felt that inept attempts at reform were doing untold damage to their party's prospects.[1] * To Tilden he wrote privately:

. . . I am living in an atmosphere that is full of mischief, and where the whirl is so great that one is inclined sometimes to doubt whether he comprehends his associates, or fully understands anything of what he is about.[2]

Tilden, the old spokesman of the Democratic Party, conceded that a moderate administrative reform was now in order, but argued that this must be carried out with a view to buttressing the party against the future, and notably the followers of Tilden among them. In other words, Tilden desired a very moderate reformation on "practical" lines. Their President was to improve the bureaucracy but must also take care to manage well the institutional interests of the Democratic Party. It is significant that Tilden in March, 1885, busied himself examining the record of Thomas Jefferson on the subject of Federal appointments, and in a paper that he prepared at this time showed how the first immortal Democratic President had removed opponents of his policies in good number from government office—"for none resign and few die," he observed. Jefferson's letter defending his dismissal of the collectors of customs at New Haven had been acquired by Tilden and printed in Joseph Pulitzer's *World*, to bring pressure upon the White House.[3] The New York *World* warned:

* Nevins holds that no such friction existed, though without giving reasons for this view. Manning's resignation, ostensibly on account of very bad health, was ready six months before it was made public in February, 1887.

"Cleveland must remember the obligations which an Administration elected by a great historical party owes to that party." [4] Moreover, both Manning and Whitney openly showed that they "heartily approved of the *World's* editorials." [5]

Cleveland in his first moves retained in office some able Republicans, especially the Postmaster and the Naval Officer of New York City. It was the "example" given by this action which troubled so conservative a reformer as Tilden, and outraged Secretary Manning as well as the Tammany contingent. For, the election over, the professional leaders and "workers" in Cleveland's party made plain their real conception of reform. As one Senator expressed it, "they felt that the civil service reform for which they had voted . . . meant the turning-out of office of Republicans and putting honest Democrats in their places." [6]

There were 100,000 deserving Democrats, long-suffering partisans, who might at last be placed in office, and by the protective rules of the civil-service law even made secure in their tenure thereafter from Republican reprisal. This was the grand notion of reform that they proclaimed as they besieged this President, like Lincoln before him, day and night in the White House. Besides, in the Inner Circle of the new Administration, men like Postmaster General Vilas, Senator Gorman, and Vice-President Hendricks exerted themselves to the utmost to balk the extension of the merit system. It was of these men that an apologist for Cleveland relates:

> Over and over again his friends broke party pledges in the belief that the President would never know. . . . The Vice-President, and at least half the Democratic Senators, and nearly all the Democrats of the House banded themselves together to break down the President . . . and force him to do their bidding.[7]

Cleveland in his letters to friends reported that he lived as in a "nightmare . . . this dreadful, damnable, office-seeking hangs over me and surrounds me." And again he exclaims: "The d—d everlasting clatter for offices continues . . . and makes me feel like resigning and hell is to pay generally." [8]

While Cleveland appeared to be making bold moves for reform, certain key places in the bureaucracy had been quietly turned over to the strongest regional bosses. The chief of appointments in the Treasury Department under Manning was a member of Gorman's Maryland machine; the new Collector at the New York Custom House, Hedden, was the alter ego of Hubert Thompson, boss of the city's anti-Tammany Democratic Organization. When the President, informed by newspaper attacks of dishonesty or incompetence at these points, moved to correct the appointments, there was an uproar among the machine men. Manning was alarmed at all the "mischief abroad." Thompson, a leader of the old Tilden "reform machine," who in despair was taking heavily to drink, wrote letters of wild and intoxicated protest to Manning, in which the threat of blackmail was aired:

Mr. Cleveland, who you Mr. Tilden, and myself made President, and you recollect all the circumstances, wrote Francis Lynde Stetson a letter asking him to get Mr. Hedden's resignation, simply and solely, and entirely because the *New York Times* and the *Evening Post* had abused Mr. Hedden for not being a strong civil service man. In spite of my feeling against Mr. Cleveland I have held my peace. . . . It means my political destruction, it means the destruction of every man who supported Cleveland in New York, it means absolute ruin all round. I must appeal to you, I must ask you to intercede. This thing must not be done. You know that I do not want to threaten. I do not want to do what is unwise or thoughtless, but if Mr. Cleveland does this dirty, dastardly act, I think I will be justified in going to any extremity that I see fit. . . . I will be compelled to publish him in the papers to show what a cowardly knave and fraud he is. I have facts, which you know of yourself . . . which could show him in a shape that would ruin him.[9]

When the President's slowness to award spoils to his party's regular "workers" became manifest, a prolonged outcry arose against him from that quarter; Pulitzer's New York *World* and Watterson's Louisville *Courier* thundered against his "ingratitude" to those who had "delivered the vote."

Thereupon he beat a retreat and proceeding with his reforms more "slowly, cautiously, practically," as McElroy puts it, he attempted to placate the professionals. Ward heelers, spoilsmen, even thieves and some individuals charged with murder, as was afterward learned, now found their way into Federal posts within Gorman's bailiwick of Baltimore.[10] Republican postmasters, as in Indiana, were removed more rapidly and without "cause," and replaced with faithful Democrats who belonged to the Hendricks machine. Late in 1885, Nevins relates,

under the full impact of party demands, Cleveland began to modify his position on appointments. . . . There was no . . . surrender of vital principles. But party leaders were permitted to state their cases to . . . [his secretaries], and a steady flow of suspensions and removals followed.

Cleveland had promised that, in accordance with the terms of the Pendleton Act, his policy would be to replace officeholders after they had been in office for four years. Thus by the end of his term there would be a "clean sweep" of almost all the Republicans; while the process could be hastened as Postmaster General Vilas did, by singling out a large percentage of Republican officials who might be charged with "offensive partisanship." Within six months Vilas had replaced 6,300 out of 49,000 fourth-class postmasters and supplanted the personnel of almost a fourth of the 2,300 "presidential" post offices. By midsummer of 1886 the President was more "generous," politicians "felt distinctly better, and the party revolt was subsiding." [11]

Here and there, also, powerful capitalists who were closely related to the party were discreetly rewarded. James Hill, the Northwestern railroad captain who became "close personal friends" with the President, saw to it that "the patronage of the Northwest was turned over substantially to two men in St. Paul who were staunch Democrats and good friends of Mr. Hill." [12] Hill thereupon came to "control" the several States which his railroad traversed. Thanks to similar favors, a boss like Gorman was able to get himself re-elected to the Senate in a tense struggle in 1887 and continue his dark and double labors in local and national affairs. "The triumph of the spoilsman Gorman was complete." [13]

But now from the other camp of the reformers and purists there arose a cry of bitter disappointment, whose chorus was swelled by the regular Republican leaders as well. Schurz, the zealous watchdog of reform, who had given Cleveland such strong aid from the platform in the recent campaign, delivered himself both in letters and in the press of some unsparing criticisms of the President's "errors."

Cleveland swung the other way, attempted at times to revoke blundering appointments, but, being also short of temper, he ended by being angrier with the reformer than with the spoilsmen. In a letter to Dorman B. Eaton, formerly a Civil Service Commissioner, he flung back at the "supercilious self-righteousness" of "carping" critics who demanded "in the affairs of government . . . complete and immediate perfection." [14] He made plain to Schurz also that he was not conducting the Federal Government "merely for the purpose of civil service reform," and finally in his annual message to Congress, December, 1886, dwelt upon the "misguided zeal of impracticable friends." Whereupon Schurz (who acted as the conscience of Presidents for thirty years) gave him a warm answer:

Your attempt to please both reformers and spoilsmen has failed. I warned you more than once that your principal danger was to sit down between two chairs. I am afraid you are virtually there now.[15]

Cleveland now severed relations with Carl Schurz and the Mugwumps, even going so far as to order one Federal officer not to attend a meeting of the Civil Service Reform League in New York. One of the reform leaders, Dudley Foulke, has shown how disingenuous the tactics of the President now became. Writing directly to 193 suspended postmasters in Indiana, and over 100 in other States, Foulke ascertained that in only 2 cases had any inquiry preceded removal. When he went to the honest man in the White House with his findings, he was told that the President approved of this course, holding that it was "impractical to inform the [suspended Republican] postmasters of charges against them." [16]

All of the older historians of the time, Dewey, Rhodes, and Oberholtzer, have agreed with the Republican view of Cleveland's blundering and inept reforms—that he was trying to serve God and the Democratic Party at the same time; that he alternately sought to please reformers and spoilsmen, and succeeded in making no one happy. Dewey finds a certain unsolved "mystery" in the tortuous procedure of the President and his relation to the great spoilsmen of his party. In Nevins's view, Cleveland, for all his "fumbling and uneven" record, made some gains, but was overwhelmed by the immensity of the task.

The difficulties were huge. But the real contradictions in Cleveland's course spring from the conflict between his sincere principles—at this time those of a Liberal Capitalist—and the needs of the party institution. He honestly hoped, as did other Liberal Capitalists, that the time would come "when all our people will see the advantage of a reliance . . . upon merit and fitness, instead of upon the caprice or selfish interest of those who impudently stand between the people and the machinery of their government." Then Cleveland found that if he made a drastic purge the Organization of his party would disintegrate behind him, and he turned to compromises. When the compromises brought mischance or scandal, he would veer about and sometimes exclaim to his spoilsmen friends out of the torment of conscience: "Well, do you want me to appoint another horse-thief?" [17] *

When four years had passed it was seen that the machine, now lubricated by the "oil" of reform—which was reputed to have a more pleasing smell—had done its task well: some two-thirds of the total number of 120,000 officeholders in the Federal bureaucracy had been changed. Of the chief Federal officers, including fourth-class postmasters, collectors, and land officers to the number of 58,000, about three-quarters were replaced. There was a "clean sweep" of all 85 politically important internal-revenue collectors; and of the heads

* But during this transition period of our politics many privileged capitalists were patently unwilling or unready as yet to rely entirely upon "merit and fitness" or impartiality in public officials. The new controls which must replace the old ones held by masters of patronage had not yet been perfected; and they refused to relinquish entirely the spoils system.

Henry B. Payne at this time pursued an amazing campaign in Ohio to elect himself to the Senate. The actual scale of direct bribery, with satchelfuls of Standard Oil money seen in the saloons of the State capital, surpassed anything that even Ohio politics had ever known. Later Republican leaders such as Hoar challenged Payne's right to a seat in the Senate, and all but succeeded in impeaching him on voluminous evidence of bribery. Payne, the father-in-law of Secretary Whitney, had used not only money but also patronage, availing himself of changes ordered by President Cleveland in Ohio post offices, which brought jobs to Payne's men. One notes a profuse letter of thanks from the notorious Payne, not only for Federal appointments in Ohio but for "reforms" leading to the placing of Payne men in Washington, as in the Public Printer's office. Cf. Cleveland Papers, H. B. Payne to Cleveland, Aug. 13, 1886.

of customhouses, 100 out of 111 were removed.[18] Cleveland, as a reformer, was "not without a becoming sympathy for the Democratic leaders and their point of view." [19] On the other hand, he had extended considerably the classified civil service, so that 27,380 Federal job-holders, "as against 14,000 under Arthur," were now protected from party assessments and removal on partisan grounds. Such a change, even though limited, was to have a very serious effect upon the nature of party control itself.

During the first two years of Cleveland's term numerous disgruntled Democratic politicians carried on an uproar of criticism and recrimination aimed at their own President. This internal dissension created a most unfortunate impression of the new ruling party, which Mr. Cleveland's want of tact and deficiency as a popular leader but augmented. He swung from intense scruples to disingenuous compromises; or, suspecting sometimes that close friends were deceiving him by "lying and treacherous representations," he would fall into moods of stubborn anger and self-assertion, and refuse even reasonable requests with ill grace—with a stubborn jaw, and a heavy fist pounding the table. The confusion in party affairs reflected itself at once in the leaderless, purposeless character of a divided Congress. This was heightened by the harrying tactics of the Republican Opposition.

Having a small preponderance in the Senate, the Republicans were able to block Administration measures, and especially important presidential appointments. The Republican Senators themselves were not surprised at the "rolling of heads" that followed the coming into power of their opponents, but what outraged them was the hypocritical pretext of reform advanced as a cover for such action. Since this virtuous Chief Magistrate had announced that changes of office would be based on evidences of corruption, incompetence, or "offensive partisanship" rather than on partisan expediency, the thousands of Republicans who had been dismissed protested with justice that they stood silently accused of these vices, while having been given generally no hearing or trial. The system of removals upon secret charges in the Post Office Department especially "was evidently the joint offspring of the President's desire for civil service reform and the clamor of his party for spoils. . . . It encouraged spies and informers; slander, falsehood, and suspicion. The [Democratic] political retainers all understood that they were to get the offices by some underhanded method." [20] Hence the ejected Republicans now clamored for public "vindication"; and a determined band of Senators, including Sherman, Edmunds, and Ingalls, in the autumn of 1885 invoked on their behalf the old Tenure of Office Act that had been used against Andrew Johnson. They demanded of the President evidence and proof, the reasons for suspensions from office, before they would give their confirmation. A struggle between the President and the Senate followed, which enlivens somewhat the fruitless years of Cleveland's first term, and wherein the issue for the stubborn President became that of saving the independence of his executive office from senatorial domination.

The Republican leaders saw the matter otherwise, simply as the business of calling a spade a spade. They contended that they were not trying to prevent the Administration from replacing Republicans with Democrats, "but were merely insisting that Cleveland should admit he was doing it, in the main, for partisan reasons." They would confirm his appointments promptly if he made plain his real motives. [21]

As in the conflict between President Hayes and Conkling, nothing came of these obstructive maneuvers except long delays and high words; for the President had the power to make "interim" appointments, repeatedly, until the Senate was forced to confirm them. By the spring of 1886 the hostile Senate was forced to yield; yet a finger had been pointed at the essential hypocrisy of the new regime, which consisted, as an old Tammany sachem cleverly defined it, of "pandering to reform." As the debate drew to its end, Senator John J. Ingalls, the waspish orator from Kansas whose words usually "scorched like drops of vitriol," had set his colleagues and the country at large to rocking in gales of laughter as with serious mien he gave an epopee upon the nature of reformers. As a group, he theorized, their devious, underhanded ways showed that they belonged to "a third sex." They were

effeminate without being either masculine or feminine; unable to beget or to bear; possessing neither fecundity nor virility; endowed with the contempt of men and the derision of women, and doomed to sterility, isolation, and extinction. [22]

II

The period of Democratic power in the Government during Cleveland's first term was one of exciting change and momentous events outside of national politics. While the wars of the "robber barons" were fought for the prizes of monopoly, industrial warfare also burst forth, especially in the West, and reached a climax with the Haymarket bombing. Flurries of panic and prosperity swept over the country; huge crops were harvested and exported to fill the world's markets; then drought came to the arid uplands of the Mississippi Valley; and afterward, new discontent, agitation for silver money, for tariff reform, railroad regulation, Trust laws, and the single tax.

In these vivid, hurried years, the masterly inactivity of the politicians was something wonderful to behold. The weakness of the political Government seemed less accident than design, as C. E. Merriam has pointed out; design that suited better the purpose of the rising business class. Moreover, the Democratic Party, as the party that traditionally professed to espouse laissez faire and "the least government," seemed an admirable instrument for such inactivity.

It had found itself, for the first time in long years, charged with the full responsibility of government. But it came to its task

not as a united body, having a clear programme and a settled platform of principles . . . but with very marked divisions . . . on all the leading issues . . . the leaders of the party are not even agreed on the question of what is the leading issue.[23]

The Democratic Speaker Carlisle in the House of Representatives found the utmost difficulty in making up the various congressional committees without splitting his followers into warring clans. There was no agreement among Eastern, Western, and Southern Democrats upon the tariff question, or upon the currency question. At critical moments Carlisle "could never depend upon his party for harmonious action." A quorum would actually be lacking upon the day when the Speaker of the House must be chosen. In Congress the Democratic Party made an unfortunate impression of inconsistency and indiscipline. With the one exception of the historic Interstate Commerce Act, passed as a bipartisan measure, little more than petty legislation issued from Washington in these years.

Nor did the Democratic President contribute any initiative. He believed that under a Government of "divided authority" he must not seek to lead Congress, but must confine himself to the execution of the laws and routine administration. For three years he shut himself up in the White House, his influence showing itself chiefly in negative or obstructive action, when he used the veto power to block wasteful pension bills or appropriation bills. Such recommendations as Cleveland chose to convey to Congress, as for instance a letter favoring the stoppage of silver coinage (before his inauguration; February 24, 1885), and a message on the same subject in December, 1885, were generally ignored or even flouted by his own partisans at the Capitol. Through Manning, and his Assistant Secretary Charles Fairchild, who succeeded him as Secretary of the Treasury, Cleveland supported a conservative and traditionally unpopular financial policy which succeeded in offsetting the mildly inflationary effects of the silver-coinage law of 1878.

Meanwhile the industrial transformation of the American society hurried forward; the rise of monopolies brought forth inevitably, in the early 1880's, renewed and most ambitious efforts at organization of the toolless laborers. With John Hay, author of the anonymous, widely read, antilabor novel *The Breadwinners*, many Americans believed that the European class struggles between proletarians and property-owners were soon to be duplicated here.

The Noble Order of Knights of Labor, which by 1886 embraced 700,000 members (according to many reports) in an industrial union, aroused fear and trembling by the systematic manner in which it waged strikes. Following a successful attack upon the Western Union Telegraph Company, which was controlled by the well-hated Jay Gould, the Knights called a sudden strike against the Missouri Pacific Railroad in February, 1886. The fiery district leader, Master Workman Martin Irons, provided inspired leadership; and the railway men pushed their struggle with revolutionary energy, as in 1877. Hundreds of engines were "killed," transportation was paralyzed throughout several of the Southwestern States along 6,000 miles of track, and large cities were deprived of coal and other supplies, while towns at certain points were occupied by armed laborers who fought bloody battles with local police authorities. For eight weeks it was "war," the militant leader, Irons said, and war, he held, that was clearly provoked by the property-owners.[24]

The striking railway men were beaten by police force and militia driving armed trains through their lines, as well as by hunger. But the significant thing was the degree in which popular sympathy now supported their side. In the affected regions of Kansas, Texas, and Missouri, the newspapers, the farming population, even the people of large cities such as St. Louis and Kansas City, aided the workers. In the subsequent investigation ordered by Congress the testimony of many intelligent, apparently impartial rural citizens described the overt acts of the Gould railroad, the widespread discontent with its service. Many straightforward witnesses went so far as to advocate the government ownership of Mr. Gould's and other railroads as the only possible solution.[25]

The leaders of both parties warily avoided expressions on this dangerous question—or upon the eight-hour day—although Senator Logan, as was now his wont, arose on April 16, 1886, to call in an alarmist speech for a standing army of double the previous size, so as "to kill off the malcontents." That year strikes violent and bitter raged on the Third Avenue Elevated Railway in New York, among the miners of Pennsylvania, the dock workers of Chicago, and the workers at the McCormick Reaper plant. The whole movement was brought to a tragic denouement by the bombing incident at Haymarket Square in Chicago. Out of the passions roused by the trial of the seven anarchists in Chicago came a break in the ranks of labor, but also the astonishing labor rising in New York led by Henry George, who seemed to be their hoped-for leader, a celebrity giving himself to the cause of the proletariat. In the battleground of the Eastern metropolis, George proceeded apparently to the formation of a veritable working-class party, saying: "I believe, and have long believed, that through politics was the way, and the only way, by which anything real and permanent could be secured for labour." [26] It needed all the resources of Chief Croker and Boss Platt of the Republican and Democratic machines in combination to defeat the inspired campaign of the Antipoverty men in New York that season.

Amid so much lower-class unrest, Cleveland remained silent, ostrichlike; the investigation of the Southwestern strike by a congressional committee was ineffectual and meaningless, though the testimony in itself had value. The party in power was suspected of not being sincere in its inquiry, and little attention was paid to it by the country.[27] President Cleveland, in a halfhearted move, recommended the establishment of a "voluntary" board of arbitration for labor disputes, although he knew well how fruitless this would be.

Violence, to which the American people with their frontier moods were so freely given, often led in the labor conflict to tragedy and emotional exhaustion. From the press and the pulpit strong sermons upon law and order were preached; and the leading journalists, using the ideology of liberty, gave warning that a "secret government" of tyranny and boycotts, directed by Martin Irons or Terence Powderly, would never be tolerated by the respectable middle class.[28]

The capitalists of railways and factories now organized themselves secretly for defense, especially at Chicago, where the Railway Managers' Association was directed by the heads of the principal trunk lines, after 1886. Measures were also taken to strengthen the State militia. As a movement toward industrial unionism, the Knights of Labor lost favor and declined steadily in strength, following sore defeats; while the craft-union organization, the American Federation of Labor, under Samuel Gompers's leadership gained rapidly by its more opportunist tactics. Both labor groups, however, professed themselves nonpartisan; and both divided their strength between the two major parties, without developing a decisive influence over them.

The uproar over the railway strikes illuminated clearly the public temper toward these corporate monsters, against whose extortions several of the Western States had years before passed so-called Granger laws regulating railways and their associated grain elevators and warehouses. But in this same year, 1886, came the celebrated Supreme Court decision (in Wabash versus Illinois) striking down all regulation by States of interstate railroads. This decision roused a political storm, and brought matters to a head. The congressional leaders of both parties, each of which had promised in 1884 some form of interstate control over railroads, now felt that they could delay no longer. In the upper chamber Senator Shelby Cullom, Republican, who as Governor of Illinois had actively studied the railroad problem, prepared one measure, while in the lower house Representative Reagan of Texas, a Democrat, prepared another.

During the summer of 1886, the Cullom Committee of the Senate, charged with investigating complaints and preparing a report for the Senate, held hearings in various parts of the country. Its membership, including Chairman Cullom, was drawn from the most conservative sections of both parties. Arthur Gorman was one of the Democratic counselors there, determined to have a law of some kind, but without clauses that might take any real effect; Senator Orville Platt of Connecticut was another Republican member who opposed the inclusion of an antipooling clause; Warner Miller of New York was the henchman of Blaine, who had put him in the Senate; while Isham Harris of Tennessee, the former Confederate Brigadier, showed only a passing interest in any of the proceedings.

Elaborate efforts were made by those two magicians of committee conference, Allison and Aldrich, to manage things so that the proposed Interstate Commerce Commission would have no power to make rates, force proper accounting, or change "long and short haul" rate differentials. At length, after much wrangling between both chambers and bad moments when the Cullom Bill was all but strangled in the house of its friends, a measure making some creditable appearance of regulating interstate commerce, forbidding rebates, rate discrimination, and pooling, emerged from the joint committee and was passed. On the floor of the Senate, Aldrich had declared that the bill was tantamount to a "revolution"; that it would cripple both internal and external commerce. Finally, in a more candid vein, Aldrich protested at the hypocrisy of the measure; it was "a delusion and a sham . . . an empty menace to great interests, made to answer the clamor of the ignorant and the unreasoning." [29] Cullom himself said, in recollection, that the act of 1887 "was conservative legislation," but passed for a radical measure in Congress and before the people. Mr. Cleveland, who had taken no part in the controversy and shown no enthusiasm at any point, signed the historic Interstate Commerce Act "with reservations" as to its legality, and fears that "the cure might be worse than the disease."

Cleveland also showed a certain tenderness toward the Pacific railroads, which once more were being asked by Congress to return the great sums advanced them. A part of the press, reflecting agrarian sentiment, urged that the mortgages be foreclosed and the land grants revoked. Cleveland had taken no action until 1886, when he advised making terms with the railroads which permitted them lower rates of interest for their sinking fund, and an extended period of eighty years in which to retire their debt to the Government. But Congress paid no attention, as usual, to the President's recommendations. The sensational exposures appearing in the New York *World* in January, 1887, soon led to the appointment of the Pacific Railway Commission by Congress to hold inquiries into the affairs and accounts of Huntington, Stanford, and Gould. These hearings, with their striking testimony as to large-scale lobbying in the national and State legislatures, and the expenditure of millions of dollars of railroad funds (without accounting) in purchasing legislative "influence," made, when published, a most instructive historical document.

When the Pacific Railway Commission reported its recommendations for a lenient settlement for the sum of approximately $100,-000,000 still owing to the Government, the minority member, Pattison of Pennsylvania, in a dissenting report proposed prosecution and jail sentences as the only fitting treatment for the railroad-owners. Yet Cleveland once more had the courage to take the side of the unpopular conservatives, and advocated the milder course of the majority's proposal.[30] Mr. Cleveland's moderation toward the Railway Barons seemed highly incongruous.

On fundamental questions of the relation of private property or industry to Government, Mr. Cleveland, as time went on, revealed more and more a spirit that was individualistic and "liberal" only in the most narrowly "bourgeois" sense. Cleveland worthily vetoed the Invalid Pension Act, by which Logan schemed to spread some $50,000,000 more a year even to the ninety-day recruits of the Grand Army. But the philosophy of this thrifty steward or "trustee of the people" is best illustrated in one of his petty executive actions, the veto of the Texas Seed Bill early in 1887.

In response to the pleas of many sufferers from drought in urgent need of seed grain, Congress had passed that season a bill affording the meager appropriation of $10,000 for such relief. At once the watchful Executive (who had permitted certain very dubious public-works or "pork" bills to pass unmolested) pounced upon the relief measure and with a strongly worded protest vetoed it (February 16, 1887). Nothing in the Constitution, he argued, warranted such an appropriation, adding smugly enough:

I do not believe that the power and duty of the General Government ought to be extended to the relief of individual suffering which is in no manner properly related to the public service or benefit. A prevalent tend-ency to disregard the limited mission of this [government] power and duty should, I think, be steadfastly resisted, to the end that the lesson should constantly be enforced that *though the people support the Government the Government should not support the people.*

Then other phrases, which have been echoed again and again on behalf of the same philosophy, reminded us that

Federal aid in such cases encourages the expectation of paternal care on the part of the Government and weakens the sturdiness of our national character. . . . The friendliness and charity of our countrymen can al-ways be relied upon to relieve their fellow-citizens in misfortune.*

Cleveland's "liberalism" toward great railroads might win approval in editorials of the *Nation,* but it provided little consolation for liberty-loving farmers at the frontiers of Texas, Kansas, and Ne-braska, who that year suffered severely from droughts. To these he offered only that mockery of the principle of equality which Anatole France epitomized in his reflection that the poor and the rich alike had the "right" to sleep under the bridges of Paris. It was a con-sistent coincidence that the vetoes or recommendations of Mr. Cleve-land usually brought relief to a Jay Gould and gloom to the masses of the people. Woodrow Wilson in 1913, when he entered the White House as a progressive Democrat, believed sincerely that he was the first Democrat to reach this place since James Buchanan. "This

* It was the same thrifty Cleveland who, as Mayor of Buffalo, had vetoed a tiny appropriation for the city firemen's Fourth of July picnic, donating a small private contribution of his own and asking others to do likewise. Senator Carter Glass, in a speech in 1936, cited Cleveland's veto of the Texas Seed Bill—as repre-senting the ideology of the old "Cleveland Democracy"—against that of President Franklin D. Roosevelt.

country has never had a Democratic administration since the Civil War," he exclaimed to a group of Senators visiting him. "You may think Cleveland's administration was Democratic. It was not. Cleveland was a conservative Republican." [81]

III

The thrifty liberalism of Mr. Cleveland and his policy of laissez faire, laissez passer, appealed to the most conservative businessmen. Laissez faire, at certain phases, appeared to be a conception of strong conservatives who sought the minimum of political control. Even so learned a man as William Graham Sumner argued that "the social order is fixed by laws of nature precisely analogous to those of the physical order." Should we mar their operation? But "business," that is, large-scale business, in its rapidly growing phase of the 1880's "wanted chiefly non-interference, which it was able to obtain either from governmental inertia or when necessary by the process of influence, intimidation or of corruption." [82]

Progress was made in improving the civil service and introducing "business principles" into at least a part of our bureaucracy; but such measures, while pleasing to the scrupulous middle classes, did not relieve deep-rooted distress; nor did the President's introduction of reforms, so far as they went, please the rank-and-file politicians of Cleveland's own party. "Merely respectable influences," as Chester Arthur had said, were never enough to "bring out the vote"; to win elections a mood of pleasurable anticipation and enthusiasm must be spread among the "men in politics." Here Cleveland had failed, and his partisans in Congress privately spoke much ill of him. In England parliamentary leadership or oratorical eloquence was of consequence, as Tilden pointed out at this time. But in America "the government must be carried on by popular leaders, and a capacity for party leadership is essential." [83]

Tilden died in 1886; Manning retired in broken health, soon to follow him. Certain of the associates of these old leaders now formed an Inner Circle around the President and the cabinet members: Whitney, Vilas, Fairchild, and Daniel Lamont (Cleveland's private secretary) and from outside the Administration, the wealthy Don M. Dickinson of Michigan, and Francis L. Stetson, the corporation lawyer who served J. P. Morgan for many years. These were the most trusted advisers. Whitney, who by his wealth dominated Washington society, was the salient personality. "He could accomplish more in one day," Cleveland said of him, "than any other man I ever saw could do in ten." He had an astonishing capacity to concentrate on a given task when necessary, throwing himself into the work with "every power of his mind . . . [sacrificing] social life, personal business—all." [34]

Whitney, while building a modern, steel-clad navy in time for an approaching war, managed party patronage with a quick and light hand. His connections with Tammany, through his mysterious business partner, Thomas Fortune Ryan, were now close. Although prodigious stock-market adventures in whisky, tobacco, and tractions also absorbed Whitney's attention, he extended his political influence and became a commanding figure of the party.

A strong rival for the leadership of the Eastern Democrats had recently appeared in the shape of David B. Hill, who as Lieutenant Governor succeeded Cleveland at Albany in 1885. Hill, the "Sage of Wolfert's Roost," resourceful lawyer, lively stump orator, and wily negotiator, followed in his career the familiar pattern of New York Machiavellianism. From the band of Tweed he had shifted quickly to the position of lieutenant in the Tilden Organization, serving later as one of the architects of Cleveland's victory. But unlike Cleveland, he preached openly "party regularity, the management of men, and reliance upon a personal organisation . . . composed of men moved like himself by self-interest, who, in conventions and on election days, could produce majorities." [35]

"*I am a Democrat,*" Hill would say meaningfully. Among the rank-and-file political "workers" who heartily disliked Mr. Cleveland, Hill grew in favor by promising always the prompt distribution of the spoils of victory, in order to "conserve the virility of the party." Where Cleveland by his restrained use of patronage weakened his party lieutenants in the New York field, Hill allied himself again with Tammany, strengthened his own faction by strident, demagogic appeals to the Irish, the saloon following, and illiterate naturalized citizens. But after elections he would devote himself soberly, in the manner of the great modern State bosses, to administering special privilege to the large monopolistic corporations of his State.[36]

The recent re-election of Hill as Governor, with the moneyed support of 35,000 saloonkeepers, and funds diverted from contracts for public works—but entirely without the President's aid or encouragement—was a heavy blow to the reformist faction in the party and threatened to eliminate Cleveland eventually from his official leadership. The great State of New York was once more in the hands of spoilsmen of the traditional type.

Cleveland's Civil Service Commission, meanwhile, showed little energy and a wholesome fear of the politicians. Two of its members were political hacks, and one of these brought his office into contempt by making campaign speeches in Maryland for Gorman's Organization.[37]

The members of the new Interstate Commerce Commission were of better caliber; but if their appointment to office was expected to end the discontent of the public with railroad service, and the especially high rates in the farming regions, there was soon great disillusionment. The Interstate Commerce Act, after an interval of excited competition and rate-cutting by the competing trunk lines, came to be ignored, and rebates, discrimination, secret rates, and pooling of traffic facilities for various sections were resumed more or less openly. When it was seen that the Interstate Commerce Commission itself had no power of action, and that the Federal courts were loath to support it, the railroads formed combinations even closer than before. Soon the new act came to be seen as a safeguard rather than a menace to great railroad properties. As a leading lawyer of Boston, Richard Olney, later explained to C. E. Perkins, the railroad-owner, the existing commission "satisfies the popular clamor for a government supervision of railroads, at the same time that that supervision is almost entirely nominal." It thus became "a sort of barrier between the railroad corporations and the people and a sort of protection against hasty and crude legislation hostile to railroad interests." [38]

The election returns of 1886 indicated revived morale in the Opposition; the Democratic majority in the lower house at Wash-

ington was visibly reduced, while the Senate became more strongly
Republican. Middle-class reform was making slow progress. It was
time that Cleveland, quitting his routine administrative labors, attempted some bold stroke to capture the lagging interest of the
people; for one must have votes to encompass re-election. As Talleyrand remarked: "To have said and done nothing is a tremendous
power; but it should not be abused."

In his first approaches to national financial questions, Cleveland
had noticed the increasing surplus in the government Treasury. Secretary Manning at first tried by various means to force out the even
more rapidly increasing hoard of silver, under the silver-coinage act
of 1878, although, like Republican Secretaries before him, he used
executive discretion to avoid making Treasury payments in that coin,
and held the dollar to its parity with gold. In the meantime the
rigid budget and taxation system accumulated a huge surplus—as
high as $150,000,000—in gold, owing to heavy receipts from the
1883 protective tariff. This surplus was accumulated at a time of
contraction or "scarcity" of money, which was heightened by the
action of national bankers in redeeming their circulating banknotes.

By 1887 the redeemable public debt was retired, and the Administration had no way of using its surplus except in buying back—that
is, anticipating the retirement of—its own unmatured bonds at a high
premium. At the discretion of the President and the new Secretary
of the Treasury, Fairchild, part of the surplus was then used to
purchase noncallable 4 per cent bonds at the tremendous premium
of 128 to 129 in the open market. Thus the great sums "which by
means of the tariff and internal revenue taxes had been collected
from the consuming population, and above all from the . . . poor
wage earners and farmers, were used to pour into the pockets of the
investing classes, especially in the East, a heavy unearned increment." [39] At times, one-third of the country's circulating money was
locked up in the Treasury, though Fairchild managed to "farm out"
part of this occasionally to the large bankers. Between 1888 and 1890
some $45,000,000 was actually paid out in the high premiums now
demanded by investors in government bonds. This extravagant
method of extinguishing the debt was not only profoundly unjust,
it was shaking the economic structure. [40] To President Cleveland's

Administration it was also a source of great embarrassment, as agitation spread against the "bloated bondholders" and against the subservience of the Administration to the "Shylocks" of Wall Street and Lombard Street.

Cleveland's very conservatism led him to considering ways of lowering the Government's ponderous surplus, a temptation in itself to politicians, by reducing taxation. Blaine, with his disposition toward government largesse, now urged that the surplus money should be spent on public works, harbor improvements, fortifications, and "pork" bills, or simply be given away to the different State governments. But to Cleveland, with his honest, saving, middle-class spirit, the needless surplus accumulating from high customs duties seemed more and more abhorrent. Thus he was led logically to explore the possibilities of lowering the tariff rates on imports.

The Democratic Representative William Morrison of Illinois had framed a tariff-reduction bill in 1886, and had won the moderate support of Cleveland; but despite the presence of a Democratic majority in the House, the bill actually failed of introduction, the Protectionist Democrats under Randall joining with Republicans to block it. With justice the Republicans had charged the Democratic Party with inconsistency and insincerity. But by the summer of 1887 the problem of the surplus "clogging" the Treasury was more pressing than ever, and made necessary the reform of a cumbersome revenue system which taxed imported necessities for the masses of the people while leaving luxuries virtually untaxed.

The President in 1887 was plainly in search of a Live Issue, but the tariff was always a nettlesome question, and he knew nothing about it. Carl Schurz relates that shortly after his election, in December, 1884, the future President had asked him

with characteristic directness . . . what big questions he ought to take up when he got into the White House. I told him I thought he ought to take up the tariff. I shall never forget what then happened. The man bent forward and buried his face in his hands on the table before him. After two or three minutes he straightened up and, with the same directness, said to me: "I am ashamed to say it, but the truth is I know nothing about the tariff. . . . Will you tell me how to go about it to learn?[41]

For three years Cleveland had hesitated; now in the autumn of 1887 he stayed up late at night, studying and learning. Although the need of a Live Issue was great, the canvassing experts of the party advised him to "go slow." Whitney, one of his most intimate counselors, strongly urged him that "it was not the right time to push it." [42] But Cleveland, who often followed his own counsel, said with an honesty that reflected the best side of his nature: "What is the use of being elected or reëlected if you don't stand for something?" For indeed there was now no other course, save the "suicidal" one—according to traditional political technique—of seizing a Live Issue by the horns.

CHAPTER ELEVEN

"FRYING THE FAT": THE PLANNED ALTERNATION OF THE PARTIES

MR. CLEVELAND'S annual message to Congress on December 6, 1887, upon the "state of the country" was entirely devoted to the tariff question, this in itself a bold departure from precedent. It was the sensation of many days and seasons, and as a public paper was reckoned the most inspiring since Lincoln's time.

Presidents and political leaders do not as a rule commit themselves irrevocably upon fundamental economic questions. But Cleveland had something of the brave tyro in him. The forthright and combative spirit in which he called for a reduction of unsound taxation upon imports showed all the stubborn "character" in him when he was aroused and had blood in his eye. Despite its labored prose locutions and split infinitives, there was a generous indignation in this paper that touched the masses of the people, and especially the liberal middle class. Cleveland for a moment raised the tone of our party politics and cleared the air; he made a "historical transformation" of the inchoate Democratic Party, as many supposed at the time, and brought it at last to "stand for something." [1]

". . . Our present tariff laws, the vicious, inequitable and illogical source of unnecessary taxation, ought to be at once revised and amended," he argued. The increased cost of living fixed by selfish industry in the tariff system was "a burden upon those with moderate means and the poor, the employed and unemployed, the sick and well, and the young and old . . . a tax which with relentless grasp is fastened upon the clothing of every man, woman, and child in the land." Moreover, competition, he continued, alluding to crying evils of the time, under the sheltering tariff wall was "too often strangled by combinations . . . frequently called trusts, which have for their object the regulation of the supply and price of commodities."

But for all its humanitarian or liberal accents, this tariff message, as we measure it, was also dictated by a coldly prudent financial logic. It was occupied from beginning to end with the alarming congestion of the Federal Treasury in recent years. Estimates showed that within six months, by June 30, 1888, the total accumulated surplus in the Treasury would rise to $140,000,000; at that time approximately one-third of the nation's circulating capital would be locked up in the vaults of the Government, removed from trade, with money for crops scarce and interest rates high. To "farm out" such sums to the banks appeared risky and politically unpopular. Meanwhile the surplus, from the point of view of Cleveland's old-fashioned, middle-class principles, provided sore temptations to politicians, against which he strove incessantly.

The alarm of the financial community over the swollen surplus in the Treasury, the Treasury Octopus, as it was called, Cleveland had shared since 1885. Like Samuel Tilden, he wished to depart from a "grasping centralization" of the Government, which accumulated vast sums idly in its Treasury for the benefit of special interests, to allow more uninterrupted play, more "liberty," for the economic life of society, even a lower cost of living, an approach eventually to a certain measure of freer trade. For Cleveland saw that for every surplus dollar accumulating in the Government Treasury at least as much was garnered by the protected industrial Trusts, whose prices were held up to the level of the tariff schedules. For every dollar in import duties paid, far more was taxed from the men in the factories or on the farms by the added price of domestic goods they must purchase.

In the divided counsels of the capitalists at this time, the extremists clamored for an ever higher Chinese wall of Protection, while the conservatives, usually the bankers, the finance capitalists, and the merchants, in their counsels held that a moderate lowering of government revenues from import duties (which was all that the President advocated) would be a prudent measure.

Moreover, Cleveland's old-fashioned petty-bourgeois nature revealed itself unconsciously in phrases that draw a kind of moral distinction between "the realization of immense profits," insured to the Trusts by Protection, and the legitimate or "moderately profitable returns" to be won in a freer market through a lower tariff scale. Thus a true conservatism, inherent in the old Liberal Capitalism, underlay Cleveland's famous message, which to the more orthodox

Republican Senators seemed like so much low "demagogy." In this spirit he gave prophetic warning in one of his concluding passages:

Opportunity for safe, careful, and deliberate reform is now offered; and none of us should be unmindful of a time when an abused and irritated people, heedless of those who have resisted timely and reasonable relief, may insist upon a radical and sweeping rectification of their wrongs.

The "radical and sweeping rectification of . . . wrongs" was the one eventuality which Cleveland's nature feared, and which he assumed the ruling caliphs, and the middle class as well, would seek to avoid.

While liberals and reformers applauded the President's outspoken appeal for tariff revision, the Inner Circle of Democratic Party managers was instantly cast down with anxiety and gloom. It would be difficult to educate the great public to lower tariff views, as they saw; the rich manufacturing capitalists would unite in a solid bloc, throwing their full financial power against the Democracy this year. For Grover Cleveland's manifesto, it must be noted, was little more than the opening gun in a wordy electoral contest. No Democratic tariff bill could possibly pass in the Republican Senate. But the Democrats were to be rallied to the reform standard, and in the debate over such a measure the whole issue would be laid squarely before the electorate.

To Blaine, the old Republican fire horse, the Democratic challenge was like the sudden ringing of an alarm bell. For years, whether in active service or in semiretirement, during which he never lost touch with the political market place, Blaine had persistently tried to maneuver party contests onto the ground of the tariff issue. He too had wished, in spite of habitual evasions by both parties, to make the struggle one over principles, principles by which he might enlist the strongest capitalists decisively upon the side of his own party. There must be no further weak Republican talk of moderate "readjustment" of the protective system by its "friends." Blaine now rose to the splendid opportunity offered to him.

He had been, during the autumn of 1887, the guest of the Steel Baron Andrew Carnegie at the latter's huge feudal castle in Scotland, a castle which nowadays often figured in public debates over the profits of tariff-protected industries. It was from Paris, however, on December 7, that Blaine directed his prompt counterblast. This had the form of an interview, an aggressive partisan attack upon Cleveland's message; it was published, via the cable, in the faithful New York *Tribune* and reprinted throughout the country.

Blaine adroitly showed himself "especially interested in the comments of the English papers" on the President's message. They inferred that it was a "free trade manifesto." As a consequence of such recommendations they anticipated already an enlarged export market for their goods. Thus, Blaine argued, the Democratic President by his doctrines favored British manufacturers and discriminated against American capitalists and laborers alike. There would follow, after the cutting of the tariff, a lamentable shrinkage of the home market and domestic trade between thirty-eight States and eight Territories; our labor would compete with cheap European labor; our farmers in turn would suffer from their loss. Blaine rang all the changes upon the old themes, also invariably distorting his opponent's statements. Cleveland, he concluded, had done well to precipitate "a full and fair contest on the question of protection." The Democratic Party in power was a "standing menace," and "that menace should be removed." [2]

To the Republican camp followers, Blaine's "Paris Letter" attested his continuing leadership of the party and, as John Hay wrote him, was "the clear blast of the trumpet, declaring battle and bringing the fighting men into well-ordered ranks." Hay concluded: "You have given us our platform for next year." [3] In this season of danger the extreme advocates of Protection would now rally to form a compact "trade-union," where they had previously differed or competed with each other on divers aspects of the tariff issue. Senator Justin Morrill, author of the Civil War tariff bill, wrote complacently at this time of Cleveland's message: "It will insure election of a Republican president." [4]

II

From the winter of 1888 to the last hours before election day in November, the great tariff debate raged, in and out of Congress. The diverse interest groups of the country aligned themselves uneasily, one might say unpredictably. Intelligent members of the middle class and the professions generally championed a step toward Free Trade; importing and some manufacturing capitalists in the East, such as Abram Hewitt, who favored free or cheap raw materials for their finishing mills, supported the Democratic argument. The principal bank presidents of New York "divided almost evenly" upon the tariff question.[5] Certain elements among the farmers favoring lower costs of finished products desired a reduced tariff; but other farmers, especially those in Ohio who raised sheep, were led to fear the competition of "free wool" from abroad. In the ranks of labor, now organized into two rival federations, indifference ruled as to the arguments for lower tariffs. The question of whence government taxes must be raised does not arouse decided or enthusiastic convictions among laborers, as does the question of the eight-hour day or that of the right to collective bargaining, matters upon which Mr. Cleveland and his friends were usually silent. Though Henry George, Labor candidate for the New York Mayoralty in 1886, now championed Free Trade, the Knights of Labor in many sections officially espoused Protection. The laborer was generally given to understand that a lowered tariff would be made the pretext for lowered wages, which would affect him immediately.

There was for the first time since 1860 a dividing issue between the two great political corporations. But the issue of the tariff seemed to move at a tangent from the questions raised by farmers and laborers nowadays: the need for improved credits, or for better wages and better working-conditions. In any case, the maneuvers in Congress that year, the action of the Democratic Party leaders in presenting their tariff measures, demonstrated glaringly the difference between theory and practice.

Mr. Cleveland had spoken fair words; and Representative Roger Mills of Texas, the new Chairman of the Ways and Means Committee, to whom was entrusted the framing of a reform bill, spoke even fairer words in his speeches. But that which followed in Congress was sadly undeceiving.

The Mills Bill, introduced in the House in 1888, observed the principle of very mild average reductions in duties upon finished goods, of about 7 per cent ad valorem, while seeking free or cheap raw materials such as wool, lumber, and flax. It was soon seen, however, that the project was far from idealistic. Thanks to the presence of a rich Democratic Party patron upon the Ways and Means Committee—Representative W. L. Scott, the Pennsylvania coal operator—the rates upon iron and iron ore were little changed, while coal was left protected. Democratic sugar-producers were also tenderly regarded, while Republican wool and steel were chastised. Soon it was seen that the projected reductions would not lower the government revenues enough to exorcise the troublesome Treasury Octopus. The bill, which had Administration support, was full of sectional favoritism, and the caustic Thomas Reed was led to remark that it plainly wanted in all Democratic idealism. "This bill, far from being philosophical, is political from one end to the other." [6]

The great debate of the summer of 1888 in the lower house was, of course, a setting for party stump speeches, in which the orators—Mills and Carlisle for the Democrats, and Reed and McKinley for the Republicans—made partisan appeals to the voters. Messrs. Mills and Carlisle were more morally earnest and learned, but Mr. McKinley was often on the verge of tears at the plight of poor Ohio workers under Free Trade, while Mr. Reed, as usual, employed his irreverent wit and sarcasm to good advantage. Both parties knew full well that talk was the sole end of the proceedings.

Seven months after Mr. Cleveland's historic message, July 21, 1888, the Democratic tariff measure known as the Mills Bill was passed by the House and sent to the Senate. Here the Republican Senators behind the breastworks of their committees had quietly been waiting for the bill ever since May. Their plans had been carefully matured, with the aid and advice of the textile and iron lobbies, led by J. L. Hayes and James Swank respectively. Swank, secretary of the Iron and Steel Association, after having formerly worked to detach Southern industrial interests by protective bait, with a certain cynicism had urged the venerable Justin Morrill to appeal to labor during this season of violent strikes:

> As the labor element is now fermenting, it would be most judicious to call attention to the fact that the Republican party has been the faithful friend of the poor man. The Homestead bill and the Morrill Tariff bill have done more for him than all previous economic legislation combined. [7]

The iron and textile men informed the Republican Senators that they must at all costs block action by Congress upon the Mills Bill. True, the Democrats in Congress were ready to make astonishing concessions. But, Swank argues, no concessions of any kind must be accepted; the Finance Committee of the Senate (Aldrich, Allison, Morrill, Sherman) must simply devise its own bill, according to its own ideas, continuing high import duties and reducing internal-revenue taxes upon whisky and tobacco instead.

To amend the Mills Bill in the Senate (in any form) would be a victory for the Democrats, who would make the most of it in the Presidential campaign. No matter how nearly perfect the Senate might make the Mills Bill it would still be the Mills Bill.[8]

The Republicans were virtually ordered never to concede that import duties might be safely reduced in order to reduce the surplus.

In the Senate Aldrich worked coolly to devise a bill which the Democrats might never compromise on in view of Cleveland's stand. With loud and long wrangling, many set speeches, and no little laughter, each house of Congress defeated the other's revenue bill. The deadlock prolonged itself, and at length faded out, as before a superimposed film, into the larger scene of the national election campaign.

III

The raising of the tariff issue had caused at once the most intense emotion among the protected capitalists of the high-tariff leagues. The Association of Woolen Manufacturers, the Iron and Steel Association, the Protective Tariff League, the Industrial League (of Pennsylvania), whose activities extended into nearly all the States, proceeded at once to issue torrents of pamphlets and Protectionist speeches against Cleveland's "Free Trade rot." Many of the manufacturers who had been reluctant in support of Blaine in 1884, and thereby contributed to the Republican defeat, now repented of their error and formed themselves into a determined bloc, assembling all the resources of the new Match Kings, the Steel Barons, and the textile men, to bring about a reversal of party control.

These same men now doubted no longer to which party they must turn. The Republican platform was marked out in advance by the industrial lobbies. As James Swank declared in an officially published ultimatum of the American Iron and Steel Association, the party must stand this year "upon an out-and-out platform *of protection for the sake of protection.*" [9] This thesis, with its opportunity to appeal for the "American system" and to cajole or intimidate labor, was readily accepted by the party managers, who had formerly been at a loss for Live Issues.

Upon ideology there was ready agreement between the capitalists and the professional party officers. But who would be the standard-bearer? Whereas the Democrats, in spite of their secret disagreements, would surely renominate Cleveland without delay, on the other side a series of booms for Native Sons wrought confusion during the springtime nominating season.

Blaine, during the whole decade after 1880, whether he dwelt in Maine or in Scotland, figured easily as the party's national leader. Now in a letter from Florence, where, for the sake of his health, he remained "out of politics," he wrote on January 25, 1888, to Chairman B. F. Jones of the Republican National Committee that his retirement from the contest for the presidential nomination was final on grounds "entirely personal to myself." [10] Actually, as Blaine made clear to one of his confidants, he desired to run, but only if there were a unanimous demand that he be "drafted." Having once been defeated, he could not again be a claimant appealing to the party to *try* him. Actually, Blaine and his agents, by all accounts of what followed, strove by indirection to bring about either the "stampeding" of the party convention of 1888 and the "drafting" of Blaine, or, this failing, the choice of a Dark Horse who would be the pawn of the old leader.

Meanwhile, the booming of divers Native Sons by various State Organizations this year favored both these designs. The numerous aspirants—General Russell Alger, the politician-industrialist of Michigan, Chauncey Depew of New York, William Allison of Iowa, John Sherman of Ohio, Judge Walter Gresham and Governor Benjamin Harrison of Indiana—all advanced their causes with the apparent support of their regional bosses and wings of the party. But the extraordinary thing about the convention that opened in June was the manner in which it "was dominated by a man three thousand miles away and apparently indifferent to the result." [11]

It is worth noting that before leaving New York Blaine's host that winter, Andrew Carnegie, had arranged with B. F. Jones and Stephen Elkins a cipher cable code permitting private communication concerning the names of all the important Republican candidates. With or without Blaine's knowledge, Carnegie was working for him. [12]

IV

Of the old-time Republican leaders and bosses who had been mighty in war and Reconstruction, Ulysses Grant, Roscoe Conkling, John Logan, Garfield, and Arthur had all died in recent years— Morton and Zach Chandler earlier. Only Blaine and Uncle John Sherman, a perpetual candidate, still possessed the authority of veterans in the party councils. New leaders pursuing new tactics had arisen to fill the ranks of the old Inner Circle: Thomas Platt, the "Easy Boss" of New York State, Matthew Quay, who had succeeded to the Camerons of Pennsylvania, Foraker of Ohio, Clarkson of Iowa, Alger of Michigan. Moreover, the sweep of civil-service reform during the 1880's, following Garfield's assassination and the popular outcry against spoilsmen, had deeply changed the nature and form of party Organization. Between 1887 and 1888 the loss of Federal patronage, the diminution of assessments as large numbers of officials were classified under the merit system, and declining revenues from sales of offices had all driven the Republican Organization to discover new sources of revenue. Momentous transformations, far more important than the tariff struggle, were taking place under the surface. These changes, which flowed from the very reform of the party institution itself, resulted in the end in the marked strengthening of the reorganized machines, which came to be wholly, rather than partially, devoted to the service of the large corporations in their regions that required political privileges. The latter-day bosses, representing an advanced professionalism, a new, specialized technique of party management, now converged upon the Chicago convention in June, 1888. It is worth pausing to mark the changes that have come over them.

The modern party manager depends less than ever before on

mere rhetoric and exhibitionism, as the new leaders, Tom Platt and Matt Quay, show us at the first glance. The men of long hair and breast-beating orations upon universal rights and the Bloody Shirt have given way to trim, quiet-spoken, indefatigable executives who run their centralized political bureaus in the manner of large business corporations. The irresponsible Robin Hood spirit of a William Tweed has also subsided. In short, the "stump politician" has been replaced by the "desk politician."

In the career of Quay of Pennsylvania the very evolution of the old-fashioned war-party leader could be marked in clear phases. He was born in 1833, of mixed Indian ancestry; his troubling physiognomy, with its aquiline nose, sharp chin, and "almondlike" eyes (one of which drooped as the result of a wound received in the late war), suggested all the superior cunning of his type. We have it upon Tom Platt's authority that Quay was, technically, "the ablest politician this country ever produced." After war service, he had educated himself for the Pennsylvania bar, directed a rural newspaper in York County, raised himself as a member of the State legislature step by step to strategic office in the State government and in the Cameron Organization, until as Secretary of the Commonwealth and Recorder of Philadelphia he held the key posts controlling the purse strings of the State. By 1879 he had become chairman of the Republican State Committee, which is to say first lieutenant in the Cameron spoils machine.

Though Quay's personality suggested a curious learning and philosophy—to young neophytes from Harvard—he was given to a scandalous private life, according to common report, in which rum, women, cards, and horses figured largely. His philosophy in dealing with his followers was based, in fact, upon the lowest possible view of human nature. It was Quay who coined the phrase "shaking the plum tree," which referred to the distribution of bureaucratic fruits following an electoral victory. One of his disciples, W. H. Kemble, probably invented the famous Pennsylvania aphorism "Addition, division—silence!" Quay controlled men by his refined understanding of their private vices; those who rebelled he often menaced with scandal, whose blight upon his own fame he himself never seemed to fear.

The early, crude devices of Quay, whereby the sinews of war were raised for the Harrisburg Ring, included the control of State deposits in various banks whose officers acted as his confederates. These paid the Commonwealth Secretary 2 per cent for funds, and charged their borrowers usually 8 per cent, dividing the proceeds with the ring. On one occasion, owing to speculative losses by which $400,000 of State treasury funds, "borrowed" on unsecured notes from complaisant banks, disappeared forever, a great public scandal brought Quay and his friends to the very gate of the penitentiary. They were saved, however, by the personal means of Don Cameron. Quay retired into obscurity for a few years; but soon the irrepressible man emerged, sought "vindication" in a magnificent campaign (1885), and placed himself once more in charge of the State treasury. Two years afterward, an obedient legislature raised him to the United States Senate, acknowledging his unchallenged mastery of the State Organization.

In this later metamorphosis, Quay's methods were vastly improved. The clients of his close-knit machine were railroads, notably the Pennsylvania, men of the Iron and Steel Association, and all public-utility corporations that were in the market for charters or franchises touching waterworks, gasworks, or streetcar lines. All legislative measures providing profits for such groups Quay called "revenue-producers," since a portion was always faithfully returned to the party chest.

To obtain the regular and punctual passage of such franchise bills, Quay exercised a command over the legislature that was uncanny. In his office at Harrisburg there reposed a voluminous card-index system, holding data on the private life and business connections of each member of the legislature. The dossiers of "Quay's coffins" contained the fruit of a lifetime of political experience. A hapless Representative who might be caught stealing from a brothel at dawn would be promptly dragooned into voting for a water-power franchise or a new gasworks by Senator Quay, the sad-eyed, cynical humorist.[13]

In olden days the Pennsylvania Railroad must needs buy a majority of the Pennsylvania Legislature, an uncertain, often unpleasant business. Now it transacted all its political business through the office of the specialist Mr. Quay, whose word, it was found, could be trusted. The measures desired by corporations were passed, it was said, in a manner that seemed always innocent and accidental—and in almost no way traceable to Mr. Quay.

In the electoral canvas Quay was expert in "catering to the masses," as he phrased it. "He exhibited consummate skill in calculating political quantities." [14] He would know to the last fraction how many voters he had with him and where he could get those he needed. He could shift with each change of the situation, setting up a new field organization for each contest. But always he labored in the interests of the railroad and manufacturing corporations, whose profits it was now his mission to protect. Thus Quay himself earned large rewards, though these alone did not satisfy his instincts, which were dominated by an overwhelming passion for gambling in political forces, markets, and human nature with greater and greater daring. Unlike the cold-hearted accumulators of money who paid him well, this masterful tactician, who directed affairs of a tremendous scope, strictly observed a code of honor with his associates; Quay was generous with his money, and died poor. [15]

In the neighboring commonwealth of New York the order of things was also deeply changed since the days of "Turkey Gobbler" Conkling. Here too a notable sociological progress had been registered. No longer did a Jay Gould feel that he must, as he said, "make the Legislature with my own money." Nor need it be said any longer—in the terms which Elihu Root, Mr. Havemeyer's lawyer, used to describe the old Black Horse Cavalry—that

> Good men, good citizens, honest law-abiding men, justified themselves in the directorates of . . . railroads and other public service corporations in spending the money of the corporations to elect senators and assemblymen who would protect them against strike bills. [16]

Nowadays these good men and citizens needed only to go to the Amen Corner of the Fifth Avenue Hotel in New York, where the Easy Boss, actually a student, a specialist in corporate problems, Platt, conducted his "Sunday school." Here, as Chauncey Depew, the president of the New York Central Railroad, related, "were made governors, state senators, supreme court judges, judges of the

Court of Appeals, and members of Congress. . . . State conventions would meet at Rochester, Syracuse, or Saratoga, but the eight hundred members would wait before acting to hear what had been decided upon in the Amen Corner." [17] *

By 1888 the affable, "mousy" Platt possessed a rich experience extending over a quarter of a century of Organization politics. Reviving his fortunes vigorously after his disasters in 1881, he had gradually eliminated rival claimants and won for himself Conkling's place in command of a hierarchy of lieutenants, Mayors of Republican upstate towns, important city and district bosses, officeholders, and a whole army of county chairmen. Platt knew well how to control conventions and legislative assemblies. But above all Platt knew that "party funds were available to those regarded as 'safe' by the big business interests." He "had held in turn practically every position in the committee hierarchy of his own party." [18] And for some twenty years longer he was to hold command over the New York Republican machine, not merely through his political acumen, but through his knowledge of men's weaknesses and ambitions. The satellites who revolved regularly around him—Black, Odell, Woodruff, Levi Morton, Lou Payn, T. W. Barnes—were the future Governors, Lieutenant Governors, Vice-Presidents, Congressmen, cabinet members, and Ambassadors. But Platt held them in leash—though without the arrogance of a Conkling. He was the supreme party leader, as Elihu Root called him, "elected by no one, accountable to no one, bound by no oath of office, removable by no one."

The electoral technique under Platt had grown more elaborate. Nowadays every inch of the State's ground was gone over, every hour of work planned, while the citizens slept. Five hundred speakers, fifteen hundred meetings, orations and pamphlets in twenty foreign languages, were not unusual for a gubernatorial contest. Thus the New York Legislature was manned with local statesmen who owed their elevation to Platt, and whose campaign expenses were defrayed generously by Platt. And in turn Platt's control of

* The Amen Corner, as Depew relates, was so named because of the manner in which the party lieutenants from all parts of the State attending Mr. Platt's conferences on Sundays exclaimed without dissent "Amen!" whenever the leader announced his conclusions as to nominations, policies, platform. *Cf.* Gosnell, *Boss Platt,* pp. 57-58, footnote.

the legislature was complete: the Speaker of the Assembly, the floor leader, the chairmen of committees, all labored faithfully to "put bills to sleep," to choke off others, or to advance those which were approved by industrial corporations or great insurance companies and banks subject to State laws.[19] (The cost of so much "subsoil" work after 1881 was presumably borne chiefly by the rich banker Levi Morton, whose ambitions Platt thoroughly understood.)

The new natural monopolies of gaslighting and street railways rising everywhere, the railroads, insurance companies, and banks, also tended to remove their lobbying agencies from Albany and conveniently transact all their affairs through the political clearinghouse at the Amen Corner of the Fifth Avenue Hotel. Platt moreover had improved his own situation, had become president of the United States Express Company, a bank director, a director of the Erie Railroad, an owner as well of a casualty company nourished by political privilege. He had many friends among the mighty men of Wall Street, where his own business office was situated. When Platt went forth among his neighbors, hat in hand, asking for contributions from "those well able to pay," he was generally well received. He was trusted; money given to him was not stolen or wasted, but a larger portion of it than ever before worked to win results.

In these days faithful and efficient services such as were given under Platt's and Quay's regimes in the two rich, neighboring commonwealths grew costlier. The constant increase of political professionalism made electoral campaigns more than ever expensive; the needs of professional politicians, like those of other parasites upon the body politic, increased up to the highest levels of the resources they could command. But the flow of donations most fortunately— at a time when levies of assessments upon officeholders diminished— grew ever larger.*

* It is not to be assumed that the regional bosses abandoned at once the collection of assessments from Federal and State officers. Under the Quay machine during the 1880's and 1890's the salaries of Congressmen and their secretaries, mint and customhouse employees, those in the Navy Yard and Federal courts, and above all the men of 8,122 post offices in Pennsylvania, represented a grand total of $7,609,911 per annum. (Ostrogorski, *Democracy and the Organization of Political Parties*, Vol. II, pp. 398-400.) Assessments in Pennsylvania would yield, then, upwards of $150,000 each year, though it was increasingly difficult under civil-service statutes to collect all of this. Most of the lower-rank officials in this body were under clear

Throughout the Union, except for differences in degree and weight, the same advancing centralization of power through alliance of the State machines with big business was to be seen. The contemporaries of Quay and Platt were now as competent in knowledge of corporate finance as in the management of county bosses and district captains. In States of smaller population, such as Iowa and Michigan, similar leaders—here Clarkson and Alger (who was also a captain of industry)—ruled unchallenged. In Ohio, although Sherman was the Elder Statesman of the party Organization, Governor Joseph Foraker busied himself with the details of management and business alliance. While Platt had Depew, the railroad president, and Morton, the Wall Street banker, as his patrons, Foraker had (up to 1888) Mark Hanna, the Cleveland magnate of coal, shipping, and street railways.

But Hanna, the tall, heavy-jowled, blunt-spoken Businessman in Politics, was in himself a new phenomenon and somewhat in advance of his times. In Ohio's affairs he rose rapidly to the position of a rival operator who threatened to overshadow Foraker himself.

From an early period of his business career, Mark Hanna had shown a desire to associate himself with large political events and achievements, as his biographer, Herbert Croly, relates. What is clearer still is that it became increasingly necessary for him to control such political events. At first, it is interesting to note—toward 1882, when the reaction to the Garfield tragedy was widespread—Hanna too had joined a civil-service reform movement in Cleveland. Men who had large stakes in businesses or public utilities considered seriously whether impartial, responsible officials in city and State bureaucracies might not serve their ends better than the old, obnoxious spoilsmen and job-brokers. But soon Hanna had found the reformers irksome, promising little relief. He had turned instead to setting up an Organization of his own in Cleveland. This was based in part

orders to "bring in the vote" in their districts, and were generally assessed in secret as well. But with the spread of civil-service reform even into local government, the old fountains dried up, and providentially the new sources, the donations of the Standard Oil, the Pennsylvania Railroad, the American Sugar Refining Company, and the steel companies—to mention only a few corporate groups—which began to be tapped freely and regularly, nowadays vastly exceeded the former revenues from assessments.

upon the Republican businessmen's clubs, of which he was the moving spirit, and in part upon his Cleveland street railways, whose personnel worked regularly for the election of city councilmen.[20]

He purchased a newspaper, tried to elect Mayors, furnished money generously to local politicians, turned over his opera house gratis to party meetings—all with poor results at the start. The rank-and-file politicians disliked his highhanded tone; they had ways of imposing upon him or tricking him, which he must learn to overcome at great cost.

As tenacious as he was ambitious, Mr. Hanna eventually learned all the mysteries of his new trade—though the city of Cleveland itself was often lost during his apprenticeship—and, with the support of the Standard Oil magnates, had himself recognized as the Republican boss of his city. Owing to his lively admiration of the young Governor Foraker, Hanna placed the local Organization and funds at the latter's disposal. Since he had shown himself already an unrivaled collector of funds, his alliance was welcomed by both Foraker and Sherman, though in a somewhat patronizing manner at the outset. For the party convention of 1888 he was given the honor of acting as personal representative, manager, and financial backer of Senator Sherman's quadrennial "boom."

With Blaine in ostensible retirement, Sherman was thought at last to have an excellent chance for the presidential nomination. In reality, the Ohio Organization, whose emissaries arrived in Chicago early in June, was divided into two rival factions which bowed to the two "rising suns," Foraker and McKinley; its support of Sherman was diplomatic rather than emotional. But Mr. Hanna, as an ardent Protectionist, had his heart set upon the election of an orthodox Republican leader.

V

The Republican Party, starved for Federal office and spoils, was nevertheless internally strengthened in 1888 by the close bonds established between its underlying regional machines and the great corporate groups. At the convention that now opened there was something new in the air, something that had a golden ring in the direct participation, as candidates or leaders, of numerous business magnates, such as Russell Alger, Chauncey Depew, Levi Morton, Stephen

Elkins, Joseph Wharton, and Mark Hanna himself, though the last was as yet little known outside of Ohio. Even John Wanamaker, the widely advertised Dry Goods King, who had had little to do directly with politics, was present as an interested delegate-at-large from Pennsylvania. The crisis produced by Mr. Cleveland's tariff message had called forth the flower of American industrial capital, whose representatives rushed to the Republican ranks.

But the nature of the party system and the nominating convention, with all its formal democratic procedure, was still such that great uncertainties lay in the old method of choosing a President through a free-for-all struggle between powerful regional bosses. This, and the shady bartering of prospective cabinet offices, embassies, and consulships for votes of delegates, were relics of inefficient, antediluvian political traditions, which seemed to have no place in the Age of Big Business. Amid brave music and colorful parades before the opening of the convention, there began again the time-honored horse-trading by political agents who with their brandy and cigars pursued the representatives of the Southern "rotten boroughs." Each faction beat the drum for its Native Son, yet each listened for the best terms, the most fruitful pledges of patronage offered in return for abandonment of this same Native Son.

At the Sherman headquarters, Mr. Hanna too was busied in the brisk, competitive bidding for the tickets of Negro delegates. So well did Mr. Hanna play this game that Mr. Foraker, who caught him red-handed in the hotel room, professed himself "greatly surprised" and indignant.[21] Foraker was to make the nominating oration for Senator Sherman again, but quite apparently had ulterior or secret designs which pointed to the engineering of a last-moment "stampede" for Mr. Blaine and a plot to make himself Vice-President.[22] Knowing something of Foraker's hardened nature, we feel that he was less shocked than alarmed lest Hanna succeed in his purpose.

Mark Hanna was revolted by Foraker's pretended piety and real duplicity, and a bitter quarrel now flared up between the two Ohio leaders. But in the meantime General Russell Alger, the monopolist of matches, directing his agents in a daring raid upon the body of Negro delegates, persuaded them, for a consideration of $50 each, to unpledge themselves to Mr. Sherman and commit their votes to him.[23] Alger's agents made the highest bids. He had promised also that if nominated, he would devote $5,000,000 to his campaign, a prospect that intoxicated the professionals. Such colossal disbursements were to be recouped through a new and higher tariff upon matches.[24] Thus the convention horde, diverted by outward disorders and inward intrigues, rumbled through its contests over credentials for the seating of delegates, its committee hearings upon platform planks, its orgy of nominating orations, and got down to the business of choosing a candidate.

In the whole field of candidates only one possessed a character which would have rendered him worthy of the Presidency. This was Federal Judge Walter Q. Gresham of Indiana, an Independent Republican, a learned jurist, an incorruptible magistrate. In his youth Gresham had served as one of the bravest generals in Grant's Army of the West. Recently he had served for a short interim period as Secretary of the Interior under President Arthur, though he had formerly refused such appointments. Gresham's reformist tendencies were appreciated among Middle Western liberals; but he had risen to new national fame by his action as Federal judge in the Wabash Railroad receivership. On behalf of defrauded investors and ill-used clients, Gresham had administered a stern check upon the Napoleonic financier Jay Gould, and given an example to the whole country of what honest men might do.

A spontaneous and scattered nation-wide—rather than regional— support in the Gresham delegation showed that idealistic Republicans nearly everywhere would have welcomed Gresham as a candidate. But Gould through the newspapers had carried on an unremitting campaign to inflame the corporations and politicians against him; while the Blaine Legion, according to the *Nation*, was ready "to fight to the last ditch to block Gresham." [25] In his own State of Indiana the regular Organization had been quickly wrested from him with the aid of Blaine's men, and turned over to another native General, Governor Benjamin Harrison, the grandson of old Tippecanoe, a successful lawyer of an extreme orthodoxy in politics. The nomination of Gresham would have won no financial support from the Railroad Barons—though, as his spokesman claimed, it was demanded "in the sighs of heaven that come from harvest-laden prairies waiting the garner's sickle to feed a hungry world." At a conference of New York politicians Chauncey Depew said in a flashing epigram: "Nominate Gresham, and he will Wabash all of us." [26]

Of the Elder Statesmen who had served country and corporations long and well, Senator William Allison of Iowa, a parliamentary leader in Congress for twenty-five years, was a man of proved ability. He was a man who sought always tactful compromises, so that dirt-farmer constituents returned him regularly to Congress, while the iron and textile lobbies made good reports of him.* But lately Allison's Fabian tactics had not been able to prevent Iowa from going "to the extreme of radical legislation," as Chauncey Depew reasoned in the New York councils of the party, "which threatens the investment in securities of her [Iowa's] railroads . . . and that makes Allison impossible." [27] Coming from one of the Granger States, he would have no support in "capitalistic" New York, Depew concluded.

Uncle John Sherman, whom Mr. Hanna, with his own keen desire for personal prestige and power through President-making, sponsored fervently, remained the strongest candidate, though scarcely strong enough. He was held to be "cold" by fellow politicians, and had a record of compromises which reflected upon his courage. As the balloting began on Friday, June 22, Sherman had the support of Quay's machine as well as Ohio's, and other allies, bringing him 229 votes out of 830; Gresham was given 111; Chauncey Depew, who was a cover for Platt's further purposes, was given 99, as New York's Favorite Son; Russell Alger, 84; Harrison and Allison, 80 and 72 respectively. Blaine, who had made repeated declinations, had been given a small, honorary vote; his supporters were discreetly scattered behind convenient cover in the field, ready to be called together, and Blaine's shadow and the uncertainty concerning him overhung the

---

* According to a story told by Foraker, Allison was notorious for his fear of committing himself to any proposition. "A flock of sheep were driven in front of a farmer's house where he [Allison] was stopping. Someone said to him: 'Mr. Allison, there go some very fine sheep.' To which he answered: 'While I am not a sheep expert, yet I can see that they do appear to be a very fine flock indeed.' Thereupon the other party ventured the further remark, 'They have been recently sheared.' To which Mr. Allison responded, 'Yes, they do appear to have been sheared; [then added in afterthought] at least on this side.'" (Foraker, *Notes of a Busy Life*, Vol. II, pp. 6-7.)

convention to the last moment. On Thursday, June 21, newspapers had published a statement of Mr. Carnegie's on behalf of his guest:

> If Mr. Blaine is nominated he will not refuse. . . . If the Republican party finds that it cannot agree on a leader, and then calls on its former leader to lead it again, it goes without saying that it would be his duty to do so (and Mr. Blaine has never failed to do his duty), more especially since it is now clear that the campaign is to be fought on the issue of protection versus free trade.

Here was the required formula for the "drafting" of Blaine, and some 400 delegates, almost enough to nominate, were ready for the command to begin the "stampede." Blaine's two sons, Walker and Emmons, were on the ground; his managers were known to have approached Foraker with offers of second place.[28] The air was thick with intrigue; and the break was expected to come after the fourth ballot, when, by a sudden move of Platt's, 58 of the New York votes for Depew were swung to Harrison, making his total 217; Sherman, in four ballots, had developed no further strength and led now by a scant margin. The Ohio delegation was reported to be ready to crumble in pieces. It was still believed, as the recess took place over the week end, and Platt went for a long carriage ride with Blaine's lieutenant, Stephen Elkins, that the "covered" votes for several Native Sons, such as Alger, Depew, and Harrison, would be swung over to the Blaine "stampede" at the end. Sherman, though seeing his case hopeless, was convinced that the secret Blaine movement would win if he retired.

Rumors of a possible compromise choice in the shape of the champion of high-tariff Protection, William McKinley, then flew about; and Mark Hanna and other Ohio men telegraphed to Sherman seeking his authorization for this move in order to "save the party from the Blaine lunatics." Sherman was bitter and obdurate. McKinley, who had come as a lieutenant of Sherman's and who remembered well the evils which had befallen Garfield in similar circumstances, made an outspoken and loyal refusal of votes for himself, which did him honor.[29] The stalemate continued. The nocturnal consultations were pursued on Friday until four in the morning, and were resumed on Saturday night by a weary major staff. Meanwhile two cables from Blaine arrived on Saturday, June 23, giving his unqualified refusal.

In the meantime the party's Inner Circle had considered Harrison seriously. Aldrich, the high priest of Protection, vouched for his former colleague in the Senate. According to the account of Nicholas Murray Butler, the group headed by Aldrich during the week end pressed for an "understanding" with Harrison, and Harrison "offered a way out if they felt that they understood him and he them." So "the emissaries went to [near-by] Indiana and came back satisfied." These emissaries included agents of Mr. Platt, who by his own persistent accounts and Sherman's was promised the post of Secretary of the Treasury for himself and control of the Federal patronage at New York. Platt, moreover, by further provisions of this "corrupt bargain," as Sherman called it, was allowed to name Levi Morton for Vice-President.[30] * There is little doubt also that Platt negotiated at great length with Blaine's man, Elkins, during their long carriage drive, for the propitiation of the Blaine forces.

It was at a secret gathering on Saturday night, June 23, 1888, in the Grand Pacific Hotel, that Harrison was named as the compromise choice of Aldrich, Platt, Elkins, Quay, and Clarkson.[31] "The nomination was ours to give, certainly it was ours to keep," wrote Mrs. Blaine regretfully afterward.[32]

From Scotland there came also on Sunday (in response to final pleas from Elkins) a confirming cable in Andrew Carnegie's secret code containing the message that sealed the bargain: "Too late Victor [Blaine] immovable. Take Trump [Harrison] and Star [Phelps]."[33] On Monday, June 25, the pawns of Platt, Quay, Alger, Clarkson (earlier supporting Allison), and a hundred of Sherman's delegates were moved en masse to the Harrison column. He was quickly nominated, and Levi P. Morton of New York was named for Vice-President.

Yet in those tense hours in the room of the Grand Pacific Hotel the Republican magnates must have weighed carefully the disad-

* In response to demands for an unmistakable pledge, a rather discreetly worded letter passed from Harrison to his manager, Michener, June 12, 1888: "I have today and heretofore fully explained to you my views on certain questions, and you are authorized on occasion to explain them to my friends."

vantages as well as the advantages of Blaine's public reputation. His case was remarkably like that of the "lost leader" Henry Clay. He had strength enough to defeat another, but not quite enough to nominate himself, except through such a desperate fight as would have alienated a large section of his party and lost the election. Once more the judgment of the great capitalists, whom he had served so well, in the decision of the Chicago hotel-room conference passed over Blaine.

Blaine, at all events, had acted as the Warwick of the 1888 convention. It was as if, one of the resentful Sherman men said, a President were named "at the brisk dictation of the autocratic ruler of the Republican Party as he goes coaching over the Highlands." [34]

VI

At St. Louis, two weeks before the Republican convention, Grover Cleveland, who had redeemed himself before the people by his brave words in the message on the tariff, was the inevitable choice for renomination. Yet certain unseemly incidents pointed to rifts in the fraternal harmony simulated at the convention. Cleveland's coolness to the up-to-date Democratic machine boss who was Governor of New York had been returned in the form of underground plots to place David Hill in nomination against him, intrigues that had been blocked by respectable elements in time to prevent scandalous dissensions. Croker, the new boss of Tammany, moreover, had taken a conciliatory course between the quarrelsome factions in the Democratic camp. For the sake of peace, Cleveland too bore the petty insults of Hill and his faction in silence, though he was by nature not a forgiving man. In any case, the banking interests and finance capitalists among the Democrats favored Cleveland. "Business men liked his civil courage and moderation"; and the merchant class approved of him because

business had not been affected by the change to a Democratic administration. . . . So the delegates renominated the President by acclamation, although many smiled derisively and indulged in sinister comments when his name excited far less applause than the mention of Horatio Seymour or Samuel Tilden.[35]

The platform of The Democracy fully reflected Cleveland's strong stand on the tariff question, and called for a popular overthrow of the Republican Congressmen who had obstructed the Mills Bill. It avowed in most vigorous terms that the immense majority of

industrious freemen . . . including every tiller of the soil, gain no advantage from excessive tax laws, but the price of nearly everything they buy is increased. . . . All unnecessary taxation is unjust taxation . . . the interests of the people are betrayed when, by unnecessary taxation, trusts and combinations are permitted to exist which, while unduly enriching the few that combine, rob the body of our citizens by depriving them of the benefits of competition.

The Republican net to catch voters was cunningly woven of many-colored strands. While the Democracy at St. Louis had appealed chiefly to the numerous middle classes in the terms of Liberal Capitalism, the Republican ideologues pursued the old system of accumulating fractions and wings nearly everywhere, of cutting across class lines, and uniting upon immediate, even transient causes groups in society which were fundamentally opposed to each other in ultimate interests.

To the capitalists of heavy industry they proclaimed their will to preserve the protective-tariff structure at all costs, even if free whisky should follow as a consequence:

We are uncompromisingly in favor of the American system of protection. We protest against its destruction, as proposed by the President and his party. They serve the interests of Europe; we will support the interests of America. . . . We denounce the Mills bill as destructive to the general business, the labor, and the farming interests of the country . . . we favor the entire repeal of internal taxes, rather than the surrender of any part of our protective system.

Such terms ensured the enthusiastic support of the new monopolistic captains of industry, who nowadays with such sensational effect and speed worked to organize great combinations of copper, lead, wire nails, cordage, oil, sugar, wax, rubber goods, oilcloth. By 1888 the whole people had become painfully aware of the new Trusts, which according to widespread belief among capitalists themselves then required the defense of a Chinese wall of tariff.

Therefore, having granted the demands of the Trusts, the Republican philosophers next made appeal to the masses of consumers who suffered from their exactions—though in terms that were suitably vague:

We declare our opposition to all combinations of capital, organized in trusts or otherwise, to control arbitrarily the condition of trade among our citizens, and we recommend to Congress and the state legislatures, in their respective jurisdictions, such legislation as will prevent the execution of all schemes to oppress the people by undue charges on their supplies, or by unjust rates for the transportation of their products to market.

Such a plank represented a mere "talking point" and apparently in no way checked the enthusiasm of the industrial monopolists for the Republican Party. Capitalists, however, might well have paid closer attention to a further plank of the platform, which reflected upon Cleveland's financial conservatism. This was inserted at the urging of shrewd Western politicians who were keen to win over the agrarian-inflationist vote:

The Republican party is in favor of the use of both gold and silver as money, and condemns the policy of the Democratic administration in its efforts to demonetize silver.

Western Congressmen had insisted that their constituents would tolerate an increase of the tariff if in return they could be assured of an expansion in silver currency which might inflate credit and prices. Finally, in response to the demands of other sagacious politicians, a hint was given in the platform that the embarrassments of the government surplus should be eliminated by the payment of pensions to soldiers more generous than anything previously known.

While a majority of the farmers in the North cared little for high tariffs, the older Middle West was becoming strongly industrialized, and did favor Protection. The settlers of the farther Mississippi Valley, on the other hand, felt a hunger for "soft money"; and it pleased them that the more "patriotic" party, to which they were habitually devoted, accorded this. In no previous platform had the Republican Party made such extravagant and contradictory promises. Throughout the West a fervent patriotism or nationalism, which

Turner has analyzed, was exceedingly strong among the farmers and settlers. Though General Benjamin Harrison was known in Indianapolis as a frigid Presbyterian deacon whose professional eminence had won him almost no intimate friends, his name aroused heart-warming memories of the old Indian fighter Tippecanoe, and stirred chords of history and tradition.

In the private councils of the party's major staff at Chicago, Chauncey Depew had remarked that Harrison's grandfather had had

> one of the most picturesque campaigns in our history. There are enough survivors of that "hard cider and log cabin" canvass to make an attractive contribution on the platform at every meeting, and thus add a certain historic flavor to General Harrison's candidacy.[36]

It was exactly as if the wily Depew understood that this important campaign, which promised an era of mounting tariffs and corporate profits, required more than ever a suitable ideological superstructure, all the mitigating, decorous effects of patriotic tradition and "historic flavor."

VII

With the two national political guilds evenly matched since 1880, the preponderance of money on the side of Harrison and Morton was expected to turn the balance. Yet, to leave no stone unturned, it was felt that the campaign must be carried out by means of political expertness as well as money. The convention over, Swank, general manager of the American Iron and Steel Association, telegraphed at once to Harrison's managers that only Senator Matthew Quay of Pennsylvania would have the approval and support of the heavy industries as chairman of the Republican National Committee.[37] Thus the specialist Quay—somewhat against his will, since he habitually shrank from publicity—became the generalissimo of the Republican campaign of 1888.

From Eastern headquarters in New York Quay together with Tom Platt laid the grand lines of the electoral battle. The chances for winning New York with the assistance of the Republican "Moneybags" Morton as vice-presidential candidate were bright. Indiana, where "every three out of four citizens is a natural-born politician," was no less important. Here Colonel William W. Dudley, the one-legged veteran of many military and party battles, and manager of the Star Route Ring's boodle canvass of 1880, was made the responsible head. Dudley was the associate and personal representative of Governor Harrison, it must be noted. It was said of him in 1880 by a defeated Democratic candidate for the Governorship of Indiana: "In the effective use of money for the purchase of purchasable votes there is no man in the country superior to Colonel Dudley." For this reason, no doubt, he was chosen treasurer of the Republican National Committee. To set the keynote Dudley swore a great oath that there would be "a fair election," adding meaningfully, "The Rebels and Copperheads can't steal this election from us as they did in 1884 without getting hurt." [38]

The extraordinary feature of the Harrison campaign of 1888, as we have noted, was the direct, open, and aggressive participation of the country's leading capitalists and the new techniques they brought to politics. Of these John Wanamaker of Philadelphia and Mark Hanna of Cleveland played the most important parts. Wanamaker, "the great American shopkeeper," pious founder of Sunday schools and Young Men's Christian Associations, had been a Stalwart Republican since the Civil War, in which his dry-goods emporium had benefited so remarkably. Like A. T. Stewart, his predecessor, this genius of bargain sales and advertisement dreamed his little dream of crowning a commercial career with political glory. Returning from the national party assembly at Chicago, where he had figured as a delegate, Wanamaker at once made a forthright public statement that Harrison's prospects were not good unless the party woke up. "The outworn methods of campaigning, which party leaders seemed disposed not to change," he predicted, would fail.

At once Chairman Quay telegraphed him, urging that he take an active part in the struggle and holding up to him the promise of exalted office and honor in reward. Wanamaker's apologist then relates that he consented to serve on condition that the National Committee would agree to the creation of an advisory board of businessmen alone, with its own treasurer and unrestricted power to raise money and decide upon its expenditure. The board was to be very large and representative, covering the whole country, its efficiency depending upon a small executive committee which carried on the real action.

The proposal was accepted. The God-fearing merchant became chairman of the Republican Party's finance committee. Wanamaker and Thomas Dolan, the Philadelphia street-railway and gas king, at once called a meeting of ten prominent citizens of Philadelphia, "each one of whom subscribed $10,000." [39] According to legend, the first $100,000 was raised in ten minutes.

"We want money and we want it quick!" ran Wanamaker's confidential circulars to manufacturers. In others he outlined roughly to each prospective beneficiary how much he might expect to gain from a drastic increase of the tariff on his product, demanding a share of this as ransom payment in advance for the Republican war chest.

The country was then organized by districts with businessmen's subscribing committees representing each district. Mark Hanna, in charge of western Ohio, though greatly cast down by Sherman's defeat, showed himself as always a magnificent collector. For the "holy work" of preserving the protective tariff, Hanna raised $100,000 in short order.[40] In New York Platt, the "Begging Chief," drove downtown in a carriage and interviewed a long list of capitalists, headed by J. Pierpont Morgan, receiving from many of these, who always trusted him implicitly, checks of $10,000 each.

The conversion of the Republican Party to extreme capitalist policy, as James Blaine had long ago foreseen, was making fortune for it, and binding the richest industrialists of the nation to its cause. The party's directorate, influenced by its powerful new recruits, shifted its tactics and levied openly upon those who would most benefit from the Republican "bulwark of prosperity." These donors or great shareholders in turn contributed new methods, a more centralized Organization, to the old party institution.

It was during May, 1888, while the merits of Free Trade or Protection were still being debated in Congress, that James P. Foster, president of the Republican League of the United States, a high-tariff association, sounded a slogan that made the canvass of that year memorable. He wrote in a letter, with utmost candor, that it was the turn of the protected manufacturers to pay and pay freely:

. . . I would put the manufacturers of Pennsylvania under the fire and fry all the fat out of them.[41]

Immediately thereafter the insistent cry for "fat" resounded in all the board rooms of the country's industries. Never before had the political managers used such good arguments for making the capitalists "give up." The sum of $1,000,000 was raised for the acknowledged expenses of the Republican campaign alone, four times that reported by the Democrats. But men spoke in whispers of a colossal secret fund of $2,000,000 more.[42]

In this centennial year of the constitutional republic a sweeping change, long in preparation, had come over its party politics. Some fifty years before (to glance back for a moment), in response to democratic and even idealistic tendencies in the American society, a more popular control of the parties had been introduced, which gave them their formally representative government by local, State, and national conventions of elected delegates. Then in turn the parties, by a hierarchical development, had come to be even "more vigorous and more thoroughly organized than the government." [43] The inner committee control—in the absence of public or mass participation—became the mechanism for absolute direction by professional leaders or bosses; and the spoils system, with its regular exploitation of patronage and taxation upon officeholders, brought about the entrenchment of this control.

During the General Grant Era the disasters of the spoilsmen and the vexations they produced caused the struggle for popular or truly democratic government to assume the form of an irresistible demand for civil-service reform. Such reform offered the greatest menace to the existence of the old party control, eager for its own perpetuation. The party professionals under the whip of civil-service reform now turned in a more systematic manner to new fields.

Under Jackson the cry had been raised "To the victors the spoils of office!" Now the call to the men of the party "to fry the fat" from protected and favored capitalists drowned out the small talk of government place and patronage. There had, of course, always been corrupt pressure by important capitalists or greedy promoters, swarming about the legislatures; there had always been many a Maecenas of politics ready to advance the career of a noted statesman, or make a free gift to his party chest. But these had had no regularity or system; in some years, as in 1876, they were not dependable. Henceforth, after 1888, there was nothing voluntary or seemingly accidental about the contributions of businessmen, which assumed progressively the character of *regular retainers* for definite and regular rather than occasional political services.

It was during the convention and campaign of 1888 that the long-shaping tendencies leading to the most nakedly direct relations between party politics and business—a union of money with a highly advanced professionalism—openly declared themselves. The great bourgeois republic of the West entered into its final nineteenth-century phase: a kind of invisible revolution, wherein the party institution, the living core of the political Government, was to be completely adapted or made over in accordance with the needs of an advanced, large-scale capitalism.

VIII

Yet on the surface the campaign was quiet and "very languid" until late in the summer, as George W. Curtis wrote to Schurz, who had stumped Ohio and dealt mighty blows to Blaine in 1884, and was now vacationing in his native Germany. The political situation seemed "extremely unsatisfactory," the old fire horse of reform admitted. His own impulse, as he wrote to Curtis in reply, was "not to have anything to do with the campaign at all." [44]

The interest of reformers in this campaign was unusually weak. Democratic pretensions to superior purity were embarrassed by the current campaign of Governor Hill for re-election in New York, Hill being most odious to the Mugwumps. Cleveland's failure to endorse Hill, on the other hand, increased the rift within his party and the chance of losing New York's heavy vote in the Electoral College. But when Blaine, who took the stump vigorously in August upon his return, cited from Republican newspapers that Cleveland had "appointed 137 men to office who have been indicted and convicted of crime"—two of them murderers, five duelists, seven forgers, some keepers of houses of ill fame, and the rest petty thieves—Independents and reformers were downcast.

The Democratic campaign this year lacked the aggressiveness and resourcefulness which Gorman, Manning, and Whitney had supplied in 1884. William A. Barnum, the chairman of the Democratic National Committee, showed in truth a lukewarm interest in tariff reform, being himself a member of the American Iron and Steel Association; while Calvin Brice, later a Senator for Ohio, who served as chairman of the executive committee for the campaign, was a friend of Whitney, H. B. Payne, and the Standard Oil family, a clever corporation lawyer and railroad promoter, with a penchant for cynical pleasantries rather than for laborious reformation. The arduous "campaign of education," which was held necessary for the low-tariff movement, was carried on earnestly enough through the speeches and writings of David A. Wells, Arthur P. Latham, and William G. Sumner, spokesmen of the Free Trade League. But the time was too short. Cleveland himself had admitted knowing nothing about the tariff question in 1885; to the electorate it was even more difficult and perplexing a matter.

The Republican strategists, moreover, did their best to promote confusion and even fear in the people. Harrison, who was a competent and even impressive public speaker, addressed large gatherings in the West, and made ninety-four speeches "without a slip," while Cleveland made but a single public appearance when in September he read his letter of acceptance. To the war veterans Harrison appealed by promising to make amends for Democratic stinginess in pensions. The laborers of the cities he warned against the abolition of Protection, which would bring "less work and lower wages" for them. The manufacturers he gratified by saying:

I am one of those uninstructed political economists who have an impression that some things may be too cheap; that I cannot find myself in full sympathy with this demand for cheaper coats, which seems to me necessarily to involve a cheaper man and woman under the coat.[45]

This was casuistry worthy of a successful lawyer.

Blaine in a "swing around the circle" was at his best, as he hailed small-town citizens by their proper names, and ever apt, quick, and full of raillery, made hay with the views of the President and his party. With one stroke he would try to detach the Irish vote, on the ground of a presumed Democratic leaning to Great Britain; with another he mocked at the agitation over Trusts. Trusts were "largely private affairs," with which neither President Cleveland nor the citizens had any right to interfere. In fact, they were more apt to be owned by Democrats than by Republicans. But then, in gloomier vein, he would charge that the Democrats had precipitated a depression by raising the tariff issue. Soon factories would be closed, half-wages would be paid, grass would grow in the streets.

According to the preachings of the New York Central's president, Depew, only "scare" tactics, only a "cyclone of fear," could win the day. The large manufacturers in New York and in the Middle West worked in concert to intimidate their employees. Through them the party Organization struck at the pocketbooks of proletarian voters. From Buffalo and Troy in the closing weeks of the canvass came reports that workers in big iron and textile mills were being provoked to panic by threats of unemployment. In Indiana certain manufacturers terrorized their workmen, exacting pledges from all known Democrats that they would switch to the support of Harrison, and threatening to close up for the winter in the event of Cleveland's success.[46]

Quay, who led the battle unsleepingly and flew everywhere making "deals," "propositions," and "trades," left no stone unturned to carry the urban vote of the East. The Knights of Labor, who loved not Grover Cleveland, were persuaded to endorse Harrison and Protection. Common report attributed this move to the bribing of Secretary Litchman of the Knights of Labor by Matt Quay. In New York the streetcar workers were coerced into declaring themselves in opposition to Cleveland.

The Democrats, moreover, were victimized by a pretty piece of fraud which Quay executed in the final weeks of the campaign. In September, a man who called himself Murchison wrote from California as a naturalized citizen of English birth to the dull-witted British Minister, Sir Lionel Sackville-West, a decoy letter, asking him which of the presidential candidates was regarded more favorably in the fatherland. To which Sackville-West, falling into the trap, replied on September 13 advising a vote for Cleveland, marking his letter "Private." In good time Quay, to whom the letter found its way, released it to the press, on October 22, as a sensation of nine days.

THE BRITISH LION'S PAW THRUST INTO AMERICAN POLITICS

ran the headlines. It was too near election time to offset the effects of the fraud, and Cleveland's angry dismissal of the British Minister did little good.

Nevertheless, the real apathy of the public toward both parties was so marked that no ordinary measures seemed to count for much.

Quay and Platt were confident that Mr. Cleveland's home State would be wrested from the Democratic column. But when the advance "sixty-day poll" was taken in Indiana, the bailiwick of Benjamin Harrison, it was confidentially predicted to the Republican managers that Harrison's compatriots, who had known him too well, would return a clear Democratic majority. The local Republican machine was thrown into panic, and appealed desperately to New York headquarters for additional funds. Quay, in a statement which he permitted to reach the ears of his opponents indirectly, reminded the Indiana men that they had promised to carry their State with their own resources if Harrison were named. He pretended to be wholly concerned with the capture of "pivotal" New York, for which all his funds would be necessary. Actually Chairman Quay and Treasurer Dudley of the Republican National Committee— Dudley himself a leader of the Indiana machine—kept the closest watch upon Indiana developments. Soon Indiana was wrought to a frenzy of debates, picnics, and barbecues, as well as processions and floats of model Log Cabins, cider barrels, and beaver-hatted pioneers. At this time the interest of "pivotal" Indiana's citizens in national elections was often felt to be more than theoretical. Thousands of Hoosier floaters from year to year regularly shifted their allegiance from one party to the other; and this phenomenon was a standing national joke.

John C. New, an Indiana member of the Republican National Committee, stated publicly on September 21, 1888, that he was on the alert for the floaters: "A complete poll shows where the floaters are, and you can depend on it we will not lose any of that element." [47] Even President Cleveland heard of strange doings, and wrote to a party leader in Indiana, September 29, 1888, asking that special precautions be taken to see that "all our men are in line, and touching elbows." [48]

The floater vote in Indiana had been estimated at 10,000 in 1880, 15,000 in 1884, but was now reckoned at 20,000. In Indiana, as in New York, all depended upon the raising of sums of money vaster than ever used before, and the accuracy with which this money was used. For the final days of the campaign Wanamaker in a last appeal raised a quantity of cash reported variously as from $400,000 to $700,000. He related afterward:

> We raised the money so quickly that the Democrats never knew anything about it. They had their spies out supposing that we were going to do something, but before they knew what it was we had them beaten.

Quay carefully kept the final disposition of his money and the direction of attack a deep secret. The Democrats "were not beaten in November, nor in October, but *long before that,*" Wanamaker said.[49] What they were doing as early as June 26, immediately after their national convention, is indicated by a confidential letter written by a party agent to George Bliss, a Republican leader of New York, and a banking partner of Levi Morton:

> Sen. O'Brien can control a very large independent Democratic vote, and also can make connection with the organized workers of this county [New York]. *I think an arrangement can be made to give it to Harrison and Morton.**

This document throws light on the amusing reports made by Colonel E. M. Shepard, editor of the *Mail and Express* (Republican), that the Republican National Committee paid through a State

---

* Levi Morton Papers, W. H. Marston to G. C. Bliss. Italics mine. This letter, found in a confused mass of the Morton private papers, substantiates largely the charges, previously somewhat vague, that portions of the Tammany vote were purchased many months in advance of the election.

We may remark, for example, how costs of election management in Indiana were rising perpendicularly: in 1872, $50,000; in 1876, $100,000; in 1880, about $200,000; in 1888, $400,000—in round numbers, according to statements of the time.

leader (perhaps Platt) $150,000 for the purchase of three local Democratic political clubs or "movements," each having from 10,000 to 30,000 votes, though complaint was made afterward that not all these votes were delivered.[50] It was also uncanny how the voters in these Democratic movements "scratched" the name of the Republican candidate for Governor, Warner Miller, and re-elected Hill while voting in a Republican President.

According to statements of numerous reporters and eyewitnesses at the time, Democratic managers were seen conferring at great length in the back rooms of Republican headquarters in Kings County (Brooklyn). One leader, it was said, took $25,000 to deliver 3,500 votes in six wards to Harrison—this alone accounting for more than half the Republican majority in the State.[51] It was widely believed that Platt and Quay had made, long in advance, their "trade" with Governor David Hill, whereby the latter's followers and lieutenants "knifed" the head of the Democratic ticket, Cleveland, in return for the desertion of Warner Miller (whom Platt disliked and feared as a rival) by the Republican State machine. "The electoral votes of the State of New York were sold by Governor Hill," the New York *Times* asserted, "to ensure his own election as Governor." [52]

The scenes in Indiana had been even more lurid. Hundreds of "foreign" voters were transported into the Hoosier State. "Many loyal sons of Pennsylvania," normally Republican followers of Senator Quay, were reported to be suddenly "migrating en masse" via freight cars of the Pennsylvania Railroad.[53] From Colonel Dudley, Republican Party treasurer, came final instructions to all his leaders in the field, in a famous letter written under the National Republican Committee letterhead:

HEADQUARTERS REPUBLICAN NATIONAL COMMITTEE

Executive Committee
91 Fifth Avenue
New York, Oct. 24, 1888

DEAR SIR:

I hope you have kept copies of the lists [of the floating vote] sent me. Such information is very valuable and can be used to great advantage. It has enabled me to demonstrate to friends here that with proper assistance

Indiana is surely Republican for Governor and President, and has resulted as I hoped it would in securing for Indiana the aid necessary. Your committee will certainly receive from Chairman Huston [of the Indiana Republican organization] the assistance necessary to hold our floaters and doubtful voters, and gain enough of the other side to give Harrison and Morton 10,000 plurality. . . . Divide the floaters into blocks of five and put a trusted man with the necessary funds in charge of these five and make him responsible that none get away and that all vote our ticket . . .

(signed) W. W. Dudley, Treas.[54]

Thus provided for, the henchmen of Dudley solicited floaters from all parts of the State, gathered them in gangs of five men, kept them under lock and key, and marched them under guard to the polls. In those days before the Australian ballot was first widely adopted (1892), the ballots were printed by the party Organizations. These were given to the men in one moment, as the press reported, "and in the next the wages of their depravity." As against a price of $2 to $5 in preceding campaigns, payments of "brand-new twenty dollar bills" or of three shiny new gold pieces of $5 was made for each vote. The Democratic watchers at the polls were overwhelmed.[55]

Dudley's "blocks-of-five" letter was discovered by a Democratic mail agent and broadcast in Democratic newspapers as early as October 31. Even Quay was frightened, but quickly recovering his aplomb, shouted in angry denial: "Forgery! A Democratic lie." Dudley brazenly instituted libel suits against the various newspapers which had published his letter—suits, however, which were later dropped.*

In the meantime the fortunes of the day favored Harrison in Indiana by a scant 2,300, the earlier trend of the State having been overcome by herculean efforts and an expenditure reckoned at as much as $400,000. In New York State, which was also needed to offset the Democratic Solid South, Harrison led Cleveland by some

---

* When the Republican leaders in Indiana, and Harrison particularly, showed that they intended to disavow Dudley, try him in an Indiana court, and make him the "scapegoat," as he termed it, that worthy threatened to "explode a lot of dynamite" and expose "the entire inside workings of the Republican National Committee." Eventually Dudley, brought before a Federal judge who was a Republican, escaped punishment on legal grounds. *Cf.* Gresham, *Life of Walter Q. Gresham*, Vol. II, pp. 608-18.

12,000 out of 1,300,000 ballots, while Hill, Democratic candidate for Governor, exceeded Warner Miller's total by 19,000, a most peculiar affair. The results were inconclusive as far as the political issues were concerned: Harrison had an electoral majority, but a clear minority of the total votes, 100,000 less than those cast in the country for Cleveland. In addition, over 400,000 votes for independent parties opposed his election.

When Chairman Matthew Quay journeyed to Indianapolis to congratulate the President-elect upon the verdict of the people, he found the usually self-possessed Harrison deeply stirred, and in pious Presbyterian fashion inclined to thank his God for having favored the Republican Party. "Providence has given us the victory," he exclaimed in deep and solemn tones.

The Pennsylvania chieftain assented out of habitual politeness, but afterward imparted to his friend, Colonel A. K. McClure, the thought that Harrison was doubtless a "political tenderfoot" and made a poor impression upon him.

"Think of the man," Quay exclaimed. "He ought to know that Providence hadn't a damn thing to do with it." And he added emphatically that he supposed Harrison "would never know how close a number of men were compelled to approach the gates of the penitentiary to make him President." [56]

CHAPTER TWELVE

POLITICAL PROFIT-SHARING

I tell you frankly that I am for "the old flag and an appropriation" for every old comrade who needs it.
CORPORAL TANNER OF THE G.A.R.

THE Republicans of 1888 fervently embraced the widespread, though unspoken, belief that the American system was a "huge profit-sharing concern." The Administration and Congress, both houses of which were now controlled by the victorious party, were to distribute the "profits" as speedily as possible. As to the mode of distribution "the only interests consulted . . . were the special interests thereby benefited." [1]

These were prosperous and carefree times, in which an enormous volume of trade was carried on throughout the American interior and with all parts of the world. The government Treasury was burdened with a swollen surplus of idle money. Well, Republican spokesmen said, was not a surplus easier to handle than a deficit? A leader of the pensioned war veterans, sounding the hopes of an important wing of the Republican army which converged upon Washington in March, 1889, cried: "God help the surplus!"

The Fifty-first Congress, which now largely represented the friendly competition, the affectionate give and take of special interests, soon became known to history as the Billion Dollar Congress. Thomas Reed, the new Speaker, as he presided over the auctioning of immense sums and of public privileges greater still, cheerfully remarked that this was "a billion-dollar country," was it not? Among the cohorts of the G.O.P. there was heard again the familiar refrain "The old flag and an appropriation."

In their eagerness for victory, the Republican Party had made promises to every wing and section. To the industrial capitalist of the East a high protective tariff had been pledged. To rural sections the party had made appeal by hinting in its platform at a renewal of silver-money inflation. To the war veterans, angered by Cleve-

land's vetoes of pension bills, Harrison promised an annuity for all
who were unable to earn a living, whether the disability originated
in the service or not. When he thought of the increasing age of the
Union veterans, a brigade of whom he himself had led with stern
courage in the war, "the minor tones of sadness and pathos" entered
his speech at "the mighty appeal of service and suffering." Then to
the spoilsmen, as we have seen, hints were quietly conveyed of the
government departments and the patronage to be placed in their
hands; while to the reformers reform was promised: "The reform
of the civil service auspiciously begun under the Republican Administration should be completed." Seldom in our history had such
hostages been given to fortune by a political party. Would the new
President be equal to appeasing so many appetites, satisfying so many
different claims?

The roulette wheel of the party system throws up all sorts of
average citizens, one of whom must be chosen to play the extremely
exacting and sometimes tragic role of Chief Magistrate. Enormous
power comes to his hand. He must be alert and sensitive, yet wear
a thick skin; he must possess almost acrobatic capacities to please
everyone, use the honest and the dishonest, balance jealous factions,
leave no openings for adversaries, hold the party columns in order,
serve the great interest groups dominating the country and thus—in
the light of the political economy of the age—serve people and
country. All this and more. For the President who as a candidate,
before November, is concerned solely with the means to election,
thinks after November of his human ambitions, of his place in history, of his chances of assuming an actual as well as a de jure leadership of his Administration and the party institution. His latent personality, hidden for diplomatic reasons, emerges more and more,
and becomes a factor. Hence foreign philosophers of politics have
often marveled at the risks taken by our party system in choosing
at times an unknown quantity, a "man of unknown smallness" by a
machinery of wirepullers and blowers.[2]
The explanation lies in the fact that the "personality" of the
President may or may not be a factor of risk for a fixed period of
four years; but the party managers, whose hands and tongues guide,

advise, or check the new ruler at every turn, exercise power for indeterminate periods, unchecked by laws or the people. A Harrison or a Cleveland may hold office for four or eight years at the most; but a Simon Cameron, a Tom Platt, an Arthur Gorman, may rule within the party government for a generation or a half-century.

On the last Sunday before his inauguration, Deacon Benjamin Harrison, as always, passed the plate for the weekly collection at his Presbyterian church in Indianapolis, of which he had been a member for forty years. He was a man who possessed a considerable fund of character and strength. He was the descendant of a distinguished family, the grandson of old Tippecanoe; he had also given proof of his own capacities at the bar. He had worked hard; and Chauncey Depew of the New York Central Railroad considered Harrison "the profoundest lawyer of the time." Senator George Hoar thought him able and intelligent, but of a nature which repelled sympathy. The observant people of Indianapolis were impressed by Harrison, but loved Judge Walter Gresham or even Judge McDonald, a Democrat, better. For while these men were prone to a humane liberalism, and even at moments to sympathy with the lower classes, Harrison suggested an intense, unswerving conservatism, and a self-righteousness which less religious souls seldom bring to their credos.

From his very youth, before the war, Benjamin Harrison had joined the Abolition Republicans who had risen in the West, and "as a party of revolt against the established order . . . won their way to political power as a party of the people." Like the other political generals, Logan, Butler, and Garfield, he had been wont to mingle soldiering with politics, hurrying from the scene of Sherman's battles in Georgia to the home front, where at the behest of Oliver Morton he campaigned from the stump. The iron of war was brought into those earlier party contests, and Harrison doubtless learned to condone many things, even the depredations at the ballot boxes of Colonel Dudley, his fellow soldier. But in its old age, as Max Farrand has written, the Republican Party had "gradually shifted over until it became the party of business interests . . . of bankers and manufacturers of the cities of the East, rather than the party of the agricultural states of the West." [3] Harrison, too, with age had shifted over. His Republicanism was intensely partisan and orthodox, and he could shut his eyes, puritan that he was, to the irregularities of "venal" Indiana's Organization politics, through whose grades he had climbed steadily to the Senatorship, the Governorship, and the White House.

The work of the war, the success of the Republican Party, the system of Protection, and the sacredness of great property interests all became part of Harrison's militant Calvinist creed. His conservatism and the fact that he came from the West, and would therefore propitiate better the Mississippi Valley wing of the party, had made him the choice of the convention managers in 1888. Another son of Indiana has commented:

The late President Benjamin Harrison had the exclusive distinction of having served the railway corporations in the dual capacity of lawyer and soldier. He prosecuted the strikers [in 1877] in the federal courts . . . and he also organized and commanded a company of soldiers during the strike. . . . Ten years later he was elevated to the presidency of the United States.[4]

Nevertheless it was not thinkable that this stubborn, self-controlled man of pure life, who had long taught a Bible class on Sundays, would comfortably tolerate new Whisky Rings and Star Route frauds. Blaine, Matt Quay, and Platt found him from the outset inflexible, distant, suspicious. These men were mighty in electoral battle; but in the peace that followed, concessions to their demands might bring ruin and disgrace—not for them, but for the President. Yet their claims upon him could not be ignored. Harrison brooded silently for long weeks over the problems raised by the disposition of cabinet posts in the Administration, his debts to the party chieftains, and his fear of them.

The contradictions in policy, the effect of being pulled hither and thither, the confused direction and "want of determined statesmanship" attributed by historians to the Harrison regime, all flowed from the clashing impulses which alternately governed it. The professional politicians found that the lawyer who spoke so vigorously before 10,000 persons was a "human iceberg" in private. He would grant a request, but "in a way which seemed as if he were denying it," while Blaine could refuse one as if he were conferring a favor.[5]

A powerful party hack, Senator for a great State, would publicly complain that when he called at the White House he was not even invited to have a chair.[6] Tom Platt, discontented like Quay, soon felt that Harrison "forgot or ignored the men most responsible for his victory."[7] But his burdens were truly great; the gross compromises, the conflicting and treacherous pledges his party had given, provided dilemmas that would have perplexed greater barristers than Mr. Harrison.

II

"When I came into power I found that the party managers had taken it all to themselves," Harrison once said in an intimate talk at which Theodore Roosevelt was present. "I could not name my own Cabinet. They had sold out every place to pay the election expenses."[8]

Promptly after his nomination, Harrison had written to Blaine and acknowledged that "only the help of your friends made success possible." He intended, moreover, to show his "high appreciation of the efficient and conclusive support" the Blaine men had given him.[9] Harrison had been the third successive Republican candidate whose nomination was dictated by Blaine. For Blaine's extremely popular stumping in 1888—he was then a legendary figure, a Prince Hal of politics to a generation which had known him from its infancy—had clearly helped to win the day. Yet the President-elect, after many secret misgivings, doubtless, over an "uncrowned king" or a "power behind the throne" in his Cabinet, had permitted ten weeks to pass before sending the Gentleman from Maine a brief, formal invitation to serve as his Secretary of State. The conventional offer was accompanied also with a "private" covering letter in which Harrison, after discussing points of policy, ended by admonishing and lecturing Blaine upon the need of preserving harmony in the party and conducting the Administration "without any selfish thought or ambition."[10] Harrison bowed before Blaine's dreadful power over the party, but apparently thinking of the tragic strife that had followed his service in the Garfield Cabinet, held him at a distance, and marked the limits of his influence.

Blaine, on terms of politeness rather than of affection (as with Garfield), accepted the brilliant office which could not have been refused him. Thereafter he busied himself chiefly with the grand designs of a "spirited" foreign policy leading to the economic penetration of Central America and South America. With reason England feared Blaine as an old enemy who cultivated a burgeoning American imperialism—somewhat neglected after the Civil War—that was spreading into the Pacific as far as the South Seas. Yet most American enterprisers, still lacking adequate capital and credit with which to exploit fully their own inexhaustible interior market, followed Mr. Blaine only reluctantly into strange seas. The rather farsighted plans for reciprocity which he now pushed were a decade in advance of his time, though they brought him a measure of brief glory for his old years.

The rest of his Cabinet Harrison allotted according to the old pattern of "geographical" distribution among the regional bosses. Some lesser offices, on the other hand, were filled according to a nepotistic system, by which personal followers and a goodly number of relatives were installed as a sort of political bodyguard. But the pretensions of the Eastern "Goldbug" Tom Platt to the command of the Treasury were ignored. Platt persistently claimed that "a positive pledge" had been given him, although the President stoutly denied this. Behind the altercation lay not only the spoils motive but the desire of the Eastern capitalists to control the Treasury policy. Platt relates:

It was a portfolio for which I believed myself to be better equipped than for any other. I had from my college days made an assiduous study of financial questions. As president of express, railroad, coal and iron, and other corporations, I had learned a great deal about how to manage fiscal affairs. Indeed, I had for many years been very ambitious to conduct the Government finances.[11]

To be sure, an attempt was made to conciliate Platt by making his law partner, General Benjamin Tracy, Secretary of the Navy. But Platt was inconsolable, and resolved never again to "trust men from Ohio," for Harrison, too, had been born there.

The Treasury was awarded instead to William Windom, formerly a Senator from Wisconsin, a politician who had long divided his time between financial ventures in New York and Organization politics in

the Northwest. Secretary Windom's advent was in itself a symptom
of cleavage in the party between the Eastern and Western wings,
and resulted from the strange bargain for more radical or more inflationary silver legislation. To satisfy this troublesome pledge, Windom, a man of "obscure and confused" notions, was soon engaged
in framing a compromise silver-coinage law which outraged the
orthodox Eastern financiers.[12]

For Secretary of War Harrison chose Redfield Proctor, head of
the Vermont Marble Company, and a leader of the high-tariff
leagues; the Attorney General was W. H. H. Miller of Indiana,
the President's law partner; while the most famous appointment of
all in this Cabinet of mediocrities was that of John Wanamaker as
Postmaster General. Thus Harrison's Cabinet, which also included
Vice-President Levi Morton, was known as the Businessmen's
Cabinet.

The Wanamaker appointment was made in payment for Wanamaker's donation of $50,000 to the party war chest, the Democrats
contended. The great shopkeeper was known everywhere for his bargain sales, his slogans of "One Price" and "Money Back." But what
capacities had he for government administration? Would he not proceed (with measuring tape over one arm, and calling "Cash!" as the
cartoonists of the day pictured it) to hold a bargain sale of the post
offices, a sale at which the Pennsylvania machine and its sinister boss,
Matt Quay, would be the chief beneficiaries?

Although Wanamaker, with his sweet and open countenance,
seemed a tyro in party politics, he soon showed that his pieties did not
embrace civil-service reform. He heeded, at the beginning, the advice of Quay, and of the other professionals who held minor cabinet
posts under him, such as Clarkson of Iowa. According to his official
biographer, Wanamaker even stayed his President from the blunder
of too drastic reforms, insisting that "full weight be given to congressional claims of patronage." [13] There was nothing distasteful to
him in the idea of the spoils belonging to the victor.

In his gracefully written inaugural address, President Harrison,
small, erect, and firm in his bearing, spoke of the prosperity and

progress of our land "so magnificent in extent, so pleasant to look upon, and so full of generous suggestion to enterprise and labor. God has placed upon our head a diadem and has laid at our feet power and wealth beyond definition and calculation. But," he added in admonition, "we must not forget that we take these gifts upon the condition that justice and mercy shall hold the reins of power."

On the score of the government service he had declared that his officers would be expected to enforce the Civil Service Law "fully and without evasion." He hoped to do more than his obvious duty in this regard. Then in measured words that bespoke the conflict in his nature, he concluded: "The ideal, or even my own ideal, I shall probably not attain."

Thereafter the claims of Congressmen from all parts of the country were taken care of. Through Clarkson, who actually directed Wanamaker's department, the doors of the government offices were opened to an army of party "workers" frenzied by four years of famine. The "headsman" Clarkson had taken his minor cabinet post temporarily in the interests of the party Organization. He began with a sickening decapitation of 15,000 fourth-class postmasters. The Iowa boss was described as working night and day in Washington, with his coat off and shirt sleeves rolled up, while party organs exhorted him literally: "Go to it, Clarkson! Out with the whole 55,000 by January 1!" Early in 1890 he could say that he had changed 31,000 fourth-class postmasters.

. . . I expect to change 10,000 more before I finally quit. I expect before the end of the month to see five-sixths of the Presidential postmasters changed. Then I can paraphrase old Simeon and say: "Let thy servant depart in peace." [14]

At a time when the government departments greatly increased their personnel the Businessmen's Cabinet found ways of installing a horde of the party's camp followers. Harrison watched this process in silence. By his extension of civil-service classification and the merit system great numbers of the new appointees became entrenched in office thereafter, thus saving them from Democratic vengeance in later years. Such were the "alluring possibilities" of reform to the Outs. In their turn, when in power, the Democrats by a "discretionary" handling of the government-service procedure would continue the process until the lists were virtually filled.

When the outcry over Clarkson became intolerable, the President swung to the other side, and lent encouragement to his Civil Service Commission. Thievery must be held within bounds, official frauds and scandals prevented.

At the insistence of Representative Henry Cabot Lodge, and (very oddly) in return for his active help to Matt Quay in the late campaign, Theodore Roosevelt was made a member of the Civil Service Commission. This young man in search of a career had with his friend Lodge quit the Independents and Mugwumps in disgust, yet the reputation of a reformer still clung to him. Determined to make the commission a living force, as he told Lodge, Roosevelt was soon embroiled in loud quarrels. He found that advance was to be made only "in the teeth of the fiercest opposition." The system of patronage was deeply embedded in the habits of the people and the parties. He found Wanamaker (behind whom Clarkson operated) an "evasive hypocrite," while the President himself remained impassive or merely tactful before Roosevelt's complaints of gross corruption.

The President desired strength and harmony for his party Organization, and on the other hand safeguards against extreme corruption, which Roosevelt and his fellow commissioners provided. Spoilsmen and reformers held a tug of war, as Roosevelt recalled. Once, in an appeal for his aid, Roosevelt told "the little grey man" Harrison the story of the backwoodsman who set out to kill a bear, but prayed in advance for success to his mission: "Oh, Lord, help me kill that bar; and if you don't help me, oh Lord, don't help the bar." The President laughed good-humoredly, yet his curious restraint amounted virtually to "an announcement that hereafter no man need fear dismissal for violating the law." [15]

Roosevelt, as Cleveland afterward said of him, now appeared to be "looking to a public career . . . studying political conditions with a care that I had never known any man to show." [16] His altercations with the Postmaster General, Wanamaker, brought a congressional investigation of certain scandals, and some publicity for himself, though few tangible results. His negligences also brought upon him, from the enemy press, the epithet of "canting young humbug." For all of Roosevelt, Quay and Clarkson had their way with many a customhouse and post office; the President himself could not be deterred from placing relatives in useful posts and adding to his personal following by appointing to public office certain editors who were his apologists in the late campaign.

The Harrison Administration, with its overt professions in favor of reform and its covert yieldings to the narrowest forms of partisanship, earned the dislike both of the reformed and of the unregenerate spoilsmen, and made a picture that was highly confusing to the popular mind. Only now and then a voice arose to complain of so much obscure, unhappy compromise. The sharp-tongued Senator Ingalls of Kansas, in a public interview of September, 1890, railed at all concessions to the civil-service reformers who, in politics, were but a product of "tea-custard and syllabub dilettantism and frivolous sentimentalism." Then, in a forthright demonstration of the working axioms of party life, he added:

The purification of politics is an iridescent dream. Government is force. Politics is a battle for supremacy. Parties are the armies. The Decalogue and the Golden Rule have no place in a political campaign. . . . To defeat the antagonist and expel the party in power is the purpose.

Hence it was lawful to "deceive the adversary, to hire Hessians . . . to mutilate, to destroy." For what commander would dare to lose a battle "through the activity of his moral nature"? [17]

III

The more active intervention of wealthy capitalists in local politics toward 1888 produced special effects which were beginning to be noticed. The management of elections and the purchasing of votes, instead of diminishing, seemed to grow more systematized and efficient. It was said nowadays that floaters were paid for their votes *after* they were delivered, as the new corporate groups participating in elections inspired high confidence that payments agreed upon would be forthcoming.*

* A Michigan correspondent's letter to the *Nation*, Jan. 3, 1889, read: "Give me $100,000 and a reliable man at each polling-place, and I will, at any general election, contract to purchase 20,000 votes for any political organization in this State."

Owing to the increasingly rigid controls over State legislatures by the Quays and Platts, it became a fairly simple matter for men who had acquired large capital to enter the upper chamber of Congress during the 1880's and 1890's. The United States Senate thenceforth came to be known as the Millionaires' Club. But more important still was its metamorphosis, in the sense that Nelson Aldrich of Rhode Island had always desired, from a body representing geographical units to one representing economic entities, such as lumber. oil, sugar, silver, copper, or steel.

These latter-day statesmen came from distant points of the country which offered strong contrasts with each other in climate and customs; yet they might be seen in the Capitol at Washington pursuing the same interests, speaking familiarly the same language. From Michigan in 1889 came two lumber Senators, McMillan and Stockbridge, while Russell Alger, the Match King (who had nearly bought his way to the Presidency) ruled as Governor at the State capitol. From Ohio a drastic political overturn had brought two Democratic Senators, Calvin Brice, director of great banks and railroads, and H. B. Payne, a member of the Standard Oil family. From the newer mining States, such as Nevada, came James Fair, the Bonanza King, and John P. Jones, the silver magnate; while California was represented by George Hearst, owner of gold mines and patron of newspapers, and Wisconsin by the nearly illiterate Lumber Baron Philetus Sawyer. These joined the Eastern grandees of banking, railroads, and public utilities—Donald Cameron, Nelson Aldrich, and Stephen Elkins, men already old in political experience.

Then later, in a steady procession, came more men of money: Hale of Maine, Kean of New Jersey, Thomas Platt and Depew of New York, Henry Cabot Lodge and W. Murray Crane of Massachusetts, and Mark Hanna of Ohio; until by the turn of the century some twenty-five multimillionaires, or enough to control all legislation through the mechanism of the committee system and party Organization, sat in the upper chamber of Congress.

Toward 1889 a United States Senator had come to represent "something more than a state, more even than a region," as William Allen White has said. "He represented principalities and powers in business." One stood for the Union Pacific Railroad, another for the

New York Central, one for the insurance interests of New York and New Jersey and Connecticut combined. From the Far West there came not one but a whole group representing the Southern Pacific; while another group from the Northwest "flaunted the golden chains" of Jim Hill. The Santa Fe "divided, with the Gould system, an interest in another. Coal and iron owned a coterie from the Middle and Eastern seaport states. Cotton had half a dozen senators." [18]

The Senate came for a time to serve not only as a rich men's club but as an Olympus where the demigods of the market, the victors in the fierce competitive race for capital, the most admired and envied accumulators of the country, stood shoulder to shoulder to guide the destinies of the nation. A hint of what these money lords in the Senate thought of their mission and of each other is given in an anecdote concerning the aged George Hearst related by Cullom of Illinois. Senator Hearst, on one occasion, gave an elaborate dinner to twenty-five of his colleagues, and after dinner in the smoking-room downstairs thought out a little speech, in which he said:

I do not know much about books; I have not read very much; but I have travelled a good deal and observed men and things, and I have made up my mind after all my experience that the members of the Senate are the survival of the fittest.[19]

A far more important part, in all probability, was played by those members of the Senate who were pre-eminent as lawyers for the leading corporations. These, whether Democrats or Republicans, often "had campaign contributions directly from the great business interests which they openly championed; or the attorneys for those interests, controlling state conventions and legislatures, named these senators, and so owned them." [20] Such were the close friends of Nelson Aldrich, chairman of the Senate Finance Committee: William Allison of Iowa, John Spooner of Wisconsin, Orville H. Platt of Connecticut, and Arthur Gorman of Maryland, corporation lawyers all, who proudly wore the "collar" of the financial interests they represented. Spooner, Allison, and O. H. Platt, who were members of Aldrich's "Philosophers' Club," were the acknowledged masters of caucus and committee machinery in the Senate, without whom almost no legislation might pass.*

It is in the committee rooms, behind closed doors, that the real legislative work of Congress is done. Aldrich and Gorman, the parliamentary leaders of their parties, moving noiselessly through these committee rooms, perfected the process which has come to be known as "invisible government." According to many legends, Aldrich needed "but to whisper in the committee rooms" of either House that laws and tariff bills might be promptly enacted or delayed.[21] His influence over his colleagues was immense and remained so during most of his thirty years in the Senate. His voice reached to distant regions, deciding where funds for aspiring Representatives or Senators might be placed, so that many lavish letters of thanks, even from Western States, gathered among his dossiers: "I am under obligations to you. . . . I will pull through and hope to have a complimentary majority."

In the opposition party, Arthur Gorman exercised almost the same power as Aldrich; he, however, was a partner of Aldrich's in certain business ventures, was united with him in a "community of interests," and formed the left arm of capitalism, as Aldrich was its right arm.[22]

The elder Robert La Follette, then a young, inexperienced Representative from a Wisconsin farming constituency, observed the working of "invisible government" in the party caucus with wonder. The caucus meeting took three and a half minutes by his watch: a presiding officer was appointed, a committee on committees was appointed, and adjournment was voted.

Then and there the fate of all the legislation at this session was decided. . . . If you will scan the committees of this Senate, you will find that a little handful of men are in domination and control of the great legislative committees of this body.[23]

In the lower house the average Representative found himself usually under the close supervision of the Senator-boss or corpora-

* When Albert Beveridge of Indiana came to Washington in 1899, he found the Senate "dominated (as he testifies in his private papers) by a 'marvelous combination' composed of Aldrich as manager, Allison as 'conciliator and adjuster,' Spooner as floor leader and debater, and [Orville] Platt as 'designer and builder.'" (Bowers, *Beveridge and the Progressive Era*, p. 138.)

tion lawyer who headed his State party. La Follette, who had arrived at Washington by building with Mrs. La Follette's aid an "independent machine," was cautioned one day about his opposition to land-grabbing or town-jobbing bills, which were demanded by the St. Paul Railroad or the Chicago & Northwestern. *"Those are your home corporations,"* he was told by Senator Sawyer, Wisconsin's boss. When he urged a colleague from Wisconsin to resist such a measure, he received the reply: "Sawyer . . . insists on my voting for the bill. . . . He has loaned me money; he has a mortgage on everything I possess." [24] On one occasion Senator Sawyer also tried to bribe La Follette directly; the latter, with his passionate temper, provoked a sensational scandal, the result of which was that La Follette's—and not Sawyer's—public career was definitely halted. His political friends at once abandoned him, because he had broken an unwritten code and ignored the "good of the party." For long years the brilliant La Follette was relegated to the private practice of law in Wisconsin, while the sordid Sawyer continued to sit in the Senate.

Between 1887 and 1890, as the embittered La Follette recollects, there was launched a renewed and tremendous offensive campaign for more and more rights and privileges by the "struggling railways," the "infant industries," and aggregations of private capital, everywhere nourished and grown strong upon government favor and now gathered in a solid community of interests. Not only did they seize upon natural resources and strategic monopolies, but parties, legislatures, courts. Congress was "overwhelmed." [25]

With the election of Harrison the recently formed industrial Trusts surpassed themselves in boldness, and set about eliminating "ruinous competition" in almost every commodity, from cordage and codfish to whisky. Early in 1890, as the McKinley Tariff Bill was being debated, some $188,000,000, an unheard-of sum, was invested directly in the combination of four new Trusts.[26] New wire-nail and tin-plate combinations, and their new mills, were set up in control of the domestic market, with "plenty of money forthcoming," as one of the promoters wrote to McKinley, on the assurance *"that the Republicans will continue to govern this country in the future."* [27] It was a significant historical conjunction that at the same time, reassured by the triumph of Republican orthodoxy, J. Pierpont Morgan in the winter of 1889-90 organized the famous "gentlemen's agreement" among the heads of the largest railroad trunk lines— though the ink had scarcely dried on the Interstate Commerce Act, whose statutes forbade such a combination.

The deep changes taking place in a society which was being "centralized" by irresistible economic forces were marked by parallel shiftings, not only in the unofficial party government, but also in historic parliamentary customs of the Government itself. The "bear garden" of Congress, which held even a sprinkling of agrarian "anarchists," such as La Follette, was still a cumbersome and inefficient legislative machine. It threatened delays for the community of interests which waited impatiently to enact their own wealth-sharing laws after March, 1889; hence this department of the Government too must undergo reorganization and "co-ordination."

The forehanded Mark Hanna of Cleveland was among those who had given thought to such problems. Before the new session of Congress opened, he had gone to Washington to work among the brethren of the Republican caucus for the election of his new protégé, William McKinley, as Speaker. However, Eastern interests brought about the selection of Thomas B. Reed of Maine, by a close vote. Reed was a curious and memorable figure in Congress, with his keen little eyes, his small, round, bald head, forever bobbing neckless over his fat, misshapen body. A giant in girth, crafty and iron-willed, he towered in mind as well as in body above his colleagues.

The Republican Party held the Presidency and a majority of both houses of Congress for the first time since 1875. But in the House of Representatives it held its majority by one vote, representing barely a quorum of 166. The death of one Republican Congressman early in the session placed the chair at a disadvantage for the conduct of business by removing the scant quorum and leaving him at the mercy of all manner of obstruction and filibustering. Owing to the partisan temper that prevailed, there was little likelihood of the transaction of any except the most formal business by the agreement of both sides. Meanwhile important legislative operations, upon which interested groups of capitalists counted heavily, must wait. But Speaker Reed had foreseen this, and carefully planned to meet the emergency. He was ready to overturn congressional precedent, by which there were preserved for long years the historic rights of the minority, in this case comprising 154 Democratic Congressmen. Should his own party, every man of which was now needed, fail to sustain his venture, Reed was ready to resign and retire.

On January 29, 1890, upon the raising of a question, only 163 members responded to the Speaker, the Democrats holding their tongues. The House then should have embarked upon a succession of fruitless roll calls in quest of a quorum—these sometimes running for eight days and nights. But now Speaker Reed suddenly gave the calm order: *"The Chair directs the clerk to record the names of the following members present and refusing to vote."* He thereupon began to call the names of enough Democrats to complete a quorum.

At once the House of Representatives exploded in a storm of verbal violence exceeding anything known in the Capitol since the eve of the Civil War. The Outs saw their ancient privilege to offer legal resistance as a minority party wrested from them. At moments certain hot-headed Southern Democrats advanced toward the Speaker as if to assault him physically, but Mr. Reed stood his ground, folded his arms over his chest, and stared them out of countenance. When, in a lull of the storm, one indignant member arose to deny the right of the Speaker to count him present, citing from the book of parliamentary law, Reed drawled deliberately: "The Chair is making a statement of fact that the gentleman from Kentucky is present. Does he deny it?" [28]

Amid the rioting and shouting that lasted for three days Reed reiterated tirelessly his thesis that the object of a parliamentary body was "action, and not stoppage of action." Beyond his judicial function the Speaker represented the will of the majority of the House, and where maneuvers pointing solely to delay could be recognized clearly, it was his duty to "take the proper course" in the interests of Congress, as of the community at large.

In the end, Reed had his ruling on the quorum question embodied in a House rule, and afterward sustained as constitutional by the Supreme Court (as well as by a subsequent Democratic Speaker). Thereafter the unruly lower chamber was held firmly in its strait jacket by "Czar" Reed's rule, as well as by limitation upon debate.

Congress was now reorganized in keeping with the times. Under the iron rule of Reed, who dragooned members taking their ease in the barbershop or cloakrooms of the Capitol in order to make up his quorums, the legislative machine rushed forward with the speed of one of Mr. Jim Hill's modern locomotives. The Fifty-first, or Billion Dollar, Congress, with an unheard-of expedition placed upon the statute books a whole series of economic decrees demanded by industrial monopolies, thousand-mile-long railways, and other friends of the ruling party.

IV

The Republican leaders in Congress now moved to perform their part of the bargain made with the industrial capitalists during the late successful campaign. Representative William McKinley, after failing to be elected Speaker, was appointed by Reed chairman of the Ways and Means Committee and entrusted with the management in Congress of the proposed tariff act. Upon him fell the mantle of old Pig-Iron Kelley, now in his last lingering illness. In the Senate Finance Committee Aldrich occupied himself even more thoroughly with the details of the new revenue bill. J. L. Hayes, the manager of the textile lobby, was ever at his side, a permanent occupant of a desk in Aldrich's committee room.

New concepts of taxation governed the lawmakers and the manufacturers' associations who appeared at lengthy hearings before McKinley's and Aldrich's committees during the winter of 1890. There must be "protection for the sake of protection." Wherever possible, rates upon imports were to be fixed not merely to offset the competition of cheap European labor, but to eliminate such competition. It was to be not only a protective tariff, but a *prohibitive* tariff; for in recent years the notion had been advanced—and by a Democratic leader, Randall—that if import duties were raised high enough, revenues would be cut off, and the problem of a government surplus would disappear: "No imports, no revenues."

The general plan was to raise an already high tariff scale by an ad valorem increase running from 4 per cent up; in addition raw sugar, which brought in heavy revenues to the Government, was to be made free of duty. Then "infant industries" were to be encouraged; and in one case, that of tin plate, long supplied from excellent cheap sources abroad, an industry as yet unborn in America was to be "guaranteed protection before he [the infant] was born." [29]

The McKinley Tariff Bill had aspects pleasing to silver-tongued political ideologues and to hard-fisted industrialists alike. First of all it was "American," it was patriotic: it encouraged domestic prosperity and the maintenance of an "American standard" of wages. McKinley, with his honest face and mellow voice, said in behalf of his bill in a closing speech, May 7, 1890:

I believe in it . . . because enveloped in it are my country's highest development and greatest prosperity; out of it come the greatest gains to the people, the greatest comforts to the masses, the widest encouragement for manly aspirations, with the largest rewards, dignifying and elevating our citizenship, upon which the safety and purity and permanency of our political system depend.[30]

In previous speeches McKinley had railed at the idea of having "cheap" goods. "Cheap" he had said "is not a word of hope; it is not a word of inspiration! It is the badge of poverty; it is the signal of distress." To the average American wage worker or farmer earning $2 a day or less such propositions were not only absurd but insulting. It was said of this sleek Congressman, who was the apostle of Ohio's heavy industry: "He had the art . . . of throwing a moral gloss over policies which were dubious, if not actually immoral, and this he did with a sort of self-deceiving sincerity." [31]

The principle of laying heavy import duties upon goods that had never yet been produced successfully here involved plainly more than "protection." It was equal to the award of great bounties or subsidies, charter rights, to monopoly, such as feudal monarchs gave to their favorites for the manufacture of a kingdom's salt or the exploitation of the Indies. Thus through Republican beneficence new Tin Plate Kings arose after the passage of the McKinley Act in 1890; and new overlords of kindred heavy industries in wire nails or structural shapes established monopolies in their markets by privilege and franchise of the commonwealth.

Here was a new form of political largesse which the party in power was free to dispose of, vaster than anything in the way of purse and patronage, government contracts, or lands given before. Moreover, this was done with an air of playing the patriot, of upholding the "American system" of wages and native enterprise. Mr. McKinley might well speak in impassioned tones of the benefits he sought for the American workers, but what he really had in his eye was the promotion of eighty-six new tin-plate mills, which were to cover the domestic market, and whose projectors were in constant touch with him, whose letters and prospectuses he cited before Congress as evidence of the industrial miracles to come.

"The Tariff is the mother of Trusts," said Mr. Havemeyer, a famous monopolist of the epoch. The belief that the Trusts were created by the tariffs was based upon the increased speculation in goods and securities of the new industrial combinations that followed new tariff acts, and the factor of mounting prices under concealed Trust control. In reality the protective tariffs were but a temporary instrument of capital, to be used and thrown aside when no longer serviceable. The underlying trend to concentration in nation-wide monopolies, arising from competition and the need for expansion of capital and profits, dominated capitalists everywhere, with or without benefit of tariffs—as in the case of Rockefeller's petroleum combination. The tariffs were stimulants, to be sure, during a cycle of expansion, encouraging price-raising and speculation, but insuring in no way against drastic deflations and subsequent cycles of falling prices. Yet most industrial capitalists, especially those who observed temporary gains from tinkering with the tariff, secretly shared Havemeyer's view. In any case, by their intervention from time to time in the political government's revenue program they felt that they were exercising a favorable control over their profit margins.

In the tariff act of 1890, the Republicans also extended the system of Protection to farmers, for the first time. Not only was a sufficient duty placed on raw wool, but also upon agricultural products, such as eggs, potatoes, bacon, and barley, very little of which was ever imported into our immense granary. "Let us cheerfully lend legislative assistance to the million farmers who own sheep in the United States," McKinley said. The "freeing" of raw sugar, on the other hand, was also held to be a move that would please farmers and small consumers, while reducing the surplus revenues. (It was also pretended that this measure would curb the power of Havemeyer's Sugar Trust, which by 1890 controlled most of the native refining.) Yet to appease the small number of Americans who then produced cane and beet sugar, a bounty of 2 cents per pound was then awarded them for their protection. In the adjustment of this clause, Aldrich from his Senate Committee saw to it that a duty of 1 cent per pound upon refined sugar was retained, arranging a *differential* (between price levels of raw and refined sugar) directly "playing into the hands of the Sugar Trust." [32] Thus one by one the different interest groups rushed forward to demand their share of an increment created through the Government's taxing power. During the logrolling orgy among these interested parties, as McKinley himself said, he and his colleagues accepted much higher increases in duties than were originally intended, "to get my bill passed." [33] Among the lobbyists, highest credit for the "management of the McKinley Tariff Bill" was given to the indefatigable and silent Nelson Aldrich.

Secretary of State Blaine was at this time deeply involved in his plans for inaugurating a system of reciprocity that would permit the penetration of Latin American markets by our industries. Counseled by the shipping magnate W. R. Grace of New York, Blaine fixed his eye upon the vast territories of South America, where 40,000,000 potential consumers of North American products were congregated. The Pan-American Congress, which he finally organized in the fall of 1889, was intended to bring about the mutual abatement of import duties, the South American wares being tropical goods, while ours were manufactured products, hence largely noncompetitive. But Blaine's enthusiastic schemes for expanding foreign trade to the south —plans that were not supported as yet by industrialists still occupied with a boundless domestic market—were doomed by the very nature of the McKinley Tariff Bill. The placing of raw sugar on the free list removed the chance to bargain with the Latin countries for reciprocal remissions of duties, and the new duties on hides were "a slap in the face to the South Americans with whom we are trying to enlarge our trade," as Blaine wrote to McKinley. Moreover, aware of the temper of the Mississippi Valley, and always a sensitive judge of "political quantities," Blaine himself now believed that the increased duties were in some cases excessive. He warned McKinley that the new tariff would

> benefit the farmer by adding 5 to 8 per cent to the price of his children's shoes. It will yield a profit to the butcher [Beef Trust] only—the last man that needs it. The movement is injudicious from beginning to end. . . . Such movements as this for protection will protect the Republican Party only into speedy retirement.[34]

Before the Finance Committee of the Senate Blaine exclaimed: "Pass this bill, and in 1892 there will not be a man in all the party so beggared as to accept your nomination for the Presidency."[35] With much justice he argued that to foster foreign trade with the tropical nations chiefly by keeping the power to bargain over sugar duties would increase the outlets of the American farmer, especially for breadstuffs, which those nations did not produce. There were numerous paragraphs in this bill, he prophesied, which while losing markets would also lose many votes.

The Senate, nevertheless, held its ground, unwilling to accord an unwonted treaty-making and economic bargaining power to the President. In the end, only a negative power to punish by increasing rates upon tea, coffee, sugar, molasses, and hides—rather than by negotiating favors—was incorporated in the McKinley Bill as a gesture toward reciprocity.

V

The men in the counting-rooms deal in ciphers, calculate precisely the effect of 5 cents per pound impost on one product, or 2 cents on another, and lay their precise demands before their political agents. But the politician is engaged in a human art, full of surprises and mysteries. While keenly desiring to respect the claims of business, he desires also to preserve his own political life. Hence an inward conflict or contradiction rages always in the breast of the politician. Having drawn up the daring McKinley Tariff Act, the politicians turned about and in fear and trembling enacted a series of compromise measures whose form they themselves could not have foretold, measures designed to "compass their election."

Reciprocity, a doctrine that aroused the interest of Western farmers, had been a "syrup" used by Blaine to sweeten the tariff medicine.

But this was scarcely enough. The veteran John Sherman had noticed from the beginning that a strategically placed group of Senators, including 17 Republicans and 1 Democrat, showed marked indifference to the pending tariff legislation. These were the men from the newly admitted territories of North Dakota, South Dakota, Montana, Washington, and from five other mountain States, rich in metal mines, and favoring the more liberal purchase and coinage of silver. They too demanded that Congress "do something" for their constituents, as the party platform itself had promised; and their claims could scarcely be ignored, since as a bloc they held "a very decided advantage in tariff legislation." [36]

The historic inflationary trend in the country, by which creditors and debtors were instinctively divided, was rising again by 1890. It assumed also the traditional form of a sectional conflict, the predominant lower middle classes west of the Mississippi, farmers, miners, and settlers, ranging themselves against the moneyed class, which presumably dominated the politics of the Eastern regions. Early in 1890, conventions were held in a score of Middle Western and Far Western cities which passed resolutions demanding new silver inflation. A great Silver Convention, secretly organized by mining-exchange interests, was held in St. Louis in the spring of 1890, and aroused the intense interest of farmers from Kansas and Nebraska, who had recently suffered from both drought and falling prices. This gathering also declared for the unrestricted coinage of silver. In the Senate the bloc of Western politicians now deliberately withheld their approval of the McKinley Tariff Act, while veteran party leaders grew frightened at the deadlock and the danger of losing the Western wing of the party.

Here was expressed a profound division of class-economic interest within the ruling party. The West, with its increasing output of raw materials, foodstuffs, and minerals, desired monetary inflation through silver coinage, the mining of which now reached enormous proportions and brought a long decline in the price of silver. Silver was but one product of the West, yet it became the symbol of all the varied mineral and agricultural goods—from copper and lead to beef on the hoof—whose value might gain in measure with the expansion of the currency. The East, on the other hand, desired the fixed gold standard gained by resumption in 1879 as the unwavering yardstick by which goods and securities were to be measured. Around the opposing symbols of silver and gold the creditor-debtor conflict, over-laid with a strong sectional hostility, expressed itself.

Do something for silver, the Western Republican Senators said in effect, and we will help you with your tariff. If relief were refused, they threatened to combine with the Democrats to enact a much dreaded "unlimited" silver-coinage act. It was not even certain that President Harrison, who had criticized Cleveland's Sound Money views, would risk his future to veto such an act.[87]

The conservative Connecticut Yankee Senator Orville Platt now gave warning that the party might be broken up, and the West and Southwest arrayed against the East. "We cannot afford that split," he declared in genuine alarm. In December, 1889, Secretary of the Treasury Windom, who hailed from Wisconsin, had proposed a makeshift silver-coinage bill of his own devising, providing for the issue of silver certificates against bullion; but no faction was satisfied. John Sherman, however, with his well-known talent for compromise, devoted himself to the task, and soon had a measure which conceded what he felt to be "a thoroughly bad principle in order to avoid the enactment of that principle in still more vicious form." [38]

Previously, by the terms of the Bland-Allison Silver Coinage Act of 1878, the Government had been purchasing and coining $2,000,000 of silver each month, conservative leaders holding this a necessary evil whose effects upon credit could be restrained. But now the silver men wanted all the national output of silver purchased and coined by the Treasury. Windom's bill had proposed coining each month $4,500,000 in silver bullion, at market value. But Sherman, evidently foreseeing the downward trend of silver in value, proposed instead the purchase of 4,500,000 *ounces* of silver per month, against which silver certificates or notes were to be issued, redeemable, however, "in gold or silver, at his [the Secretary of the Treasury's] discretion." The Sherman Silver Purchase Act, as it was called, like previous legislation drawn by this inveterate compromiser, was extremely obscure in its provisions, leaving to executive control the question of whether the country's money was to remain upon a gold or a silver basis.

The bill at any rate did not admit unlimited silver coinage, which was so greatly feared by Eastern finance capital. To reassure those who dreaded the depreciation of our currency, the act declared that it was the established policy of the Government to maintain the two metals, gold and silver, "at a parity"—although actually the ratio was constantly changing, the gold value of a silver dollar having fallen from 93 cents in March, 1889, to 72 cents in December, 1889. This clause was afterward interpreted by the Secretary of the Treasury as a "virtual promise that the notes shall always be redeemed in gold or its exact equivalent." [39] As the price of silver fell, the annual additions to the currency became even smaller than under the earlier Bland-Allison Act of 1878, and less actual inflation was involved. Here lay the supreme cleverness of Sherman, to whom is attributed the substitution of the word "ounces" for "dollars."

Yet disastrous consequences for the frail Republican politicians flowed from this hybrid measure. When it appeared as a queer bedfellow of the McKinley Tariff Act, it left the Western inflationists bitterly dissatisfied, while at the same time it aroused great concern and disappointment among the Eastern moneylenders, as involving for them a dangerous principle. Sherman himself admitted voting for the bill with disgust: "the day it became a law I was ready to repeal it, if repeal could be had without substituting in its place absolute free coinage," he said later.[40] As for President Harrison, who admitted that he did not understand it, he signed it largely because Sherman, Aldrich, and Windom assured him that he could safely do so.[41]

The pro-industrialist policy of the majority party lent impetus to the growth of larger manufacturing units and centralized control of whole industries. Between 1880 and 1890 the number of woolen mills diminished by one-third, and the number of steel and iron mills by the same proportion, while by 1890 annual output had advanced to a volume half again higher than in 1880. In the field of farm implements and shoe manufacture, as in meat-packing, large-scale production methods were introduced, ownership became concentrated in fewer hands, and new machinery displaced thousands of workers. On the Eastern seaboard seven coal-carrying railroads controlled nearly all the hard coal of the country. The Sugar Trust, of which the public was now keenly aware, was generally execrated, while the Standard Oil, as even a Congressman from Maine had recently avowed, represented "a power which makes itself felt in every inch of territory in this whole republic, a power which controls business, railroads, men and things." [42]

Now that a Chinese wall of tariff was to yield such favor to the industrial Trusts, it was repeatedly urged by the politicians of both parties that a bill seeking to curb or regulate monopolies should be passed at the same time. As one disingenuous Senator remarked, such a measure would serve as a "good preface to an argument upon the protective tariff."

Amid painful excitement over duties upon tin plate and glassware and the coinage of silver, Uncle John Sherman, by request, introduced an Anti-Trust Bill early in December, 1889. Such a law had been advocated in the platforms of both parties; it proposed, under the interstate-commerce clause of the Constitution, to punish Trusts which acted in restraint of trade, persons injured by such monopolistic combinations being permitted to recover three times the damage sustained.

As the bill was framed in committee and discussed (somewhat frivolously) in Congress, its language was rendered progressively awkward, verbose, and ambiguous. Certain humorists, such as Ingalls and Gorman, even attempted to introduce "jokers" prohibiting trade in options on produce exchanges—amendments which, as Sherman argued, were intended to bring the bill into contempt and by indirection into defeat. [43]

The curious provisions of the so-called Sherman Anti-Trust Act were this time not actually the work of the old compromiser, whose interest in the affair was due (according to rumor) to some special personal pique.* It was Hoar and Edmunds, working quietly in the

* He was believed to have sought vengeance against a certain industrial baron who had blocked his march to the White House in 1888. "John Sherman has fixed General Alger [the Match King]," Harrison is reported to have said when the bill was passed. (Gresham, *Life of Walter Q. Gresham*, Vol. II, p. 632.)

"mausoleum" of the Senate Judiciary Committee, who designed the characteristic provisions of this "legislative monstrosity." The bill "was totally reconstructed in the Judiciary Committee," Hoar related. "I do not think he [Sherman] ever understood it." [44] The important change made was that of giving to the Federal courts—and not to the Executive, through a commission—the jurisdiction to punish "contracts and combinations in restraint of commerce among the several States or with foreign nations." Collusion within State lines was exempted, a further loophole. Moreover, one provision attempting to define Trusts and combinations, written by Edmunds and Hoar, furnished, as it was said, "guide-boards for persons desiring to evade the law." [45] In after years these eminent lawyers and constitutionalists, Hoar and Edmunds, both pursued a most lucrative practice of advising combinations, pools, and Trusts exactly when their contractual arrangements were valid and would be upheld by the courts and when they contravened statutory prohibitions. [46]

The Sherman Anti-Trust Act was passed after three months of fantastic wrangling in both houses, July 2, 1890, barely in time to "go to the country" with it in an election campaign. Meanwhile the Trusts, which had used the device of delegated control for a whole industry vested in a board of trustees, dissolved quickly, and were soon reborn under "a new sign" and agreements more secret still. Henceforth they existed as *owning* corporations under licenses granted by complaisant State legislatures, such as those of New Jersey and Delaware. Out of a series of eight Trust cases tried in almost three years of Harrison's term, seven were lost by the Government before the Federal courts, while the eighth, although won by it, was so unsatisfactory and limited as a precedent as to be well-nigh futile. Moreover, for the majority of citizens the privilege of bringing suit at their own cost against giant corporations and their batteries of skilled lawyers in our Federal courts was at best an illusory form of relief.

Senator Cullom of Illinois, who had managed the passage of the Interstate Commerce Act, voted for the Anti-Trust Act, although he believed that "if it were strictly . . . enforced, the business of the country would come to a standstill." He adds: "It was never seriously enforced" for many years. [47]

During the debate in the Senate, the intelligent conservative Orville Platt of Connecticut made serious charges that the Anti-Trust Act had been carelessly drawn and hastily promoted:

> The conduct of the Senate . . . has not been in the line of the honest preparation of a bill to prohibit and punish trusts. It has been in the line of getting some bill with that title that we might go to the country with. The questions of whether the bill would be operative, of how it would operate . . . have been whistled down the wind in this Senate as idle talk, and the whole effort has been to get some bill headed: "A Bill to Punish Trusts" with which to go to the country.[48]

Through tortuous compromises and weird half-measures on other issues the Republican majority in the Billion Dollar Congress of 1889-91 moved steadfastly enough toward its object of doing away with the large government surplus which the thrifty Grover Cleveland had left. By readjusting the sugar duties, some $60,000,000 in revenue per annum was lost to the Government, a fair part of this remaining, however, to the American Sugar Refining Company. President Harrison, too, had promised that he would not be found ungenerously "weighing the claims of old soldiers with an apothecary's scales." This served to spur on to extravagance a Congress which needed no encouragement. Soon the pension allowances were greatly extended. Applications increased tenfold; the number of pensioners was doubled and reached almost 1,000,000, while expenditures under the head of pensions advanced from $88,000,000 in 1889 to $159,000,000 a year by 1893. President Harrison had finally appointed as head of the Pension Bureau the "loud-mouthed Grand Army stump-speaker" Corporal James Tanner, who upon taking office made the following pronunciamento:

> For twenty years I have been able to only plead, but now I am thankful that at these finger-tips there rests some power, and . . . I propose just as soon as possible to call in every one of the certificates of pension [33,871 at $3.75 per month] . . . no man ought to be down on the pension roll . . . for less than the miserable pittance of one dollar per week, though I may wring from the hearts of some the prayer, *"God help the surplus!"* [49]

To the cry of "The old flag and an appropriation!" the Fifty-first Congress enacted also a long series of public-works bills, acts for the improvement of rivers, harbors, coast defense, ships of war—and all that passes under the name of "pork-barrel" legislation, until the total sum of approximately $1,000,000,000 by various measures had been signed away, and the great Treasury surplus turned into a deficit. The unuttered doctrine that the Government was a "profit-sharing concern" was being carried to grotesque extremes under a Republican Administration, which sank every day in prestige.

V I

The industrial capitalists had taken the most aggressive part in the campaign of 1888, and seen to the reinstallation of a Republican regime in the three branches of the Government—for under Harrison interesting appointments to the Supreme Court bench were made. They had also established much more explicit and close relationships with the unofficial party government and its professional leadership. Yet the results, especially in a parliamentary sense, appeared most disappointing and full of melancholy surprises two years later. The controls had proved inadequate. Politicians were still an unpredictable element.

In democracies, bodies of popular deputies have often provided sensational disappointments to those whom they represent; and political philosophers have often raised the theoretical question of whether the assemblage of a group of deputies in a parliament or convention is an effectual representation of the general or sovereign will of a nation. Is not a parliament or a Congress rather the grouping of several hundred representatives of private interests, who, once elected, may prove as unfaithful to their paymasters as to their constituents?[50] Republican return to power, under the Protectionist banner, had brought a handsome increase of the tariff. But within a few months it was seen that the drop in revenues which was to follow enactment of the "prohibitive" McKinley bill had been grossly underestimated. The Billion Dollar Congress, with its uncontrollable appetite for pensions and "pork," for dredging channels, rivers, and harbors, had exhibited a colossal extravagance—while the President seemed to have exercised no leadership over it. Then to cap their blunders the politicians had, with abject motives of party gain—rather than of sound capitalist policy—enacted the new Silver Purchase Act, which to bankers and bondholders in the East was a legislative Frankenstein.

Although it was in itself neither fish nor fowl, and a "cowardly compromise," as financial leaders termed it, the Sherman Silver Purchase Act increased the demand liabilities of the Government and created a Treasury strain at once in 1890, as the first chill of a cyclical depression was felt. In September, 1890, the failure of the great Baring Brothers Bank in London, comparable to that of Jay Cooke in 1873, brought heavy liquidation by the English of their securities in American enterprises. Grain, cotton, and all commodity markets began to decline; manufacturing and employment slackened; and the favorable movement of gold to this country was reversed. John Sherman and his friends had been convinced that the increasing wealth and population of the country would absorb a little more silver, in the long run, without bringing inflation. But for the short term a squeeze developed—as the Treasury accumulated silver and followed its "discretionary" Sound Money policy of paying its obligations only in gold. The reserve dwindled steadily, until in 1892 there was on hand something less than the minimum gold reserve, traditionally considered to be $100,000,000.

Finance capitalists were outraged at the "lack of determined statesmanship" which had led to temporizing with inflation. They felt:

If the president, supported by senators and representatives from the East . . . opposed to the free coinage of silver without an international agreement, had fought the silver propositions at every step, it would have been impossible to pass the silver-purchase bill.[51]

The business class had given the politicians their orders in 1888 for favoring tariff legislation; but the all too human politicians had paid a price for new Protection that was out of reason. It was as if they said: Here is Protection, but we had to take much bad silver in order to get it.

Nor had the politicians of the majority party succeeded in their efforts to please all their friends. The reformers were vexed at the beginning of Harrison's term by his apparent yielding to spoilsmen like Quay and Clarkson and the "rolling of heads" in the Post Office Department, over which Wanamaker nominally presided. But soon, as elections approached, Mr. Harrison's intrinsic character showed itself as stubborn as Cleveland's. Though ready to appoint relatives and friends to pleasant offices, he would permit no stealing. As an administrator he was abler and more energetic than Cleveland in bringing about improvements in the government service, and a house-cleaning of revenue and customs offices. Here he ended by snubbing powerful bosses and party leaders. Hanna was refused the appointment of a lighthouse master at Cleveland. Sherman declared himself "weary and discouraged—weary from pressure based upon the opinion that I can do something for my friends, and discouraged because I have not been able to do anything." [52] Quay, at Harrison's wish, was driven from the Republican National Committee upon publication of facts concerning his earlier misappropriations of Pennsylvania State funds, while Tom Platt was wholly alienated. Blaine, having been given "the head of the table," as his wife felt, was permitted no further privileges whatsoever for that reason, and labored in the Cabinet under increasingly strained relations. [53] As a political leader, Benjamin Harrison, coldly following his own ambitions and scruples, forfeited the support of Republican chieftains in Congress and in the party Organization.

Meanwhile other, humbler friends whom the party leaders in Congress had tried to conciliate, especially the agrarian and frontier wing, became embittered over the mess of pottage which had been sold to them as a silver-coinage act. There had been a brief flurry of speculation in silver during the summer of 1890, when its ratio to gold rose to 19.76 to 1 (19.76 ounces of silver to 1 ounce of gold). But immediately thereafter came a continuous downward movement of silver, which by 1893 brought the ratio to 26.49 to 1. Silver production increased enormously, while gold, as if by a "conspiracy," became scarcer and dearer; and the disparity between the buying power of both metals became wider than ever before, the bullion in a silver dollar being worth less than 60 cents in 1893. The Sherman Silver Purchase Act, while unpleasing to the East, by its gross deceptions embittered the West, and gave edge to a sectional insurgence scarcely less passionate than that which preceded 1861.

McKinley, Reed, Blaine, and Harrison had pledged themselves in 1888 to the "sacred protection of American labor." Yet in July, 1889, following the Protectionist victory, the Carnegie Steel Company (which was protected by a tariff duty of $17 per ton for steel rails), at the order of Henry Frick suddenly locked out thousands of its workers at the Pittsburgh mills, quickly defeating a strike. Frick forced the labor union to accept a 20 per cent reduction and a sliding-scale system of wages. Even the conservative E. L. Godkin of the *Nation* now asked what "protection" was being given to mill workers.[54]

McKinley, the orator of Protection, had expressed much solicitude lest his fellow citizens turn into "cheap men" in a "cheap country." But the wives of his constituents acted as if they did not see eye to eye with him. For coal, blankets, carpets, tableware and kitchenware, women's and children's dresses, all became suddenly dearer; fresh fish paid 1 cent a pound duty now; every cabbage cost 3 cents more, the duties on oranges and lemons were trebled after July, 1890.[55] Even articles of tin plate, which received no tariff increase until the following year, were raised in advance, and workingmen were forced to pay higher prices for canned goods and tin buckets. "The women . . . heard in every store the clerks behind the counters explain how this article or that could not be sold hereafter at the former price because of the McKinley Bill." [56]

Never had there been such an uproar along the countryside. The gloomiest prophecies of farm leaders as to what would follow unbridled Protection were borne out in humble facts. The Democrats seized their opportunities, and in McKinley's own district sent tin-peddlers all about offering coffeepots at $1.50, and tin cups worth 5 cents at 25 cents or more.[57] While the great paymasters of parties looked on in troubled hesitation this autumn, political discussion waxed fierce in the kitchens and the people came forth to turn the Republicans out in a new Tidal Wave.

Great was the slaughter. Throughout the Northern States the majorities of Republican Ins were replaced by majorities of Democratic Outs. Traditionally Republican provinces such as Ohio, Michigan, Illinois, Wisconsin, Kansas, and even Massachusetts sent mostly Democrats to the House of Representatives, which for the new session of 1891 held 235 Democrats and 9 outright Populists against only 88 Republicans, the smallest contingent since the Civil War. Besides, nearly 40 of the Democrats were Farmers' Alliance men, that is, owed their election to the intervention of the immensely strengthened farm organizations in the West.

The Senate was Republican, though by the sharply reduced majority of 8. But a score of the Republican Senators were Free Silver men from the new frontier States; two Populist Senators, the Reverend James Kyle of North Dakota and William Peffer of Kansas, also graced the upper chamber of Congress. It was symptomatic that the veteran Ingalls, who had jested too long concerning his political principles, was flung out at last by the people of Kansas, while Peffer, fierce-looking, black-bearded editor of a farm journal, took his seat.

What was most alarming behind the statistics which told the story of the 1890 upheaval was the evidence that not only the Republican Party was losing in its old strongholds, but also that both of the historic political corporations appeared to face a menace of a new kind. The sundering of old "institutional" bonds under the shock of new sectional and class-interest forces was audible above the uproar. That which the canny conservatives, such as Platt of Connecticut, had most feared, that which all the art of compromise and the party system itself was called upon to resist, had come to pass: the break between East and West, between men who lived from industry and men who lived from agriculture, between the City and the Land.

Between 1890 and 1896 the American people were as implacably divided by the Mississippi River as they had been divided in 1860 by Mason and Dixon's line.

After 1890, a crevasse was opened in the American party system. To the professional politicians and their business allies it was a widening abyss, at which they stared in terror and into which their whole structure of privilege and convenience, all the comfortable and profitable habits, devices, connections, built by long years of work, might at any instant roll down all together. The mixture of brazen extravagance and wretched compromise which had passed for policy under the ruling Republican Administration had but pressed their whole system nearer to its final catastrophe.

But social earthquakes, though arriving suddenly, are natural phenomena which prepare themselves, not invisibly, over a period of time. We must glance back for an interval if we would know something of the sequence of conditions and movements which preceded the uprising of the 1890's.

CHAPTER THIRTEEN

THE NEW JACOBINS

In God we trusted, in Kansas we busted!
SLOGAN OF PIONEERS

IN the last third of the nineteenth century the most spectacular development in United States history was the progressive, continuous opening and exploitation of the new frontier lands west of the Mississippi and north of the Missouri. Between 1860 and 1900 the prairies of the "Middle Border"—comprising western Kansas, western Nebraska, Minnesota, the Dakotas, and the mountainous States beyond them—were rapidly settled. With more than 400,000,000 acres opened to the plow, the domain of the American farmer was doubled, and the harvest of his crops increased proportionately as well as absolutely. In this era the main wheat-growing region of the country moved west of the Mississippi River, and the center of population, as Western politicians delighted to point out, shifted beyond the Appalachians toward points of the Middle West.

The complexion of America was changed; it no longer bore the stamp of the original thirteen Atlantic States and their dozen or two of cousin States or offspring colonies beyond the seaboard. It was a continental nation, whose characteristic traits would be the sweep and distances of its central plain. American wheat, the chief product of the States beyond the Mississippi River, now flowed in a groaning torrent through the new central port of Chicago out to the seven seas. The development of the Mississippi Valley assumed the proportions of a world event, equivalent to that of the Nile Valley in ancient times. The abundance and cheapness of foodstuffs contributed to the increase of European population and permitted the diversion of this population as a standing army of labor, hastening the Industrial Revolution in the Old World and bringing in turn masses of landless immigrants to America.

Outwardly an air of cheerful industry filled the new grain regions, as railroads pushed into newly built towns, and profitable machine farming of single crops increased harvests anew—until by 1900 American farm exports reached the value of about $700,000,000. Yet, picturesque and successful as the material growth of the hinterland appeared, its whole development was attended with tremendous reverses and hardships.

After the "boom" of 1879-80, eastern Europe, South America, and even the Orient increased their production of wheat; tariffs were raised against the American crop; prices underwent a sustained downward movement in world markets, wheat falling from an average level of more than $1 per bushel in the decade following the war to an average which approached 70 cents in the 1890's. In the great Southern crop of cotton, too, there was a picture of production doubled and prices halved during the forty years following the Civil War. Under such conditions the farmers who lived in the East or the older sections of the Middle West, raising varied rather than single crops, near large cities and enjoying cheap transportation, flourished tolerably well, while the lot of the Western and Southern farmers, despite their abundant harvests, was plainly worsened.

The settlement of the more arid regions, formerly known as the Great American Desert, had been hurried and wasteful. In western Kansas and north of the Missouri River, a fearful winter befell the settlers in 1886; then a crop failure, drought, grasshoppers, came in succeeding years. Thousands of the ruined frontiersmen returned from the western rim of the Middle Border, or recrossed the Missouri into Iowa, leaving whole towns with new opera houses, schools, and churches to bleach in the desert sands. Their covered wagons bore the legend:

IN GOD WE TRUSTED,
IN KANSAS WE BUSTED [1]

The American farmers produced and sold their goods in an unprotected, a free, world market; they purchased railroad service, clothing, farm machinery, and household articles in a closed, a "protected," even a monopolized, market. Capital they borrowed at painfully usurious rates from the agents of Eastern banking and insurance institutions. During good times loans were pressed upon the settlers at from 8 to 12 per cent interest, often at 30 to 40 per cent by devices of indirection. But in hard times the moneylender curtailed his credit cruelly, while land and houses fell under the hammer of the auctioneer.

The instability, the hazardousness, of agricultural undertakings at the frontier became notorious. An "act of God," a season of plague, was enough to send the settlers wandering again in search of new lands, which nowadays grew scarcer. Those who hung on, at subsistence level, in the central portion of the Western grain States, contending with the evil of dwindling crops and falling prices, were filled with a bitterness and gloom which seems to rise from the vast, lonely plains themselves and which is caught in memoirs such as Ed Howe's and Hamlin Garland's. They strove to make two blades of grass grow where one had grown before, but at the end they found that in the terms of debts or mortgages or railway services, the two blades begot no more than one. As one of their spokesmen said:

> We went to work and plowed and planted; the rains fell, the sun shone, nature smiled, and we raised the big crop that they told us to; and what came of it? Eight cent corn, ten cent oats, two cent beef and no price at all for butter and eggs—that's what came of it. Then the politicians said that we suffered from overproduction.[2]

The first efforts of the Federal Government to regulate railroad combinations brought little relief to the remoter farm sections, suffering from heavy rates between interior points and railroad terminals, rates which often equaled the total wholesale value of the wheat being shipped. The farmers, moreover, were keenly aware of collusion between the railroads and the middlemen who operated warehouses and grain elevators. They were compelled not only to sell through the railroad-owned warehouse and elevator companies, but were forced to endure unfair trade practices by which high-grade wheat often received the valuation of lower-grade wheats at the elevators. And when in years of money scarcity, stemming from Eastern or European money centers, credit for crops was unobtainable on any terms, then the iron circle of the conspiracy of expropriation, to the mind of the Western agrarian, seemed complete.

Most Western farmers who reflected upon their misfortunes came to believe that the root of the "conspiracy" which ruined and ex-

propriated the small producer lay in the private control of money
and credit by capitalists in the financial centers of the Eastern States
and in Europe. Jeremiah ("Sockless Jerry") Simpson, who became
Governor of Kansas, had in his youth been an industrious pioneer
farmer in the Middle West. He had worked hard, prospered for a
time, then saw all his land and goods lost to creditors and mortgagors in a year of panic. Then Simpson had turned perforce to the
practice of law and politics. Throughout the farm country, whether
of corn or of cotton, the experience was the same. From the uplands
of South Carolina there came also the "poor-white" leader Ben Tillman, who told how for years after the Reconstruction period he had
operated a successful farm, made money, bought more land, mules,
guano. In 1881 he had thirty plows, and as he related, the devil
tempted him to buy a steam engine and other machinery amounting
to $2,000, all on credit. There followed a season of drought and
crop failure; he had "sickening prices" to pay nevertheless to merchants and bankers. All was lost at one stroke. Then Ben Tillman
sought new light on the science of agriculture, and attempted to
start anew; but nothing availed. In the end he too had entered
politics; a stout, combative, and vituperative fellow, he devoted himself to overthrowing the old Bourbon Democratic machine and building, as he said, a state in the name of farmers.

The summer and harvest season of 1890 brought a remarkable
illustration of the "international conspiracy" of the capitalists against
the American yeoman of the West. Following a mild winter, there
was fine growing weather throughout the year, and a bumper crop of
grain was harvested and exported to Europe, which was experiencing
shortage again. But once more money was scarce and dear, owing to
the failure of the London banking house of Baring Brothers. Wheat
sank to low levels at a moment when, owing to the McKinley Tariff
just enacted, the industrial Trusts made sharp increases in the price
of wire, clothing, machinery, twine, and shoes which the farmer
must buy. The sturdy, self-reliant American settler, whom our folklore had so long exalted as "the bone and sinew of the nation,"
suffered from good crops and Hard Times; he endured poverty in
the midst of plenty. In comparison with the oppressed peasants of
Europe, the American farmer lived well, and was intrinsically strong

and free. But he felt that he was bearing the brunt of the cost of the expansion of industry and the accumulation of capital; he sensed that there was something fundamentally wrong in the political economy under which he lived.

In truth, agriculture at the frontier performed for the Eastern manufacturing States, under the Republican protective tariff, the function of colonialism for European nations, providing cheap raw materials and foodstuffs in exchange for finished articles, and furnishing capital profits enough for a magnificent expansion of industrial and financial institutions.[3] The frontier had produced an independent "peasant proprietor," who lived and worked as a small individual producer and escaped for a time the wage system which capital in its growth everywhere imposes. Thus had arisen in the earlier republic of American memories and ideals a society marked by an amazingly high degree of true democracy and equality. But the spread of large-scale production causes the land to be exploited more rapidly, introduces machine agriculture, and exhausts the land. After the Civil War large-scale capitalism, with its system of division of labor, had gained a new, unobstructed footing, and expanded with the greatest speed. Free land or cheap land dwindled, or was squandered shamelessly, or was appropriated by speculative land companies and railroads; until by 1893, as Frederick J. Turner noted, the "frontier" was gone. Immigration continues unchecked, but the newcomers find less and less free or cheap land where they can live as their own masters, that is, as individual producers; instead they form a standing army of labor in the cities. "No longer is the great republic the promised land for emigrants," as Marx comments, nor for pioneers and settlers. Thus capitalism completes the process which involves, in Marx's words, "the necessary annihilation . . . of self-earned private property."

How the efforts of the masters of capital here with iron determination pressed toward this end was shown in more than one unguarded admission or allusion. When in the autumn of 1890 the misfortunes of the agriculturists and their protests were being heard everywhere in the country, William Walter Phelps, an Eastern Republican leader, who was not only a member of his party's Inner

Circle but an outstanding capitalist in his own right, said publicly at New York:

The export of agricultural products must find a limited and failing market; the export of manufactured articles must find an increasing and permanent market. The lowest grade of labor can raise corn and wheat and pork. It does not require the intelligence and skill and invention in which American labor surpasses the world. *Ultimately, then, we must lose these markets for our wheat, but not for our wares.*[4]

What Phelps, who was one of the best informed of the Republican spokesmen, was implying with such candor was that the whole fiscal and taxation policy of the Government must be directed to furthering the growth of capitalist production, while accepting a relative decline for agriculture, a kind of doom for the independent farmer, to whom Phelps refers in terms of unconcealed contempt. He was implying that the chief function for American farming, under a policy which frankly fostered the expansion of large-scale capitalism, was to provide cheap food for American industry.*

The truths which the Congressman and foreign diplomat Phelps revealed by 1890 were terribly clear to the farm leaders of the West. These, who were still the carriers of Jacksonian Democratic ideals befitting their independent and individualistic middle-class way of life, saw, after long hesitations and misgivings, "an altered nation and changed ideals." They saw, as Turner says, "the sharp contrast between the traditional idea of America, as the land of opportunity, the land of the self-made man, free from class distinctions and from the power of wealth, and the existing America, so unlike the earlier ideal."[5] They saw capital, industries, railroads, banks, and labor itself consolidating into great combinations whose force burst over State lines and threatened to control all the processes of economic life. At last, in deep alarm, they were led to turn against their own pioneer and libertarian doctrines of government, which had nourished so well the dragons who were devouring them. Many strange new voices

---

* Many years of residence as a neighbor of small farmers has convinced me that the raising of corn, wheat, and pork requires a highly skilled, resourceful, intelligent labor, as well as a fund of strong character. Yet the false notions of capitalists such as Phelps have continued to be disseminated and form the basis for the enduring injustice which has been done to our farming class.

among them demanded, for their very existence, the extension of the power of the National Government rather than its restraint. The National Government, they said, must now invoke its power to regulate the railway net effectively, to curb monopolies, to extend credit to small producers, to establish postal savings banks, to own the telegraph system, to control currency, to fix income taxes upon the rich, to reclaim lands monopolized by railroads and land companies. In short, the National Government must use its supreme power to halt the sweep of capitalist centralization which took from the farmers the lion's share of their harvests.

The breach with the tradition of Federal limitation, woven long ago into the constitutions of the thirteen States, was an easy one for the men of the frontier and the Middle Border to effect. Their view as recent settlers had always been a national one rather than one bound by the narrow borders of the old Eastern States. They had fought with an impassioned nationalism under Lincoln for the defense of the Union. From the National Government in turn they had won free land and homesteads. Now by an easy logical transition they sought to "free" money, they sought to "nationalize money," as the old Greenback leader James Weaver phrased it, in order to remove it from the control of a few domestic and foreign bankers.

II

The obsession with monetary inflation dominated all the farm movements, and indeed the mass movements generally, of a country which had always faced inexhaustible resources, but which up to the twentieth century lacked the gold and capital to exploit them. There were many discordant voices among the militant farmers of the 1880's and 1890's. The single-tax ideas of Henry George, who would by taxation take all land from railroads and speculators and place it in cultivation, that is, in use, seemed to attack the ground-rent evil at its root and won thousand of supporters after 1881. Like George's *Progress and Poverty*, Bellamy's *Looking Backward* in 1888 gained converts by the thousands, who formed Bellamy Clubs, or Utopian and Nationalist groups.

Some factions then urged the development of co-operatives, both for purchasing supplies and for marketing; others proposed strongly a "subtreasury scheme" which would cause government warehouse credits to be issued against stored grains and cotton. Yet the prevailing and extremely simple doctrine, to which the leaders of the principal farmers' organizations always returned, was that "fair prices" must somehow be won all around for the tillers of the soil, and that the one means to this was by money inflation.

With the resumption of specie payment after 1879 the thought and discussion of the Western farmer almost invariably centered upon the monetary problem. In terms of the value of his produce money had indisputably become "dearer." To repay a debt of $1,000 upon his land, contracted some years before, he must raise not 1,000 bushels of wheat or 10,000 pounds of cotton, but 1,500 bushels of wheat or 15,000 pounds of cotton, or even more. Remembering the demonetization of silver in 1873, he could not put out of mind the notion of a "conspiracy" of all the creditor and bondholding classes against the tillers of the soil. This had been the battle cry of the Grange, and of the Greenback Party, which mustered 1,000,000 votes in 1878; it was the leitmotiv of the new semi-secret, fraternal National Farmers' Alliance of the 1880's which, succeeding the Grange, was soon led by events to work for the creation of a new nation-wide political party of farmers and small producers.*

After the discovery of the Comstock Lode, which caused an immense outpouring of silver, the miners of silver, copper, and other metals from the mountain States joined in the agitation for free coinage which might bring to them also a "fair price." The mining interests were as one with the Farmers' Alliance spokesmen in agitating against a presumed conspiracy of the "Great Money Power" of Europe and of the Eastern financial centers in America against the producers of the Great West. The political vehicle of the third party was ready to hand, in the form of the Greenback and Anti-Monopolist

---

* Economic conditions strongly favored political upheaval in 1890. For example: "In Kansas 60 per cent of the taxed acreage, in 1890, was under mortgage; in Nebraska, 55 per cent; in Iowa, 47 per cent. . . . The average annual value of the corn crop during the years 1885-1889 was $70,000,000 less than that in the preceding five years. . . . On wheat land the acreage value of the yield fell from $11.10 to $8.83," or some 20 per cent. (Dewey, *National Problems*, pp. 233-34.) The agriculturists thus felt a very marked "increase" in the value of money and in their debt burden.

Organization, which had been for long years a permanent fixture of politics in the Western tier of States.

The farm organizations and lodges, which were essentially educational and fraternal movements and only secondarily political, had occasionally worked with the existing parties, usually in the North with the glorious and patriotic Republican Party, to which most of the Middle Border was loyal. As one account of the period runs:

They elected lawyers and other professional men to represent them. . . . They appealed to their party leaders. They sought to interest the press in their behalf. They brought their case before the courts . . . before the bar of public opinion.[6]

Yet they had met with deception and disappointment. Then they determined through one or the other of the established political guilds to elect their own people, dirt farmers, to the legislatures or to Congress. But:

If the farmer went to the capital fresh from the plow, among a crowd of lobbyists, he was as clay in the hands of the potter. If his constituents kept him there year after year, until he learned the ways of legislation, then he ceased to be a farmer and became a member of some other class, perhaps a stockholder in a great railroad, or manufacturing corporation, with interests in common with the opponents of agricultural classes.[7]

By 1890 the masses of the Farmers' Alliance had lost all hope or patience with the bosses and "ringmasters" of both old parties; and at last, in the spring of that year there went forth the call by various minority or third-party leaders, powerfully supported by the Alliance men, to a national convention at Topeka, Kansas, for the purpose of organizing a People's Party.

The response to the call was tremendously enthusiastic. State after State along the Middle Border of the Great West held rousing "Independent" conventions to instruct delegates for the People's Party. Leaders too arose and flocked to the agrarian cause, men and women who had been scornfully called in the East "wild jackasses" *

---

* This epithet was based upon a legend of the wild burros of the South American pampas, who, threatened by enemies, always formed a circle with their heads together at the center and defended themselves by kicking out with their hind legs. (Bryan, *First Battle*, p. 456.)

or "calamity howlers" or "political rainmakers" as they lectured up and down the land. These became the inspired, invincible organizers of regional victories over political machines.

The gathering at Topeka in 1890 was less a political convention, as a native historian has related, than "a religious revival, a pentecost of politics in which a tongue of flame sat upon every man, and each spake as the spirit gave him utterance." Such unbridled passion, such free rein to honest indignation, in itself suggested a striking departure from long-established American party traditions. From puritan Kansas, which seemed now to play the role of Massachusetts in an earlier revolution, there came two statesmen, Jeremiah Simpson and William A. Peffer, men of long chin whiskers, broad-brimmed hats, and heavy boots, but strong and devout in their agrarian rebellion, and mighty orators on the subject of railroad monopolies and Goldbugs. From Minnesota came Ignatius Donnelly, benign of face and with a silvery beard. Twenty years before he had served as a lobbyist for Jay Cooke's Northern Pacific, but today he was the "Sage of Nininger, Minnesota," known everywhere as the transported philosopher of silver inflation and the torrential orator of the new Populism. As of old, General Weaver, the incorruptible Iowa radical, was in the forefront of the movement. But in addition there were the fanatical temperance crusaders, who lent a special tone to the proceedings, Kansas women "with skin tanned to parchment by the hot winds, with bony hands of toil, and clad in faded calico," who could talk as well and even straighter to the point than the men.[8]

Of the latter Mrs. Mary Ellen Lease became deservedly famous as a political apparition. She was actually a woman of parts; the mother of four children, she had become a member of the bar and a successful public lecturer as well. In appearance she was handsome and distinguished, though the Eastern public would not believe this when they heard of her immortal epigram: "What you farmers need to do is to raise less corn and more *Hell!*" Mrs. Lease's line of attack was simple and direct and took the convention by storm:

Wall Street owns the country. It is no longer a government of the people, by the people and for the people, but a government of Wall Street, by Wall Street and for Wall Street. The great common people of this country are slaves, and monopoly is the master. The West and South are bound and prostrate before the manufacturing East. Money rules, and our Vice-President is a London banker. Our laws are the output of a system which clothes rascals in robes and honesty in rags. The parties lie to us and the political speakers mislead us . . . the politicians said we suffered from overproduction. Overproduction when 10,000 little children, so statistics tell us, starve to death every year in the United States, and over 100,000 shop-girls in New York are forced to sell their virtue for the bread their niggardly wages deny them!

Mrs. Lease, like a true daughter of Kansas, made moral earnestness her battle-ax. She paused for breath while the crowd gave thunderous encouragement; then continued:

There are thirty men in the United States whose aggregate wealth is over one and one-half billion dollars. There are half a million looking for work. . . . We want money, land and transportation. We want the abolition of the National Banks, and we want the power to make loans direct from the government. We want the accursed foreclosure system wiped out. . . . We will stand by our homes and stay by our firesides by force if necessary, and we will not pay our debts to the loan-shark companies until the Government pays its debts to us. The people are at bay, let the bloodhounds of money who have dogged us thus far beware.[9]

The agrarian revolt rose to its crest in the years when the area of free land was disappearing; its storms raged from 1890 to 1896 at the heart of the last interior frontier of new lands, the so-called Middle Border. The "significance of the frontier" in our history, beyond that which Turner has given to it, lies in the space it allowed and the "period of grace" it afforded against the inevitably closing iron circle of capitalist concentration and the wage system. For long periods men had been able to escape from Europe or the clogged cities of the Eastern seaboard to free or cheap land, to individual ownership of as much of the means of production as a man could personally manage. Such was the grace, such the climate of liberty, the incalculable boon which America certainly offered for generations, until the settlers reached the parched zone of the Great American Desert. At this moment also the industrial revolution had overtaken the land movement, and encompassed virtually the whole continent with its railroad net and its industrial-financial institutions. It was now that the people of the West changed their ideas and

urged limitation of the economic freedom which, they formerly believed, was sufficient in itself to realize the economic equality of a society of small producers. Where formerly they demanded the abolition of all political restrictions and privileges, they now wanted them restored in the interest of the independent small producers.[10]

The Free Soil farmers of the Mississippi Valley, in the name of human liberty and progress, had formerly joined with the Northern capitalists to crush Southern landholders and save the Union. But it was the Northern capitalists who had won the lion's share; it was their policies which had triumphed. Now the Western farmers, in revolt against the selfsame interest group which they had helped to raise to power, were ready even to join with the South, abolishing sectional lines, to overthrow the class which threatened their small properties and enterprises. As the Populist leader Senator Allen of Nebraska said, the old political parties had been "divided on Mason and Dixon's line." Northern people were always told that their Southern brethren sought power to destroy the Union, and

while we were following the banner of the Republican party on the one hand, and of Bourbon Democracy on the other, the gold power of the world, represented by its agents in the United States, was fastening the chains of an industrial slavery on the people so firmly that it will take a generation to strike them off.[11]

But the democracy of the Middle Border envisaged no fundamental change of the social system itself. It was imprisoned "within the circle of capitalist relations," made up as it was of small producers, or petits bourgeois. These pretended that men might somehow be held to a commerce and a capitalist production of small size, although the law of profit and the market which determines capitalist relations led always to larger ventures, larger accumulations, and the elimination of small enterprisers. They were divided in views except upon the object of money inflation, which was expected to redress the balance of prices for them. They were hostile instinctively to the labor movement, which after 1886 was believed to be "tainted" with anarchism; and they looked with disfavor upon the current agitation for the eight-hour day; while for their part the leaders of organized labor, such as Samuel Gompers, warned their followers to keep free of entanglements with the "employing farmers" and seek wages in solid money. Henry Demarest Lloyd, the Chicago idealist who advocated now a broad alliance of farmers and laborers, which would bring about "the repossession by the people of the property of the people," was doomed to early and repeated disappointments. The "Alliance ideas" in politics were most limited, as one of the most progressive of the farmers' leaders, Representative John Lind of Minnesota, now observed, and would be found wanting if put to the test of administration. Lind felt that "the gist of the farmer's complaint was not that he was poor or suffering but that others who labored and deserved less received the greater share of the profit on his products." [12]

As one of them said jestingly, what was wanted above all was *"a debt-paying system of finance."* The money question overshadowed railroads, monopolies, tariffs, in their minds. "The money question must be kept to the front," as the chairman of the party, Taubeneck, contended, and leaders like Weaver and Donnelly agreed that it must be the "great central idea" to which the others were tributary.

The menace of the Populists lay, then, not so much in their doctrines as in the determination which they showed to dispense with both of the two national political corporations—which had too long pretended to satisfy all factions and classes—and to build a separate class party of their own. It would be not a proletarian party, but one akin to the Jacobins, a party of small proprietors and petits bourgeois. But it would lead to the disarrangement, perhaps the destruction, of the long-existing, highly formalized party institution, with all its nice mechanisms for the outward alternation of power by an interior cabal. It would establish, as in Europe, the pattern of the class interest or "belief" party in a republic which had contented itself with professional patronage parties.*

* Owing to the inner contradictions of their position, being themselves capitalists, yet the most exploited or doomed section of the capitalist class, the petite bourgeoisie have often formed the vanguard of the parties of progress.

All the slogans or campaign songs of the Populist movement between 1890 and 1894 stress this rebellion against the old professional parties and the crying need for a truly independent political organization. The Populists, former Democrats or Republicans, sang "Good-Bye, My Party, Good-Bye!" Or, to the tune of "The Girl I Left Behind Me," they sang of "the party left behind me." To the tune of "Save a Poor Sinner like Me" they sang of how "The railroads and old party bosses together did sweetly agree" to deceive "hayseeds like me." [13]

The enthusiasm, the energy, engendered at Topeka had borne fruit in the Tidal Wave of 1890, which rudely overwhelmed the Republican officeholders throughout the country. The Populists, especially in the Middle Border, after throwing up hastily their district and State Organizations, disputed with the veteran Democrats on even terms the gains from Republican failure, capturing virtual control of five States. In the South, where the Southern Alliance men ran as Independent Democrats, Ben Tillman arose as Governor of South Carolina, farmers' partisans headed the governments of Georgia, Tennessee, and Texas. In Kansas the People's Party won an overwhelming majority of the State legislature as well as the Governorship. Fantastic reports and fears of the insurrection of agrarian "anarchists" spread through the East, whose feeling was summed up by Godkin of the *Nation*, when he wrote: "We do not want any more States until we can civilize Kansas." [14]

I I I

While the "Silver whirlwind" of the 1890's spread destruction west of the Mississippi and fear mounted among the moneylenders, the existing Republican regime gave a lamentable display of weakness. In its short or Lame Duck session the discredited Fifty-first Congress in 1891 seemed to have got entirely out of hand. A faction in the Senate led by the vacillating Sherman made an abortive attempt to repeal the compromise Silver Purchase Act of 1890. But in the House, working at cross purposes, the same majority of Republicans who had voted reactionary measures in perfect discipline a year before now came close to passing a free-coinage bill, the resistance of the iron-willed Speaker, Reed, staving this off at the last hour. The rank-and-file politicians in Congress seemed unnerved by the uproar among their constituents.

When the new Congress convened, the lower chamber was Democratic by an overwhelming and unruly majority, which in itself was divided over the silver issue, while the Senate was still Republican. Legislation was blocked by partisan maneuvers, the Democrats contenting themselves with "popgun" measures aimed to discredit the Republican Administration, which were usually vetoed in the Senate.

Nor did the ruling President count for much as a leader of his party Organization. Following the congressional defeat of 1890, Harrison veered to reform policies in appointments and in the administration of the civil service. The "headsman" Clarkson retired from his minor cabinet post in the Post Office Department and by 1891 the classified list of officials under the merit system was increased some 20 per cent, to the number of 34,000. Defeated for re-election in the following November, by March, 1893, Harrison brought the number of Federal officials under the classified civil-service list to 42,000 before he retired.

Harrison, with his austere temper, was not made to please the more fleshly professional chieftains. Former President Hayes, in his diary, quotes a Chicago judge describing him as a typical Presbyterian deacon: "stiff, cold, distant. They are the elect of God—by faith, not works, to be saved." [15] The disposition to arbitrate independently and coldly between opposing wings and interest groups, to administer the government service with probity, to accept in the spirit of true conservatism even the responsibility of conciliating or pacifying the people—as shown by Harrison's leaning to inflation—all this, combined with an unfortunate piety of manner, led to disaster as far as party harmony was concerned. Boss Quay broke publicly with Postmaster General Wanamaker, who yielded always to Harrison's wishes, and announced himself disgusted with "Sunday-school politics"; he formed, together with Platt, an anti-Harrison wing.

The "foot soldiers" of party politics were wont to sing soft complaints of the puritan spirit of President Harrison, who was often pictured as a devotee of family life and a doting grandfather, with Baby McKee in his arms. Wanamaker, who sacrificed his leisure to

religious movements such as the Y.M.C.A., and Vice-President Levi
Morton, who, though a devout Yankee, owned the profitable Shore-
ham Hotel in Washington, a convivial rendezvous for politicians,
also troubled the political minds. In a ditty which Elihu Root recalled, they sang:

> The baby runs the White House,
> Levi runs the bar,
> Wanny runs the Sunday school
> And dammit here we are![16]

Here they were—and it would have been merely funny if the
disturbance of the party machinery had not led to a sort of prostration of the Government itself. A decade of Good Government and
middle-class bureaucratic reform had elapsed since Garfield's death,
and left little more than popular discontent and damaged political
reputations.

The theory has been advanced recently that though a stanch conservative, Harrison was independent-minded enough to attempt a
respectable middle course; at this, not only the spoils politicians, but
the more predatory capitalist groups, who exerted always secret pressure to command avenues of information, influence, or privilege,
fought him. Blaine found himself unable to meddle in other departments of the Government than his own; very ill in his last years, he
seemed to know little of what was happening within the cabinet
council, and was sometimes even rudely opposed in the affairs of the
State Department.[17] Financial New York was at sea, especially with
regard to the Treasury policy, upon which the preservation of the
gold standard hung, and mistrusted the President. One by one the
great party chieftains turned their guns upon him.

The procedure of punishment that follows, as a veteran political
journalist explains, is almost invisible:

No threats are made, no open opposition shown, but the President suddenly discovers that the wheels are not turning. . . . Nominees are not
confirmed . . . departments don't function, strange rumors seep into
official gossip. There is an inertia that he cannot overcome, and for which
no definite reason can be given. It creeps over everything like an incoming
tide.[18]

Reports of conflict between the President and his Secretary of State were also heard. During a prolonged illness of Blaine Harrison himself carried on the work of the State Department, and took occasion to inject his own bellicose notes into certain petty foreign incidents, such as the discreditable dispute with Chile and the adventure in Hawaiian annexation which was now set on foot. Harrison complained aloud that he was forced at times to carry Blaine's "knapsack," but was repaid with little gratitude from the great party leader.[19] On the other hand, Mrs. Blaine's vivacious letters show an animus against the "oracle of the White House" which is unmistakable. His suspicion, his deliberate efforts to restrict Blaine's influence, were hotly resented; the muffled quarrel became a public contest when Blaine resigned his office three days before the opening of the Republican nominating convention, June 4, 1892. It marked the climax of Republican internal dissension.

The spoils element and the businessmen as well were looking to Blaine once more, as Boss Clarkson said, to foster prosperity, and to his famous magnetism and popularity to check the Populists in the West.[20] Yet, whether Blaine or Harrison was nominated, the prospects for the disorganized Republicans were poor indeed this year.

While the Government was afflicted with dissension and inertia, the country experienced a severe financial squeeze. The drain of gold in the first six months of 1891 had been offset temporarily by the marketing of a bumper crop in the autumn; but in 1892 the adverse trade movement was renewed; by May the Treasury's gold surplus, which had approached $200,000,000 under Hayes, had declined to $114,000,000. The British pound sterling rose appreciably; secret gold-hoarding by banks increased, and this sharpened the pinch. It was well known in banking circles in 1892 that only fear of political disaster restrained the Harrison Administration from making new government loans in order to build up the gold reserves.[21]

The circle of embarrassment was now complete. By the summer of 1892 the Treasury "practically abandoned" further gold payments to the New York clearinghouse banks against government notes presented to it for redemption. That is, the Secretary of the Treasury, now Charles J. Foster, would make "patriotic appeals" to the bankers which persuaded them, for the moment, to postpone their demand for specie. But bankers' patriotism, when there is question of gold, is notoriously short-winded. The bankers could not use paper money or Legal Tender to cover their commitments due abroad and payable in foreign specie. True, they had certain supplies of gold themselves; but these they kept hoarding against the day of possible inflation; in the meantime, being in need of sterling currency to pay for import accounts, they returned again and again to press the Treasury to redeem more government notes and Legal Tender. "Gold was virtually hoarded, both by the banks and by the Government," and this in itself constituted a "first step in the depreciation of the currency." [22]

"After all, it can only be a question of time . . . before we shall be upon a silver basis," wrote the New York banker Jacob H. Schiff, in a private memorandum for the Secretary of the Treasury. This outcome, according to the head of Kuhn, Loeb & Co., was being forced surely and steadily by the tactics of the bankers themselves— and apparently not by the fierce-sounding but quite penurious agrarian politicians of the West.[23] By hoarding approximately three-fourths of the floating supply of gold, and draining the government Treasury of its remaining gold, the bankers themselves were precipitating the very crisis they feared.

For years past, as for years to come, the agrarian radicals dwelt with passion upon the "bankers' conspiracy in the two continents," by which gold was cornered, prices were driven down, and American farmers were impoverished. Such accusations were as regularly branded by the other camp as the fantasies of "boy orators" from the frontier, the farrago of windy Populist imaginations. It was but a subterfuge by which thievish "repudiators" and defaulters hoped to get something for nothing, or hoped to pay a $1 debt with 70 cents of money. The nostrum of silver coinage, as Carl Schurz contended, was one of those fallacies "having a streak of rascality in them" which happened to appeal to the American people.[24] It is therefore in mere justice to the simple-minded peasants of Kansas that we cite from the papers of the banker Jacob H. Schiff evidence of the concrete reality of the often mentioned banking conspiracy.

What was being done by the bankers was of course no conspiracy, but simply a response on their part to the law of profit. If by the signs, which they could read as well as any politician, the country were one day to drop from the fixed gold standard, then gold owned by themselves would receive automatically and overnight a higher valuation and create immense profits in terms of paper or silver money. Schiff, in his letter and private memorandum of June 27, 1892, furnished at Secretary Foster's request, reported frankly that just such profit-seeking and "cornering" tactics were being pursued to the embarrassment of the Government and the country's trade.

The banks have no gold obligations, and if, as is no doubt being done, they use their machinery for the purpose of accumulating gold and furnishing Treasury Notes instead of Gold Certificates when demanded for export purposes, it results practically in an attempt to "corner" the Treasury. All legitimate means should be used to accumulate the country's stock of gold in the Treasury for the protection of the national currency, and not in the banks, whose stockholders would be made the beneficiaries of any accumulations of gold, should the latter ever go to a premium.[25]

"Patriotic persuasion" must be continued, he argued, though profit knew no country. Schiff urged that the Government should put pressure upon the banks "through legislation, if it must be," to halt the hoarding tactics. Temporary obstacles to gold exports also might be erected through the increase of subtreasury charges; but short of a general banking reform, involving the repeal of the Sherman Silver Purchase Act and creation of a central banking system (such as the present Federal Reserve) nothing but temporary relief might be won.

The Government followed stopgap measures of the nature advised by friendly bankers. Meanwhile the uneasiness of capitalists everywhere was further intensified by the extraordinary progress which the Populist and Alliance movement continued to register in the interior of the country. The farm leaders throughout the West and the South were furiously busy in 1892 with preparations for the launching of a well-organized, independent national party. A preliminary convention was held in Cincinnati, May 15, 1891, then finally at a great gathering of representatives of twelve national organizations in St. Louis, February 22, 1892, the People's Party chose its chairman and executive committee, and issued a call for a presidential nominating convention to be held at Omaha.[26] The revolutionary enthusiasm with which the movement proceeded promised clearly that the new party might play a decisive part in the balance between the two old professional parties, and might have a career similar to that of the Republican Party after 1856. The new young Jacobins who appeared, even as nominal Democrats or Republicans, men like Senator "Pitchfork Ben" Tillman of South Carolina, or the "Boy Orator" Representative Bryan of Nebraska, were thoroughly infected with the prevailing silver "heresy" and infected their fellows all about them. Free-silver bills were introduced in Congress and narrowly defeated, while flurries of panic ran through Wall Street's financial community. Early in the winter of 1891, when the bewhiskered Populist William Peffer of Kansas, a veritable figure of earth, entered the Senate, E. L. Godkin reminded his readers: "The times are revolutionary in the West." In the excited pen pictures with which the Washington correspondents strove to frighten the little children of Eastern capital, this gentle man who possessed much learning was described as a hairy anarchist, demanding—in a "gruffly hoarse but low-toned voice issuing from a sea of long, dark beard flowing nearly to his waist"—the distribution of unlimited quantities of money by the Government to the people.[27]

CHAPTER FOURTEEN

THE RETURN OF THE OUTS: THE CANALIZATION OF DISCONTENT

. . . While we were following the banner of the Republican party on the one hand, and of Bourbon Democracy on the other, the gold power . . . was fastening the chains of an industrial slavery on the people so firmly that it will take a generation to strike them off. SENATOR WILLIAM ALLEN OF NEBRASKA

THE industrial capitalists, as we have seen, had taken a most enthusiastic part in the canvass of 1888, even organizing themselves as a "trade-union" on behalf of the Republican Party and "prohibitive" Protection. But by 1892, with the "silver whirlwind" devastating the West, and the warning symptoms of an approaching financial crisis already felt, they stared at the prospect of what was for them financial chaos, counting their corporate profits in silver or paper money of the most uncertain value. Currency debasement, the emergency remedy of hard-pressed governments since Biblical times, does not impoverish industry, but rather "inflates" and stimulates it as with the effect of a drug. Yet it is a drastic medicine, of usually momentary effect, offering always the dangers of the unknown as against the certainties of fixed values. Moreover, the developing complexity of the American economic structure, its enormous savings in fixed-income securities and government bonds, its banks, insurance, and trust companies, all its elaborate affiliations with European financial centers, required defense of the international gold standard against the menace of an inflationary "earthquake." Better to continue the process of deflation, which had begun late in 1890, better to cling to the safe anchorage of the gold standard as marked in 1879, cost what it might, than to embark upon unknown economic adventures.

Sophisticated in their political ideas, the great capitalists like the Rockefellers, Havemeyer, Gould, James Hill, and others who "moved obscurely in the background" of party action nowadays admittedly paid their money to both parties. In all regions and all elections they worked by using the tactics of alternation, as one of them said, for "the party of business," and operated as a kind of interior cabal, untouched by the theatrical triumphs or defeats which the professional political adversaries administered to each other. Ostensibly Republican in their sympathies in 1888, the men of the Standard Oil clan, for instance, were believed to own also a large share of stock in the Democratic Party, through Senator Henry B. Payne and the former Secretary of the Navy, W. C. Whitney. The Sugar Trust had its Republican champion in Senator Aldrich, but a Democratic agent as well, it was understood, in Senator Gorman. A great railroad magnate might shift his affections like some heartless cocotte, who would sleep for a night with anyone who rewarded her. Jim Hill, master of the Great Northern Railroad, had paid heavily for Cleveland's election in 1884; but in 1888 reports of his fabulous offers of money to the Harrison campaign chest in return for the privilege of controlling one of the cabinet posts had been repeatedly heard. Henry Villard, another great Railroad Baron of the time, had been in other years a passionate Abolitionist Republican, the pupil of Horace Greeley, but in 1892 he, like many others of his class, "switched" to the support of the Democratic Party and Grover Cleveland. Four years later, in 1896, it was another story.

Villard's motives and action, as a pattern of the capitalist mind at work in the crisis of the 1890's, are worth studying. The owner of railroad and industrial securities and also the agent of powerful German banks in Frankfort and Berlin which held large investments in America, Villard intended that their securities should continue to be payable in gold of the existing standard, and not in silver or paper. The newspapers which he subsidized, the *Nation* and the New York *Post*, therefore, kept up a withering fire at the "senseless Silver Purchase Act" which disordered the money markets. Following a tour in 1891 of the Northern Pacific Railroad, which ran through the disaffected Granger States, Villard became convinced that a currency crisis and depression was inevitable; he then warned his friends in advance, as he relates, "to put their houses in order . . . and prepare for the worst." [1] To the German financiers, Villard communicated his fears for the future of American securities,[2] as well as his disgust at the course of the Government.

Throughout the whole West, he reported, the agrarian legislators were fomenting "an epidemic of dishonesty . . . manifesting itself in the most outrageous legislative violence to railroads and the free silver coinage infatuation." [3] The Republicans, however, were responsible for the McKinley Tariff of 1890, which was so unpopular with the masses of the voters, and for the Sherman Silver Purchase Act, which bankers abhorred. Doubtless the Republicans would be beaten in 1892, but what would the Democrats do? They were no better; and a large bloc of the Democratic Congressmen, as is shown by their attempts to pass a free-coinage measure, were completely "heretical."

On February 10, 1891, from his retirement as a private lawyer, Grover Cleveland had issued his challenge to the silver movement in a public letter, ranging himself with "those who believe that the greatest peril would be initiated by . . . the unlimited coinage of silver." Villard now saw the light. He and his friends had been "very blue," as he wrote Bryce, but Cleveland's letter would "compel the rank and file of his party to suppress its silver inclinations and go right in that respect." [4] Cleveland had made a powerful appeal to the masses by his demand for tariff reform in 1887 and 1888; a reform which Villard as a Liberal Capitalist also favored; now he also went "right" in the respect of sound money. Villard and his two propagandists of Liberal Capitalism, Carl Schurz and E. L. Godkin, were also strongly in favor of civil-service reform, with which Cleveland was identified. In the view especially of German bankers, who looked at America as an investment, all that was needed to make of this country a paradise of capitalism was a measure of tariff reform, sound currency, and the kind of permanent, responsible, clean bureaucracy which the German Empire had already established.[5] To make head against the "wild radicals" of the West, to defend his railroad and his adopted country—the two were indistinguishable in his mind—and to win favoring conditions for international finance capitalism, Villard, like certain other wealthy Americans, gave himself over almost entirely to the great game of President-making. He relates in his memoirs that there was but one way of saving the country and the road [the Northern Pacific] from a ruinous catastrophe, viz., by the earliest possible repeal of the Sherman [Silver Purchase] Act, and the election of a President in 1892 who could be relied on to exert executive influence for the repeal of the Act as well as for the establishment of the gold standard.

Through the autumn of 1891 and the winter and spring of 1892 Villard lobbied tirelessly in Washington against the Free Silver movement. He felt himself drawn "against his wish into the political whirlpool"; he became "a hard-working politician," arranging conference after conference between leading statesmen and leading capitalists. The emergency was great; the Republican Party was discredited and Harrison was distrusted. He reasoned: *"Only a Democrat, entirely sound on what seemed to Mr. Villard to be the two main issues, could meet the emergency."* [6]

Discontent was abroad in the land; its impulse would injure the Ins and benefit the Outs, the Democrats. Therefore a "sound," that is, a conservative, Democrat placed at the controls of the movement would serve to canalize discontent. Only a conservative Democrat could, by carrying the Solid South and the financial East, offset the menacing advance of the agrarians in the West. This Democrat, once more, could only be Cleveland. Villard called on Cleveland and obtained his consent to the early promotion of his candidacy. Early in 1892 he addressed a gathering of twenty-eight Congressmen at Speaker John Carlisle's home in Washington, declaring that Cleveland was "the only Democrat who could be elected," and assuring them that a strong and rich group of New Yorkers would back his nomination.

From the coffers of Villard-controlled public-utility and railroad corporations certain moneys now went forth to points in the Northwest wherever Villard's political agents might gain support (especially among German constituents) for party delegates pledged to Cleveland and the gold standard. To a request for cash, apparently, from a Democratic Party manager in Milwaukee, Villard's private secretary wrote, March 12, 1892:

I have your confidential note. Of course, we are not [that is, the local company] in a very flourishing condition, and do not feel like spending much money. Still, we can see the desirability of being on good terms with your political friends. If you will please indicate the minimum amount you think would be acceptable, we will let you hear from us.[7]

Some three weeks later, long before the Democratic convention, Villard informed the same Western organizer that the New York group behind Cleveland was "probably the strongest [Organization] the party ever had in this state" and could "easily command all the funds they need for carrying on the campaign against Hill." [8]

Villard with his newspapers, his hired publicists, his corporations, and his important German and Mugwump connections as well, had made a good beginning. But soon afterward, the legionaries of the whole determined Eastern Gold Democracy, whose fortunes were firmly attached to Cleveland's—whether they loved him or not— rallied about him conscious "of the threat which was rising beyond the Alleghenies." Their zeal was augmented by their confidence "that he would stand like a rock against financial vagaries" to which more devious, demagogic politicians, such as David Hill, might succumb.

Grover Cleveland's earlier career had been associated with the movement for bureaucratic reform which Liberal Capitalism demanded for its own health. His second candidacy had been based upon the appeal for tariff reform, another and very popular aspect of Liberal Capitalism. But in his later period, as he faced his third candidacy, while still holding the loyalty of reformers by his reputation as a liberal, he was governed by the "principle of unyielding conservatism in all that affected finance and business . . . more than ever before he was gaining the allegiance of frightened Eastern capitalism." [9]

The later Cleveland, according to Henry Watterson, was a much changed man. He had married and had children; he frequented the society of mighty nabobs, social leaders, and "supermen" of the American metropolis. For four years, during his retirement to private life, he labored as a corporation lawyer in downtown New York, associated, though unofficially, with the important Wall Street law firm of Bangs, Stetson, Tracy & MacVeagh. At this time Francis Lynde Stetson, head of the firm, was mainly occupied as counsel to

the banking house of J. Pierpont Morgan. One perceives the cultivated and rather crafty Stetson, in moments when he was not busy
with Morgan's railroad reorganizations, holding the former President's ear, talking with him for long hours, during these silent years,
as friend and mentor. For the selection of profitable investments
Cleveland had the advice not only of Stetson but also of one of the
most powerful speculative leaders in Wall Street, William C. Whitney, formerly his Secretary of the Navy and political field marshal.
Another financial magnate who became his intimate friend was
"Commodore" E. C. Benedict, a native of Connecticut. Cleveland
speculated in stocks and accumulated a middle-sized fortune by
following in the tail of a dauntless band of corsairs, Whitney,
Thomas Fortune Ryan, Oliver H. Payne, and James R. Keene—
though there were occasional reverses which troubled his prudent
nature.[10] Other capitalists who figured in the intimate circle of the
former grocery clerk and sheriff were men like Oscar Straus, the
department-store millionaire, and Charles S. Fairchild, the lawyer
who had been Secretary of the Treasury in his Cabinet and was now
a leading New York banker. These men, who prepared to carry him
again to the White House, guarded and defended Cleveland; in
a sense they insulated him. "Behind Fairchild stood the great banking interests; behind Whitney . . . a large part of Wall Street; and
the Straus brothers represented rich mercantile interests." [11]

The later Cleveland, then, was no more the jovial, ruddy-faced
giant of Buffalo's taverns, who knew how to sit down and drink beer
with the laborer and conciliate proletarian discontent. He had come
to embrace the views of the magnates and social leaders who surrounded him, that "the people must be molded" by the "supermen"
of business and politics. Perhaps he shared more and more the ideas
of his dashing friend Whitney, who said in a pointed phrase of a
private letter at this period that the object of Good Government
was "to allow the public and private interests to subserve each
other." [12]

The rise of the Populist movement Cleveland watched with a
frightened fascination. He feared that his party "would become a
sort of political Cave of Adullam to which would report 'everyone

that was in distress, everyone that was in debt, and everyone that was discontented.' " [13] For such as these Cleveland now had even less sympathy than that which he showed for the victims of drought in Texas to whom once he refused government relief. To the demands of "agitators" his powerful friends knew that he would turn a face of granite. It was this man, who, as members of his own party charged, made "his friends and counsellors among the plutocrats of the land," who was marked to lead again the party of opposition.[14]

II

William C. Whitney, who had shown such remarkable promise as a political manager during Cleveland's first term, had divided his time recently between the breeding of monopolies in whisky, tobacco, and tractions, and the raising of thoroughbred horses. Lately he had made a turn in Wall Street together with Thomas Fortune Ryan, whereby the surface railways of New York, fallen from the hands of the dying corruptionist Jacob Sharp, had all been gathered together, reorganized, and recapitalized overnight, at a profit to himself of some $5,000,000. But Cleveland and the Gold Democrats now called on him to lead the preconvention contest and, turning from the nightmares of the market place, Whitney not only assumed command of the Cleveland battalions in the fight for the nomination, but furnished the money.[15]

Although he had a domineering spirit, was occasionally arrogant and sometimes malicious, men seemed almost to enjoy being cheated by Whitney. Impeccably dressed, always cool in manner, he had nevertheless depths of emotion, intense nervous sensibility, and the intuition of a great gambler. Those who knew him found him endlessly entertaining and kind. Leaders had confidence in his judgment. Opponents, such as David B. Hill, "believed he would betray any man who stood in his way." He was "undoubtedly a master at political wire-pulling and intrigue. . . . But he had vision . . . a receptive, alert mind, and . . . the rare gift of doing things quickly." [16]

Another trait which endeared him to many followers was his possession of inexhaustible supplies of money, which he dispensed with prodigal liberality—money which came to him as if conjured up by his magician's fingers, and which he strewed about with a lordly hand.* It was but a medium of power which he stinted not to use, which embellished his life and made its swift passage as diverting to himself as it was meteoric to others. In the craft of politics Whitney displayed genius, and developed himself as a national boss who worked behind the scenes, the forerunner of others who studied his handiwork. This was something which the crisis of capitalism and the inchoate, divided Democratic Party sorely needed.

The chief danger for the Gold Democrats lay in the presidential bubble of David Hill, former Governor and now United States Senator and boss of New York State. Hill had stepped into Cleveland's place and promptly exploited all the resources of the spoilsman while Cleveland labored for administrative reform. His alliances were firmly cemented with the leading city bosses, Croker of Tammany in New York, McLaughlin of Kings County, Sheehan of Buffalo, and others. "I am a *Democrat!*" he would exclaim, leering over his black, curling mustachios, as he disposed of public-works, canal, or aqueduct contracts and cheap liquor licenses to his retainers. But lately the Sage of Wolfert's Roost had added to his other talents the arts of the demagogue, preaching the justice of the eight-hour day, and declaring himself a convinced bimetallist who sought an increased coinage of silver—if only by international agreement. The designs of such a slippery man upon the Presidency frightened respectable capitalists everywhere. When, with his henchmen marching in close formation, Hill ousted the Cleveland men, gained control of the New York Democratic State Committee, and called a prematurely early state convention to elect delegates for the Chicago national party convention, panic spread among the Cleveland band. The so-called Snap Convention (February 22, 1892), engineered through hurried primaries called with insufficient notice, and carried out under the unit rule, was to launch Hill's boom in

---

* One day in Paris Whitney met a rich acquaintance "who had been nibbling at the Democratic nomination for Governor of New York," but debated with himself over the possible expenses involved. Asked for his opinion of the matter Whitney exclaimed: "Why, of course you ought to run. Go ahead, make your preliminary canvass, and when you have put up $200,000 or more, you will have become so much interested that you will . . . spend some more money." (Parker, *Recollections of Grover Cleveland*, p. 163.)

earnest and give notice that the former President had lost control of his own great State of New York.[17]

William Whitney, however, was equal to the emergency. At his own cost he organized a massive demonstration of respectable citizens and reform leaders at an "Anti-Snapper's Convention," and thoroughly exposed Hill's designs in the press, arousing tremendous indignation among the people. Hill's overreaching tactics acted as a boomerang. Whitney's energetic offensive smashed his bubble in time; the "spontaneous enthusiasm" for Cleveland engendered by the "unlimited funds" of money, to which Henry Villard alluded at this moment, completed the work.[18]

Before leaving New York for the nominating convention at Chicago, scheduled for June 9, 1892, Whitney set up the skeleton of a nation-wide party organization, following a secret conference with twelve national delegates, leaders from "strategic" parts of the country, such as Vilas of Wisconsin, Morss, a newspaper publisher of Indiana, Don Dickinson of Michigan, and F. L. Stetson of New York. These men, who embodied either wealth or a concentrated political influence in their sections, together with Whitney made "consummate preparations," so that all the properties and leading roles, all the scenery and "peasants and soldiers," for the convention's grand opera (in the shape of committees, resolutions, and temporary chairman who would manage the meetings) were fully rehearsed in advance.[19]

Opening splendid headquarters at the Palmer House in Chicago, Whitney plunged into his labors of intrigue, bartering, negotiation, and conciliation. To Hill and Tammany Hall, whom he had balked, he now offered terms of peace and "recognition." Offensive coalitions of rabid Western or Southern Silverites were headed off; in good time plots by clever conservatives such as Senators Brice and Gorman, who were personal enemies of Cleveland, were broken up or outflanked.

It was not easy work. The "poor-white" followers of Pitchfork Ben Tillman, who seemed Democrats in name only, had sworn that they would never accept Cleveland. It would mean "a prostitution of the principles of Democracy . . . and a surrender of the rights of the people to the financial kings of the country," as their spokes-

men with curious foreknowledge said publicly.[20] Yet even these men
had been soothed. After all, Cleveland "could win," as Senator Vest
of Missouri, himself a Silverite, had urged, on the sole ground of
tariff reform; and good party men "should be willing to postpone
the silver question to prevent Republican success."[21]

In the end Whitney held the whole convention in his hand. Over
the door of his hotel suite the word "Cleveland" blazed in an incan-
descent arch, and as eyewitnesses recalled, he mingled familiarly
with all visiting delegations. But in a room at the rear he "talked
Richard Croker into an attitude of benevolent neutrality; won a
. . . concession from Brice; cultivated . . . relations with Gorman,"
conquered Indiana, gathered wavering delegates under his banner,
and scattered a formidable coalition of silver states. All this was
done with an ease which seemed incredible to the politicians present
as they saw Whitney "lounging in the rooms of the opposition, or
silently and calmly adjusting his eyeglasses" while the convention
hall shook and thundered with hate, vituperation and violence. "I
can't keep the votes back," Whitney exclaimed jubilantly to associates
who complimented him. "They tumble in at the windows as well
as at the doors."[22]

Wherever Whitney passed, there rumors of "soap" used among
the uninstructed or unpledged delegates were usually rife. Sometimes an accidental slip revealed the methods at work. At the close
of the first ballot, according to one story by a newspaper correspondent, when it seemed that Cleveland might still be short of the
requisite two-thirds vote, a noisy row broke out among the Democratic representatives from the Indian Territory, some of whom
claimed that "they had not received all that had been promised."[23]
Promptly, a Whitney agent appeared among the malcontents and
"everything was arranged in a satisfactory manner." Thus the votes
kept tumbling in and the road was opened again for a responsible
Federal bureaucracy and "sound" financial policies. The people's
delegates quickly chose as their leader a statesman characterized as
one who chose his friends and advisers from among the great capitalists, who believed firmly that "corporations created by State or
Nation are not amenable to the control of their creator," and who
opposed all measures for bimetallism which might "enlarge the cur-

rency of the world." [24] What was even more remarkable was the manner in which Whitney, at least for this season, had united clashing professional elements and hostile economic classes in a party that was chronically torn by dissension.

III

While the nomination had been machine-made, and settled upon the first ballot, behind the doors of the Resolutions Committee a fierce dispute over the platform showed the internal divisions between groups. On the Burning Issue of silver coinage and inflation, the official position was made as equivocal, as noncommittal, as possible: the party declared in favor of using "both gold and silver," both metals to be held at a "parity"—although lately this had been impossible because of the huge increase in silver production. The Democrats moreover pledged themselves to obtain international bimetallic agreements with the principal foreign governments, fixing the ratio of silver to gold in world markets. This proposed, in effect, a kind of pegging of silver which realistic students of finance were willing to talk about while knowing well that it could probably never be arranged. Then, to conciliate further the radical wing, A. E. Stevenson of Illinois, a strong Free Silver champion, was nominated for the Vice-Presidency.

Concerning the "iniquitous" Republican protective tariff which Cleveland four years earlier had attacked so bluntly, the real plan of the party managers was to say as little as possible. The original resolution, as written by Whitney and Vilas and sanctioned by the former President, eschewed all that Free Trade ardor which had moved the hearts of the common people, and treated only of judicious revision to be made without injury to "any domestic industries . . . at every step regardful of the labor and capital" which had relied on tariff legislation.[25] This was precisely the official position of the Republicans for the last twenty years, the doctrine that the tariff system was to be improved or "reformed" only by its friends and beneficiaries.

But Henry Watterson, the erratic journalistic star of the party, and Congressman Tom L. Johnson of Cleveland conducted a powerful opposition which was finally brought out of committee to the floor of the convention, where the arch wirepuller, Whitney, was at a disadvantage. By open debate the dead-hearted tariff resolution was turned into a fighting slogan denouncing the McKinley Tariff Act as "the culminating atrocity of class legislation," and promising to the masses free raw materials and cheaper manufactured goods. This clause also called attention to the heavy reductions in wages which had recently followed the enactment of the highest iron and steel duties which the country had ever seen. Watterson boasted that

over the protest of Whitney, his organizer, and Vilas, his spokesman, I had forced him [Cleveland] to stand on that gospel [of tariff reduction]. He flew into a rage and threatened to modify, if not to repudiate, the plank in his letter of acceptance.[26]

Cleveland, on the advice of his managers, was now determined to use only the most Fabian tactics. Want of caution, he feared, might lead to Democratic "wandering in the dark wilds of discouragement for twenty-five years." [27] He was concerned no longer with tariff reform and the ills of the plain people; he desired to offend no powerful vested interests. Obsessed as he was with the danger of the silver movement and the secret hope of rallying conservative forces to its defeat, the last shreds of liberalism seemed to have fled from the chambers of his mind, making him, as Charles A. Dana said, the "stuffed prophet" of a naked conservatism.

This season, gold-minded Republican industrialists, ignoring the rhetorical or platform pebbles of Democratic politicians which rattled about their heads, willingly "switched" their affections to the party of the Outs. Andrew Carnegie himself wrote to express his sympathy with Cleveland, saying:

You know that for several years my chief anxiety in public matters has been in regard to the "silver question" and that I stated in the North American Review that if I were called upon to vote for a Free Trade Democrat who supported sound money, or a Tariff Republican who was not sound upon money, I should vote for the former.[28]

At the Republican National Convention at Minneapolis, beginning June 7, love and harmony were as notably lacking as enthusiasm. Much mystery has been made of Blaine's decision to break openly with President Harrison three days before the party's nominating convention. Was it because Mrs. Blaine disliked Mrs. Harrison?

The old leader suffered from declining health, which actually made the adventure of a presidential race impossible. Inscrutable and silent, he watched the opening of the nominating convention, which it was hoped once more might "draft" him. There is strong evidence that he did not desire the nomination. Why, then, did he permit his name to be entered so late in the day? With the hardest fighting needed to offset the patronage advantage of the reigning President, Blaine's manager, Tom Platt, conducted what witnesses have described as a torpid and motionless convention campaign utterly unworthy of his reputation for wiliness.[29] Or were Blaine's motives, as others have suggested, those of vanity and personal vengeance?[30]

Such a political "mystery" can scarcely be solved so long as we cling to conventional, Fourth Reader concepts of history and of the party institution. But when we follow the reasoning of two so widely different political philosophers as Edmund Burke and Friedrich Engels, who agree that both of the great professional parties in the long run tacitly function as one, and work toward the common social ends, then the meaning of Blaine's unorthodox action in its incidence and timing becomes unmistakable.

For the party in power to refuse its President a renomination is to repudiate its own Administration and cast discredit upon itself. The Republican President, if he has been energetic enough, comes to the convention with his regiments of officeholders manning the strategic posts in the party Organization throughout the country, and the "dummies" from Southern Republican "rotten boroughs" usually pledged to him. Thoroughly aroused and pugnacious by nature, Mr. Harrison had made a vigorous fight indeed, left nothing to chance, and had his renomination assured on the first ballot. Blaine's half-hearted opposition could not halt this result, but could only serve to heighten the discord which ruled among Republicans and open the way to their foreseen defeat. It was like a secret act of apostasy by the most hardened of the old partisans, significant indiscipline of a leader who had always hitherto accepted party discipline.

To the "Old Guard" of regional bosses, Platt, Quay, Clarkson, and Foraker, it was of course a clear signal that they too might relax their efforts. These veteran chieftains had long been disaffected, and had carried on a covert resistance to the Chief Magistrate and his clique. His selection, as Platt recalls,

caused a chattering of the teeth among the warm-blooded Republicans of the East . . . many of the New York delegates, including myself, wrapped ourselves in overcoats and ear-muffs, hurried from the convention hall, and took the first train for New York. I had repeatedly uttered warnings that Harrison's renomination spelled disaster.[31]

Platt opposed the renomination of Levi P. Morton, the Money-bag of the party Organization, for the Vice-Presidency. He advised Morton, to whom he held out the bait of the Presidency itself, that he must not be "sacrificed" in a hopeless campaign. Shrewd observers guessed that what Platt most feared was that "Morton would add too much strength to the ticket." [32] Matt Quay too gave clear hints in advance that the results from Harrison's renomination might be unpleasant.[33]

Once more there had been thunderous ovations at the mention of the magic name of Blaine. "Like the chorus of an anthem with measured solemnity" as William Allen White remembers it, "the galleries chanted: Blaine! Blaine! James G. Blaine!" It was the passing of Blaine. That gigantic demonstration was at once a salutation and a requiem.[34] Harrison received a majority of 533⅙ votes, Blaine had 182½, and McKinley, for whom Mr. Hanna now organized a demonstration rather than a serious contest, received 182. Whitelaw Reid was named for the Vice-Presidency, but the strong voice of his friend and mentor Blaine was not heard in that season's tournament.

There are such things as strategic retreats from which a party, like an army, may rally stronger than before. "Let them [the Democrats] meddle with the tariff . . . and let them get into the wrangle over the finances which is bound to come," commented the ardent Republican Theodore Roosevelt after the election.[35] The passiveness of the great bosses in itself promised failure for the party. They would have bowed to the yoke if they had not sensed a meaningful coldness in high quarters which formerly furnished whatever moneys were required for their expert services.

According to Parke Godwin, it was Cleveland rather than any Republican leader who was the favorite of the Union League Club in these dark days![36] As in 1884, bankers and financiers favored Cleveland. From tariff-protected corporations there came, as usual, contributions to the Republican chest, which, however, were unusually meager this year. Mr. Hanna of Cleveland, the Businessman in Politics who had served so well in 1888, was invited cordially by the President to act as treasurer of the Republican National Committee this year. But Mr. Hanna declined the honor.[37]

The uncommonly evasive, meaningless, compromising platform which the Republicans devised for this campaign angered the great capitalists of the East. To have won real support in New York, as a Republican banker afterward intimated,

the currency and financial question ought to be made paramount, but this advice was totally disregarded. . . . As a consequence, those who had given their support to the Republican Party because of their belief in its greater trustworthiness on financial questions soon became lukewarm in their actual and moral support.

On the other hand, as Jacob Schiff concluded in a letter full of implied reproaches, the responsibility of the Democratic Party and the nature of its leadership nowadays was such as to remove the fear that "Democratic ascendancy may become a threat to the prosperity of the country." [38]

The mightiest of the Republican bosses and their chief paymasters acted strangely as if they were mummers playing in a puppet tragedy, and marched without the joy of battle in their eyes. Had they forgotten all the ancient lessons of party loyalty and party duty, bred in the bones of American citizens and preached for generations by father to son? Or had new loyalties replaced the old institutional ones?

Blaine and his professional colleagues loved their party, "right or wrong," none more fervently than Blaine, one of the party's founding fathers. But more and more perceptibly these professional politicians were departing from the old "innocent" party faith. It seemed nowadays as if they loved their "country" even more than their party; that is, their economic *patrie* which had nourished and reared them to fame, wealth, or power, and in whose services they had come to dedicate the party itself. If, perchance, the higher interests of their "country" needed the immolation of party, must they not then prove equal to this most touching of sacrifices? *

IV

The two professional political parties, as was their custom, both "straddled" the key question of the time. But the new "class party" of peasant proprietors, the Populists, were silent about nothing. At the national convention, opening at Omaha, July 2, 1892, some 1,300 accredited People's Party delegates, together with thousands of their adherents, gathered to answer the call. They came by wagon and oxcart, and even by train, though the hostile railroad masters, by a crafty oversight, refused the usual picnic-fare reductions to Populists.[39]

The spirit of the Jacobins which seethed in this crowd overwhelmed all moderate counsels. Cleveland's nomination had made the Middle Border farmers all the more determined to run a national ticket for this campaign and strive for a balance of power between the Republicans and the Democrats. All of the Northern Farmers' Alliance, the remnants of the Grange, the "Wheel," Miss Frances Willard's temperance movement, and even the Knights of Labor were represented at Omaha. Only the Southern Alliance men, who, below Mason and Dixon's line, continued as a "white men's movement" to work within the single-party system, were absent.

With prayer, music, and frenzied cheering this strange party convention, so unlike the mechanical performances of its rivals, was opened by Ignatius Donnelly, Minnesota philosopher, who read the preamble to the platform:

. . . we meet in the midst of a nation brought to the verge of moral, political, and material ruin. Corruption dominates the ballot-box, the legis-

* One of the good contemporary comments upon the "listless" Republican-Democratic contest in 1892 was to the effect that "each side would have been glad to defeat the other if it could do so without electing its own candidate." (Muzzey, *James G. Blaine*, p. 481, fn.)

lature, the Congress, and touches even the ermine of the bench. The people are demoralized. . . . The newspapers are largely subsidized or muzzled; public opinion silenced; business prostrated; our homes covered with mortgages; labor impoverished and the land concentrating in the hands of the capitalists. The urban workmen are denied the right of organization . . . a hireling standing army, unrecognized by our laws, is established to shoot them down. . . . The fruits of the toil of millions are boldly stolen to build up colossal fortunes for the few. . . .

A vast conspiracy against mankind has been organized on two continents, and is rapidly taking possession of the world. If not met and overthrown at once, it forebodes terrible social convulsions, the destruction of civilization . . . despotism. . . .

We have witnessed . . . the struggles of the two great political parties for power and plunder. . . . They have agreed together to ignore in the campaign every issue but one. They propose to drown the outcries of a plundered people with the uproar of a sham battle over the tariff, so that capitalists, corporations, national banks, rings, trusts, watered stock, the demonetization of silver . . . may all be lost sight of.

In conclusion the keynote orator, Donnelly, expressed the essential doctrine of the new party as the belief that the "powers of government . . . should be expanded . . . to the end that oppression, injustice, and poverty shall eventually cease in the land." He proclaimed that "we seek to restore the government of the Republic to the hands of 'the plain people.' " [40]

The extremely radical platform laid before the convention, incorporating what would now still, some forty years later, be held a most enlightened program, demanded first of all the expansion of the currency by the free and unlimited coinage of silver.* Then came demands for government ownership of railroad, telegraph, and telephone systems; for a graduated direct income tax; for the direct election of Senators. Such were the principles of the "cranks, lunatics and idiots" of the frontier (as the Eastern press called them), which were received with derision by the leaders of both professional parties.

But principles and platform counted for much among the enthusi-

* It is now widely acknowledged that credit or banking facilities in the 1890's were woefully inadequate and inelastic in the interior of the country.

asts of the People's Party, and their demonstrations over Donnelly's eloquent address and over the various planks of their creed, proclaimed one by one, resembled to onlookers a mass manifestation of 1789 at the gates of the Bastille. A frightened Eastern journalist wrote home:

And when that furious and hysterical arraignment of the present times, the incoherent intermingling of Jeremiah and Bellamy, the platform, was adopted, the cheers and yells which rose like a tornado from four thousand throats and raged without cessation for thirty-four minutes, during which women shrieked and wept, men embraced and kissed their neighbors, locked arms . . . leaped upon tables and chairs in the ecstasy of their delirium,—this dramatic and historical scene must have told . . . that there was something back of all this turmoil more than the failure of crops or the scarcity of ready cash. And over all the city during that summer week brooded the spectres of Nationalism, Socialism and general discontent.[41]

For their presidential candidate the People's Party, after failing to win the liberal Judge Walter Gresham to their cause, named again the old Greenbacker General James Weaver. Weaver in his nation-wide tour that year attacked day by day the Senate, the Supreme Court, the industrial monopolies, the two professional parties, and argued strongly for what is respectably known nowadays as a "managed currency." The Populist organizers made large inroads into the Republican Party strength in the West, so that the electoral outcome seemed more confusing and incalculable than ever before to the experts. The Republican organ of Whitelaw Reid, the New York *Tribune*, especially sounded notes of discouragement and observed "a modern tendency toward socialism everywhere."

As the day approached for the national presidential plebiscite of 1892, the irruption of the crude Populists and their unorthodox doctrines caused anxious heart-searching in the counting-rooms of Eastern and Middle Western cities, as in the headquarters of party machines. The Republican Party, which was held in the West nowadays to be more closely connected with corporate wealth, was less infected with the silver "heresy" than the Democratic Party, whose Southern wing was almost completely captured by the Alliance following of Tillman and Thomas Watson.

The contest was considered to be close. Whitney was aware that the Populist strength would be taken largely from the Republican column in the Western tier of States and in the new mountain States, and would better by that much Cleveland's chances of election. The men in real command of the party—Whitney, Henry B. Payne, August Belmont, Henry Villard, Croker, respectively stock speculator, oil monopolist, banker, Railroad Baron, and city boss—for all their loathing of inflationary doctrine, now forced themselves to make a strange bargain with the Populist devils. A fusion between these two parties was therefore quickly arranged. In two states, Kansas and North Dakota, it was formal; in three others, Colorado, Idaho, and Wyoming, it was unofficial, the Democrats simply refraining from nominating Electors. Fusion also was carried out in Oregon and Nevada.[42]

This "unholy union" was a stratagem worthy of Whitney, who loved to proceed by indirection toward his ends. But for the usually honest and outspoken Cleveland to combine with hated foes was a strange role, especially in view of his full awareness of what the party's Inner Circle expected him to do about currency inflation.

V

"I do think—indeed I know," wrote Cleveland immediately after his nomination, "that Whitney should nominally, if not really and actively, be at the head of the committee to manage the national campaign. . . . It is more essential and vital to success than any other one thing." [43]

The titular chairman of the campaign committee was an inoffensive politician from Pennsylvania; Whitney, after much urging, agreed to become the real commander. It was he who had done everything to assure Cleveland's renomination; now he must see to it that his man was elected.

Whitney was not to be made a member of the Cabinet, nor was he offered an Ambassadorship for his pains. Now one of the richest of Americans, his services to Cleveland and to his party were devoted, selflessly one might almost say, to the interests of his class. For the moment the American presidential race absorbed him as much as the British Derby. This President-maker, who was known as Cleveland's "political agent," worked among the jealous to create unified effort, to gather campaign funds, and to direct the expenditure of these funds. The fruit of victory for him would not be public honor, but an all-pervasive "influence" over the National Government during eventful years, which he knew how to turn to account.

The strategy of the Democratic campaign demanded first that the rift between Cleveland's faction and the great city bosses of New York State be closed. The spoilsmen wing of the New York party, led by David Hill, must be placated and the malignant Hill himself neutralized. Croker of Tammany lent himself to Whitney's designs; but Sheehan of Buffalo, and the powerful Edward Murphy of Albany, the party's New York State chairman, demanded of the "Great Reformer" distinct pledges of a certain kind.

It was not easy to wheedle the impolitic, unforgiving Cleveland into doing his bit in such transactions. These were the men who but yesterday had done their best to "scuttle" him, as he said. Yet without their expert collaboration in the canvass, New York would be lost. "They have the organization and the power," and were indispensable, as Whitney repeatedly pointed out.[44]

Cleveland was fat, heavy-handed; and Whitney must struggle constantly to infuse him with some of his own mental suppleness if Organization harmony were to be achieved. Whitney must now cajole him, now pull him along by main force. We find Whitney pleading with the candidate to make overtures to bosses like Murphy of Albany and, for the sake of avoiding mischance, writing out whole letters for Cleveland to sign and address. "You may think it cheeky my suggesting it," he writes to Cleveland, who is summering at Cape Cod, "but it is to get the tone in which I hope you will write to him [Murphy]." Then follows the proposed draft of an affectionate letter to the treacherous Murphy:

As I am the candidate and you are the State Chairman can't you come into the harbor [at Falmouth] some day and pay me a visit? . . . I regret very much to hear that your other daughter's health is requiring your attention. I hope it is nothing that will cause you anxiety. We are entering upon a campaign which in my honest judgment is full of the gravest consequences to the people of this country. . . . Let us sink all our personal feelings in the greater interests involved.[45]

Here the brilliant Whitney even apes the clumsy locutions of Cleveland's style of correspondence.

Tirelessly he forces Cleveland to compromise with his foes within the party, if he would avoid the loss of whole States. He urges him to come to New York. "You can heal lots of sores by patting a fellow on the back." [46] "You could help the campaign by being where men could see you now and then," [47] for Cleveland, in fear of blundering, held himself silent at his seashore retreat, aloof from the "dirty work" that must be done. Cleveland's instincts bade him keep free of entanglements with the plunderers who would ruin the clean bureaucratic system which he hoped to build. Yet at last Whitney persuaded the obstinate statesman that he must come to New York to "smooth out the recalcitrants." The private dinner at a hotel in New York, September 8, 1892, with the disgruntled bosses Sheehan, Murphy, and Croker, took place under conditions of strain and ill will which were difficult enough. But the meeting itself, and Cleveland's concession in coming and talking to the bosses around a table, together with Whitney's indefatigable peacemaking efforts, paved the way for "uniting the full organization strength" in New York, as Whitney reported afterward.[48] Cleveland's visit, he summed up, had done "a world of good."

Although the Democratic candidate was a man of quite colorful, roughhewn character, his mind and his mode of expression often appeared coarse and dull. Even in details of expression, his alter ego, Whitney, must guard over him, warning him not to write too many commonplace letters, and to do so only when he means "to strike a blow." Enemies in the press, Whitney writes, were trying to use Cleveland's ordinary correspondence "in order to familiarize the public with you in a commonplace character." [49]

While the West and the South fermented with "heretical" doctrines and listened to the strange new prophets of Populism, the purpose of Cleveland and the Democratic Party management was as yet a dark secret. Whitney, the real leader of the hated "Eastern money power," as he traveled about the country grew keenly aware of the deep discontent among the masses and the unpopularity his man enjoyed. In 1891 he had strongly advised Cleveland, though in vain, not to write his outspoken letter on the perils of Free Silver. Now this infinitely clever master of stock speculation coaxed the candidate to make in his few public statements some demonstrations of liberalism and humanitarianism that might allay discontent. He actually requests Cleveland to strike up a Populist tune! He reports:

> In the South the impression of you got by the people is that you do not appreciate their suffering and poverty (and these are the real sources of the Alliance movement) and have your ideas formed by the Eastern money power, etc.—*the usual twaddle*. I think having this in view, you might write on the tariff and on silver in a mood sympathetic to them and make a great change in the South. As you said to me, it is unaccountable what ideas they get, and where they get them.[50]

Whitney was ready to turn to account the very anger of the masses at men of his own stamp. Cleveland was too blunt a man to be effective in carrying out such Machiavellian counsels. Yet he bided his time and said little until the day of his acceptance speech at New York, in September, when the chance came to experiment with Whitney's demagogic ideas.

As this evenly matched national campaign (very quiet so far as the Eastern half of the country was concerned) got under way in July, the explosion of the bloodiest labor struggle the country had ever seen, at the Homestead works of the Carnegie Steel Company, quickly changed the complexion of things. Here in western Pennsylvania, at the very heart of protected industry, where a virtual monopoly in steel had been wonderfully nourished by legislative subsidies, the organized workers (who struck and were immediately locked out) soon learned in what manner their wages were "protected" and how crushing was the power of the new corporate giants.

Andrew Carnegie appears to have favored unions and uniform wages in his industry for many years before 1891, when Henry Frick became his partner and general manager. While with his wonted hypocrisy Carnegie had won much publicity for his labor sympathies, his earlier motives were evidently prompted by the need of preventing the loss of technical and productive advantages at Pittsburgh to cheap labor used by powerful rivals in the Chicago district. But with his position now dominant enough to ignore his rivals, he decided to change front suddenly, reduce wages, and break up the union in his plants. Only the deliberate plan to annihilate the powerful Amalgamated Association of Iron and Steel Workers, then at the peak of its strength, explains the sudden departure of the philanthropist for Scotland and his leaving full authority in the hands of the relentless Frick, foe of all labor organization. Only thus can be explained also the elaborate preparations for industrial war, the erection of palisades about the mills—while the workers watched suspiciously—and the final challenge, when a band of 300 armed Pinkerton men, ordered from New York, moved upon Homestead.

The battle which began at dawn of July 6, when the Pinkertons arrived and fired a volley into the crowd at the landing-place, ended with ten killed, some sixty wounded, the invaders disarmed and driven off, and the plants held and guarded by the workers. But soon, under powerful pressure, the reformist Democratic Governor, Pattison, sent 8,000 Pennsylvania militia to impose order; "blacksheep" (nonunion) workers were brought in; the union laborers were forced to surrender after more than four months of struggle.

The whole country was aroused by the industrial warfare at Pittsburgh, especially after July 23, when Alexander Berkman made his ill-advised attempt to assassinate Frick. Discussion raged over the wickedness of monopolists who accepted their 70 per cent tariffs and sought wage reductions of from 10 to 40 per cent. The plight of the Homestead workers not only won world-wide sympathy but had numerous political repercussions. Republicans were especially fearful lest this affair, and other labor battles arising from drastic wage cuts in many industries, should bring defeat to the Harrison Administration.

Whitelaw Reid, candidate for the Vice-Presidency, suffered from the bitter hostility of organized labor in the powerful Typographers' Union, which his newspaper had frequently tried to defeat. But now, in view of so much spreading class hate, he sent telegraphic appeals to Carnegie through the cipher code of the State Department, apparently with Harrison's approval, pleading for a settlement, or peace terms, which would permit recognition of the steel union. An agent of the Republican National Committee, John Milholland, was also sent to Pittsburgh to appeal to Frick, but had the greatest difficulty even in interviewing him.

In this period of "weak" government authority, which followed the era of Reconstruction, the emissary of the Republican Party and, unofficially, of the Government itself, could be rebuffed by a Frick. The Carnegie company had declared publicly that it would never again recognize the Amalgamated or any other labor organization; and Frick stood by this pledge as he said: "If it takes all summer . . . Yes, even my life itself!" Carnegie, from the refuge of his Scottish castle, sustained Frick with a laconic cablegram of July 29, 1892, which said in part: "Tribune too old. Probably the proposition is not worthy of consideration." [51] A single corporation held in its hands the fate of thousands of workers, touched the existence of millions of Americans, while the national election itself was at stake in this season as the whole country watched the duel between Capital and Labor. Yet nothing could be done by the servile politicians. The political emissary must needs obtain permission by cable from the laird of the steel works, abroad, to see Mr. Frick. The question of who was to be the people's President was for the absentee owner Carnegie to decide. It was clearly a secondary and even trivial matter as against the consideration of defeating the largest trade-union in the country and winning, as Frick put it in confidential reports to his chief, untold future profits from present losses. "We had to teach our employés a lesson," he said when the strike had dragged to its end, "and we have taught them one that they will never forget." [52]

For the sake of such gains for decades to come, the defeat of the party of Ins, the personal reverses of Messrs. Harrison and Reid, might well be endured; their replacement by the party of Mr. W. C. Whitney could also be borne with fortitude. The Republican President, as he had previously done in Indiana labor disputes, now played an aggressive part in administering more "great lessons" and so came honestly by his political extinction. Throughout that summer and fall militant labor rebelled, marched against capital; fierce strikes were fought almost simultaneously at the mines of Cœur d'Alene, Idaho, at the railway yards of Buffalo, New York, and elsewhere.

President Harrison felt himself in honor bound to dispatch rescue parties of Federal troops in response to urgent calls. Under the guns of his soldiers at the mines of Idaho, in Tennessee, and in large Eastern cities corporate capital was protected in an immediate sense and massive strikes were broken.

While business felt an increasing pinch in 1892, the unrest of industrial labor in the mines and factories overlaid the unrest of agricultural producers in the West. In this season of insurgency, when the eyes of millions were unveiled to the hard conditions which faced them, public interest in the current party contest for possession of the National Government actually sagged to an extremely low ebb. Externally, despite the ingenious efforts pursued by both sets of wirepullers, the personalities and claims of both leading candidates left the millions of voters listless and indifferent. A Populist organ which argued that the legislation enacted by the Republican Party "has been dictated or inspired by interests localized within the plutocratic circle" dominating the Eastern seaboard States of New York and Pennsylvania and their neighbors, pointed out at the same time that "the species of Democracy known as Clevelandism seeks to get beyond the Republicans in . . . compliance with the grasping demands of the moneyed and monopolistic interests of this same circumscribed section." [53]

Nevertheless, the plan of the Democratic Machiavelli was shaped nicely toward canalizing this very unrest of farmers and wage-earners into the cul-de-sac of the alternate political corporation which he, in company with the Villards, Hills, Paynes, Strauses, and the Gormans, Crokers, and Murphys, managed behind the shield of the "honest trustee" Grover Cleveland. With the discontent of ill-used farmers turned to account by a combination with the Populists, it suited the designs of the Gold Democrats to turn to account the sudden revolt of industrial labor as well.

A few weeks after Whitney had advised him to use a "sympathetic tone" toward the advocates of silver-money inflation, Grover Cleveland stood in Madison Square Garden, New York, reading his letter of acceptance of the nomination for the Presidency. Deliberately he took occasion to turn to his own advantage the bitterness growing among the underprivileged. In his fumbling language he assailed excessive tariff taxation as a system of governmental favoritism which "is directly antagonized by every sentiment of justice and fairness," made life harder for our workingmen and farmers alike, and left "the workingmen suffering from . . . his professed friends." In one passage of clear allusion to the Homestead incident, he then observed with heavy but merited sarcasm, that the workingman "still waits for a division of the advantages secured to his employer under cover of a generous solicitude for his wages." The speech even daringly hinted at some sympathy for the worker "seeking security for his interests in organized co-operation." [54]

Upon the thorny question of inflation, Cleveland persisted in his opposition to "doubtful experiments" upon the American currency. But he added, ambiguously enough, yet sympathetically, as if leaving hope that the dire scarcity of credit would be relieved: "The wants of our people arising from the deficiency or imperfect distribution of money circulation ought to be fully and honestly recognized and efficiently remedied." Whitney himself, with his fertile ideological subterfuges and demagogic schemes, could have asked for nothing better. The speech contained gestures virtuous and ingratiating enough for "times big with danger."

The hides of capitalists are tough to the blows of orators in political tournaments; but sensitive conservative leaders resented and feared the consequences of Cleveland's tactics. Senator Orville Platt of Connecticut protested that Cleveland was acting as an "incendiary, inciting to anarchy," in order to gather in votes; and by fusion with the Populists, which this well-informed member of Aldrich's Philosophers' Club felt to be a treacherous move, he was "sowing the wind. . . . The harvest is getting ready for reaping." [55]

V I

"Election Day. The lack of interest continues," wrote the aged Republican former President Hayes in his diary. Neither candidate excited "enthusiasm with the active men in politics, the workers"— the hurrah boys—he observed. "As it is . . . the chance of Cleveland is the best. *The country can stand it.*" [56] One of the elders of the Republican Party, Senator Allison, exclaimed afterward: "It was

God's mercy to this country that Cleveland, and not Harrison, was elected President."

The receipts of the Republican National Committee agents were disappointing. Mr. Frick, of the Carnegie Steel Company, paid in only $25,000, apparently only half the sum given in 1888, and even this, as he told Elkins, he thought "a waste of money." Too late came a letter from Carnegie stipulating that he should pay no more than $10,000 this year.[57]

On the other hand Whitney, who declared himself "haunted with the money fear" and promised Cleveland "a good finance committee," set himself to raise whatever funds were needed for all exigencies.[58] What he apparently did, in effect, was to hold an informal meeting (quite like that of Wanamaker's and Quay's "fat-frying" movement) at which political "protection" was offered to the various groups in finance and industry, who were invited to make contributions in measure with the privileges they desired from the National Government.* Promise was given, for instance, to "take care of" the Sugar Trust, which paid to Mr. Whitney's campaign fund now probably the largest donation ever received in a party campaign. Such political promises are of course tacit, or secret, rather than written contracts. Since they are not necessarily revealed to the party's standard-bearer, their infallible or letter-perfect fulfillment cannot always be expected to follow, and they involve certain human risks. The contributions themselves depend upon the confidence which the payer feels in the actual influence carried by the "political agent."

Upon such terms Whitney was enabled to organize also an enthusiastic bankers' committee, whose chairman was August Belmont, and which levied contributions in Wall Street as freely as Wanamaker's committee had levied them upon the tariff-hungry manufacturers of Pennsylvania and Ohio.[59] For the bankers not only the gold standard was at stake, but also privileges in serving as government, War Department, and Navy depositories. The railroad interests, as a bloc, desired at this time chiefly "protection" from the workings of the Interstate Commerce Act, which was empowered to

---

* With the distinction that whereas the Republican "fat-friers" promised augmentations of tariff benefits, the Democratic agents now apparently promised immunity from loss of such benefits.

punish "pooling" and discriminatory rates. The manufacturing groups feared most the workings of the Sherman Anti-Trust Act, and prosecution before the Federal courts; this group also sought reassurances that the tariff schedules would not be radically changed to their loss. The Whisky Trust, with which Whitney himself was often identified, was deeply concerned with the problem of excise taxes as well as government prosecution; the Sugar Trust, through its friend Senator Gorman, also pressed its own claims before the high councils of the Democratic Party.

Pitchfork Ben Tillman in a eulogy on Senator Gorman before the Senate some years later related, concerning the campaign of 1892 and certain accusations made against Gorman:

> In the conversations I had with Democratic leaders, it was clearly brought out that the sugar refineries were ready to contribute to the Democratic campaign fund if it could be understood that the industry would be fostered and not destroyed by the Democratic Tariff policy, and I received the impression, which became indelibly fixed . . . to this day, that President Cleveland understood the situation and was willing to acquiesce in it if we won at the polls.[60]

The candidate might be in no way a party to corrupt agreements. In 1892 he was certainly not informed of all the shifts to which Whitney in his frantic search for money resorted, though he might bear the responsibility for them afterward. Mr. Havemeyer of the Sugar Trust was reported later to have turned over $100,000 to Whitney and Gorman—some reports rated his total donations to both parties at $500,000, including State campaign funds.[61] *

In another case, a New York millionaire named Van Alen, who had a reputation for stupidity, boasted publicly that he had paid to Mr. Whitney's campaign fund $50,000 in return for the promise of certain appointment to a foreign embassy, that of Italy; Mr. Cleveland, to the horror of all true civil-service reformers, would be compelled afterward to ask the Senate's approval of his appointment.

---

* Mr. Henry Havemeyer, testifying two years later before a Senate committee upon his donations to both parties, stated with great candor, "We receive a good deal of protection for our money." In other words, if the doctrines of both parties opposed each other, Mr. Havemeyer might be promised positive benefits from the managers of one party, and from the other protection or immunity from negative or injurious action!

Whitney, in 1892, made history in raising the "sinews of war." He also left no stone unturned to placate the great city bosses, not only pledging to their machines patronage for the future, but providing them with large sums of money and important places in the current campaign Organization. Cleveland, frightened at times by Whitney's "excesses" and his "deals" with treacherous spoilsmen, exclaimed privately: "I have not been consulted at all—or scarcely at all—about the conduct of the campaign"; [62] and again: "I don't seem to be running things much." [63]

But that Whitney gave him clearly to understand the necessity of reassuring the protected manufacturers and industrial Trusts is shown by the special tone of a passage in Cleveland's letter of acceptance, whose "line" Whitney helped to establish in numerous conferences. Departing from the spirited party plank on tariff reform, with its Free Trade animus, and from the bellicose tone of his own earlier papers, Cleveland said:

. . . we wage no exterminating war against any American interests. We believe a readjustment can be accomplished . . . without disaster or demolition . . . we contemplate a fair and careful distribution of necessary tariff burdens rather than the precipitation of free trade. . . . We will rely upon the intelligence of our fellow countrymen to reject the charge that a party [the Democratic] . . . is planning the destruction . . . of American interests; and we know they cannot be frightened by the spectre of impossible free trade. [64]

This was almost precisely the terminology used by the Republican politicians. At signs of such a clear change of front, such a concession by the champion of low tariffs, the tariff-protected industrialists who were approached for donations might well believe in Whitney's "influence" and capacity to shape events.*

At the polls some 5,500,000 votes were cast for Cleveland, giving him a plurality of 400,000 over his adversary. The electoral majority was more crushing still, with Republican Illinois, Wisconsin, and

* Whitney was continually consulted on the writing of the letter of acceptance, in which the candidate expresses his doctrines. (Cleveland Papers, July-Sept., 1892.) "Big Business was behind him [Cleveland] and there was no end of campaign money" whether to make converts among formerly Republican Germans of Wisconsin or the Jewish voters of New York's East Side. (Dunn, *From Harrison to Harding*, Vol. I, p. 397; *cf.* Vagts, *Deutschland*, Vol. I, p. 452, on Villard's "operations.")

California added to the "doubtful" States of Indiana, New York, and New Jersey in the Democratic column, making in all 277 electoral votes to 145. In the Middle Border, in the mountain States, and on the Pacific slope, the new People's Party gathered 22 electors for Weaver, and as an analysis of the polling reports shows, drew some 63 electoral votes in addition from habitually Republican sections to the Democrats.[65] More than 1,000,000 votes were cast for the Populist ticket; in Kansas, 5 out of 7 congressional seats were won by them; in three States their candidates for Governor were elected. What was more important, many Democratic candidates for Congress, such as William Bryan of Nebraska, were elected by their support, and were pledged to Populist doctrines.

The Populists had not won the "balance of power," but in twelve Western States (of the Middle Border and the Rockies) they had cast almost 35 per cent of the total vote. The results were not clear: in the South, the "Negro question" kept white farmers Democrats; in the East, labor did not vote for Populism. Perhaps Cleveland would have won without fusion with the Populists in the West, though the outcome might have been too painfully close to bear.

New York's social leaders, the Chamber of Commerce, and the Reform Club were jubilant, and tendered the victorious candidate a series of brilliant dinner parties, one of these being given at Sherry's on November 17, 1892, by Henry Villard, who had labored so hard in the campaign and given so much. The real purpose of this gathering, as Villard related privately, was that Cleveland might proffer to his hopeful moneyed supporters direct assurances with reference to the currency problem, which was "of the greatest weight for all civilized people." [66] The old reformer Carl Schurz, who nowadays fought almost exclusively on behalf of gold, in his toast likened Cleveland to Washington and Lincoln.

Cleveland made an extemporaneous and quite sentimental speech. "I thank God," he exclaimed in reply to the ovations of Villard, Whitney, W. R. Grace, Calvin Brice, William Steinway, Oswald Ottendorfer, and others, "that far above all doubts and misgivings . . . we may see the light of hope and of safety." ("Misgivings" alluded, no doubt, to the deeply radical color of the national vote that year.) Cleveland, however, received his illumination from "the principles of true, honest and pure Democracy, showing the way in all times of danger, leading us to the fulfillment of political duty and the redemption of all our pledges. . . . Let us not be misled to our undoing by other lights of false Democracy which may be kindled in broken faith and which, shining in hypocrisy, will, if followed, lure us to the rocks of failure and disgrace." [67]

The pledge was unmistakably given. In Cleveland's honest conviction, true and pure democracy was gold, and false democracy, silver; and the numerous millionaires present undoubtedly gathered hope and felt more safe.

In the meantime the most ruthless of the protected monopolists, Henry Frick, was writing to his partner: "I am very sorry for President Harrison, but I cannot see that our interests are going to be affected one way or the other by the change in administration." To which the vivacious Carnegie replied:

Cleveland! Landslide! Well we have nothing to fear and perhaps it is best. People will now think the Protected Manfrs. are attended to and quit agitating. Cleveland is a pretty good fellow. Off for Venice tomorrow. [68]

CHAPTER FIFTEEN

THE SECOND CLEVELAND TERM: THE BETRAYAL OF POPULAR MANDATES

You may think Cleveland's administration was Democratic. It was not. Cleveland was a conservative Republican.
                                        WOODROW WILSON

"I ONLY wish God would put it in my power," Cleveland writes after the victory, as if with a groan of anxiety, "to make known to the Democratic party what the last election means." [1] The last election had clearly been a manifestation, though distorted in part by sectional and institutional factors, of popular discontent at government favoritism toward one of the richest group of capitalists, the protected manufacturers. To a great degree also, the signs of popular feeling showed a sharp increase in the demand for monetary inflation.

But the plans fixed in the Inner Circle of the incoming party pointed, instead, to deflation, to the defense of Sound Money at all costs, to the restoration of business "confidence" in the American dollar and in government finances. These plans would oppose the simple demands of masses of farmers and small tradespeople, untutored in conservative economic doctrine but suffering from the real distress of a cruel deflation; they would lend themselves to the charge of favoring, in turn, another and even more powerful capitalist group, made up of the national bankers, the insurance companies, the great security and interest-gathering institutions of the money centers. Hence Cleveland, with his mind upon certain solemn "duties" and the fulfillment of certain "pledges" of which the voting masses knew little, anticipated bitter strife and disillusionment within his party, deeply divided as it was on the questions of the hour. Concerning the rightness and virtue of his course he held no doubts, being convinced, as he said, that we were passing through "days of wildness," and that only "conservatism and steadiness" might bring the Ship of State to a safe harbor. [2]

The first plan of the new Administration involved the most bitter pill of all: repeal of the Sherman Silver Purchase Act of 1890, and the abolition of silver as a metallic basis for our money, despite the party platform which promised the use of "both gold and silver." As a second measure, in order to cover the alarming Treasury deficit of 1892 a reform of the protective-tariff schedules was planned; to be sure, an extremely moderate downward revision, but one which would encourage rather than prohibit imports, and so raise the customs revenues of the Government. A third measure, of more temporary character, was directed to shoring up the gold reserve of the Treasury through government loans. This reserve had been dangerously depleted under Harrison, and the unpleasant job of issuing new government bonds for the purchase of more gold had been delayed up to the last hour, leaving it as an "orphan" on the doorstep of the incoming Administration.

Measures of finance, always obscure to the people and ill-understood by most politicians, absorbed the energies of the second Cleveland Administration even before it was inaugurated. The worried financiers swarmed about the President-elect and pursued him with their advice. Mr. Henry Villard, who acted as "the friend and counsellor" of the President, advised him of the coming of a "financial hurricane." Villard represented a group of German bankers who hoped to manage profitable government loans in combination with the American bankers—August Belmont, J. P. Morgan, and James Stillman—and therefore followed events closely. Cleveland was warned that he must act promptly if he would not have the future of the new Administration jeopardized by financial disasters.[3]

Two weeks before his inauguration the President-elect set on foot private preliminary negotiations with Belmont, to whom he sent Daniel Lamont. He wished to learn upon what terms $50,000,000 in Treasury bonds, at "three or four percent"—for the purpose of augmenting the government gold reserve—might be floated. The actual gold, he said, was to "be brought from abroad and put in our Treasury, and I want it done promptly and in such manner that the par value of the bonds shall be forthcoming to us free from commission." He added: "Of course we do not commit ourselves. . . . The necessity of such action may be averted. I only want you to find out in the most confidential way possible what can be done if the contingency arrives." [4]

Soon all Wall Street gossiped of forthcoming government loans. Discussion raged in the circle of the President-elect, harassed at this moment by the problem of choosing a new Cabinet. Villard, who lobbied hard in the expiring Lame Duck session of Congress during February to win repeal of the Silver Purchase Act, also addressed an unofficial meeting of the newly selected Cabinet at the Arlington Hotel, on the eve of the inauguration, pleading that an extra session of Congress should be called in order to take prompt action which would stimulate both financial "confidence" and government loans. Cleveland, the "honest steward," was highly optimistic, events proved, about the terms on which money could be borrowed. He would, in good time, be undeceived as to the mercy which international bankers showed sovereign governments in distress.

But for the moment the need for borrowing money was averted. In February and early March the great New York banks, in response to new "patriotic" appeals by government officials, deposited limited amounts of gold in the Treasury against Legal Tender notes. Foster, the outgoing Secretary of the Treasury, had come to Wall Street personally, to plead with the banks that they give up gold voluntarily in exchange for Legal Tender, obtaining thus some $6,000,000 to $8,000,000 in gold deposits to tide over the change in the Administration. [5] The impending government loan was postponed, to the disappointment of the watching international financiers. Cleveland's political advisers, John Carlisle and Walter Gresham, had urged postponement of this momentous and, in some measure, unprecedented step, without added authorization by Congress.*

II

President Cleveland's second Cabinet, balanced after much effort between Northern, Southern, and Western sections, contained at least one distinguished and independent American personality in Judge

---

* "From a strict commercial point of view"—that is, of possible profits from overnight revaluation of gold hoardings—"there was good reason why the banks should not make any such exchange." (Noyes, *Thirty Years of American Finance*, p. 183; cf. *Commercial and Financial Chronicle*, Feb. 11 and Feb. 18, 1893, editorials.)

Walter Gresham of Indiana, who was named Secretary of State. The famous jurist, who had been a lifelong Republican, had supported Cleveland against his own personal rival, Harrison, in the late elections and so helped to carry Indiana. The selection of this man of progressive views on tariff, civil-service, and railroad questions lent honor to the new Administration and gave it upon the surface a nonpartisan and even liberal air. For Gresham's very talents and scrupulous honesty had excluded him from high office within the gift of his own party, and he was not liked the more for that by professional Democrats. But by now the noble Gresham was old and tired, cast in a role for which he was less apt, and in a department where his particular talents and enlightened principles could help little, in truth, to mitigate the profoundly reactionary passion of this Administration.

John Carlisle of Kentucky, the former Speaker of the House, was also expected to be an ornament as well as a useful adjunct. For many years he had been known for his low-tariff views, upheld frequently in congressional debates. As Secretary of the Treasury he was expected to show Western sympathies rather than subservience to Wall Street or State Street, while his familiarity with taxation problems and his long parliamentary experience would stand in good stead.

Once a popular and important figure in his party, an exponent of old-fashioned democracy in his public speeches, Carlisle showed a wavering character and incapacity for his office during the difficult years in which he served. The Eastern bankers were at first suspicious of the "bluegrass" Secretary; and his course toward them at the outset showed a disposition not to yield quickly enough to their most urgent demands, while paying some heed to the intense convictions and prejudices of the Western and Southern agricultural masses. Had not Carlisle in 1875 opposed the resumption of the gold standard? In the controversy over silver and gold he would have favored a typical politician's solution of compromise. But as between compromise measures of more restricted silver coinage and outright repeal of the Silver Purchase Act, the determined President struck for absolute repeal and, under tremendous pressure himself, shouldered aside his hesitant Secretary. Carlisle suffered from the contradictions of his position; when at length he yielded to the extreme Gold

Democrats, he seemed to collapse. His actions grew more and more inconsistent, and scandal attacked him; Cleveland and his close advisers made decisions for the Treasury Department, while the once brilliant Mr. Carlisle would sometimes be picked up, befuddled and helpless, after having sought relief in nocturnal drinking bouts.

The other cabinet members were unknowns, in part mediocre political selections, in part personal friends, such as Wilson Bissell, the Postmaster General, a native of Buffalo; but their selection too was not without significance. A familiar figure from the old regime was Daniel Lamont, earlier private secretary to Cleveland at Albany and at the White House, and now named Secretary of War. Lamont had been an aide and protégé of the late New York boss, Daniel Manning, and was a master of Organization craft and lore. To Cleveland he had been an indispensable and trusted servant. During the Republican interregnum, Whitney had found the bald-headed, close-mouthed little man with the walrus mustaches most useful as a confidential aide in his stock-market forays. Whitney, with his increasingly sinister Wall Street reputation, could no longer be invited into the Cabinet any more than Henry Villard. But Lamont, considerably enriched, more secretive and silent than ever, was Whitney's alter ego in the Cabinet, the custodian of presidential secrets and the "Assistant President," as political observers called him. "Lamont in some respects filled the place of William C. Whitney in Cleveland's first Administration," and was also "the means of communication . . . between Cleveland and the big business men of the country." [6] Thus the restless hand of the uncanny Whitney still hung over the Administration for years—even more potent than if he had been present at its councils—though he held himself in the shadows now, sometimes fearing even to show himself in Washington.*

The many illuminating letters and dispatches from Whitney to Lamont, arriving almost daily at certain seasons, show what close watch Whitney kept over the affairs of the National Government, testify to his constant requests for jobs and places to be turned over to friends of the Standard Oil family, and record his demands for

---

* "Because of articles about me [in the press] intended for the annoyance of Cleveland it would be thought wrongly of at this time." (Lamont Papers, letter of June 1, 1895.)

special government favors to friendly banks, as well as his detailed advice and virtual orders in matters of taxation, tariff schedules, and financial policy. "If I want a thing I will ask for it," Whitney writes Lamont breezily at the very beginning of the new term.[7] And the mousy Lamont carries out all requests promptly, or goes noiselessly to the President's office to transmit Mr. Whitney's views as to which banking syndicate should be awarded the profitable financing of a government-bond issue, or which tariff duties should be "specific" and which "ad valorem."[8] A message comes, and Lamont sends off a War Department memorandum requesting the assignment of post-office deposits to a certain New York bank of which "Mr. Whitney is one of the largest owners."[9] One spirited communication reads:

In making plans I hope August Belmont & Co., will have the opportunity of being made the financial agents of the different departments. Brown Bros. were made so when we were in before but they did little or nothing this time and I think Belmont entitled to consideration. He took the chairmanship of the bankers' committee and gave $10,000 himself.[10]

Lamont is Secretary of War; but military duties do not occupy enough of his time. He glides from the Post Office to the White House, to the corridors of the Senate, back to the Treasury Department, where, at periods, he seems to supersede Carlisle. The advance knowledge he possesses concerning financial actions contemplated by the Administration, concerning duties on sugar or steel, upon which impassioned and notorious speculation in Wall Street largely centered in the 1890's—all this is of supreme value, giving tactical advantage to the market leader with millions at his command. Whitney, in return, gives Lamont "points" or advance "tips" upon speculative stocks: "I don't want to advise, but Col. [O. H. Payne?] and I have both bought [Metropolitan] Traction around 110."[11] Certainly in a time of peace Lamont was one of the busiest Secretaries of War the Government had ever boasted. As the unsleeping liaison officer for the magnificent Whitney and his associates, Lamont of course enjoyed an influence at the cabinet table far surpassing his official rank.

Still curiouser was the personality and the choice of Richard Olney of Boston as Attorney General, a strategic executive post in an Administration which was in duty bound to prosecute the industrial Trusts and monopolistic railroads. Olney's selection, after certain other personages had declined the embarrassing invitation, was due to "a strong New York backing," according to an intimate of Cleveland's.[12] Some unseen hand and eye which shaped the character of the new Administration as a "rock of conservatism" had certainly fished up this hard-crusted Yankee corporation lawyer from State Street, who had spent his life chiefly in the service of New England financiers and railroad captains.

Without public glory as yet, Olney's capacities were fully appreciated by men like John M. Forbes and Charles E. Perkins, the builders of the rich Chicago, Burlington & Quincy Railroad, whom he served as corporation counsel. Olney was a bank director as well as a director of two other large railroads, the Santa Fe, and the Boston & Maine, at the time of his appointment.[13] All his life had literally been passed in board rooms, trading, negotiating, counseling. Olney was admired by the great Eastern capitalists, and his selection for a cabinet office was made with a view to gaining their support for the Cleveland Administration.

But more lately he had acted together with the young Mr. Elihu Root as counsel to the Whisky Trust, prosecuted under the Sherman Anti-Trust Law. The Whisky Trust (American Cattlefeed and Distilling Company), famous at the moment for having attempted to have an independent distillery in Chicago blown up by dynamite, was under prosecution in several States at the same time, like the Standard Oil Company. But the case had been won before Federal Judge Jenkins in Massachusetts, on the afterward familiar ground that "manufacturing is not commerce"; Judge Jenkins had promptly been appointed to the United States Supreme Court by President Harrison. But among Mr. Olney's satisfied employers who had seen him "riddle" the Anti-Trust Act in court we find once more the ubiquitous Mr. Whitney, who, with the stealthy Mr. Ryan, held much stock then in the Whisky Trust. Like the protective tariff, the Trust law was to be administered by a "friend,"—indeed by "the hired man of the Whisky Trust." [14]

Olney's authorized biographer has described the man as both obstinate and cruel, of a pugnacious disposition, with a glaring bulldog physiognomy and eyes like coals. In short,

a hard-thinking, accomplishing, ruthless being like one of those modern war-tanks which proceeds across the roughest ground, heedless of opposition, deaf alike to messages from friends and cries from the foe, able to crush every person and every obstacle that gets between it and its chosen objective.[15]

A close student of his profession, he had previously shown distaste for public office, and took almost no pleasure in human company save that of his family, over whom he tyrannized. We must note also that four years earlier, in 1888, he had played a most active part in breaking a strike by the employees of the "Burlington" Railroad, to whose fortunes he seemed more attached than to any other thing.

Before accepting Cleveland's offer Olney had written at once to Perkins, president of the Burlington, asking if in his opinion it would be "to the true interest of the C.B.&Q." that he, Olney, should become the United States Attorney General.[16] The reply may have assured Olney that since he loved railroads, which were then under such heavy attack, and disbelieved in the legal force of the Anti-Trust Act, his acceptance of the post would be in the true interest not only of the Burlington but of all railroads and industrial corporations.

If Lamont was the fox of this hard-pressed, embattled Administration, then Olney, with his bold and aggressive temperament, was its lion. Yet he brought intellectual traits superior to the others which made him eventually the formidable, the dominating figure of the President's circle. Especially he showed a certain brilliance of logic which enabled him to define the self-interest of the capitalist class with a precision and clarity that few others have equaled. He would fight without giving quarter when the way was clear, but he could bide his time too.

Some weeks before Olney took office, the railroad captain Perkins, who feared government attempts to regulate railroads, sought the prospective Attorney General's aid in persuading the new Administration to abolish the Interstate Commerce Commission altogether. Olney in his reply considered various aspects of the recent reform law and expressed with utmost candor a "business and rail-road point of view" and a philosophy of government relations with business which has seldom been so wisely and honestly put. He advised:

My impression would be that looking at the matter from a railroad point of view exclusively it would not be a wise thing to undertake. . . . The attempt would not be likely to succeed; if it did not succeed, and were made on the ground of the inefficiency and uselessness of the Com-mission, the result would very probably be giving it the power it now lacks. *The Commission, as its functions have now been limited by the courts, is, or can be made, of great use to the railroads. It satisfies the popu-lar clamor for a government supervision of railroads, at the same time that that supervision is almost entirely nominal. Further, the older such a com-mission gets to be, the more inclined it will be found to take the business and railroad view of things. It thus becomes a sort of barrier between the railroad corporations and the people and a sort of protection against hasty and crude legislation hostile to railroad interests. . . . The part of wisdom is not to destroy the Commission, but to utilize it.*[17] *

During the tense opening weeks of the new Administration, Olney began to press his clear business and "railroad view of things" upon the Government. According to this the gold standard must be de-fended at all costs. He maintained close contact between the Cleve-land Cabinet and the "bankers, merchants and others in Boston," as he related. To Perkins, Forbes, and Henry Lee Higginson he sent information about where to "spend some money" in accomplishing the repeal of the Silver Purchase Act, furnishing them with a list of "doubtful Senators, who ought to be persuaded to see the thing in the right light."[18]

III

When Cleveland was inaugurated the till was bare; it was the most disheartening state of affairs since Buchanan had left office in 1861. Only the traditional gold reserve of $100,000,000 was left for the last defense of the currency. Yet of these things the President

---

* The device of setting up putative reform as a "barrier" against real reforms, suggested so unmistakably in Olney's letter to a railroad president, is a piece of political legerdemain that has been used repeatedly in the past—and by no means neglected in the present.

openly said nothing, as he said nothing of the growing financial crisis. Although Carlisle wished not to appear to yield to Wall Street, soon he too, after some hesitation, undertook journeys to Canossa and interviewed the New York bankers in person to obtain fresh deposits of gold in return for government paper currency. Thus painfully some $25,000,000 more were gathered in an early effort to dam up the flow of gold from the Treasury. The adverse trade balance, the fear of the new "radical" Congress, the rising public sentiment for inflation, all combined to make bankers reconvert their paper money into gold again at the first moment. Then "the very sight of this desperate struggle going on to maintain the public credit was sufficient to alarm both home and foreign interests." [19]

It seemed incredible, it was grotesque, that the young nation of boundless resources and capacity for growth, which had repaid the bulk of the gigantic Civil War debt in a few years, should now be "fighting for its financial life," while its energetic citizens suffered from the scarcity of capital and credit. Did the bankers actually believe that the great republic of the West was about to disappear forever in the gulf of bankruptcy? Some of them were resigned to the suspension of gold payments at any moment. At least one academic authority, Professor Taussig of Harvard, maintained that such a departure would, in the long run, alter prices or values but little, since he held that the scarcity of credit was the chief and temporary trouble.[20]

Yet the movement of the money market continued "abnormal." Though the American harvest was large in 1892 and trade active, disordered speculation had created points of weakness which pressure of liquidation from London soon uncovered. Moreover, Austria was accumulating gold for resumption, while Russia did the same for suspected war purposes, and interest rates were rising. It needed only the touch of sensational incidents to turn the steady stream of liquidation into a mad torrent in 1893.

By mid-April of 1893 the bankers were again drawing gold from the Treasury at an alarming rate. Cleveland sent the trusty Lamont to appeal for gold exchanges, but received a rebuff from James Stillman, head of the National City Bank.[21] On April 20, 1893, Secretary Carlisle in a public interview, whose motive was rather obscure, admitted that the government gold reserve had fallen below $100,-000,000, and announced that he was using his discretionary powers and would continue to pay out gold (for silver notes) "as long as he had gold lawfully available for that purpose." This was a day of panic in financial markets, following upon the sudden, unexpected passing of dividends by the National Cordage Co. The Secretary's vague expression led to rumors that he might begin at any moment to redeem paper money only in silver coin, at his discretion, as he was authorized to do under the Sherman Silver Purchase Act of 1890. A storm of anger directed itself upon him from Wall Street, echoing the general mistrust of Carlisle that Stillman had earlier expressed to the President's confidential agent, Daniel Lamont.[22]

Enormous pressure from a formidable group of moneylenders and financiers was now put upon the President. Francis L. Stetson, formerly his associate and now counsel for J. P. Morgan & Co., described to him the terror in the financial district, reporting that gold had actually gone to a premium. Cleveland must, he wrote, promptly issue a statement that would undo the harm wrought by Carlisle. Above all he must be prepared to use "every dollar of the $100,000,-000 gold reserve in meeting the government obligations"—that is, he must if need be use this up rather than attempt to hold it intact.[23]

Cleveland responded at once as requested, with an outspoken declaration that he would maintain the gold standard. Now in a flood of letters applause was showered upon him by the frightened rich, Republican and Democrat, Jew and gentile. From New York Charles Fairchild, Jacob Schiff, Andrew Carnegie, and many others wrote him that he had saved the nation's honor and credit, and above all its "industrial interests." [24] Andrew Carnegie went on to suggest a "line" that the President might take to allay the excitement throughout the country, in a public proclamation, which he made so bold as to write for him:

As long as I am President of the United States, the workingman is going to be paid in as good a dollar as the foreign banker is.

There was a political cunning in Carnegie which clearly overreached itself, and the President did nothing of the sort, even though the steel magnate assured him that "this would be good politics." Carnegie further promised him "the unanimous support of the Republican party," if he should begin the fight for repeal of the Silver Purchase Act.[25]

By May 5, 1893, the storm raging in Wall Street had reached catastrophic proportions. Certain of the new Trusts collapsed into bankruptcy at this moment, following fraudulent reports of their earnings and payment of artificial dividends. After the failure of the Reading Railroad in February, there came new sensations in May with the exposure of fraud in the Atchison, Topeka & Santa Fe Railroad, whose directors had gulled public and bankers alike to the tune of $7,000,000. Wall Street became a nightmare of downward-careening values. English and European banks, which had loaned the bulk of the capital used by our overbuilt and overcapitalized railroads, discharged their holdings of stocks and even of high-grade bonds at once, precipitating a vast bank run which swept the country. In New York money virtually disappeared; certified checks sold at a 4 per cent discount; clearinghouse bank scrip was used again for exchanges, as in 1884 and 1873.

But in the interior of the country, in the South and the West, banks in need of currency clamored in vain during May and June; the New York banks refused to discount their notes and paper, and five hundred banks failed.[26] It was a fearful "lesson" in sound finance which the Eastern bankers now administered to the agrarians, a lesson which they never forgot, and which was attended with a vast number of foreclosures of farm mortgages that year. In the South, as in the West, there were fine harvests that season; in certain regions the farmer brought his cotton to town only to find that against such security no money whatsoever could be obtained from the bank even to pay for shipment of his crop.

During the parlous days of May and June, the Treasury not only redeemed its Treasury notes in gold, but began paying its ordinary bills in gold coin, as Morgan's lawyer, F. L. Stetson, had insisted. The great financiers redoubled their efforts to force the President to call an extra session of Congress for the repeal of the Silver Purchase Act—a step which his purely political advisers sought to delay. August Belmont sent word that the British Government had ordered the

Indian mint closed to silver coinage, causing heavy losses to the United States Treasury, which had been purchasing over 50,000,000 ounces of silver a year.[27] Jim Hill reported frenzied conditions in the Northwest, with no money available for moving crops. He now advised the President to listen carefully to the proposals of that "expert financial man," Jacob Schiff of Kuhn, Loeb & Co.[28] At the very same moment, as if by collusion, Fairchild, the banker who was Cleveland's friend and former Secretary of the Treasury, brought a memorandum which he had obtained from Schiff, framing a highly plausible compromise measure for the emergency. This scheme proposed quieting the unhappy masses by appearing to yield free coinage of silver in one clause, while in another it directed that coinage must be suspended entirely whenever the gold reserve became impaired or fell below a safe stipulated figure.[29]

The financial panic grew into a business depression and spread unemployment as liquidation continued of its own momentum month after month. Bankers increased their agitation for repeal of the Silver Purchase Act of 1890, which made suspension of gold payments, in their opinion, an ever present possibility and accelerated the tendency to hoarding. Mr. Schiff wrote again in different vein, June 21, 1893. Now, he said, was the time to act; now was the strategic time to call Congress in session and repeal the Silver Purchase Act. For soon the American grain harvest would be moving to Europe and a return flow of gold in payment for it would "ease the situation temporarily and make it harder to repeal." [30] The President must act now rather than when "things seem to be on the mend."

Cleveland had up to now recoiled from calling Congress; possibly because he, like Carlisle, wished to avoid "seeming to yield to Wall Street pressure." [31] Possibly, also, out of fear of the painful step involved. The President and the Democratic majority in Congress had been elected upon a platform of tariff reform; certainly they had no clear mandate from the people to terminate the law for the purchase of silver. Moreover, most Congressmen hated Cleveland heartily; he yielded them patronage reluctantly or without political skill, while asking of them unpopular measures which might lead to their unseating when they faced their constituents again. Cleveland for his part had a singular aversion for the legislative branch of our

Government. He was the author of the expression "I have a Congress on my hands." [32] Moreover, he had deliberately withheld patronage for precisely such an emergency in order to use it as a club with which to beat the legislators until they dispatched "the duty our party owes the people." [33]

After Schiff's letter, the President no longer brooded and hesitated over his course, long marked for him by the financiers of the Eastern money centers. On June 30, 1893, he called Congress in special session for August 7 for the purpose of repealing "unwise laws" relative to the currency.*

IV

The country was more and more bitterly divided over the money issue, according to sectional feeling and according to the economic position of creditor or debtor. In the East the conservative press, led by the New York *Tribune,* the Springfield *Republican,* and the *Nation,* preached continually the great "lesson" of Sound Money. It said in effect:

You agrarians have by your agitation for the purchase of silver enacted a law destined to force a deficit upon the Treasury, and another increasing without limit the issues of silver-coin Treasury notes which are a liability upon it. Thus confidence in the national Treasury and currency has been undermined. Banks cannot meet bills of exchange due in London with silver or with Legal Tender covered by silver bullion; in a period of "adverse" trade they are forced to draw out gold and ship it abroad, while others add to this movement through justifiable fears of repudiation which you have spread; thus gold disappears from circulation; money and credit based upon gold diminish tenfold. What we must do now in the crisis (which you agrarians have brought about) is to repeal the whole wretched

---

* The pressure at times seemed intolerable. The papers of Cleveland are swollen with letters, memoranda, and dispatches from finance capitalists, day after day—while through the screen which surrounds him almost no word from Mr. Bryan's "bold yeomanry" ever penetrates. Cleveland, with admirable candor, has left us the most nearly complete private papers of any President. We must not therefore assume that he was more besieged by "Wall Street" than were Harrison, Arthur, Hayes, and Grant, who preceded him but who have left us no such complete private record. The legend of Cleveland's "courage" to execute unpopular measures desired almost exclusively by one class in the community has of course been nurtured by this same class exclusively—and has recently been resurrected to draw invidious comparison with our present Chief Magistrate, Franklin Roosevelt.

silver-buying program—restore "confidence" in our money itself, so that credit and trade may revive again.

Cleveland's vigorous appeal to Congress for a gold standard was mainly written by Richard Olney, though its belligerent phrases were softened by the President. Sharing the religious faith of all financial conservatives in the "drip theory" of economy, he urged that the purpose of repeal was to make our currency "so safe . . . that those who have money will spend and invest it in business and enterprise instead of holding it." [34]

The farmers of the West and the South, however, were up in arms against a program which would continue to its bitter end the process of contraction so immediately disastrous to them. After the stoppage of the Indian mint in June, the world market price of silver plunged downward rapidly, and concomitantly, as Representative Bryan of Nebraska noted, wheat fell from 83¾ cents a bushel on June 1, 1893, to 69½ cents in October.[35] The downward course of commodity values was explained by experts as due to improved methods of production in all goods throughout the world. But in July, as the special session of Congress prepared to convene, a great Silver Convention gathered at Denver, representing the mining interests of the mountain States, and added its voice to that of the farm leaders in demanding a halt to the gigantic international bankers' "conspiracy" to demonetize silver on two continents.[36]

Both major political parties were denounced for violating their clear platform pledges not to abolish silver coinage. "This is a life or death struggle for our Republic," one of the Western farmers' leaders wrote to the Populist Senator Allen, August 9, 1893.[37] The sectional and class lines drawn by the fierce dispute over repeal of the Silver Purchase Act split across party lines in both houses of Congress in a manner most significant and ominous. Led by Richard Bland of Missouri and Bryan, the Boy Orator from Nebraska, fully one-third of the Democrats in the House of Representatives, supported by a file of Populists, revolted against the Administration leadership. But in this emergency almost the whole Republican minority, which in 1890 had voted for the Sherman Silver Purchase Act to "prevent something worse," was now brought over by their leader, Thomas Reed, to succor the Democratic Administration. The mocking Reed evoked great laughter when he exclaimed: "We stand in a very peculiar position, we Republicans to-day!" The Republicans, he told Congress, would support a Democratic President against the irresponsible hosts of his own party in the battle for "specie payments and prosperity," for "true and solid finance." [38]

In the Senate, where limitation of debate could not be invoked, the issue was even more doubtful. Silver Republicans from the Great West, such as Teller, Jones, and Stewart, combined with the Populists Peffer, Allen, and Kyle from the Middle Border and a bloc of Southern Democrats in the battle against gold; while Eastern Republicans, under the leadership of Aldrich and John Sherman (who now expiated his sins) broke from their party lines to join the Eastern Gold Democrats led by Gorman.

During the sultry months of July and August, when preparations must be made for the parliamentary struggle and the party lash be applied to laggards by the President, Cleveland fell ill and was mysteriously absent. While a minor surgical operation upon a tumor in his palate was performed in utmost secrecy, the greatest anxiety prevailed among his circle of friends. What havoc for all markets and trade might not follow an accident to the President in this time of panic and party strife? Happily, the mammoth Cleveland recovered quickly from his ordeal, somewhat embittered by his physical suffering, more resolute than ever to defeat the "heretics." Pain, illness, the strokes of opponents, only hardened him; he fought with a martyr's fervor in the cause of gold money.

The plans of the Inner Circle were thorough. Patronage power was withheld from Senators and Congressmen until the contest was decided. Enormous pressure was brought to bear upon wavering Representatives, who were given the darkest reports of business prostration, while each man who could be reached was reminded of his responsibility to provide relief to the embarrassed Treasury and aid to commercial revival. [39] On the other hand, an influential old spoilsman like Senator Daniel Voorhees of Indiana, who had formerly been an opponent of Cleveland and a lifelong inflationist, was completely won over by being given all the Organization patronage of his region, so that he became suddenly bloated with political prosperity.*

The veteran Silverite Richard Bland, the young Joseph Bailey of Texas, and the still younger Bryan led the fight for the plain people from beyond the Mississippi.

Bryan, elected to Congress three years earlier at the age of thirty, had already attracted national attention by his powerful speech against repeal of the Silver Purchase Act at the close of the previous session. In his youth, at college in the West, he had become a debater and an orator of astonishing force. This poor, handsome young country-town lawyer possessed modest learning and uncertain information; but when he spoke in public he made points quickly and knew how to confound his adversaries and win applause. Drawn by the glamour of the rostrum, he embarked upon lecture tours, spoke in idealistic and democratic tones upon the questions of the day, and found that he could sway multitudes with ease. He was a perfect figure of a dramatic actor, six feet tall, his face pale, his head noble and expressive, with dark eyes, strong aquiline nose, and wide jaw. Returning at daybreak from one of his early speaking tours, he wakened his wife and exclaimed to her: "Mary, I have had a strange experience. Last night I found that I had power over the audience. I could move them as I chose. I have more than the usual power as a speaker, I know it. God grant that I may use it wisely." [40] His speech was lucid and studded with many a pointed anecdote. Its facile, somewhat florid and conventional poetry or metaphor, when delivered in his ringing and musical voice—which, by all accounts was of "unrivaled beauty"—enhanced the general effect. Moreover, his evangelical temper, his sincere, instinctive distrust of the Eastern money-changers, combined with a characteristic disposition to praise everywhere the humble charm and virtue of small property-holders —the "brave yeomanry" of his native prairies—made him the darling of the disaffected rural masses.

* Voorhees, as a leading member of the Finance Committee, would have been a formidable stumbling-block: "that the Voorhees 'gang' and the Voorhees family were provided for was one of the incidents of the repeal." (Rhodes, *History of the United States*, Vol. VIII, p. 403.)

From the theme of Free Trade which he had earlier espoused, Bryan had turned to the study of the silver question only recently, at the advice of his confrere Joseph Bailey of Texas. Then he had joined the American Bimetallic League, attended its convention in Chicago, heard its ideologues, and become transported by what he had learned of the "international bankers' conspiracy." Thereafter it was to be for him the burden of an unending song.

On August 16, 1893, Bryan rose to speak from prepared notes, threw them aside, and giving to passion free wing, made a soaring three-hour oration for bimetallism. He urged the need of a "second War of Independence"; for Bryan with his intense nationalism held that a plot was on foot to keep our credit and currency system subject to that of British financiers.

In an earlier speech (February 9, 1893), he had said indignantly: "Was the silver act alone cause of the depression?" But the whole world suffered. Repeal would not aid recovery, but would destroy the crop values of millions of grain and cotton farmers.

The poor man who takes property by force is called a thief, but the creditor who can by legislation make a debtor pay a dollar twice as large as he borrowed is lauded as the friend of a sound currency.

The free American farmer was no longer free. The last census showed "a real estate mortgage indebtedness in the five great agricultural States—Illinois, Iowa, Missouri, Kansas and Nebraska—of more than one billion of dollars."

Bryan had also inveighed against the treachery of his party's policy. "Does anyone believe," he asked, "that Mr. Cleveland could have been elected President upon a platform declaring in favor of the unconditional repeal of the Sherman law?"

Now, pursuing the same ideology, he aligned his countrymen in "two nations" of the poor and the rich, the Haves and the Have-Nots, who dwelt side by side. He saw them as divided not by the want or possession of property and the tools of production, but by the conflicting claims of creditor against debtor. In an emotional epopee, given with marvelous effect, he pictured on the one side, "the corporate interests of the United States, the moneyed interests,

aggregated wealth and capital. imperious. arrogant, compassionless";
and on the other,

an unnumbered throng, which gave a name to the Democratic Party, and
for which it has assumed to speak. Work-worn and dust-begrimed, they
make their sad appeal . . . their cries for help too often beat in vain
against the outer wall, while others less deserving, find ready access to
legislative halls.[41]

The House was well whipped into line by the system of ironclad
rules which a Democratic Speaker now used in the manner of Reed.
The Gold Democrats were led by the Administration floor leader,
William Wilson of West Virginia, while Reed spoke for the Republican allies in his old cynical style, declaring that nothing could
be done to relieve the sufferings of the poor except to continue to the
end the processes under way.[42] Repeal was promptly carried in the
House by methods which crushed delay or obstruction.

Bryan was a warning and an apparition; but the push of the Gold
Democrats in the Senate was continued unremittingly all summer.
Here the humanitarian appeals of Silverite Senators such as Teller,
Jones, and Stewart, accused by opponents of holding large interests
in Western mining stocks, were somewhat compromised. Subsequent
events revealed their close affiliations with Marcus Daly, William
Clark, and J. Augustus Heinze, the Copper and Silver Barons of
the Rocky Mountains. But the cause of silver coinage held other,
more disinterested adherents in the South and the Middle Border
States as well; and in the freer theater of the Senate, where parliamentary liberty of debate prevailed, the Administration forces were
driven to ruthless tactics to crush a determined filibuster.

The hero of civil-service reform, from the White House, applied
the whip of patronage unremittingly, rewarding his friends and pun-
ishing opponents. One by one vulnerable or "doubtful" Democratic
Senators were brought under discipline and acted as Cleveland
"cuckoos" who answered, as one Senator said, to the clock at the
White House. It was a supreme effort to exercise congressional leadership upon the part of Cleveland, who had always shown himself
inept for such tasks. (It was a departure from his earlier view that
Congress should make laws and the President merely execute them.)

The Sound Money Senators of both parties broke lines and stuck to each other "as close and affectionately as a stamp sticks to a love letter." Gorman and Brice, as nominal Democrats, and the Republican leaders, Sherman, Aldrich, Allison, and Orville Platt, stood shoulder to shoulder, not as party men but as representatives of the creditor classes, of the part of the country where the creditor classes were in the saddle.[43]

Yet the long deadlock continued during the torrid summer months at Washington, through September and October. The filibustering Populists made speeches which ran as long as fifteen hours, the record achieved by William Allen of Nebraska. The country was uneasy; to circumvent obstruction seemed impossible unless some basis of compromise were found with the Opposition. Even bankers in New York feared that unconditional repeal of the Silver Purchase Act was impossible.

Late in October, both Gorman and Quay in the Senate made a maneuver to bring about simply a restriction of silver-purchasing, and Secretary Carlisle, who apparently favored a politic compromise himself, brought their proposals to Cleveland.[44] But Cleveland "smote the table with his fist" and, forcing Carlisle to change his ground, held the party to "unconditional repeal."

One by one, certain Southern Senators mysteriously yielded, and the last of the needed votes was gained by October 30, 1893.[45] It was a "great personal victory" for the obstinate President; letters from capitalists and sermons in the conservative press showered their praise upon the "staunch old fellow," as the Republican leader, William McKinley, called him. Jacob Schiff and others wrote him that he had exceeded even the fondest hopes of the bankers who had been "in despair" hitherto. He had "stood like a rock" and saved the "honor of the country," though he knew, as he confided to his intimate friend, Don M. Dickinson, that he "looked full in the face" of dissension and disruption for his own party as a consequence of his policy.[46]

"You may . . . congratulate yourselves that you have laid away the free coinage of silver in a sepulcher" Bryan threatened, but it would yet "lay aside its grave clothes and its shroud. It will yet rise, and in its rising and its reign will bless mankind." [47]

From this day forth, as Bryan's warning had intimated, the radical farm wing, the inflationist masses in the West and South, prepared under secret leadership and by all means possible, as Cleveland himself afterward realized, to wrest control of the party Organization from its Eastern masters.[48]

V

Repeal of the silver-purchasing provisions of the Silver Purchase Act of 1890 did not bring the promised restoration of "confidence." The terrible deflation swept forward, as if under its own momentum or impelled by its own necessities. Banks and railroads continued to fail, factories such as the great Carnegie steelworks at Pittsburgh shut down entirely; until by the end of 1893, 642 banks had closed their doors, 22,500 miles of railway had gone into receivership, and a fourth of our heavy industries were moribund.

Bank deposits shrank $378,000,000 during 1893. The Populists and the silver factions, pointing to the fearful credit hardships of the country and the continued decline of all commodity markets, now argued that recovery itself was barred by deflationary measures and the reduction of the circulating money. The Government no longer added to its paper-money obligations by the issuance of Treasury silver notes; but its revenues fell alarmingly, the deficit mounted, and doubts as to its ability to meet even its ordinary expenses were felt.

Meanwhile, at the height of the economic storm, Mr. J. Pierpont Morgan, leader of the Wall Street bankers, proceeded unfalteringly to reorganize and to sweep into his Eastern combination certain fallen coal railroads, such as the bankrupt Reading. His great rivals, the Rockefellers, who now pooled their cash in the National City Bank, borrowed without fear and expanded their activities in new fields of railroads, copper mines, and iron mines. At the same time, it is evident that the Rockefeller-controlled National City Bank continued its gold-hoarding tactics, and paid its current obligations preferably in United States notes or certificates, according to confidential reports from the New York Sub-Treasury to Carlisle.[49]

The plan of the Cleveland Administration was to cover the government losses by borrowing money to purchase gold; as a more permanent measure and one which had been promised for the relief of the "plain people," it was intended to enact lower tariff rates, which would encourage import revenues and repair the losses brought by the "prohibitive" McKinley Tariff Act. In the autumn prices received for the 1893 harvests were extremely low; the adverse movement of gold continued, instead of reversing itself with the crop season, and the Treasury gold reserve sank to $60,000,000. It now became imperative for the Government to borrow money with which to buy gold immediately.

Secretary Carlisle, who was always "more of a theoretical Democrat" than President Cleveland, his biographer relates candidly, hesitated to increase the Government's debt during a time of peace. He found that the laws under which he could borrow money, those of the Resumption Act of 1875, were extremely awkward, providing only for long-term loans with high-interest coupons, such as 5 per cent, instead of for such low-interest, short-term "exchequer bonds" as the British Government used to meet temporary deficits. Moreover, the loss of gold was chiefly caused by the "discretion" which the Treasury used in meeting payments of silver notes in gold coin. It was a very doubtful matter legally if the Treasury could borrow additional money in order to *buy gold with which to redeem Treasury silver notes,* according to the existing Cleveland policy. Carlisle certainly differed with the President, and felt more strongly than he that further legal authorization was required from Congress; and on this point even Attorney General Olney, a fanatic of gold, supported him, though Olney hoped perhaps that Congress might be forced by the awkwardness of the situation to provide remedial legislation and authorize 3 per cent short-term bonds.

In his Treasury report at the close of 1893, Secretary Carlisle pictured the straits of the Government and stated in conclusion that "Congress alone has the power to adopt such measures as will relieve the present situation and enable the Treasury to continue punctual payments of all legitimate demands upon it." Congress, however, moved not at all, a large minority, perhaps even a majority now, hoping that the dilemma of the Government would bring inflation. The Silverites advised that the Treasury pay in the silver which it possessed in great store. Moreover, the implications of Carlisle's statement were unpleasant to high financial groups, since he cast doubts upon the legal authority of the Executive to borrow money through the Treasury Department for gold purchases. In financial diplomacy, Carlisle lacked the light touch of John Sherman.

In January, 1894, "the Government approached nearer to actual bankruptcy than at any time in the present generation," wrote A. D. Noyes, two years after.[50] Carlisle, under extreme pressure from Cleveland, reversed his position, and contradicted his own statements to Congress, assuming on January 17, 1894, the power to adopt measures of relief. He announced publicly an issue of $50,000,000 of 5 per cent ten-year bonds, to be sold at not less than 117.223, to yield 3 per cent. The Silverites in Congress denounced the Administration and especially the Secretary, who now began his unhappy career as the scapegoat for both Congress and Wall Street. A resolution was passed by the House Judiciary Committee which implied, in a degree, that the procedure of the Secretary was unlawful.*

Bankers were doubtful as to the legality of the bonds, and suspicious of their indenture, which signified them as payable simply in "coin." Besides, Mr. Carlisle had not "consulted" them nor made "confidential arrangements" in advance; he had not come to Wall Street and settled the bargain. The financial district, according to Curtis—the Assistant Secretary, whom Carlisle dispatched thither—was cold to the bonds, and it appeared that they would not be fully subscribed to. At the last moment, following urgent warnings of sabotage, Carlisle was forced to swallow his pride and go to Wall Street himself, hat in hand, to beseech the bankers for their gold. He returned disappointed, though Mr. Stillman felt better after a private interview with the Secretary.[51] Only in the last forty-eight hours did the large banks relent and manage to fill the missing subscriptions, averting disgraceful failure for the whole government loan.

The bankers furnished gold, but in order to do so, quietly presented their Legal Tender for redemption at the New York Sub-

* "No stretch of the imagination could make the grant of 1875," writes Carlisle's authorized biographer, "include the power to sell bonds for the purpose of redeeming the [Silver] Treasury notes . . . in gold." (Barnes, *John G. Carlisle*, pp. 291-92.) Nor could he use the proceeds of such loans for current expenses, it was held, without authorization from Congress.

Treasury, obtained the gold from the Government, and reloaned this same gold in effect to the Treasury at Washington. It was not of course illegal, but "an undoubted subterfuge." [52] Mr. Schiff's warnings were now justified, as the banks continued to "protect their own gold holdings": the "endless chain" had begun its operation. In a few weeks, the effect of the loan was lost. The Populists, and the Silverites, led by the long-bearded Peffer of Kansas, thundered in earnest against the "betrayal" by Cleveland and his Secretary of the millions of suffering people by selling their credit "to appease the clamor of these misers of Wall Street." [53] In an atmosphere of recrimination, hate, gloom, and financial depression, debate on the long-promised and long-postponed tariff-reform bill was now taken up in earnest.

VI

In theory, the framing of tariff legislation by Congress is a form of taxation for the purpose of obtaining revenue from import duties; in practice, tariff legislation by our politicians has notoriously been a kind of political orgy or free-for-all, the results of which have been utterly unpredictable. The Democratic position upon the tariff, as advocated for nearly seven years since Cleveland's message of 1887, had been essentially that raw materials such as wool, coal, iron ore, must be duty-free, so that costs of finished goods for the masses of consumers might be kept within bounds. Beyond this, the dominant party leadership, overriding Free Trade "extremists," had committed itself generally to "temperate reform" of duties upon semifinished and finished articles of manufacture.

But the trouble was that everybody differed as to whose raw materials should be made free. The fixing of hundreds of import duties, the planning of revenues therefrom, was never submitted to a body of technicians. The politicians charged with framing a tariff act invited the spokesmen or dominant factors of each industry to lay their demands before the Ways and Means Committee of the House. The various items were then fought over in caucuses, in committee meetings, and in private conferences at hotel rooms, while each Congressman, or each clique of Congressmen and Senators, contributed to the final result by forcing preferred treatment of his own "deestrict"—that is to say, the dominant corporations in his neck of the woods—in return for his approval of the whole bill.

After some thirty years of tariff manipulation, the technique of lobbying by special interests and logrolling by politicians had reached a high point in the 1890's. The framing of a tariff bill is the great hour of the politician; a fever possesses him; the legislative mill grinds out its debates amid mounting excitement and confusion; passionate disputes, parliamentary maneuvers, surprises and ambuscades, succeed each other.

But to the masters of the committee machinery in Congress and the managers of the party Organization, the outward disorder serves as a screen which usefully conceals their own cool and steadfast action. The problem for the key men in each party involves not only the defense of established positions, but also the fulfillment of pledges more or less explicit, made in election campaigns in return for stipulated corporate donations. At this point the play of "invisible government," as the elder Senator La Follette defined it, becomes all-important, and bosses like Gorman or Quay, intriguers and wire-pullers like Secretary Lamont and W. C. Whitney, who stood behind him, prove their mettle.

As the Ways and Means Committee in the House, under the chairmanship of William L. Wilson of West Virginia, a stanch advocate of tariff reform, labored at its appointed task during the winter of 1894, the oracles of Protection spread their propaganda actively. A Republican leader in the Senate set the keynote by arguing that now was the wrong time to reduce tariff duties, "with the prices of most products at the lowest ever known, with many workers seeking in vain for work, and with charity laboring to keep back suffering and starvation in all our cities." [54] Republican politicians' hearts also still beat warmly for labor, though the debauch of Protection in 1890 had in no way brought security to labor in 1893. Mr. Andrew Carnegie, then at the height of his fame as an example of triumphant individualism and the survival of the fittest, sounded the same tune. A short time before, he had told Mr. Cleveland that if he had to choose between Protection and Sound Money, he would take Sound Money. But repeal of the Silver Purchase Act having been won, and the gold standard having been successfully defended thus far, he underwent a change of heart and now wished Protection too. The President, he said in a public letter upon the tariff question, would surely have the good sense not to attempt at this time a "surgical operation" upon a sick nation.[55]

In each industry it was always the wrong time to reduce protective duties.* The bill which Wilson's House committee had framed by January, 1894, worked in the direction of free raw materials and very light reductions of duties which might benefit farms. But in nearly all respects it retained the overwhelmingly protective character of the McKinley Tariff, and indeed, by the timidity of its measures, provided a shock for all true tariff-reformers. Even Carnegie had expressed his relief that there was to be no "revolution" and declared himself highly satisfied with the bill as it stood, except for a few details which required changing.[56] But the bill as a whole, as Henry Watterson declared, by its cowardly concessions "struck a blow at the cause of genuine tariff reform." [57] In no way did it fulfill the demand of the people, a year before, to diminish the advantages of the industrial Trusts, nourished by tariff subsidies. But while reformers among the Democrats, such as Mills of Texas, vented disgust at the compromises woven into the Wilson Bill, other Democrats, from the iron lands of Alabama and Tennessee, the coal fields of Maryland, and the sugar plantations of Louisiana, stoutly resisted measures which aimed at cheaper or free raw materials. Numerous amendments were offered, among these, an important innovation in the shape of a direct, gradu-ated income-tax clause, long championed by the Populists, and now supported so warmly by the agrarian Democrats from the West that it was adopted. After fierce squabbling, which showed the most seri-ous divisions in the ranks of the Democratic majority, the Wilson Bill, with its income-tax clause, was passed by the House and sent to the Senate, February 1, 1894.†

---

* In earlier days in England, Sir Robert Peel had once made a great oration in Parliament on behalf of Free Trade. Upon this a canny Scottish fisherman wrote him expressing hearty approval of everything Sir Robert had said except upon the one item of smoked herring, a trade in which he feared Norwegian competition. Upon all other items—saving smoked herring—however, the Scot signed himself an enthusiastic devotee of Free Trade. (Cf. Tarbell, *The Tariff in Our Times,* p. 220.)

† Thomas Reed at this time had some meaningful observations to make for the benefit of Mr. Bryan and other "friends of the people." He said that "in power,

In the upper chamber, a majority of 44 Democratic Senators held sway; 4 Populists supported the movement for a lower tariff; while a minority of 38 Republicans were in opposition. It needed then but the insurgence of 5 Democrats to block the Wilson Bill, or force amendments of all its vital parts. This was precisely what was brought about by Arthur Gorman of Maryland.

The Wilson Bill had seemed a paltry enough gesture at tariff reform. But now the Senate Finance Committee, of which the Maryland boss was a member, got to work behind its closed doors improvising hundreds of amendments—in all 634—which left but a few shreds of the original bill as framed in the House. The chief labor of the Democratic "right wing" was to destroy the clauses making for free raw materials. Coal was to be taxed to win the approval of the "ambassador from the sovereign state of Maryland," as Gorman sometimes styled himself; iron ore must be taxed again to appease the representatives of Alabama in the Senate; while, as Reed afterward described the operation,

seventy-five millions of people are to be burdened with a tax on sugar in order to hold the votes of the sugar-producing state of Louisiana, and the sugar trust had to have its demands satisfied in order to insure liberal contributions to the Democratic campaign fund.[58]

The redoubtable Gorman, as we have seen, was posted at a bottleneck of legislation, supported by an iron guard of from 5 to 8 Democratic Senators who, with the collusion of the Republican minority, were able to block a majority vote. Senator Jones of Arkansas, who acted as official floor leader of the Democrats in the tariff struggle of 1894, has left us frank testimony of Gorman's "combination" of 8 Senators, including Brice of Ohio, Caffery of Louisiana, and Murphy of New York, all sworn "to stand by one another in their different demands." [59] Thus all paths beaten by the feet of captains of industry

even the Democratic Party has got to obey the everlasting laws of common sense. When they are in the minority they can throw their limbs about in all sorts of contortions; they can look any way that they think beautiful. But when they come into power, they have got to act according to the eternal verities and that is going to be a great shock to him [Bryan] on every occasion. He is going to see the leader of the House quail on the subject of free trade. He is going to see 'patriots' operate as some of them are going to operate to-day." (McCall, *Life of Thomas B. Reed*, pp. 185-86.)

and their lobbyists led to the door of Gorman's committee room. The demands of Steel Kings, Sugar Barons, and owners of Whisky Trusts all passed through his fine hands and were embodied in the amended bill as reported from the Senate Finance Committee in the early days of March, 1894.

Publication of the Senate's terms caused a shock to the country and a second, greater wave of popular anger. After two months of secret higgling the restoration of the old duties upon the raw materials coal, iron ore, and sugar had nearly all been forced through by Gorman's bloc. Where the Democratic majority measure in the House had sought reductions, the significant changes were nearly all *increases;* where the majority party had searched for augmented revenues by encouraging imports through lowered duties, unseen hands had turned them aside. The most glaring case was that of raw sugar, made free of duty in 1890 by the Republicans, and now given an impost of 40 per cent ad valorem. Meanwhile refined sugar, supposedly in order to maintain a required "differential," received an increased duty of ⅛ cent a pound, a pretext for the American Sugar Refining Company to raise its prices at once.

Frustrated on every side, the majority of Democrats had been led to raising revenues by levying not upon the protected Trusts, but upon the breakfast table of the great mass of citizens. "The final outcome was more than satisfactory to the Sugar Trust." [60]

When it finally emerged from "the mysterious recesses of the Democratic steering committee," the amended Wilson Bill became known as the Gorman Tariff, and was admitted even by Senator Aldrich to represent "a switch to Protection, incorporating increases in duty of from 10 to 300 percent in a long list of items." [61]

What happened? "Who killed Cock Robin?"

Andrew Carnegie, the famous lay Republican who saw "with his little eye," has left in one of his memoirs a plausible (though rather self-complacent) account of how the iron and steel duties were "arranged." Carnegie joined many others in giving chief credit to Arthur Gorman for "defeating the revolutionary features of the Wilson Bill."

Going to Washington early in the session of 1893-94, Carnegie saw Gorman and learned from him that there was much danger of the passage of tariff clauses which might "injure" steel and kindred industries.

"I can afford to oppose this bill and beat the President," Gorman confided to Carnegie; "but I cannot afford to oppose and be beaten by him." What Gorman sought, through Carnegie, was Republican co-operation (in making some concessions to tariff reform) which would permit him then "to carry a reasonable bill."

Then Gorman imparted the following advice:

. . . If you will make out a schedule of reductions in duties which you assure us can be made without injury to American industries,—for I don't want to injure one of these any more than you do,—I can carry enough of our people with me who are good Americans and feel as I do.[62]

Carnegie was thus invited as an expert to help determine what iron and steel duties were healthy for "good Americans," and soon submitted to the Senate Finance Committee his approved list, which was apparently adopted almost without question.

Yet Gorman was but a cog in the machine, a faithful officer of his party. Above Gorman stood an even greater shadowed power, the uncrowned leader of the Democratic National Organization. At these moments of stress, with Congress blockaded, responsibility divided, the President aloof or deliberately passive, the veritable leadership of the party acts to break through the deadlocks of the cumbersome democratic process, and bring decisions and the fulfillment of pledges.

At New York, W. C. Whitney is as if besieged, during the tariff debates, by all those interest groups who have something at stake. And day by day he fires off dispatches to his alter ego in the Cabinet, Secretary of War Lamont, which advise in detail as to which duties should be made specific, which ad valorem, and also as to matters of exact "classification" of many products. The patronage power of the White House, indispensable for controlling Congressmen, is manipulated by the advice of the "Assistant President" Daniel Lamont, who is under orders from Whitney. At times the Secretary of War, in the thick of the tariff intrigues, seems to move his headquarters to the Senate Building.

When the Sugar Barons Henry and Theodore Havemeyer (whose claims are most painstakingly forwarded by Whitney to Washington) at tense moments in the contest find that they must reach the President personally, they are sent directly to Lamont for the needed interview. Henry Havemeyer's secretary writes:

Sugar is fighting for life, here, now, not for big boodle. It can't get on with less than it has agreed to accept. I don't want to join with the opponents of the tariff bill. Mr. Havemeyer can show the President in half an hour's interview the exact situation.[63]

On behalf of the Whisky Trust, in which Whitney himself was interested, one significant clause was quickly inserted which fixed an increased duty of 20 cents per gallon on whisky—in theory a tax upon whisky; in practice, as it was observed, "a gift of many millions to the Whisky Trust which holds in warehouse more than a year's supply and can pocket as clear profit the 20 cents additional tax on all that it pleases to take out of bond before the Act goes into effect." [64]

Throughout the winter and spring of 1894 the Havemeyers, with their lobbyists Terrell and Searle, could be seen pursuing the Senate committeemen. According to persistent and sensational reports in the press, secret conferences on March 6 and March 9, 1894, between the Havemeyers and a group of Democratic Senators were held in a room of the Arlington Hotel, immediately before the reporting of the amended tariff bill from the Senate Finance Committee. At one of these private gatherings, Secretary of the Treasury Carlisle was reported to have been present.

The one subject of the conference which all reports agreed had been most fully discussed was the fulfillment of the pledged obligations of the Democratic Party toward the American Sugar Refining Company—in short, the promise that sugar was "to be taken care of" in the proposed new tariff bill. The corporation's claims were put by H. L. Terrell, secretary and lobbyist, and were reported to have been approved by Mr. Carlisle, according to E. J. Edwards, the Washington correspondent of the Philadelphia Press, who, under the pseudonym of "Holland," reported the whole affair.

Then, according to snoopers at a keyhole of the adjoining room, one of the Louisiana Senators, Mr. Caffery, had drafted a schedule for sugar, "Mr. Havemeyer looking over his shoulder, and the other members of the Sugar Trust watching the Senator with eyes that fairly glistened." [65]

These scandalous rumors of collusion and misconduct by Senators were also supported by news of remarkable happenings in Wall Street. On the very day of the first Arlington Hotel conference, tremendous gyrations of American Sugar stock, which rose 12 and fell 9 points within a few hours, pointed to telegraphic "leaks" from Washington of advance information.[66] A Crédit Mobilier scandal of tariff "deals" shook the country in May, 1894.*

The reports of bribery and collusion came so strong that a resolution for an investigation was adopted. Early in June a Senate committee began hearing its own accused members as well as the captains of industry implicated in the case. Here, in a melodramatic interlude which provided relief in the monotonous comedy of the tariff debate, there came the famous verbal duel between the Populist Senator Allen of Nebraska and the unabashed Henry Havemeyer.

In testimony given on June 12, 1894, which made a rich contribution to our science of politics, Mr. Havemeyer stoutly denied any special collusion with members or leaders of the Democratic Party. He had indeed no particular love for one party, but had donated sums of money to both parties. He pursued, he said, "only the politics of business." In New York State, for instance, he had contributed $10,000 to Mr. Whitney's fund for organization of a reform convention (the "Anti-Snappers") which helped bring about the renomination of Cleveland; thereafter he had also given money to the Republican State campaign. Corporations had always given money to political parties. "It is a very suitable and proper thing to do," he concluded with some heat.

---

* Lamont was known to be wonderfully informed of developments not only in secret Senate committee sessions but in the New York Stock Exchange. A government official, Lamoureaux of the Land Office, who was close to Lamont, related to the Washington correspondent, Dunn, how he had made $34,000 at this time from an investment of $5,000 in American Sugar stock. "Dan Lamont told me to buy, and said to hold on until a certain price was reached." (Dunn, *From Harrison to Harding*, Vol. I, p. 128.)

Senator Allen: Why should the American Sugar Refining Company contribute to either of the political parties in the State of New York?

Mr. Havemeyer: We have large interests in this State; police and fire protection. . . .

Senator Allen: And you contribute to both parties with the expectation of whichever succeeds your interest will be guarded?

Mr. Havemeyer: We have a good deal of local protection for our contributions. . . . It is my impression that wherever there is a dominant party, wherever the majority is very large, that is the party that gets the contribution, because that is the party which controls the local matters.

Senator Allen: Then the sugar trust is a Democrat in a Democratic State, and a Republican in a Republican State? [67]

Secretary Carlisle admitted having seen Mr. Havemeyer twice and having given him a letter of introduction to Senator Mills, a member of the subcommittee seeking adjustment of the tariff controversy. He denied indignantly having had any corrupt motive or interest. He had been in agreement with Mr. Havemeyer's views, however, because of his desire to increase the Treasury revenues. Senator Brice, accused of speculation in sugar stock, denied everything. According to one delightful legend, he had refrained from "plunging" like the others in sugar when Mr. Havemeyer refused to open his books to him. Brice had told the Sugar Baron that he was used to playing in stocks only as an "insider" himself. Senator McPherson of New Jersey admitted having written a telegram ordering the purchase of fifteen hundred shares of the stock, then seeking to recall the order as perhaps improper. But his cook had sent it off by mistake! [68]

The swarthy Matthew Quay, however, came off best of all. He had bought and sold, he said manfully, not only the stocks of the American Sugar Refining Company, but all sorts of other stocks more or less constantly since 1861. His last transaction in American Sugar was admittedly on the day that was fixed for the vote upon the sugar schedule. He concluded: "I do not feel that there is anything in my connection with the Senate to interfere with my buying or selling the stock when I please, and I propose to do so in the future."

Nothing came of the investigation by the "shirking committee," as the press called it, except education for the public. Prominent stockbrokers took sudden vacations in Europe; others refused absolutely to open their books. A single obscure lobbyist was found guilty, and a journalist who had made charges but refused to reveal his sources was punished for contempt.

Mr. Cleveland, in the White House, had followed each step of the legislative drama with mingled emotions and varying humors. Firm and courageous in the fight for gold, he seemed surprisingly reticent in the contest for free raw materials and lower costs for manufactured articles to the American consumer. At moments he appeared to give up hope that concessions for his declared doctrines could be wrested out of the deadlock between the two houses of Congress. He realized at an early stage of the affair that the Senate could not be made to abandon the highly protective features of the bill, and counseled compromise to the Administration leader, Jones of Arkansas. In Nevins's account there is a picture of Cleveland's intense disappointment at his "betrayal" by a turbulent and corrupt Congress. Yet it is significant that the President, whatever private indignation he may have expressed, exercised no such iron leadership as he demonstrated in the earlier struggle for silver repeal.

The tariff debates and scandals dragged on into July. Finally, when cunning moves were being made to shelve action upon the whole tariff bill for another year, the Administration leaders, Jones and Harris, held a conference with Mr. Cleveland, informed him fully of every step which was being taken by the supporters of the tariff bill, and examined in detail the position of every member who could possibly be influenced without humiliating concessions. The prospects were poor. Finally the President seemed to resign himself to the unpleasant fact that free coal, free sugar, and free iron ore as promised to the voters could not be obtained from the Protectionist Democrats, held in line by Gorman. He then expressed to Jones his wish that his adherents delay no longer and "go ahead and do the best they could." [69]

The Senate's Gorman Bill was then passed in July, and came to the stage of joint conference with the House, which had passed the vastly different Wilson Bill. Hope still remained that the protagonists of the House would at the last hour force more liberal measures upon the Senate in their joint conference. But here again, in the joint committee, a new deadlock developed, Gorman's friends still refusing the slightest concessions to "liberal" tariff principles. Meanwhile business was depressed by political uncertainty; the Treasury staggered under its deficits, in sore need of the added revenues promised by the proposed tariff act. Yet it appeared now that no Democratic tariff bill of any kind, no matter how adulterated, would be enacted.

The President had known upon what hard terms a tariff bill must be passed. There is a further hint of this in the confidential letter of a Washington journalist to "Assistant President" Lamont, which alludes clearly to a private conversation held some time earlier with Lamont, in which the writer "gathered that you and the President had no objection to the compromise schedule—40 percent" ad valorem duty on raw sugar.[70] Yet now he was faced with the final choice between having no tariff bill whatsoever or accepting a bill which represented a humiliating political defeat.

In a strange explosion of wrath expressed in a public letter to Representative William L. Wilson, Cleveland's notorious temper snapped. He fought to avoid the loss of the tariff bill, but at the same time, with the whole Gorman Bill to be swallowed as an alternative and the whole affair reeking with scandal, made strenuous efforts to escape responsibility for the party's disgrace. In the letter of July 2, 1894, which was read before the House of Representatives on July 19, 1894, a letter whose motives were obscure and mixed, whose terms were as awkward as they were impetuous, the President openly condemned the senatorial leaders of his own party.

He makes an allusion to "the methods and manipulations of trusts and combinations" which have attended the controversy over the tariff legislation, expressing his displeasure thereat and of course disclaiming any responsibility for the same. But he adds, in his usually heavy style, that these unfortunate incidents must not halt the party in doing their duty:

While no tenderness should be entertained for trusts, and while I am decidedly opposed to granting them, under the guise of tariff taxation, any opportunity to further their peculiar methods, I suggest that we ought not to be driven away from the Democratic principle and policy which lead to the taxation of sugar by the fear, quite likely exaggerated, that in carrying out this principle and policy we may indirectly and inordinately encourage a combination of sugar refining interests.[71]

Here Cleveland helps to hold in check the "liberal" House, which plainly balks at accepting a high sugar duty. (His misstatements, moreover, were grave, as events soon proved.) He falls once more into his familiar "courageous" role of taking the unpopular side and refusing to injure a great industrial monopoly. But at the same time he takes a stern, democratic tone toward the stubborn Senate dissidents, making "earnest appeal" for concessions on their part, for "party honesty and good faith," and adherence to promises made to the people, in the joint conference. Upon them, waiving all personal responsibility, he fixes his public censure. He concludes:

Every true Democrat and every sincere tariff reformer knows that this bill in its present form and as it will be submitted to the conference, falls far short of the consummation for which we have long labored, for which we have suffered defeat without discouragement; which in its anticipation gave us a rallying cry in our day of triumph, and which in its promise of accomplishment is so interwoven with Democratic pledges and Democratic success, that our abandonment of the cause or the principle upon which it rests means party perfidy and party dishonor.

He had done his duty, the President exclaims in effect in this belated manifesto; the others had betrayed the cause and were to blame.

For the politicians sitting in the Senate Cleveland's letter fell with the effect of an absurd stroke of puppet-show lightning. But the Senators nevertheless boiled with rage.

Gorman, who had clearly been singled out for punishment, seemed truly astounded. He delivered himself in reply on July 23, 1894, of a bitter speech whose accents have all the marks of honest and passionate indignation. Whatever was done, Gorman, who as a party boss was responsible for his word, faithfully carried out his part in an "understanding." In the world of politics, as in the world of crime, the secret understandings for which secret payments are made must be lived up to according to a professional code of honor. Hence to Gorman's consistent view it was the President who had acted in "bad" faith. The attack was as unjust as it was unethical, by the political code. The Democratic Senators were honest men, he shouted, who had fought for a Democratic tariff when "cowards in high places dared not show their heads."

Here was a clear imputation of indirection on Mr. Cleveland's part. Gorman's denunciation, one of the bitterest ever pronounced against a President of the United States, of course took the form of opposition to the encroachments of Mr. Cleveland upon the constitutional rights and prerogatives of the Senate. Waves of applause greeted him when he said that

> it was a most extraordinary proceeding, for a Democrat, elected to the highest place in the Government . . . to join with the commune in traducing the Senate of the United States, to blacken the character of Senators who are as honorable as they are, who are as patriotic as they ever can be, who have done as much to serve their party as the men who are now the beneficiaries of your labor and mine, to taunt and jeer at us before the country as the advocates of trusts and as guilty of dishonor and perfidy.[72]

Meanwhile Cleveland's lieutenants in the Senate, Messrs. Jones and Harris, sat in silence, Jones himself knowing, as Gorman had stated, that the President had been fully informed of every change, and had acted in bad faith toward them.*

Republican and Democratic Senators alike were convinced that Mr. Gorman had carried out an unwritten contract which was—whether the President knew of it directly or no—the sine qua non of party success in the last campaign. Pitchfork Ben Tillman in his eulogy of Gorman before the Senate, years later, referred to the widely discussed bargain which the party had made with the sugar-refiners and expressed the conviction (which we may qualify) that Cleveland knew of it. His charge of party perfidy was therefore "an act of the grossest wrong and cruelty to Senator Gorman" if, as Tillman understood, Cleveland knew of the negotiations in question.[73]

A distinguishing feature of the revenue bill was the clause which

---

* Nevins, citing the memorandum of Senator Jones in *Grover Cleveland*, p. 582, admits as much, reluctantly, in an account which makes no explanation of the foregoing incidents. Moreover, in citing (p. 581) Cleveland's letter on "party perfidy," which he remarks "had come just a little too late," the stupidest and most fallacious passages are omitted.

levied a direct tax of 2 per cent on all incomes over $4,000, a form of taxation which had been used only in the crisis produced by the Civil War, and was counted upon to produce greatly needed revenues. Disgust with the Wilson-Gorman Tariff Bill was in part offset by hopes for saving the income-tax provision, which Populist and Western politicians had for years championed. Thus the agrarian Democrats in the House, as Bryan has related, though outraged by the Senate's amendments, had nevertheless been forced into line because of retention of the income-tax provision, and had even celebrated its passage boisterously.

On the "right wing" a fierce, bipartisan opposition to the income tax immediately developed. The great bankers had rushed at once to their friends in the Government to put pressure against this measure. "It is an unjust discrimination," exclaims Stillman in anguish to Daniel Lamont, one moreover which would arouse bitter class feeling—in Wall Street! [74] Bourke Cochran, the theatrical orator of Tammany Hall, warned Congress that proletarians everywhere would be indignant because they could not share in this tax; while his fellow New Yorker Senator Hill gave voice to similar fears in the upper chamber. Platt of Connecticut, however, as an old-fashioned Yankee Senator, in more candid language opposed the income tax as sectional and class legislation by which the West and the South levied upon the wealth of four States: New York, Massachusetts, New Jersey, and Pennsylvania. It was, he cried, the product of an unaccountable "prejudice against the accumulation of wealth . . . by industry, enterprise, frugality, economy, and good judgment in investment." Populist demagogues alone, he said, had raised up this blind and envious agitation against so-called "Robber Barons." They would but cause the "hum of . . . wheels" to stop, the "beneficent corporations" to die! [75]

At the last moment, opposition to the income-tax clause was suddenly muffled, while quiet preparations were made to test its constitutionality in the Federal courts. The mongrel Wilson-Gorman Bill, after protracted wrangling, became law—though without the President's signature—August 13, 1894.

In letters which soon found their way into the public press Cleveland permitted himself renewed fulminations at the "machinations" of Trusts and combinations, at "the communism of pelf"—one of his happier phrases, undoubtedly—and at "the deadly blight of treason" which had overtaken certain members of his party.[76] But his own function as leader of his party had been forfeited. The strange scenes and stranger words which had accompanied the tariff contest of 1894 bespoke on the one hand the contradictions within the mind of the middle-class statesman; on the other hand they illustrated the grave defects of the machinery of party rule itself—leading to lamentable error, misunderstanding, and dissension among the principal actors, though they all might be bent upon the same ends.*

Now Congress could be seen openly quarreling with the Chief Magistrate, often blocking confirmation of his appointments, and he in turn vented his feeling upon Congress in various ways, though usually by exercising his veto power. Co-operation between the two arms of the Government became nonexistent, Mr. Cleveland earning then the title which William Allen White gave him of "His Obstinacy." This official dissension, which degenerated into petty manifestations of ill temper and meanness, would have been sport to observe were it not for the rising tide of disorder showing itself at all points in 1894 and threatening, as it seemed, the very foundations of the republic. While the fumes and the stench of scandal hung over the Capitol, and statesmen snapped at each other, there rose suddenly, as if in retribution for so much treacherous frolic and faithlessness, the whole bitter mass of the people in rebellion.

* Many of the obstructions created by dissident Democratic Senators, it appears from the keen study of Professor N. W. Stephenson, were but the indirectly transmitted commands of Aldrich, leader of the Republican Protectionists. The confusion, delay, and tortuousness arose no doubt from that "double affiliation" which Stephenson defines as a condition in which the legislators gave half their allegiance and half their minds "to a label, a tradition, a constituency that has lost its reality" and the other to a "reality": the economic constituencies of Sugar, or Coal, or Collars and Cuffs. (Stephenson, *Nelson W. Aldrich*, p. 108.)

BOOK THREE

THE UPRISING OF THE 'NINETIES

CHAPTER SIXTEEN

1894: AN ANGRY PEOPLE

*. . . You will agree with me that in these days of wild-
ness, conservatism and steadiness should not be at a
discount.* GROVER CLEVELAND

DURING the fateful spring of 1894, while the Government, divided
in its authority, fumbled with its money crisis, the nation received a
sudden, serious fright as the result of the intrusion of an uninvited,
immensely powerful stranger in the social drama. In that grim season
the people, the poor and the hungry among them, were "in movement," if not literally up in arms. From points near and far came
the early incomplete reports now of significant disorders, now of
riotous hordes of unemployed, desperate men, gathering in the West,
seizing whole railroad trains, looting food, riding across the broad
country, or marching on foot toward the Eastern cities. Now they
would disappear into the interior, then reappear, their leaders issuing
fiery pronunciamentos against the Government along the way.

From Los Angeles, California, 1,000 men under "General" Fry,
a former army officer, were said to have departed upon captured
railroad trains of the Southern Pacific. From San Francisco an army
twice as large, also said to be possessed by the frenzy of revolt, was
believed to have commandeered a Union Pacific train and sped on its
way across the mountains and prairies. In Ohio another mass had
been forming itself since March, its leader promising, with the melt-
ing of the snows, to move upon Washington with 150,000 men. Still
other bands were forming in the South and the Middle West. The
most alarming and contradictory accounts, by letter and in the press,
told of "hundreds of thousands" of unwashed and ragged recruits
joining the "anarchist" and "terrorist" armies day by day, in preparation for an American "Bastille."

A long shudder swept through the rich and respectable class, and
through the men in politics. The American people showed normally
an almost superstitious reverence for law and order. But older men

remembered how our people were given also to spontaneous mass movements and sudden manifestations of tremendous violence, especially when peaceful or lawful channels of action seemed blocked. The Know-Nothing riots, the Anti-Renters' and Barnburners' disorders, in earlier times could still be recalled vividly. But since the general railway strike of 1877 industrial warfare, ever more systematic and more violent, had been growing apace.

The winter of 1894 had been one of unprecedented suffering among the people. Conservative estimates by commercial agencies reckoned 2,000,000 unemployed, while some authorities counted as much as 3,000,000. In Chicago alone, 100,000 men walked the streets in search of work; thousands slept in public buildings, the police not daring to oust them; riots took place almost daily among the mobs of famished outcasts waiting in bitter cold before the soup kitchens furnished by the "friendliness and charity" of private citizens, as Mr. Cleveland phrased it. Over the countryside the American tramp, who had arisen in the late 1870's and 1880's, roved everywhere, usually alone or joined in small bands, in search of food or forage. But in 1894 his kind congregated in organized "industrial armies." How had the numbers of the discontented multiplied so swiftly? For this, many voices, in sermons and in editorials, blamed the "agrarian anarchists" of the Populist Party.

In the Western and Northwestern tier of States the idea of secession from the Eastern half of the country, from the "Goldbugs" and "bloated bondholders," was often heard toward 1894. Political disillusionment was at its flood.

The farmers who were burdened by mortgages and low crop prices had clamored for "soft money," at least a lowering of the tariff schedules which might relieve them by reducing the cost of the goods they commonly consumed. The Republicans had promised them a little silver inflation in 1888 if their representatives would lend support to a higher tariff. The high McKinley Tariff had come, but the compromise Silver Purchase Act of 1890 had proved a snare and a delusion so far as currency inflation or credit relief was concerned. Then in 1892 the Democrats had promised a low tariff; and the farmers had turned to them, combined forces with them—and got only that which they had least desired: repeal of the Silver Purchase Act, entrenchment of the gold standard, and a tax upon sugar, which was "a gift of $30,000,000 to the Sugar Trust." Thus whichever party the people swung to in their alternations between the two great political corporations, the scheming financiers (seen through the Western mind) appeared to emerge always the gainers, moving steadfastly toward their end, however much the fortunes of office-holding politicians might fluctuate.

A sense of extreme frustration gripped the people of the interior. The idea of direct petitions through peaceful public demonstrations had been mentioned more than once by Populist leaders. It was with the feeling that a nation-wide emergency had arisen which could be met by no slow, routine procedure, and the firm conviction that the democratic institutions of a once free people had been captured by conspirators, that "General" Jacob Coxey, a patriotic and apocalyptic spirit, formerly a Greenbacker and always an enthusiastic reformer, in the early spring of 1894 began to equip his "industrial army," the Commonwealers, for the invasion of Washington.

The owners of large properties were no less firmly convinced that a fearful emergency had come for our republic. As the armies of Coxey, Kelly, Fry, and others converged from distant and various points of the hinterland upon Washington, the most urgent appeals were sent to the National Government. "Jim" Hill, from the dark-gray, granite fortress in St. Paul which was his railroad headquarters, wrote President Cleveland:

There are between four and five thousand men between here and the Pacific Coast in parties of from two to six hundred, desiring to go to Washington. They are mainly of the worst class—men who do not want to work for a living. If they can be prevented from starting and dealt with in small squads, the matter can be settled sooner and more safely than if they are allowed to go as far East as St. Paul or Chicago.[1]

A few days later (May 5) Hill reported his whole railroad over-run by wandering bands of former miners, lumbermen, and farm hands, who appeared in force, overawed train crews, commandeered whole trains, and freely transported themselves eastward. Similar news along Huntington's Southern Pacific and the Union Pacific lines. "There seems to be absolutely no way of enforcing municipal or state authority," Hill reported for the benefit of the Federal authorities. He now claimed that a horde of 25,000 to 35,000 men in various parties was bound for the Capital, momentarily separated but planning to join up later.[2]

With Coxey's Army reported moving through Pennsylvania in the last week of April, tension rose in Washington. Newspapers advocated "strict and stern repression" by armed forces to protect the President, Congress, and the public buildings of the city. New England Senators made impassioned orations against foreign agitators and "un-American manifestations"; wealthy persons were said to be leaving Washington with their families, considering the city insufficiently guarded and policed, the Government passive, timid, or "weak." [3] Confidential reports showed embittered farmers along the route of the armies, giving ovations to the marchers or actually joining with them. Even cultivated literary men like John Hay heaped mockery and abuse upon the manifestants, though there was, in Hay's jesting reproaches to his "anarchist" friend, Henry Adams, an undertone of real anxiety for his Washington mansion.[4]

Following its display of strength in the struggle for silver repeal, the National Government had relapsed into presumably laissez-faire policies, and had shown inordinate "weakness" before the drive of industrial rings for tariff privileges. It did nothing about evidence of official misconduct and venality among Senators; and finally, as a liberal writer, Henry D. Lloyd, pointed out, Mr. Havemeyer was "still at large." That thousands of Americans in the cities walked the streets in search of work, their bowels griped by hunger, the Government also pretended not to notice.

But what of the attacks upon the property of great railroads, the seizures of trains? Could these be ignored?

To Attorney General Richard Olney, the connoisseur of railroad securities (whose market value, incidentally, was not aided by recent developments), these developments in the Western States were wholly intolerable. As our minister of justice—so he regarded his post—he summoned all the energy of the National Government to the defense of the railways; his department moved with all the promptitude and ruthlessness of his own self-righteous, ruthless, and property-loving nature.

Throughout the disturbed area, where most of the railroads were in the hands of receivers of United States courts, he employed the increasingly useful device of the injunction, which he ordered United States Marshals to obtain wherever possible. Though the Government was now running at a calamitous deficit, Olney enrolled approximately 1,000 Deputy Marshals to help track down the disturbers. Where the population and local officials openly sympathized with the "industrial armies" and Commonwealers, the mere report of this condition was answered by Olney through a presidential order sending Federal troops into the area. One affray near Billings, Montana, resulted in the death of one and the wounding of several more Commonwealers by United States Marshals. Olney's armed myrmidons, Marshals or regular soldiers, pursued "lost" trains up and down the fastnesses of the Rocky Mountains for many weeks, until the manifesting bands were broken up or arrested. By such measures the square-jowled bulldog of the Department of Justice, as he assured Mr. Cleveland, prevented the arrival and congregation of "desperate men . . . at least sixty or seventy thousand of them" at Washington.[5] True, only a minority of the citizens joined in the demonstrations but, as Olney held, it would have taken only a little more to spread a veritable insurrection, a "march of the Paris mob on Versailles."

The coming of General Coxey's legionaries, at which Washington alternately laughed and shivered, was held to offer the most formidable threat to law and property. Jacob Coxey himself merited the good opinion of his contemporaries, being a citizen of uncommon charm and originality. This one-time successful quarry-owner of Massillon, Ohio, was a philanthropist of Populist views, given to a stubborn nonconformity which often leavens our national character. He had pondered over implacable economic measures and events; he had become convinced, by his own manner of reasoning, that merciless monopolists moved the Government at their will nowadays, possessing the ballot boxes, the administrative offices, and the legislative chambers. Coxey felt an apocalyptic hate of Eastern finance capital and its gold-money doctrines.

He had conceived a fairly simple, concrete program for the national emergency. He would employ the credit of the National Government to set the unemployed to work everywhere at building and improving roads. His Good Roads Bill, for whose sake he had been broadcasting pamphlets at his own expense since 1892, would have authorized the Federal Government to issue $500,000,000 of paper currency (in noninterest-bearing bonds) against the pledged bonds of States, counties, and municipalities which desired to improve their roads, streets, or schools, the local loans in question to be retired by moderate sinking-fund operations over twenty-five years. These redemptions, in turn, would permit cancellation of the Federal paper obligations.[6] It was a project for financing public works during a great depression by methods which, with slight modifications, might well have proved feasible and provided public relief; it was a plan which has been adopted by virtually all of the great modern nations, as well as by both major American political parties, two generations after Jacob Coxey's hour.

To be sure, Coxey's methods were novel. He was convinced that our parliamentary system had broken down, that only direct though peaceful manifestations by the people themselves could win relief. He must send a "petition in boots" to the National Capital. But through no fault of their own the recruits he gathered were humble and tattered men. Among them were some former circus performers and quacks, such as Christopher Columbus Jones and one Brown, who rode invariably upon a great white horse. A historian of the movement holds that the majority were sober mechanics who had long been out of work. The atmosphere of the camp in which they were concentrated suggested the Salvation Army. Prayers were offered and hymns were sung.[7]

Coxey's efforts to win publicity for his movement often embraced the technique of the big-top circus. His language, especially on the score of "usurers," was sometimes impolitic, often perfervid. But after allowance is made for the eccentricities of Coxey's movement, one stands astonished at the torrents of abuse and defamation heaped upon this leader's gentle head. While leading a popular petition that reflected a fresh, democratic impulse from the heart of the people, he was pictured at once as a clown and as an incendiary who spread "the bacilli of anarchy." To Godkin, of the New York Evening *Post*, Coxey was an imbecile, but to Bishop Greer, preaching an inflammatory sermon to National Guardsmen at St. Bartholomew's Church in New York, he was an enemy of society.[8] Yet his "ragamuffins" asked only for work, and the country then needed good roads almost as badly as the men needed work.

As the "industrial army" set off from Massillon, with bands playing, banners flying, and the rain falling, two detectives, one of them from Mr. Olney's Department of Justice, fell into line as recruits. En route, as the army moved slowly through the Pennsylvania highlands and the Blue Ridge of Maryland, one of the spies kept Mr. Cleveland and Mr. Olney thoroughly informed of developments. There were "no known anarchists in the camp" and the body of Commonwealers numbered but 250 to 300 men, the total varying from day to day.[9] But when the Commonwealers, ragged and footsore, arrived in the District of Columbia and pitched their camp outside the gates of the capital, these small numbers had been depleted.

The public sympathy and help given to the Commonwealers troubled the minds of the politicians. In the Senate, Kyle, the North Dakota Populist, demanded that the petition of Coxey be received by Congress in friendly fashion. But such defense of the right of peaceful petition for unemployed citizens was indignantly rejected by Senator Hoar, who cried out against the effort of "Five or ten thousand men . . . to dictate to the other 65,000,000." The demonstration of masses of the people had no lawful place; only the formally elected representatives of the people could speak for the sovereign will.[10]

General Coxey, negotiating with the police authorities of Washington (who were ready and armed to the teeth), sent word in advance that his men proposed to parade peacefully before the Capitol while a committee presented their petition to Congress for the Good Roads Bill. The demonstration was to be orderly. But permission to appear before the Capitol was refused by police authorities.

Nevertheless the tatterdemalion band of Commonwealers on May 1, 1894, proceeded down Pennsylvania Avenue, with bagpipes skirling. It was noticeable that the greater part of the crowd of 15,000 or 20,000 people who lined their route showed marked friendliness for them. At the Capitol grounds a dense throng was gathered to watch the ceremonies; but here also a solid phalanx of police, almost outnumbering the marchers, barred the way. General

Coxey was ordered to halt. He lifted his hat to the police commander and declared that "he protested the order." Then as Coxey and two leaders hurried forward, walking alone across the vast square toward the Capitol, mounted police galloped after them. The petitioners jumped a stone fence and scrambled into the near-by bushes, while the police and the crowd pressed after them. After being roughly handled, Coxey and two others were arrested, though Coxey was released and returned to his followers. Brown was badly beaten, as was Christopher Columbus Jones. The crowd gave a great cheer for Coxey and his men at one moment; and the mounted police, seeming to lose their heads completely, charged, swung their clubs, until fifty or more members of the crowd and the "industrial army" were beaten and trampled down.[11]

The next morning most of Washington and the country at large laughed at its great fears of yesterday. The rout of the Coxey "insurrection" by force was held to be comic. It was also sad.

II

Nothing of Attorney General Olney's tactics in dealing with the Commonwealer disorders is without meaning. In the defense of the property interests to which he now felt himself called he showed not only an unusual fighting spirit (when many of his class were bewildered by their fright) but a certain inventiveness as well. The somewhat rare injunction procedure against labor disorders had been used previously, to be sure, in several Middle Western States by Federal courts administering receiverships. But now Olney, from Washington, extended its use over a broad area of the nation and supported it with detachments of Federal troops sent at the President's order, *though without requisitions by local or State authorities.* Moreover, United States Marshals were encouraged to call promptly on the Federal authority upon whatever legal ground was possible. A long step forward was being taken, by which our national government authority and police apparatus were being applied to the defensive needs of large capitalist enterprises. The precedents established, the legal weapons which Olney was perfecting and which were to be drawn upon more extensively after his time, "were admirably adapted," as his biographer notes, "to greater disorders."

The affair of the Commonwealers and that of the revolutionary Chicago strike which followed it almost immediately, Olney wrote to Cleveland, in 1902, "were dealt with in practically the same way." [12]

The year following the panic of 1893 found employers engaged in the most intensive wage-cutting. Whereas previous depressions, those of 1873-77 and 1884-86, had caused labor organizations almost to disappear into the ground, the workers in factories, mines, and railroads, despite divisions among them, now fought with tenacity and élan for their unions. The second Cleveland term made labor history, with strikes in 1894 involving nearly 750,000 workers.[13] These were fought with almost prodigal energy in the coal fields of Pennsylvania, Ohio, and southern Illinois, as in the mills and railroad yards of turbulent Chicago and other cities. Backward or myopic as it was in political action, the young labor movement in the United States, above all when it threw up genuine leaders, showed indomitable strength for economic action; its spirit was syndicalist rather than social-democratic.

The Administration attempted as long as possible to ignore the labor problem; party politicians shrank from speaking of the nightmare of class war which haunted men in the 1890's. Yet while no "class party" arose as the political institution of the proletarians, such as most European states now had, the mighty stresses of class struggle shook the old professional party institution from top to bottom; deep-rooted traditions of popular government, such as the people had been taught to cherish, had to be thrown overboard to face a social crisis manifested in the most malignant form. It needed all the shrewdness of masters of American political tactics to bring the grand old party system, with its amalgam of contradictions and conveniences, intact and whole through the howling storms which burst upon it.

After Homestead new lessons were implanted in the minds of younger labor leaders. Samuel Gompers, the former immigrant cigarmaker who was president of the new craft-union grouping known as the American Federation of Labor, was prompted to explore more opportunistic tactics, matching those of the party magnates and captains of industry, rather than a "futile socialism." However, Eugene

Debs, a native of Indiana who had been for several years secretary of the important Brotherhood of Locomotive Firemen, conceived rather that a single, unified industrial union must be created large enough and centralized enough to measure its strength with the railroad monopolies of the time. The Brotherhoods and the outmoded Knights of Labor—originally an industrial union itself, now hardly more than a secret lodge, extremely weak and not a little corrupt as well—would serve no longer.

Debs resigned his office after the autumn of 1892 and set to work organizing the American Railway Union as "one big union" which would overcome both the craft restrictions of the Brotherhoods (by embracing all the railway workers together) and the ineffectiveness of the Knights of Labor.[14] After a year of ardent campaigning, the A.R.U. claimed 150,000 members and 465 locals, and had the credit of a quick and successful strike against James J. Hill's Great Northern Railroad.

The railroad-owners, for their part, had not been idle. Since 1886 they had been perfecting a defensive combination of twenty-four railroads (employing 221,000 workers) called the General Managers' Association and centering its activities in the terminal city of Chicago. Somewhat secret in its action, because of its dubious legal position under the Interstate Commerce Act of 1887, it acted to assist its members in labor disputes and provide strikebreaking recruits. It strove also to impose uniform wages and hours according to the so-called Chicago scale. After 1893 it moved with vigor to check the menacing growth of the A.R.U. Thus two giant industrial combinations, organized on class lines, faced each other in the lush-grown industrial city of Chicago, their conflict a symptom of massive forces at work which neither the Fourth of July orations of politicians nor the measures enacted by legislatures took into account.

To ignite the flame of battle between these implacable adversaries it needed but the fuse of the small, exceedingly bitter strike in May, 1894, at Pullman, just outside of Chicago. Here in this "model" company-owned town, with its neat green-lawn-bordered streets and red-brick houses, the feudal notions and petty tyrannies of Mr. George Pullman, the Palace Car Baron, had badgered the tenants of his Utopia into a passionate uprising. Sharp reductions in wages during the winter of 1894 probably counted for less than the all-seeing "benevolent despotism" which hemmed in the lives of the workers between company stores and houses whose rents and taxes were exacted unfailingly, at undiminished rates. Mr. Pullman's manor hands struck, but were locked out, and all appeals for arbitration were rejected. The Pullman workers then in a body joined the "one big brotherhood" of the American Railway Union, which was believed to be invincible. In the councils of their union the Pullman men urged their fellow railway workers to a boycott of Pullman cars.

Debs, one of the ablest and most devoted of labor leaders, very pacific in temper, hoped to the last to avoid spreading the conflict, and made repeated petitions for a peaceful settlement through the A.R.U. These, however, were steadfastly rejected or even went unanswered. The General Managers' Association had come to the aid of the Pullman Company at once, pledging its support through all exigencies. In its determination to "close the door to all attempts at conciliation and settlement" it showed also the clear purpose of embracing the larger battle looming with the new railway union.* On June 21, 1894, the American Railway Union, meeting in convention, gave an ultimatum to the Pullman Company, promising that upon refusal of mediation in the period of four days following, its members everywhere would refuse to handle Pullman cars on all railroad lines where they were employed.[15]

On June 26 at noon, as the ultimatum expired, the sympathetic boycott was begun. All Pullman traffic out of Chicago and as far west as the Pacific coast was paralyzed; the affair became a national incident as the boycott led to automatic strikes and some 60,000 men ceased work along the Western railway lines. Debs inspired a remarkable solidarity and discipline in his men. His abiding fear now, as in the strike against Hill's railway, was of disorder. For a full week, from June 26 to July 3, while, progressively, twenty-two railroads were tied up, actually no violence was heard of.[16] It was called the most "colossal boycott," "blackmail" upon an enormous scale—

* As testimony in the subsequent trial showed, the chairman of the G.M.A., St. John, declared on the eve of the boycott and strike: "Gentlemen, we can handle the various brotherhoods, but we cannot handle the A.R.U. . . . . we cannot handle Debs. We have got to wipe him out, too." (Debs, *Debs: His Life*, p. 39.)

never before had the country seen a strike so large and yet so well organized. Eugene Debs's appeal to public opinion on June 29 was treated in the already frenzied press as a "declaration of war" upon society. In his proclamation addressed "To the Railway Employees of America" he declared:

The struggle with the Pullman Company has developed into a contest between the producing classes and the money power of the country.

The Pullman workers had been mortgaged body and soul to a "heartless corporation." When all peaceful petitions had failed, the union had entered the fight. Then the combination of railways had come to the rescue and gone "into partnership with Pullman . . . in his devilish work of *starving his employees to death*," making it a general contest between the solidarity of labor and the combined railway corporations.[17]

The leading newspapers of Chicago, especially the powerful Chicago *Tribune,* now raised a cry of alarm at public violence, the "tyranny of Debs" and "mob control" in Chicago, an alarm which, as the Governor of Illinois afterward explained to President Cleveland, was entirely baseless at this time. Even the *Nation,* at a time when the discipline and peacefulness of the workers seemed to promise an inevitable victory, described the action as an insurrection by railway workers against all the people, hinting plainly that after the would-be dictator Debs had roused enough people "to commit murder and arson," the Government would have to "cope with them in the old-fashioned way"; that is, we would have to "shoot them down."[18]

If the harassed President at Washington, and his now most influential counselor, Olney, had not been possessed by their inveterate fear of popular and proletarian movements, the stress of the moment, the alarm in the press reports of the first six days—though not yet reflected in the more accurate Eastern press—would have whipped them to action. On June 18, in the week before the strike began, following the panic over the Commonwealers an "anarchist plot to blow up the Capitol" had been "discovered" by the New York *Tribune* and other newspapers.[19] A French statesman, Carnot, had just been assassinated in Paris. Terror and gloom unhinged the coolest minds of men in high places or in public life.

Olney had injected himself and the Federal government power into the railway conflict from the first hours. Were not his cherished Chicago, Burlington & Quincy, his Santa Fe, as well as the whole public order, menaced by the "rebellion" and "conspiracy"? However peaceful the boycott stoppage might appear, it must be treated as "conspiracy." By his own lights, "No punishment which he [Debs] is likely to get . . . will be commensurate with his offense." [20] What was to be done? The country's railroads and industry were being paralyzed. A short time before Olney had expressed to Perkins of the Burlington his real (though secret) convictions that the Interstate Commerce Act and existing Federal laws, as they stood, could not be brought to regulate or prevent combined action "in restraint of trade" on the part of the privately owned railroad monopolies. But in this crisis, which to his mind threatened "the stability of our institutions and the entire organization of society as now constituted," he swung to a diametrically opposed legal position. The railroad to him formed a "public highway" and no mere private enterprise; its workers had "no absolute right" and only a "relative right" to quit their employment in a concerted movement and block the "public highway." In denying the workers' right to combine, Olney cited as his legal ground the very Interstate Commerce Act which he had ridiculed yesterday, and more especially the Sherman Anti-Trust Act of 1890.[21]

Flushed with his bold-handed victories over the Commonwealers, Olney rushed to the hapless President, urging him, as he tells us in his own memorandum, to use United States troops during the first days of the railway strike (before June 30) in order

to prevent the interference with the mails and with interstate commerce on his own initiative—without waiting for action by the courts and without justifying the proceedings as taken to enforce judicial decrees [that is, without waiting for injunctions].

Olney's tactics were marked by bold innovation, free and unexpected construction of a law to regulate railroads (not labor unions). They suggested also an extreme departure from traditional Democratic

Party doctrines of States' Rights, which the more prudent Cleveland feared to abandon except "in support of the judicial tribunes," that is, of injunctions previously issued by the courts.

Olney set to work vigorously upon his counterplan; first to obtain the needed judicial authority for repressive action; second, to bring into a contest between railway capital and labor the whole power and authority of the Federal Government before it had been legally requested, before any disorders had been committed, and while public opinion undoubtedly favored the peaceful strikers. John Sherman, when once questioned upon this point of law, had denied that the Anti-Trust Act, which was fashioned to protect the common people from monopolies, could be used to punish labor organizations. No Trust under the provisions had as yet been prosecuted successfully by Mr. Olney or his predecessor; but Mr. Olney was now convinced that by this same law the wretched Pullman workers, and their allies of the A.R.U., might be punished for "conspiracy" in restraint of commerce between the States.

Upon the advice of the General Managers' Association Olney quickly engaged an aggressive railroad lawyer, Edwin Walker, to act as special counsel to the Federal District Attorney at Chicago. On June 30, 1894, the fourth day of the strike, workers had shown up in force at two points and compelled the uncoupling of Pullman cars from trains, though without resort to violence. It was on this day that Olney sent extraordinary instructions to Walker:

It has seemed to me that if the rights of the United States were vigorously asserted in Chicago, the origin and center of the demonstration, *the result would be to make it a failure everywhere else and to prevent its spread over the entire country.*[22]

Further, he counts upon Walker to resort to "all legal remedies," and gives instructions to the other Federal agents not to wait for warrants under criminal statutes against persons actually guilty of illegal acts, but to file bills in equity enjoining persons by name, and all other persons co-operating with them, from interference with the mails or with interstate commerce, on the general ground, as he puts it, of violation of the Sherman Anti-Trust Act.* Finally, Olney hints

* This unexpected use of the Anti-Trust Law caused Henry D. Lloyd to call it promptly "the Anti-Trade-Union law."

that these processes are to be carried out "by a force that is overwhelming and prevents any attempt at resistance." Cleveland's minister of justice, who could find no remedy under the law for combinations of capitalists or "unions" of railroad-owners, moved to deprive railway workers of the last vestiges of the freedom of contract fixed in the historic bill of rights.

Previous existing grounds for the dispatch of Federal soldiers to troubled areas were found in the "domestic violence" clause of the Constitution, which required a formal demand for military assistance from the executive officer or legislature of the State involved. Under this clause Hayes had taken military action in 1877. There existed also ground for calling out Federal troops to suppress "insurrection" under the Revised Statutes of the United States, No. 5298, passed by Congress as a war measure in 1861, and also under a Reconstruction measure enacted in 1871 against the Ku Klux Klan, and used cautiously by Grant. But Olney himself had been numbered then among those who publicly criticized Grant for "usurpation" of sacred States' Rights and constitutional liberties.[23]

For special reasons no approaches were made to Governor John Altgeld of Illinois, who, under the authority divided by our constitutional federal system between national and local governments, was directly responsible for public order in his State. Nor did any demand for military aid come from this peculiar officer. Governor Altgeld, somewhat reluctantly, had himself used Illinois militia to stop the destruction of property during a recent miners' strike, but it was reported that his methods had been so impartial as to afford no encouragement to nonunion or "scab" workers.

Altgeld, like the Mayor of Chicago, had been elected during a historic revolt against the Republican machine in Illinois, and in the teeth of the public utilities' and railroad corporations' hostility. The Governor who had pardoned the surviving Haymarket anarchists in 1893 was regarded with definite suspicion by the General Managers' Association, of which Olney had been a founding member. Altgeld made no move; but then no single application for police protection was made to him, as he related, up to July 6, 1894, by any railroad official or any other person or officer in Cook County.[24]

Olney, however, was little concerned with propriety. He assumed in advance, as he says, that the affair at Chicago "might have to be met and dealt with by the Army of the United States." He was busy arranging a "legal picture" in such wise that the Department of Justice could "put itself in the position which had induced the President to authorize the use of troops as against the Coxey movement." [25] Federal troops were what the General Managers wanted above all: they were "efficient," and ever since 1877 they had been considered "killers," compared with the local militia. The railway managers intrigued from the outset to keep out the State militia and convert the conflict into one between the workers and the Federal Government.[26]

At Olney's order, the force of Deputy Marshals in Chicago was increased from 50 to 1,000, ultimately to 3,600. These armed recruits, who were set to guarding the railroads, were scarcely gentle characters but, according to testimony of Chicago police officials, included "thugs, thieves, and ex-convicts." Their presence on behalf of an unpopular cause, among an aroused population which had hitherto held itself in hand, soon had the desired effect.

III

The Democratic Governor of Illinois followed the proceedings at Chicago and Washington with a mind that grasped everything quickly, yet was unable to repress emotions of indignation and amazement. Henry Demarest Lloyd, Altgeld's friend, was present at Springfield during the critical July days. The Governor, despite his repugnance for such work, by July 3 had turned his office into military headquarters, wholly absorbed in the problem of preserving order, and protecting life as well as property. Tables and maps on his desk showed the disposition of State troops, held in readiness. Telegraphic calls for police protection from various points outside of Chicago, especially in southern Illinois, were promptly met, though Altgeld remarked privately of one request, not connected with the Chicago strike:

I have reason to fear that these troops are wanted at that place only to help the railroad defeat the demand of their men for higher wages, but I cannot refuse to send them in the face of allegations of public danger.

If it becomes necessary, I could and would put 100,000 men [from downstate] into . . . Chicago inside of five days! The whole State would answer to the call as one man.

Altgeld further suspected that "the railroads had everything to gain by a little well-advertised rioting" which could be attributed to the strikers.[27] For his part, the Governor regretted the dangerous course of the strike, which by its complete stoppage of traffic made merchants, and especially millions of farmers, bitter over daily losses.

During the generation in which big business came of age and took dominant power over the government apparatus, Altgeld of Illinois stands out in a place of his own, amid the procession of bullet-headed generals, cruel-lipped captains of industry, political charlatans, and machine bosses who crowd the annals of our bourgeois republic. This most calumniated and reviled political leader—the "forgotten eagle" of Vachel Lindsay's poem, a man of rare honor and Roman "virtue," over whose tale one pauses with gratitude and relief—emerges from the gloom of the period to play his part of passionate protest and humane opposition momentarily, only to be broken and hurled back, in tragic defeat, into the obscurity from which he came. For Altgeld's truthfulness, his fearless and scrupulous sense of justice, in themselves offered danger for the program being developed so boldly at Washington.

His career had been typical of the contemporary American folk legend. Brought to Ohio in 1847 as an infant of a few months, the child of Prussian immigrants, he had grown up in extreme poverty. When a mere boy he had fought in the Union Army. Then followed years of wandering and privation during which he worked as a farm laborer and managed to educate himself at the same time. A man of genuine learning, he had been admitted to the bar in Iowa, and finally achieved an extraordinary success as lawyer, judge, and businessman.

His was a proud, truthful, simple, forthright nature. His public speech, like the numerous papers and pamphlets he wrote upon questions of social justice, law, and penology, is filled with a strong logic which cuts through sham and an eloquence which has nothing of mere rhetoric. This unpolished, self-taught man, with his pale face and piercing dark eyes, was held by the Grangers to be their leader and friend during the days when he lived in Iowa. In Chicago, where as a leading figure in local politics he was elected judge of the Cook County Superior Court in 1886, labor instinctively felt in him a friend, though by hard work, savings, and bold investments in land he had become also one of the wealthier capitalists of the city. He knew the world of business, yet he never forgot the world of hungry farmers and wandering laborers.

These sympathies were shown in the many independent and wise rulings from his court, which brought him notice as one of the leading jurists of the West during the 1880's, but also won him the lasting enmity of Charles T. Yerkes, the master of street railways and public utilities. Altgeld, an individualist, who had come by his money honestly and through terrible and patient struggle in the Chicago "jungle," as he felt, had welcomed the hatred of Yerkes and his friends. In the surprises and upheavals of 1892, John Altgeld was given the Democratic nomination for the Governorship, conducted a powerful campaign by means of a "personal machine" (such as Robert La Follette was now slowly building in near-by Wisconsin), and carried the State, which had been safely Republican for forty years. Altgeld's popularity among German Republicans as well as among the masses had contributed enormously to Cleveland's election. A band of enthusiastic young men had gathered about the new reform leader, including Henry D. Lloyd and Brand Whitlock. His qualities of realism and energy, his pungent expressions, stirred up the corrupt Western commonwealth. He would say: "The greatest reformer and purifier . . . is the sun. Let sunlight into the dark places and the poisons collected there disappear." [28]

Altgeld's pardon of the anarchists surviving the Haymarket affair—whose conviction he, like half the people of Illinois, believed to be a clear miscarriage of justice—was decided upon after a long struggle with his own conscience, and, being an act of the noblest political courage, won him the censure of 99 per cent of the nation's newspapers. He had granted the pardon in a magnificent state paper knowing that he would be "killed" politically thereafter, and de-

nounced everywhere as a "foreigner," a "demagogue," an "anarchist."
The independent Governor of Illinois had thus fully earned the
mistrust not only of the General Managers' Association at Chicago,
but of the Administration at Washington, as it prepared to intervene
in the vast railway strike with its full power.

The railway strike gathered revolutionary force. Here was the
danger and the cause of its undoing. For though the laborers' demands have a limited objective, referring solely to wage conditions
at the Pullman works, the spreading results of stoppage of the
circulation of commerce over a huge part of the nation—striking at
millions of men, merchants, manufacturers, farmers, members of the
lower middle class—cleave as they paralyze society, combine all who
are injured against labor, and provoke inevitably the full fighting
force of the state to bring defeat to the workers. The strike of general
or semi-general scope (as contrasted with the strategic, localized
"flanking" strike) is essentially revolutionary; with its tremendous
economic pressure creating losses of many millions of dollars each
day, it summons, in times of peace, all the forces of organized society
to the struggle.

Almost the whole American press worked to alarm the country
over the "colossal boycott" and the "Debs Rebellion." "Mobs in
Control of Chicago," or "Chicago Faces Famine," ran the headlines.
The characteristic comment was "It makes no difference whether the
strikers are right or wrong." [29] A lone newspaper, the Chicago *Eight-
Hour Herald*, commented afterward upon

its [the local press's] insane policy of exaggeration and misrepresentation,
inflaming the passions of the people and doing its level best to arouse class
prejudices. From the first these papers have used every effort to magnify
the difficulty, and to prevent any attempts at arbitration, conciliation or
peaceful settlement. [30]

On July 2 some small disturbances took place; several cars were
turned over by strikers, the United States Marshal present was
ignored, two or three wooden boxcars were set on fire in the freight
yards. [31] But on the following day, July 3, these disorders subsided
suddenly. Debs, struggling to preserve calm and discipline, had

asked strikers and sympathizers to wear a white ribbon in order to distinguish them from agents provocateurs. Thus the nonunion rioters might easily be recognized.* But on that very day the forces of the Federal Government had already been sent in motion. Attorney General Olney had telegraphed to the special counsel, Edwin Walker, the following cryptic hint:

Advantages of bill in equity restraining unlawful combination against operation federal laws, whether under interstate-commerce law, act of July 2, 1890 [Anti-Trust Law], or on general grounds, are obvious and will doubtless be availed of by you, if practicable. Immediate, vigorous measures at center of disturbance immensely important.[32]

Thus the brilliant lawyer urged the sweeping and unprecedented use of the Interstate Commerce and Anti-Trust acts against the railway union. At the slightest sign of irritation among the tense population the "legal picture" he was designing would be filled out; the President, to use his own words, could then be "induced to move in support of the judicial tribunals."

The District Attorney at Chicago, Milchrist, and Edwin Walker grasped the hint quickly, and toiled all the night of July 1 to prepare the National Government's bill. The Federal Judges, Grosscup and Wood, abandoned their impartial judicial positions and assisted in improving the bill of indictment so that it rested upon charges of interference with the United States mails, as well as upon the novel ground of unlawful restraint of commerce. Then on the following morning, July 2, the same judges granted "the most sweeping injunction ever issued from a Federal court," ordering all persons "to refrain from interfering with or stopping any of the business of any of the railroads in Chicago engaged as common carriers," prohibiting also the "persuasion" of employees. It was a veritable "gatling gun on paper" as the General Managers' Association joyfully declared, and marked the completion of the first step in Olney's plan.[33]

By secret orders of the War Department steam was kept up for troop trains at Fort Sheridan near Chicago for two days after July 2.

---

* Few, if any, of the strikers, but rather small boys and hoodlums, were involved in these first disturbances, according to affidavits of the Mayor and Chief of Police of Chicago, furnished to the Strike Commission afterward. *Cf.* Lloyd, *Henry Demarest Lloyd*, Vol. II, p. 150.

On this day, United States Marshal Arnold, at the head of a strong body of deputies, read the new court order to a crowd gathered before the Rock Island tracks at Blue Island, on the outskirts of Chicago. He was hooted, and he and his deputies were jostled and roughhoused, though good-humoredly. He reported the incidents.[34]

Chicago and its outskirts were still comparatively peaceful.* But the effectiveness of the strike was unparalleled; factories were shutting down, stockyards preparing to close, grain and cattle movements paralyzed throughout the West, while thousands were being thrown out of work every day.

On July 3 Attorney General Olney, obviously pleased at developments thus far, telegraphed even broader hints to the District Attorney:

> Congratulate you upon the legal situation, *which is all that could be desired.* Trust use of United States Troops will not be necessary. *If it becomes necessary they will be used promptly and decisively upon the justifying facts being certified to me. In such case . . . let Walker and marshal [Arnold] and United States judge join in statement as to the exigency.*[35]

Olney had told his Federal helots precisely how to proceed (though he passes over this point in his memoirs on the subject). Immediately, upon the same day, there came a telegram in reply from Marshal Arnold, attested to by District Attorney Milchrist, by Special Counselor Walker, and by Federal Judge Grosscup, a dispatch which was highly misleading if not wholly false.

> When the injunction was granted yesterday a mob of from two to three thousand held possession of a point in the city near the crossing of the Rock Island by other roads, where they had already ditched a mail train, and prevented the passing of any trains, whether mail or otherwise. I read the injunction writ to this mob and commanded them to disperse. The reading of the writ met with no response except jeers and hoots. Shortly after the mob threw a number of baggage cars across the track, since when no mail trains have been able to move. I am unable to disperse

---

* While Chicago newspapers, such as the *Tribune,* published provocative and inflammatory reports in an incendiary manner, examination of the New York press shows no violence worth noticing during the first seven days, though the affair was followed with the greatest possible attention.

the mob, clear the tracks, or arrest the men who were engaged in the acts named, and believe that no force less than the regular troops of the United States can procure the passage of the mail trains or enforce the orders of the court. I believe people engaged in trades are quitting employment to-day, and in my opinion will be joining the mob to-night, and especially to-morrow, and it is my judgment that the troops should be here at the earliest moment. An emergency has arisen for their presence in this city.

J. W. ARNOLD,
United States Marshal

We have read the foregoing, and from that information and other information that has come to us believe that an emergency exists for the immediate presence of the United States troops.

P. S. GROSSCUP, *Judge*
EDWIN WALKER,
THOMAS E. MILCHRIST,
Attorneys [36]

As he bore this document, which was the desired "certification of an emergency," to the cabinet meeting at the White House on July 3, Mr. Olney knew a moment of triumph. The second step in his war plans was completed. All day the Cabinet discussed measures for the strike; the opposition of Secretary of State Gresham, an old liberal, and of General Nelson Miles to military intervention was overcome, Cleveland seeming in full agreement with his bellicose Attorney General and eager for drastic action to end the "reign of terror in Chicago." * That day he gave the order to move regular army troops into Chicago. Secretary of War Lamont announced that "all the land forces of the United States" would be used to uphold the law, as the first detachment of 1,200 men from Fort Sheridan rode into Chicago. And Olney, in his truculent tone, exclaimed to the members of the press:

We have been brought to the ragged edge of anarchy, and it is time to see whether the law is sufficiently strong to prevent this condition of affairs. If not, the sooner we know it the better, that it may be changed.[37]

* Blue Island, where Marshal Arnold was actually rolled in a ditch by strikers, was not within the city of Chicago.

As a fourth step in Olney's plan, District Attorney Milchrist, at Chicago, summoned a Federal grand jury at once to ask for the indictment of Eugene Debs and other railway-union leaders on the grounds of "insurrection" and "conspiracy." These indictments were promptly found on the legal ground of the Sherman Anti-Trust Act of 1890.[38]

IV

Order had been preserved surprisingly well at Chicago up to this point. As far as any direct intimation from the authorities or railway managers there was concerned, the Governor "could scarcely have known that a strike existed . . . much less that it was accompanied by disorder or obstruction of the laws." [39] The presence of large bodies of Deputy Marshals had stimulated some small disorders by July 2. But the entrance of regular soldiers on Independence Day completely changed the atmosphere of the great strike. Dense, excited throngs gathered about the railway yards and tracks. As the trains now moved again, convoyed by soldiers, the railway workers exerted themselves to block their progress. Nimbly they uncoupled the freight cars atop which the soldiers rode, and dodged back into the crowds before they could be shot down.

The burning of freight cars began in earnest on July 5 at the Rock Island Railroad yards, and soon made an inferno of overturned box-cars, ties, signal towers, and merchandise. Lurid reports of the great Western metropolis given over to anarchist mobs and bloody street fighting now filled the press. Cavalry charged, rifles and revolvers flashed. *"Is it revolution?"* asked the New York *Tribune.*

Night after night the respectable burghers of Chicago, on the roofs of their uptown homes, could stand looking toward the busy loop district, the freight yards and stockyards, gaping at the vision of their city of industry, wealth, soot, meat, blood, and misery apparently roaring up in flames. Many still recall asking themselves if a whole social order were foundering in ruins as they saw "the sky . . . lighted up with the glare of the flames of 500 or more freight cars burning in the . . . yards of the Grand Trunk road." [40] *

---

* But the masters of railroads may have known something about these salutary fires. The Mayor of Chicago, according to Henry D. Lloyd's notebook, caused forty affidavits to be procured showing that the burning of freight cars was done

After July 6, with disorder increasing, upon Governor Altgeld's suggestion Chicago authorities called for militia—the Federal regulars being too few to handle the situation now—and 5,000 Illinois National Guardsmen were sent to the scene at once by Altgeld, who, the day before, had issued his first protest against President Cleveland's unwarranted intervention. It was the Illinois militia so reluctantly ordered in by Altgeld who wrought the first bloodshed. Attacked by a maddened mob on July 7, they fired point-blank, killing between twenty and thirty persons and wounding scores of others. After four days of turbulence, July 6-9, in which crowds were fired upon every day, order was imposed as new regular regiments and more militia were rushed to the city. Some 14,000 State and Federal soldiers cowed the population. President Cleveland issued a proclamation warning all citizens of Illinois against assembling in public, ordering them to disperse after noon of July 9.[41]

Before a Federal grand jury summoned on July 10, Judge Grosscup delivered in the form of a furious diatribe instructions calling for the indictment of Eugene Debs and his fellow officers of the American Railway Union. Their indictment was found at once; the headquarters of the A.R.U. were broken into, Debs and three other officials were arrested, released under heavy bail for a few days, then rearrested on contempt-of-court proceedings and jailed.

Debs had made a strong appeal through the Chicago trade-unions, while still free, for a general strike of organized labor throughout the nation. The city-wide strike at Chicago began slowly in response; national officials of the American Federation of Labor, called to a meeting at Chicago on July 12, proved reluctant to authorize such a step, Gompers advising instead a general retreat, as more expedient under the circumstances. The spreading movement was checked; the

by "railroad men," that is, agents or detectives for the railroad companies, who also incited hoodlums in the crowd to participate. (Lloyd, *Henry Demarest Lloyd*, Vol. I, p. 152.) The total damage was estimated at approximately $350,000, giving force to Altgeld's statement later in his Cooper Union speech, Oct. 17, 1896, that the disorder, damage, and violence were far exceeded in contemporary labor outbreaks at Buffalo, New York, and in the Ohio coal fields, but were deliberately magnified by the press. It is also significant that although the city of Chicago was liable for the destruction of property by mob violence, the railroad companies refrained from pressing any claims for damages in a court at which evidence on all phases of the affair might have been made public. *Cf.* Browne, *Altgeld of Illinois*, fn., p. 147.

railway workers' ranks began to weaken before so much assembled authority and might, although strongly worded resolutions against "government by injunction" were issued by both the A.F. of L. and the Knights of Labor. All pleas for arbitration by the railway union were refused by the railroads, and over 700 union men were placed under arrest on various charges. The strike was beaten; its leaders were imprisoned. Traffic revived gradually; the powerful industrial union for railway workers, so brilliantly organized but a year before, began to disappear into the ground.[42]

During these spectacular events public opinion showed itself bitterly divided. At the height of the emergency James Kyle, the Populist Senator from North Dakota, had introduced a resolution seeking to limit the Federal court processes used against the railway workers. At this, Cushman K. Davis of Minnesota, one of the more cultivated lawyers in the upper chamber, had burst forth in a violent pronunciamento which reflected fully the passions felt now by respectable property-owners, and which was echoed through the nation's press:

My duty to the Constitution and the laws forbids me to sustain a resolution to legalize lawlessness. . . . The power to regulate commerce among the several States is vested by the Constitution in Congress. Your associates [to Kyle] have usurped that power. . . . You are rapidly approaching the overt act of levying war against the United States. . . . *You might as well ask me to vote to dissolve this government.*[43]

The press with one voice thundered its applause for Senator Davis's high words, as it now showered praise upon Cleveland and Olney. Meanwhile Eugene Debs was denounced as a "dipsomaniac" who had stirred the scum of society to revolt.

Yet many prominent men, swayed by emotions no less passionate, took up the opposing cause. In Chicago former Senator Lyman Trumbull, an octogenarian relic of the war against slavery, returned to public life after twenty years of retirement and joined with the youthful lawyer Clarence Darrow, and with Henry Lloyd and Jane Addams, in the defense of the union leaders. At Cooper Union in New York, a mass meeting to which 10,000 people came was addressed by Henry George, who exclaimed:

I yield to no one in my respect for order but there is something more important than order . . . liberty. I would rather see every locomotive in the land ditched than the enforcement by the standing army of that law which reigned in Warsaw.[44]

Furthermore, opposition, most vigorous and most embarrassing to the Washington authorities, came from the Governor of Illinois himself.

John Altgeld had watched the action of the Washington Administration with mounting anger. He had been elected as the friend of the common people of Illinois, over the resistance of the corporations and railways. In the crisis, in his cruel dilemma, little as he may have desired to turn the balance to the railway corporations, he had acted with probity, ready to defend their property. They had not called him. The sudden highhanded intervention of the Federal Government in Illinois, concerning which he was never consulted, was not only a grievous reflection upon himself but an insult to the people of Illinois, and an infringement upon their rights. The General Managers' Association had not only courted violence, as he knew, but had gone over the heads of the Chicago authorities and of the "anarchist" Governor, as they called him, to bring in Federal armed forces. Altgeld's long telegram of protest was sent to President Cleveland on July 5, the day following the arrival of Federal soldiers in Chicago. It read in part:

Sir:—I am advised that you have ordered Federal troops to go into service in the State of Illinois. Surely the facts have not been correctly presented to you in this case . . . for it is entirely unnecessary, and as it seems to me, unjustifiable. . . . I will say that the State of Illinois is not only able to take care of itself, but it stands ready to furnish the Federal government any assistance it may need elsewhere. Our military force is ample.[45]

Altgeld declared that the labor struggles in Illinois had been followed by the State authorities in the most responsible manner. He cited the frequent use of militia recently to protect mining properties in strikes; the repeated dispatching of soldiers in answer to appeals from railroad-owners against "violence" at rural points— though his officers reported to him that obstruction at these points resulted not from violence but from the complete walkout of the trained railway workers.

Nothing had happened (up to July 5), he contended, save "local disturbances," which were within the power of city police and State military forces to control. He had not sent troops to Chicago because no official or private citizen as yet had asked for them. "I repeat that you have been imposed upon," Altgeld asserted to the President. Even if the Federal intervention came within the letter of the statutes on insurrection (that is, the laws of 1861 and 1871), the Constitution forbade such exercise of police power without the request of the community and State. He continued: "I submit that local self-government is a fundamental principle of our Constitution." Such action "insults the people of this State," Altgeld concluded, "by imputing to them an inability to govern themselves, or an unwillingness to enforce the law." Without raising the question of Federal supremacy, he made formal protest and petitioned for the immediate withdrawal of the Federal troops on strike duty in Illinois. Cleveland replied at once with a laconic message in which he stated the legal grounds for his action and insinuated that Altgeld had not performed his "plain duty"—at the same time ignoring completely the issues raised by Governor Altgeld. In his later recollections of the affair, he commented that Altgeld's invocation of the bill of rights and of the principles of local authority at this juncture was "irrelevant . . . and absolutely frivolous."

On July 6, while he arranged with Chicago authorities to send at once a heavy force of Illinois militia to the city, Altgeld directed a longer, sharper, even more firmly argued message to the President. Was it true, he asked, that at any slight disturbance the Executive at Washington, overriding all local authority, might send Federal troops into any community? Such government revoked completely the principle of local rights which was a fundamental part of the American system of democracy. It was contrary to constitutional law that, in times of peace, the Federal military forces should take action in a local situation without subordination to the local civil authorities, or that military power should even take precedence over civil authority. All of the officials who had called for Federal aid were officers appointed from Washington, doing the bidding of the President, whose will would be "the sole guide." As his agents, they passed judgment upon local disorders, applied to him for military aid, and were answerable thereafter only to the President at Washington.

"Yet the autocrat of Russia could certainly not . . . claim to possess greater power than is possessed by the executive of the United States, if your assumption is correct." This "assumption as to the power of the executive" was new; it might lead, by an easy step, from a government of limited powers to the establishment by an ambitious Executive of outright military government. Where would it stop? The very unwarranted presence of Federal troops had "proved to be an irritant," and Altgeld again asked for their withdrawal, while giving fullest assurance that the State of Illinois would preserve order.[46]

Altgeld's powerful appeals on the ground of historic liberal democracy held implications of danger which not only the General Managers' Association but Cleveland and Olney as well quickly grasped. The growth of centralized nation-wide, interstate combinations in industry and transport during the recent period required more and more plainly a correspondingly centralized, national police protection. In recent years the checks given at first to such corporations by attempted supervision through local governments (the Granger laws in the West) had been fortunately overcome by the Supreme Court. Now when a nation-wide, or clearly interstate, combination of railway workers arose in turn to measure its strength with the force of the concerted railway corporations, it became imperative that the whole police power of the National Government be summoned in defense of the threatened property interests. Restraints and barriers upon such defensive action in the form of local sentiment or traditions of local rights must be overcome at all costs. In these "days of wildness" —before so menacing an attack by labor upon capital—even talk about "democracy" must be checked as so much poppycock.

By a shift in the interpretation of our constitutional government, and by a most devious usage of laws recently enacted to regulate interstate corporations, a Democratic President and his lieutenants introduced truly "revolutionary" doctrines in extending so widely "government by injunction." Professed Jeffersonian Democrats, they labored unremittingly to break down the last vestiges of States'

Rights, and make the apparatus of the National Government the supreme instrument of force in the defense of great properties.

Altgeld's reply Cleveland dubbed "a rather dreary discussion" of general constitutional principles, and with scant patience he answered curtly on July 6 that "in this hour of danger and public distress, discussion may well give way to active efforts on the part of all in authority to restore obedience to law and to protect life and property." [47]

Attorney General Olney also gave forth a ringing public statement which heaped contumely upon the Governor of Illinois. The soil of Illinois, this former "Jeffersonian" Democrat asserted, was the soil of the United States; the soldiers were there to execute United States laws; all pretended notions of local rights "became practically extinct with the close of the Civil War." [48] *

A prolonged thunder of applause now rose from the press at Cleveland's insulting message to the "anarchist" Altgeld. It was a "ten-strike," and his proclamation of order given at the same time was equally relished. "The respectable press of the country is a unit in applauding and sustaining the President," commented the *Nation* in relief. [49] The strange public controversy over democratic doctrine was drowned out in rifle fire, cheering, and bloodshed.

It remained only that the Supreme Court should sanction with all its august authority the boldly extended use of the injunction, and that the union leaders should be imprisoned. The appeal of Debs to the highest court brought a ruling a few months later which placed the use of the injunction in labor disputes at last upon a firm legal basis, at the same time, as Olney had hoped, virtually setting strikes by labor organizations outside the law, with the whole prestige and might of the Federal Government thrown against them. Later, in 1897, the so-called blanket injunction was also sanctioned. [50] The tremendous strike had been smashed everywhere by Olney's legal-military engine; and now the triumphant Olney busied himself in

---

* I submit that no consistency can ever be distinguished, upon theoretical constitutional grounds, in the veerings of our statesmen and parties between "Jeffersonian" and "Hamiltonian" doctrines, so called. But a consistent enough line, determined by attachment to the defense of property, may be found; thus alternately and adventitiously, States' Rights may be invoked by Republican authority, and Federal "centralism" by a Democratic President.

seeing to it that the thousands of Deputy Marshals who had guarded and fought for the railway properties should be paid off by the Federal Government and no further loss be borne by the railroads.[51]

In certain sections of society, Olney was admired no less than the "courageous" Cleveland. Was it true that Cleveland had been "led sadly astray . . . by his impetuous and bellicose Attorney General"? [52] With a becoming modesty, Cleveland accepts credit for actions which he admits to have been unprecedented, congratulating himself and his principal associates

on the part which fell to them in *marking out the way and clearing the path, now unchangeably established, which shall hereafter guide our nation safely and surely* in the exercise of the important functions which represent the people's trust.[53]

V

The secret sorrow of the Cleveland Administration, during the ordeals of 1894, was the continued budgetary deficit and the incessant drain of gold from the Treasury. If Grover Cleveland often suggests the character of an honest, prudent steward of the bourgeois, so his Administration, likewise, suffered from the besetting troubles of the bourgeoisie: it strove to present a decent and unworried front to all customers, but night after night it walked the floor in its torment, and bore silently the humiliating extortions of its unrelenting creditors. For while the Government fought without rest day by day in 1894 against the militancy of "industrial armies," of labor unions, and of agrarian insurgents, the very classes it defended so stoutly, the Eastern banking and commercial classes, in short, the moneylenders and interest-gatherers, appeared to be the first to withdraw their confidence and, at moments, to desert it utterly.

"The path of duty is unusually rugged," wrote Cleveland at this time to his friend and political supporter, Don M. Dickinson.[54] Little wonder that his private correspondence at this period contains many an unchecked groan and lament. Stubbornly he and his counselors moved forward on the "path of duty" marked out beforehand, in the face of mounting difficulties and a weight of popular hostility and denunciation such as few Administrations had ever borne. Proposals for measures which would have experimented with compromise, or softened a little the anger of large sections, in the matter of currency reform were rejected. "Cleveland opposed anything new," Hoke Smith, a member of his second Cabinet, observed. He trusted few men. "Cleveland considered all great questions only with his chosen advisers." These were Olney and Daniel Lamont of his Cabinet, and the financiers Stetson, Charles Fairchild, E. C. Benedict, and Whitney, all of whom assured him in so many words that the popular condemnation of his course was but the expression of "blatherskites." [55]

The episodes of the Commonwealers and the "Debs Rebellion" had aroused the deepest misgivings concerning the future of the republic in European money centers. These unpleasant scandals in the middle-class republic of endless wealth and resources were likened to the intense class struggle which rent the older continent at this time. But whereas Europe, with its entrenched hierarchies, its military landowning caste, had peculiar resources for fighting revolution, it was believed that the newer society of America was wanting in them. Here, wrote privately an American diplomat from abroad, was "the test of our institutions such as has been often malignantly predicted, and there was on every hand evidence of hopes or fear that our Republic might not be able to bear such a strain without serious injury." [56]

But if the American proletarians and farmers seemed unruly, then our capitalists too had shown themselves both extravagant and shifty. Unpleasant exposures concerning false bookkeeping by two of the largest railroads, and the disposition of promoters of new Trusts to declare lavish extra dividends purely for their effect upon the stock market, a few days before they were plunged into bankruptcy—such excesses also increased the frightened liquidation of English, Dutch, and German investments, which brought the adverse movement of gold to its maximum by 1895.

The depression entered its most acute phase in the autumn of 1894. The sun shone, the rain fell, right well the farmer toiled, and a bumper crop was brought forth. Wheat fell to 50 cents per bushel, the record low price for the century; at the same time Western corn, an indispensable article of export which usually brought much foreign specie here, suffered from sirocco and was heavily damaged. Distress haunted the American "yeomen" as they went to the ballot boxes that autumn. But over the counsels of the Administration at Washington, over the Treasury Department, the counting rooms of New York, there hung anxiety and bewilderment almost as strong.

In the midst of an election contest the Administration had not dared to borrow new money by floating new bond issues. By August, 1894, the proceeds of the recent loan were exhausted; the gold reserve sank to $52,000,000. The only recourse left for Secretary Carlisle was to go humbly to Wall Street and use "persuasion" again, beseeching the bankers to deposit sums of gold in the sub-treasuries in return for Legal Tender. This was not easy. A year before, when President Cleveland had made a "patriotic" call for help to the great clearinghouse banks, James Stillman had merely written to Daniel Lamont:

> I can hardly sufficiently express my disappointment at not being able to, at least, try and render the President some slight assistance at this juncture in the finances of the country, and I trust that you will convey to him my great disappointment in not being able to respond to his call.[57]

The gold-hoarders were vexed with Carlisle. They had heard of his private view that if the bankers would not co-operate with the Government in defending the gold standard, it was as much their misfortune as the Treasury's; the country perhaps would not "go to the dogs" if specie payments were suspended for a time. Stillman that summer wrote Lamont that

> it is reported that the Secretary feels no concern; does not see any necessity for issuing bonds to increase his gold reserve, and was reported as saying . . . that the New York banks were obliged to take the action they were taking for their own and not the Treasury's protection. . . . The opinion is that the Government's finances are getting into a very weak and dangerous condition, and that the time will come when the reserves of the New York banks will be the only bulwark to prevent disaster to the financial interests of the country.[58]

In August, 1894, the bankers, torn between their appetite for gold profits and their fear of suspension of specie payments, grudgingly yielded to Carlisle and deposited $15,000,000 in gold with the Treasury as a temporary maneuver.

The November elections saw the consummation of the worst fears of the Gold Democrats. The voters in great part attributed their privations to the party in power. Embittered labor, joining with the farm vote in the Middle West, turned Democrats out of Congress en masse. Moreover, the hardy Republican Party showed signs of revived leadership.

In Ohio the year before William McKinley had become the protégé of Mr. Mark Hanna of Cleveland, and with a vigorous stump-speaking campaign gained an overwhelming plurality of 80,000 for the Governorship. In 1894 Mr. Hanna, taking advantage of Democratic discord, had displayed his protégé everywhere before the country in election campaigns, heralding him in the press and in cartoons with the sun rising behind his Napoleonic head, as "The Advance Agent of Prosperity!" In the East and North, new alignments and new attractions were placed alluringly before the conservative classes which had backed the Cleveland Democracy, while discontent was ingeniously canalized again toward the party of the Outs.

Upon the left wing, in the Middle Border States and the Great West, however, far more menacing developments took place. The Populists, abjuring fusion with the now discredited Democrats, made the highest advance of their history, receiving almost 1,500,000 votes and electing 6 United States Senators as well as 7 Representatives. The intransigeance of the Populists this season helped to return many seats to Republicans in Congress, giving them a decisive majority in both houses; but here too there were complicating factors, for many of the Republican Congressmen were more or less openly pledged to silver inflation. On this issue of monetary inflation, now that silver purchase was abolished and no business recovery followed, the "regular" Democratic leadership had earned overwhelming unpopularity and the party itself was divided. In formerly conservative States, such as South Carolina, men like Ben Tillman (the "Marat" of the agrarian revolution) swept everything before them upon anti-Cleveland tickets, and stood in control of the local party machines. In Nebraska the ambitious William Bryan, campaigning for the Senatorship in a predominantly Republican State, upon an anti-railroad, prosilver, and prolabor platform of his own devising, came so near victory that it did him much honor, while leaving the regular leadership of his party, as well as the opponents of bimetallism in Washington and Wall Street, badly frightened.

The "sudden uprising of discontent," as observers in the field reported, pervaded the Republican masses as well as the Democrats. Not only Hard Times, but a deep sense among the electorate of *the betrayal of popular mandates by the Democratic Party* was given by the press as the cause of the "avalanche" of November 7, 1894.[59]

The Cleveland Administration now harvested the bitter fruits of hated policies. Leaders of the party vied with each other in publicly disavowing the Executive; vituperation could go no further than in the speech of the naturally gifted Ben Tillman, who styled Cleveland a "tyrant." The "tyrant" and the "Judas from Kentucky," Carlisle, remained silent under the storm, and with nothing more to fear, devoted themselves in the teeth of full congressional obstruction to the unpleasant tasks which the financial oracles of the time had decreed as stern duty.

On November 14, 1894, Carlisle repeated the action of January, issuing a circular inviting public bids for a second loan of $50,000,000, in the shape of 5 per cent ten-year bonds. The New York bankers and their international allies who made a specialty of government financing could scarcely hide their displeasure at these terms. Privately (for they could not make such claims publicly) they had been pressing Cleveland and his advisers to take measures to overcome the technical awkwardness of the provisions of the Resumption Act of 1875, under which the Executive borrowed money to obtain gold. They wanted the bonds made "payable in gold" expressly rather than in "coin"; they wanted to avoid awkward "premium" bonds, with their high coupon rates; they preferred confidential arrangements made privately with the banking syndicate, so that the marketing of the bonds might be more easily and profitably controlled. They wanted above all firmer assurance of specie payment than the mere established policy of the Treasury (during four presidential terms) to redeem paper money in gold even when silver payment was optional. These were the hard terms discussed in numerous private letters to Cleveland from Stetson, Fairchild, J. and W. Selig-

man, the Strauses, and other financiers. They were also outlined in a
frank public interview given by J. Pierpont Morgan.[60]

Carlisle's arrangements for the new loan had ignored these demands, which, at all events, he could not have met without being
impeached by Congress. He took special precautions to consult the
bankers well in advance and prevent the withdrawal of Treasury
gold by the very banks who subscribed to the loan, as had happened
in January. He threatened to publish the names of such "unpatriotic"
bankers. At this, several bankers, in high dudgeon, withdrew their
contemplated subscriptions, among them Mr. Cleveland's friend and
former Secretary of the Treasury, Charles S. Fairchild. Rumors of
secret strife between Cleveland and Carlisle over the terms of the
bond issue were also heard at this time, and formally denied.[61]

The bankers, as much for their own protection as for the Government's, supported the second Cleveland loan, though with dead
hearts. When the bids were opened by Secretary Carlisle, the offer
of the Morgan-Belmont syndicate, on an "all-or-none" basis, was
found most advantageous, offering terms similar to those of the last
loan, at slightly more than 3 per cent yield. But the syndicate actually
found it difficult to retail the bond issue at any substantial profit.
According to James Stillman of the National City Bank, Morgan
would have been seriously embarrassed had not Stillman hurriedly
raised some $20,000,000 of Standard Oil gold from foreign and
domestic sources, to fill out the required sums.[62]

Whereas the previous loan had tided things over for ten months,
the gold proceeding from the second loan vanished from the government Treasury within ten weeks! Once more the "endless chain" was
at work; the bankers "took flight," their withdrawals of gold reaching in January the record figure of over $43,000,000.

In furnishing the Government with gold, the large subscribers had
this time tacitly agreed not to obtain their gold from Treasury redemptions, but from other sources or from Europe. They had, however, quietly borrowed the necessary gold on thirty-day gold notes
from other domestic banks, then afterward repaid these gold obligations through Treasury redemptions. As before, this was done, financial experts observed, to protect themselves against an imminent peril

of the Treasury and the banks alike being precipitated upon the silver basis.[63] *

The complete failure of the second loan threw the President into extreme alarm lest default might be near at last. In his annual message to Congress in December, 1894, he now came out bluntly with the demands which the bankers in his intimate circle had been pressing for two years, but which no politicians believed Congress would accord. The existing fiscal provisions of the Resumption Act of 1875 he held obsolete and senseless. With the Government running at a deficit, efforts to replenish its gold reserve brought an "endless-chain" into operation, since the gold borrowed was soon paid out again for Legal Tender, and the Legal Tender reissued by the Treasury could be presented again and again for redemption in gold. Cleveland therefore suggested that Congress pass an act pledging the Government to repay its bonds specifically in gold, so that abundant gold credits might be forthcoming. Otherwise he must continue to defend the nation's credit under the existing statutes, by repeated, wasteful loans.

Congress made no move to aid the Executive, its majority of bimetallists trusting that out of the Government's dilemma might come the long-awaited specie-payment suspension.

Late in January the gold reserve was again far below the "sacred" limit of $100,000,000; confidential memoranda from Treasury officials showed that a few large demands for sums of gold would cause the subtreasuries to suspend specie payments at any moment. At the same moment the New York Dry Goods Magnate Isador Straus brought word that panic tactics might be expected in Wall Street; with European interests "selling their holdings in American investments as rapidly as the market will take them," gold withdrawals would come in a new and greater torrent. The only thing left to be done in this emergency, he urged, was for the Administration to concentrate all effort "on legislation that will authorize the

---

* Out of withdrawals of approximately $69,000,000 from the Treasury gold stock between Nov. 22, 1894, and Jan. 26, 1895, only $28,861,855 had gone abroad to meet exchange balances, while over $40,000,000 remained hoarded privately at home. The banks were not compelled to make gold payments on their deposits, but simply insured themselves against missing profits from an impending inflation. *Cf.* New York *World*, Feb. 1, 1895.

issue of gold bonds—the retirement of the Greenbacks and Treasury Silver Notes and the permission to national banks to issue currency up to the par value of the bonds." [64]

Cleveland bestirred himself at once, and on January 28 presented the New York merchant's proposals in a special message to Congress which had the nature of an ultimatum. He sought authorization now for 3 per cent long-term bonds, to be repaid only in gold, as well as drastic currency reforms permitting cancellation of the irredeemable Greenbacks and Treasury silver notes and their replacement proportionately by national banknotes, secured in turn by government gold bonds. In Congress, Representative Springer on behalf of the Administration quickly introduced a bill incorporating these measures.

The gold-obsessed finance capitalists in the East warmly applauded Cleveland's message, J. Pierpont Morgan saying: "The President is absolutely right. The only remedy is the one he recommends—the issuance of a gold bond . . . payable specifically in gold." [65] The war between Silver and Gold was now on in earnest.

Amid stormy scenes in the House, a Democrat from Pennsylvania denounced the President as a creature of mere *"belly and brass."* In the Senate Vest, who had worked hard as leader of the Administration wing in Congress, declared dramatically that he felt compelled at last to part company with the President.

The President of the United States has issued a declaration of war against silver, and he seeks now . . . to make those of us who do not believe in a single gold standard accessory to the destruction of silver. . . . I wish to say for one that never, never, in a time of profound peace, will I vote to issue one bond by this Government for the purpose of securing . . . the gold standard. . . . Sir, it is not pleasant to differ with the head of my party. I have for months remained silent, so that it might not be said that I had added to the discord . . . in the . . . party. But we have come to the parting of the ways.

The Silver Republican Senator Teller of Colorado cried: "There is no emergency here at all. . . . This country is not going to the dogs. . . . We are suffering to-day because the American people can not consume, because they are poor." [66] An insurgent Congress defeated Springer's bill, and demanded that the Treasury pay its obligations in silver, of which it held such ample supplies. The Democratic Party was now broken in two; the bipartisan voting followed a sectional boundary, generally almost the entire South and the States west of the Mississippi opposing the Northeastern and North Central States.

VI

The President and his Cabinet had not been waiting idly; the rebellion of Congress was foreseen. While the stump politicians on the evening of January 30, 1895, vied with each other in denouncing an "international bankers' conspiracy," an experienced emissary of the Treasury Department, Assistant Secretary William E. Curtis, was conferring secretly in the Sub-Treasury Building at New York with August Belmont, the American partner of the Rothschilds.[67] Curtis telegraphed to Secretary Carlisle that Belmont appeared discouraged, thinking "we have overstayed our time," while other leading bankers, including James Stillman, George F. Baker, and even Charles Fairchild, seemed to hold themselves aloof. Only an immediate and very large loan of $100,000,000 could save the day. Meanwhile a daily loss of $3,000,000 in gold was reported from the New York Sub-Treasury.[68]

On the following morning, January 31, the conference was renewed, J. Pierpont Morgan appearing now and taking the lead in the negotiations. Morgan insisted that "it would be absolutely impossible to secure gold by public advertisement." What the Government needed was to borrow gold from abroad, and to make sure that the gold obtained for its bonds would be imported from outside, that is, from Europe, and therefore not redeemable instantly for Legal Tender. Morgan made the following proposal:

I will undertake to get the gold necessary abroad, provided it is left in my hands to undertake and, if I succeed, that you will make a private contract for the gold.[69]

The tentative provisions of a contract with the Government were discussed. Curtis, Carlisle, and apparently Olney also had decided to use the authority of an unfamiliar Civil War statute (Section 3700, Revised Statutes, 1862) permitting a private sale of bonds for gold.

These propositions Curtis brought back to Washington that night, agreeing to report promptly to the bankers.

On February 2 the Treasury Department emissary again went to New York and negotiated with Morgan and Belmont. The New York bankers had made their dispositions with their European correspondents for a loan of $50,000,000 and proposed an interest rate of 3.75 per cent. Apparently all difficulties were settled at this meeting, pending only the action of Congress. Rumors in the financial district indicated as much. A large foreign shipment of gold destined for Europe was halted; the dollar grew stronger.[70]

The terms of the Morgan syndicate seemed hard. The size of the loan was too small, the interest rates astonishingly high compared with current interest rates on other government bonds. Moreover, the insistence upon a private contract by which they were to control and "turn over" the bonds on their own terms—rather than a public sale of bonds with open bidding—deeply alarmed Carlisle. This man of chronic indecision "desired to make a popular loan . . . and he hoped that even yet Congress might be induced to come to his rescue by authorizing a sale. The scraps of messages written in his own hand . . . are indisputable evidence as to the agitated state of his mind." [71] For several days Cleveland, Carlisle, Lamont, and Olney debated the matter continually at the cabinet table. At length, on February 3, Carlisle wrote Morgan and Belmont rejecting their offer.

In greatest alarm, feeling or indeed knowing that a popular bond sale would be doomed to failure, and that a mere public announcement indicating the failure of the private negotiations would be followed by renewed financial panic, Morgan urged his Democratic confrere Belmont to hurry to Washington. Then, learning that a public advertisement of a bond sale was to be made that very afternoon, February 4, Morgan telephoned to Carlisle and urged him "in the strongest terms not to do this, and at least to delay its issue until Mr. Belmont and myself should have an interview with the President." [72] Negotiations must not be broken off at this point, he insisted, without further discussion. Taking with him his partner Robert Bacon and his lawyer and Cleveland's friend Stetson, Morgan left at once for Washington by private train.

The President, flanked by Carlisle and Olney, confronted the international banker on Tuesday morning, February 5. Both were "bull-necked" men. Cleveland felt his dilemma keenly. At the moment, as he imparted to confidants, he was embittered by the proceedings of the bankers. However, in later recollections he forgot this and praised them.[73] Their terms seemed impossible; though refusal also seemed well-nigh impossible at this juncture. Yet he repeated his preference for a public offering of bonds, open to all bidders.

Morgan argued that "an immediate supply of gold from Europe was the only means of averting panic and widespread disaster." He insisted firmly upon a thirty-year 4 per cent bond, at 104½ or par to the syndicate, yielding interest of 3.75 per cent. The highest guess in the press at the moment was a 3.50 per cent yield, or a price of approximately 111 for such a bond.[74] The price was high, but Morgan would undertake to corner the sterling or gold market and control it during the duration of the bond financing, which involved, as he now determined, a provision of $65,000,000 in gold.

It was a bold plan worthy of this monopolist of banking; and even bolder was his offer to lower his charges by 20 per cent if Congress would yield on the matter of a specific pledge of gold repayment. This would net the Government a saving of roundly $16,000,000 in interest upon a thirty-year loan. No such demand had been made by any Government-bond syndicate for a generation. Morgan made this offer as "a safe proposition," knowing there was not the least likelihood that Congress would pass an act authorizing a gold bond.

Nothing came of this first conference on Tuesday, while the debate over the bond and currency bill raged in Congress. Burning curiosity waxed among the whole press and public; Cleveland postponed action again, his mind undecided, troubled, fearsome. It was agreed that Morgan and his associates were to wait at New York and return toward the end of the week, as soon as the Administration bill was voted upon.

The interest rates demanded by the hard-fisted, red-nosed banker, and reflecting the impaired credit of the United States were a sore point; yet from within the Treasury Department constant pressure was apparently put upon Cleveland and Carlisle to ratify the proposal. "The difference in price . . . is nothing compared with panic and suspension," urged the confidential negotiator of the whole contract, Curtis. "Morgan . . . thinks the situation the most critical since the war." [75] *

Thursday night, February 7, the Administration's financial bill was overwhelmingly defeated in the House. Several hours earlier, during the afternoon, Morgan, Bacon, and Stetson, fully informed of the expected outcome, had already left New York by private car for Washington. Just why or how J. Pierpont Morgan chose to go to Washington on the evening of Thursday, February 7, to see the President is not clear.† He was closely in touch hour by hour at this period with persons who figured in the Inner Circle of the Administration. The President, still wrestling with his soul, had not asked for him again. But the indomitable Morgan had clearly resolved that delay could no longer be borne; the moment had come to force the hand of the Government.

At the railway station that evening, by what could scarcely be a coincidence, the Secretary of War and "Assistant President" Daniel Lamont met the Morgan party. The inscrutable little man behind whom the shadowy figure of Whitney always stood played his own mysterious part in these great transactions.‡ He appeared everywhere, in touch with everyone and everything. He informed the banker that the President was still undecided, and refused to see Morgan that evening. An angry scene followed, in which "Jupiter" Morgan, accustomed to riding down all opposition, heatedly expressed his disgust, and announced his intention of returning at once

---

* Brisbane wrote: "If a man wants to buy beef, he must go to the butcher; if he wants to buy great quantities of beef, he must go to the big butcher. If Mr. Cleveland . . . wants much gold, he must go to the big banker." (New York *World*, Feb. 8, 1895.)

† T. A. Barnes in his study of John Carlisle, examining the private papers of the Assistant Secretary of the Treasury, Curtis (later a prominent New York banker), indicates that Morgan came largely of his own volition, without any formal invitation.

‡ From Whitney he had been receiving constant communications, such as the following: "Personally I think it very fortunate that there is such an alliance to be had by the government as Morgan and his great power. I do not presume to advise, but I think the only thing hanging over the country is the fear of the Government's financial condition. . . . If I were the President, whatever I did I should do with Morgan.—It will fail of the effect otherwise and the President will not be credited with good judgment in the matter." (Lamont Papers, Whitney to Lamont, Jan. 3, 1896.)

to New York, come what might. Olney wrote Lamont some years later:

> You were present at all the important conferences between the President and the bankers. Do you remember coming with Messrs. Morgan, Belmont, and Bacon to my house in the evening—when Morgan stated that they despaired of accomplishing anything in Washington and were going to return to New York that night and let things take their course? I think you and I persuaded them to hold on and try the result of an interview with Mr. Cleveland the next morning, which we felt certain we could bring about.[76]

While the President deliberated in the White House, the magnate went to his hotel and during the long hours of this gloomy winter night sat up over a game of solitaire. The financial centers, the markets of the world, waited; the fate of statesmen and parties waited upon the end of the night.

"The next morning," continues Olney's recollection, "the interview took place in the President's Room at the White House." Cleveland had finally been persuaded to treat with Morgan, and thrust aside the cautious counsels of Carlisle.

The conference of Friday, February 8, 1895, was even more tense and heated than that of the Tuesday preceding. It was as if the trusty steward of the people at every step rued the consequences of his pact with the international banker. Cleveland and Carlisle strove to soften the terms of the bond; Morgan yielded nothing. According to an account which Morgan has given, the President fully appreciated the kind of public reaction which would follow their bargain. A prey to intense excitement, walking up and down the room, he cried: "You are trying to force me into doing what I do not want to do." [77]

At one psychological moment of the contest, a telephone call came from a Treasury official who reported that there was less than $9,000,000 in gold coin at the New York Sub-Treasury. Whereupon Morgan is said to have remarked: "Mr. President, the Secretary of the Treasury knows of one cheque outstanding for twelve million dollars. If that is presented today; it is all over." [78] The implied threat in Morgan's words was unmistakable. An indecisive, bewildered man faced a resolute and dangerous one.

Presidential resistance gave way; the Administration placed itself in the hands of the bankers' syndicate. Cleveland had found Mr. Morgan, he recollected, a formidable fellow, "a man of large business comprehension and of remarkable knowledge and prescience," with a mind which (compared with his own) appeared to move "with lightning-like rapidity." [79] Much of the Morgan "prescience," however, may have flowed from the helpful and protective screen of counselors and advisers, the Lamonts, Stetsons, and Olneys, who surrounded the President.

When the question was raised of legal justification for such a private contract as Morgan demanded, the banker answered "with lightning-like rapidity," referring to the obscure act of 1862, by which the Government might buy gold from private sources and pay for it with bonds. "This was a proposition entirely new to me," Cleveland recalled. It may have been equally new to Morgan, "who had been coached by Olney." [80] Olney attests to this by saying that he had been called upon to give an opinion upon this point before the meeting.[81]

The final contract called for the sale of 3,500,000 ounces of gold or $65,116,244 (half of which was to come from Europe) to the Government in return for $62,000,000 par value of thirty-year 4 per cent bonds at 104½. Morgan had forced upon the Government substantially the terms fixed in his secret conference at New York earlier with Assistant Secretary Curtis. Morgan, thereupon, gambled boldly on improving trade conditions and a change in the adverse gold movement, which he had foreseen. His syndicate borrowed exchange in London, on its own credit, and thus sold bills for American currency, pegging the world exchange rate of the dollar at a point favorable to their gold operations. Morgan also supervised and controlled for several months the gold reserve of the Treasury. Every banking house and exchange dealer in New York having important European connections was bound to the undertaking by being given an allotment of the syndicate's bonds at profitable rates. For the frightened bankers, Morgan provided leadership and engendered confidence at last. It was a tremendous undertaking, and its success in turning the financial tide for the moment was spectacular. Markets rallied upon the news; the public subscription price was set at 112¼

—against 104½ to the syndicate—making a "spread" of seven and three-fourths points, worthy of a loan for a "banana republic." In some twenty minutes the loan was subscribed to sevenfold, and the bonds soon sold at 119, ultimately at 123. The government gold reserve mounted from $42,000,000 to $107,000,000 again, while the Morgan-Rothschild syndicate earned overnight a minimum profit of $5,000,000, though some reckoned it as high as $9,000,000.[82]

Unpleasant comments were made at once on the harsh terms imposed during the emergency, and the difference between the rates of this loan and existing bond rates, yielding such handsome profits to the bankers for no real service and without risk on their part— profits "gratuitously given by the Administration in a secret conference, and . . . paid out of the public Treasury."[83] Yet our "horses and cows alone," an infinitesimally small fraction of our wealth, were worth nearly $2,000,000,000.

When word was brought to Congress on February 8 of the bond contract, with its offensive provision for heavy reduction in costs if Congress would pass legislation within ten days authorizing repayment specifically in gold, a new explosion of rage burst forth from the people's representatives. The alternate offer of "Shylock" Morgan was spurned on the instant. Bryan of Nebraska gave the alarm:

What is this contract? . . . It is a contract . . . with the representatives of foreign money loaners. It is a contract made with men who are desirous of changing the financial policy of this country . . . they come to us with the insolent proposition, "we will give you $16,000,000, paying a proportionate amount each year, if the United States will change its financial policy to suit us." Never before has such a bribe been offered to our people by a foreign syndicate.[84]

Bryan upon this occasion threw down a challenge which sounded remarkably like those menaces of sectional rebellion pronounced forty years earlier: "The West and the South will unite successfully to resist the cruel demands of the East."

Popular condemnation and hatred of the President and his chosen counselors rose to new heights in the early days of 1895. But once he had taken the great plunge, Cleveland held firm, ignoring the cries of foes, as courageous as ever in his unpopularity. Meanwhile an effusion of laudatory statements and letters came from the finance capitalists who continually surrounded this President, the men who oversaw his little personal investments, the very men who yesterday without "confidence" or patriotism and for fear of missing gold profits had been draining away the Treasury's gold. These men, always most nauseating in their allusions to the "national honor," assured him once more with unmitigated compliments that in saving the gold standard he had saved virtue, and that the severe conditions demanded by the mortgagors were due solely to the "infamous inaction" of "blatherskites" in Congress.[85] Finally he was told that "all the people of brains, wealth and influence" were henceforth "one solid mass of admirers." A trickle of applause from these quarters provided such measure of consolation as Cleveland might have.

Yet at moments even the stout Cleveland appears forlorn, as he tells Ambassador Bayard. Though he had saved the gold dollar and thereby served God, as he felt, he seemed to have lost the country. Even his closest political friends in the Senate trust him no more. His Cabinet, to be sure, is composed of loyal men. "I sometimes feel guilty when I recall the troubles I have induced them to share with me. In our hand to hand conflicts our triumphs are many," he reflects—thinking doubtless of the rout of General Coxey, the imprisonment of Debs, the successful bargain with Morgan—"but I am afraid, as we triumph, our party loses and the country does not gain as it should; and yet what would the condition be without us?" [86]

CHAPTER SEVENTEEN

THE PEOPLE CAPTURE A PARTY

In the midst of plenty we are in want!
"COIN" HARVEY

BETWEEN 1892 and 1896 the Cleveland Administration "stood like a rock" in defense of the gold standard despite a furious popular opposition which led the legislative department of the Government to range itself against the Executive. Finance capitalists, bankers, the heads of insurance companies, as well as widows and orphans, could all sleep soundly in the knowledge that their securities would never undergo devaluation so long as the Gold Democrats held the fort. Industrial capitalists, on the other hand, found the structure of the protective-tariff system largely unaltered during this interim; while the more monopolistic members of this group, who had feared the effects of the Anti-Trust Act, also found themselves pleasantly reassured. So busy was Mr. Olney's Department of Justice in prosecuting Eugene Debs and his fellows, or in making strikes of labor unions "a failure everywhere," that railway combinations, Sugar Trusts, and Octopuses of Oil all felt themselves not merely immune to prosecution, but actual gainers by Mr. Olney's application of the law.

Fears had often been expressed by conservative oracles that our Constitution contained a bill of rights which was too "strong," that our "loose" federal form of government, with its puzzling lacunae or overlapping areas of divided authority, gave too great a scope to dangerous popular or class movements and the militancy of organized labor. Yet in the crisis of 1894 the Cleveland Administration had closed the breach—no mean achievement in itself, involving a striking departure from traditional policies of laissez-faire or "weak" government in peacetime. Under Cleveland and Olney the use of the military and police power of the central Government had been greatly extended; the might and prestige of the whole Federal Government had been thrown into a crushing counteroffensive aimed at the destruction of the power of labor organization. Finally, the trial of

Eugene Debs, and the hearing of his appeal before the Supreme Court in May, 1895, as a sequel to the dramatic events at Chicago, became a cause célèbre.

The Supreme Court, with its vast latent powers as marked for it since John Marshall's time, had lain dormant, in effect, for almost a generation.*

This unique institution of our Government cannot be said to have been revered as a "father symbol," least of all by the older Republican leaders, Lincoln and Grant. What a famous Democratic leader thought of it is suggested in a passage of one of Grover Cleveland's letters of this period, touching his plan to nominate for a vacancy in that court Mr. William Hornblower of New York:

> You will, I know, agree with me, that a man should not be rejected for the place simply because corporations are among his clients, and I hope you will agree with me that in these days of wildness, conservatism and steadiness should not be at a discount.[1] †

But the question of whether the Supreme Court members were immortals, to be regarded with superstition, or simply successful corporation lawyers who had passed the party test—as might be judged from the wavering opinions of the 1870's and 1880's—seems inconsequential. What is important here is that by a series of fateful decisions in 1895, with which it intervened boldly in the controversies of the age, the Supreme Court assumed once more an initiative and legal authority beyond the dreams of John Marshall, and assumed the commanding role in our Government. It was a kind of legal "revolution" or coup d'état; and much of the religious reverence which now attaches to the Supreme Court, forty years later, dates from its history-making defense of corporate property in the 1890's.[2]

The majority opinion in the Debs case, written by Mr. Justice

---

* The Legal Tender Decision of 1870, an attempt to halt the postwar money inflation, was resisted as premature by industrial and railway interests, who may have counseled the Stalwart Republican President, Grant, to "pack" the Supreme Court. This he did, as many students believe, by his new appointments, which led to a prompt reversal of the previous court decision.

† But Mr. Hornblower had once helped prosecute a corrupt henchman of Senator David Hill of New York; and by the system of "senatorial courtesy" the nominee must pass not only an economic catechism but a party test—until a candidate no less conservative, but "offensive to no one" in the party Organization, as Hill said, was named.

Brewer, "a stern defender of property rights," and issued May 27, 1895, completely upheld the sweeping injunctions issued by the lower Federal court. These were novel tactics, rising usually in a suit in equity, which seeks to "enjoin" one party from injuring the property of the other. But in the case of labor action involving no direct damage to property, it became necessary for the Justices to base elaborate legal argument upon the property value of "expectancies" and of "goodwill" in employer-employee relationships and employer-customer relationships, which were held to be irreparably injured by the boycott and strike. Yet was not the quitting of work or the refusal to patronize a given entrepreneur within the complete legal right of American citizens? Could these "rights" of man be restricted? Here the Supreme Court wholly accepted Olney's charge of "malicious conspiracy" to restrain interstate commerce, as defined in the recent acts to regulate railroad and industrial combinations. The court was plainly embarrassed by the constitutional problem of denying a laborer's right to quit his work, which Olney had openly raised, and to his disappointment evaded this issue. But it condemned in the strongest terms actions (of labor) which blocked the "public highways" and interstate traffic moving upon them. To punish or suppress such "conspiracy" the highest tribunal of the land asserted that the whole power of the National Government might lawfully be invoked. The questions raised by Governor John Altgeld were answered.[3]

The decision represented not only a complete vindication for Olney and Cleveland, but as Cooley, the famous jurist who was to enter the Supreme Court later, remarked, "a great and valuable lesson in constitutional construction . . . settled for all time." [4] This historic decision sanctioning the use of court injunctions filled American labor leaders with dismay. It was a formidable legal weapon, making possible imprisonment for contempt of court without a hearing, and without trial by jury, of those who organized labor action. As the independent Springfield *Republican* remarked of the Debs decision, it represented "a palpable usurpation of despotic powers." Moreover, the representatives of discontented labor were threatened with the suspension of "every bill of popular rights written since Magna Charta." [5] Debs pointed out that, as would have happened doubtless in the Imperial Russia of the Czars, he was denied a jury trial by the autocrats whom he had offended. Compelled to languish in jail, removed from action on behalf of the poor and the oppressed to whom alone he declared himself devoted, this "criminal" began to read the writings of Karl Marx brought to him by a socialist admirer. Here he fell, as he relates, upon one doctrine which was then novel to him, but which seemed at last to throw a powerful illumination upon his experiences: the doctrine that the modern state, the courts, police, executive, and legislature were in the last resort only the instruments of defense for capital.

Debs had "interrupted traffic" for a time and was punished; but it was remarked that Armour, directing the Beef Trust, and Havemeyer, dominating the Sugar Trust, not only interrupted or restrained traffic, but "virtually killed" competition in defiance of the law; yet they went unpunished and undisturbed.[6]

The advance of industrial combinations had been quickened under the Cleveland Administration, though nowadays these took the form of single large corporations (instead of Trusts), designed by skillful lawyers under State charters in New Jersey and Delaware. In the new fields of gaslighting and traction, however, monopolies of an especially offensive character were set up overnight through seizure of public franchises. Whitney, Ryan, Yerkes, Mark Hanna, and William Rockefeller, in collusion with local and State party Organizations, had invaded this field with astonishing speed. But the debauch of local government ended by affronting middle-class opinion once more. Storm over the monopolies raged intermittently in Illinois, where Altgeld day and night fought the "eternal monopoly" bills of Yerkes; and in Ohio, where Mark Hanna's domineering tactics roused up the friends of Good Government. Since the passage of the Sherman Anti-Trust Act, certain State officials, in response to sharpening public complaints, now resumed the attack upon the most malignant of the industrial combinations. The prosecution of the Standard Oil Company begun in Ohio caused Mark Hanna to write his impetuous lines to the State's Attorney: "You have been in politics long enough to know that no man in public office owes the public anything." In New York during this new campaign against monopolies, Havemeyer's Sugar Trust had been found guilty of unlawful practices, but had appealed the judgment to the Supreme Court, where it stood trial late in 1894.

The case of the United States *versus* E. R. Knight, Philadelphia, subsidiary of the American Sugar Refining Company, had been inherited from the closing year of the Harrison Administration, and was now to be prosecuted by Attorney General Richard Olney. Olney but a short time before elevation to public office had "torn to pieces" the Anti-Trust Act before a Federal court in Boston. Now, after extended delays, he proceeded against the monopolists of sugar in what seemed a most "lackadaisical" manner, especially when we remember his bearing toward the Commonwealers and the American Railway Union. It was "like setting a wolf to guard a sheepfold," the New York *World* sardonically observed.[7]

While the case was still pending in the Supreme Court, Olney expressed privately at a dinner party his belief that "a mere combination of manufacturers" was not in contravention of the Sherman Anti-Trust Act. Secretary of State Gresham, among those present, himself a famous jurist, argued that it would take but "a scintilla" of evidence for the Supreme Court to infer collusion in buying and selling between the States by such combinations.[8] Yet evidence of sales or price control, easily obtainable, was never brought forward in the high court by Olney. His charge was not designed to prove combination or conspiracy in buying or selling, but simply in manufacturing. It seemed the weakest case that could have been made; and the former Trust attorney was accused thereby (in the reformist press) of having had "manifestly and even almost avowedly no desire to enforce any law in restraint of trust conspiracies." [9]

The Supreme Court on January 20, 1895, dismissed the bill against the sugar refineries on precisely the ground which Olney had laid in his briefs as a corporation lawyer; that "manufacture was not commerce and that, although the products of manufacture were intended to be sold and might be sold beyond the State of manufacture, no interstate commerce would be involved until the goods were actually en route.[10]

The decision, as a momentous test of the law, caused jubilation among the promoters of monopolies; and immediately following it came an outburst of reported "mergers" in which the new General Electric Company, the American Tobacco Company, and the American Telephone Company extended their operations throughout the country, while J. Pierpont Morgan undertook in earnest the financing of national combinations in heavy industries as well as railroads.[11] * Olney, however, was in happiest spirits over his defeat, as he wrote privately to a friend:

> You will observe that the Government has been defeated in the Supreme Court on the Trust question. I always supposed it would be, and have taken the responsibility of not prosecuting under a law I believed to be no good—much to the rage of the New York World.[12]

Following the absolution of the notorious Sugar Trust, the Supreme Court turned to deliberate over the income tax clause of the Wilson-Gorman Tariff Act of 1894. This measure, providing for a direct levy of 2 per cent on incomes above $4,000 a year, was inserted, under popular demand, to offset the unjust balance created by heavy taxes on imported goods borne by the masses of the consumers.

The most violent protests had been raised against the income tax as "discriminatory" taxation aimed at the Eastern States. Ward McAllister, the mentor of New York's "Four Hundred," threatened that he and other members of society would exile themselves to Europe and dwell forever in Monte Carlo. Was it possible, Bryan asked in retort to these threats, that there were people in the country "whose patriotism was less than 2 per cent. deep"?[13] And if there were such people, could not the country well spare them?

But solid men all rallied against this "communistic" threat to property rights and civilization, and summoned a brilliant staff of lawyers to conduct a test suit by which the constitutionality of the income-tax law was to be determined before the Supreme Court. Should it be sustained again, however (as the Supreme Court had done after the Civil War), the consequences promised to be un-

* The free American citizen must now, without let or hindrance, as Henry Lloyd declared, eat the bread of the Flour Trust, the meat of the Beef Trust, live by the light of the Oil Trust, and die and be buried by the Coffin Trust.

pleasant: rebellious threats of stirring up "the old [Boston] tea-party spirit" in resistance to tyrannical Federal tax-collectors, were nowadays heard among owners of large incomes.[14]

The noted corporation lawyer Joseph H. Choate, who with former Senator George Edmunds directed the legal attack upon the income tax, was wholly "inspired by the impulse of the patriot," if we are to believe his official biographer. He feared lest "a rampart around the rights of property" would finally be broken and civilization itself imperiled by Populist and other barbarous atrocities. Against the constitutionality of the measure he argued on various legal grounds; but like many great lawyers, he counted in the last resort on an emotional appeal. Once we began in this way, he pleaded, taxes would be imposed principally upon wealth; it was "the beginning of socialism and communism"; it would bring "the destruction of the Constitution itself." It implied not only an assault upon the rich, but a discriminatory levy principally upon the four States of Massachusetts, New York, Pennsylvania, and New Jersey.[15] Then in an eloquent peroration, as David Graham Phillips reported it, he made great moan that

Most of the widows and orphans, most of the helpless . . . had their small capital invested in corporations, and the income tax robbed them. "We speak for them," he said. "In striking at the corporations, in attempting to confiscate their property, you injure, not the wealthy—they can now stand it—but the widow and orphan." [16]

It remained for the energetic Attorney General to defend the Government's case and make head against Choate's skillful appeal to class fear and money greed in the breasts of Supreme Court Justices. Yet once more Olney fought as with a dead heart.[17]

The hearings were protracted; the attention of the whole country hung in April and May on this case. When the majority opinion was announced on May 20, 1895, as adverse to the Government by a narrow vote of 5 to 4, rumors that one of the Justices had been persuaded to change his mind at the last moment deepened the anger and gloom of the people. The majority decision was marked by prodigious legal quibbling over the question of the form in which a "direct tax" and not a "tax on rent" might be permissible to the

Federal Government. Such a tax, it was contended, could only be levied "by apportionment among the States, on the basis simply of population, like a poll tax." But underneath the tortuous syllogisms by which the court chose to nullify the act of Congress the genuine emotions of the majority Justices were revealed, at moments, as is shown in the accents of Justice Field. Fearful of an oncoming social revolution, yet unwilling to die or to quit his seat, this aged Justice wrote in warning words which echoed Choate's oration:

> The present assault upon capital is but the beginning. . . . It will be but the stepping stone to others, larger and more sweeping, till our political conditions will become a war of the poor against the rich; a war growing in intensity and bitterness.[18]

Justice Harlan in his dissenting opinion, however, held that the decision of the majority struck "at the very foundations of National authority," denied powers vital to the general Government and the preservation of the Union, and did "monstrous, wicked injustice to the many for the benefit of the favored few in particular States." Many an editorial sermon of the day represented the Supreme Court decision overthrowing the income tax as "the triumph of selfishness over patriotism." The great and rich corporations, which the Government had recently strained its last resources to defend from harm, had, by hiring the ablest lawyers possible and fighting desperately, escaped from their just share of taxation due this same Government.[19] To Western and Southern farmers, whose earnings were drawn into Eastern financial centers by railroad and banking charges, it was the final evidence of the alliance between the highest tribunal and the rich. When, they asked, would the people elect a President who would "appoint somebody besides corporation attorneys to the Supreme Court bench"?[20]

On the other hand the organs of possessors of large incomes, like Whitelaw Reid's New York *Tribune*, were exultant at our escape from "communistic revolution":

> The fury of ignorant class hatred, which has sufficed to overturn absolute power in many other lands, and even now renders the maintenance of a Government of law uncertain in some, has dashed itself in vain against the Constitution of the United States.[21]

Telling phrases which showed how the Constitution, to the wealthier class, had something of "absolute" or divine powers of endurance, standing as a fortress against class rebellion, and manned by the vigilant and august tribunal of the Supreme Court Justices. But, on the other hand, should the oracles of the Constitution have sustained the income tax, then, as the *Nation* cynically intimated, the ark of our covenant would have seemed less than divine; owners of property and income might well have turned to violence themselves, and taken part in a modern revival of "the old tea-party." [22] *

II

Step by step the moves of the Administration and the high court—while Congress stood divided and baffled—seemed to draw an iron ring, forged by the new necessities of an industrialized society, around the old liberties of the American people. Thousands of poor farmers in the interior of the country were convinced (from highly circumstantial evidence) that the President was actually in the pay of two or three great international moneylenders; while those who championed organized labor were no less certain that the Administration and the high court alike were bound over to the railroad and industrial corporations.

When Henry D. Lloyd, after a decade of devoted labor, published his dispassionate and ironical tract upon the monopolies, *Wealth versus Commonwealth*, in the autumn of 1894, W. D. Howells, the novelist, wrote to him in the mood of the times that it was a graphic picture of how "prosperity was destroyed and law baffled and justice bought in lands where freedom never was, but surely not in this home of liberty!" [23]

The surprising thing was the passiveness and apparent good humor of the people under so much provocation and real suffering. "Think . . . how many times since the Crédit Mobilier," wrote a friend of Lloyd's, . . . "the alarm has been sounded to the American sheep by faithful shepherds and how placidly the sheep has gone on feeding, and being fed upon!" For Lloyd's book, with its patient, ob-

* Heaven forfend that such a horrid example should have been set by our best citizens for "ignorant labor"! Happily, the Supreme Court averted this melancholy outcome—though by a decision that was uncomfortably close: five to four.

jective tone and its want of positive solutions, made but a modest stir in its day.

Yet humble, obscure, though intelligent men among the masses were reflecting more intensely than ever before upon events and their meaning. To one of these, a small property owner evidently, Lloyd now wrote:

One thing which . . . accounts for the apathy of the working men, the farmers, and the middle class in the cities, is that with that logic which the people seem to possess by instinct they divine that the problem of our times is a much more complicated one than the various vendors of specific panaceas would have them believe. They . . . are not likely to move until they have got a pretty clear idea of how the evil is to be attacked at its roots and then not until they are aroused by some dramatic event.[24]

The people waited for the expression of simple, clear doctrines. Of dramatic events fitted to give these point there had been not a few. One of the events which fixed itself indelibly in the public memory was undoubtedly the secret conference of President Cleveland with Morgan and Belmont which immediately preceded the private gold loan of January, 1895. The mistrust and anger of the masses of people was gradually focused upon this incident and its principals rather than anything else, and led them by natural steps to an inevitable partisanship in the contemporary struggle between Silver and Gold.

Out of overwrought Chicago there had appeared suddenly in 1894 a mighty pamphlet which dramatized the principles of bimetallism for the men of the 1890's as the *Contrat Social* or *Uncle Tom's Cabin* had marched before earlier revolutions. This was the little treatise by William H. ("Coin") Harvey, entitled *Coin's Financial School,* said to have been read within the year by half a million readers. In this lucid, vigorous, cleverly illustrated discussion, arranged in the form of lectures (with interpellations) by the young financial "expert" Coin to leading capitalists and editors of Chicago, such as Joseph Medill, Lyman Gage, Armour, and H. H. Kohlsaat, Harvey endeavored to "locate the seat of the disease that threatens the life of the nation." His moral is embodied clearly in the illustrative cartoon at the opening of the book, showing a naked chained man (labeled "American Industry") struggling in vain to reach a banquet table groaning with good fare. The caption read: "In the Midst of Plenty We Are in Want!"

Coin pictured the trials of the period in strongly compassionate terms:

> Hard times are with us; the country is distracted; very few things are marketable at a price above the cost of production; tens of thousands are out of employment; the jails, penitentiaries, workhouses and insane asylums are full; the gold reserve at Washington is sinking . . . a huge debt hangs like- an appalling cloud over the country . . . hungered and half-starved men are banding into armies and marching toward Washington; the cry of distress is heard on every hand . . . riots and strikes prevail throughout the land; schemes to remedy our ills when put into execution are smashed like box-cars in a railroad wreck, and Wall Street looks in vain for an excuse to account for the failure of prosperity to return since the repeal of the silver purchase act.[25]

There was the rub; the adoption and defense of the gold standard seemed only to have deepened the depression. Values remained low, money was still scarce, and spasmodic minor panic movements recurred within the major cycle of deflation. To Coin Harvey the whole history of our success and failure, of our prosperity and want, is seen in terms of money abundance and scarcity. Ever since silver, "the money of the people," had been abolished by the "Crime of '73" the circulation of currency had been insufficient, property values and commodity values sank, while gold was "cornered," and "rose" incessantly in value. Yet all the gold in the world, when melted into blocks, could be placed behind the counter of one of Chicago's large banks. It was nothing less than a "conspiracy"—here Coin touches a universal instinct to simplify complex problems by pointing to evil design. It was a conspiracy against the farmer, the debtor. "Our debts like a great sponge come West and soak up the Money." The West paid interest upon an ever increasing debt to the East, and could only pay by (1) selling its products or (2) borrowing. But now they could neither sell goods nor borrow money, and their products were worth but half their value of a decade before.

On one hand the law of the land says these debts must be paid, and there are the courts and sheriffs to enforce it. On the other hand, the people cannot pay, as a new monetary unit makes it impossible. . . . The people will retaliate. . . . Under the effects of this legalized robbery . . . the future of the republic looks serious and threatening.[26]

Thus Coin Harvey (by his quantitative theory of bimetallism) narrowed the whole problem of cyclical depression under capitalism to one of a contest between creditor and debtor. Let us have a more ample "primary money" at the basis of our credit system—that is, use abundant silver as well as gold as the redemption basis—and credit would multiply, money would circulate plentifully, prices would rise, the debtor would no longer be disadvantaged by his creditor. Coin Harvey's plea for monetary inflation, at its best, contained the concept to which statesmen were to return, two generations later, of a "managed currency" or "commodity money." But while the people cried for inflation, through silver coinage at the old ratio of 16 to 1 for gold—this would now make for a 60-cent dollar by 1894-95 silver values—a conspiracy of Goldbugs barred the way, kept "property . . . standing still and gold . . . going up." [27] *

Harvey's explanation of the paradox of "want in the midst of plenty" made the most irresistible appeal to millions of farmers, miners, merchants, millers, and even workers. Against their just aspirations he ranged the sinister "East" with its finance capitalists hugging their bags of gold, and its politicians, such as Cleveland, Carlisle, and John Sherman, who were pictured as vultures preying upon mankind. But behind "the East" stood the menace of a hideous "English Octopus" spreading its tentacles over the globe itself, stretching out to every sea and continent, covering the British Isles with its evil refulgence—the Rothschilds.

At this moment, various missions and projects were under way for an international bimetallic congress of the leading powers, by which the ratio of silver to gold was to be fixed and production allotted. But the proposed "pegging operations" were repeatedly postponed.

---

* Coin Harvey expressed under the bimetallic dogma what is recognized as the disparity, or inequality, between falling commodity prices and wages on the one hand, and on the other, fixed interest charges, rents, insurance, freight charges, and taxes which decline slowly or almost imperceptibly.

J. P. Morgan himself held talks with Sir William Harcourt at this time in London with a view to "taking silver out of politics." England, after ordering the mints of India closed to silver, was believed to have barred such agreements at every step. Must we wait then upon England's pleasure? Harvey asked.

Whenever property interests and humanity have come in conflict, England has ever been the enemy of human liberty. . . . A war with England would be the most popular ever waged on the face of the earth. If it is true that she can dictate the money of the world, and thereby create world-wide misery, it would be the most just war ever waged by man.[28]

The English were the interest-gatherers of the world, and they demanded payment in gold. In the struggle for world markets, American inflation through unlimited silver coinage would conquer world markets and wrest financial domination from England. Harvey cried:

Shall we wait while the cry of the helpless is heard on every hand? Shall we wait while our institutions are crumbling? This is a struggle for humanity. For our homes and firesides.[29]

Other men in recent years, such as the Populist leader Ignatius Donnelly, had expounded bimetallism. But none so lucidly as Coin Harvey, whose call rang over the continent. The American people, especially its rural masses, were deeply disposed, by environment and mode of production, to embrace the simple monetary device of silver inflation rather than the laborious, self-denying way of disciplined class organization and class action which the Marxists preached. A mere device, they fondly imagined in 1895 and 1896, a mere stroke of the pen, following a mandate of a free people, would transport them into the promised land.*

III

Politicians, John Altgeld has said,

are not the leaders of our progress and of our civilization. As a rule they do not gaze into the firmament or measure the stars; their vision is limited

* At this instant, the opening of the Rand gold fields in South Africa, in addition to the current discovery of the cyanide process for treating low-grade ores,

to the weather vane on public buildings. They never give the order for advance on any great question, they wait to be commanded to move, and then hesitate until assured that it is the voice of the majority calling to them. They wait until the leaders of thought have captured the stronghold of a wrong, and then they try to plant their flag over the ramparts that were stormed by others.[30]

Through 1895 and 1896 the "silver craze" swept across the West "like a prairie fire." The subtleties and mysteries of primary money and bank money, the rhythms of gold movements and their relationship to credit and commodity prices, were discussed by amateurs at the forks of ten thousand country roads. Now professional politicians of both parties, though predominantly, or more notably, in the ill-controlled, disaffected Democratic Party, heard voices calling them, voices of vast majorities of their constituencies. It was late in the day. But they turned upon the established central leadership; they shunned Mr. Cleveland and all his works as if their very political lives hung on repudiation of their President.

What happened now was anomalous in the history of the parties. The Democratic Party controls, the committee posts, all the administrative and appointive powers, were still vested in the old leadership —that of the Gold Democrats; but in effect few obeyed the old command any more. The unity and continuity of effort which through the party Organization give energy and direction to our extremely formalized and compartmented Government was broken. The Gold Democrats at the top of the party hierarchy had completely impaired their usefulness under the existing system as "brokers" between the people and special interests. The Administration no longer spoke the same language as the ordinary Congressman; Congress remained hostile and blocked measures of the Executive; and the regional bosses, who usually managed to reach the Senate, virtually ostracized the man in the White House.

"Think of it," Cleveland himself wrote to Ambassador Bayard, "not a man in the Senate with whom I can be on terms of absolute confidence." [31]

prepared the way for a tremendous increase in the world gold supply, augmenting new capital, creating new credits and buying power, repairing the ravages of depression in the early 1890's by 1897.

When Cleveland's annual message upon the state of the nation, containing also proposals for further conservative financial reforms, was read to Congress, December 3, 1895, only four persons applauded, two of them, Democrats; "both looked surprised," shook their heads, and clapped again despondently.[32]

Of the old Southern leaders, Vest, Jones, Harris, and Bland in 1895 became outright opponents of the orthodox party leadership upon the silver issue. Uniting with Western Silver Republicans, they tried to regain their influence through planned demonstrations for free-coinage bills. Even in Wall Street, late in 1894 Stetson, the Morgan lawyer, had heard through scouts of plans by the insurgent Democrats to force through a Free Silver bill at the next session. "They expect your veto," he wrote Cleveland, "but do not care for it, as they are making the plan for 1896, when the Silver party shall have swallowed the Populists as the Republican Party did the Free-Soilers. We are on the eve of a very dark night unless a return of commercial prosperity relieves popular discontent," he concluded sadly.[33]

New men arriving in Washington even sought quick paths to celebrity by violent tirades against the President. In the House, Champ Clark of Missouri now likened Cleveland to Benedict Arnold and Aaron Burr, naming him as one of the three greatest traitors our country had ever known.[34] And Tillman during his whirlwind campaign for the Senatorship in South Carolina had declared: "Send me to Washington, and I'll stick my pitchfork into his [Cleveland's] old ribs!"[35] Arriving in triumph at the Capital, he was as good as his word, and delivered his greatest piece of vituperation before the Senate, sounding the keynote for the party insurrection.

The country appealed in vain to the "bull-necked and self-idolatrous man who holds the reins of power," he cried. "We . . . [Democrats] had fondly hoped for relief. We elected a President to give the people bread and he gave them only stones."

In defiance of the popular mandates, in betrayal of party pledges, this "besotted tyrant" proceeded to pay out "gold instead of coin," and borrowed money in order to continue to do so, "giving no heed to the interests of any but his *moneyed* friends—I might say his owners or partners. . . . Wall Street and his connections with wealthy men have debauched his conscience and destroyed all sympathy with the masses." [36]

The action of the repudiated Administration, facing a hostile, divided, and turbulent Congress, could be only defensive henceforth. Within the government departments themselves secret moves by the enemy to capture the machinery of organization and control had to be warded off continually. Cleveland himself related to a confidant:

> It was some time before we discovered that, in a large number of the Congressional districts of the middle and further West, some of the most active silver men were getting into post-offices. . . . It became evident, later, that a plan had been formed to use the patronage to promote their own ideas, so that the administration, in addition to business depression, the Chicago strike, and an unusual popular unrest, found some of its [Democratic] appointees turned against itself. Among these active men, none was more industrious in seeking places for his followers than Mr. Bryan.[37]

After 1895, the Gold Democrats were engaged in a losing struggle to hold the party in one State Organization after another. The Southern and Western States fell from their hands quickly, South Carolina, and Virginia like Missouri and Nebraska. Carlisle, once hailed as "the great Kentuckian," was sent on a speaking tour in his native State, but was received in his home town of Covington with a shower of rotten eggs.

What was most alarming was the bipartisan character of the uprising. Among the Republicans, the veteran Senator Teller of Colorado prepared to lead his Western followers into the new crusade, as he declared in a bitter passage with Aldrich. "We can get along without the party as well as the party can get along without us," he threatened.[38] Meanwhile firm hands reached for the leadership of the mass movement. In the spring of 1895, Governor Altgeld, who dominated the powerful Democratic Organization of Illinois, after some hesitation took a decided position on the great issue of the day and warmly espoused a Silver Convention of Illinois Democrats, held in June that year. The tariff issue he argued was now "a dead horse." In a prophetic statement which fixed the new "line," he said:

If our party takes a firm position on this subject (silver coinage) and the Republican party straddles the question, as it will be obliged to do, we will sweep the country and achieve a greater victory than we ever have.[39]

Whereas if the Democrats were to "stand for nothing," there was no object even in making a campaign.

Despite the unremitting propaganda of hate against Altgeld in the great press, the workers and farmers of Illinois idolized him; he continued to hold a large and enthusiastic majority of his State party under his resolute command, and it was feared now in Eastern financial centers that Altgeld rather than the President would emerge as the dominant national leader in his party councils.

The "war of the poor against the rich" which Mr. Justice Field had predicted and himself stimulated, in words bitter with class hatred, had finally taken the form of a struggle of Silver against Gold. The issues of the hour were carried to the people in Altgeld's clear challenge: "The continuation of the single gold standard means the permanent degradation of the great toiling and producing masses of this country." [40] In the new session of Congress, convened in early December, a free-coinage bill had been introduced once more with every prospect of final success when a wholly unexpected political cataclysm struck the country.

IV

With his blunt, bellicose message to Congress, December 17, 1895, upon the Venezuela boundary dispute, President Cleveland suddenly exploded a bombshell and offered the most dangerous provocation to a great foreign power. The controversy with England over a boundary in the jungles of South America flared up under the most perplexing and even suspicious circumstances.

In our foreign relations the doctrine of a Manifest Destiny overseas, advocated by Seward, Blaine, and Captain Mahan, had been pursued neither consistently nor aggressively as yet, though in the closing decades of the nineteenth century the Great Powers intrigued or raced with each other, throughout the world, for imperial territorial acquisitions. Attempted adventures in Santo Domingo and Cuba by American freebooters had been checked by public opinion and by the continued indifference, thus far, of our most important capitalist groups. In the obscure negotiations over Hawaii, the intrigues or "deals" for annexation begun under Harrison were repudiated for a time by Secretary Gresham; the Cleveland policy showed itself in 1893 both scrupulous and pacific, though at the end the direction was reversed. Discreet dispositions looking to the eventual absorption of the Pacific Island were made—"to the utter consternation of the moralists who had thus far applauded his [Cleveland's] course." [41]

But meanwhile a long, dreary dispute over the frontier between British Guiana and the republic of Venezuela, dating from 1876, caused intermittent attempts by our Government—at the invitation of Venezuela—to bring about a settlement by arbitration. As in his first term, so in his second, in 1894 Cleveland reported to Congress diplomatic negotiations on this question looking toward a long-delayed arbitration. But the worthy Gresham died of a sudden illness in May, 1895, and Mr. Cleveland, admiring the diplomatic traits of his Attorney General, had promptly promoted him to the State Department.

Within a few weeks the cables vibrated with a thunderous message (though still secret) such as Olney would have sent to a labor union, calling Her Majesty's Government sharply to account "upon the point whether Great Britain will consent or will decline to submit the Venezuelan Boundary Question in its entirety to impartial arbitration." [42] It was a very free, very bold, and very broad construction of the historic Monroe Doctrine, one which the British Government and even various American jurists were scarcely prepared for.

The firing (on July 20, 1895) of this unpublished "twenty-inch gun" of Olney's, as Cleveland dubbed it, had the latter's entire approval, as "the best thing of the kind I ever read." [43] Though the Monroe Doctrine had been regarded hitherto as a declaration of policy to resist new territorial expansion by Europe in the Western Hemisphere, Olney now applied it to a boundary dispute between established governments in South America; and further, in belligerent phrases intimated that the United States regarded as "unnatural and inexpedient . . . any permanent political union between a European and an American state." Finally, he gave warning that though we had hitherto been a pacific nation, avoiding the extensive use of arms, "with the powers of Europe permanently encamped on American [that is, South American] soil, the ideal conditions we have thus far enjoyed cannot be expected to continue." The United States on this continent is "practically sovereign and its fiat is law," he added menacingly.[44]

Our own Ambassador, Bayard, was consternated as he transmitted this "bumptious" and exasperating message to the British Foreign Minister. The Government at London, in process of changing, appeared greatly taken aback and proceeded to withhold its reply with almost insulting deliberation and delay. After four months a refusal of arbitration, though in diplomatic language, came to Washington.

The traditional view of the affair holds that President Cleveland and Olney were outraged or emotionally aroused by the studied discourtesy shown our Government. The private correspondence of the two statesmen, however, does not suggest passionate haste or strong feelings. Cleveland, departing on December 3, 1895, for a duck-shooting expedition while the British message was known to be on its way, asked Olney to hold it secret when it arrived, and prepare a message which was to await his return. Cleveland's closing, somewhat cryptic words were:

If I were here I would not be hurried in the matter even if the Congress should begin grinding again the resolution-of-inquiry-mill.[45]

At this moment a Senate committee was investigating the Chicago strike and its defeat by the Government; another committee contemplated the investigation of the President's contract for a loan from an international, or "British," banking syndicate. Morgan himself would soon be hailed to the witness stand in Washington. Cleveland later (December 29, 1895), in a qualifying private letter to Bayard, alluded to the "tides of jingoism" which he honestly struggled to stem! But what needed stemming was class and sectional passion aroused by the arrogant behavior of the Executive and the Supreme Court rather than "jingoism." What cause for haste, what urgency was there, in distracting politicians and citizens alike by the warlike public message on the Venezuela question which came December 17, and without the consultation of the rest of the Cabinet, usual in so grave a case?

The President here boldly reasserted the Monroe Doctrine in its broader application, according to Olney. His own rewritten version, his rephrasing of Olney's paper, was if anything more pugnacious. He insisted in effect that arbitration must be forced upon the disputants; he asked Congress for authorization to appoint a commission which would investigate the boundary claims. When its report would be completed and accepted, it would be "the duty of the United States," he avowed, "to resist by every means in its power, as a willful aggression upon its rights and interests," any territorial appropriations (by Great Britain) not agreeing with the American view. He continued:

> In making these recommendations I am fully alive to the responsibility incurred and keenly realize all the consequences that may follow . . . there is no calamity which a great nation can invite which equals that which follows a supine submission to wrong and injustice and the consequent loss of national self-respect and honor, beneath which are shielded and defended a people's safety and greatness.[46] *

A wave of excitement, a thrill of passion, now swept through the country, spreading from bold-faced type in the press to mass meetings in the large cities, to financial panics and bank runs. Throughout the confused, dissentient nation, the man in the street showed his ready disposition to strike a pose of belligerency and defiance in company with the larger herd. The obscurer, muddier tribe emotions were aroused quickly to a flaming war spirit. "The country is with the President." "He has struck a strong chord of patriotism"; he had made "a strong and brave" exhibition of "American backbone" worthy of the late Jim Blaine—these were the typical expressions of approval in a press which the night before had given no fragment of a thought to our troubles in Venezuela.[47]

Congress, which had shown a stony hostility to the President's message on financial reform two weeks before, fell over itself in its haste now to encourage him, furnishing instantly an appropriation for the expense of a boundary commission, together with a resolution of approval. Naturally, in such a juncture the people, Congress,

---

* Olney afterward explained that he had sought "words the equivalent of blows" in order to waken the English. (James, *Richard Olney*, p. 140, letter to Knox, Jan. 29, 1912.)

do not side with "the enemy"—England, and its "bank rule"—whom our bimetallists had been denouncing almost daily.

But in both countries the voices of Christian ministers and of clear-sighted leaders were also raised to stay the war madness. On Monday, December 23, 1895, a huge peace meeting in New York was addressed by Henry George and Dr. Lyman Abbott. It was mobbed by a horde of jingoes. Joseph Pulitzer, the nabob of the newspaper world, then at the height of his journalistic power and still in a pacific phase, denounced the bellicose message as an atrocious blunder, which had the design of a coup d'état by Olney.[48] The New York *Post*, reflecting capitalist dismay at the sudden panic in the security markets, frankly accused the Administration of using the threat of a foreign war as a political dodge.[49] Once before, in April, 1861, under Secretary Seward, it had been attempted, when this statesman proposed to Mr. Lincoln that they "change the question before the public" as a way of staving off the slavery issue!

That such thoughts may not have been unknown to an Administration often accused of submission to "English bank rule," and especially to its new Secretary of State, is suggested by a most curious letter from Representative Paschal of Texas to Olney. This communication, which arrived a little earlier, at a moment when some leaks from the State Department or British sources caused unpleasant mention of the current diplomatic strain with England, read as follows:

You are right, now go ahead. Turn this Venezuela question up or down, North, South, East or West, and it is a "winner"—pardon the slang—morally, legally, politically, or financially, your attitude at this juncture is the trump card. It is, however, when you come to diagnose the country's internal ills that the possibilities of "blood and iron" loom up immediately.

Why Mr. Secretary, just think of how angry the anarchistic, socialistic, and populistic boil appears on our political surface and who knows how deep its roots extend or ramify? One cannon shot across the bow of a British boat in defense of this principle will knock more *pus* out of it than would suffice to inoculate and corrupt our people for the next two centuries. . . .

I believe scarcely a discordant voice will be heard 'mid the welcoming chorus of applause this country will send up from ocean to ocean, from Lakes to Gulf, the hour the stars and stripes bid defiance to British greed, aggression and insolence.

A war with England would finally, the author concluded, be a good chance to test our immigrant population, and show whether our "free Republican institutions are to be submerged by hordes of modern Goths and Huns among us." [50]

While the British remained silent, and gloom hung over both countries for a fortnight, from December 17 to New Year's Day, enlightened leaders of opinion such as Bryce and Joseph Chamberlain on the one side, Carl Schurz, John Bassett Moore, and others on this side, worked to still the clamor for a war which finance capital was unprepared for. [51] *

Moreover, the difficulties which England faced with the German Emperor, William II, following Jameson's raid into the Transvaal early in January, 1896, diverted its anger. A tribunal of arbitration was agreed upon after several months. The war scare subsided quickly, and Cleveland and Olney, who had talked so loud, proved surprisingly accommodating in subsequent negotiations. [52] Three years later, in 1899, nearly all of the English contentions with respect to the Venezuela boundary were quietly conceded by arbitration, and almost nothing of Guiana was lost to Britain. This curious outcome of so absurd a quarrel was afterward considered by Woodrow Wilson a "diplomatic triumph" for Cleveland. [53]

The President had borne lately many trials and humiliations. But the sudden diplomatic sortie, so much like a military diversion whatever may have been its motive, did little to allay the deep-seated torment of domestic issues, the financial illness of the time, which soon returned in a form even more malignant than before, rendering the closing year of Cleveland's second term a harrowing nightmare.

V

During 1895 the pressure against the American currency, through redemptions of paper money at the Treasury, tended to relax gradu-

---

* The New York Chamber of Commerce passed a resolution urging conciliatory treatment of Britain, Jan. 2, 1896. (Nevins, *Cleveland*, pp. 645-46.) Wall Street condemned the message.

ally. The Morgan loan provided support for nearly the full year, while the dollar remained "pegged." But in the autumn gold exports were resumed, the "corner" in exchange seemed to give way, and the Treasury gold reserve dwindled again, though more slowly than before. With the explosion of the Venezuela incident, withdrawals of gold assumed the proportions of a run on the Treasury. " 'The Philistines are upon us'—in other words private hoarding has begun," the New York Sub-Treasury head reported to Secretary Carlisle, December 20, 1895.[54]

Once more the President sent a special message to Congress asking for enabling legislation which would permit short-term Treasury loans and the expansion of national banknotes. But the bimetallists of Congress were as stubborn as ever, and prepared instead a free-coinage bill, which was defeated largely by Republican votes. Again the Administration faced the choice between a new loan through a bankers' syndicate which would be politically ruinous, and a popular loan which might win poor support.

Fully informed of the Government's position, Morgan organized during December, 1895, another huge banking syndicate which was intended to distribute a government gold loan of from $100,000,000 to $200,000,000, through German, British, and French as well as American participants. On December 23, 1895, Morgan and his lawyer, Stetson, were reported prowling about Washington again. Morgan's offer to Secretary Carlisle was reported to be for $200,-000,000, on the same hard terms as in February, 1895.[55]

The financing of loans to sovereign governments is, of course, one of the richest trades known, and one most eagerly sought for by great moneylenders. But for the movement of such ponderous sums of gold elaborate advance arrangements are required. In a sense, Morgan forced the hand of the Government as he, with the aid of Stillman, aligned the great New York banks and their foreign correspondents under his orders, before the Government had indicated its purpose. His advance preparations were certainly not made from entirely "patriotic" motives, and rendered a possible attempt at a popular loan, if the Government should so decide, all the more difficult; while the low bid which he offered, after having placed most of the other potential bidders under his orders, seemed now "unwarranted," and brought upon him severe criticism.[56]

On January 3, 1896, the shadow of the colossal banker hovered over Washington again. He was seen to call upon the "Assistant President," Lamont, who, inviting him into his little study, there had him meet "accidentally" with Secretary Carlisle.[57] On that very day one of Whitney's pressing dispatches had been sent to Lamont, urging that "Morgan and his great power" be used. None else but Morgan should be treated with, otherwise failure would be invited.[58] Meanwhile James Stillman, who loaned money for the current speculations of both Whitney and Lamont, also urged acceptance of the Morgan offer, to which he was a partner.[59]

But the climate had now changed. The New York *World*, with which the Newspaper Baron Joseph Pulitzer carried on prodigious circulation campaigns, acted as a watchdog for the people, and began giving the alarm as early as December 24, 1895, in boldface headlines which read: "No More Bond Scandals." Its "newshawks" shadowed the New York bankers continually. While Whitney pressed the cause of the Morgan syndicate through the back doors of the Government the adventurous Pulitzer attacked in the open. Early in January, 1896, the presence of Morgan and Stetson in Washington was again detected, and the *World's* front page thundered every day for a popular loan, denouncing presumed plans for a private contract with Morgan:

SMASH THE BOND RING

GO TO THE PEOPLE

SAVE THE COUNTRY FROM THE MISCHIEF, THE WRONG, THE SCANDAL
OF THE PENDING BOND DEAL WITH THE MORGAN SYNDICATE.

Pulitzer sent a daring challenge to the country when he offered to lend $1,000,000 in the name of the *World*, and dispatched telegrams everywhere to form a list of subscribers for a popular loan distributed directly throughout the country.[60]

The final broadside was the cartoon of January 4, 1896, entitled "Our Modern Robber Barons," in which the sinister-looking pirate (Morgan) and his mates, clad in feudal costumes, were shown demanding ransom in the amount of $12,000,000 from Uncle Sam, for his "sorrowing sweetheart" (The National Credit). Joseph Pulitzer, who now regaled a huge audience by his theatrical exposures of the wicked rich, was undoubtedly responsible for the defeat of the banking syndicate's plans and for the moment "rendered a real service to the country." [61]

The *World* well expressed popular feeling when it said:

The people of this country do not want to see the Government cornered again by a syndicate of bankers. They do not want bonds worth 120 sold for 104½, and especially they do not want to see this done in a secret and evidently prearranged manner through the agency of a recent partner of the President.[62]

The bankers were frightened. Stillman complained sadly to Lamont at having his "motives misinterpreted and reviled," and reported that his friends were now disposed to withdraw their offerings.[63] The head of the House of Morgan, upon the day when he was pilloried in the *World,* wrote to Cleveland offering his fullest support for a popular loan.[64] *

Whatever the President had intended to do, he now had no choice. In a letter which was soon made public and reflected a certain embarrassment, he declared that he had contemplated only a public sale of bonds; the accusations of a "maliciously mendacious and sensational newspaper" had been unfounded.[65]

The fourth Cleveland loan of $100,000,000, announced January 6, 1896, became an affair of popular subscription. Issued at more favorable terms than its predecessor, at a price of 110½, it raised the Treasury gold reserve quickly to $128,000,000. By now the world gold supply was increasing again; moreover, the outstanding redeemable paper currency was reduced by one-fifth; the inflationary pressure had been checked.[66] The gold standard was safe. But the voters

* The image of Morgan as a "Robber Baron" soon became further fixed in the popular eye and memory when in mid-June the great banker came reluctantly to Washington to testify before a Senate committee as to his part in the private gold loan of 1895. Questioned about his profits, he stoutly and repeatedly said: "I decline to answer." What he had done had been done from "patriotic" motives solely. But the price at which the bonds in question were disposed of he stubbornly refused to reveal. They had become his "personal property" and thereafter concerned the public no more.

and the politicians, in full cry, were to be heard from as the quadrennial presidential plebiscite opened in 1896.

VI

For a whole year preceding the national conventions of 1896 both great parties had been skirmishing for a position of advantage upon the money question, the Republicans hesitating to speak openly, the new Democratic leaders, on the other hand, waiting for their opponents to commit themselves, as expected, to a single gold standard. The growing Populist Party, with its 1,500,000 votes in 1894, dominating a huge territory in the West and the Southwest, had been distinguished for its logical championing of regulative or "leveling" laws in the interests of all agrarian property-holders, for its demands for railway and corporate reforms, increased diffusion of credits, and equalization of the tax burden. But after 1895 the spread of Coin Harvey's ideas, and the hue and cry over the "Robber Baron" syndicate combined to aid the skillful intrigues of the Silver and Copper Kings, Marcus A. Daly, J. Augustus Heinze, William A. Clark, and the Hearst Estate, in bringing a sudden shift from the uncompromising reform position of the Populists.

The new "line" demanded that the silver issue be advanced at all costs, and a practical working alliance be made with Silverites of both older parties. "Keep the money question to the front" was the word of order given by the national chairman, Taubeneck, to various Populist State conventions; "it is the only living issue before the people. I hope your state convention will build a platform making the 'money question' the great central idea." Weaver, Ignatius Donnelly, and Senator Allen of Nebraska also urged going before the people in 1896 "with the money question alone." [67] The plan of simplifying their appeal and focusing it on the one Burning Issue of the day, if only to "win this time," allured the more practical Populist leaders, while the intervention of the Mining Kings, acting now as a socially irresponsible capitalist group (in search of immediate gain through inflation of metal prices), promised fruitful sources of campaign contributions which few Organization leaders could overlook.

The agents of the Anaconda and other Rocky Mountain mining

groups were careful to stress at many a bimetallist gathering the gains which inflation would bring in farm prices, when their over-weening interest was of course in the price of copper and silver and lead. The mine-owners acted as a powerful leaven in a movement which worked to wean the Populists from their more radical doc-trines, and bore them toward a united front with the mass of the Democrats and the Western wing of the Republicans. Thus the silver movement of the 1890's, like the antislavery movement of 1860, promised to sweep over the old party alignments, swallowing up one whole party and splitting the other. The meaning of such a revolu-tionary realignment for the nation was fully understood by Sound Money leaders of both parties who could read the signs: it betokened nothing less than a class struggle—if not purely of the proletarian workers in the cities against their masters, certainly between the "two nations," the poor and the rich, a Gracchian uprising of debtor against creditor, of the people of the land against the people of the great cities.

Within the Democratic national Organization a silent contest raged, in which the old ruling group of Gold Democrats was forced to retreat step by step. The choice of Chicago over New York as the site of the approaching nominating convention was in itself an evil omen.[68] The followers of Bland and Vest, the Silverite leaders, and a new figure, Governor Boies of Iowa, captured one State conven-tion after another from the Gold Democrats; so that these latter hoped no more for a majority of the party, but solely to obstruct action through the historic unit or two-thirds rule. Secretary Carlisle himself had gone forth again in the spring of 1896 to warn the workingmen of Chicago against the "free-silver foolishness," but Altgeld, who the Cleveland Administration had thought was ruined in 1894, answered Carlisle on May 16 with a ringing call for silver inflation, and won over the Illinois State Organization. "We must relieve our people," was Altgeld's watchword.

When the Illinois Republicans, moreover, "straddled" the money issue and nominated a ticket dictated by Yerkes and his associates, the Democratic Party placed itself firmly in support of Altgeld. The stormbird of Middle Western politics saw himself renominated for the Governorship by a great majority; he was vindicated before his own people, while national delegates from his large State were instructed to vote for "the free and unlimited coinage of silver at 16 to 1." [69] Altgeld, having the status of a naturalized citizen, could not aspire to the Presidency. With fortune and health broken by four years of fierce political combat, he wished to refuse office, but leadership of the Silver Democrats was thrust upon him.

John Altgeld commanded the crowd not so much by extravagance of oratory as by hard-hitting argument and blazing sincerity. His rise to dominant leadership in his party despite torrents of calumny directed at him increased the dismay of the Gold Democrats, who now feared lest they might lack even a sufficient minority to furnish resistance under the two-thirds rule.

At this very time there had come news of the Republican nominating convention at St. Louis and the adoption of an uncompromising gold plank. Governor William McKinley, termed by his adversaries the "suit of clothes" for the Ohio magnate and rising party boss Mark Hanna, had been awarded the Sound Money nomination at once by a complaisant party convention.

Altgeld immediately, in an explosive public interview, charged that the Republican convention had been "monopolized" like others of Mark Hanna's Trusts. It was a gathering, he said, comparable to those select circles which once flourished along the frontier, where no man who had not committed homicide or stolen a horse might be admitted. "So, in that St. Louis convention only a man who had manipulated Congress or ravished a legislature or seduced a judge" was eligible for membership. The logic of the situation called for a bold assumption of the whole silver program by the Democratic Party.[70]

In this election year, it was observed, the Democrats would have all the "principles," the heavy brass bands, the sentiment of the masses of voters. All that they needed was a "Moses." Altgeld, the idol of the Middle Western masses, was a Prussian by a margin of three months, and hence ineligible; Richard Bland, of Missouri (a strategically weak Border State), was in the ripeness of age; Vest was a Southerner; other new arrivals were too little known. With the collapse of the Cleveland wing, no experienced Eastern politician would be "available" at the forthcoming convention. Was there some

Lincoln, or some "unknown Altgeld" for this "irrepressible conflict" which gathered itself—a man fresh from the people, whose call to millions of farmers and laborers might be combined with the electric summons of revolutionary change?

On the eve of the Democratic State Convention in New York, President Cleveland was persuaded to make one more public appeal to his party on behalf of Sound Money. He wrote in a public message:

> I refuse to believe that . . . there will be engrafted upon our Democratic creed, a demand for a free unlimited and independent coinage of silver. . . . The Democratic party is neither unpatriotic nor foolish.

His voice carried no more authority, it aroused no surprise. Only a few Eastern strongholds, New York, Pennsylvania, New Jersey, Massachusetts, were still held by the old hierarchy of Gold Democrats.

In this dark hour, new hope was suddenly kindled upon the "right wing" when the press at New York announced that William C. Whitney, "the popular Democrat and great tactician," on the eve of sailing for Europe had suddenly decided to remain at home and join in a great effort to lead the Sound Money forces. "Whitney Enters the Fight" ran the heartening news.

"A great crisis is upon the Democratic Party" read the statement in which the secretive man now openly addressed the nation. If a free-coinage plank were adopted, "disruption of the Democratic party . . . the worst panic and distress" would certainly follow. The creditor classes, he argued, would not be the worse off, "but wages would be paid in silver, the sufferers as usual being the poorer classes." Then, in a still more subtle vein, Whitney said that he entertained the highest hopes that an international bimetallic agreement was near, making silver coinage (at a fixed ratio to gold value) possible and safe again.* But if the Democratic Party waited not until a sound form of bimetallism was possible, then Whitney prophesied for it "the most disastrous defeat that any party has ever had in this country."

---

* This was the will-o'-the-wisp project for "pegging" world silver, often held up at election seasons, though nothing came of it.

Whitney further alleged that he acted solely from "patriotic" motives. He would proceed to Chicago not as a delegate but simply "to use his personal influence." Nor was he in any sense a candidate, as some immediately deduced. He concluded:

I am not foolish enough to suppose that any Eastern man could be nominated by this convention, much less that I could be. I sympathize thoroughly with the feeling in the South that has caused the uprising and that will find expression in Chicago; but as to the principles . . . and the issues being framed, I entirely disagree.[71]

The decision of the brilliant Whitney, who was not only the richest but "the ablest Democratic politician," as the Philadelphia *Times* said, to enter the lists and undertake a "most heroic" battle, revived many drooping spirits.[72] It was the promise that he would "use his personal influence" that caught the eye of the experienced men. This "influence" had twice made a President. Politicians in the interior scouted the idea that Mr. Whitney could go to Chicago "and do like the wise men of the East who went to St. Louis—buy up enough delegates to make a gold platform." [73] But with his money, his verve, and his remarkable popularity among professional politicians, who could tell what might happen? Whitney never lost battles. This political miracle-worker, who at this crisis, virtually for the first time, fought in the open, might alone turn the tide.

A few days later, June 24, Whitney, aided by the swart David Hill, managed the New York State Convention at Saratoga with his old skill. A platform which in appearance departed from Cleveland's hated single gold standard in advocating "international bimetallism" was adopted by a lackluster body of party delegates, whose ovations were chiefly tendered to Whitney.[74] Now, gathering about himself the Eastern party bosses and statesmen, he prepared quickly to march on Chicago.

These were turbulent and dangerous hours for the bourgeois republic, when the people, as Mr. Cleveland felt, seemed to let reason fly from its chambers, when "strange heresies" and "false prophets" beckoned to them. Masses of poor farmers clamored for more abundant credit and money; organized labor demanded the suppression of "government by injunction"—the curbing of the Federal courts themselves! Mr. Cleveland had seen these dangers as imminent after his election in 1892; but the harsh lessons he had taught and the still harsher ones taught by the Supreme Court had only lent scope to disillusionment. The poor, the debtor class, the smallholders, saw as if their eyes were opened for the first time the painful contrast between historic ideas of liberty, of human rights, between good American expectations of opportunity or prosperity, and the bleak realities of the time. The old political leadership appeared to have destroyed itself. The discipline, the continuity, with which party tradition and party Organization had known how to master popular passions and avoid class-sectional conflagrations now seemed irreparably lost.

Mr. Whitney himself was not confident of victory. Indeed, the elaborate massing of money and force on the Republican side this year, as we shall see, had forecast clearly up to the spring of 1896 one of our periodic alternations of the party control in the Government. Mr. Whitney's precipitate and open return to the management of convention politics took place under circumstances which had suspicious connections with new, unforeseen prospects of Democratic Party success under the Free Silver standard.

The fearful danger looming now was not that the Democratic Party might lose, but that it might win and the gold standard might be lost. At this period, the plans of the Gold Democrats depended much upon the aid of the clever young Governor of Massachusetts, William E. Russell, who had recently distinguished himself by winning his office in a habitually Republican State. Whitney wrote to Governor Russell on June 18, 1896:

> Now is the time. Come with me to Chicago and we will do one of two things—either beat down this craze or save the *esprit de corps* of the Eastern Democracy by most emphatic action. *This last is probably all we can do, but there is more duty in that at the present time than in anything else.*[75]

What did Mr. Whitney propose to do with the Eastern Democracy once he had saved its esprit de corps?

Russell, at all events, had responded heartily, but asked that his name should not be presented as a candidate, for the moment. But Whitney insisted that Russell leave his name open, as a possible means of rallying the Gold Democrats. He held out hope to Russell's ambitions:

> The fight we make will help any man around whom it centers. Unless you wish it we will not make it on you, but do not take any action without we have had a chance to talk. Show this to any friend you choose. I haven't time to argue or discuss at this moment.[76]

The veteran of many political battles, resourceful and ruthless, Whitney knew the temper of conventions before they opened, as he knew the pulse of the markets which he made or smashed. Surely, skeptical as he was, he had not turned back from his beloved Derby in England to assume the large burdens and expenses of a convention struggle with the hope of nominating a Hill of New York, or a Russell of Massachusetts, in the face of the gathering horde of silver "fanatics." His own admission that no Eastern man could win casts further doubts over his motives and his behavior—which in the end mystified, as it disappointed, Governor Russell.

On Thursday, July 1, the New York newspapers signalized the departure of a "Gold Train" made up of three luxurious cars which Mr. Whitney had ordered and prepared to accommodate the notables of the Eastern Democracy on their voyage to the Chicago front. The Gold Train was equipped with rich and ample store of food and liquids. To the popping of champagne corks, cheering themselves up as well they might, a resolute but convivial little band rode together out of New York. It included Mr. Whitney and his partner, Thomas Fortune Ryan, David Hill, Senator Smith of New Jersey, Frederic Coudert, Boss "Billy" Sheehan of Buffalo, divers Tammany leaders, journalists such as George Harvey and Charles Miller, and several aides-de-camp.[77]

Within a few minutes after the arrival of their train at the station in Chicago, as they jostled their way toward their hotel quarters through a hostile crowd flaunting silver badges and uproarious as if in preparation for some violent action, the Gold Democrats' good spirits were severely dampened. On every hand they saw strange, uncouth faces which were not often like the smooth ones of politicians. What they saw and heard in the hours before the Chicago convention opened led one of the party, it was related, to remark seriously to Whitney: "For the first time I can understand the scenes of the French Revolution!" [78]

CHAPTER EIGHTEEN

THE RISE OF A NATIONAL BOSS: MARK HANNA

There won't be any revolution.
MARK HANNA

THE beautiful convenience of the American party system consisted in its reversible character: while one of its two component parts performed unpleasant tasks and so earned for itself unpopularity, the other could make ready to accept the benefits of all the negative discharges which the process rhythmically produced.

Between 1880 and 1896 the composition of both great professional parties was fairly identical, the difference being composed of political nuances only. The adversaries were evenly balanced and alternated regularly in control of the National Government.

After 1894, the Republicans in Congress, for instance, neglected no chance to use their timeworn partisan and harrying tactics. The extreme difficulties of 1893-94, which they had gladly shirked, were now fully "turned to account." The clever Mr. Reed, no longer Czar of the House—in the pinch—helped to defend the gold standard whenever the Democratic majority failed Mr. Cleveland. But the emergency past, he would use again his great gifts of sarcasm to expose the blunders, compromises, and "traditional" incompetence shown by the Democrats in power. At the final vote for the Wilson-Gorman bill he had said tauntingly:

> You are going to enact a bill which you believe not to be an honest bill, and you are going to accompany it with a parade, which you also know is not honest. . . . You are going to give us free sugar.—Yes, in your minds. [Laughter.] You are going to give us free coal.—Oh, my friends! And then you are going to give us free iron, and you are going to do it in a bold and manly way, like the backdown you are making here. [Laughter and applause on the Republican side; the Democrats nevertheless preparing to lift Mr. Wilson to their shoulders for a victory parade.] . . . Now how do you like the whole programme? You are going to vote it; say how you like it.[1]

The Republicans, under Reed's leadership, while helping in Mr. Cleveland's fight for Sound Money, escaped the odium of that bitter contest, and prepared confidently for restoration to complete national power in 1896. Their attitude during the collisions of these stormy years which had shaken the whole country had been negative, or ostrichlike. They had not been compelled to remit an iota of their so-called principles, which as before favored Sound Money, generous subsidies in the form of Protection for industrial capitalists, and a tolerant policy of laissez faire toward monopolies in railroads and heavy industry.

It is doubtful whether the Republican professionals had absorbed any special lessons from the class upheavals of recent days. They proposed simply to carry on the work of the blunt Cleveland and his "regular" Eastern Democracy, though with Republican finesse. In addition, it was firmly believed in those days by the Republican leaders that the fillip of Protection would encourage again a rise of prices and inaugurate a cycle of prosperity, something of which would inevitably dribble or leak downward to the uneasy masses.

Republican leadership, as typified by Mr. Tom Platt, Mr. Matt Quay, and Mr. Mark Hanna, had grown gradually more "business-like" since 1888, especially in the management of national party work. Ambitious and irresponsible adventurers in political patronage, who might prey indiscriminately upon the wealthy (as well as the poor) as in the General Grant Era, were curbed—partly owing to the extension of civil-service reform. The great State bosses in charge of their efficient, centralized bureaus or clearinghouses of political privilege were answerable directly, as we have seen, to the banking, railroad, and insurance companies, and spared these the expense of maintaining separate lobbying or bribery agencies in the State capitals. Meanwhile, the most prominent capitalists and most important corporations, instead of giving donations out of friendship or to further the career of some military captain or political orator, paid regular fees annually for regular professional services. The members of the party machine, the army of political "workers" who managed the electorate at the polls, now depended mainly upon the war chest gathered from regular corporate fees and infinitely less upon uncertain assessments upon officeholders. This alliance between political professionalism and large-scale corporate capitalism had become especially close and effective since the "fat-frying" Protectionist campaign of 1888.

The "System"—as many now vaguely named it in 1896—reflected a much improved centralization of the machinery of popular political action, yet there was room and pressing need for substantial further improvements still. The Republican Party, for instance, resembled at times a symphony orchestra whose instruments often played out of tune. Elements of serious hazard still existed even under the improved controls. Thus the national convention of 1888 had witnessed spectacular dissension, a riot of selfish ambitions, with the result that a disagreeable compromise had been forced and a Dark Horse of uncertain potentialities named for the Presidency. Then conflicting pledges had been given and treacherous bargains reached even with the Silverite faction from the West. Such leadership had ended by losing control of its own party. The national party control, expressed in the management of delegated representative authority at the presidential convention every four years, according to the process developed during fifty years of machine politics, was still subject to too much chance, intrigue, surprise; it was still an affair, largely, of last-moment, impromptu horse trades between the great regional bosses, out of which anything might come. Politics was still in good measure an inexplicable "art" rather than a department of exact knowledge, at a moment in our history when only the maximum efficiency and the firmest control of the existing machinery might hope to win the day.

It was at this point, during the social upheavals of the 1890's, that a momentous change in party politics produces itself which is properly associated with the emergence of Ohio's Businessman in Politics, Mark Hanna, on the national scene. Some twenty years before, the businessmen had extended their activity in local or State politics, until during the 1880's they held as a group a fixed dominant position over the State machines. But under Hanna, in the 1890's, they moved to overhaul the antiquated controls of national party life. The old, outworn devices gave way to new machinery fitted for the Age of Big Business—machinery pictured vividly by the epithet "steam roller," the road-building monster which forty years ago summoned up as much terror as do our war tanks today.

Mark Hanna, the descendant of industrious Scotch-Irish settlers, the former grocery clerk of Cleveland who rose to be a "lord of the Great Lakes," was usually caricatured in the partisan press of his time as a beetle-browed Irish bully, clad in a suit checkered with dollar marks, smoking a big cigar, drinking out of a dark whisky bottle, and driving his heel into the prostrate, writhing skeletons of proletarian women and children. He was pilloried as a cruel employer, a greedy monopolist whose only notion of political activity was "to go out and buy somebody." [2] It was true that he appeared to the casual glance "bullet-headed, cruel-lipped, dynamic." He towered large, and carried an imposing paunch firmly before him, so that when he strode into the Union League Club he was recognized at once for what he was.

Yet juster, more lifelike portraits of the time show Hanna's physiognomy, though gross, full of keen interesting lines and ridges, and eyes alive with cunning intelligence, suggesting rather a wellfed merchant prince from an old Dutch masterpiece than the ignorant bully of contemporary legend. It was true that he drank, but only water. He was hard in a trade; but so were the other Yankee neighbors in New Connecticut, the Rockefellers, the Paynes, the Flaglers, and even the eccentric Tom L. Johnson (before he turned Single-Taxer), among whom Hanna passed a life of incessant struggle and acquisition. According to Tom Johnson, who was for a time Hanna's rival as a streetcar magnate, the man's belligerency was impersonal, a product of his social climate rather than of constitutional inhumanity. "Life meant war to Mark Hanna. . . . And he made war, not to bend men but to break them." [3] He wanted power, and only money was the symbol of power in his world; while "instinct told him" that the easy way to make money was through the seizure, and protection by law, of natural resources, railways, publicutility corporations. Law-made wealth was easy and sure. "He believed in monopoly more honestly than most men believed in religion." [4]

Hanna's wealth was not pyramided upon a single conquered industry but spread broadly through the industrial Middle West. He was a great merchant, whose fleets transported every year an increasing tonnage of coal and iron ore along the shores of our inland chain of lakes, the North American Mediterranean; he was president of a large bank, hence on intimate and responsible terms with a whole community of Middle Western capitalists; his street railways led him to give strict regard to local politics, his employees serving as organizing agents in elections; finally his opera house attested to his imaginative feeling for public meetings, for dramatic and theatrical events, and his lifelong devotion to Shakespeare.

Far more outspoken than his fellow industrialists in expressing the feudal notions of his class, Hanna was said to believe, in effect: "Some men must rule; the great mass of men must be ruled. Some men must own; the great mass of men must work for those who own." [5] The state to him was "a business state." He talked in public, as in private, a little too freely of the use of money in politics, and suffered for this.[6] A group of dinner companions were scandalized by him one day when he remarked bluntly that "all questions of government in a democracy were questions of money." [7]

His political education was rich. Expansion into the street-railway and utility fields had made much of his wealth dependent directly upon State and municipal franchises, that is, upon the constant pursuit of political privilege. During the 1880's he had already shown inventiveness as a pioneer of businessmen's political associations and parades. Being persistent, and learning much from various reverses and harsh experiences, Hanna steadily extended his political influence, held the confidence of his business friends, and as an unrivaled collector of funds became a dominant personage in Ohio's party life and election campaigns.

He had been attached to Governor Joseph Foraker and opened his purse to him in 1885 and 1887, just as Whitney had done for Governor Grover Cleveland. Hanna had also supported John Sherman's aspirations to the Presidency, and gained much knowledge from the discordant party convention of 1888, where our multimillionaire amateur of professional politics figured for the first time as one of the principals in the game of President-making, the most expensive of American sports.

Here Hanna had clearly shown aptitude. All his life he had shown a characteristic passion for machinery; his life, indeed, was bound up with the twin forces of money and machinery.[8] In the convention hotbed of wirepulling and intrigue, he all but succeeded in carrying Uncle John Sherman to the White House, despite the great man's chronic unpopularity.

The lessons borne in upon him from the defeat of 1888 concerned the tortuous procedure and indiscipline of his friend Foraker—impelled by no one knew what obscure private ambitions. On the other hand, a prominent associate in the Ohio Organization, Congressman William McKinley, had given a public display of Roman virtue and discipline when he thrust away the proffered crown of the Dark Horse on behalf of his superior. Now "loyalty" is as precious a quality in party politics as "honor" is among thieves. If McKinley may forsooth have been astonished a little at his own "moderation," Hanna was even more impressed with the Major's shining qualities in responsible and confidential affairs, and a beautiful, historically important friendship now rose upon the ruins of that which had been entertained for Foraker. The bargain was struck, the pact was made between the two men; plans were laid, discussed, ripened, far in advance, over long years.

"You could have been President!" Hanna is believed to have said to McKinley with something of awe. (Though sometimes, in after years, he grew impatient at signs of weakness or stupidity in the Major, Mr. Hanna firmly believed that his friend was "morally" a better man than he was.) Then his thought may have run at the time somewhat after this fashion:

Anyway, old Sherman is finished now; and you are going to be the biggest man in Ohio. Republican presidents will continue to be chosen from the Middle West and from Ohio, its most important State. You are known to the business class of the country as a champion of Protection. You will continue to fight for Protection, for the good of business, for the people. (Hanna earnestly defined his relationship to the common people as a "work-giver.") Your chance will come again. I will work for that chance.

The idea of planning an action far in advance was of course more familiar to Mark Hanna, man of large enterprises and long-term investments, than to most politicians. If he had learned anything from the reverses of 1888, it was that far too much had been left to chance and accident. The Constitution itself had left a good deal to chance in the matter of popular elections of officers of the Government. The party machinery had then been created to eliminate chance from this democratic operation. But even after nearly a hundred years it was plain that party decisions were still subject to lamentable accidents rising from feigned or real contests between rival factions, or even from the still too democratic nature of the party process itself, which a more perfect mechanism would finally remove.

The attempt to have McKinley chosen Speaker of the House in 1889, which failed by so narrow a margin, was part of the long-pull plan which Hanna conceived. Delay or obstruction which is met by well-laid plans and their directors seems but to fit them the better for the right moment. McKinley had figured in 1890 as chairman of the Ways and Means Committee, having his name attached to the highest protective tariff ever passed. While this "holy work" was being carried out, the protected manufacturers, especially those in western Pennsylvania and Ohio, had linked their future firmly with that of their standard-bearer, McKinley, and his patron.

Defeated for re-election to Congress in November, 1890, by Democratic gerrymandering of his district, McKinley was awarded the nomination for the Governorship in 1891. Despite the strong popular current running against the Republican Party, he was elected, his victory being due, as everyone recognized, to the aggressive management of Mark Hanna.

Money had been used without stint. Hanna not only contributed freely himself and "tapped" the local capitalists, but also made pilgrimages into near-by Illinois and Pennsylvania, warning industrialists there of the larger calamities which might follow for the protected from the loss of the Ohio elections. Moreover, the unusually big sums raised were most efficiently managed. Hanna measured well the men who worked under him. Lieutenants who by long specialized experience knew "political quantities" and reported precisely how many votes were required to carry a county or a district were given the sums they required, sometimes as much as $10,000 for two or three counties, and the results were as promised.[9] The fact that a powerful wing of the Republican force held itself undefeated in a year of general disaster was the "only bright spot" of the campaign and was attributed by the well-informed to Mr. Hanna's talent for organization.

Following the State elections, the shifty Foraker, whose strength was chiefly based upon the notorious Cincinnati machine, had determined to stand for the United States Senatorship against Uncle John Sherman. The elimination of Sherman from public life, after his long and distinguished services, by so undependable a character, the declared opponent of McKinley and Hanna, offered serious danger to the further plans of the "regular" Ohio Organization. In the State legislature Hanna, with whom political management now became a ruling passion, personally directed a fierce struggle for the re-election of Sherman. In the closing weeks of the contest, money appeared in abundance at Columbus; recalcitrant legislators were hunted down everywhere in the State by Hanna's hard-driven agents and persuaded to change their minds. Uncle John was awarded the victory once more, and a stinging lesson in discipline (though at great cost) administered to Fire-Alarm Joe Foraker.[10] Thereafter rulership in the party councils was evenly divided between the wily professional boss, Foraker, and the Businessman in Politics, an alliance required by party harmony and deeper business interests but reflecting little mutual trust.

Thereafter, as a former member of the Ohio Legislature has said, Mark Hanna's law firm of Cleveland dominated the lobbying in Ohio.

No bill was permitted to come out of committee [in the State legislature] until Mr. Hanna's lawyers had first examined and approved it. . . . Money was rarely used. It was not necessary. . . . But . . . there was something behind the [Hanna] lobby that worked with clocklike precision and extended over the entire State. It included the local press and the press agencies, the Chambers of Commerce and the county rings. . . . Ohio, in short . . . was ruled by business. Not by all business, but by bankers, steam-railroads, public-utility corporations. . . . When crises arose, Senator Hanna marshalled his supporters, Senator Foraker marshalled his, and the Democratic bosses delivered a sufficient number of votes to insure the desired result.[11]

Under Hanna, the efforts of manufacturers and financiers to influence government directly became "an orderly branch of politics." The scattered power of business became co-ordinated, purposeful. He devoted his life to building "a steel-ribbed, fire-proof machine . . . the like of which was never known before, for it was held together not by the politicians but by the business interests. . . . It was the first mobilization of class-conscious industrialists." [12]

At the convention of 1892 McKinley, who possessed much political astuteness of a traditional kind, assumed the correct attitude of being "overtly favorable" to the renomination of President Harrison, while Hanna, in command of the Ohio delegation and its friends, conducted a sort of dress parade on behalf of his protégé. Harrison's defeat provided its problems for the two schemers; but with the increasing difficulties of the Democratic regime, and its failure to bring about a true tariff reform, the way was opened for a return to the old policies and the standard-bearer of Protection. Much depended upon the second gubernatorial campaign of McKinley, in 1893, when suddenly this good man, like thousands of other Americans, found himself in serious business difficulties as the endorser of notes, in large sums, owed by a ruined business associate. In his despair he considered abandoning his political career, on the eve of the new campaign, and returning to the private practice of law so that he might some day repay his creditors.

The Hanna "syndicate," with a splendid esprit de corps, came at once to the Governor's rescue. The confusion of the Governor's affairs and the size of the outstanding notes, circulating in many hands in a gross sum of $130,000, required that Mr. Hanna should be put in complete charge. Men of purse and property, men who had profited richly by Mr. McKinley's labors, steel and machinery manufacturers and ironmasters, bankers and railroad-owners, were quickly called together, and induced to form a pool which in utter secrecy subscribed the full amount of the statesman's obligations. The select circle of Western millionaires—including Hanna, Myron T. Herrick, H. H. Kohlsaat, John Hay, Andrew Carnegie, Henry Frick, Philander C. Knox, Charles Taft, Samuel Mather, Judge William Day—embraced several future cabinet members and Ambassadors, who acted in concert to save a valuable political property from shipwreck. Care was even taken that the unhappy McKinley should not know the names of his benefactors nor the amounts they donated.[13] The bonds which held him to Hanna and his "syndicate" were now forged forever.

II

In William McKinley, the "Napoleon of Canton, Ohio," our latter-day craft of professional American politics might be said to have reached its finest flower. "He was deeply, essentially a politician," as William Allen White has written.[14] His antecedents, his record, his "regularity," were of an impeccable and orthodox Republicanism, ranging from patriotic war service in his youth long ago to his most recent orations on behalf of iron duties and "infant industries." He knew the rules of the game and played it carefully, "like a gentleman," keeping always on high ground. In politics, as William Allen White said, "the first maxim is to take care of yourself, the second maxim is to take care of your crowd." McKinley, as a politician of the better grade, sometimes put the second maxim first, and was the more appreciated for it. As to doctrines or principles, he had none "except the bundle of jargon and prejudice known as Republican principles in that day." [15]

His appearance also was ideal. He had the handsome, dignified presidential mask which appeals to many voters, though John Hay detected in his face the inscrutability of "a genuine Italian ecclesiastical face of the fifteenth century." [16] To William Allen White this face, with its broad, noble brow and firm steady eye, was "the statesman's face, unwrinkled, unperturbed: a face without vision but without guile." It was the "mask of a kindly, dull gentleman . . . a cast most typical to represent American politics; on the whole decent, on the whole dumb, and rarely reaching above the least common multiple of the popular intelligence." [17] Moreover, thirty years of professional politics seemed to have "galvanized" McKinley "with a coating of publicity" so that: "He became as one 'affected by public use.' He walked among men like a bronze statue . . . determinedly looking for his pedestal." [18] He was amiable and kindly to all men, yet his friendships were like "public relations." He was reluctant usually to commit himself on any issue; his letters were most guarded, ambiguous or blank, as if he had his future biographer in his eye. When he spoke it was with fluency, with an old-fashioned, florid rhetoric, having a sort of self-deceiving sincerity which concealed the most selfish and interested motives. At any rate, this perfect public man—who, as White remarks, "hid his cigar from the camera lest the picture should corrupt youth!"—lent himself beautifully to the necessities of a complex, democratic political system (more so than cleverer men, such as Sherman and Reed), and was perfectly suited to the designs of the Hanna "syndicate" which ransomed him from the bankruptcy court in 1893.[19]

The McKinley "boom" was organized by Hanna, early in 1895, to display the "spontaneous" or "irresistible" will of the people to have Governor McKinley as their President. The planned "boom" of course implies a cynical denial of spontaneity or democratic procedure and choice, while paying its respects to the outward forms of democracy. Mr. Hanna believed as unblushingly in advertising as his brilliant predecessor, Mr. Barnum, master of the Greatest Show on Earth. "Just as the Circus King used to placard the fences and barns of the Atlantic States with marvelous posters bearing the announcement, 'Wait for Barnum,' so Mark Hanna sprinkled through the press of the country seductive references to the Major." [20] For long months before the nominating convention of 1896, the billboards were hung with posters heralding the coming of "McKinley: The Advance Agent of Prosperity," until hardened political "workers," and especially Southern delegates, were filled with enthusiasm when they arrived at St. Louis. The "hippodroming" of Governor Mc-Kinley was also managed, at Mr. Hanna's expense, through the use of a private car which helped display the Governor upon all possible political occasions, up and down the country, from Maine to Minnesota.[21]

1894 was a year which promised Republican restoration. Toward the end of this year Mark Hanna had come to the remarkable decision to withdraw from active direction of the house of M. A. Hanna & Co., to which he had given nearly thirty years of his life, and devote all his time to advancing the presidential aspirations of his friend the Governor. His business interests were turned over now to the care of his brother, Leonard Hanna, and some eighteen months

before the national convention of 1896 he set in motion the steam
roller which he had long been devising in his mind.

These were parlous times, when men in high places spoke of a
coming revolution, or of a drift to state socialism which was no less
ominous.[22] The voices of young spokesmen of discontent rolled across
the country from the western rim of the Mississippi Valley and from
the deep South, "told the money-owners of the East that they were
driving the producing South and West into solid union against
them."[23] The conversation of men of substance gathered in the
Union League Club of Cleveland, as well as in that of New York,
was often studded with nervous questions as to the objects of "revolutionaries" such as Altgeld and Tillman. On one such occasion at
which Hanna was present, these ever present fears were broached
and Samuel Mather, the Cleveland steel master, remarked hopefully
that "all the country needed was some protection for its industries
and solid money." Whereupon Mark Hanna took his cigar out of
his mouth and grunted: "Sam's right. There won't be any revolution.
You're just a lot of damn fools."[24]

There was the man, with all his confidence, his arrogance, which
made his herd follow him. "He did not confer, he gave orders.
He neither understood nor brooked opposition."[25] As it had suited
the private ends of himself and his associates to capture the Cleveland City Council, so it behooved them now in these trying times to
control the national Administration. The course which Mr. Hanna
was pursuing to many adversaries and reformers smelt freely of corruption. But his corruption was rational. It flowed from the very
nature of our society and its laws, Hanna himself intimated on divers
occasions. His actions embodied boldly, and with considerable native
"smartness," the practical rationalizations of the business class, the
new industrial barons; and because of his outspokenness and his characteristic scorn for bookish men and tender consciences, because of his
very want of hypocrisy—for which we tend now to accord him some
respect—he became the target, the most visible object of hatred
among his fellows.

"*There won't be any revolution.*" The Populists and "anarchists"
must be crushed. The Republican Party must win, the Gold Demo-

crats having lost control of their following. It must win with a Western candidate, his candidate, McKinley of Ohio. There would follow increased Protection, rising prices, Sound Money, and prosperity. But unlike the other industrial barons, who were not always public-spirited or even "class-conscious" enough, Hanna was willing not only to contribute a large part of his own fortune toward the desired end, but to see the affair through by his own hard work.

At the beginning of 1895, Mark Hanna set aside a very large sum of money, usually estimated at more than $100,000, and engaged a winter home at Thomasville, Georgia, ostensibly to escape the rigors of the Northern winter. Here he kept open house; Governor McKinley soon joined him, and made excellent company, while groups of white and colored gentlemen came every day to sit on the porch, partake of the Hanna cigars, and pay their respects to the Ohio statesman.

McKinley usually made friendly and tactful little talks. Then while McKinley looked the other way Mark Hanna made his deals with these gentlemen, which he spoke of as "combinations," and effected his briberies, which he defined to his friend as "arrangements." For these were the local Southern politicians, who, while never hoping or dreaming of Republican victory in their States, exploited to the full the representation for their "pocket boroughs" at the national party assembly. They were the "dummy delegates" who every four years delivered or pledged their votes in advance in return sometimes for money, sometimes for Federal patronage, sometimes for both.

Hanna had marked well the frenzied bidding and counterbidding for Negro delegates at the convention of 1888. He saw to it now that the work should be "so well done, that . . . able and unscrupulous" opponents could not undo any of it.[26] All preliminary arrangements for the separate State conventions in the South, at which delegates were to be instructed, were "fixed" in advance. Hanna saw to it that the State chairmen and secretaries of State committees and their associated wirepullers were all "the right kind of men," certifying the election of delegates pledged to McKinley.

All this entailed the most painstaking detail work. For weary months two lieutenants of Governor McKinley, together with Hanna's agents, were "on the road" throughout the South, attending pre-liminary conferences and being present on the ground even at the various local conventions to see that the program was carried out as stipulated.[27] A solid bloc of nearly 200 Southern delegates was thus added quietly to the Northern strength of the candidate a year in advance. The agents of rival candidates, such as Reed and Allison, when they began to make their preliminary inquiries found that they were too late; at the local conventions they could not reach the floor; chairmen would be unaware of their existence and continue running their meetings even when a quorum was lacking.

Should the anti-McKinley groups, however, bolt or, holding their own conventions, name their own delegates, as happened in several States, then it remained, at the outset of the presidential convention, for the Credentials Committee of the Republican National Com-mittee to pass upon their "regularity" or the justice of their com-plaints. But here Hanna, by a master stroke which involved super-human organizational labors, again was beforehand.

For a year he had been seeing, or sending his agents to, the Republican National Committeemen throughout the country. These men, either prominent capitalists or active politicians who represented their States in the party's hierarchy, had a judiciary power over the matter of delegates' credentials. Thirty-five out of fifty of the com-mitteemen, according to an experienced political journalist, Dunn, had been enveloped, persuaded, convinced—by promises of "recogni-tion" or by something that talked wonderfully—that they must "stand firm for the right," that is, find in the end all but the Mc-Kinley delegates from the South irregular.[28] These tactics had been used before, in a measure; but Hanna combined, perfected them. He invented the steam roller, which ran over the opposition and passed on. The Easy Boss, Tom Platt of New York, commented afterward with admiration:

Hanna . . . had the South practically solid before some of us awak-ened. Then he picked off enough Western and Pacific Slope States, before the convention met, to render him and McKinley invincible.[29]

The Eastern admirers of that able and clever Goldbug, Reed of Maine, found themselves hopelessly outdistanced many months before the convention opened. The dominant State bosses, Platt and Quay, who usually grouped numerous satellite State Organizations with their own, and brought forth Favorite Sons (if only for bargaining advantages), understood at once that they were beaten. There is a legend that these two gentlemen offered peace and laid their terms for cabinet and department posts before Mr. Hanna in the autumn of 1895. With their partnership, Hanna could well afford to coast to the finish line, and so he brought their propositions to his man, McKinley.

The Governor, at this juncture, is reported by his official biographer to have said: "Mark, there are some things that come too high. If I were to accept the nomination on those terms it would be worth nothing to me, and less to the people." [30] Mark Hanna was impressed.

No bargains were struck, because no bargains were needed. When Tom Platt, Quay, Clarkson, and the manager for Reed were reported on January 7, 1896, to be combining their forces in a "Stop McKinley" movement, it was understood by Mr. Hanna, who was a sharp trader himself, to be but a bold bluff. Unseen by the public, and holding already a clear majority of the convention in his hands, the proprietor of Cleveland's opera house could afford to pause in his unremitting labor and chuckle at the dramatic picture which the Eastern leaders made for him. Governor McKinley, with his pronounced moral and geographical advantage, "the overwhelming popular choice" of the people, was opposed only by the bosses and the Goldbugs of the East. Mr. McKinley and Mr. Hanna continued on their way, refusing to commit themselves on the question of silver or gold standard, which underlay the maneuvers and demands of the party's Eastern wing.[31]

During the raging controversy over gold and silver in the winter and spring of 1896, urgent queries came to Hanna and McKinley for the truth as to their future monetary policies. The anxiety of the capitalists in the East was given point when they recalled that as a member of Congress McKinley had repeatedly voted for augmented silver coinage between 1878 and 1891; and once even for a Free Silver bill. Yet only silence came from the voluble Ohio orator. "Why should he speak?" said H. H. Kohlsaat, a member of Hanna's group. "He has 600 delegates, and will be nominated before the end of the first ballot." [32] The question was, of course, not one of principle but purely one of tactics or timing.

But John Hay, at any rate, spread some light on the McKinley-Hanna financial policies when during a visit to England in May, 1896, he gave a public interview to the London press predicting confidently the nomination and election of McKinley, and asserting further that McKinley was not a Silverite, but would defend the gold standard.[33] Here were certainties which, at the moment, owing to Mr. Hanna's superior cunning, but few of the American voters or even of the leading Republican statesmen possessed.

Mark Hanna's steam roller rolled forward, giving an air of "irresistibility" to the McKinley campaign. The slipshod politicians, who worked usually with brass bands, claques, and tom-toms "to swarm their bees, were astounded to see a campaigner use the exact, business-like methods of a general manager of a railroad." [34] In February, 1896, the convention of Indiana, an important Middle Western State, was quickly overpowered. As to the methods used here, concerning which historians give but the barest inkling, they were held to be shockingly ruthless even by local professionals.*

Early in April important Western State conventions were conquered by Hanna, Wisconsin and Nebraska being added to Ohio (where Foraker had meekly surrendered) and the Southern "rotten boroughs." Then, with a deliberate display of audacity, Hanna suddenly raided the New England bailiwick of Reed and Henry Cabot Lodge, and had Vermont's delegates instructed for Governor McKinley. A ring of high Protectionists, including Senator Redfield Proctor (head of the Vermont Marble Works), Alger of Michigan, and Fairbanks of Indiana, aided powerfully in the cause.

The fight was all but won when the Reed combination appeared

---

* In the private papers of the late Senator Albert Beveridge of Indiana, one finds a friendly letter from L. T. Michener, a veteran Organization lieutenant, warning the rising young stump orator to shun Mr. Hanna's nominating convention: "There is likely to be a very nasty mess, and I don't want you connected with it," he writes, "especially as the supporter of a man whose nomination will be succeeded by scandal after scandal." Then, alluding to the outright purchase of delegates and rank-and-file politicians, he closes: "My dear boy, I want you to realize that our party never yet has sold a nomination, either wholly or partially." (Bowers, *Beveridge and the Progressive Era*, p. 59.)

unable to hold the full support of its own part of the country. But desiring a spectacular success in an important State, Hanna entered McKinley's name for the contest in Illinois, where a strong local machine determinedly supported the Favorite Son, Senator Shelby Cullom. To raise up an opposing organization, Hanna enlisted the services of the young Charles G. Dawes of Chicago, son of a former Congressman and a friend of McKinley's. Dawes, under Hanna's tutelage, soon proved himself a brilliant lieutenant, and after a sharp fight, the outcome of which was in doubt during several days and nights, won over the Illinois delegation.[35] Mark Hanna, who at the final stage had clung to the telephone in his Cleveland headquarters from noon to night, could now sleep with the assurance that his project of eight years was successfully accomplished.

Mr. Thomas Platt still carried on a pretended opposition to McKinley, probably for tactical reasons. As late as May 11, 1896, he said in a private circular to his lieutenants, that Governor McKinley was

not a well balanced man as Governor Morton is. . . . He is not a trained and educated public man as Senator Allison is. He is not an astute political leader as Senator Quay is. He is simply a clever gentleman, much too amiable and impressionable to be safely intrusted with great executive office; whose desire for honour happens to have the accidental advantage of the association of his name with the last Republican protective tariff . . . on the money question nobody can look at McKinley's record and read the flabby things he has said without perceiving that he has no fixed opinions, but has been turned and twisted by changing public opinion.[36]

III

Nevertheless, the leaders, soldiers, sutlers, and camp followers of the Republican army, as always before, gathered together at St. Louis in mid-June for a national party assembly—at which the voice of the people was to be heard. Music and banners provided once more their strong notes of sound and color. The professional politicians buzzed about in the lobbies of hotels and drank in the bars to the health of a Favorite Son or a secondary choice. There was literally nothing more for them to do. The nomination had really been settled since the autumn of 1895, when McKinley and Hanna had felt strong enough to refuse the "proposition" offered by the Eastern bosses. There remained, however, the question of the formal party resolutions touching the great, underlying economic issues which must be faced at this convention, matters which are generally beyond the mental capacity or concern of the common or garden variety of political "worker." With public opinion inflamed, with Silver Democrats and Silver Republicans alike issuing daily blasts at the international financiers and "Robber Barons," overwhelming interest centered in the "line" to be marked for the party platform that year.

The finance capitalists, the international bankers, the heads of huge insurance companies and their allies, as we have seen, were now swinging over en masse to support the party of the Outs at a time when their Democratic champion, Cleveland, and his faction approached the term of their usefulness. The deepest wish of this faction now was to bulwark the threatened gold standard. On the other hand, the typical industrial capitalists who invariably backed the Republican Party seemed obsessed once more with the idea of a new crusade for Protection and the higher price levels it would permit. Democratic bungling with the tariff schedules, it was felt, had failed to relieve the country or improve its Treasury finances; and to the industrial barons, whose spokesman was McKinley, the opportunity to reaffirm and extend the principles of Protection was a golden one. As for the matter of the currency, the manufacturers were less concerned on this score than the finance capitalists; in the last resort they could compile their augmented and protected profits in the terms of an inflated, as well as a contracted, a paper as well as a gold, currency, as they had done during the periods of war and Reconstruction. "I can live in a balloon as well as the other fellow," old Zach Chandler had said after the Civil War.

The strategy of the seasoned campaigner McKinley was to "straddle" the whole issue of bimetallism by advocating an ambiguous Sound Money program, while building everything upon the question of a protective tariff "for American workers," so many of whom were now in distress. In this matter Hanna appeared to yield to his friend's judgment for the time. Part of the support which came to the Major from some of the Far Western States—Wyoming, for instance, instructed its delegates for "Free Silver and McKinley"—seemed to justify such tactics of evasion or conciliation. The prudent "line" was, then, to hold the party together on the doctrine of Protection, which most Republicans agreed upon, while escaping dissension over the bitter question of bimetallism, which divided them. It was, in short, a Micawberlike position, biding one's time, saying as little as possible about the true issue, and trusting that "something would turn up" later to ease the unpleasant crisis. McKinley had stuck to it during a long conference of August, 1895, with Mark Hanna and Russell Alger of Michigan, in which they had urged in vain commitment to the gold standard.[37]

That such typical tactics of compromise, used in 1888 and 1892 by the G.O.P., must suddenly be thrown aside this year is evidence of the "higher" stage of developing capitalism in the United States in 1896. Finance capitalism—the direction of gigantic, combined banks; the combination·of smaller units of industry into Trusts, recapitalized under "absentee ownership" and managed by investment bankers who floated their securities—this was the new order dominating our industrial society. The great investment bankers and promoters such as J. P. Morgan or the Standard Oil group (after 1893) were ready for the more centralized scheme of control over industry which is identified with finance capitalism, and which was closely linked with international banking powers. At this stage the inconveniences of a fluctuating currency in which values and exchange must be measured offered serious barriers to financial expansion. For the huge investment operations foreseen at home and abroad, and especially with a view to overcoming the fears of allied bankers in Europe and winning the further use of their capital, the American money basis must be made not only "as good as gold," it must *be* gold. The financiers of the East were now up in arms. They were in fact "class-conscious," and determined to accept the challenge of a fierce class struggle. They made it plain that they would not loosen their purse strings unless the Republican Party became, once and for all, the avowed champion of the gold standard. From the autumn of 1895 to the spring of 1896 their confidential agents swarmed about the camp of Hanna and McKinley. One such agent, the lawyer William C. Beer, for years "political observer" for the great New York Life Insurance Company and for other allies of the House of Morgan's financial hierarchy, has given us in his private papers—consisting of patient, detailed reports to his employers—a clear glimpse of the persistent, secret pressure exerted upon Mr. Hanna and his candidate.[38]

In his conversations with Mr. Beer, Hanna's diffidence in facing such a Burning Issue seems pronounced, and with good reason. He had made a tremendous investment, so to speak, in large-scale party and electoral machinery for the control of millions of votes, and was reluctant to risk this over the matter of a few words which might serve as a wanton provocation. We see Hanna for the moment even playing at being a Western bimetallist. He ends, however, by advising the enthusiastic insurance corporation lawyer Mr. Beer to go forth and work among the brethren, so that hardened Silverite politicians such as Teller of Colorado and Pettigrew of North Dakota might be brought to see the light. To this end he promises Beer also liberal expense money.[39]

Hanna, like McKinley, by his plentiful field reports was more fully informed of the threatened split in the Republican Party than was the aggrieved Mr. Morgan, and was resolved at least to postpone this disaster as long as possible. The less time Mr. Teller was given for his work of destruction, the better. Actually a tentative draft of the Republican currency plank had been prepared by the friends of McKinley some ten days before the opening of the party festival at St. Louis, and privately approved by McKinley.[40] Here there was clear mention of maintaining the "existing standard," which meant the same thing as using the phrase "gold standard," but the ambiguity still permitted holding the Western Silver Republicans in the McKinley column. Such was the position which Hanna steadfastly took during conferences in high Republican circles; while H. H. Kohlsaat, the Chicago publisher, and others as stubbornly demanded the insertion of the word "gold." "I am just as strong a gold-man as you are," Hanna exclaimed to Kohlsaat.[41]

Behind the scenes the bitter struggle over the question of language or wording continued as the sole problem before the Republican leadership. Feeling ran high; the pressure from Eastern financial powers was unremitting. At this very moment, we must recall, Mr. J. Pierpont Morgan, who was a very unforgiving man, was preparing to appear before a committee of the Senate in Washington and testify as to his presumed "conspiracy" in government gold loans. Whitelaw Reid early in June had paid a quiet visit to Canton, communicated New York opinion to the Governor, and brought back with him a copy of the memorandum upon a currency resolution already approved by McKinley. This Reid showed to certain moneyed Republicans of the metropolis, and above all to Mr. Morgan, who discussed with him the all-engrossing questions of inserting into the resolution the word "gold." Mr. Morgan then wrote a draft of a proposed currency plank himself in which he, most meaningfully, changed the phrase "existing standard" to "existing *gold* standard." This draft Whitelaw Reid instantly forwarded on June 13, 1896, to McKinley, at Canton, Ohio, with the following explanation:

The anxiety here, on the whole subject of the money plank to be adopted next week, can hardly be exaggerated. There seems to be no doubt that the most conservative bankers are extremely apprehensive that any hesitation on our part to take the squarest sound money ground would bring a great and probably sudden depression in values. On the other hand, there is no doubt that the enclosed plank—which practically says nothing we were not fully agreed upon at Canton—will be followed by an appreciation in values.[42]

With the "enclosed plank," which came almost directly from the famous corner of Wall Street, the letter carried quite plainly an ultimatum to the wavering politician. Put in the word "gold," it was implied by signs from the highest financial circles in the country, and a boom will follow; leave it out, dare to "straddle" the issue this time, and there will be a depression, perhaps panic.

In view of the existing state of opinion, the word "gold" would be a flaming provocation to millions of voters. Yet with stubbornness, even vindictiveness—which reflect a well-known side of Mr. Morgan's character—this was demanded at all costs, as a matter of principle, perhaps one of vindication as of necessity. With the passing of Mr. Cleveland, the great defender of gold, a determination no less firm must be shown by the imminent Republican Administration.

Such was the unanimous message brought by numerous confidential agents, political bosses, statesmen, hurriedly converging upon St. Louis from the Eastern money centers, and from Cleveland and

Chicago, before the opening day: a currency plank embodying the defense of the gold standard in words which could never be unsaid, which pledged that literally and explicitly, must be proclaimed this year.

Fresh from State Street, Boston, came Senator Henry Cabot Lodge, the "scholar in politics," and now a Massachusetts boss in his own right. The man of letters handed the burly, perspiring Hanna his memorandum for a gold plank, saying, according to one account, in the tones of a dangerous jingo "activist" such as he and Theodore Roosevelt now delighted to use: "You'll put this in the platform or we'll rip you up the back!" [43] Hanna asked:

"Who in hell are you?"

"Senator Henry Cabot Lodge, of Massachusetts."

"Well, Senator Henry Cabot Lodge, of Massachusetts, you can go plumb to hell. You have nothing to say about it." [44]

Foraker, now the lawyer for Mr. Morgan's Southern Railway, arrived from Cincinnati, Aldrich came from Providence, Thomas Platt, the Easy Boss of New York, hurried in, all with the same urgent message: all threatening to fight the Ohio candidate to the last ditch if they were not heeded.

To make sure of what the Republican resolutions would say, the American Bankers' Association had raised a special fund of $85,000, which an officer of the National Union Bank of New York, Oscar E. Leach, "took to St. Louis . . . and gave to Thomas C. Platt . . . to use in preparing a sound money platform." Mr. Platt thereupon "gathered many black and some white delegates to his bosom," and their voices were added to the Sound Money chorus.[45]

Behind the scenes, in the Resolutions Committee before the opening day, the simulated controversy prolonged itself, centering upon the use of words and the phrasing of the currency plank. This time the paymasters of the party would take no chances with their politicians, but would pin them down. The actual words used were dictated by the strongest finance capitalists in the country, yet most of the politicians and capitalists present in St. Louis did not even know how to spell correctly! But out of this secret war of words came, as Lodge rightly and triumphantly assumed, a historic change of ground for the party of Lincoln, Seward, and Sumner.

Because of the tremendous consequences which followed the decision, several of the participants and advisers—Tom Platt, Lodge, Foraker, Kohlsaat and McClure, the newspaper publishers—claimed the glory of having written the finally adopted plank. Each insisted that he alone had forced it down the throats of the "careful cowards" Hanna and McKinley, thus precipitating the calamitous and revolutionary struggle of the 1896 political campaign. Tom Platt said, "It was in 1896 that I scored . . . the greatest achievement of my political career. That was the insertion of the gold plank in the St. Louis platform." [46] In truth many hands collaborated toward the same predestined end. At this juncture of history, the logic of events was overwhelming for the party of capitalism. Hanna had foreseen this, and with his consummate shrewdness had played a waiting game while the convention forces gathered and tested their strength. At the last moment he unmasked himself. Thus his candidate, known as a bimetallist, had the air of being overborne on the money issue instead of hastening in advance to do the bidding of the great Eastern capitalists and their political bosses.

On Friday night, June 13, the council of political bosses, capitalists, and financial advisers, with the aid of Melville E. Stone, head of the Associated Press—who knew how to spell the word "inviolably"— made the fateful decision; the final plank as adopted by the convention was written out, and McKinley's acceptance gained by telegraph. The leader of the would-be "straddlers," Hanna, had his hand forced, exactly as he had wished, and no sooner than he had wished. "The whole thing was managed in order to succeed in *getting what we got*," he wrote to A. K. McClure afterward.[47] All through Saturday and Sunday, June 14 and 15, two days after everything had been finished, the Eastern grandees had continued to force his hand, while he played the ignorant fool. "Herrick and he had it all arranged when they came to St. Louis. . . . Mr. Hanna was right to let it seem that the eastern end of the party forced his hand in declaring for the gold standard," wrote one who had watched events from close by.[48] The Eastern Sound Money press, on June 16, promptly announced a "victory" over the "shifty" bimetallists from Ohio, and the ringing words of the Republican money plank, voted by a large majority of the convention in the teeth of the Western Silverites, said unequivocally:

The Republican Party is unreservedly for sound money. . . . We are unalterably opposed to every measure calculated to debase our currency or impair the credit of the country. We are, therefore, opposed to the free coinage of silver, except by international agreement with the leading commercial nations of the world, which we pledge ourselves to promote, and until such agreement can be obtained the existing gold standard must be preserved. All our silver and paper currency must be maintained at parity with gold, and we favor all measures designed to maintain inviolably the obligations of the United States and all our money, whether coin or paper, at the present standard, the standard of the most enlightened nations of the earth.[49]

The nomination of McKinley on the first ballot by a vote of 661½ was followed with routine enthusiasm, but absolutely without surprise. It was the adoption of the so-called gold plank that precipitated the only dramatic exhibitions in this completely machine-made convention.

Senator Teller of Chicago, leader of the Silver Republicans, who had stormily and vainly opposed the money plank in the Resolutions Committee, mounted the rostrum on June 19 and in a moving address announced that 34 delegates, representing Montana, Utah, Colorado, Idaho, and South Dakota, were bolting the convention and leaving their party. This too was a historic development: one of the founding fathers of the Republican Party was leading the whole bloc west of the Mississippi out of the camp. As the oratory of Teller's swan song rose to its epopee, the expression of Hanna, who sat perspiring in the front row, changed "to a vicious iron glare." Then in a tumultuous scene following the "parting-of-the-ways" speech, the majority rose, howled and shouted at the small silver minority: "Go! Go! . . . Go to Chicago! Take the Democratic train!" Hanna's voice was heard above the uproar shouting, "Good-by! Good-by!" Then, when the platform was voted in, jubilation seized the throng, the future seemed assured and golden, ten thousand throats sounded the notes of "America," while Hanna was seen with his head back, singing away, his face beaming with joy.[50]

In the press stand at this hour sat former Congressman William J. Bryan of Nebraska, as correspondent for the Omaha *World-Herald*, of which he was editor. Besides attending to his journalistic duties all during the week he had also been conferring earnestly with the Silverites in the Republican camp, urging them to bolt if the gold plank passed. Well informed as he was, he knew that the "silver crowd" meant to combine a Republican wing with the Democratic and Populist parties. "I had foreseen this outcome," he says in his memoirs. "The convention turned out as I expected, and the looked-for bolt took place. I felt sure that the action of this convention would have a large influence at Chicago." [51] When Teller's bolt took place, Bryan seemed beside himself with suppressed excitement, according to a journalist who sat working nearby, and climbing over the tops of the desks, moved to the front of the stand the better to see. Like Hanna, though for different reasons, he too seemed happy. "There was a gleam of joy in Bryan's eye and the least smile of satisfaction flitted across his face." [52]

CHAPTER NINETEEN

THE BRYAN CAMPAIGN

Free Silver is the cow-bird of the reform movement.
HENRY D. LLOYD

NEWS of the sweeping "gold victory" at the St. Louis convention at once electrified and united all the diverse, scattered factions throughout the country which had been taking the popular side in recent controversies; those who had differed in their preferred reforms, those who had favored the popular silver idea in varying degree, now found it possible to combine quickly upon the one issue. The Republican decision was Democracy's opportunity, as the *World* said, June 20, 1896. Would they be bold enough?

Altgeld, who had never been a fanatic of monetary inflation, had spoken out as one of the first leaders to commit the regular Western Democratic Organizations to the cause of "the toiling and producing masses." In Nebraska the Free Silver forces won complete control of their State convention and, in a turbulent outburst, voted down a resolution approving Cleveland's Administration.[1] The Populist leaders, Senator Allen of Nebraska, Weaver, and Taubeneck (chairman of the party), simultaneously aligned themselves beside the regular Western Democrats upon this one issue. "The honest yeomanry of the land," Taubeneck said, were ranged squarely "against the pampered owners of wealth." On behalf of Southern sentiment, now nearly unanimous for bimetallism, Senator Richard (Silver Dick) Bland, of Missouri, who had led the silver movement in the House and the Senate during twenty years, accepted the Republican challenge, declaring in an interview:

> The coming fight . . . is to be between the productive masses of the United States, and what might be called the fund-owning classes. The toilers of the East are just as deeply concerned as the toilers of the West and South.[2]

On the other hand, the Gold Democrats, led in close formation by Whitney and bearing their compromise resolution on international bimetallism, which was intended actually, as Bryan's Omaha *World-Herald* said, "to stem the tide of genuine bimetallism," offered their concerted opposition.[3] But against the danger from Whitney's men there arose the welcome, the rare, almost unprecedented example of the Silver Republican bolters, who under the lead of the old Stalwart Senator Teller of Colorado threw party loyalty to the winds and marched toward Chicago as volunteers for the silver movement.

Even before the date set for the Republican convention at Chicago, the Populist leaders had known positively that Mr. Teller and his Silverite friends would bolt. Taubeneck wrote confidentially to Ignatius Donnelly from St. Louis:

> The Democrats had a large and influential lobby here, moving heaven and earth to get the bolting Republicans to join the Democratic party and go to the Chicago Convention. Bryan was here the entire week. Bland also had a strong lobby on the ground.[4]

In New York, Mr. Pulitzer's *World* during the ensuing summer's fighting veered unaccountably, and threw its powerful voice to the side of Sound Money, charging a conspiracy of Silver Kings to control the Government and double the value of their metal. It was above all "a conspiracy against American labor," by a Silver Trust holding $616,000,000 of mining property.[5]

Mr. Teller, the conservative press quickly pointed out, owned some $2,000,000 in silver, lead, and copper-mining securities; the Bonanza Kings of the Pacific slope, John Mackay and Fair, and the gilded California youth William Hearst, heir of the gold-mining Senator, each possessed fortunes in mining properties reckoned at from $20,-000,000 to $40,000,000. Then Senators Jones and Stewart of Nevada were likewise rich mine operators, while the Montana Copper Barons, William A. Clark, J. Augustus Heinze, and Marcus Daly, were also not to be counted among the unwashed poor.

The fears and calculations of the *World* were vastly exaggerated, young Mr. Hearst's newspapers promptly answered. But the intrusion of the great mining interests certainly added to the complexity of the class-sectional movement for Free Silver in 1896. Nearly two years before, the picturesque Marcus Daly, owner of the fabulous Anaconda mines, had entered the fight for the "people's money" in earnest. Through the American Bimetallic League, which employed Bryan as a lecturer and which Daly largely subsidized, powerful, constant, though secret aid was given to the "embattled farmers" who struggled against Eastern "despotism" and "British tyranny." After his death, Daly's books revealed that he and his associates, Heinze and the Hearst Estate, expended no less than $289,000 in securing delegates pledged to Free Silver for the Democratic convention in 1896.[6] During the campaign he gave $50,000 more in one check, according to the statement of Senator J. K. Jones, the Democratic national chairman. Thus the mining operators seem to have acted as an irresponsible, or insurgent, capitalist group at odds, momentarily, with the dominant financial order; they seemed bent on adventures of their own which might lead to an overnight inflation of all commodity and metal values—in which their economic stake was indeed a huge one. The Western mining interests (which obviously hoped to unload their greatly enhanced mining shares upon the New York stock market) added their own special influence and gave an increased "sectional" twist to the class upheaval of 1896. The political champions of the Jacksonian farmers acquired a group of moneyed supporters in the Mining Barons in addition to the mass enthusiasm they already possessed.

The form that the conflict now takes is the traditional one in which the two great divergent interests of society, the classes attached to two different material conditions of existence, two different forms of property, have often fought for supremacy; that of the country against the town, landed property against capital. In the revolution of the Civil War, Northern capital allied with free farmers had fought the domination of the landed economy—more for its own liberation than for the liberation of slaves. Thenceforth out of this Second American revolution, from the emancipated factories of the capitalists and the colossal war debt owed their masters had come new, grievous burdens and inequalities, which the farmers and smallholders now stared at in the 1890's, once more as through a torn veil. The "embattled farmers," West and South, now entered into the fight against new inequalities which were expressed to them in the disparity between the unchanging level of their debts and fixed costs and the falling prices of their goods. They fought, as they declared, for the "cause of humanity" once more, but in reality they fought also for higher wheat, corn, and cotton prices. Here were the limits of their insurgence, and here the points of similarity in interest with the mysterious handful of bimetallist paymasters, who fought for humanity while they intrigued for higher silver, copper, and lead.

The egalitarian doctrines so strongly nourished on the frontier now broke rudely upon our formal, feigning party contests with unheard-of force. Yet, behind the characteristic ideas, habits of thought, and *Weltanschauungen* which F. J. Turner attributed to the frontier, we must mark also the economic circumstances which conditioned them. The trade movement of the country moved then (as still now in great degree) upon the East-West axis; the inner continental region of the West and South as well functioned still under the economy of a colonial relationship with the industrially advanced Northeastern seaboard and Great Lakes region. (Comparable, it has been remarked, to the relations between the backward raw-materials colonies of Africa and the Orient and imperial Britain.) [7] The "free" settlers of the frontier, the "bold peasantry" among whom Peffer, Weaver, Mary Lease, and Bryan were reared, were small independent landholders for the most part, cultivating as much land as their unaided strength could manage, and still resisting the completed, implacable wage system of the older Northeastern communities, the rulers of which moreover "exported" capital to the West, "seized" resources there, sold machinery and railroad, banking, or entrepreneurial services at their own terms. In these social and economic differences between the sections lay the root of the difference in ideology which Turner has described, but before which his analysis stops. The militant ideology of the frontier now gave its own "sectional" tone to the class struggles of the 1890's, to the Tidal Wave in which independent settlers, small proprietors and shopkeepers, organized laborers, and silver-mine or copper-mine owners together moved toward the Democratic Party.

The conflict of profoundly material interests gave, then, a "revolutionary" character to the war of ballots in 1896—especially as compared with preceding party combats over nuances in taxation, bureaucratic reform, or "personalities." Hence Henry George, writing from the Western battle front, asserted:

The Democratic Party . . . is not the Old Democracy that has existed so long. It is really a new party. . . . Win or lose, the old party lines have been broken.[8]

Yet we must not deceive ourselves as to the true character of the "revolution of the land" in the 1890's. As in the case of the capitalist revolution against "the South" in 1861, so now again we must penetrate behind the ideology and the verbiage of the political orators to the real interests at stake, noting well the limits marked for this uprising. As Marx warns us in his political reflections, in the struggles of history we must distinguish between "the superstructure of sentiments, illusions, habits of thought, generalities," and the facts of property interests and material conditions upon which this superstructure is built.

The British landed aristocracy too, as Marx reminds us, when faced with the Industrial Revolution, had insisted that they were fighting for eternal principles of truth, for ancient, constitutional rights and liberties—rather than land rent. While the liberal John Bright, leader of the Manchester industrialists, in turn demanded increased rights and liberties for the lower classes when, in fact, as the Tory philosopher Bagehot points out, he sought "properly enough" increased rights for his own class.

So in America in 1896 the spokesmen of the "Jacksonian farmers," feeling their people to have become exploited "colonists" of the interior, under the yoke of Eastern and foreign financiers, believed, as Bryan told them, that they were engaged in "a fight for the common people." In reality they were fighting for the power and "might" of the corn and wheat lands of the Mississippi Valley and the frontier. But some of their professional brethren, in the Democratic Party and even the Populist Party, while proclaiming the "new battle for freedom" on behalf of the producing masses, were knowingly fighting for the Anaconda mines, for the wealth of the Comstock Lode, for Bonanza Kings, for Daly, Clark, Heinze, Hearst, and others.

Many streams, swollen to torrential size and all flowing together at last, contributed to make the "great silver flood" in which Mr. Whitney and his hopeful little band of Gold Democrats found themselves engulfed promptly upon their arrival in Chicago. The old

Tilden-Cleveland hierarchy of the party managers had been completely outmaneuvered. Powerful interests were now at work to carry the masses of the Populist Party as well, with its estimated 2,000,000 voters, into fusion with the silver movement—over the protests of intelligent radicals, such as Lloyd, who mistrusted the "temporary monetary issue."

Under the tumultuous surface excitements, celebrations, parades, and *feux d'artifices* of the eve of the Chicago convention, the organized battalions of professionals carried on their planned and paid work, furnishing brass bands, pennants, or "spontaneous" blood-curdling demonstrations, as the occasion required. Even the most naïve of the silver ideologues who spoke there commented with surprise on the perfect unison and discipline with which the audience responded "like a trained choir" to his arguments.[9] This effect Bryan attributed, as he hints, to his own eloquence rather than to a large claque, carefully organized by the Bimetallic League and following a premeditated plan. Yet it is true also that natural and life forces may burst over the banks laid for them; history too sometimes surprises, and exceeds the schemes, the frames, set by wirepullers and their claqueurs at party conventions.

II

The "logic of events," the tactics for the electoral campaign, as envisaged since the autumn of 1895, had pointed to an unqualified demand for Free Silver and the breaking of the political alliance made between the capitalistic Eastern Republicans and the Western farmers in 1860. The silver movement after capturing the Democratic Party must take over a portion of the Republican Party as well. This was what Altgeld meant in the spring of 1895 when he remarked that half of the Republicans in his own State of Illinois were Free Silver men, and predicted that by taking a clear stand for silver the Democrats would win their greatest victory. This step, moreover, was made unavoidable after the adoption of an outright "gold plank" in June by Mr. Hanna's convention at St. Louis.

Many witnesses testify that from the opening of the Democratic convention (from which Bland, as a candidate, was absent) Altgeld became its dominating spirit, its "brain and will." He headed the

Illinois delegation, which was pledged to the Free Silver cause. In intelligence he towered above the others easily; none equaled him in firmness, courage, and practical political sagacity. The men of the press came to him more than to anyone else for information on the tide of the battle. Each candidate wooed Altgeld for support of his nomination; Jones of Arkansas, Tillman, Bryan, and the other Silverite leaders present all worked with him for the capture of the necessary two-thirds majority of the convention.

In Free Silver conferences and secret caucuses before the convention opened it was carefully arranged that when the contesting Nebraska delegations came up with their credentials, the Bryan delegation should be seated in place of the Gold Democrat delegation.[10] Then by the unseating of four of the Michigan delegation (through legalistic methods), and by augmentation of the number of delegates from the Territories, a two-thirds majority was to be assured. Altgeld was the prime mover in these preliminary maneuvers. Cajoled, threatened, or challenged by leaders of the different factions, the man whom President Cleveland had insulted, and the whole Eastern press had tried to crush with calumny, led the Democratic Party relentlessly to the adoption of the "new heresies" of silver money.

Teller, the Republican bolter, was seriously considered by Altgeld for the presidential nomination as a means of breaking old party lines. Naming the former Republican would have set "principle" above party, as in 1860; but he would not have been a popular choice among the rank-and-file politicians. Hence Bland was the predominant choice of the Western men. Yet it was a handicap that he was a "Southerner," represented Missouri, and that his wife was a Catholic. Senators Jones and Vest were old men. Governor Boies of Iowa was one of the stronger of several Favorite Sons, but he also came under the onus of having been a Republican up to recently. Among lesser Favorite Sons was Bryan, too young at thirty-six, with only Nebraska and several Indian Territory delegates as his following, though the politicians as well as the silver-mine owners behind the scenes felt well disposed toward him because of his speaking power and his faithful services to the American Bimetallic League. There is reason to believe that Altgeld at first favored him for the Vice-Presidency as a running mate to Bland.[11]

In the contest for the post of temporary chairman to preside over the convention, Bryan, eager for this office, was passed over as a matter of seniority. He was rewarded, however, by being named to speak in the debate over the platform; then, by a last-minute shift of the program, he was selected for the strategic last place, closing the whole debate on the silver resolution. All these positions were carried over the desperate opposition of Whitney and David Hill. As the convention opened preliminary arrangements were carried out as expected, with the vital steering committees and subcommittees in the hands of the "radicals." Whitney and his friends were in despair. They could make at best only a demonstration to "save the esprit de corps," that is, hold together the party's Eastern wing for future emergency action. At the convention the once invincible Whitney seemed to abandon the fight completely.

William Bryan of Nebraska, the poor country-town lawyer, had for eight years been carving out a career in politics after an old American pattern. The mind of this born elocutionist, in the view of William Allen White, who knew him, may well have been stuffed with the spirit of old steel engravings such as covered the walls of his library in Lincoln, Nebraska—engravings of Jefferson, Jackson, Lincoln, Webster, and above all, of Henry Clay, "towering almost ten feet high in foreground, badly out of perspective, pleading with the lilliputian senators—all in stocks and tail coats . . . all dignified and serious, wrapped in improving meditation. . . . Bryan all his life seemed to draw from this picture his fine Fourth Reader views . . . of life." [12] It may have been true likewise, as others felt, that Bryan was: "Not really able nor even clear headed, lacking capacity as a thinker"; that his abstinence from drink and tobacco, his religious piety and ill-concealed evangelism, made him a little "the humbug" to hardened professional colleagues, upon whom he too must depend in the last resort. [13]

Yet Bryan's very "simplicity" led him to embrace historic opportunities which the wise old men of the East could not, or would rather not, see. In his campaigns, in his lecture tours on behalf of the American Bimetallic League, he saw with his own eyes the force stirring at the "grass roots" of the republic. Then his evangelism, his single-minded fanaticism, like Cromwell's, was suited to the revolutionary times, and lent point and astonishing force to his speech.

On the other hand, by his own convictions Bryan was far from being the "dangerous revolutionary" whom his frightened adversaries pictured. The limits of his protest (like the limitations of his thought) were well defined, and became more evident later as his career extended itself prosaically, after the glamour, the excitation, the intoxicated rhetoric of his great hours in 1896 had passed. He mourned at the bier of the pure-hearted Lyman Trumbull, but differed strongly with the old war Republican's later socialistic views. He flirted successfully with the Populists in Nebraska and won their co-operation in his creditable, though unsuccessful, fight for the United States Senatorship in 1894. Ignatius Donnelly of Minnesota said of him: "We put him to school, and he wound up by stealing the schoolbooks." [14] He worked with the Populists, they believed him one of them; yet he was not of them.

The Populists, the radical wing of the farmers of the Middle Border, were bent on reversing the old Jacksonian and libertarian doctrines, which had sought free land, freedom from governmental or authoritarian restrictions, and now sought rather increased national government support to guarantee their old liberties. They clamored for a "paternalistic" Federal ownership of monopolies in railroads and grain elevators, for the extension of government Treasury facilities in farm credits and warehousing. Monetary inflation was but incidental, a means to an end of sweeping and rational reform. Here Bryan did not follow where they led. On these radical demands he was vague or silent.

It was the singular role of this "evangelist and crusader, with a great musical, vibrant voice, fashioned for political purposes," to check the impetus of the Farmers' Alliance (Populist) movement, divert its logical drive for genuine land reform, and shift the objective of the land uprising to the monetary issue solely. Glozing over the laborious reforms demanded by the agrarian radicals, this young Christian Statesman led his followers to the social impasse of monetary inflation, from which he promised them untold benefit—above all, a longed-for redistribution of wealth—would certainly flow.

Bryan, finally, saw no harm in carrying on an opportunistic collaboration with the Silver and Copper Barons, feeling sincerely that attainment of their objectives would aid his own people too. Such a compromise was perfectly typical of the Puritan temperament. The aggressive mining interests that worked behind the scenes, according to some observers, seriously considered Bryan as the most likely figure for the plan of a "stampede," whose outcome none as yet could foretell. For Bryan, though less known than the older politicians, attracted the Populists, and might provide the best bridge leading to fusion with their important voting strength. "Bryan is a Populist in all but the name," one of the agrarian leaders wrote to Weaver, in the early spring of 1896.[15] He proposed that Bryan should head the Populist and Democratic tickets both.

While without modesty about his ambitions, there was something meek and patient as well as practical in the way in which Bryan advanced his cause. His humility avoided enmities. Numerous politicians and delegates recalled afterward that Bryan spoke to them seriously in asking their support at the 1896 convention; although, as Champ Clark afterward said, he seemed to be the only one who believed in his chances. But hopefully he persisted, like other Favorite Sons, in reaching as many people as he could, holding himself the most available "regular" Democrat from a "doubtful" Northern State, and destined to be chosen by elimination. Bryan and his wife wrote thousands of letters to leaders and members of State Organizations concerning platform resolutions, pledges, and the support of his own incredible candidacy. "I perhaps was personally acquainted with more delegates than any other man who was mentioned as a candidate," Bryan observed.[16]

Carefully the young man wheeled himself into position to be struck by presidential lightning. He was delighted when he contrived to appear in the momentous debate over the silver plank, serving as one of the "keynoters" of the Western silver uprising within the party. It was a further stroke of luck that he was the last speaker for the silver faction, and was given additional time in return for augmented speaking time asked by the opposing Gold Democrats—Hill, Vilas, and Russell. Bryan's speech was long prepared, woven from old strands of ideas and phrases used in lectures throughout the South and the Mississippi Valley.

As he waited for his hour, a friend, Clark Howell, editor of the Atlanta *Constitution*, sent him a note scribbled on an envelope: "This is a great opportunity." Bryan, according to his own recollections, wrote in reply: "You will not be disappointed," and sent the envelope back.

III

Though the external behavior of the "revolutionary mob" which overran the Chicago convention may have been enough to frighten the Eastern Democrats, inwardly the convention's action reflected order and a firm command. Altgeld, its directing spirit, though a semi-invalid, sat quietly in his place among the delegates, always holding himself impassive, as under an iron control.

On Tuesday, July 7, the recommendation of the party's national committee—which traditionally was followed—that Senator David B. Hill act as "temporary chairman," that is, preside over the proceedings of the nominating convention, was voted down uproariously by a majority of 556 to 349, John W. Daniel, of Virginia, an ardent bimetallist, receiving the office. It was the opening blow and a finishing stroke: "the sceptre of political power passed from the strong, certain hands of the East to the feverish, headstrong mob of the West and South." [17] The too crafty Hill was like a man who was out of his element.

On the following day the credentials of the Nebraska prosilver delegates, Bryan at their head, were passed upon, and with the Territorial delegates a two-thirds majority was achieved for Free Silver, and the obstructive power of the minority eliminated.

While the convention, waiting for further business, gave itself over to celebrating the overthrow of the Goldbugs, Altgeld was called by tremendous, sustained ovations to make an impromptu speech. In a brief, vigorous statement, he set the keynote: "no compromise" in the party resolutions. "With his sharply chiselled French Revolution face, his high, ringing voice, his bitter vehemence of manner, and his facility for epithet," as a hostile journalist described him, Altgeld figured largely in the horrific myth of a bogeyman which gripped all the conservative classes. He was pictured as the most dangerous influence in the convention [having] the stamp of the agitator who, when the bludgeon had failed of its full work, would be ready with the poisoned knife, and who, in leading a victory-drunken mob, would not hesitate to follow pillage with the torch.[18]

Yet the vast majority of the audience applauded to the echo their hero who might have had the nomination if he had been eligible. It was the music of consoling vindication for Altgeld.

Thursday, July 9, which began with the reading of the platform by Senator J. K. Jones on behalf of the Resolutions Committee, saw the climax of the convention. By its platform the new Democratic Party which was being born took the unprecedented step of disavowing the ruling national Administration of its own President. Mr. Cleveland was denounced in so many plain words for making private contracts for bond sales to the Morgan banking syndicate and increasing the national debt in time of peace; he was condemned for his highhanded use of the court injunction and Federal troops; more, the august "House of Lords," our Supreme Court, for its recent decisions was also visited with the party's disapproval. Then the silver plank was read before listeners, tense, bitter or jubilant:

We are unalterably opposed to monometallism, which has locked fast the prosperity of an industrial people in the paralysis of hard times. . . . We demand the free and unlimited coinage of both silver and gold at the present legal ratio of 16 to 1, without waiting for the aid or consent of any other nation.

There was to be no compromise. Pitchfork Ben Tillman, as arranged, began the debate upon the platform resolutions with a fierce castigation of the President, in a style which recalled plainly the secessionist days of 1860. The men of the South, he cried, were up in arms against their exploiters:

We of the South have burned our bridges behind us so far as the Eastern Democrats are concerned. . . . We denounce the Administration of President Cleveland as undemocratic and tyrannical. . . . A plutocratic despotism is sought to be established.

In answer, Hill of New York rose to the defense of this old rival, Cleveland, and spoke also for the minority opposing Free Silver coinage. With his usual smacking emphasis upon the word "Democrat" he began:

I am a Democrat, but I am not a revolutionist. My mission here to-day is to unite, not to divide—to build up, not to destroy. . . . My friends, I speak more in sorrow than in anger. You know what this platform means to the East. . . . We want the principles of Jefferson and Jackson. We want no greenback currency. . . . We want no paper currency.[19]

Hill, the most conciliatory speaker for the Gold Democracy, was little heard by the tempestuous men of the Chicago convention. Even less Senator Vilas, of Wisconsin, Cleveland's former Postmaster General, though he gave warning of a bloody debacle to come: "Perhaps somewhere in this country there lurks a Robespierre, a Danton, a Marat?" Nor did the delegates and the spectators, by turns turbulent, hostile, or bored, give heed to the sickly Governor Russell of Massachusetts, who, after pleading in a weak voice against repudiation, exclaimed finally that "our country, if not this convention, will listen to our protest."

Bryan of Nebraska now strode toward the platform "two steps at a time." He had the bearing of "a strong-limbed, strong-lunged" athlete as he stood for an instant facing "the wild crowd. . . . It had been known for hours that the convention might be stampeded for the Nebraskan. . . . Ear-splitting noises were heard; waves of scarlet fans danced in the galleries." [20] The whole convention, the moment, demanded impatiently a voice to express its purpose, its hope. Bryan had himself marvelously well in hand, as he relates, having been thoroughly prepared since the night before; in his mind was the epopee of the "cross of gold" which he had been saving for such an occasion, "recognizing its fitness for the conclusion of a climax." [21] Many of those who were present also attest to the "miracle" of the young speaker's mastery over the crowd, as we remember the enchantment of a great actor in our youth. With a gesture he silenced the long roar of applause that had greeted him; the clear, soaring voice began its work.

His opening words were as modest as they were courteous. He

was not so "presumptuous" as to measure himself against the more distinguished gentlemen who preceded him; but, he cried:

The humblest citizen in all the land, when clad in the armor of a righteous cause, is stronger than all the hosts of error. I come to speak to you in defense of a cause as holy as the cause of liberty—the cause of humanity.

He passed over the bitter personal issues raised by the reigning President. "The individual is but an atom; he is born, he acts, he dies; but principles are eternal; and this has been a contest over a principle." Thus Bryan, "with . . . the zeal which inspired the crusaders who followed Peter the Hermit," clothed the interests of the silver Democrats in the noblest ideology.

In the face of so much legend that the sense of Bryan's appeal was "socialistic," we must note the precise line of his reasoning, even at the emotional crest of his oratory. In its essence it reflects not a landless, toolless proletarian opposition, but the mentality and social relationships of the lower middle class, the numerous body of small-holders, artisans, country lawyers, and shopkeepers at crossroads to whom Bryan belonged and whom he would lead in a crusade against the *big* property-holders and *big* capitalists. Thus with a significant and deeply characteristic stroke of dialectics—paradoxical and falla-cious at once—he defined the businessman anew in a passage which he was proud of and inserted at the last moment as the only new ma-terial among his old silver arguments. The Eastern Democrats had accused the silver men of "disturbing business," and Bryan, turning to the gold delegates, said:

. . . we reply that you have disturbed our business interests by your course. We say to you that you have made the definition of a business man too limited in its application. The man who is employed for wages is as much a business man as his employer, the attorney in a country town is as much a business man as the corporation counsel in a great metropolis; the merchant at the cross-roads store is as much a business man as the merchant of New York; the farmer who goes forth in the morning and toils all day—who begins in the spring and toils all summer—and who by the application of brain and muscle to the natural resources of the country creates wealth, is as much a business man as the man who goes upon the board of trade and bets upon the price of grain; the miners who go down a thousand feet into the earth . . . and bring forth from their hiding places the precious metals to be poured into the channels of trade are as much business men as the few financial magnates who, in a back room, corner the money of the world. We come to speak for this broader class of business men.[22]

With a reasoning familiar to our own age also, Bryan drew a line of cleavage between the small or petit-bourgeois capitalist and the great finance capitalists of the world money centers. In such argument, as in such a "revolution," there is confusion and contradiction, just as there is latent discord, jealousy, and sectional hostility among the conglomeration which forms the party of the middle class, the landed interests and producing interests, fused by an hour of crisis and opportunity. Thus, unlike Bebel in Germany and Jaurès in France, rational economic doctrinaires who were at this time directing the Social Democratic movement of the working class in Europe, Bryan addressed himself to numerous divisions and groups in the body politic, offering something to each. For the producing and toiling masses he seems to attack the ruling financial class, and proposes a redistribution of wealth, saying:

There are those who believe that, if you will only legislate to make the well-to-do prosperous, their prosperity will leak through on those below. The Democratic idea, however, has been that if you legislate to make the masses prosperous, their prosperity will find its way up through every class which rests upon them.

But repeatedly he turns to his dominant theme, the defense and exaltation of the landed interest; he apotheosizes the frontiersman, the pioneer. Once more Jefferson's "chosen" people and Jackson's "embattled farmers" are fighting for cheaper money and relief from their debts. He extols

the hardy pioneers who have braved all the dangers of the wilderness, who have made the desert to blossom as the rose—the pioneers away out there (pointing to the West), who rear their children near to Nature's heart, where they can mingle their voices with the voices of the birds— out there where they have erected schoolhouses for the education of their young, churches where they praise their Creator, and cemeteries where rest the ashes of their dead—these people, we say, are as deserving of the consideration of our party as any people in the country. It is for these that we speak. . . . Our war is not a war of conquest; we are fighting in the defense of our homes, our families, and prosperity.

It is significant how he passes over in the most general terms concrete issues of tariff, of statism, of the regulation of monopolies, raised by the truly radical farm leaders, while harping on the theme of cheap money.

Did the great cities favor the gold standard? But the great cities themselves

rest upon our broad and fertile prairies. Burn down your cities and leave our farms, and your cities will spring up again as if by magic; but destroy our farms and the grass will grow in the streets of every city in the country.

As the measured words of the orator rolled over the great hall the tense crowd responded rhythmically with crashes of applause to the points brought home. At one climax, Bryan's voice rose, and he gesticulated in graceful pattern:

We have petitioned, and our petitions have been scorned; we have entreated, and our entreaties have been disregarded; we have begged, and they have mocked when our calamity came. We beg no longer; we entreat no more; we petition no more. [A dramatic pause.] *We defy them.*

The last words, "We defy them!" were flung out with a most impressive movement of the speaker's whole body; they rang with an accent of "superb disdain," and were followed by an outburst of mad cheering from 20,000 throats.[23] Then amid renewed silence, in more subdued but intense accents, Bryan launched into the famous conclusion of his speech, whose meaning has been much overlooked, closing with an appeal to patriotism in the face of the traditional enemy, England. The mixed sectional-class conflict was given a memorable nationalistic or jingo hue. Must we wait for England to decree bimetallism in the world before we moved, he asked? It was the "issue of 1776" again.

If they dare to come out in the open . . . we will fight them to the uttermost. Having behind us the producing masses of this nation and the world, supported by the commercial interests, the laboring interests, and the toilers everywhere, we will answer their demand for a gold standard by saying to them: *You shall not press down upon the brow of labor this crown of thorns, you shall not crucify mankind upon a cross of gold.*

The hall awoke from its hypnotic silence in a bedlam of cheering and parading which lasted for half an hour. The Goldbugs were undone. The Western Democracy had found its leader. The various State delegations forming in processions gathered before the Nebraska section and dipped their flags before the Nebraska standard. Only the Eastern gold men sat sullen before this largely spontaneous uproar, and in the vote upon the platform which followed cast their minority ballots in a dying opposition. According to the conservative press of New York and Chicago, it was a "political debauch," an "orgy," likened to the opening of the Reign of Terror in Paris. "Hell was broken loose in Chicago," Wickham Stead cabled to London.[24]

Other more discriminating observers noted the unusual enthusiasm and spontaneity which marked this convention, an unfamiliar phenomenon at our popular political gatherings, and utterly absent at the preceding Republican convention at St. Louis. One wrote, in London:

It was essentially the most genuine and impromptu political movement that has been known for many a decade. It was really the birth of a new party—a party devoted in spirit, whatever its mistakes of method, to human rights and human progress, to the welfare of the common people, to the promulgation of a newer and truer Democracy.[25]

Bryan of Nebraska—his words had been flashed throughout the country by telegraph, making a profound or a terrifying impression —had introduced a new spirit into the formal contests of the parties, evoked a national, quasi-revolutionary impulse on behalf of silver-money inflation of a scope which few men, least of all the rather shifty mine operators who originally sponsored silver coinage, could have calculated in advance. The little-known Western politician, by the "miracle" of his speech, was as a consequence to be catapulted into the presidential nomination and an electoral contest which would shake the very foundation stones of the republic. Bryan might have been nominated by acclamation at the moment his speech ended; but the balloting which was to follow the adoption of the silver platform was held over until the next day.

"Bryan, Bryan! No crown of thorns, no cross of gold!" the paraders and revelers sang.

Bryan, whose candidacy had been "amusing" on the morning before July 10, was second only to Bland in the first three ballots and assumed the lead on the fourth. Another adjournment, and a hasty conference was called by the leaders and wirepullers; then on the fifth ballot the "break" came, and a majority was won by the Boy Orator and "tribune of the people." On the following day the press significantly reported:

The Democratic National Convention nominated William J. Bryan of Nebraska for President. . . . Withdrawals . . . brought the gold reserve . . . below $100,000,000.[26]

A man of wealth, Arthur Sewall, a banker, shipbuilder, and railway director who .happened to believe in Free Silver, was then named as the vice-presidential candidate.

The hysterical crowds who came to his hotel carried the Nebraskan upon their shoulders and called for a speech. "My friends," he responded, "I feel this is going to be a campaign of sentiment. This is to be a fight for the common good."

IV

News of the unheard-of proceedings at Chicago aroused consternation in high Republican circles. Not only was the choice of the young Silverite orator from the Northwest drastic in itself, but what was worse, the party's disavowal of its own Democratic Administration as "plutocratic" and "despotic" upset traditions, broke all the established rules of the chivalric tournament of party politics. The insurgent Democratic leadership had exchanged the wooden lances of fictive election debates for the sharpened scythes and pitchforks of class-sectional issues. Where the Republican strategists had counted that they would pass the summer good-humoredly in recounting the errors of the party in office, blaming Hard Times, poor prices, blundering tariff laws, even unfavorable weather, on the incompetence of the opposition, where they had trusted fondly that even a Republican "rag doll" would be carried into office by the rhythmically recurrent negative discharges of the biparty system, they must now literally battle for their lives.

So Mr. Hanna felt. The Republicans had committed themselves, to be sure, to the gold dollar. But their campaign tactics, as outlined on the morrow of the St. Louis convention, involved mentioning as little as possible this unpleasant item. "I am a Tariff man, standing on a Tariff platform," the Major had said at once to his counselors. "This money matter is unduly prominent. In thirty days you won't hear anything about it." Mark Hanna, who had very properly been chosen chairman of the Republican National Committee, had expressed thorough agreement with this view. But Judge William Day, an active associate who was present at the conference, had remarked: "In my opinion, in thirty days, you won't hear of anything else." [27]

With the young Mr. Bryan fanning general discontent and offering an "immediate cure" for all the nation's ills, they were confronted not with a political campaign but with a "revolution." Hanna, who had planned an agreeable yachting vacation to Nantucket after so much hard work, wrote to McKinley July 16:

> The Chicago convention has changed everything. It has knocked out my holiday and cruise along the New England coast. [The campaign will be] work and hard work. I consider the situation in the West quite alarming as business is all going to pieces and idle men will multiply rapidly. With this communistic spirit abroad the cry of "free silver" will be catching.[28]

In conferences of late July, the Republican managers agreed to forget the tariff question and face the currency issue squarely. This meant a "campaign of education" upon the financial question, hard ungrateful work among broad masses of people who were ill equipped to learn or understand; enormous efforts and enormous sums of money must be expended to this end. Moreover, this year, instead of carrying on work in a half-dozen "doubtful" States, they must fight up and down the whole country.

It was a discouraging prospect. The air was thick with gloom—markets sank, stocks fell, gold began to be drawn freely from the government Treasury. Hanna now resolutely made Organization plans upon a larger scale than he had anticipated. He arranged for two national headquarters instead of one—at Chicago as well as at New York. Then, on July 26, he left Canton and Major McKinley and came to New York on a first, secret mission of the campaign.

The decision taken at the People's Party convention at St. Louis, in mid-July, seemed but to augment the alarming class-sectional character of the struggle this year. To St. Louis also the agents of the silver cabal quickly repaired, bent as they had been for two years on achieving fusion between the Populists and the Democrats. This to Marcus Daly, and to allied Silverite politicians like Senators Stewart, Jones of Nevada, and Pettigrew, as to the veteran People's Party leaders, Weaver, Allen, and Sockless Jerry Simpson, would break the bonds between the rural West and the financial Northeast, and with it the hegemony of the Eastern Goldbugs.

These men now contrived to manage the Populist convention by means of wirepulling as effective as any party assembly ever saw. Henry Demarest Lloyd in a letter of the time reflected on how curious it was that "the new party, the Reform party, the People's party, should be more boss-ridden, gang-ruled, gang-gangrened than the two old parties of monopoly." [29] But yesterday this well-meaning reformer had joined the Populists with enthusiasm and worked to bring about a coalition between farmers and union labor, convinced that "the people are about to take possession of the property of the people." Today bitter doubts assailed him.

The veteran Populist and Farmers' Alliance organizers were now within sight of victory, power, and office, after so many years of wandering in the wilderness. Did they not have the substance of what they wanted in Bryan? asked Simpson of Kansas. Bryan was a Populist in all but name, and what did the party name matter?

Amid scenes of emotional storm usually attending the farmers' party conventions, while the highly extroverted Mary Elizabeth Lease nearly burst a blood vessel, and the chairman burst his galluses out of sheer excitement, Senator Allen, the "incorruptible" Weaver, and other leaders steered the convention toward fusion, despite a stubborn opposing minority. This consisted in part of clear-sighted prolabor radicals such as Lloyd, in part of the idealistic Southern

Populists who had faced prejudice and violence in their efforts to erect a truly progressive third-party organization, free from Southern Bourbonism and official corruption. (It was becoming really a second "white man's party" in a region devoted to the single-party system.)

"By the time this money question is settled," argued Senator Marion Butler of North Carolina, . . . the great transportation question—that great question which stands side by side with the money question—will be upon you." The problems of transportation, the trusts and monopolies—these were what the People's Party had come into existence to fight, he urged.[30]

Other opponents of fusion felt that the moment was a turning-point in their young party, which had grown in a few years to 1,500,-000 votes and dominated a half-dozen Western and Southwestern States. Would it not be the "death knell" of their movement, they asked, if they were swallowed up in the Democracy?

The People's Party, as we have remarked, had risen as a "peasants' party" of the Middle Border and the South, advocating carefully studied land reforms, popular credit institutions and co-operative marketing measures, which at the period represented a realistic view of their problems. Slowly, despite special difficulties, it approached coalition with trade-union groups and even socialists of various colors. Must whatever gains in educational and cohesive force the persistence of their Organization promised be now jeopardized, gambled away by the opportunists who cried with Weaver and Allen *"Win this time"*?

The minority stoutly urged a course defined in an unfortunate phrase: to stick to "the middle of the road," that is, drive between the two big parties. But the answer from Allen carried the day:

Do you want . . . a President who is in favor of . . . Government ownership of railroads and telegraphs?

I do not want [my constituents] to say to me that the Populists have been advocates of reforms, when they could not be accomplished, but when the first ray of light appeared and the people were looking with expectancy and anxiety for relief, the party was not equal to the occasion; that it was stupid; it was blind; it kept "in the middle of the road" and missed the golden opportunity.

Weaver for his part welcomed the "new Pentecost," and would not refuse the proffered assistance of 3,000,000 Silver Democrats and 1,000,000 Silver Republicans "simply because they have shown the good sense to come with an organized army ready for battle." Bryan was a champion of the people. Let us go to the rescue of this gallant knight, "assailed . . . by the sleuth hounds of the money power of the world," he exhorted.[31]

At the last moment, after having agreed to nominate Bryan of Nebraska by acclamation, the veteran Populists gagged at approving of Sewall, the banker and railroad man, for the Vice-Presidency. The fire-eating Thomas Watson of Georgia was proposed instead. A tense contest was fought over this issue, in the midst of which came a somewhat chivalrous telegram from Bryan, refusing the Populists' nomination if his running mate were not also named by them. But this dispatch was highhandedly withheld from the convention by Senator Allen, and the Populists, in ignorance, proceeded to name Bryan and Watson for their ticket.[32]

In their platform, too, the Populists showed radical deviations from the Democrats, demanding besides free and unlimited coinage of silver the establishment of postal savings banks, direct election of Senators and of Presidents and Vice-Presidents, the initiative and referendum, government ownership of public utilities, and Federal public-works expenditure for the unemployed. In this anomalous manner they responded to the "bugle call" of fusion, amid frenzied demonstrations, singing, and waving of the American flag.

Lloyd, a bitter observer of the last minute proceedings, wrote on July 18, 1896:

. . . The poor people are throwing up their hats in the air for those who promise "to lead them out of the wilderness" by way of the currency route. . . . The people are to be kept wandering forty years in the currency labyrinth, as they have for the last forty years been led up and down the tariff hill.

He reflected further that this "fortuitous collection of the dissatisfied" lacked all grasp of any fundamental principle which might keep a genuine party movement together.

The Free Silver movement is a fake. Free Silver is the cow-bird of the Reform movement. It waited until the nest had been built by the sacrifices and labour of others, and then it laid its eggs in it. . . . The People's party has been betrayed. . . . No party that does not lead its leaders will ever succeed.[33]

The intense division of opinion in the press during the 1896 campaign showed how the nation was split into two great sections. South of Mason and Dixon's line and the Ohio River generally, and west of the Mississippi, Mr. Bryan was a Tribune of the People; he was leader of a "new battle for freedom" to the Duluth *Herald*; and a true knight of the West "fighting for the people," according to the Kansas City *Times*.[34]

But north and east of this boundary, the press and the pulpit thundered in a voice of fury against Bryan and his followers: "Down with the fanatics!" called the Springfield *Republican*; "National dishonor, private robbery, the exaltation of anarchy . . . the damnation of the Constitution," were the patent objects of the silver movement to the Philadelphia *Inquirer*. In Chicago, now the financial metropolis of the older Middle West, the press generally echoed McKinley's partisan denunciation of the Democratic convention as "an aggregation of populism, socialism and idiocy," precipitating a crisis "greater than the Civil War." But in New York's newspapers emotion strained mere words; the Bryan movement was commonly treated as

the hysterical declaration of a reckless and lawless crusade of sectional animosity and class antagonism. . . . No wild-eyed and rattle-brained horde of the red flag ever proclaimed a fiercer defiance of law, precedent, order, and government.[35]

The gentle souls who edited the family journal *Harper's Weekly* held that the spirits of Danton, Robespierre, and Marat (in the form of Bryan, Altgeld, and Tillman) had risen again to impose the Revolutionary Terror of 1793. Bryan, moreover, the "baby orator," was "clay to the hand of the potter"—John Altgeld, who was portrayed in caricature almost each week of the campaign as a ruffianly Catiline, concealing a torch in his gown (!) and using the head of Bryan as his mask.

In the East, the New York *Morning Journal* alone, among important newspapers, spoke for the Democratic side. Against the advice of his editors, the young William Hearst, whose father was Marcus Daly's late partner, threw himself into the silver movement with all his resources, and regaled a large public with Homer Davenport's savage cartoons of Mr. Hanna, and Henry George's bugle blasts for the new crusade.

Bryan himself emphasized the sectional nature of the conflict from the beginning when he alluded, in an unfortunate phrase, to the East, and to New York particularly, as "the enemy's country," which he intended to invade.

Professor Frederick J. Turner, at the time, wrote also of the upheavals of the day as a sectional conflict. The West, he said, was a debtor region; the West had been built up with borrowed capital. But now, not only was money scarce, but free or cheap land as well; "profoundly dissatisfied," eagerly agitating the problem of the monetary unit, "discontent is demanding an extension of governmental activity in its behalf." [36]

The West still engendered its separate ideology. Despite an occasional Collis Huntington, or a Jim Hill, there was relatively less inequality of station and property in the prairies of the Granger States, the Middle Border, and the plateaus and slopes of the Rocky Mountains. The factory, with its "wage slavery," was still a weaker element in the Western economy; men clung to an older, simpler American concept of democracy, and made in the West a last gallant stand against the triumph of high capitalism.

It was in New York City, where the inhabitants of monstrous shadowed slums dwelt within a stone's throw of the Gothic or Renaissance castles of brownstone built for financial nabobs, it was here, where in all their contrasting extremes of grandeur and misery the "two nations" were to be seen side by side, that the old American doctrines of democracy appeared weakest. It was here, in the financial and social center of the country, that the old Eastern leadership of the Democrats reached the momentous decision to abandon their party.

Party loyalty and party discipline had been fed to our political leaders with their mothers' milk. Yet now Whitney, from his palace on Fifth Avenue, denounced the majority Democrats. After the convention Whitney stated publicly that he would support neither his party's candidate nor its platform. He and the other men of capital who had been patrons of the Democratic Party had discovered that they were "men of principle" first, and Democrats afterward. It was a "fight for the preservation of National Honor," Whitney asserted. What troubled him was the slowness of the Republicans to "grasp at once the seriousness of the situation." He advised that they give up the irrelevant tariff issue and concentrate upon the money question. Else, a Sound Money Democratic Party must be launched at once.[37]

President Cleveland, sitting in the White House alone, feeding upon his bitterness, as he has been described, also underwent a crisis of "class consciousness." This "man of the people" was soon to leave his office considerably richer than when he arrived, twelve years before, thanks to his association with Whitney, Stetson, and Benedict; and he too discovered that it was time to place principle above party and forego all compromise. The Silverites were "madmen," or "criminals" worthy of the penitentiary, he burst out in a private letter to one of his friends at this point. To another he said with feeling: ". . . It will be our duty to stand by our guns and let the party go."[38]

A *formula* was sought by which the Eastern wing of the Democratic Party could, in a body, desert and go over to the enemy. Great financiers, such as Whitney, railroad masters and bankers, who had worked with the party's Inner Circle since the days of Tilden, men such as Belmont, Charles Fairchild, Jim Hill, and the more recent convert Henry Villard, having failed to hold their party, prepared to destroy it from within. The project of a new frank class alignment which was implicit in their plans was most bluntly expressed by the banker Fairchild, who insisted that a third ticket must be put in the field, saying:

We want to see the defeat of the Democratic ticket, and we shall try to draw away as many votes as we can from it. . . . Of course, we shall find no fault with those of our friends who cast a straight vote for McKinley.[39]

The problem was a delicate one; it was intended that any new party should not draw strength from the Republicans. In fact Stillman, of the National City Bank, strongly urged his friends among the Eastern Democrats not to run a separate candidate.[40] Dickinson of Michigan and Senator Vilas of Wisconsin, however, busied themselves with Mr. Whitney's party of Gold Democrats, which in the Border Southern States was to answer the pretended partisan scruples of their followers. A rather stillborn party of Gold Democrats was hastily set up (at a very tame "national convention") and a ticket, consisting of Senator John Palmer of Illinois and General Buckner of Kentucky, was offered to the electorate. This party of bolters, Bryan declared, were "in the employ of trusts and syndicates and combinations," and were "leaving their party for their party's good." Yet they accumulated 135,000 votes in November, and in at least one important State helped to tip the balance of the votes for the Republicans. Moreover, the esprit de corps of the Eastern wing was thus held together, as Whitney had hoped, for revival of the old control in the event of Bryan's defeat.

Many of the Cleveland Democrats, however, wasted no time over the Gold Democrats, but went wholeheartedly over to Mr. Hanna's party. Henry Villard, one of the earliest deserters, launched the National Sound Money League, which numbered William Rockefeller as one of its chief subscribers. James J. Hill brought his political power in six Northwestern States to the Republican Party. To J. Pierpont Morgan he wrote on July 15, 1896:

There is an epidemic craze [for free silver] among the farmers, and to some extent among those who receive wages or salaries. . . . [The McKinley managers] should get to work *at once*. . . . I will do anything or everything in my power to further the end we all have in view.[41]

Once more, as in the Jacksonian Era, there were ranged on the one side, as Parton said, "nearly all the ancient wealth, nearly all the business activity, nearly all the book-nourished intelligence, nearly all the silver-forked civilization of the country." Noting this cleavage and the abandonment of the Democratic Party by its old leaders and its men of talent and wealth, Bryan exclaimed: "At last we have the line drawn, so that a man can take his place on one side or the other." [42] Upon his side, it seemed literally as if there were only "the common people."

V

Full of hope and joy, yet bearing himself everywhere with marked poise, moderation, and courtesy, the Boy Orator proceeded from Chicago to his home in Nebraska in mid-July. The aura of a dramatic national fame hung over him. At railroad stations of every town and village along the way immense throngs came to do honor to the newly risen hero; banners waved and flowers were strewn for him. The people burst through windows or climbed upon telegraph poles to see him and cheer him. "To the excited crowds who pressed about him," wrote the historian Woodrow Wilson at the time, "he seemed a sort of knight errant going about to redress the wrongs of a nation."

Yet after the long procession of what passed for "statesmen" since the Civil War, was it surprising that the young Bryan engendered enthusiasm in the masses? He had given noble voice to their anger and to their hopes. Consciously or unconsciously, Bryan, in his great hour, introduced a new democratic spirit, wanting in our political life since the historic debates and campaigns of Lincoln.

He had the advantage of surprise. His magnetic power over crowds suggested at once to his advisers, as to his own temperament, the scheme of a vigorous, unconventional, even theatrical personal canvass. He would "go to the people" up and down the land, to as many as possible, in a speaking tour such as no one had attempted before, but which the speed and convenience of the modern railroad now permitted.

With his sheer youthful strength and tireless voice, Bryan rivaled the effect of the modern radio broadcasts as he journeyed some 18,000 miles, made over six hundred speeches within three months, and addressed in person over 5,000,000 listeners. It was a circuslike performance; it was also unprecedented, since tradition held that the candidate for the highest office in the land must dissemble his wish for that honor, and appear not to seek the office overtly.

The prodigious pilgrimage by railroad began in the first week of August when the Democratic candidate, instead of receiving formal notification of his nomination at home, set forth to make his speech of acceptance in New York, "the heart of the enemy's country." Here Bryan, reading a carefully prepared address at Madison Square Garden, before 20,000 persons, exhorted them to join with him in the campaign of "the struggling people" against "the money-owning and money-changing class." He had thought to attack the intellect rather than the heart of New York. His long elucidation of the doctrine of bimetallism was probably less effective when read than would have been an emotional exhibition such as he had given at Chicago. Opposition newspapers announced that his "invasion" had fallen flat, that his argument was unconvincing, while a friendly one noted "whirlwinds of enthusiasm" among the electorate. The streets leading to his hotel were blocked by thousands of New Yorkers; to pass through, he was compelled repeatedly to make impromptu addresses to them from his carriage.

In the hostile territory east of the Alleghenies, Bryan was disposed to speak softly. He sought to assure his audience that he was neither a "wild revolutionary" nor a socialist. "Distinctions" of wealth and education, he held with Andrew Jackson, would always exist.

Our campaign has not for its object the reconstruction of society. We cannot insure to the vicious the fruits of a virtuous life . . . we do not propose to transfer the rewards of industry to the lap of indolence. Property is and will remain the stimulus to endeavor and the compensation for toil.[43]

But, he closed, when great aggregations of wealth were trespassing upon the rights of individuals, the time had come to ignore those who had a "pecuniary" interest in noninterference, and to take action.

The new leader of the Democratic Party on this occasion also formed a friendly alliance with Tammany Hall, saying: "Great is Tammany! And Croker is its prophet!" [44] Bryan never affected a horror of simple, patronage-seeking politicians. The shrewd boss of New York's proletarian voters, for his part, could not appear to resist the glamorous candidate of his party, though Tammany's organizing power was permitted this year to be less prominent than its enthusiasm.

During August, Bryan launched his campaign in earnest. Night after night he rolled across the country, prayed to his God kneeling on the floor of his sleeping-car, slept soundly, and arose refreshed to address himself, during twenty or thirty halts, to as many as 100,000 persons in a day. He spoke spontaneously, with his wonted earnestness and power, and often with native wit. To the crowds he appeared "godlike" as he placed himself at the head of the greatest rising of the poorer classes and the equally numerous middle classes which the country had ever known.

From his train platform, vividly and with abandon, before crowds of Ohio hog farmers or wheat-growers in Illinois (the "Sucker State") he would paint the evils of mortgage foreclosures. He would exclaim: "It is because your legislation has been making the farmer's life harder all the time; it is because the non-producing classes have been producing the laws." At St. Paul, Minnesota, the principality of Jim Hill, he attacked railroad-wreckers and Coal Barons who exacted tribute from every fireside, "from those who desire to be protected from the cold of winter." Then in the towns he addressed himself to the merchants and the millers, asserting that with the silver dollar, the great flour magnate would "get nearly twice as many of such dollars for his product and . . . pay wages that will buy as much as the wages paid today and still make as much profit as he does now." To businessmen in general he preached deliverance from the tyranny of the banks. Before city laborers, in great industrial centers such as Chicago, he assailed the monopoly-ridden Government, which used armed force in strikes; denounced government by injunction (which trade-unions now fought as their greatest danger); advocated the direct income tax upon wealth, recently barred by the Supreme Court.

Rumors of attempted intimidation among workmen were rife, and Bryan advised them openly to conceal their intentions, as was lawful, under the secret ballot: to hold their jobs and march in Republican parades if commanded to do so, but to vote according to their convictions.[45]

As a figure of American politics, Bryan has been charged with failing to make an "all-class combination of the type so frequently effected by Theodore Roosevelt" and so frequently effective in our party life today, while appealing instead to disparate groups and sections and especially those of the agrarians, labor, and the lower middle-class.[46] Where a Theodore Roosevelt endeavored to neutralize important factions among the big capitalists, while attacking others, Bryan—if we except the friendly Silver Cabal, with its limited resources—certainly seems to clash with all enterprises of the larger type and the greater bosses of the East identified with them. He seems to bring down all their concerted, unmitigated hostility. Yet careful reading of his speeches shows that he himself had no coherent class program—wished for no naked "class struggle"—but shifted his emphasis, in turn, to attract highly diverse groups, ranging from the religious, rural pietists to the merchants and organized laborers of the towns.

In general he expounded the notion that the free coinage of silver would increase the circulation of capital and the redistribution of wealth: "When there is more money in circulation there is a better chance for each man to get money than there is when money is scarce."

But to intelligent laborers it seemed doubtful that all their ills would be removed with the revaluation of the gold standard. As one Socialist spokesman, De Leon, said, there was no little fear that labor might be crucified anew "upon a cross of silver." Yet Bryan's assaults upon the "money power" carried conviction; the party platform opposing court injunctions was designed to win over organized city labor. Eugene Debs, like Samuel Gompers of the American Federation of Labor, stumped vigorously for the silver crusade; and from Chicago, embittered by economic strife, Hanna's Republican agents reported:

The labor organizations are against us to a man. Impossible to teach them. They are more interested in the question of Federal jurisdiction over strikes than the money question.[47]

Whether or no Bryan willed or foresaw the outcome, it was a militant mass, ever rising in numbers, that followed him, formed of groups geographically and socially diverse, having in common chiefly the fact that they were groups "out of the center of control and striving to make themselves more effective in the national . . . political life."[48] The people marched and sang revolutionary hymns,

and even offered violence to the opposition; in certain large cities—
in Chicago, and even in New Haven—adherents of Bryan, roused to
a dangerous pitch, stoned Republican Sound Money paraders.

Among the marching crowds in that torrid summer of 1896, the
legend of the "Great Commoner" as the embodiment of earlier
American ideals of democracy was created, to endure for many years.
As he toured the country, an innovator of modern mass leadership,
hostile newspapers accused Bryan of a want of dignity unfitting him
for the office of President. He replied in a manner which convinced
and delighted his followers:

> . . . I would rather have it said that I lacked dignity than . . . that
> I lack backbone to meet the enemies of the Government who work against
> its welfare in Wall street. What other Presidential candidates did they
> ever charge with lack of dignity? (*A voice:* "Lincoln.") Yes, my friends,
> they said it of Lincoln. (*A voice:* "Jackson.") Yes, they said it of Jackson.
> (*A voice:* "And Jefferson.") Yes, and of Jefferson; he was lacking in
> dignity too.[49]

The peregrinations of the young Tribune of the People through the
older Middle West to the Northwest, as far as the highest Rockies,
and back to the Southern "border" States and Chicago, created a
mobile democratic forum by which the masses felt themselves engaged directly in a discussion of the Burning Questions of the day.
The price of wheat and corn, the cost of mortgage debt and crop
loans, the need for regulating railroads and industrial corporations,
for curbing our Supreme Court, for leveling the inequalities of wealth
by an income tax—all these immediate (rather than partisan or
fictive) issues were agitated day by day in the continuous and vast
democratic symposium which the champion of the silver dollar conducted.

By such novel methods, astounding the professional politicians,
the masses of the people were directly reached everywhere; enormous forces of sympathy, of fraternal emotion, of hope, were stirred
as in a great "democratic debauch" or folk festival. It was an effort
worthy of a more certain and clear-visioned leadership, a more
rational program of social reorganization than mere unaided monetary inflation, which—after its interval of economic confusion—would

have left all social relations of property, all sources of inequality, unaltered.

Meanwhile, the storm blew hard over the country. In September the professional politicians who knew how to measure popular trends were in despair. Yet keener minds among them, like Hanna's, noted that Bryan promised too much: "He's talking Silver all the time." [50] He promised by silver inflation an improved distribution of wealth. There were glaring fallacies in the claims of this "Christian Statesman" who believed simply that "the great political questions are in the last analysis moral questions"; and it was upon these weaknesses that the heaviest attacks were centered.

VI

Democrats or Republicans, the big capitalists and the rentier class were agreed upon the common end they had in view; they were moreover terribly determined. Yet their unaided votes alone might well prove insufficient for the battle at the polls. The first field reports in late July and August, attesting to the Great Commoner's popularity, caused pessimism to run rampant in Republican circles for several weeks, as Mr. Hanna arrived in New York to take charge of the national campaign.

History is made of classes and economic forces in conflict; but history, as all recognize, is also full of heroes and fools who serve for a moment to impede or divert the stream of events or hasten the solution of a foredoomed crisis. Bryan was a voice and, in a sense, an American conscience who gave freer reign to the discontent and impulses of the Have-Nots, lending them an ethico-religious ("fundamentalist") and sectional form. But Mark Hanna was a political generalissimo of genius, risen suddenly from the councils of the leading capitalists, to meet and checkmate the drive of the masses by summoning up the berserk fighting power latent in his class. John Hay wrote now to a friend in Paris:

I never knew [Mark Hanna] intimately until we went into this fight together, but my esteem and admiration for him have grown every hour. . . . He is a born general in politics, perfectly square, honest and courageous, with a *coup d'œil* for the battle-field and a knowledge of the enemy's weak points which is very remarkable.[51]

The financial metropolis saw him go to work at once at the Eastern national headquarters (which he established, wisely enough, in the building of the Metropolitan Life Insurance Company), and was soon able to measure the brusque force, the "iron will" of this "plain Western business man." [52] No sooner was he off the train than he was in touch with everything and everyone; he was seen ordering supplies and "literature," making appointments, arranging conferences with the veteran politicians, Platt of the New York hierarchy, Quay (a constant counselor), Redfield Proctor of Vermont, Fassenden of Connecticut, Joseph Manley of Maine, all of the national committeemen who could be reached. Hanna's energy and resolution compelled confidence and respect. "You make me think of a lot of scared hens," he is said to have exclaimed to a group of pessimistic capitalists at the Union League Club.

In a sense—and his craftiness here can scarcely be underestimated —Hanna actually exploited the prevailing pessimism. Bryan was absurd, but the farmers swallowed his fallacies and there was a tremendous work to be done; it would be madness to shirk it or miscalculate it. As he moved with Mr. Cornelius Bliss among the groups of bankers, industrialists, and insurance-company magnates, he unfolded the plan of his "educational campaign," involving a direct canvass (paralleling Bryan's vast effort) of the voters in every town and hamlet of thirty Northern States. This would need far more money than anyone had ever conceived of as needed for a political campaign. To parody the famous words of Danton upon the need of boldness in revolution, Hanna frankly said to the American capitalists in 1896: What we need is money, more money, and still more money. A Republican leader wrote to William Beer, the lawyer for the New York Life Insurance Company:

I wish that Hanna would not talk so freely about money. But I know that we are going to need more. It is disappointing that a Democrat like McCall [president of the New York Life Insurance Company] has more sense of the real situation than Mr. Depew [president of the New York Central Railroad].[53]

But at the Union League Club Mr. Hanna continued to preach to the New York capitalists the need for "three million more dollars for the campaign fund," and for thousands of speakers, brass bands, and educational pamphlets on Sound Money by the ton. Not only Republicans, but many an affluent Democrat, such as Cleveland's former Secretary of the Treasury Charles Fairchild, and the shipping magnate W. R. Grace, were seen by newspapermen conferring with Hanna at his headquarters.[54] The financiers were consternated; Hanna exacted almost as much money as they might lose to Bryan! A million or two had been enough previously; but now there was private talk, apparently, of $10,000,000 or $15,000,000, colossal sums such as no political leader had ever before been trusted with.

When Mark Hanna left for the West in August, he had made a good beginning, but bewilderment and fright still ruled in the East. At Western headquarters in Chicago, which was to be the real front for the field workers, trusted Hanna lieutenants such as Charles G. Dawes, Charles Dick, and W. M. Hahn and Henry C. Payne of Wisconsin were placed in charge of the work.

Hanna set up a complete machinery for modern political warfare. The Republican National Committee, which he headed, instead of being a sort of clearinghouse, a kind of central agency (chiefly for receiving appeals for funds from State bosses worried about their districts), became the general staff of the whole army. Its orders were carried out by the State committees automatically, as if they were the branch offices of one of the modern, centralized industrial Trusts in oil, steel, or sugar. A loose confederation of Republican regional leaders and ward heelers was whipped into the shape of a machinelike army, under a single leader who oversaw everything, who infused all its men, from top to bottom, with his confidence and resolution.

At Canton, Hanna arranged also a careful program with the amiable Major McKinley, who, the reader must bear in mind, was still the candidate for the Presidency. McKinley, a student for many years of the blunders of Blaine, Hancock, Harrison, and other candidates of his generation, was a master of the mot juste. He would make no break in public over some chance phrase such as "rum, Romanism and rebellion," but planned all details in advance. The Boy Orator might tour the country and make his one speech twice or ten times a day, but Mr. McKinley would keep his ingratiating personality before the public as much as Bryan—by remaining at home. McKinley and Hanna carefully plotted their celebrated "front-porch" tactics, by which large organized delegations of editors, ministers, prominent citizens, war veterans, temperance societies, Presbyterians, farmers, railroad workers, wholesale merchants, Catholics, Germans, Negroes, like so many trained seals, with their expenses paid in advance, were induced to make pilgrimages to the home of the Napoleon of Canton, Ohio. There the visitors gazed upon their candidate, paid him honor, and asked him certain leading questions of the day (as written out beforehand by the McKinley staff), and received from him a gracious welcome and a prepared answer, which was forthwith published by the press of the nation.

The front porch in Canton became a national sounding-board. It is related that the leaders of proposed delegations would announce their intention to New York headquarters or to McKinley, or even come on a preliminary visit. McKinley would then say: "You are going to represent the delegation and make some remarks. What are you going to say?" Any old thing? That would scarcely do, and might be gravely inconvenient. McKinley would then ask to see the address in advance, censor it, and send it back in the form he desired. In one case at least, a speech was blue-penciled twice over and virtually dictated by the candidate, so that it had the precise effect desired "from the party's standpoint," as McKinley expressed it.

The mock ceremony would take place at the appointed time, one, ten, or twenty a day. McKinley would come forth in all his dignity, with his round decent paunch, his unruffled white vest and cutaway, and a conventional politician's black hat; he would shake hands, smile warmly as he knew how to smile, and burst into "spontaneous" oration in answer to his guests:

. . . this year is going to be a year of patriotism and devotion to country. I am glad to know that the people in every part of the country mean to be devoted to one flag, and that the glorious Stars and Stripes (great applause); that the people of the country this year mean to maintain the financial honor of the country as sacredly as they maintain the honor of the flag.

What we want, no matter to what political organization we may have belonged in the past, is a return to the good times of years ago. We want good prices and good wages, and when we have them we want them to be paid in good money . . . in dollars worth one hundred cents each.[55]

With an air of the most unctuous patriotism, McKinley, the Civil War veteran, attacked the suggestion of sectional strife raised by his opponent, saying: "We know no 'enemy's country' in this fair land of ours." Nor did he neglect, as usual, to repeat his old familiar appeals to American workmen; he extolled the "dignity of labor," and gave dire warnings of the consequences of a "cheap dollar" for wage-earners. Finally, his addresses emphasized ever and again the destructive class antagonisms stirred up by the Silver Democrats. "In America," he said, "we spurn all class distinctions. We are all equal citizens and equal in privilege and opportunity."

This front-porch game was played all summer and fall at increasing tempo. After having ordered immense quantities of engravings of his friend William labeled: "The Advance Agent of Prosperity," Mark Hanna returned on August 15 to his labors over the supply problem behind the front in New York.

Meanwhile Bryan was stumping through western New York and the near-by Middle West. McKinley will lose Ohio! observers predicted.[56] Panic rose; gold was being hoarded or exported; stocks had sinking spells; and money was wanting still for the trainloads of pamphlets and the exhaustive canvass which Hanna designed in all its detail, with agents penetrating into every election district. The period from mid-August to early September, when the advance "sixty-day" polls were taken, was the low ebb of Republican hopes. Hanna's second visit to the East "is being wholly devoted to getting funds," the press gossiped.[57] It was at this point that James J. Hill came East from his railroad headquarters in St. Paul to join his efforts with those of Mr. Hanna and Cornelius Bliss, treasurer of the Republican National Committee.

Hill, coming fresh from the frenzied Northwest of Common-wealers and Populists and Silverites, conducted Hanna promptly to the "high places" of Wall Street. During the week of August 15, the press noted daily the progress of the carriage containing Mr. Hill and Mr. Hanna, uptown and downtown, from Wall Street to the

Pennsylvania Railroad offices, and to the New York Central offices. At the House of Morgan, at Kuhn, Loeb's, Hill corroborated Hanna's testimony as to the reality of the danger threatened; it was not a politician's scare for the sake of making free with the banker's money, but an emergency. Hanna could be trusted to use to the full political donations, unlike professionals who by common report wasted half the sums given them. Hill, who had bought large quantities of coal for the Great Northern Railroad from Hanna, vouched for his friend's integrity. Thus there came into use, in greatly expanded form, the device of the *political assessment upon corporate wealth* used in 1888.

After these mad cab rides of Jim Hill and Mark Hanna up and down New York, the morale of the Republican army improved wonderfully. "The feeling about Mr. H[anna] has changed," writes one of the general staff from the field of action. "He had made a lot of these people see that he knows what he is doing. But there is a bad scare here." [58]

Once again "Dollar-Mark" Hanna's contribution to American political science has the stamp of genius and fresh invention, carrying further, perfecting, tendencies and devices partly used or foreshadowed. Working in Ohio under the orders of Matt Quay in the famous boodle and "fat-frying" campaign of 1888, Hanna had studied well the handiwork of a master, had become himself adept in the "little shows of sharp practice and most of the big schemes of fine politics now in use by the Republican National Committee." [59] But instead of appealing to or wheedling the protected manufacturers who were privileged by the tariff subsidy, Hanna organized thoroughly the business of collecting contributions on the ground that the very life of business and credit was at stake. Responsible men were appointed to act as local agents in all the large cities, soliciting and receiving funds.

Mr. Hanna always did his best to convert the practice [of fund-raising] from a matter of political begging on the one side and donating on the other into a matter of systematic assessment according to the means of the individual and institution. [In the case of the banks and trust companies] a regular assessment was levied, calculated . . . at the rate of one-quarter of one per cent of their capital, and this assessment was for the most part paid.[60]

The Standard Oil (admitting a valuation now of $100,000,000), through Mr. Archbold and William Rockefeller, who knew Hanna well, turned in $250,000; J. P. Morgan did likewise; the four great meat-packing houses of Chicago were reported to have given altogether $400,000. Mr. McCall, of the New York Life Insurance Company, was called upon again and again. George W. Perkins, both a Morgan partner and an insurance-company officer, and William H. Hyde of the great Equitable company, testified some years later (in the Hughes investigation) that they gave freely large portions of their clients' premiums toward aiding the Republican campaign of 1896. This was equivalent to a bank's giving up part of its depositors' money for a political campaign.

Thus a war chest equal to all demands was gathered by Hanna, a sum which Croly modestly estimates at $3,500,000 (as officially recorded), but which other estimates have placed at from $10,000,000 to $16,500,000.* Never had politicians wallowed in such a golden stream as now poured forth for them, and which increased in abundance up to the closing days.

The printing of 120,000,000 copies of 275 different pamphlets in English, German, Italian, Polish, Yiddish, Greek, Swedish, and other languages was pushed forward, and their distribution in carlots organized. The speeches of McKinley, Thomas Reed, John Sherman, and John Hay were broadcast to the millions. Willing academicians also, such as J. Lawrence Laughlin of the Rockefeller-endowed University of Chicago, were hired for the occasion and painted the uncertainties of monetary inflation in the darkest colors.[61] All arguments were pointed to a concrete appeal to people of small means: first, upon the question of the future purchasing power of the dollar; second, upon the immediate effect of silver inflation on savings, pensions, insurance, and small investments.

* The expenditures in the final days of the canvass throughout the country for getting out the vote are never officially recorded or made public. Croly does not include these in his estimates. Joseph Foraker frankly ridiculed Croly's estimate, saying only that Mr. Hanna's war chest was of a size "which would have made a very popular man out of any distributor of it." (Foraker, *Notes of a Busy Life*, pp. 445-47.)

Nor did the high command of the Republican campaign halt at provoking the most violent class hate. Aggressive young Republican orators, such as Henry Cabot Lodge and Theodore Roosevelt, then the Police Commissioner of New York, and even respectable ministers of the church, attempted to outdo with their billingsgate firebrands like Tillman. Altgeld was chosen as the main target of attack; he was "the crowned hero and worshipped deity of the anarchists of the Northwest," who used the pliable Bryan as his pawn, said Dr. Lyman Abbot.[62] On October 16, 1896, before a crowd of 15,000 in Altgeld's own city of Chicago, Theodore Roosevelt, who this season distinguished himself as a picturesque stump orator, characterized the Governor of Illinois as "one who condones and encourages the most infamous of murders," and "would substitute for the government of Washington and Lincoln . . . a red government of lawlessness and dishonesty as fantastic and vicious as the Paris Commune. . . . Bryan . . . would steal from the creditors of the nation half of what they have saved."[63] The sophisticated John Hay delivered himself of a coldly conceived piece of vituperation entitled "The Platform of Anarchy," which was broadcast by the Eastern press; while more innocent personages, such as Dr. Charles H. Parkhurst of New York, also pointed their fire upon the menace of "anarchy" raised by the reform projects of Bland, Altgeld, and Bryan.

It was not the first time that the cry of "anarchy" had been raised in America against levelers and egalitarians. This constituted, in fact, tried and tested tactics. Under Washington and Hamilton the Federalists had wielded such arms fiercely against Jefferson's Democratic-Republicans; later, in the 1830's, Clay and the men of the United States Bank had raised a similar alarm against the Jacksonians. Now again the hue and cry was raised against the new Jacobins and their program of "chaos and cupidity," their promises of "boodle" to farmer, laborer, and miner.[64] American political discussion was as traditionally given to violence of pre-election epithet as the people were given to post-election respect for the laws and peaceable behavior. One wonders sometimes what epithets would be employed for a truly radical political movement designed to eliminate a large portion of existing privilege.

While appealing to historic tradition and "principle," Republican Party strategy itself did not ignore the immediate appeal of "boodle." In addition to the circulation of colored lithographs of McKinley, bearing a Full Dinner Pail and entitled "The Advance Agent of Prosperity," a sudden and rather mysterious rise in the price of wheat, from 64 cents a bushel in July, to 82 cents in October, was also used to point its moral.[65] "Now do something for corn," said voices from the agricultural States.

Early in September even Hanna had been thoroughly alarmed at learning, through careful private polls, that the sure Republican State of Iowa held some 30,000 "bolters" and with Populist aid would go decisively for Bryan. In this and other "doubtful" States he ordered the most elaborate advance polls, without regard to cost. Through September and half of October Hanna directed his attention upon Iowa and other Granger States; his speakers and "drummers," armed with campaign literature and other "substantial arguments," were sent into every town and village, ordered not to return until the hurrah for Bryan had been converted into a hurrah for McKinley, gold, and Protection. The work was well done. A second private canvass, toward October 15, showed that Iowa was "saved," and Hanna turned to concentrate his attack upon Illinois, Ohio, and Michigan.[66]

Yet new danger appeared in October again when organized labor, spurred by Altgeld and Debs, was shown to be swinging irresistibly toward the Democratic candidate. Roused by inhuman insult and libel, Altgeld came to New York and in a three-hour speech at Cooper Union sought to vindicate his actions in 1894 and the platform of his party. He seemed beside himself with passion, as were so many others in this season of hate. But during his speaking tour none knew of his frequent fainting spells, from which he rose resolutely, at the risk of death from a heart attack, to fight again. Never had he spoken so clearly, so seriously, so tellingly as at New York on October 17, 1896, when the plain people of the city received him with tremendous ovations. It is toil that makes civilization and not the cutting of coupons, he said. "The American people are called on this year to *make a new Declaration of Independence to mankind.*" [67]

On the other hand, during a Republican rally in Brooklyn, Mark Hanna was greeted "like a President," and in response to many noisy, good-humored calls, was finally introduced as the "Warwick of the West." The tall magnate, his face wreathed in smiles, gave a pleasant impromptu talk, in which he said meaningfully: "If I have been successful in anything in this campaign, it is in knowing enough not to talk too much." [68] Hanna's final moves were made without any talk whatsoever.

Under the surface an ugly spirit of coercion and intimidation suddenly showed itself in the late stages of the campaign. For some time agents of the great insurance companies from New York and Connecticut had gone about quietly informing their debtors that "if McKinley were elected, [their] mortgages would be extended for five years at a low rate of interest." [69] *

But toward the end of September, when Bryan seemed far in the lead, the tactics of more and more direct coercion spread quickly and quite openly—as if by a prearranged signal, one might have said, everywhere, East, West, North—upon a greater scale than ever before in an electoral contest. Large "contingent" orders were sent to iron manufacturers and shipbuilders, with the proviso that they be canceled if Bryan were elected. [70] † Gold-payment clauses were written into bank loans. Important employers now came before their workers with gloomy warnings that if McKinley were defeated there would be a dearth of business, their factories would run on half-time or would be shut down entirely for the coming winter. A workingman entered Democratic headquarters in Chicago weeping, and crying aloud for all to hear that he had been threatened with dismissal;

---

* The *St. James Gazette* of London, Nov. 6, 1896, in an article signed "Observer," described the use of money to turn the farmers' vote in the pivotal central Western States: "The eastern insurance companies who own mortgages on the farms in Iowa, Indiana and Illinois, and the neighboring states, have their agents in every hamlet almost, and six weeks ago, fearing things were running in favor of Bryan, sent these agents to see personally every farmer and come to an understanding that if McKinley were elected they would grant five years' extension of the loan at a low rate of interest."

† The Wilmington (Delaware) *Morning News*, Nov. 3, 1896, reported: "The Harlan and Hollingsworth Company of this city have received a contract for a boat costing $300,000. One clause in the contract provided that in the event of Bryan's election the contract shall be canceled. If the boat is built here $160,000 of its cost would be paid to Wilmington workmen for wages." (Williams, *William Jennings Bryan*, p. 195.)

his family would starve because he had been a leader in his district Democratic campaign.[71]

In September also some of the railroads began to circularize their employees with printed statements in each pay envelope, warning them that the roads would be ruined if they were compelled to pay bond interest in gold while earning depreciated American money; rolling stock, it was predicted, would come to a standstill everywhere if Bryan were elected.

"Who are these men who are so solicitous about your wages?" ran one of the Democratic circulars in answer. Mr. Carnegie, Mr. Hanna? Had not those gentlemen reduced workingmen's wages and compelled them to accept these reductions by force of police and soldiers?[72] But the tactics of intimidation were now spreading like a disease.

On October 19, Chairman Jones of the Democratic National Committee made a strong public protest that "the great corporations, with scarcely an exception, and many of the large employers of labor are engaged in a concerted effort to coerce their employees to vote against their convictions. . . . The workingman is being robbed of his 'rights' as an American citizen by an appeal to force and fraud." On October 20, Hanna replied publicly that the accusation was absurd; Republicans, he added cynically, could not possibly resort to such "un-American" measures. He himself would help in tracking down such malefactions if they actually existed.

Two days later, Jones reported that numerous Chicago manufacturers were threatening their workers with dismissal or cuts in wages. He then cleverly advised all employees to petition their masters for guarantees of a raise in wages in the event of McKinley's election. Hanna replied in a vehement outburst on October 24 that the Democrats were the ones using coercive methods in "a bold attempt to excite workmen against their employers."[73]

In the final fortnight, tension grew unbelievably high, especially in centers such as Chicago. Bryan, speaking there on October 28, 1896, for a last time before the balloting, brought the whole city into the streets. From his open carriage he reviewed hundreds of thousands, passing among them as "the incarnation of triumphant revolution," according to the Eastern press. Once more street fight-

ing and rioting broke out in Chicago, where Republican paraders
were attacked and McKinley billposters torn from walls and burned.[74]
In a Kentucky town the Democratic "traitors" Palmer and Buckner,
the Gold Democrat candidates for the Presidency and the Vice-
Presidency, were surrounded by a mob and roughly handled. Cities
trembled with commotion; families and parishes were divided by
hate. Nervous police took special precautions throughout the country
as election day approached, especially at New York, where Republicans prepared a monster "victory parade" for Saturday, October 31,
preceding the election.

All expert reports now indicated that Mr. Bryan would probably
be defeated; but none would guarantee that he might not win. Since
mid-October, when the coercive measures had been undertaken in
earnest, the game was really up. "It is all over," Hanna wrote confidently on October 28 to a friend who had contributed a check, which
he returned. "Reports are satisfactory just where we wanted them
most." [75] Two days before, the dependable Boss Cox of Cincinnati
had reported a complete reversal in "doubtful" Ohio. The systematic
tactics of coercion applied everywhere, added to the dragnet which
swept every tiny rural community for floaters or possible added votes,
had completed the task.

On the Saturday evening before election, Democratic headquarters
at Chicago, where hope for victory still ran strong, were startled by
a press dispatch announcing that the leading railroads and the great
manufacturers had determined upon a final united ultimatum to their
employees for Monday, November 2, to the effect that none need
return to work if Bryan were elected.

"Men, vote as you please," the head of the Steinway piano works
is reported to have said, in terms which were repeated throughout
the country, "but if Bryan is elected tomorrow the whistle will not
blow Wednesday morning." [76]

An excited discussion arose among the Democratic leaders,
Jones and Teller among them, as to what was to be done on the instant. Some present held that this final shameless "un-American"
threat would serve as a boomerang, since it would be secretly resented. But the venerable Senator Teller shook his head sadly and
said: "Boys, I am afraid it beats us. If I were a working man and

had nothing but my job, I am afraid when I came to vote I would think of Mollie and the babies." [77]

The highly organized Sound Money parade and victory demonstration by the Republicans at New York, on October 31, included by most estimates 150,000 people and was witnessed by perhaps 1,000,000 more. All that Saturday afternoon and all evening, while the city was brilliantly illuminated and bedecked, the marchers with tin horns and flags, wearing costumes or riding in floats, filled the streets. As before, trade associations, moving in battalions, with banners marking them as wine and spirit dealers, or lawyers, or railroad officials, sang songs in the characteristic vernacular of the time. Thus the railroad men:

> Hully-gee! Who are we?
> Erie! E—ee—rie!

The stockbrokers and bank clerks passing before the Union League Club cheered and shouted: "We want Morgan!" [78] The final mass meeting of the Democratic Party, too, was an occasion for speeches, fireworks, and celebrations up to a late hour, until the great city, strewn with rubbish, broken papier-mâché, colored bunting, and campaign buttons, sank to sleep in exhaustion.

In the last hour's preparations for "getting out the vote," for rounding up the floaters all over the country and in all closely disputed regions, nothing had been overlooked by Mr. Hanna's superb Organization. Moral enthusiasm was to be beaten at every point in the line by a machinelike domination of the actual polling. This department had been prepared by Mr. Hanna and his aides for weeks in advance, and its storming parties waited impatiently for their hour. In some thousand precincts the Republican district leaders and their henchmen were provided for by a last distribution of gold pieces. As one veteran political journalist related, every person having a vehicle on wheels was hired to transport voters from their homes to election booths and back:

Voters who were at work and possibly subject to loss of time while going to the election were paid for their time, many of them upon a very liberal basis. Farmers who had to leave their fields were recompensed for their loss of time and for the loss of time of their hired hands. . . . Every voter, no matter in what condition he may have been, was sought out. . . . Every county chairman, district chairman, precinct captain . . . lieutenants, and all other willing workers, were supplied with money to get out the votes.[79]

In Ohio there was one vote cast for every four living persons (with women then not voting), surpassing all previous records by 25 per cent. In Indiana there were 30,000 floaters reported by watchers as receiving besides sandwiches and liquor only $5 a head in this year of depression. The Democratic district captains in Indiana, according to their leaders, suffered from a lack of "political mechanics" to handle the vote, and stood by watching helplessly.[80] In one Western district having only 30,000 registered voters some 48,000 voted, by an oversight of Mr. Hanna's men. Reports of Negroes imported by trainloads across Mason and Dixon's line were heard at many points. "The very graveyards were robbed of the names on their tombstones." [81] The Democratic Party funds, finally, which were officially estimated at $425,000, were countered with a Republican war chest probably ten times greater, and unofficially reckoned at twenty or thirty times greater.

The leaders of the reborn Democratic Party, as they measured the sweep of the early returns, realized, as Altgeld said, that while they had been able to make "the most heroic political fight ever seen," the odds had been too great. The Party, Altgeld said, was

confronted by all the banks, all the trusts, all the syndicates, all the corporations, all the great papers. It was confronted by everything that money could buy, that boodle could debauch, or that fear of starvation could coerce. . . . It was confronted by a combination of forces such as had never been united before and will probably never be united again; and worse still, the time was too short to educate the public.[82]

An enormous vote had been brought forth, the greatest outpouring in our history, of which Bryan—"repudiation," "anarchy" and all—had nearly 6,500,000 (more than had ever before voted for a President), while McKinley had some 7,000,000. The Republican electoral majority, however, was decisive, standing at 271 to 176. But the change of 14,000 votes, it has been estimated, distributed in six States (some of which were carried by but a few hundred votes)—

California, Oregon, Kentucky, Indiana, North Dakota, and West Virginia—would have yielded a clear Democratic-Populist victory. The supreme importance of Hanna's strategy and dynamic Organization was thus proved beyond a doubt.

"God's in his Heaven, all's right with the world!" Mr. Hanna telegraphed to his friend William, who knelt and prayed for joy in his bedroom at Canton. Mr. Hanna had made a President, and prepared for a long reign in which there would be gold and privilege, protective tariffs high enough for the most ambitious of manufacturers, and in consequence, a Full Dinner Pail for contented, submissive labor. The nightmare of Altgeld as a power in the country was ended. And Bryan, as the New York *Tribune* thundered,

the wretched, rattle-pated boy, posing in vapid vanity and mouthing his resounding rottenness . . . goes down with the cause and must abide with it in the history of infamy. . . . Good riddance to it all . . . to the foul menace of repudiation and Anarchy against the honor and life of the Republic.[83]

Mr. Bryan, to be sure, was not to pass his life "abiding in infamy," but became instead the idol of Western Democracy, and for almost two decades his party's dominant leader. The silver question vanished with the increase of gold production in 1896 and 1900 and the approach to "elastic" currency under a central banking system. The Democratic Party, having lost completely the favor of "the big bankers, the big manufacturers, the big masters of commerce," under Bryan, wandered in the wilderness of defeat for long years, as had been predicted; it was long a minority party of opposition, supported normally by Bryan's Western agrarians, the Solid South, and an aggregation of professional city machines in the Northeast. In their voting, city laborers certainly showed no decided preference for the Democratic Party, especially during the years of Theodore Roosevelt, who took lessons from the Boy Orator in mass leadership. Thus the farmer-labor class alignment, which made 1896 so dramatic, disappeared, and the great parties reverted to type, on the whole resuming their old character of identical parts within our traditional party institution. This status held good after the upheavals of the "New Freedom" under President Wilson, 1912-16, as after the social upheavals over silver, 1893-96, thus revealing the amazing persistence and strength of the institution. Its greatest test came undoubtedly with the profound depression of the 1930's and the class alignments of 1936.

But on November 4, 1896, the men who carried on in the Republican Party the essentially unchanged tradition of Hamilton and Webster, seeing in themselves the triumph of "wealth and talents," apparently glimpsed something of the scope of their victory, the long years of unchallenged sway, the glittering opportunities before them and, humanly enough, "let joy be unconfined."

When the returns of November 3 indicated McKinley's certain election, in a certain Chicago club, long after midnight,

one of the world's greatest merchants started the old boyhood game of "Follow the Leader." He was joined by bank presidents, merchants, Chicago's foremost men; they went over sofas, chairs, tables, up-stairs and down-stairs, and wound up with dancing in each other's arms.[84]

And in this agreeable humor of their great hour we may charitably leave our Republican friends, facing strange years of war and peace, growth and change.

BIBLIOGRAPHY

Numerous collections of the private papers of leading personages treated here are not open to scholars as yet, or are accessible only under severe restrictions. But enough have been made available, fortunately, to yield us a clear insight into the unofficial, informal thought of the principal actors—as contrasted with their official public declarations of motive. Since our purpose was to observe "the difference between that which men in politics say and that which they mean," the study of unpublished sources, in various test cases, has played an important part in determining our judgment of what happened and how things were done.

A fair amount of unpublished material has already been sifted by recent historians and biographers cited here, though the deductions implicit in this material have not always been drawn.

For use of unpublished material not hitherto available to the public, special acknowledgments are due to the late Dr. Harry Garfield, who gave permission to study the valuable collection of the James A. Garfield Papers and Private Diaries; to the Library of Harvard University for the Villard Papers; to Professor P. P. Chase of Harvard University for certain letters of W. C. Whitney contained in the William E. Russell Papers.

A selective list of sources follows. Newspaper and periodical material, and Government reports and documents, are indicated in the Reference Notes.

PRIVATE PAPERS, MANUSCRIPTS, UNPUBLISHED LETTERS

William E. Chandler Papers, Library of Congress. A voluminous collection, treating of machine politics in the General Grant Era.

Grover Cleveland Papers, Library of Congress. Voluminous and candid, furnishing a striking picture of the 1880's and 1890's. (A portion of President Cleveland's letters have been published in one volume, edited by Allan Nevins.)

Charles S. Fairchild Papers, New York Historical Society

James A. Garfield Papers and Diaries, Library of Congress. A very rich and helpful collection.

Ulysses S. Grant Papers and Letterbooks, Library of Congress

Walter Q. Gresham Papers, Library of Congress. Relating to national politics and reform movements.

Daniel S. Lamont Papers, Library of Congress. Valuable for national politics of the 1890's.

Daniel Manning Papers, Library of Congress

Justin M. Morrill Papers, Library of Congress. Treating of tariff politics.

Levi P. Morton Papers, Manuscript Division, New York Public Library

Richard Olney Papers, Library of Congress

William E. Russell Papers, in the possession of Professor P. P. Chase, Harvard University. Documents of the 1896 campaign.

Carl Schurz Papers, Library of Congress. Voluminous and candid.

John Sherman Papers, Library of Congress

Charles Sumner Papers, Library of Congress

Henry Villard Papers, Library of Harvard University

Elihu B. Washburne Papers, Library of Congress. National machine politics of the 1860's and 1870's.

MEMOIRS, HISTORICAL WORKS, BIOGRAPHIES, PUBLISHED LETTERS

Adams, Henry, *The Education of Henry Adams,* Houghton Mifflin Company, 1918

—— *Letters, 1858-1891,* ed. by W. C. Ford, Houghton Mifflin Company, 1930

Adler, Cyrus, *Jacob H. Schiff: His Life and Letters,* Doubleday, Doran & Company, 1928, 2 vols.

Alexander, De A. S., *A Political History of the State of New York,* Henry Holt & Company, 1906-23, 4 vols. Vol. IV is *Four Famous New Yorkers.*

Altgeld, J. P., *Live Questions,* Donohue, Henneberry & Co., Chicago, 1890

Badeau, Adam, *Grant in Peace,* S. S. Scranton & Co., Hartford, 1867

Bagehot, Walter, *The English Constitution,* rev. ed., D. Appleton & Company, 1930

Barnes, J. A., *John G. Carlisle,* Dodd, Mead & Company, 1931

Barr, E. N., "The Populist Uprising" (pamphlet), in Vol. II, *A Standard History of Kansas and the Kansans,* University of Chicago Press, 1918

Barron, C. W., *More Told to Barron*, Harper & Brothers, 1931

—— *Told to Barron*, Harper & Brothers, 1930

Beale, H. K., *The Critical Year: A Study of Andrew Jackson and Reconstruction*, Harcourt, Brace and Company, 1930

Beard, C. A., *American Government and Politics*, 7th ed., Macmillan Company, 1933

—— *The American Party Battle*, Macmillan Company, 1928

—— *Contemporary American History, 1877-1913*, Macmillan Company, 1921

—— and M. R., *The Rise of American Civilization*, Macmillan Company, 1927, 2 vols.

Beer, Thomas, *Hanna*, Alfred A. Knopf, 1929

Beveridge, A. J., *Abraham Lincoln, 1809-1858*, Houghton Mifflin Company, 1928, 2 vols.

Bigelow, John, *The Life of Samuel J. Tilden*, Harper & Brothers, 1895, 2 vols.

Bishop, J. B., *Presidential Nominations and Conventions*, Charles Scribner's Sons, 1916

Blaine, H. S., *The Letters of Mrs. James G. Blaine*, Duffield & Co., 1908, 2 vols.

Blaine, J. G., *Life and Character of James A. Garfield: Memorial Address*, Government Printing Office, 1882

—— *Twenty Years of Congress*, Henry Bill Publishing Co., Norwich, Conn., 1884, 2 vols.

Bowers, Claude, *Beveridge and the Progressive Era*, Houghton Mifflin Company, 1932

—— *The Tragic Era—The Revolution after Lincoln*, Houghton Mifflin Company, 1929

Bradford, Gamaliel, *Union Portraits*, Houghton Mifflin Company, 1916

Browne, W. R., *Altgeld of Illinois*, Viking Press, 1924

Bryan, W. J., *The First Battle: Story of the Campaign of 1896*, W. B. Conkey Co., Chicago, 1896

—— *Memoirs*, John C. Winston Company, 1925

Bryce, James, Viscount Bryce, *The American Commonwealth*, 3d ed., Macmillan Company, 1893, 2 vols.

Caldwell, R. J., *James A. Garfield: Party Chieftain*, Dodd, Mead & Company, 1931

Carlson, Oliver, and Bates, E. S., *Hearst, Lord of San Simeon*, Viking Press, 1936

Cary, Edward, *George William Curtis*, Houghton Mifflin Company, 1894

Chapman, J. J., *Causes and Consequences*, Charles Scribner's Sons, 1898

Chidsey, D. B., *The Gentleman from New York: A Life of Roscoe Conkling*, Yale University Press, 1935

Cleveland, Grover, *Letters*, ed. by Allan Nevins, Houghton Mifflin Company, 1933

—— *Presidential Problems*, Century Co., 1904

Commons, J. R., and others, *History of Labour in the United States*, Macmillan Company, 1921-35, 4 vols.

Conkling, A. R., *The Life and Letters of Roscoe Conkling, Orator, Statesman, Advocate*, Charles L. Webster, 1889

Coolidge, L. A., *An Old-fashioned Senator: Orville H. Platt*, G. P. Putnam's Sons, 1910

—— *Ulysses S. Grant*, Houghton Mifflin Company, 1917

Corey, Lewis, *The Decline of American Capitalism*, Covici-Friede, 1934

—— *The House of Morgan*, G. Howard Watt, 1930

Cortissoz, Royal, *The Life of Whitelaw Reid*, Charles Scribner's Sons, 1921, 2 vols.

Crawford, T. C., *James G. Blaine: A Study of His Life and Character from the Standpoint of a Personal Witness of the Principal Events in His History*, Edgewood Publishing Co., Philadelphia, 1893

Croly, Herbert, *Marcus Alonzo Hanna*, Macmillan Company, 1912

—— *The Promise of American Life*, Macmillan Company, 1909

Cullom, Shelby, *Fifty Years of Public Service*, A. C. McClurg & Co., 1911

Curtis, G. W., *Orations and Addresses*, ed. by C. E. Norton, Harper & Brothers, 1894, 3 vols.

Davenport, Walter, *Power and Glory: The Life of Boies Penrose*, G. P. Putnam's Sons, 1931

Debs, Eugene, *Debs: His Life, Writings, and Speeches*, ed. by M. S. Reynolds, Appeal to Reason, Girard, Kan., 1908

Dennett, Tyler, *John Hay: From Poetry to Politics,* Dodd, Mead & Company, 1933

Depew, Chauncey, *My Memories of Eighty Years,* Charles Scribner's Sons, 1922

Dewey, D. R., *Financial History of the United States,* 11th ed., Longmans, Green & Company, 1931

—— *National Problems: 1885-1897,* Harper & Brothers, 1907

Dorfman, Joseph, *Thorstein Veblen and His America,* Viking Press, 1937

Du Bois, W. E. B., *Black Reconstruction,* Harcourt, Brace and Company, 1935

Dunn, A. W., *From Harrison to Harding,* G. P. Putnam's Sons, 1922, 2 vols.

Dunning, W. A., *Reconstruction, Political and Economic,* Harper & Brothers, 1907

Eckenrode, H. J., *Rutherford B. Hayes: Statesman of Reunion,* Dodd, Mead & Company, 1930

Farrand, Max, *The Development of the United States from Colonies to a World Power,* Houghton Mifflin Company, 1918

Feinstein, Isidor, *The Court Disposes,* Covici-Friede, 1937

Foraker, J. B., *Notes of a Busy Life,* Stewart & Kidd Co., Cincinnati, 1916, 2 vols.

Ford, H. J., *The Rise and Growth of American Politics,* Macmillan Company, 1898

Foulke, W. D., *Fighting the Spoilsmen,* G. P. Putnam's Sons, 1919

—— *Life of Oliver P. Morton,* Bowen-Merrill Co., Indianapolis, 1899, 2 vols.

Fuess, C. M., *Carl Schurz: Reformer,* Dodd, Mead & Company, 1932

George, Henry, Jr., *The Life of Henry George,* Doubleday, Doran & Company, 1930

Gibbons, H. A., *John Wanamaker,* Harper & Brothers, 1926, 2 vols.

Gompers, Samuel, *Seventy Years of Life and Labor,* E. P. Dutton & Co., 1925, 2 vols.

Gosnell, H. F., *Boss Platt and His New York Machine,* University of Chicago Press, 1924

Gresham, Matilda, *Life of Walter Q. Gresham,* Rand McNally & Company, 1919, 2 vols.

Hamilton, Gail (Mary Abigail Dodge), *Biography of James G. Blaine,* Henry Bill Publishing Co., Norwich, Conn., 1895

Haney, L. H., *A Congressional History of Railways in the United States, 1850-1887,* University of Wisconsin, Economic and Political Science Series, Vol. 3, No. 2; Vol. 6, No. 1, 1908-10, 2 vols.

Harris, W. C., *The Public Life of Zachariah Chandler,* Michigan Historical Commission, 1917

Harvey, G. B. McC., *Henry Clay Frick the Man,* Charles Scribner's Sons, 1928

Harvey, W. H., Coin's Financial School, Coin Publishing Co., Chicago, 1894

Haworth, P. L., *The Hayes-Tilden Disputed Presidential Election of 1876,* Burrows Bros. Co., Cleveland, 1906

Hayes, R. B., *Diary and Letters,* ed. by C. R. Williams, Ohio State Archaeological and Historical Society, 1925, 5 vols.

Haynes, F. E., *Third Party Movements since the Civil War,* State Historical Society of Iowa, 1918

Hendrick, B. J., *The Life of Andrew Carnegie,* Doubleday, Doran & Company, 1932, 2 vols.

Hesseltine, W. B., *Ulysses S. Grant: Politician,* Dodd, Mead & Company, 1935

Hibben, Paxton, *The Peerless Leader: William Jennings Bryan,* Farrar & Rinehart, 1929

Hicks, J. D., *The Populist Revolt,* University of Minnesota Press, 1931

Hoar, G. F., *Autobiography of Seventy Years,* Charles Scribner's Sons, 1903, 2 vols.

Hovey, Carl, *The Life Story of J. Pierpont Morgan,* Sturgis & Walton, 1911

Howe, F. C., *The Confessions of a Reformer,* Charles Scribner's Sons, 1925

Howe, G. F., *Chester A. Arthur: A Quarter-Century of Machine Politics,* Dodd, Mead & Company, 1934

Howe, M. A. De W., *Portrait of an Independent: Moorfield Story,* Houghton Mifflin Company, 1932

Hudson, W. C., *Random Recollections of an Old Political Reporter,* Cupples & Long, 1911

James, Henry, *Richard Olney and His Public Service,* Houghton Mifflin Company, 1923

Julian, G. W., *Political Recollections, 1840 to 1872,* A. C. McClurg & Co., 1884

Kautsky, Karl, *Demokratie und Parlamentarismus,* Leipzig, 1911

Kendrick, B. B., ed., *The Journal of the Committee of Fifteen on Reconstruction,* Columbia University Press, 1914

Kent, F. R., *The Democratic Party: A History,* Century Co., 1928

—— *Political Behavior,* William Morrow & Company, 1928

Kerr, W. S., *John Sherman: His Life and Public Services,* Sherman, French & Co., Boston, 1908, 2 vols.

Kohlsaat, H. H., *From McKinley to Harding,* Charles Scribner's Sons, 1923

La Follette, R. M., *Autobiography,* La Follette Co., Madison, Wis., 1913

Larson, H. M., *Jay Cooke, Private Banker,* Harvard University Press, 1936

Lloyd, C. A., *Henry Demarest Lloyd,* G. P. Putnam's Sons, 1912, 2 vols.

Lloyd, H. D., *Wealth against Commonwealth,* Harper & Brothers, 1894

Logan, M. S. (Mrs. John A.), *Reminiscences of a Soldier's Wife,* Charles Scribner's Sons, 1913

McCall, S. W., *The Life of Thomas Brackett Reed,* Houghton Mifflin Company, 1914

McClure, A. K., *Old Time Notes of Pennsylvania,* John C. Winston Company, 1905, 2 vols.

—— *Our Presidents and How We Make Them,* Harper & Brothers, 1900

McDonald, John, *Secrets of the Great Whiskey Ring,* W. S. Bryan, St. Louis, 1880

McElroy, Robert, *Grover Cleveland the Man and the Statesman,* Harper & Brothers, 1923, 2 vols.

McLaughlin, A. C., *The Courts, the Constitution, and Parties,* University of Chicago Press, 1912

McMurry, D. Le C., *Coxey's Army,* Little, Brown and Company, 1929

Martin, E. S., *The Life of Joseph Hodges Choate,* Charles Scribner's Sons, 1920, 2 vols.

Merriam, C. E., *American Political Ideas,* Macmillan Company, 1920

Merriam, C. E., *Four American Party Leaders*, Macmillan Company, 1926

Merriam, G. S., *The Life and Times of Samuel Bowles*, Century Co., 1885, 2 vols.

Michels, Robert, *Zur Soziologie des Parteiwesens in der moderne Demokratie*, Leipzig, 1910

Milton, G. F., *The Age of Hate: Andrew Jackson and the Radicals*, Coward-McCann, 1930

Muzzey, D. S., *James G. Blaine: A Political Idol of Other Days*, Dodd, Mead & Company, 1934

Nevins, Allan, *Abram S. Hewitt*, Harper & Brothers, 1935

—— *Grover Cleveland: A Study in Courage*, Dodd, Mead & Company, 1933

—— *Hamilton Fish: The Inner History of the Grant Administration*, Dodd, Mead & Company, 1936

Nicolay, J. G., and Hay, John, *Abraham Lincoln: A History*, Century Co., 1890, 10 vols.

Norton, C. E., *Letters of Charles Eliot Norton*, ed. by Sara Norton and M. A. De W. Howe, Houghton Mifflin Company, 1913, 2 vols.

Noyes, A. D., *Thirty Years of American Finance*, G. P. Putnam's Sons, 1900

Oberholtzer, E. P., *A History of the United States since the Civil War*, Macmillan Company, 1917-37, 5 vols.

—— *Jay Cooke, Financier of the Civil War*, George W. Jacobs Co., 1907, 2 vols.

Olcott, C. S., *The Life of William McKinley*, Houghton Mifflin Company, 1916, 2 vols.

Ostrogorski, M., *Democracy and the Organization of Political Parties*, Macmillan Company, 1902, 2 vols.

Pacific Railway Commission Report, U. S. Congress, Senate, 50th Cong., 1st Sess., Documents, Vol. V; Vol. VII of report

Paine, A. B., *Thomas Nast: His Period and His Pictures*, Macmillan Company, 1904

Parker, G. F., *Recollections of Grover Cleveland*, Century Co., 1909

Parton, James, *Life of Jackson*, Jas. R. Osgood & Co., 1860

Peck, H. T., *Twenty Years of the Republic*, Dodd, Mead & Company, 1906

Pennypacker, S. W., *Pennsylvania in American History*, William J. Campbell, Philadelphia, 1910

Phelps, M. N., *Kate Chase, Dominant Daughter*, Thomas Y. Crowell Co., 1935

Pierce, E. L., *Memoirs and Letters of Charles Sumner*, Roberts Brothers, 1893, 4 vols.

Platt, T. C., *Autobiography*, B. W. Dodge & Co., 1910

Poore, B. P., *Perley's Reminiscences of Sixty Years in the National Metropolis*, Hubbard Bros., Philadelphia, 1886-87, 2 vols.

Pringle, H. F., *Theodore Roosevelt*, Harcourt, Brace and Company, 1931

Pyle, J. G., *The Life of James J. Hill*, Doubleday, Page & Co., 1917, 2 vols.

Rhodes, J. F., *History of the United States from the Compromise of 1850*, Macmillan Company, 1893-1925, 10 vols. (earlier volumes first published by Harper & Brothers)

Richardson, J. D., ed., *A Compilation of the Messages and Papers of the Presidents, 1789-1897*, Government Printing Office, 1896-99, 10 vols.

Robinson, E. E., *The Evolution of Political Parties*, Harcourt, Brace and Company, 1924

Robinson, W. A., *Thomas B. Reed: Parliamentarian*, Dodd, Mead & Company, 1930

Roosevelt, Theodore, *Theodore Roosevelt: An Autobiography*, Macmillan Company, 1913

—— and Lodge, H. C., *Selections from . . . Correspondence*, Charles Scribner's Sons, 1925, 2 vols.

Russell, C. E., *Bare Hands and Stone Walls*, Charles Scribner's Sons, 1933

—— *Blaine of Maine: His Life and Times*, Farrar & Rinehart, 1931

Salter, J. T., *Boss Rule*, McGraw-Hill Book Co., 1935

Schlesinger, A. M., *The Rise of the City, 1878-1898*, Macmillan Company, 1933

Schurz, Carl, *Speeches, Correspondence and Political Papers*, G. P. Putnam's Sons, 1913, 6 vols.

—— *Reminiscences*, McClure Co., 1907-08, 3 vols.

Seitz, Don, *Joseph Pulitzer: His Life and Letters*, Simon & Schuster, 1924

Sherman, John, *Recollections of Forty Years,* Werner Co., Akron, Ohio, 1895, 2 vols.

—— and William, *Sherman Letters,* ed. by R. S. Thorndike, Charles Scribner's Sons, 1894

Smith, T. C., *The Life and Letters of James Abram Garfield,* Yale University Press, 1925, 2 vols.

Stackpole, E. J., *Behind the Scenes with a Newspaper Man,* J. B. Lippincott Company, 1927

Stanwood, Edward, *A History of Presidential Elections,* 3d ed., Houghton Mifflin Company, 1892

Stephenson, G. M., *John Lind of Minnesota,* University of Minnesota Press, 1935

Stephenson, N. W., *Nelson W. Aldrich, a Leader in American Politics,* Charles Scribner's Sons, 1930

Stevens, Thaddeus, *Reconstruction,* Lancaster, Penna., 1865 (pamphlet in the Ford Collection, New York Public Library)

Stoddard, H. L., *As I Knew Them: Presidents and Politics,* Harper & Brothers, 1927

Tarbell, I. M., *The Tariff in Our Times,* Macmillan Company, 1911

Taussig, F. W., *The Silver Situation in the United States,* G. P. Putnam's Sons, 1893

—— *The Tariff History of the United States,* 8th ed., G. P. Putnam's Sons, 1931

Thayer, W. R., *The Life and Letters of John Hay,* Houghton Mifflin Company, 1915, 2 vols.

Turner, F. J., *The Frontier in American History,* Henry Holt & Company, 1920

Usher, E. B., *The Greenback Movement of 1875-1884,* privately printed, Milwaukee, 1911

Vagts, Alfred, *Deutschland und die Vereinigte Staaten in der Weltpolitik,* Macmillan Company, 1935, 2 vols.

Villard, Henry, *Memoirs,* Houghton Mifflin Company, 1904, 2 vols.

Watterson, Henry, *"Marse Henry": An Autobiography,* George H. Doran Company, 1919, 2 vols.

Weber, Max, *Wirtschaft und Gesellschaft,* Tubingen, 1922, 6 vols.

Weed, Thurlow, *Life, Including His Autobiography,* Houghton Mifflin Company, 1883-84, 2 vols.

Welles, Gideon, *Diary*, Houghton Mifflin Company, 1911, 3 vols.

Werner, M. R., *Bryan*, Harcourt, Brace and Company, 1929

Whisky Frauds Report, U. S. Congress, House of Representatives, 44th Cong., 1st Sess., Document 186

White, Horace, *The Life of Lyman Trumbull*, Houghton Mifflin Company, 1913

White, W. A., *Masks in a Pageant*, Macmillan Company, 1928

Williams, C. R., *The Life of Rutherford Birchard Hayes*, Houghton Mifflin Company, 1914, 2 vols.

Williams, W. C., *William Jennings Bryan*, G. P. Putnam's Sons, 1936

Winchester, Paul, *Men of Maryland since the Civil War*, Arnold Pub. Co., Baltimore, 1923, 2 vols.

Yellen, Samuel, *American Labor Struggles*, Harcourt, Brace and Company, 1936

REFERENCES

FOR the convenience of readers, the references are given in the shortest form that will identify the book. For full bibliographical details, see the Bibliography.

CHAPTER I

[1] Bradford, *Union Portraits*, p. 180.
[2] Sherman, *Letters*, p. 248.
[3] Blaine, *Twenty Years*, Vol. II, pp. 48-49.
[4] Marx, *Eighteenth Brumaire*, p. 55.
[5] Blaine, *Twenty Years*, Vol. I, p. 198.
[6] *Ibid.*, Vol. I, p. 207.
[7] Beard and Beard, *Rise of American Civilization*, Vol. II, p. 35.
[8] Bradford, *Union Portraits*, p. 155.
[9] Beard, *Contemporary American History*, p. 91.
[10] Beard and Beard, *Rise of American Civilization*, Vol. II, p. 7.
[11] Beale, *Critical Year*, p. 73.
[12] Dunning, *Reconstruction*, p. 87.
[13] Hoar, *Autobiography*, Vol. I, p. 212.
[14] Pierce, *Sumner*, Vol. IV, p. 229.
[15] Dunning, *Reconstruction*, p. 87.
[16] Pierce, *Sumner*, Vol. IV, p. 229.
[17] Beale, *Critical Year*, p. 359.
[18] Stevens, *Reconstruction*, speech at Lancaster, Pa., Sept. 7, 1865 (pph.), p. 8.
[19] *Ibid.*, p. 7.
[20] *Ibid.*, p. 8. Italics mine.
[21] Pierce, *Sumner*, Vol. IV, p. 229.
[22] U. S. Senate, 39th Cong., 1st Sess. (1865-66), Document No. 2, pp. 42-43.
[23] Beale, *Critical Year*, pp. 63-64; Sumner Papers, Stevens to Sumner, June 3, 1865.
[24] Pierce, *Sumner*, Vol. IV, pp. 267-68.
[25] Williams, *Hayes*, Vol. I, pp. 277-78.
[26] Welles, *Diary*, Vol. II, pp. 385-87, 392.
[27] Blaine, *Twenty Years*, Vol. II, pp. 75-76.
[28] *Ibid.*, Vol. II, pp. 115-16.
[29] Schurz, *Speeches*, Vol. I, p. 374.
[30] *Congressional Globe*, Dec. 18, 1865.
[31] Milton, *Age of Hate*, p. 291.
[32] Oberholtzer, *History*, Vol. I, pp. 415-17. *Cf.* Milton, *Age of Hate*, pp. 372-74.
[33] Welles, *Diary*, Vol. II, p. 426, footnote.
[34] *Ibid.*, Vol. II, p. 645.
[35] Ostrogorski, *Democracy*, Vol. II, p. 127.
[36] Conkling, *Roscoe Conkling*, pp. 276-77.
[37] Blaine, *Twenty Years*, Vol. II, p. 232.
[38] Foulke, *Morton*, Vol. I, pp. 474-75.
[39] Blaine, *Twenty Years*, Vol. I, p. 380.

[40] Welles, *Diary*, Vol. II, p. 645; Dec. 24, 1866.

[41] Larson, *Jay Cooke*, p. 200.

[42] Oberholtzer, *Jay Cooke*, Vol. II, p. 28; letter of Henry to Jay Cooke, Oct. 12, 1867.

[43] Smith, *Garfield*, Vol. I, p. 424.

[44] Beale, *Critical Year*, pp. 8, 9.

[45] Oberholtzer, *Jay Cooke*, Vol. II, p. 28.

[46] Welles, *Diary*, Vol. III, p. 358.

[47] Cf. Hesseltine, *Grant*, p. 95 ff.

[48] Badeau, *Grant*, p. 14.

[49] Logan, *Reminiscences*, pp. 224-25.

[50] Washburne Papers, J. L. Camp to Washburne, Jan. 27, 1867.

[51] Hesseltine, *Grant*, p. 99.

[52] Oberholtzer, *History*, Vol. I, p. 489, citing the Philadelphia *Ledger*, Feb. 10, 1868.

[53] Williams, *Hayes*, Vol. I, p. 331, citing Hayes's diary, July 9, 1868.

[54] Washburne Papers, J. L. Camp to Washburne, Jan. 27, 1867.

[55] Foulke, *Morton*, Vol. I, p. 479.

[56] *Congressional Globe*, Feb. 5, 1866, pp. 685-86.

[57] Du Bois, *Black Reconstruction*, p. 214.

[58] Sumner Papers, letter of July 7, 1865.

[59] Kendrick, *Journal of the Joint Committee of Fifteen*, p. 26.

[60] Beard, *Contemporary American History*, p. 73.

[61] Kendrick, *Journal of the Joint Committee of Fifteen*, p. 85.

[62] *Ibid.*, p. 29 ff.

[63] *Ibid.*, p. 34. Italics mine.

[64] Welles, *Diary*, Vol. II, pp. 548-49.

[65] *Ibid.*, Vol. III, p. 474.

[66] *Ibid.*, Vol. III, pp. 425-26.

[67] Hamilton, *Blaine*, p. 286.

[68] Hoar, *Autobiography*, Vol. I, pp. 65-66.

[69] Washburne Papers, Chandler to Washburne, Oct. 19, 1868. Italics mine.

[70] Tarbell, *The Tariff*, p. 22.

[71] *Ibid.*, pp. 37-38.

[72] Oberholtzer, *Jay Cooke*, Vol. II, pp. 27-28.

[73] *Ibid.*, Vol. II, p. 40, fn.

[74] *Ibid.*, Vol. II, p. 56, fn.

[75] Larson, *Jay Cooke*, p. 202; Chandler to Jay Cooke, Sept. 1, 1867.

[76] *Ibid.*, p. 463, p. 20, fn.

[77] Poore, *Perley's Reminiscences*, Vol. II, p. 218.

[78] Washburne Papers, M. B. Brouns to Washburne, Dec. 9, 1867.

[79] Rhodes, *History*, Vol. IV, p. 533.

CHAPTER II

[1] Blaine, *Eulogy of Garfield*, p. 31.

[2] McLaughlin, *The Courts*, p. 152.

[3] Parton, *Jackson*, Vol. III, p. 149.

[4] Stanwood, *Presidential Elections*, p. 102.

[5] Parton, *Jackson*, Vol. III, p. 149.

[6] Ostrogorski, *Democracy*, Vol. II, p. 52.

[7] Bryce, *American Commonwealth*, Vol. II, p. 90.

[8] Ostrogorski, *Democracy*, Vol. II, pp. 128-29.

9 *Ibid.*, p. 92.
10 Julian, *Political Recollections*, pp. 13-14.
11 Bryce, *American Commonwealth*, Vol. II, p. 23.
12 White, *Trumbull*, p. 183.
13 Welles, *Diary*, Vol. II, p. 250.
14 Hay and Nicolay, *Lincoln*, Vol. V, p. 128.
15 *Cf.* Russell, *Blaine*, Chap. XX.
16 White, *Trumbull*, p. 184.
17 Adams, *The Education of Henry Adams*, p. 264.
18 Badeau, *Grant*, pp. 156-57.
19 Welles, *Diary*, Vol. III, p. 547.
20 *Ibid.*, p. 557.
21 Hesseltine, *Grant*, p. 152.
22 Hoar, *Autobiography*, Vol. I, p. 248.
23 Hesseltine, *Grant*, p. 153, citing the *National Republican*.
24 *Ibid.*, pp. 190-91.
25 Nevins, *Fish*, pp. 118-19.
26 Bowers, *Tragic Era*, pp. 245-46.
27 Norton, *Letters*, Vol. I, p. 413.
28 Harris, *Chandler*, p. 116.
29 Coolidge, *Grant*, p. 386.
30 Foulke, *Morton*, Vol. II, p. 156.
31 *Ibid.*, p. 265.
32 *Cf.* J. D. Cox, "How Judge Hoar Ceased to Be Attorney-General," *Atlantic*, August, 1895.
33 Rhodes, *History*, Vol. VI, p. 378.
34 Foulke, *Morton*, Vol. I, p. 58.
35 Harris, *Chandler*, p. 109.
36 Conkling, *Roscoe Conkling*, p. 510.
37 Gosnell, *Boss Platt*, p. 25.
38 Ostrogorski, *Democracy*, Vol. II, p. 148.
39 Grant Papers, Letterbook, Porter to Murphy, July 13, 1870.
40 White, *Trumbull*, p. 363; *Congressional Globe*, Dec. 11, 1871, p. 51.
41 U. S. Congress, House of Representatives, 43rd Cong., 1st Sess., Miscellaneous Documents, No. 264, May 2, 1874.
42 Howe, *Arthur*, p. 49.
43 Russell, *Blaine*, p. 115.
44 U. S. Congress, House of Representatives, 43d Cong., 1st Sess., Executive Document No. 132. *Cf.* Hoar, *Autobiography*, Vol. II, pp. 2-3.

CHAPTER III

1 J. D. Cox, "The Civil-Service Reform," *North American Review*, January, 1871, p. 85.
2 Larson, *Jay Cooke*, p. 290.
3 *Cf.* Pacific Railway Commission Report, Vol. VII, p. 3738.
4 Larson, *Jay Cooke*, pp. 291-92.
5 *Pacific Railway Commission Report*, Vol. VII, p. 3854, Huntington to Colton, Jan. 14, 1876.
6 *Ibid.*, letter of Nov. 10, 1875.
7 Larson, *Jay Cooke*, pp. 291-92, citing Cooke Papers, Apr. 23, May 10, 1870.
8 *Ibid.*, p. 292, Chandler to Jay Cooke, May 11, 1870.
9 Blaine, *Eulogy of Garfield*, p. 31.

[10] Welles, *Diary*, Vol. II, p. 250.
[11] Muzzey, *Blaine*, pp. 232-33.
[12] Hamilton, *Blaine*, p. 239.
[13] Russell, *Blaine*, p. 192.
[14] Hamilton, *Blaine*, p. 263; letter of Nov. 12, 1871.
[15] *Ibid.*, p. 195.
[16] Smith, *Garfield*, Vol. I, p. 474.
[17] Caldwell, *Garfield*, pp. 192-93.
[18] Smith, *Garfield*, Vol. I, p. 456.
[19] *Ibid.*, Vol. I, p. 456; letter to Hinsdale, Dec. 3, 1870.
[20] Taussig, *Tariff History*, p. 299.
[21] Tarbell, *The Tariff*, pp. 66, 77.
[22] Hamilton, *Blaine*, p. 238.
[23] Oberholtzer, *Jay Cooke*, Vol. II, p. 349.
[24] Russell, *Blaine*, p. 297.
[25] *Ibid.*, pp. 297-98.
[26] Oberholtzer, *Jay Cooke*, Vol. II, p. 354.
[27] Larson, *Jay Cooke*, p. 275, citing Jay Cooke Papers.
[28] New York *Tribune*, Feb. 27, 1873.
[29] Hamilton, *Blaine*, p. 491; letter to Garfield, Dec. 10, 1880.
[30] Nevins, *Fish*, p. 184, and p. 921, memorandum of Fish.
[31] *Harper's Weekly*, Mar. 18, 1876, p. 222. *Cf. Congressional Record*, 44th Cong., 1st Sess., Vol. IV, Pt. 7 (Belknap Trial).
[32] Nevins, *Fish*, pp. 588, 656-57.
[33] Larson, *Jay Cooke*, p. 232; Jay Cooke to Henry Cooke, Nov. 27, 1866.
[34] New York *Tribune*, Sept. 20, 1873.
[35] *Cf.* U. S. Congress, House of Representatives, 41st Cong., 2d Sess., Report No. 31, pp. 152-53.
[36] *Cf.* Nevins, *Fish*, p. 285.
[37] Larson, *Jay Cooke*, p. 269; letters of Henry Cooke to Jay Cooke.
[38] Smith, *Garfield*, Vol. I, p. 449; letter to Hinsdale, Jan. 10, 1870.
[39] New York *Tribune*, January-March, 1872; U. S. Congress, Senate, 42d Cong., 2d Sess., Report No. 227, speech of Carl Schurz.
[40] Caldwell, *Garfield*, p. 241. *Cf.* U. S. Congress, Senate, 43d Cong., 1st Sess., Report No. 453, Vol. II, p. 1075.
[41] Smith, *Garfield*, Vol. I, p. 566.
[42] Dunning, *Reconstruction*, p. 281.
[43] Nevins, *Fish*, p. 466, citing Fish's diary, Oc*. 4, 1870.
[44] Smith, *Garfield*, Vol. I, p. 462; letter of Oct. 26, 1870.
[45] *Ibid.*, Vol. I, p. 465; letter to Cox, Feb. 7, 1870.
[46] Hesseltine, *Grant*, p. 376.
[47] Chandler Papers, Gen. Dodge to Morgan, Aug., 1872. Italics mine.
[48] Hamilton, *Blaine*, p. 491, Blaine to Garfield, Dec. 10, 1880.
[49] Garfield Papers, Blaine to Garfield, Feb. 13, 1880.
[50] Hesseltine, *Grant*, p. 208.
[51] McDonald, *Secrets*, p. 47. *Cf. also Whisky Frauds Report.*
[52] Hesseltine, *Grant*, pp. 379-80, citing Fairchild Papers, T. O. Howe to Fairchild, June 14, 1875.
[53] *Whisky Frauds Report*, pp. 3, 6.
[54] *Ibid.*, pp. 3, 11, 33; McDonald, *Secrets*, pp. 114-20.
[55] McDonald, *Secrets*, p. 35.
[56] *Ibid.*, pp. 17-18. Italics mine.
[57] *Ibid.*, p. 51.

[58] *Whisky Frauds Report*, pp. 353, 355, 369-72, testimony of Bluford Wilson.
[59] White, *Trumbull*, p. 341.
[60] Gresham, *W. Q. Gresham*, Vol. I, p. 346.
[61] Foulke, *Morton*, Vol. II, pp. 173, 213. Italics mine.
[62] Smith, *Garfield*, Vol. I, p. 465.
[63] Harris, *Chandler*, p. 119.
[64] Foulke, *Morton*, Vol. II, p. 215.
[65] *Ibid.*, pp. 267-68.
[66] Harris, *Chandler*, p. 103.

CHAPTER IV

[1] Rhodes, *History*, Vol. VI, p. 383.
[2] Pierce, *Sumner*, Vol. IV, pp. 433-39; Poore, *Perley's Reminiscences*, Vol. II, p. 280.
[3] Hoar, *Autobiography*, Vol. I, p. 386.
[4] Fuess, *Schurz*, p. 165, fn.
[5] Foulke, *Morton*, Vol. II, pp. 163-64.
[6] *Ibid.*, Vol. II, p. 163.
[7] New York *Tribune*, Dec. 22, 1870.
[8] Foulke, *Morton*, Vol. II, p. 172.
[9] Fuess, *Schurz*, p. 169.
[10] Merriam, *American Political Ideas*, p. 28.
[11] Rhodes, *History*, Vol. VI, p. 403, citing the New York *Times*, Jan. 3, 1871.
[12] *Nation*, Sept. 29, 1870, p. 199.
[13] Paine, *Nast*, p. 144.
[14] *Ibid.*, p. 164.
[15] Alexander, *Political History*, Vol. III, p. 268.
[16] Paine, *Nast*, pp. 188-89.
[17] Alexander, *Political History*, Vol. III, p. 311.
[18] *Cf.* New York *Tribune*, Sept. 16, 1871.
[19] New York *Tribune*, Jan. 3, 1872.
[20] *Ibid.*, Jan. 3, 5, 11, 1872; White, *Trumbull*, p. 364.
[21] White, *Trumbull*, p. 366.
[22] Foulke, *Morton*, Vol. II, p. 218.
[23] *Ibid.*, pp. 215-16.
[24] Fuess, *Schurz*, p. 213.
[25] Foulke, *Morton*, Vol. II, pp. 247-48.
[26] *Ibid.*, Vol. II, p. 241.
[27] New York *Tribune*, June 1, 1872.
[28] *Nation*, Apr. 18, 1872, p. 249. Italics mine.
[29] Adams, *Letters*, p. 273; to Carl Schurz, Feb. 14, 1876.
[30] Alexander, *Political History*, Vol. III, p. 284.
[31] Smith, *Garfield*, Vol. I, pp. 494-95.
[32] Julian, *Political Recollections*, p. 336.
[33] Smith, *Garfield*, Vol. I, p. 494.
[34] *Ibid.*, Vol. I, p. 529.
[35] Washburne Papers, Chandler to Washburne, July 19, 1872.
[36] Sherman, *Letters*, p. 338.
[37] Taussig, *Tariff History*, p. 180 ff.
[38] Foulke, *Morton*, Vol. II, p. 264, fn., citing the Chicago *Tribune*.
[39] *Ibid.*, Vol. II, pp. 266-67.
[40] Chidsey, *Conkling*, p. 168.

[41] Conkling, *Roscoe Conkling*, p. 336.
[42] *Ibid.*, p. 429.
[43] Oberholtzer, *Jay Cooke*, Vol. II, pp. 352-54, 357.
[44] Hesseltine, *Grant*, p. 281, fn.
[45] Merriam, *Bowles*, Vol. II, pp. 195-96.
[46] Chandler Papers, Dodge to Chandler, Sept. 19, 1872.
[47] *Ibid.*, G. C. Tichenor to Chandler, Oct., 1872.
[48] *Ibid.*, Dodge to Edwin Morgan, Aug., 1872.
[49] *Ibid.*, Morton to E. D. Morgan, Aug. 7, 1872.
[50] *Ibid.*, Dodge to Morgan, Aug., 1872.
[51] D. B. Eaton, "Political Assessments," *North American Review*, Sept., 1882, p. 198.
[52] McDonald, *Secrets*, p. 51.
[53] Williams, *Hayes*, Vol. I, p. 469.
[54] McDonald, *Secrets*, p. 52.
[55] Julian, *Political Recollections*, pp. 342, 335-36.
[56] Smith, *Garfield*, Vol. I, p. 529.
[57] Stanwood, *Presidential Elections*, p. 297.
[58] Adams, *Letters*, p. 274.
[59] Caldwell, *Garfield*, p. 224.

CHAPTER V

[1] Merriam, *Bowles*, Vol. II, p. 266.
[2] Merriam, *American Political Ideas*, p. 28.
[3] Salter, *Boss Rule*, p. 254.
[4] Cortissoz, *Reid*, Vol. II, p. 17.
[5] Chidsey, *Conkling*, pp. 84, 90.
[6] *Ibid.*, p. 91.
[7] Foulke, *Morton*, Vol. II, p. 178, fn.
[8] Hamilton, *Blaine*, p. 491; letter to Garfield, Dec. 10, 1880.
[9] Foulke, *Morton*, Vol. II, pp. 390-91.
[10] Smith, *Garfield*, Vol. I, pp. 531-32, citing J. A. Garfield, *Review of the Transactions of the Crédit Mobilier Company*.
[11] *Poland Committee Report*, p. 7.
[12] Smith, *Garfield*, Vol. I, pp. 538-39.
[13] Caldwell, *Garfield*, pp. 221-30.
[14] Russell, *Blaine*, p. 252.
[15] Hamilton, *Blaine*, p. 286.
[16] *Wilson-Hoar Report*, p. xvii.
[17] *Congressional Record*, Mar. 23, 1874, p. 2354.
[18] Hesseltine, *Grant*, pp. 329-30.
[19] Foulke, *Morton*, p. 319.
[20] Noyes, *American Finance*, p. 20.
[21] Kerr, *Sherman*, Vol. I, p. 357.
[22] Caldwell, *Garfield*, p. 200.
[23] Hesseltine, *Grant*, p. 330.
[24] New York *Times*, Mar. 21, 1874.
[25] Nevins, *Fish*, p. 713, citing Fish's diary, Apr. 21, 1874.
[26] Hoar, *Autobiography*, Vol. I, p. 206.
[27] Foulke, *Morton*, Vol. II, pp. 346-48.
[28] Hamilton, *Blaine*, p. 246; Gen. R. A. Schenck to Blaine.
[29] Noyes, *American Finance*, p. 21.

[30] Rhodes, *History*, Vol. VII, p. 70.
[31] *Cf.* Sherman, *Recollections*, Vol. I, pp. 509-20.
[32] Noyes, *American Finance*, p. 21.
[33] Hesseltine, *Grant*, p. 337, citing Chandler Papers, Apr. 10, 1874.
[34] *Whisky Frauds Report*, pp. 5-6, 11, 30.
[35] *Ibid.*, p. 355; McDonald, *Secrets*, pp. 105-10.
[36] *Cf.* Gresham, *W. Q. Gresham*, Vol. II, p. 439 ff.
[37] U. S. Congress, House of Representatives, 44th Cong., 1st Sess., Miscellaneous Document No. 186.
[38] *Whisky Frauds Report*, p. 369 ff.
[39] *Ibid.*, p. 399.
[40] Grant Papers, Letterbook, Grant to Pierrepont, July 17, 1875.
[41] Nevins, *Fish*, p. 797 citing Fish's diary, Feb. 8, 1876.
[42] *Nation*, Nov. 25, 1875.
[43] Merriam, *Bowles*, Vol. II, pp. 253-54.
[44] Paine, *Nast*, p. 326.
[45] Rhodes, *History*, Vol. VII, p. 191.
[46] Bowers, *Tragic Era*, p. 473.
[47] Alexander, *Political History*, Vol. III, p. 332.
[48] Hoar, *Autobiography*, Vol. I, p. 308.
[49] Muzzey, *Blaine*, p. 76.
[50] Russell, *Blaine*, pp. 267, 270-71.
[51] *Ibid.*, p. 268.
[52] Merriam, *Bowles*, p. 250.
[53] Hamilton, *Blaine*, p. 378.
[54] Caldwell, *Garfield*, p. 249.
[55] Muzzey, *Blaine*, p. 84.
[56] Smith, *Garfield*, Vol. I, p. 599; letter of Apr. 18, 1876.
[57] *Nation*, Apr. 27, 1876, p. 269.
[58] U. S. Congress, House of Representatives, 44th Cong., 1st Sess., Miscellaneous Document No. 176, pp. 95, 123.
[59] *Ibid.*, pp. 98, 105-08, 110.
[60] Garfield Journal, May 27, 1876.
[61] *Congressional Record*, June 5, 1876, p. 3604.
[62] *Ibid.*, p. 3608.
[63] Rhodes, *History*, Vol. VII, pp. 203, 204.
[64] *Nation*, June 15, 1876, p. 373; New York *Tribune*, June 7, 1876.
[65] New York *Sun*, June 12, 1876.
[66] Ingersoll, *Works*, Vol. IX, pp. 59, 60.
[67] Alexander, *Political History*, Vol. III, pp. 333-34.
[68] Adams, *Letters*, p. 288.
[69] Hamilton, *Blaine*, p. 418.
[70] Alexander, *Political History*, Vol. III, pp. 108-10.
[71] Paine, *Nast*, p. 165.
[72] Alexander, *Political History*, Vol. III, pp. 274-75.
[73] Nevins, *Hewitt*, p. 304.
[74] Bowers, *Tragic Era*, p. 487.
[75] Williams, *Hayes*, Vol. I, p. 406, citing Hayes's diary, Oct. 12, 1875.
[76] Paine, *Nast*, p. 459.
[77] Williams, *Hayes*, Vol. I, p. 469, fn.
[78] *Ibid.*, Vol. I, p. 479, citing Hayes's diary, Aug. 13, 1876.
[79] *Cf.* Bigelow, *Tilden*, Vol. II, pp. 21, 31, 54-55.
[80] Williams, *Hayes*, Vol. I, p. 481; letter to Edwards Pierrepont, Sept. 16, 1876.

[81] Hamilton, *Blaine*, p. 422. Italics mine.
[82] Ingersoll, *Works*, Vol. IX, pp. 157, 158, 160.
[83] *Nation*, Oct. 19, 1876, p. 237.
[84] Gresham, *W. Q. Gresham*, Vol. II, pp. 459-60.
[85] *Nation*, Mar. 1, 1877, p. 124.

CHAPTER VI

[1] Rhodes, *History*, Vol. VII, p. 284.
[2] Bigelow, *Tilden*, Vol. II, p. 12.
[3] *Ibid.*, Vol. II, p. 13.
[4] Chandler Papers, T. W. Osborne to "Dear Gorn," Nov. 9, 1876.
[5] Bigelow, *Tilden*, Vol. II, p. 17 ff.
[6] *Ibid.*, Vol. II, p. 21.
[7] Chandler Papers, Chandler to E. F. Getchell, Nov. 22, 1876.
[8] Bigelow, *Tilden*, Vol. II, p. 19.
[9] Chandler Papers, Vol. 43, copy by Chandler.
[10] *Ibid.*, Nov. 20, 1876.
[11] U. S. Congress, House of Representatives, 44th Cong., 2d Sess., Miscellaneous Documents, pp. 138, 144-45.
[12] Bigelow, *Tilden*, Vol. II, p. 95, quoting from Tilden's Secretary's diary.
[13] *Nation*, Mar. 8, 1877, pp. 142-43; Paine, *Nast*, pp. 399-403; *Potter Committee Report*, 1879.
[14] Bigelow, *Tilden*, Vol. II, p. 74, fn.
[15] Nevins, *Hewitt*, p. 387.
[16] Garfield Papers, Dec. 13, 1876.
[17] Smith, *Garfield*, Vol. I, p. 643.
[18] *Ibid.*, Vol. I, p. 644.
[19] *Cf.* Bigelow, *Tilden*, Vol. II, pp. 54-56; Rhodes, *History*, Vol. VII, p. 289.
[20] Sherman Papers, J. H. Van Alen to Sherman, Feb. 16, 1877.
[21] Williams, *Hayes*, Vol. II, pp. 79-80.
[22] Howe, *Arthur*, pp. 65-75.
[23] Phelps, *Kate Chase*, p. 245.
[24] Gosnell, *Boss Platt*, p. 22.
[25] New York *Sun*, Sept. 27, 1877.
[26] *Harper's Weekly*, Mar. 11, 1876, p. 202; *cf.* also Apr. 8, p. 282; Apr. 15, p. 302; June 17, p. 486.
[27] Alexander, *Political History*, Vol. III, p. 368.
[28] *Ibid.*, p. 369.
[29] New York *Sun*, Sept. 27, 1877.
[30] Alexander, *Political History*, Vol. III, p. 32.
[31] Conkling, *Roscoe Conkling*, p. 414. Italics mine.
[32] *Ibid.*, p. 540; "man milliners" was in the original speech, but is omitted by A. R. Conkling.
[33] *Ibid.*, pp. 540-41.
[34] *Ibid.*, p. 541. Italics mine.
[35] *Ibid.*, p. 549. The whole speech is given (pp. 538-49) except that the most "sarcastic" passages are omitted; they are quoted in the New York *Tribune*, Sept. 28, 1877.
[36] Cary, *Curtis*, p. 258.
[37] New York *Tribune*, Sept. 27, 1877.
[38] *Nation*, Oct. 18, 1877, p. 233.
[39] New York *Tribune*, Dec. 13, 1877.

[40] Williams, *Hayes*, Vol. II, pp. 87-88.
[41] Howe, *Arthur*, p. 82.
[42] *Nation*, Feb. 6, 1879, p. 93.
[43] Alexander, *Political History*, Vol. III, pp. 409-10.
[44] Gompers, *Seventy Years*, Vol. I, pp. 139-40.
[45] Haynes, *Third Party Movements*, p. 221.
[46] Rhodes, *History*, Vol. VIII, p. 46.
[47] *Cf.* New York *Sun*, July 23-25, 1877.
[48] Gresham, *W. Q. Gresham*, Vol. I, p. 382.
[49] *Ibid.*, Vol. I, p. 383 ff.
[50] Commons and others, *History of Labour*, Vol. II, p. 191.
[51] *Nation*, Aug. 2, 1877, p. 68.
[52] Rhodes, *History*, Vol. VIII, p. 48.
[53] Commons and others, *History of Labour*, Vol. II, p. 189 ff.
[54] *Nation*, July 26, 1877, p. 50; *cf. ibid.*, Aug. 9, 1877, pp. 84-85.
[55] Conkling, *Roscoe Conkling*, pp. 412-13.
[56] Blaine, *Garfield*, p. 10.
[57] Sherman, *Recollections*, Vol. II, p. 662.
[58] Haynes, *Third Party Movements*, p. 139.
[59] See Haynes, *Third Party Movements*, pp. 122-27, for the platform.
[60] Sherman, *Recollections*, Vol. I, pp. 593-94.
[61] Noyes, *American Finance*, p. 32.
[62] Garfield Journal, Feb. 22, 1878.
[63] Sherman, *Recollections*, Vol. II, pp. 604, 607.
[64] Article "Allison," Dictionary of American Biography.
[65] Sherman, *Recollections*, Vol. II, p. 621.
[66] Williams, *Hayes*, Vol. II, p. 123, citing Hayes's diary, Feb. 26, 1878.
[67] Haynes, *Third Party Movements*, p. 128.
[68] Usher, *Greenback Movement*, p. 24-28.
[69] Haynes, *Third Party Movements*, pp. 92-93.
[70] *Ibid.*, p. 117.
[71] *Ibid.*, p. 120.
[72] Smith, *Garfield*, Vol. II, p. 664; journal and letter to Austin, Mar. 3, 1879.
[73] *Congressional Record*, Apr. 2, 1878, p. 2200; Apr. 8, 1878, p. 2333.
[74] *Ibid.*, Apr. 9, 1878, p. 2373-5.
[75] Smith, *Garfield*, Vol. II, p. 681, speech of Apr. 4, 1879.
[76] Hayes, *Diary*, Vol. III, pp. 570-71, Aug. 14, 1879.
[77] Howe, *Arthur*, p. 95.
[78] Alexander, *Political History*, Vol. III, p. 427.
[79] Williams, *Hayes*, Vol. II, p. 97.
[80] For a full account of the trial, see "Star Route Trial," Appleton's Annual Cyclopaedia, 1882, pp. 753-67; 1883, p. 777.

CHAPTER VII

[1] Hicks, *Populist Revolt*, p. 16.
[2] Cortissoz, *Reid*, Vol. I, p. 394.
[3] Kerr, *Sherman*, Vol. II, p. 33.
[4] Sherman, *Recollections*, Vol. II, p. 737.
[5] Hesseltine, *Grant*, pp. 435-36.
[6] Badeau, *Grant*, p. 316.
[7] Alexander, *Political History*, Vol. III, pp. 435-36.
[8] *Letters of Mrs. James G. Blaine*, Vol. I, pp. 161-62.

[9] Smith, *Garfield*, Vol. II, p. 951.
[10] *Cf.* Caldwell, *Garfield*, pp. 278-82, 286-90.
[11] Conkling, *Roscoe Conkling*, p. 592.
[12] *Ibid.*, pp. 599-600.
[13] Smith, *Garfield*, Vol. II, p. 975.
[14] Hoar, *Autobiography*, Vol. I, p. 397.
[15] Stanwood, *Presidential Elections*, p. 361.
[16] Muzzey, *Blaine*, p. 172.
[17] Hudson, *Random Recollections*, p. 98.
[18] *Nation*, June 17, 1880, p. 445.
[19] Smith, *Garfield*, Vol. II, p. 991.
[20] Robinson, *Political Parties*, pp. 198-99.
[21] Kerr, *Sherman*, Vol. II, p. 33.
[22] New York *Tribune*, Oct. 29, 1880.
[23] Stanwood, *Presidential Elections*, p. 364.
[24] Smith, *Garfield*, Vol. II, p. 1028.
[25] *Ibid.*, Vol. II, p. 1012; Aug. 5, 1880.
[26] Howe, *Arthur*, p. 117.
[27] Garfield Papers, Garfield to Townsend, Sept. 2, 1880; Townsend to Garfield, Sept. 3, 1880.
[28] *Ibid.*, Garfield to Townsend, Sept. 7, 1880.
[29] Depew, *My Memories*, p. 110.
[30] Croly, *Hanna*, p. 115 ff.
[31] *Ibid.*, pp. 116-17.
[32] Cortissoz, *Reid*, Vol. II, p. 35.
[33] Smith, *Garfield*, Vol. II, p. 997.
[34] *Ibid.*, Vol. II, pp. 996-97.
[35] *Ibid.*, Vol. II, p. 1053.
[36] *Ibid.*, Vol. II, p. 1001.
[37] *Nation*, July 15, 1880.
[38] Smith, *Garfield*, Vol. II, p. 1008; letter of July 24, 1880.
[39] *Ibid.*, Vol. II, pp. 1009-10; letter of July 26, 1880.
[40] *Ibid.*, Vol. II, p. 1011.
[41] Cortissoz, *Reid*, Vol. II, pp. 63-64.
[42] Smith, *Garfield*, Vol. II, p. 1012; journal of Aug. 4, 1880.
[43] Platt, *Autobiography*, p. 127.
[44] *Ibid.*, pp. 127-32.
[45] Conkling, *Roscoe Conkling*, p. 612.
[46] Smith, *Garfield*, Vol. II, p. 1015; Aug. 9, 1880.
[47] Howe, *Arthur*, pp. 119-20.
[48] Platt, *Autobiography*, p. 135.
[49] Caldwell, *Garfield*, p. 303.
[50] Smith, *Garfield*, Vol. II, pp. 1034-35; letter of Sept. 29, 1880.
[51] *Harper's Weekly*, Nov. 15, 1884, p. 748.
[52] *Nation*, Feb. 24, 1881, p. 122.
[53] Muzzey, *Blaine*, p. 186.
[54] Garfield Papers, Journal, Jan. 7, 1879.
[55] Hamilton, *Blaine*, p. 309; letter of Dec. 5, 1873.
[56] *Ibid.*, pp. 490-95.
[57] *Ibid.*, p. 502.
[58] *Ibid.*, p. 1086.
[59] Thayer, *Hay*, Vol. I, p. 447.
[60] Cortissoz, *Reid*, Vol. II, p. 47; letter of Jan. 1, 1881, p. 50.

[61] New York *Tribune*, Jan. 3, 1881. *Cf.* Alexander, *Political History*, Vol. III, p. 464.

[62] Cortissoz, *Reid*, Vol. II, p. 50; letter of Reid to Garfield, Jan. 16, 1881.

[63] Garfield Papers, Journal, Mar. 3, 1881.

[64] *Ibid.*, Mar. 20, 1881.

[65] St. Louis *Globe-Democrat*, Mar. 29, 1881, cited in Smith, *Garfield*, II, 1106.

[66] Smith, *Garfield*, Vol. II, p. 1082; letter of Jan. 23, 1881.

[67] Garfield Papers, letters from Blaine to Garfield, Mar. 20, Apr. 5, and May 5, 1881.

[68] J. L. Connery, "Secret History of the Garfield-Conkling Tragedy," *Cosmopolitan*, June, 1897, pp. 146-47.

[69] Smith, *Garfield*, Vol. II, p. 1110.

[70] Cortissoz, *Reid*, Vol. II, p. 61.

[71] *Nation*, May 12, 1881, p. 329.

[72] Cortissoz, *Reid*, Vol. II, p. 64; letter of Apr. 11, 1881. Italics mine.

[73] Hamilton, *Blaine*, p. 514.

[74] *Cf.* New York *World*, July 2, 1881.

CHAPTER VIII

[1] Russell, *Blaine*, p. 385.

[2] *Letters of Mrs. James G. Blaine*, Vol. I, p. 228. Italics mine.

[3] Weber, *Wirtschaft und Gesellschaft*, Vol. I, pp. 675, 661-70.

[4] *Congressional Record*, Dec. 12, 1882, p. 354.

[5] U. S. Civil Service Commission, *First Annual Report*, 1884, p. 10.

[6] Howe, *Arthur*, pp. 191-92.

[7] Tarbell, *The Tariff*, pp. 100-01.

[8] Muzzey, *Blaine*, p. 268.

[9] Stephenson, *Aldrich*, p. 431, fn.; speech of Feb. 6, 1883, before the Tariff Commission.

[10] *Ibid.*, p. 60.

[11] Olcott, *McKinley*, Vol. I, p. 130.

[12] Stephenson, *Aldrich*, pp. 42, 50-51, 63.

[13] Taussig, *Tariff History*, p. 232 ff.

[14] Sherman, *Recollections*, Vol. II, p. 854.

[15] Stephenson, *Aldrich*, p. 60.

[16] Morrill Papers, Wharton Barker to Morrill, Dec. 20, 1882.

[17] *Ibid.*, Hayes to Morrill, Mar. 1, 1883.

[18] Howe, *Arthur*, p. 226.

[19] Tarbell, *The Tariff*, p. 126.

[20] McCall, *Reed*, p. 110.

[21] Howe, *Arthur*, p. 211, citing a conversation of 1878. First italics mine.

[22] Alexander, *Political History*, Vol. III, p. 493.

[23] Cortissoz, *Reid*, Vol. II, p. 77; letter of Oct. 28, 1881.

[24] Morrill Papers, Swank to Morrill, Dec. 1, 1886.

[25] Cortissoz, *Reid*, Vol. II, pp. 81, 82.

[26] *Bulletin of the American Iron and Steel Association*, Nov. 7, 1883, p. 305.

[27] Dorfman, *Veblen*, pp. 45, 60-62.

[28] American Iron and Steel Association, special pamphlet, Feb., 1883, in the Morrill Papers.

CHAPTER IX

[1] Hamilton, *Blaine*, pp. 622-23.
[2] *Letters of Mrs. James G. Blaine*, Vol. II, pp. 90-91.
[3] H. D. Lloyd, "The Story of a Great Monopoly," *Atlantic*, March, 1881, p. 318.
[4] *Idem*, "The Political Economy of Seventy-three Million Dollars," *Atlantic*, July, 1882, p. 70.
[5] *Cf.* Russell, *Bare Hands*, pp. 38-41.
[6] Cortissoz, *Reid*, Vol. II, p. 99, Watterson to Reid, Nov. 21, 1884. Italics mine.
[7] *Pacific Railway Commission Report*, p. 3721, Huntington to Colton, May 1, 1875.
[8] Nevins, *Cleveland*, pp. 79-80.
[9] *Ibid.*, p. 82.
[10] McElroy, *Cleveland*, Vol. I, pp. 41-42.
[11] Nevins, *Cleveland*, p. 5.
[12] Alexander, *Political History*, Vol. IV, p. 33.
[13] Croly, *Promise of American Life*, pp. 116-18.
[14] *Ibid.*, pp. 123, 124.
[15] Hudson, *Random Recollections*, p. 148.
[16] Alexander, *Political History*, Vol. IV, p. 19.
[17] McElroy, *Cleveland*, Vol. I, p. 62.
[18] Nevins, *Cleveland*, p. 137.
[19] McElroy, *Cleveland*, Vol. I, p. 52.
[20] *Ibid.*, Vol. I, p. 54.
[21] Nevins, *Cleveland*, p. 117.
[22] Cortissoz, *Reid*, Vol. II, p. 96.
[23] Foraker, *Notes*, Vol. I, pp. 165-66.
[24] *Ibid.*, Vol. I, pp. 167, 168.
[25] Roosevelt and Lodge, *Correspondence*, Vol. I, pp. 72, 86-87, 121.
[26] *Nation*, June 12, 1884, p. 495.
[27] Fuess, *Schurz*, p. 288.
[28] Pringle, *Roosevelt*, p. 81.
[29] *Ibid.*, pp. 87-89.
[30] Nevins, *Cleveland*, p. 156.
[31] Winchester, *Men of Maryland*, p. 44.
[32] Hudson, *Random Recollections*, pp. 162-64.
[33] *The Education of Henry Adams*, p. 347.
[34] Chandler Papers, July-September, 1884.
[35] Muzzey, *Blaine*, p. 291.
[36] Rhodes, *History*, Vol. VIII, p. 233.
[37] Bryce, *American Commonwealth*, Vol. II, p. 208.
[38] Pyle, *Hill*, Vol. I, p. 426.
[39] *Cf.* Oberholtzer, *History*, Vol. IV, pp. 343-44.
[40] McElroy, *Cleveland*, Vol. I, p. 98.
[41] Hudson, *Random Recollections*, p. 241.
[42] Adams, *Letters*, p. 360; letter to C. M. Gaskell, Sept. 21, 1884. Italics mine.
[43] *Nation*, Aug. 7, 1884, p. 106.
[44] Hudson, *Random Recollections*, p. 190.
[45] Muzzey, *Blaine*, p. 299.
[46] Howe, *Storey*, p. 151.
[47] *Nation*, Nov. 6, 1884, pp. 388, 390.
[48] *Cf.* Oberholtzer, *History*, Vol. IV, pp. 208-09.

[49] *Cf.* New York *Times*, Oct. 19, 1884.

[50] Hudson, *Random Recollections*, pp. 205-06.

[51] Rhodes, *History*, Vol. VIII, p. 225.

[52] New York *World*, Oct. 30, 1884.

[53] "Thoughts on the Causes of the Present Discontents."

[54] *Nation*, June 21, 1888, p. 497.

[55] New York *World*, Oct. 2, 1884.

[56] *Nation*, July 26, 1888, p. 64, citing statement in *Iowa State Register*.

[57] Levi Morton Papers, W. H. Marston to George Bliss, June 26, 1888.

[58] The original telegram is in the possession of William G. Rice, Albany, N. Y., who has kindly authorized its use here.

CHAPTER X

[1] Hudson, *Random Recollections*, pp. 268-69.

[2] Bigelow, *Tilden*, Vol. II, p. 316, letter of Dec. 21, 1885.

[3] *Ibid.*, Vol. II, pp. 298-300.

[4] New York *World*, Sept. 10, 1885.

[5] Nevins, *Cleveland*, p. 243.

[6] Rhodes, *History*, Vol. VIII, p. 245.

[7] McElroy, *Cleveland*, Vol. I, p. 146.

[8] *Ibid.*, Vol. I, p. 149.

[9] Manning Papers, Thompson to Manning, July 18, 1886.

[10] New York *Tribune*, Nov. 25, 1886.

[11] Nevins, *Cleveland*, pp. 246, 248.

[12] Pyle, *Hill*, Vol. I, pp. 426, 427.

[13] Dewey, *National Problems*, p. 38.

[14] Cleveland, *Letters*, p. 75.

[15] Schurz, *Reminiscences*, Vol. III, p. 413.

[16] Foulke, *Fighting the Spoilsmen*, p. 39.

[17] Rhodes, *History*, Vol. VIII, p. 250.

[18] Dewey, *National Problems*, pp. 35-36.

[19] Oberholtzer, *History*, Vol. IV, p. 333.

[20] Foulke, *Fighting the Spoilsmen*, p. 39.

[21] Nevins, *Cleveland*, p. 255.

[22] *Congressional Record*, Mar. 26, 1886, p. 2786.

[23] *Nation*, Jan. 14, 1886, p. 21.

[24] *Cf.* F. W. Taussig, "The South-western Strike," *Quarterly Journal of Economics*, January, 1887, pp. 208-22; *Nation*, Mar. 25, 1886, p. 247; Apr. 29, 1886, p. 349.

[25] *Cf.* U. S. Congress, House of Representatives, 49th Cong., 2d Sess., Report 4174.

[26] George, *Henry George*, p. 467.

[27] *Cf.* Dewey, *National Problems*, pp. 43-44.

[28] *Nation*, Apr. 1, 1886, p. 267; Apr. 29, 1886, p. 349.

[29] Stephenson, *Aldrich*, p. 68.

[30] *Cf.* Nevins, *Cleveland*, p. 354; *Pacific Railway Commission Report*, especially Pts. 6-7.

[31] Barron, *They Told Barron*, p. 237, citing the Rev. N. D. Hillis.

[32] Merriam, *American Political Ideas*, p. 27.

[33] Bigelow, *Tilden*, Vol. II, p. 312; letter to Watterson, Mar. 26, 1885.

[34] Parker, *Recollections of Cleveland*, pp. 493-94.

[35] Alexander, *Political History*, Vol. IV, p. 64.

[36] *Ibid.*, Vol. IV, pp. 105, 111, 127, 389-91.

[37] *Cf.* Dewey, *National Problems*, pp. 37-38.
[38] Olney Papers, letter of Dec. 28, 1892.
[39] Nevins, *Cleveland*, p. 279.
[40] *Cf.* Noyes, *American Finance*, pp. 125-26.
[41] McElroy, *Cleveland*, Vol. I, p. 268.
[42] Cleveland Papers, Whitney to Cleveland, Dec. 11, 1887.

CHAPTER XI

[1] *Cf. Nation*, Dec. 8, 1887, p. 447; July 26, 1888, p. 61.
[2] New York *Tribune*, Dec. 8, 1887.
[3] Muzzey, *Blaine*, p. 367; letter of Dec. 8, 1887.
[4] Morrill Papers, letter of Jan. 7, 1888.
[5] Nevins, *Cleveland*, p. 387.
[6] Tarbell, *The Tariff*, p. 159.
[7] Morrill Papers, letter of Dec. 1, 1886.
[8] *Ibid.*, Swank to Morrill, Apr. 20, 1888.
[9] *Nation*, Mar. 22, 1888, p. 228.
[10] Hamilton, *Blaine*, p. 604.
[11] Muzzey, *Blaine*, p. 374.
[12] Hendricks, *Carnegie*, Vol. I, p. 328.
[13] Davenport, *Penrose*, pp. 73-75.
[14] Platt, *Autobiography*, p. 211.
[15] *Cf.* Stackpole, *Behind the Scenes*, pp. 92-109; Pennypacker, *Pennsylvania*, Vol. II, pp. 193, 299.
[16] Gosnell, *Boss Platt*, p. 265.
[17] *Ibid.*, p. 58.
[18] *Ibid.*, pp. 37, 38.
[19] *Ibid.*, pp. 156-58.
[20] Croly, *Hanna*, p. 148.
[21] Foraker, *Notes*, Vol. I, pp. 363-64.
[22] Croly, *Hanna*, pp. 133, 136-37.
[23] Stephenson, *Aldrich*, p. 71.
[24] Gresham, *W. Q. Gresham*, Vol. II, pp. 632-33.
[25] Gresham Papers, J. W. Foster to Gresham, May 11, 1888; *Nation*, May 10, 1888, p. 375.
[26] Gresham, *W. Q. Gresham*, Vol. II, p. 589.
[27] Depew, *My Memories*, pp. 131-32.
[28] Foraker, *Notes*, Vol. I, p. 368.
[29] Sherman Papers, telegrams of Halstead, Hanna, and Hoar, June 23, 1888.
[30] Sherman, *Recollections*, Vol. II, p. 1029.
[31] Stephenson, *Aldrich*, p. 434, fn. 8.
[32] *Letters of Mrs. James G. Blaine*, Vol. II, p. 182.
[33] *Cf.* Hendricks, *Carnegie*, Vol. I, p. 328.
[34] Muzzey, *Blaine*, p. 380, fn.
[35] Alexander, *Political History*, Vol. IV, p. 110.
[36] Depew, *My Memories*, p. 132.
[37] Tarbell, *The Tariff*, p. 175.
[38] New York *Times*, Oct. 31, 1888; New York *World*, Nov. 25, 1888.
[39] Gibbons, *Wanamaker*, Vol. I, pp. 257, 258.
[40] Croly, *Hanna*, p. 149.
[41] *Nation*, July 26, 1888, p. 64.
[42] New York *World*, Nov. 25, 28, 1888.

[43] McLaughlin, *The Courts*, p. 155.
[44] Schurz Papers, letters of Aug. 13, Sept. 24, 1888.
[45] *Nation*, July 5, 1888, p. 4.
[46] Cleveland Papers: Sheehan to Cleveland, Oct. 3, 1888; S. S. Cary to Cleveland, Aug. 4, 1888; Edward Murphy to Lamont, Oct. 9, 1888; New York *World*, Nov. 25, 1888.
[47] Gresham, *W. Q. Gresham*, Vol. II, pp. 603-04.
[48] Nevins, *Cleveland*, p. 435.
[49] Gibbons, *Wanamaker*, Vol. I, p. 259.
[50] *Nation*, Nov. 29, 1888, pp. 425, 429; Mar. 7, 1889, p. 190.
[51] New York *World*, Nov. 8, 1888.
[52] New York *Times*, Nov. 15, 1888.
[53] *Ibid.*, Oct. 29, 1888.
[54] Gresham, *W. Q. Gresham*, Vol. II, p. 602 ff.
[55] New York *World*, Nov. 25, 1888; *Nation*, Nov. 22, 1888, p. 406.
[56] McClure, *Old Time Notes*, Vol. II, p. 573.

CHAPTER XII

[1] Croly, *Hanna*, pp. 152, 151.
[2] Bagehot, *English Constitution*, pp. 94, 99.
[3] Farrand, *United States*, p. 284.
[4] Debs, *Debs; His Life*, p. 105.
[5] Hoar, *Autobiography*, Vol. I, p. 414.
[6] Cullom, *Fifty Years*, p. 249.
[7] Platt, *Autobiography*, p. 210.
[8] Gibbons, *Wanamaker*, Vol. I, p. 269, Bull Moose letter of Roosevelt, 1912.
[9] Hamilton, *Blaine*, p. 646.
[10] Muzzey, *Blaine*, p. 389.
[11] Platt, *Autobiography*, p. 206.
[12] Noyes, *American Finance*, p. 140.
[13] Gibbons, *Wanamaker*, Vol. I, pp. 299-300.
[14] *Nation*, Feb. 27, 1890, p. 168; cf. June 20, 1889, pp. 495, 500.
[15] Roosevelt and Lodge, *Correspondence*, Vol. I, p. 87.
[16] Parker, *Cleveland*, pp. 250-51.
[17] Stoddard, *As I Knew Them*, p. 195.
[18] White, *Masks*, p. 79.
[19] Cullom, *Fifty Years*, p. 235.
[20] White, *Masks*, p. 79.
[21] *Cf.* D. G. Phillips, "The Treason of the Senate," Pt. II, *Cosmopolitan Magazine*, April, 1906.
[22] Stephenson, *Aldrich*, pp. 105, 206, 207.
[23] Beard, *American Government*, p. 268.
[24] La Follette, *Autobiography*, pp. 72, 82.
[25] *Ibid.*, p. 89.
[26] Noyes, *American Finance*, p. 118.
[27] Tarbell, *The Tariff*, p. 193, letter of F. G. Niedringhaus.
[28] McCall, *Reed*, pp. 167-68. Cf. Dewey, *National Problems*, p. 153.
[29] Olcott, *McKinley*, Vol. I, p. 172.
[30] McKinley, *Speeches*, p. 430.
[31] Thayer, *Hay*, Vol. II, pp. 136-37.
[32] Taussig, *Tariff History*, p. 276.
[33] Olcott, *McKinley*, Vol. I, p. 127.

[34] Tarbell, *The Tariff*, p. 204.
[35] Muzzey, *Blaine*, p. 445.
[36] Sherman, *Recollections*, Vol. II, p. 1085.
[37] *Nation*, May 8, 1890, p. 365.
[38] Noyes, *American Finance*, pp. 149-50.
[39] Dewey, *Financial History*, p. 437.
[40] Sherman, *Recollections*, Vol. II, p. 1070.
[41] Article "Benjamin Harrison," by A. T. Volwiler, Dictionary of American Biography.
[42] *Congressional Record*, July 22, 1886, p. 7323.
[43] Kerr, *Sherman*, Vol. II, pp. 201-03.
[44] Hoar, *Autobiography*, Vol. II, p. 22.
[45] Kerr, *Sherman*, Vol. II, p. 203.
[46] *Cf.* Foraker, *Notes*, Vol. II, p. 345.
[47] Cullom, *Fifty Years*, p. 254.
[48] Coolidge, *O. H. Platt*, p. 444.
[49] *Nation*, May 30, 1889, p. 439; July 25, 1889, p. 64.
[50] *Cf.* Kautsky, *Parlament und Demokratie*, p. 65.
[51] Dewey, *National Problems*, p. 227.
[52] Croly, *Hanna*, p. 154.
[53] *Letters of Mrs. James G. Blaine*, Vol. II, pp. 256-57.
[54] *Nation*, July 18, 1889, p. 41.
[55] Dewey, *National Problems*, pp. 179-80.
[56] Rhodes, *History*, Vol. VIII, p. 366.
[57] Olcott, *McKinley*, Vol. I, p. 180.

CHAPTER XIII

[1] Hicks, *Populist Revolt*, p. 32.
[2] *Ibid.*, p. 57.
[3] *Cf.* Corey, *Decline of Capitalism*, p. 51.
[4] *Nation*, Oct. 9, 1890, p. 275. Italics mine.
[5] Turner, *Frontier in American History*, p. 239.
[6] C. S. Walker, "The Farmers' Movement," *Annals of the American Academy of Political and Social Science*, Vol. IV, p. 795.
[7] *Ibid.*, p. 796.
[8] Barr, *Kansas*, Vol. II, pp. 1148-49.
[9] Hicks, *Populist Revolt*, p. 160.
[10] Corey, *Crisis of the Middle Class*, pp. 129-30.
[11] Bryan, *First Battle*, p. 265.
[12] Stephenson, *Lind*, p. 68.
[13] Hicks, *Populist Revolt*, pp. 168-70.
[14] Haynes, *Third Party Movements*, p. 239.
[15] Hayes, *Diary*, Vol. V, p. 91.
[16] Gibbons, *Wanamaker*, Vol. I, p. 328.
[17] A. T. Volwiler, review in *American Historical Review*, Vol. 41, April, 1936, pp. 554-57.
[18] Stoddard, *As I Knew Them*, p. 178.
[19] Cullom, *Fifty Years*, p. 252.
[20] Muzzey, *Blaine*, p. 470, letter of Jan. 15, 1892.
[21] Noyes, *American Finance*, pp. 167-68.
[22] *Ibid.*, p. 170.
[23] *Cf.* Adler, *Schiff*, Vol. I, pp. 262, 263-64.

[24] *Nation*, Jan. 22, 1891, p. 59.
[25] Adler, *Schiff*, Vol. I, p. 264.
[26] *Cf.* Haynes, *Third Party Movements*, pp. 259-60.
[27] *Nation*, Feb. 5, 1891, p. 104.

CHAPTER XIV

[1] Villard, *Memoirs*, Vol. II, p. 359.
[2] Vagts, *Deutschland*, Vol. I, p. 451.
[3] Villard Papers, Villard to James Bryce, Feb. 24, 1891.
[4] *Ibid.*, Villard to James Bryce, Feb. 24, 1891.
[5] Vagts, *Deutschland*, Vol. I, p. 452.
[6] Villard, *Memoirs*, Vol. II, pp. 360-61. Italics mine.
[7] Villard Papers, C. A. Spofford to E. C. Wall, Mar. 12, 1892.
[8] *Ibid.*, Villard to E. C. Wall, Apr. 2, 1892.
[9] *Cf.* Nevins, *Cleveland*, pp. 480-81.
[10] Barron, *More They Told Barron*, p. 9.
[11] Nevins, *Cleveland*, p. 481.
[12] Lamont Papers; Whitney to Lamont, undated (ca. 1893).
[13] Parker, *Cleveland*, p. 208.
[14] Alexander, *Political History*, Vol. IV, p. 175.
[15] Parker, *Cleveland*, p. 155.
[16] Alexander, *Political History*, Vol. IV, p. 172.
[17] *Ibid.*, Vol. IV, pp. 127, 195.
[18] *Cf. Ibid.*, Vol. IV, pp. 145, 173.
[19] *Cf.* Parker, *Cleveland*, p. 156, fn.
[20] Haynes, *Third Party Movements*, p. 266.
[21] Dewey, *National Problems*, p. 243.
[22] Alexander, *Political History*, Vol. IV, p. 173.
[23] Dunn, *From Harrison to Harding*, Vol. I, p. 96.
[24] Alexander, *Political History*, Vol. IV, p. 175.
[25] Stanwood, *Presidential Elections*, p. 468.
[26] Watterson, *"Marse Henry,"* Vol. II, p. 134.
[27] *Ibid.*, Vol. II, p. 141.
[28] Cleveland Papers, Apr. 22, 1893.
[29] Russell, *Blaine*, p. 428.
[30] *Cf.* Muzzey, *Blaine*, pp. 470-80.
[31] Platt, *Autobiography*, pp. 246-47.
[32] Alexander, *Political History*, Vol. IV, p. 187.
[33] Dunn, *From Harrison to Harding*, Vol. I, p. 98.
[34] White, *Masks*, p. 101.
[35] Roosevelt and Lodge, *Correspondence*, Vol. I, p. 129; letter of Nov. 16, 1892.
[36] Cleveland Papers, Apr. 5, 1893.
[37] Croly, *Hanna*, p. 165.
[38] Adler, *Schiff*, Vol. I, p. 304.
[39] Hicks, *Populist Revolt*, pp. 230-31.
[40] Stanwood, *Presidential Elections*, pp. 474, 475.
[41] F. B. Tracy, "Menacing Socialism in the Western States," *Forum*, May, 1893, p. 332.
[42] Stanwood, *Presidential Elections*, pp. 329-30.
[43] Cleveland Papers, letter to W. Bissell, June 30, 1892.
[44] *Ibid.*, letter of Aug. 22, 1892.
[45] *Ibid.*, letter of Aug. 11, 1892.

[46] Cleveland Papers, letter of July 10, 1892.
[47] *Ibid.*, letter of Aug. 30, 1892.
[48] *Ibid.*, letter of Sept. 15, 1892.
[49] *Ibid.*, letter of July 20, 1892.
[50] *Ibid.*, letter of Aug. 30, 1892.
[51] Harvey, *Frick*, pp. 151, 152.
[52] *Ibid.*, p. 178.
[53] *National Economist*, May 14, 1892, p. 130.
[54] For the whole speech, see New York *World*, Sept. 27, 1892.
[55] Coolidge, *O. H. Platt*, pp. 498, 423-24.
[56] Williams, *Hayes*, Vol. II, p. 376. Italics mine.
[57] Harvey, *Frick*, pp. 156-57.
[58] Cleveland Papers, letter of Aug. 11, 1892.
[59] Lamont Papers, Whitney to Lamont, undated (ca. 1893).
[60] Cullom, *Fifty Years*, p. 267.
[61] New York *Tribune*, May 14, 15, 1894.
[62] Cleveland, *Letters*, p. 296, Cleveland to W. Bissell, July 24, 1892.
[63] *Ibid.*, p. 311, Cleveland to R. W. Gilder, Sept. 25, 1892.
[64] New York *World*, Sept. 27, 1894.
[65] McClure, *Our Presidents*, p. 359.
[66] Villard Papers, Villard to L. H. Bamberger, Nov. 18, 1892.
[67] New York *World*, Nov. 19, 1892.
[68] Harvey, *Frick*, p. 157.

CHAPTER XV

[1] Cleveland, *Letters*, p. 311; to D. M. Dickinson, Nov. 21, 1892.
[2] *Ibid.*, p. 331, letter of Aug. 25, 1893.
[3] Villard, *Memoirs*, Vol. II, pp. 363-64.
[4] Cleveland, *Letters*, p. 319; letter of Feb. 19, 1893.
[5] *Cf.* Noyes, *American Finance*, pp. 183-85.
[6] Dunn, *From Harrison to Harding*, Vol. I, p. 106.
[7] Lamont Papers, letter of Apr. 4, 1893.
[8] *Ibid.*, Whitney to Lamont, Jan. 3, 1896.
[9] *Ibid.*, War Department Memo.
[10] *Ibid.*, undated; probably early in 1893.
[11] *Ibid.*, undated; probably 1894.
[12] Parker, *Cleveland*, p. 178.
[13] Poor's Manual of Railroads for 1894; Board of Directors of Chicago, Burlington & Quincy, as of Mar. 4, 1894; directors elected for Boston & Maine, Dec. 11, 1893.
[14] New York *World*, Jan. 23, 1895; Dec. 24, 1895, editorial.
[15] James, *Olney*, p. 12.
[16] Olney Papers, Letterbook, Feb. 16, 1893.
[17] *Ibid.*, Dec. 28, 1892. Italics mine.
[18] *Ibid.*, letter to Carlisle, July 5, 1893.
[19] Noyes, *American Finance*, p. 185.
[20] Taussig, *The Silver Situation*, p. 75 ff.
[21] Lamont Papers, Stillman to Lamont, Apr. 22, 1893.
[22] Barnes, *Carlisle*, pp. 236-38.
[23] Cleveland Papers, Stetson to Cleveland, Apr. 20, 1893.
[24] *Ibid.*, numerous letters, Apr. 22, 1893.
[25] *Ibid.*, letter of Apr. 22, 1893.

[26] *Cf.* Noyes, *American Finance,* pp. 190-94.
[27] McElroy, *Cleveland,* Vol. II, p. 26; Cleveland Papers, June 24, 1893.
[28] Cleveland Papers, May 20, 1893.
[29] Adler, *Schiff,* Vol. I, pp. 268-69, citing Schiff memorandum.
[30] Cleveland Papers, Schiff to Cleveland, June 21, 1893.
[31] Nevins, *Cleveland,* p. 524.
[32] *Cf.* Dunn, *From Harrison to Harding,* Vol. I, p. 118.
[33] Cleveland, *Letters,* pp. 314-15.
[34] Cleveland Papers, Cleveland to Governor Northern of Georgia, Sept. 25, 1893.
[35] Bryan, *First Battle,* p. 118.
[36] *Public Opinion,* July 22, 1893, p. 364.
[37] Hicks, *Populist Revolt,* p. 310.
[38] *Congressional Record,* Aug. 26, 1893, p. 955.
[39] *Cf.* Dewey, *National Problems,* p. 263.
[40] Werner, *Bryan,* p. 21.
[41] Bryan, *First Battle,* pp. 81, 110, 113-14.
[42] Robinson, *Reed,* pp. 288-92.
[43] Stephenson, *Aldrich,* pp. 105, 107.
[44] Barnes, *Carlisle,* pp. 236-37.
[45] Dunn, *From Harrison to Harding,* Vol. I, p. 121.
[46] Cleveland, *Letters,* p. 337, letter of Oct. 9, 1893.
[47] *Congressional Record,* Nov. 1, 1893, p. 3066.
[48] *Cf.* Parker, *Cleveland,* p. 214.
[49] Barnes, *Carlisle,* pp. 297-98.
[50] Noyes, *American Finance,* p. 209.
[51] Lamont Papers, letter of Stillman to Lamont, Jan. 29, 1894; *cf.* Barnes, *Carlisle,* pp. 315-16.
[52] Noyes, *American Finance,* p. 215.
[53] Nevins, *Cleveland,* p. 599.
[54] Cullom, *Fifty Years,* p. 254.
[55] New York *Tribune,* Feb. 8, 1894.
[56] *Ibid.,* Jan. 3, 1894.
[57] *Cf.* Taussig, *Tariff History,* Chap. VI.
[58] Tarbell, *The Tariff,* p. 236.
[59] Nevins, *Cleveland,* p. 573.
[60] Taussig, *Tariff History,* p. 313.
[61] New York *Tribune,* May 9, 1894.
[62] Andrew Carnegie, "My Experiences with, and Views upon, the Tariff," *Century,* December, 1908, p. 199.
[63] Cleveland Papers, H. L. Terrell to Lamont, Mar. 6, 1894.
[64] New York *Tribune,* Mar. 22, 1894.
[65] Philadelphia *Press,* May 14, 17, 1894.
[66] New York *World,* Mar. 7, 9, 1894.
[67] U. S. Senate, 53d Cong., 2d Sess., Report No. 606, pp. 351-52.
[68] Dunn, *From Harrison to Harding,* Vol. I, p. 127.
[69] Tarbell, *The Tariff,* p. 234.
[70] Lamont Papers, R. Wightman to Lamont, 1894.
[71] *Congressional Record,* July 19, 1894, p. 7712.
[72] *Ibid.,* July 23, 1894, p. 7805.
[73] Cullom, *Fifty Years,* p. 267.
[74] Barnes, *Carlisle,* p. 324.
[75] Coolidge, *O. H. Platt,* pp. 450, 453.
[76] McElroy, *Cleveland,* Vol. II, p. 117; letter to Catchings, Aug. 7, 1894.

CHAPTER XVI

[1] Pyle, *Hill*, Vol. II, pp. 79-80.
[2] Cleveland Papers, letter of May 5, 1894.
[3] *Ibid.*, numerous letters, Apr. 30, 1894; Army and Navy Register, Apr. 20, 1894.
[4] Thayer, *Hay*, Vol. II, p. 112.
[5] James, *Olney*, p. 39; memorandum, pp. 36-39.
[6] McMurry, *Coxey's Army*, pp. 25-29.
[7] *Ibid.*, pp. 38-39, 66.
[8] *Cf.* New York *Tribune*, Apr. 30, 1894.
[9] Cleveland Papers, confidential memorandum, Apr. 20, 1894.
[10] *Nation*, May 3, 1894, p. 319.
[11] McMurry, *Coxey's Army*, pp. 116-19; *cf.* New York *Sun*, May 2, 1894.
[12] James, *Olney*, p. 40.
[13] Commons and others, *History of Labour*, Vol. II, p. 501.
[14] *Cf.* Debs, *Debs: His Life*, p. 7.
[15] Commons and others, *History of Labour*, Vol. II, p. 502.
[16] *Cf.* New York *Tribune*, June 27-July 4, 1894.
[17] *Nation*, July 5, 1894, p. 1.
[18] *Ibid.*, July 5, 1894, p. 1.
[19] New York *Tribune*, June 18, 1894.
[20] Olney Papers, letter to Edwin Walker, July 7, 1895.
[21] *Ibid.*, letter to Justice Harlan, Aug. 26, 1894; letter to Bellamy Storer, July 12, 1894.
[22] James, *Olney*, p. 47. Italics mine.
[23] Browne, *Altgeld*, p. 169, citing the Boston *Post*, Jan. 16, 1875.
[24] *Ibid.*, p. 144.
[25] James, *Olney*, p. 201, citing Olney's memorandum.
[26] Browne, *Altgeld*, pp. 136, 137; Yellen, *American Labor Struggles*, p. 117.
[27] Lloyd, *H. D. Lloyd*, Vol. I, pp. 148-49, 150.
[28] Browne, *Altgeld*, p. 71.
[29] Atlanta *Constitution*, cited in *Public Opinion*, July 12, 1894, p. 331.
[30] Cited in *Public Opinion*, July 19, 1894, p. 361.
[31] New York *World*, July 3, 1894. *Cf.* Yellen, *Amercian Labor Struggles*, pp. 118-19.
[32] U. S. Attorney General, *Annual Report, 1896*, Apx., p. 61.
[33] New York *Tribune*, July 3, 1894.
[34] U. S. Attorney General, *Annual Report, 1896*, Apx., p. 66.
[35] *Ibid.*, p. 65. Italics mine.
[36] *Ibid.*, p. 66.
[37] New York *Tribune*, July 5, 1894.
[38] *Ibid.*, July 11, 1894.
[39] Browne, *Altgeld*, p. 134.
[40] New York *Tribune*, July 7, 1894.
[41] *Cf.* New York *World*, July 7-10, 1894.
[42] *Cf.* Commons and others, *History of Labour*, Vol. II, pp. 503-04.
[43] *Nation*, July 12, 1894, p. 19. Italics mine.
[44] New York *Times*, July 13, 1894.
[45] Browne, *Altgeld*, p. 154 ff.
[46] *Ibid.*, p. 161.
[47] *Ibid.*, p. 162.
[48] James, *Olney*, p. 56.

[49] *Nation*, July 12, 1894, p. 19.
[50] Commons and others, *History of Labour*, Vol. II, p. 508.
[51] Olney Papers, letter to Edwin Walker, Dec. 31, 1894.
[52] Nevins, *Cleveland*, p. 627.
[53] Cleveland, *Presidential Problems*, p. 117. Italics mine.
[54] Cleveland Papers, letter of Mar. 18, 1894.
[55] Dunn, *From Harrison to Harding*, Vol. I, p. 108, 105-106; Cleveland Papers, Feb. 15, 1895.
[56] Vagts, *Deutschland*, Vol. I, p. 278, citing A. D. White to Gresham.
[57] Lamont Papers, Apr. 22, 1893.
[58] Barnes, *Carlisle*, p. 348.
[59] New York *Times*, Nov. 8, 1894.
[60] Cleveland Papers, January-February, 1895.
[61] Barnes, *Carlisle*, pp. 358, 361-62.
[62] Corey, *House of Morgan*, p. 185.
[63] *Cf.* New York *Journal of Commerce*, Nov. 22, 1894.
[64] Cleveland Papers, letter of Jan. 24, 1895.
[65] *Public Opinion*, Feb. 7, 1895.
[66] *Congressional Record*, Jan. 29, 1895, pp. 1478, 1479.
[67] New York *World*, Feb. 1, 1895.
[68] Barnes, *Carlisle*, p. 373, letter of Curtis to Carlisle, Jan. 30, 1895.
[69] *Cf.* U. S. Congress, Senate, 54th Cong., 2d Sess., Doc. 187, p. 296.
[70] New York *World*, Feb. 2, 1895.
[71] Barnes, *Carlisle*, p. 376.
[72] *Ibid.*, p. 378.
[73] McElroy, *Cleveland*, Vol. II, p. 87.
[74] New York *World*, Feb. 6, 1895.
[75] Barnes, *Carlisle*, p. 380, letter of Feb. 5, 1895.
[76] Lamont Papers, Olney to Lamont, May 13, 1904.
[77] Rhodes, *History*, Vol. VIII, p. 435.
[78] Hovey, *Morgan*, p. 178.
[79] Parker, *Cleveland*, p. 325.
[80] Rhodes, *History*, Vol. VIII, p. 431.
[81] Lamont Papers, May 13, 1904.
[82] Corey, *House of Morgan*, p. 189.
[83] *Cf.* New York *World*, Feb. 9, 1895.
[84] Bryan, *First Battle*, p. 137.
[85] Cleveland Papers, E. T. Randolph, G. S. Williams, C. S. Fairchild, to Lamont, Feb. 21, 1895; E. C. Benedict, Feb. 20, 1895.
[86] *Ibid.*, Feb. 13, 1895.

CHAPTER XVII

[1] Cleveland Papers, letter to D. M. Dickinson, Aug. 25, 1893.
[2] *Cf.* Feinstein, *The Court Disposes*, Chap. VIII.
[3] Frankfurter, *The Labor Injunction*, pp. 17-24.
[4] *Nation*, May 30, 1895, p. 413.
[5] Cited in *Public Opinion*, June 6, 1895, p. 628.
[6] New York *World*, May 29, 1895.
[7] *Cf. Ibid.*, Jan. 23, 1895.
[8] Gresham, *W. Q. Gresham*, Vol. II, p. 652.
[9] New York *World*, Jan. 23, 1895.
[10] James, *Olney*, p. 209 (Olney memorandum).

[11] *Cf.* Josephson, *Robber Barons,* p. 381 ff.
[12] Olney Papers, Olney to Stephenson, Jan. 22, 1895.
[13] Werner, *Bryan,* p. 52.
[14] *Nation,* Feb. 21, 1895, p. 138.
[15] *Cf.* Martin, *Choate,* Vol. II, pp. 1-17.
[16] *Ibid.,* p. 15, citing the New York *World,* Mar. 30, 1895.
[17] *Cf.* James, *Olney,* p. 75.
[18] Martin, *Choate,* Vol. II, p. 9.
[19] *Public Opinion,* May 23, 1895, p. 562.
[20] *Cf.* New York *World,* May 22, 1895.
[21] New York *Tribune,* May 21, 1895.
[22] *Nation,* Feb. 21, 1895, pp. 138-39.
[23] Lloyd, *H. D. Lloyd,* Vol. I, p. 197.
[24] *Ibid.,* Vol. I, p. 201, letter to F. F. Murray.
[25] Harvey, *Coin's Financial School,* p. 3.
[26] *Ibid.,* p. 120.
[27] *Ibid.,* p. 109.
[28] *Ibid.,* p. 132.
[29] *Ibid.,* pp. 146-47.
[30] Browne, *Altgeld,* p. 70.
[31] Cleveland Papers, Feb. 13, 1895.
[32] New York *World,* Dec. 4, 1895.
[33] Cleveland, *Letters,* p. 369, letter of Oct. 7, 1894.
[34] Dunn, *From Harrison to Harding,* Vol. I, pp. 143-44.
[35] Peck, *Twenty Years,* p. 459.
[36] *Congressional Record,* Jan. 29, 1896, pp. 1075, 1076, 1078.
[37] Parker, *Cleveland,* p. 214.
[38] *Congressional Record,* Feb. 25, 1896, p. 2101.
[39] Browne, *Altgeld,* pp. 261-62.
[40] *Ibid.,* p. 263.
[41] Beard and Beard, *Rise of American Civilization,* Vol. II, p. 362.
[42] James, *Olney,* p. 109.
[43] Nevins, *Cleveland,* p. 634.
[44] James, *Olney,* pp. 108, 109.
[45] Cleveland, *Letters,* p. 416, letter to Olney.
[46] James, *Olney,* p. 120.
[47] *Public Opinion,* Dec. 26, 1895, pp. 840-42.
[48] *Cf.* New York *World,* Dec. 24, 1895.
[49] New York *Post,* Dec. 24, 1895.
[50] Olney Papers, Oct. 23, 1895.
[51] Vagts, *Deutschland,* Vol. I, pp. 512-13.
[52] Rhodes, *History,* Vol. VIII, p. 452.
[53] Woodrow Wilson, "Mr. Cleveland as President," *Atlantic,* March, 1897, p. 299.
[54] Barnes, *Carlisle,* p. 405.
[55] New York *World,* Dec. 24, 1895.
[56] Barnes, *Carlisle,* pp. 413-14.
[57] New York *World,* Jan. 4, 1896.
[58] Lamont Papers, Jan. 3, 1896.
[59] *Ibid.,* Dec. 25, 1895.
[60] New York *World,* Jan. 3, 1896.
[61] Barnes, *Carlisle,* p. 414.
[62] New York *World,* Dec. 25, 1895.
[63] Lamont Papers, Jan. 3, 1896.

[64] Nevins, *Cleveland*, p. 686.
[65] Cleveland, *Letters*, pp. 422-23, Cleveland to Senator Caffery, Jan. 5, 1896.
[66] Noyes, *American Finance*, p. 241 ff.
[67] Hicks, *Populist Revolt*, p. 344.
[68] New York *World*, Jan. 17, 1896.
[69] Browne, *Altgeld*, pp. 264-67.
[70] New York *World*, June 20, 1896.
[71] *Public Opinion*, June 25, 1896.
[72] Cited in *Public Opinion*, June 25, 1896, p. 814.
[73] *Ibid.*, June 25, 1896.
[74] *Ibid.*, June 25, 1896.
[75] W. E. Russell Papers, Whitney to Russell. Italics mine.
[76] *Ibid.*, letter of June 22, 1896.
[77] New York *World*, July 2, 1896.
[78] Nevins, *Cleveland*, p. 700.

CHAPTER XVIII

[1] McCall, *Reed*, p. 208.
[2] *Nation*, Oct. 8, 1908, p. 328.
[3] Howe, *Confessions*, p. 147.
[4] *Ibid.*, p. 151.
[5] *Ibid.*, p. 147.
[6] Rhodes, *History*, Vol. IX, p. 7.
[7] Beer, *Hanna*, p. 168.
[8] *Ibid.*, p. 46.
[9] Croly, *Hanna*, p. 161.
[10] Foraker, *Notes*, Vol. I, p. 445.
[11] Howe, *Confessions*, pp. 172-73.
[12] White, *Masks*, pp. 163, 166-67.
[13] Olcott, *McKinley*, Vol. I, pp. 289-92.
[14] White, *Masks*, p. 154.
[15] *Ibid.*, p. 155.
[16] Thayer, *Hay*, Vol. II, p. 153.
[17] White, *Masks*, p. 166.
[18] *Ibid.*, p. 155.
[19] *Ibid.*, p. 166.
[20] Thayer, *Hay*, Vol. II, pp. 138-39.
[21] Croly, *Hanna*, pp. 167, 171; *Nation*, May 21, 1896, p. 387.
[22] Peck, *Twenty Years*, p. 478.
[23] Denver *News*, cited in *Public Opinion*, Feb. 21, 1895, p. 166.
[24] Beer, *Hanna*, p. 134.
[25] Howe, *Confessions*, p. 152.
[26] Croly, *Hanna*, p. 176.
[27] Dunn, *From Harrison to Harding*, Vol. I, p. 172.
[28] *Ibid.*, Vol. I, pp. 171-73.
[29] Platt, *Autobiography*, p. 331.
[30] Olcott, *McKinley*, Vol. I, p. 300.
[31] Beer, *Hanna*, p. 142.
[32] *Nation*, May 21, 1896, p. 387.
[33] Dennett, *Hay*, pp. 174-75.
[34] White, *Masks*, p. 207.
[35] Cullom, *Fifty Years*, p. 273; Croly, *Hanna*, p. 183.
[36] Alexander, *Political History*, Vol. IV, p. 251.

[37] Croly, *Hanna*, p. 194.
[38] Beer, *Hanna*, pp. 305-25; memorandum to President McCall of the New York Life Insurance Company.
[39] *Ibid.*, pp. 138-42.
[40] Croly, *Hanna*, pp. 195-99.
[41] Kohlsaat, *From McKinley to Harding*, p. 36.
[42] Cortissoz, *Reid*, Vol. II, p. 206.
[43] Dunn, *From Harrison to Harding*, Vol. I, p. 177.
[44] Kohlsaat, *From McKinley to Harding*, p. 37.
[45] Seitz, *Pulitzer*, p. 225.
[46] Platt, *Autobiography*, p. 310.
[47] Croly, *Hanna*, p. 199.
[48] Beer, *Hanna*, pp. 143-46.
[49] New York *World*, June 16, 1896.
[50] *Cf.* Dunn, *From Harrison to Harding*, Vol. I, p. 181; White, *Masks*, pp. 212-15.
[51] Bryan, *Memoirs*, p. 100.
[52] Dunn, *From Harrison to Harding*, Vol. I, p. 181.

CHAPTER XIX

[1] Hicks, *Populist Revolt*, p. 347.
[2] New York *World*, June 30, 1896.
[3] *Public Opinion*, July 2, 1896, p. 8.
[4] Hicks, *Populist Revolt*, p. 351.
[5] *Cf.* New York *World*, Aug. 18, 19, Sept. 28, 1896.
[6] Seitz, *Pulitzer*, p. 226. *Cf.* Carlson and Bates, *Hearst*, pp. 81-82.
[7] *Cf.* Corey, *Decline of Capitalism*, pp. 420-21.
[8] New York *Journal*, July 11, 1896.
[9] Bryan, *Memoirs*, p. 115.
[10] *Cf.* Hibben, *Bryan*, pp. 183-84.
[11] Hibben, *Bryan*, pp. 182-83.
[12] White, *Masks*, pp. 251-52.
[13] Kent, *Democratic Party*, pp. 339-40.
[14] Hicks, *Populist Revolt*, p. 356.
[15] Werner, *Bryan*, pp. 58-59.
[16] Bryan, *Memoirs*, p. 102.
[17] New York *World*, July 8, 1896.
[18] F. E. Leupp, "The Democratic Convention," *Harper's Weekly*, July 18, 1896, p. 714.
[19] *Public Opinion*, July 16, 1896, pp. 70-71.
[20] New York *World*, July 10, 1896.
[21] Bryan, *Memoirs*, p. 103.
[22] Bryan, *First Battle*, speech on pp. 199-205.
[23] Peck, *Twenty Years*, p. 500.
[24] Browne, *Altgeld*, p. 277.
[25] *National Review*, London, December, 1896, p. 454.
[26] New York *Tribune*, July 11, 1896.
[27] Olcott, *McKinley*, Vol. I, p. 321.
[28] Rhodes, *History*, Vol. IX, pp. 18-19.
[29] Lloyd, *H. D. Lloyd*, Vol. I, p. 259.
[30] Bryan, *First Battle*, p. 261.
[31] *Ibid.*, pp. 269-70, 279.

[32] Dunn, *From Harrison to Harding*, Vol. I, pp. 191-92.
[33] Lloyd, *H. D. Lloyd*, Vol. I, pp. 260, 264.
[34] *Public Opinion*, July 16, 1896, pp. 79, 75.
[35] *Ibid.*, p. 75, citing the New York *Mail and Express*.
[36] F. J. Turner, "The Problem of the West," *Atlantic*, September, 1896, p. 296.
[37] *Public Opinion*, July 30, 1896; interview of July 23, 1896.
[38] Parker, *Cleveland*, p. 212.
[39] Bryan, *First Battle*, p. 356.
[40] Lamont Papers, Stillman to Lamont, Sept. 4, 1896.
[41] Pyle, *Hill*, Vol. I, pp. 496-97.
[42] Bryan, *First Battle*, p. 452.
[43] *Ibid.*, p. 316.
[44] Werner, *Bryan*, p. 93.
[45] Bryan, *First Battle*, pp. 536, 541, 571-72.
[46] Merriam, *Four American Party Leaders*, p. 71.
[47] New York *World*, Sept. 12, 1896.
[48] Merriam, *Four American Party Leaders*, p. 71.
[49] Bryan, *First Battle*, p. 477.
[50] Beer, *Hanna*, p. 153.
[51] Croly, *Hanna*, p. 228.
[52] *Cf.* New York *Tribune*, July 31, Aug. 2, 1896.
[53] Beer, *Hanna*, p. 152.
[54] New York *Tribune*, July 31, 1896.
[55] New York *Times*, July 24, 1896.
[56] New York *Journal*, Sept. 26, 1896.
[57] New York *World*, Aug. 20, 1896.
[58] Beer, *Hanna*, pp. 155-56; W. C. Beer to Harvey Fleming.
[59] New York *World*, Oct. 6, 1896.
[60] Croly, *Hanna*, p. 220.
[61] Kohlsaat, *From McKinley to Harding*, p. 52.
[62] Browne, *Altgeld*, pp. 286-87.
[63] *Ibid.*, p. 287; *cf.* also Williams, *Bryan*, p. 187.
[64] New York *World*, Oct. 4, 1896.
[65] New York *Tribune*, Oct. 17, 1896.
[66] Croly, *Hanna*, p. 217.
[67] New York *World*, Oct. 18, 1896.
[68] New York *Journal*, Sept. 26, 1896.
[69] Peck, *Twenty Years*, p. 511.
[70] Hibben, *Bryan*, p. 201.
[71] New York *World*, Sept. 10, 1896.
[72] *Ibid.*, Sept. 9, 1896.
[73] *Public Opinion*, Oct. 22, 29, 1896.
[74] New York *World*, Oct. 28, 1896.
[75] Beer, *Hanna*, p. 165.
[76] Williams, *Bryan*, p. 195.
[77] *Ibid.*, p. 190.
[78] *Cf.* New York *World*, Nov. 1, 1896.
[79] Dunn, *From Harrison to Harding*, Vol. I, p. 195.
[80] New York *World*, Oct. 31, 1896.
[81] Hibben, *Bryan*, p. 201.
[82] Browne, *Altgeld*, p. 295.
[83] New York *Tribune*, Nov. 4, 1896.
[84] Kohlsaat, *From McKinley to Harding*, p. 53.

INDEX

293, 355, 357, 358, 366, 381, 426, 442. *See also* Republican Party

Lincoln, Abraham, 4; reconstruction plans, 5-7; 8, 11, 13, 14, 16, 29; advocates convention system, 73; Dark Horse, 76, 77; 79

Little Rock & Ft. Smith Railroad, 209-212. *See also* Blaine

"Live Issues," 72, 74, 396, 397

Lloyd, Henry Demarest, 343, 344, 479, 562, 574, 576, 581, 582 *fn.*, 583, 612, 613, 667, 681, 683

Lobbying, 55, 103-108, 111, 112, 115-116, 126, 181, 326, 327, 330, 331, 403, 404, 450, 542, 547

Lodge, Henry Cabot, 278, 356, 357, 442, 444, 652; champions gold standard, 658, 659; 700

"Log-Cabin," as symbol, 74, 75, 77, 289, 429

Logan, John A., head of G.A.R., 36, 45; supports Grant, 47, 59, 60, 80, 88; Illinois boss, 91, 98; as "Railway Congressman," 107, 116, 118; 121; and Whisky Ring, 134; fights civil service reform, 139; 143, 170, 173, 184, 238; favors inflation, 190, 193, 194; favors deflation, 195; defends Whisky Ring, 200, 202, 203; for "restoration" of Grant in 1880, 273, 274, 279; 295, 297; alliance with Blaine, 336; candidate for Vice-President, 1884, 360, 372; calls for army in labor disputes, 387; 406

Logrolling, 331, 333

Louisiana (in 1876 election), 227-231, 233, 236, 237

Mackay, John, 663

Madison, James, 63-65; 256, 239

Manifest Destiny, 620

Manning, Daniel, as Tilden's lieutenant and Democratic boss, 217, 347, 348, 351-353, 358; in campaign of 1884, 359, 362, 363, 367; as Secretary of the Treasury, 376, 377, 386; opposes Cleveland's civil service reforms, 378, 379; 392, 395, 427, 522

Marble, Manton, 221

Marx, Karl, 252, 471, 607

Mather, Samuel, 645

Matthews, Stanley, 230, 235, 236

McAllister, Ward, 609

McClure, A. K., 659

McCulloch, Hugh, 39, 40, 191

McDonald, John A., and Whisky Ring, 133-136, 169, 198-201, 222

McGarrahan Claim, 129, 130

McKee, William, and Whisky Ring, 134, 201

McKinley, William, enters Congress as Protectionist, 328, 329, 332; 403, 413; refuses nomination for President in 1888, 417; and McKinley Tariff, 447, 450-454, 464; as Hanna's protégé, 448, 591; 500, 537; Governor of Ohio, 642-646; presidential boom, 647-650; waverings on silver issue, 651-655; campaign of 1896, 680, 684, 695-699, 701; elected President, 706, 707

McKinley Tariff Bill, 447, 450 *ff.*, 464, 470, 489, 498, 539, 560. *See also* Tariff

McPherson, J. R., 549

MacVeagh, Wayne, 238, 304, 313

Merritt, E. A., 250 *fn.*, 309

Michener, L. T., 418 *fn.*, 652 *fn.*

Milchrist, Thomas E., and railway strike, 1894, 578-581

Miller, Warner, 389, 431, 433

"Millionaires' Club," Senate as, 444-445

Mills, Darius Ogden, 370

Mills, Roger Q., and tariff revision, 402-404; 543, 549. *See also* Tariff

"Minor Cabinet," 131-132, 222, 274, 301

Missouri-Pacific Railroad, strike against, 386-388. *See also* Labor Movement

"Molly Maguires," 252

Monroe Doctrine. *See* Venezuela Boundary Dispute

Monroe, James, 65

Morgan, Edwin (Governor of New York), 60

Morgan, J. Pierpont, 77, 261, 393; aids Republican fund in 1888, 424; combines railroads by "gentlemen's agreement," 448; 492, 519, 538; and bond issues under Cleveland, 593-603; 609, 613, 616, 622; and 1896 bond issue, 626-628; 655; demands gold plank in Republican platform, 1896, 656-657; 687; contribution to McKinley campaign fund, 698, 699